THE WORKS OF
WILLIAM CONGREVE

EDITED IN THREE VOLUMES BY

D. F. McKENZIE

PREPARED FOR PUBLICATION BY

C. Y. FERDINAND

Volume III

OXFORD
UNIVERSITY PRESS

OXFORD
UNIVERSITY PRESS

Great Clarendon Street, Oxford OX2 6DP

Oxford University Press is a department of the University of Oxford.
It furthers the University's objective of excellence in research, scholarship,
and education by publishing worldwide in

Oxford New York

Auckland Cape Town Dar es Salaam Hong Kong Karachi
Kuala Lumpur Madrid Melbourne Mexico City Nairobi
New Delhi Shanghai Taipei Toronto

With offices in

Argentina Austria Brazil Chile Czech Republic France Greece
Guatemala Hungary Italy Japan Poland Portugal Singapore
South Korea Switzerland Thailand Turkey Ukraine Vietnam

Oxford is a registered trade mark of Oxford University Press
in the UK and in certain other countries

Published in the United States
by Oxford University Press Inc., New York

British Library Cataloguing in Publication Data

Data available

Library of Congress Cataloging-in-Publication Data

Congreve, William, 1670–1729.
[Works. 2010]
The works of William Congreve / edited in three volumes by D. F. McKenzie; prepared
for publication by C. Y. Ferdinand.
p. cm.
Includes bibliographical references and indexes.
ISBN-13: 978-0-19-811884-8 (alk. paper)
ISBN-10: 0-19-811884-8 (alk. paper)
I. McKenzie, D. F. (Donald Francis) II. Ferdinand, C. Y. (Christine Y.) III. Title.
PR3361.M395 2006
822'.4—dc22 2006027154

Typeset by SPI Publisher Services, Pondicherry, India
Printed in Great Britain
on acid-free paper by
CPI Antony Rowe, Chippenham, Wiltshire

ISBN: 978-0-19-811884-8 (Vol. I)
ISBN: 978-0-19-929747-4 (Vol. II)
ISBN: 978-0-19-929746-7 (Vol. III)
ISBN: 978-0-19-920254-6 (Set)

1 3 5 7 9 10 8 6 4 2

CONTENTS

VOLUME III

INCOGNITA:

OR,

LOVE

AND

DUTY

RECONCIL'D.

A

NOVEL.

Licens'd Decemb. 22. 1691.

LONDON,

Printed for *Peter Buck*, at the Sign
of the *Temple*, near *Temple Bar*
in *Fleet-street*, 1692.

TO THE
Honoured and Worthily Esteem'd

Mrs. *Katharine Leveson*.

Madam,

A Clear Wit, sound Judgment and a Merciful Disposition, are things so rarely united, that it is almost inexcusable to entertain them with any thing less excellent in its kind. My knowledge of you were a sufficient Caution to me, to avoid your Censure of this Trifle, had I not as intire a knowledge 5 of your Goodness. Since I have drawn my Pen for a Rencounter, I think it better to engage where, though there be Skill enough to Disarm me, there is too much Generosity to Wound; for so shall I have the saving Reputation of an unsuccessful Courage, if I cannot make it a drawn Battle. But 10 methinks the Comparison intimates something of a Defiance, and savours of Arrogance; wherefore since I am Conscious to my self of a Fear which I cannot put off, let me use the Policy of Cowards and lay this Novel unarm'd, naked and shivering at your Feet, so that if it should want Merit to challenge 15 Protection, yet, as an Object of Charity, it may move Compassion. It has been some Diversion to me to Write it, I wish it may prove such to you when you have an hour to throw away in Reading of it: but this Satisfaction I have at least beforehand, that in its greatest failings it may fly for 20 Pardon to that Indulgence which you owe to the weakness of your Friend; a Title which I am proud you have thought me worthy of, and which I think can alone be superiour to that

Your most Humble and 25
Obliged Servant
CLEOPHIL.

THE
PREFACE
TO THE
READER.

Reader,

SOME Authors are so fond of a Preface, that they will write one tho' there be nothing more in it than an Apology for its self. But to show thee that I am not one of those, I will make no Apology for this, but do tell thee that I think it
5 *necessary to be prefix'd to this Trifle, to prevent thy overlooking some little pains which I have taken in the Composition of the following Story. Romances are generally composed of the Constant Loves and invincible Courages of Hero's, Heroins, Kings and Queens, Mortals of the first Rank,*
10 *and so forth; where lofty Language, miraculous Contingencies and impossible Performances, elevate and surprize the Reader into a giddy Delight, which leaves him flat upon the Ground whenever he gives of, and vexes him to think how he has suffer'd himself to be pleased and transported, concernd and*
15 *afflicted at the several Passages which he has Read, viz. these Knights Success to their Damosels Misfortunes, and such like, when he is forced to be very well convinced that 'tis all a lye. Novels are of a more familiar nature; Come near us, and represent to us Intrigues in practice, delight us with Accidents*
20 *and odd Events, but not such as are wholly unusual or unpresidented, such which not being so distant from our Belief bring also the pleasure nearer us. Romances give more of Wonder, Novels more Delight. And with reverence be it spoken, and the Parallel kept at due distance, there is*
25 *something of equality in the Proportion which they bear in reference to one another, with that between Comedy and Tragedy; but the* Drama *is the long extracted from Romance*

*and History: 'tis the Midwife to Industry, and brings forth
alive the Conceptions of the Brain.* Minerva *walks upon the
Stage before us, and we are more assured of the real presence of* 30
Wit when it is delivered viva voce—

Segnius irritant animos demissa per aurem,
Quam quæ sunt oculis subjecta fidelibus, & quæ
Ipse sibi tradit spectator.—

Horace. 35

Since all Traditions must indisputably give place to the
Drama, *and since there is no possibility of giving that life to
the Writing or Repetition of a Story which it has in the Action,
I resolved in another beauty to imitate* Dramatick *Writing,
namely, in the Design, Contexture and Result of the Plot.* 40
*I have not observed it before in a Novel. Some I have seen
begin with an unexpected accident, which has been the only
surprizing part of the Story, cause enough to make the Sequel
look flat, tedious and insipid; for 'tis but reasonable the Reader
should expect it not to rise, at least to keep upon a level in the* 45
*entertainment; for so he may be kept on in hopes that at some
time or other it may mend; but the 'tother is such a balk to a
Man, 'tis carrying him up stairs to show him the Dining-Room,
and after forcing him to make a Meal in the Kitchin. This I
have not only endeavoured to avoid, but also have used a* 50
*method for the contrary purpose. The design of the Novel is
obvious, after the first meeting of* Aurelian *and* Hippolito *with*
Incognita *and* Leonora, *and the difficulty is in bringing it to
pass, maugre all apparent obstacles, within the compass of two
days. How many probable Casualties intervene in opposition to* 55
*the main Design, viz. of marrying two Couple so oddly engaged
in an intricate Amour, I leave the Reader at his leisure to
consider: As also whether every Obstacle does not in the
progress of the Story act as subservient to that purpose, which
at first it seems to oppose. In a Comedy this would be called the* 60
*Unity of Action; here it may pretend to no more than an Unity
of Contrivance. The Scene is continued in* Florence *from the
commencement of the Amour; and the time from first to last is
but three days. If there be any thing more in particular
resembling the Copy which I imitate (as the Curious Reader* 65

will soon perceive) I leave it to show it self, being very well satisfy'd how much more proper it had been for him to have found out this himself, than for me to prepossess him with an Opinion of something extraordinary in an Essay began and
70 *finished in the idler hours of a fortnight's time: for I can only esteem it a laborious idleness, which is Parent to so inconsiderable a Birth. I have gratified the Bookseller in pretending an occasion for a Preface; the other two Persons concern'd are the Reader and my self, and if he be but pleased*
75 *with what was produced for that end, my satisfaction follows of course, since it will be proportion'd to his Approbation or Dislike.*

INCOGNITA:

OR,

Love & Duty
RECONCIL'D.

*A*URELIAN was the only Son to a Principal Gentleman of *Florence*. The Indulgence of his Father
prompted, and his Wealth enabled him, to bestow a
generous Education upon him, whom, he now began to
look upon as the Type of himself; an Impression he had   5
made in the Gayety and Vigour of his Youth, before the
Rust of Age had debilitated and obscur'd the Splendour of
the Original: He was sensible, That he ought not to be
sparing in the Adornment of him, if he had Resolution to
beautifie his own Memory. Indeed *Don Fabio* (for so was   10
the Old Gentleman call'd) has been observ'd to have fix'd
his Eyes upon *Aurelian*, when much Company has been at
Table, and have wept through Earnestness of Intention, if
nothing hapned to divert the Object; whether it were for
regret, at the Recollection of his former self, or for the Joy   15
he conceiv'd in being, as it were, reviv'd in the Person of his
Son, I never took upon me to enquire, but suppos'd it
might be sometimes one, and sometimes both together.

Aurelian, at the Age of Eighteen Years, wanted nothing
(but a Beard) that the most accomplished *Cavalier* in   20
Florence could pretend to: he had been Educated from
Twelve Years old at *Siena*, where it seems his Father kept
a Receiver, having a large Income from the Rents of several
Houses in that Town. *Don Fabio* gave his Servant Orders,
That *Aurelian* should not be stinted in his Expences,   25
when he came up to Years of Discretion. By which means
he was enabled, not only to keep Company with, but also to
confer many Obligations upon Strangers of Quality, and

Gentlemen who travelled from other Countries into *Italy*,
30 of which *Siena* never wanted store, being a Town most
delightfully Situate, upon a Noble Hill, and very well
suiting with Strangers at first, by reason of the
agreeableness and purity of the Air: There also is the
quaintness and delicacy of the *Italian* Tongue most likely
35 to be learned, there being many publick Professors of it in
that place; and indeed the very Vulgar of *Siena* do express
themselves with an easiness and sweetness surprizing, and
even grateful to their Ears who understand not the
Language.

40   Here *Aurelian* contracted an acquaintance with Persons
of Worth of several Countries, but among the rest an
intimacy with a Gentleman of Quality of *Spain*, and
Nephew to the Archbishop of *Toledo*, who had so
wrought himself into the Affections of *Aurelian*, through
45 a Conformity of Temper, an Equality in Years, and
something of resemblance in Feature and Proportion, that
he look'd upon him as his second self. *Hippolito*, on the
other hand, was not ungrateful in return of Friendship, but
thought himself either alone or in ill Company, if *Aurelian*
50 were absent: but his Uncle having sent him to travel, under
the Conduct of a Governour, and the two Years which
limited his stay at *Siena* being expired, he was put in
mind of his departure.

His Friend grew melancholy at the News, but
55 considering that *Hippolito* had never seen *Florence*, he
easily prevailed with him to make his first Journey
thither, whither he would accompany him, and perhaps
prevail with his Father to do the like throughout his
Travels.

60   They accordingly set out, but not being able easily to
reach *Florence* the same Night, they rested a League or two
short, at a *Villa* of the great Duke's called *Poggio Imperiale*,
where they were informed by some of his Highness's
Servants, That the Nuptials of *Donna Catharina* (near
65 Kinswoman to the great Duke) and *Don Ferdinand de
Rovori*, were to be solemnized the next day, and that
extraordinary Preparations had been making for some

time past, to illustrate the Solemnity with Balls and
Masques, and other Divertisements; that a Tilting had
been proclaimed, and to that purpose Scaffolds erected   70
around the Spacious Court, before the Church *Di Santa
Croce*, where were usually seen all Cavalcades and Shews,
performed by Assemblies of the Young Nobility: That all
Mechanicks and Tradesmen were forbidden to work or
expose any Goods to Sale for the space of three days;   75
during which time all Persons should be entertain'd at the
Great Duke's Cost; and publick Provision was to be made
for the setting forth and furnishing a multitude of Tables,
with Entertainment for all Comers and Goers, and several
Houses appointed for that use in all Streets.   80

This Account alarm'd the Spirits of our Young
Travellers, and they were overjoy'd at the prospect of
Pleasures they foresaw. *Aurelian* could not contain the
satisfaction he conceiv'd in the welcome Fortune had
prepar'd for his dear *Hippolito*. In short, they both   85
remembred so much of the pleasing Relation had been
made them, that they forgot to sleep, and were up as soon
as it was light, pounding at poor Signior *Claudio*'s Door (so
was *Hippolito*'s Governour call'd) to rouse him, that no
time might be lost till they were arriv'd at *Florence*, where   90
they would furnish themselves with Disguises and other
Accoutrements necessary for the Prosecution of their
Design of sharing in the publick Merriment; the rather
were they for going so early because *Aurelian* did not
think fit to publish his being in Town for a time, least his   95
Father knowing of it, might give some restraint to that
loose they design'd themselves.

Before Sun rise they entred *Florence* at *Porta Romana*,
attended only by two Servants, the rest being left behind to
avoid notice; but, alas! they needed not to have used half   100
that caution; for early as it was, the Streets were crowded
with all sorts of People passing to and fro, and every Man
employ'd in something relating to the Diversions to come;
so that no notice was taken of any body; a Marquess and his
Train might have pass'd by as unregarded as a single   105
Fachin or Cobler. Not a Window in the Streets but

echoed the tuning of a Lute or thrumming of a Gitarr: for,
by the way, the Inhabitants of *Florence* are strangely
addicted to the love of Musick, insomuch that scarce
their Children can go, before they can scratch some
Instrument or other. It was no unpleasing Spectacle to
our Cavaliers (who, seeing they were not observ'd,
resolv'd to make Observations) to behold the Diversity of
Figures and Postures of many of these Musicians. Here you
should have an affected Vallet, who Mimick'd the
Behaviour of his Master, leaning carelesly against the
Window, with his Head on one side, in a languishing
Posture, whining, in a low, mournful Voice, some dismal
Complaint; while, from his sympathizing *Theorbo*, issued a
Base no less doleful to the Hearers. In Opposition to him
was set up perhaps a Cobler, with the wretched Skeleton of
a Gitarr, battered and waxed together by his own Industry,
and who with three Strings out of Tune, and his own
tearing hoarse Voice, would rack attention from the
Neighbourhood, to the great affliction of many more
moderate Practitioners, who, no doubt, were full as
desirous to be heard. By this time *Aurelian*'s Servant had
taken a Lodging and was returned, to give his Master an
Account of it. The Cavaliers grown weary of that ridiculous
Entertainment, which was diverting at first sight, retired
whither the Lacquey conducted them; who, according to
their Directions, had sought out one of the most obscure
Streets in the City. All that day, to the evening, was spent
in sending from one Brokers Shop to another, to furnish
them with Habits, since they had not time to make any
new.

    There was, it happened, but one to be got Rich enough
to please our young Gentlemen, so many were taken up
upon this occasion. While they were in Dispute and
Complementing one another, (*Aurelian* protesting that
Hippolito should wear it, and he, on 'tother hand,
forswearing it as bitterly) a Servant of *Hippolito*'s came
up and ended the Controversie; telling them, That he had
met below with the *Vallet de Chambre* of a Gentleman, who
was one of the greatest Gallants about the Town, but was at

this time in such a condition he could not possibly be at the
Entertainment; whereupon the Vallet had designed to dress
himself up in his Master's Apparel, and try his talent at
Court; which he hearing, told him he would inform him
how he might bestow the Habit for some time much more 150
to his profit if not to his pleasure, so acquainted him with
the occasion his Master had for it. *Hippolito* sent for the
Fellow up, who was not so fond of his design as not to be
bought off it, but upon having his own demand granted for
the use of it, brought it; it was very Rich, and upon tryal, as 155
fit for *Hippolito* as if it had been made for him. The
Ceremony was performed in the Morning, in the great
Dome, with all magnificence correspondent to the wealth
of the great Duke, and the esteem he had for the Noble
Pair. The next Morning was to be a Tilting, and the same 160
Night a Masquing Ball at Court. To omit the Description
of the universal Joy, (that had diffus'd it self through all the
Conduits of Wine, which convey'd it in large measures to
the People) and only relate those effects of it which concern
our present Adventurers. You must know, that about the 165
fall of the Evening, and at that time when the *æquilibrium* of
Day and Night, for some time, holds the Air in a gloomy
suspence between an unwillingness to leave the light, and a
natural impulse into the Dominion of darkness, about this
time our Hero's, shall I say, sally'd or slunk out of their 170
Lodgings, and steer'd toward the great Palace, whither,
before they were arrived, such a prodigious number of
Torches were on fire, that the day, by help of these
Auxiliary Forces, seem'd to continue its Dominion; the
Owls and Bats apprehending their mistake, in counting 175
the hours, retir'd again to a convenient darkness; for
Madam Night was no more to be seen than she was to be
heard; and the Chymists were of Opinion, That her
fuliginous Damps rarefy'd by the abundance of Flame,
were evaporated. 180

Now the Reader I suppose to be upon Thorns at this and
the like impertinent Digressions, but let him alone and he'll
come to himself; at which time I think fit to acquaint him,
that when I digress, I am at that time writing to please my

185 self, when I continue the Thread of the Story, I write to
please him; supposing him a reasonable Man, I conclude
him satisfied to allow me this liberty, and so I proceed.
   If our Cavaliers were dazled at the splendour they beheld
without doors, what surprize, think you, must they be in,
190 when entering the Palace they found even the lights there
to be but so many foils to the bright eyes that flash'd upon
'em at every turn.
   A more glorious Troop no occasion ever assembled; all
the fair of *Florence*, with the most accomplished Cavaliers,
195 were present; and however Nature had been partial in
bestowing on some better Faces than others, Art was alike
indulgent to all, and industriously supplyed those Defects
she had left, giving some Addition also to her greatest
Excellencies. Every body appear'd well shap'd, as it is to
200 be supposed, none who were conscious to themselves of
any visible Deformity would presume to come thither.
Their Apparel was equally glorious, though each differing
in fancy. In short, our Strangers were so well bred, as to
conclude from these apparent Perfections, that there was
205 not a Masque which did not at least hide the Face of a
Cherubim. Perhaps the Ladies were not behind hand in
return of a favourable Opinion of them: for they were both
well dress'd, and had something inexpressibly pleasing in
their Air and Mien, different from other People, and
210 indeed differing from one another. They fansy'd that
while they stood together they were more particularly
taken notice of than any in the Room, and being
unwilling to be taken for Strangers, which they thought
they were, by reason of some whispering they observed
215 near them, they agreed upon an hour of meeting after the
company should be broke up, and so separately mingled
with the thickest of the Assembly. *Aurelian* had fixed his
eye upon a Lady whom he had observ'd to have been a
considerable time in close whisper with another Woman;
220 he expected with great impatience the result of that private
Conference, that he might have an opportunity of engaging
the Lady whose Person was so agreeable to him. At last he
perceived they were broke off, and the 'tother Lady seem'd

to have taken her leave. He had taken no small pains in the
mean time to put himself in a posture to accost the Lady, 225
which, no doubt, he had happily performed had he not
been interrupted; but scarce had he acquitted himself of a
preliminary bow (and which, I have heard him say, was the
lowest that ever he made) and had just opened his Lips to
deliver himself of a small Complement, which, nevertheless 230
he was very big with, when he unluckily miscarried, by the
interposal of the same Lady, whose departure, not long
before, he had so zealously pray'd for: but, as Providence
would have it, there was only some very small matter
forgot, which was recovered in a short whisper. The 235
Coast being again cleared, he took heart and bore up, and,
striking sail, repeated his Ceremony to the Lady; who,
having obligingly returned it, he accosted her in these or
the like words:

'If I do not usurp a priviledge reserved for some one 240
more happy in your acquaintance, may I presume, Madam,
to entreat (for a while) the favour of your Conversation, at
least till the arrival of whom you expect, provided you are
not tired of me before; for then upon the least intimation of
uneasiness, I will not fail of doing my self the violence to 245
withdraw for your release.' The Lady made him answer,
she did not expect any body; by which he might imagine
her Conversation not of value to be bespoke, and to afford
it him, were but farther to convince him to her own cost.
He reply'd, 'She had already said enough to convince him 250
of something he heartily wished might not be to his cost in
the end.' She pretended not to understand him; but told
him, 'If he already found himself grieved with her
Conversation, he would have sufficient reason to repent
the rashness of his first Demand before they had ended: for 255
that now she intended to hold discourse with him, on
purpose to punish his unadvisedness, in presuming upon
a Person whose dress and mien might not (may be) be
disagreeable to have wit.' 'I must confess (reply'd
Aurelian) my self guilty of a Presumption, and willingly 260
submit to the punishment you intend: and though it be an
aggravation of a Crime to persevere in its justification, yet

I cannot help defending an Opinion in which now I am
more confirm'd, that probable conjectures may be made of
265 the ingenious Disposition of the Mind, from the fancy and
choice of Apparel.' 'The humour I grant ye' (said the Lady)
'or constitution of the Person whether melancholick or
brisk; but I should hardly pass my censure upon so slight
an indication of wit: for there is your brisk fool as well as
270 your brisk man of sense, and so of the melancholick.
I confess 'tis possible a fool may reveal himself by his
Dress, in wearing something extravagantly singular and
ridiculous, or in preposterous suiting of colours; but a
decency of Habit (which is all that Men of best sense
275 pretend to) may be acquired by custom and example,
without putting the Person to a superfluous expence of
wit for the contrivance; and though there should be
occasion for it, few are so unfortunate in their Relations
and Acquaintance not to have some Friend capable of
280 giving them advice, if they are not too ignorantly
conceited to ask it.' *Aurelian* was so pleased with the
easiness and smartness of her Expostulation, that he
forgot to make a reply, when she seem'd to expect it; but
being a Woman of a quick Apprehension, and justly
285 sensible of her own Perfections, she soon perceived he
did not grudge his attention. However she had a mind to
put it upon him to turn the discourse, so went on upon the
same Subject. 'Signior (said she) I have been looking round
me, and by your Maxim I cannot discover one fool in the
290 Company; for they are all well drest.' This was spoken with
an Air of Rallery that awakened the Cavalier, who
immediately made answer: ''Tis true, Madam, we see
there may be as much variety of good fancies as of faces,
yet there may be many of both kinds borrowed and
295 adulterate if inquired into; and as you were pleased to
observe, the invention may be Foreign to the Person who
puts it in practice; and as good an Opinion as I have of an
agreeable Dress, I should be loth to answer for the wit of all
about us.' 'I believe you (says the Lady) and hope you are
300 convinced of your error, since you must allow it impossible
to tell who of all this Assembly did or did not make choice

of their own Apparel.' 'Not all (said *Aurelian*) there is an
ungainness in some which betrays them. Look ye there
(says he) pointing to a Lady who stood playing with the
Tassels of her Girdle, I dare answer for that Lady, though   305
she be very well dress'd, 'tis more than she knows.' His fair
unknown could not forbear laughing at his particular
distinction, and freely told him, he had indeed light upon
one who knew as little as any body in the Room, her self
excepted. 'Ah! Madam, (reply'd *Aurelian*) you know every   310
thing in the World but your own Perfections, and you only
know not those, because 'tis the top of Perfection not to
know them.' 'How? (reply'd the Lady) I thought it had
been the extremity of knowledge to know ones self.'
Aurelian had a little over-strain'd himself in that   315
Complement, and I am of Opinion would have been
puzzl'd to have brought himself off readily: but by good
fortune the Musick came into the Room and gave him an
opportunity to seem to decline an answer, because the
company prepared to dance: he only told her he was too   320
mean a Conquest for her wit who was already a Slave to the
Charms of her Person. She thanked him for his
Complement, and briskly told him she ought to have
made him a return in praise of his wit, but she hoped he
was a Man more happy than to be dissatisfy'd with any of   325
his own Endowments; and if it were so, that he had not a
just Opinion of himself, she knew her self incapable of
saying any thing to beget one. *Aurelian* did not know well
what to make of this last reply; for he always abhor'd
any thing that was conceited, with which this seem'd to   330
reproach him. But however modest he had been heretofore
in his own thoughts, yet never was he so distrustful of his
good behaviour as now, being rally'd so by a Person whom
he took to be of judgment. Yet he resolved to take no
notice, but with an Air unconcerned and full of good   335
humour entreated her to Dance with him: She promised
him to Dance with no body else, nor I believe had she
inclination; for notwithstanding her tartness, she was upon
equal terms with him as to the liking of each others Person
and Humour, and only gave those little hints to try his   340

Temper; there being certainly no greater sign of folly and
ill breeding, than to grow serious and concerned at any
thing spoken in rallery: for his part, he was strangely and
insensibly fallen in love with her Shape, Wit and Air;
345   which, together with a white Hand, he had seen (perhaps
not accidentally) were enough to have subdued a more
stubborn Heart than ever he was master of; and for her
Face, which he had not seen, he bestowed upon her the best
his Imagination could furnish him with. I should by right
350   now describe her Dress, which was extreamly agreeable
and rich, but 'tis possible I might err in some material
Pin or other, in the sticking of which may be the whole
grace of the Drapery depended. Well, they danced several
times together, and no less to the satisfaction of the whole
355   Company, than of themselves; for at the end of each Dance,
some publick note of Applause or other was given to the
graceful Couple.

   Aurelian was amaz'd, that among all that danced or stood
in view he could not see *Hippolito*; but concluding that he
360   had met with some pleasing Conversation, and was
withdrawn to some retired part of the Room, he forbore
his search till the mirth of that Night should be over, and
the Company ready to break up, where we will leave him
for a while, to see what became of his adventurous Friend.
365   *Hippolito*, a little after he had parted with *Aurelian*, was
got among a knot of Ladies and Cavaliers, who were
looking upon a large Gold Cup set with Jewels, in which
his Royal Highness had drank to the Prosperity of the new
married Couple at Dinner, and which afterward he
370   presented to his Cousin *Donna Catharina*. He among the
rest was very intent, admiring the richness, workmanship
and beauty of the Cup, when a Lady came behind him and
pulling him by the Elbow, made a sign she would speak
with him; *Hippolito*, who knew himself an utter Stranger to
375   *Florence* and every body in it, immediately guessed she had
mistaken him for her acquaintance, as indeed it happened;
however he resolved not to discover himself till he should
be assured of it; having followed her into a set Window
remote from Company, she address'd her self to him in this

manner: 'Signior *Don Lorenzo* (said she) I am overjoy'd to   380
see you are so speedily recovered of your Wounds, which
by report were much more dangerous than to have suffered
your coming abroad so soon; but I must accuse you of great
indiscretion, in appearing in a Habit which so many must
needs remember you to have worn upon the like occasion   385
not long ago, I mean at the Marriage of *Don Cynthio* with
your Sister *Atalanta*; I do assure you, you were known by
it, both to *Juliana* and my self, who was so far concerned
for you, as to desire me to tell you, that her Brother *Don
Fabritio* (who saw you when you came in with another   390
Gentleman) had eyed you very narrowly, and is since
gone out of the Room, she knows not upon what design;
however she would have you, for your own sake, be advised
and circumspect when you depart this place, lest you
should be set upon unawares; you know the hatred *Don*   395
Fabritio has born you ever since you had the fortune to kill
his Kinsman in a Duel': Here she paused as if expecting his
reply; but *Hippolito* was so confounded, that he stood mute,
and contemplating the hazard he had ignorantly brought
himself into, forgot his design of informing the Lady of her   400
mistake. She finding he made her no Answer, went on. 'I
perceive (continued she) you are in some surprize at what
I have related, and may be, are doubtful of the Truth; but I
thought you had been better acquainted with your Cousin
Leonora's Voice, than to have forgot it so soon: Yet in   405
Complaisance to your ill Memory, I will put you past
doubt, by shewing you my Face'; with that she pulled off
her Mask, and discovered to *Hippolito* (now more amaz'd
than ever) the most Angelick Face that he had ever beheld.
He was just about to have made her some answer, when,   410
clapping on her Mask again without giving him time, she
happily for him pursu'd her Discourse. (For 'tis odds but
he had made some discovery of himself in the surprize he
was in.) Having taken him familiarly by the Hand, now she
had made her self known to him, 'Cousin *Lorenzo* (added   415
she) you may perhaps have taken it unkindly, that, during
the time of your indisposition, by reason of your Wounds,
I have not been to visit you; I do assure you it was not for

want of any Inclination I had both to see and serve you to
420 my power; but you are well acquainted with the Severity of
my Father, whom you know how lately you have
disobliged. I am mighty glad that I have met with you
here, where I have had an Opportunity to tell you what
so much concerns your Safety, which I am afraid you will
425 not find in *Florence*; considering the great Power *Don
Fabritio* and his Father, the Marquess of *Viterbo*, have in
this City. I have another thing to inform you of, That
whereas *Don Fabio* had interested himself in your Cause,
in Opposition to the Marquess of *Viterbo*, by reason of
430 the long Animosity between them, all hopes of his
Countenance and Assistance are defeated: For there has
been a Proposal of Reconciliation made to both Houses,
and it is said it will be confirm'd (as most such ancient
Quarrels are at last) by the Marriage of *Juliana* the
435 Marquess's Daughter, with *Aurelian*, Son to *Don Fabio*:
to which effect the old Gentleman sent 'tother Day to
Siena, where *Aurelian* has been Educated, to hasten his
coming to Town; but the Messenger returning this
Morning, brought word, That the same day he arriv'd at
440 *Siena*, *Aurelian* had set out for *Florence*, in Company with a
young *Spanish* Nobleman, his intimate Friend, so it is
believ'd, they are both in Town, and not unlikely in this
Room in Masquerade.'

Hippolito could not forbear smiling to himself, at these
445 last words. For ever since the naming of *Don Fabio* he had
been very attentive; but before, his Thoughts were wholly
taken up with the Beauty of the Face he had seen, and from
the time she had taken him by the Hand, a successive
warmth and chillness had play'd about his Heart, and
450 surpriz'd him with an unusual Transport. He was in a
hundred Minds, whether he should make her sensible of
her Error or no; but considering he could expect no farther
Conference with her after he should discover himself, and
that as yet he knew not of her place of abode, he resolv'd to
455 humour the mistake a little further. Having her still by the
Hand, which he squeez'd somewhat more eagerly than is
usual for Cousins to do, in a low and undistinguishable

Voice, he let her know how much he held himself obliged
to her, and avoiding as many words as handsomely he
could, at the same time, entreated her to give him her   460
Advice, toward the management of himself in this Affair.
Leonora, who never from the beginning had entertain'd the
least Scruple of distrust, imagined he spoke faintly, as not
being yet perfectly recovered in his strength; and withal
considering that the heat of the Room, by reason of the   465
Crowd, might be uneasie to a Person in his Condition; she
kindly told him, That if he were as inclinable to dispense
with the remainder of that Nights Diversion as she was,
and had no other engagement upon him, by her consent
they should both steal out of the Assembly, and go to her   470
House, where they might with more freedom discourse
about a business of that importance, and where he might
take something to refresh himself if he were (as she
conceiv'd him to be) indisposed with his long standing.
Judge you whether the Proposal were acceptable to   475
Hippolito or no; he had been ruminating with himself how
to bring something like this about, and had almost
despair'd of it; when of a suddain he found the success of
his design had prevented his own endeavours. He told his
Cousin in the same key as before, That he was unwilling to   480
be the occasion of her Divorce from so much good
Company; but for his own part, he was afraid he had
presumed too much upon his recovery in coming abroad
so soon, and that he found himself so unwell, he feared he
should be quickly forc'd to retire. *Leonora* stay'd not to   485
make him any other reply, only tipp'd him upon the Arm,
and bid him follow her at a convenient distance to avoid
Observation.

Whoever had seen the Joy that was in *Hippolito*'s
Countenance, and the Sprightliness with which he   490
follow'd his Beautiful Conductress, would scarce have
taken him for a Person griev'd with uncured Wounds.
She led him down a back pair of Stairs, into one of the
Palace Gardens which had a Door opening into the Piazza,
not far from where *Don Mario* her Father lived. They had   495
little Discourse by the way, which gave *Hippolito* time to

consider of the best way of discovering himself. A thousand
things came into his Head in a minute, yet nothing that
pleased him: and after so many Contrivances as he had
500 formed for the discovery of himself, he found it more
rational for him not to reveal himself at all that Night,
since he could not foresee what effect the surprize would
have, she must needs be in, at the appearance of a Stranger,
whom she had never seen before, yet whom she had treated
505 so familiarly. He knew Women were apt to shriek or swoon
upon such Occasions, and should she happen to do either,
he might be at a loss how to bring himself off. He thought
he might easily pretend to be indisposed somewhat more
than ordinary, and so make an excuse to go to his own
510 Lodging. It came into his Head too, that under pretence of
giving her an account of his Health, he might enquire of her
the means how a Letter might be convey'd to her the next
morning, wherein he might inform her gently of her
mistake, and insinuate something of that Passion he had
515 conceiv'd, which he was sure he could not have
opportunity to speak of if he bluntly revealed himself. He
had just resolv'd upon this Method, as they were come to
the great Gates of the Court, when *Leonora* stopping to let
him go in before her, he of a suddain fetch'd his Breath
520 violently as if some stitch or twinging smart had just then
assaulted him. She enquired the matter of him, and advised
him to make haste into the House that he might sit down
and rest him. He told her he found himself so ill, that he
judged it more convenient for him to go home while he was
525 in a condition to move, for he fear'd if he should once settle
himself to rest he might not be able to stir. She was much
troubled, and would have had a Chair made ready and
Servants to carry him home; but he made answer, he
would not have any of her Fathers Servants know of his
530 being abroad, and that just now he had an interval of ease,
which he hop'd would continue till he made a shift to reach
his own Lodgings. Yet if she pleased to inform him how he
might give an account of himself the next morning, in a line
or two, he would not fail to give her the thanks due to her
535 great kindness; and withal, would let her know something

which would not a little surprize her, though now he had
not time to acquaint her with it. She show'd him a little
Window at the corner of the House, where one should wait
to receive his Letter, and was just taking her leave of him,
when seeing him search hastily in his Pocket, she ask'd him   540
if he miss'd any thing; he told her he thought a Wound
which was not throughly heal'd bled a little, and that he
had lost his Handkerchief. His design took; for she
immediately gave him hers: which indeed accordingly he
apply'd to the only Wound he was then griev'd with; which   545
though it went quite through his Heart, yet thank God was
not Mortal. He was not a little rejoyc'd at his good Fortune
in getting so early a Favour from his Mistress, and
notwithstanding the violence he did himself to personate
a sick Man, he could not forbear giving some Symptoms of   550
an extraordinary content; and telling her that he did not
doubt to receive a considerable Proportion of ease from the
Application of what had so often kiss'd her fair Hand.
Leonora who did not suspect the Compliment, told him
she should be heartily glad if that or any thing in her power   555
might contribute to his recovery; and wishing him well
home, went into her House, as much troubled for her
Cousin as he was joyful for his Mistress.

Hippolito as soon as she was gone in, began to make his
Remarks about the House, walking round the great Court,   560
viewing the Gardens and all the Passages leading to that
side of the Piazza. Having sufficiently informed himself,
with a Heart full of Love, and a Head full of Stratagem, he
walked toward his Lodging, impatient till the arrival of
Aurelian that he might give himself vent. In which   565
interim, let me take the liberty to digress a little, and tell
the Reader something which I do not doubt he has
apprehended himself long ago, if he be not the dullest
Reader in the World; yet only for orders sake, let me tell
him I say, That a young Gentleman (Cousin to the   570
aforesaid *Don Fabritio*) happened one night to have some
words at a Gameing House with one *Lorenzo*, which
created a Quarrel of fatal Consequence to the former,

who was killed upon the Spot, and likely to be so to the
latter, who was very desperately wounded.

Fabritio being much concerned for his Kinsman, vow'd
revenge (according to the ancient and laudable custom of
Italy) upon *Lorenzo* if he surviv'd, or in case of his death (if
it should happen to anticipate that, much more swinging
Death which he had in store for him) upon his next of Kin,
and so to descend Lineally like an *English* Estate, to all the
Heirs Males of his Family. This same *Fabritio* had indeed
(as *Leonora* told *Hippolito*) taken particular notice of him
from his first entrance into the Room, and was so far
doubtful as to go out immediately himself, and make
enquiry concerning *Lorenzo*, but was quickly inform'd of
the greatness of his Error, in believing a Man to be abroad,
who was so ill of his Wounds, that they now despair'd of his
recovery; and thereupon return'd to the Ball very well
satisfied, but not before *Leonora* and *Hippolito* were
departed.

So, Reader, having now discharg'd my Conscience of a
small Discovery which I thought my self obliged to make to
thee, I proceed to tell thee, that our Friend *Aurelian* had by
this time danced himself into a Net which he neither could,
nor which is worse desired to untangle.

His Soul was charm'd to the movement of her Body: an
Air so graceful, so sweet, so easie and so great, he had never
seen. She had something of Majesty in her, which appear'd
to be born with her; and though it struck an awe into the
Beholders, yet was it sweetned with a familiarity of
Behaviour, which rendred it agreeable to every Body.
The grandeur of her Mien was not stiff, but unstudied
and unforced, mixed with a simplicity; free, yet not loose
nor affected. If the former seem'd to condescend, the latter
seem'd to aspire; and both to unite in the centre of
Perfection. Every turn she gave in dancing snatcht
Aurelian into a Rapture, and he had like to have been out
two or three times with following his Eyes, which she led
about as Slaves to her Heels.

As soon as they had done dancing, he began to complain
of his want of Breath and Lungs, to speak sufficiently in her

Commendation; She smilingly told him, he did ill to dance so much then: Yet in Consideration of the pains he had taken more than ordinary upon her account, she would bate him a great deal of Complement, but with this Proviso, That he was to discover to her who he was. *Aurelian* was unwilling for the present to own himself to be really the Man he was; when a suddain thought came into his Head to take upon him the Name and Character of *Hippolito*, who he was sure was not known in *Florence*. He thereupon, after a little pause, pretended to recal himself in this manner: 'Madam, it is no small demonstration of the entire Resignation which I have made of my Heart to your Chains, since the secrets of it are no longer in my power. I confess I only took *Florence* in my way, not designing any longer Residence, than should be requisite to inform the Curiosity of a Traveller, of the rareties of the Place. Whether Happiness or Misery will be the Consequence of that Curiosity, I am yet in fear, and submit to your Determination; but sure I am, not to depart *Florence* till you have made me the most miserable Man in it, and refuse me the fatal Kindness of Dying at your Feet. I am by Birth a *Spaniard*, of the City of *Toledo*; my name *Hippolito di Saviolina*: I was yesterday a Man free, as Nature made the first; to day I am fallen into a Captivity, which must continue with my Life, and which, it is in your power, to make much dearer to me. Thus in obedience to your Commands, and contrary to my Resolution of remaining unknown in this place, I have inform'd you, Madam, what I am; what I shall be, I desire to know from you; at least, I hope, the free discovery I have made of my self, will encourage you to trust me with the knowledge of your Person.'

Here a low bow, and a deep sigh, put an end to his Discourse, and signified his Expectation of her Reply, which was to this purpose—(But I had forgot to tell you, That *Aurelian* kept off his Mask from the time that he told her he was of *Spain*, till the period of his Relation.) 'Had I thought (said she) that my Curiosity would have brought me in debt, I should certainly have forborn it; or at least

have agreed with you before hand about the rate of your
discovery, then I had not brought my self to the
Inconveniency of being censur'd, either of too much
655   easiness or reservedness; but to avoid, as much as I can,
the extreamity of either, I am resolv'd but to discover my
self in part, and will endeavour to give you as little occasion
as I can, either to boast of, or ridicule the Behaviour of the
Women of *Florence* in your Travels.'
660   *Aurelian* interrupted her, and swore very solemnly (and
the more heartily, I believe, because he then indeed spoke
truth) that he would make *Florence* the place of his abode,
whatever concerns he had elsewhere. She advised him to be
cautious how he swore to his Expressions of Gallantry; and
665   farther told him she now hoped she should make him a
return to all the Fine Things he had said, since she gave
him his choice whether he would know whom she was, or
see her Face.
          Aurelian who was really in Love, and in whom
670   Consideration would have been a Crime, greedily
embrac'd the latter, since she assured him at that time he
should not know both. Well, what follow'd? Why, she
pull'd off her Mask, and appear'd to him at once in the
Glory of Beauty. But who can tell the astonishment
675   *Aurelian* felt? He was for a time senseless; Admiration
had suppress'd his Speech, and his Eyes were entangled
in Light. In short, to be made sensible of his condition, we
must conceive some Idea of what he beheld, which is not to
be imagined till seen, nor then to be express'd. Now see the
680   impertinence and conceitedness of an Author, who will
have a fling at a Description, which he has Prefaced with
an impossibility. One might have seen something in her
Composition resembling the Formation of *Epicurus* his
World, as if every Atome of Beauty had concurr'd to
685   unite an excellency. Had that curious Painter lived in her
days, he might have avoided his painful search, when he
collected from the choicest pieces the most choice Features,
and by a due Disposition and Judicious Symmetry of those
exquisite parts, made one whole and perfect *Venus*. Nature
690   seem'd here to have play'd the Plagiary, and to have

molded into Substance the most refined Thoughts of
inspired Poets. Her Eyes diffus'd Rays comfortable as
warmth, and piercing as the light; they would have
worked a passage through the straightest Pores, and with
a delicious heat, have play'd about the most obdurate   695
frozen Heart, untill 'twere melted down to Love. Such
Majesty and Affability were in her Looks; so alluring, yet
commanding was her Presence, that it mingled awe with
love; kindling a Flame which trembled to aspire. She had
danced much, which, together with her being close   700
masked, gave her a tincture of Carnation more than
ordinary. But *Aurelian* (from whom I had every tittle of
her Description) fancy'd he saw a little Nest of Cupids
break from the Tresses of her Hair, and every one
officiously betake himself to his task. Some fann'd with   705
their downy Wings, her glowing Cheeks; while others
brush'd the balmy Dew from off her Face, leaving alone a
heavenly Moisture blubbing on her Lips, on which they
drank and revell'd for their pains; Nay, so particular were
their allotments in her service, that *Aurelian* was very   710
positive a young Cupid who was but just Pen-feather'd,
employ'd his naked Quills to pick her Teeth. And a
thousand other things his transport represented to him,
which none but Lovers who have experience of such
Visions will believe.   715
     As soon as he awaked and found his Speech come to him,
he employ'd it to this effect:
     ''Tis enough that I have seen a Divinity—Nothing but
Mercy can inhabit these Perfections—Their utmost rigour
brings a Death preferable to any Life, but what they give— 720
Use me, Madam, as you please; for by your fair self, I
cannot think a Bliss beyond what now I feel—You
Wound with Pleasure, and if you Kill it must be with
Transport—Ah! Yet methinks to live—O Heaven! to
have Life pronounced by those Bless'd Lips—Did they   725
not inspire where they command, it were an immediate
Death of Joy.'
     Aurelian was growing a little too loud with his
Admiration, had she not just then interrupted him, by

730 clapping on her Masque, and telling him they should be observed, if he proceeded in his Extravagance; and withal, that his Passion was too suddain to be real, and too violent to be lasting. He replied, Indeed it might not be very lasting, (with a submissive mournful Voice) but it would 735 continue during his Life. That it was suddain, he denied, for she had raised it by degrees from his first sight of her, by a continued discovery of Charms in her Mien and Conversation, till she thought fit to set Fire to the Train she had laid, by the Lightning of her Face; and then he 740 could not help it, if he were blown up.

He begg'd her to believe the Sincerity of his Passion, at least to enjoin him something, which might tend to the Convincing of her Incredulity. She said, she should find a time to make some Trials of him; but for the first, she 745 charged him not to follow or observe her, after the Dissolution of the Assembly. He promised to obey, and entreated her to tell him but her Name, that he might have Recourse to that in his Affliction for her Absence, if he were able to survive it. She desired him to live by all means; 750 and if he must have a Name to play with, to call her *Incognita*, till he were better informed.

The Company breaking up, she took her leave, and at his earnest Entreaty, gave him a short Vision of her Face; which, then dress'd in an obliging smile, caused another 755 fit of Transport, which lasted till she was gone out of Sight. *Aurelian* gathered up his Spirits, and walked slowly towards his Lodging, never remembring that he had lost *Hippolito*, till upon turning the Corner of a Street, he heard a noise of Fighting; and coming near, saw a Man make a 760 vigorous Defence against two, who pressed violently upon him. He then thought of *Hippolito*, and fancying he saw the glimmering of Diamond Buttons, such as *Hippolito* had upon the Sleeves of his Habit, immediately drew to his Assistance; and with that Eagerness and Resolution, that 765 the Assailants, finding their unmanly odds defeated, took to their Heels. The Person rescued by the Generous Help of *Aurelian*, came toward him; but as he would have stoop'd to have saluted him, dropp'd, fainting at his feet. *Aurelian*,

now he was so near him, perceiv'd plainly *Hippolito*'s
Habit, and step'd hastily to take him up. Just as some of 770
the Guards (who were going the Rounds, apprehensive of
such Disorders in an Universal Merriment) came up to him
with Lights, and had taken Prisoners the Two Men, whom
they met with their Swords drawn; when looking in the
Face of the Wounded Man, he found it was not *Hippolito*, 775
but his Governour *Claudio*, in the Habit he had worn at the
Ball. He was extreamly surpriz'd, as were the Prisoners,
who confess'd their Design to have been upon *Lorenzo*;
grounding their Mistake upon the Habit which was known
to have been his. They were Two Men who formerly had 780
been Servants to him, whom *Lorenzo* had unfortunately
slain.

They made a shift to bring *Claudio* to himself; and part
of the Guard carrying off the Prisoners, whom *Aurelian*
desired they would secure, the rest accompanied him 785
bearing *Claudio* in their Arms to his Lodging. He had not
patience to forbear asking for *Hippolito* by the Way; whom
Claudio assured him, he had left safe in his Chamber, above
Two Hours since. That his coming Home so long before
the Divertisements were ended, and Undressing himself, 790
had given him the Unhappy Curiosity, to put on his Habit,
and go to the Pallace; in his Return from whence, he was set
upon in the Manner he found him, which if he recovered,
he must own his Life indebted to his timely Assistance.

Being come to the House, they carried him to his Bed, 795
and having sent for Surgeons *Aurelian* rewarded and
dismissed the Guard. He stay'd the dressing of *Claudio*'s
Wounds, which were many, though they hop'd none
Mortal: and leaving him to his Rest, went to give
Hippolito an Account of what had happened, whom he 800
found with a Table before him, leaning upon both his
Elbows, his Face covered with his Hands, and so
motionless, that *Aurelian* concluded he was asleep; seeing
several Papers lie before him, half written and blotted out
again, he thought to steal softly to the Table, and discover 805
what he had been employed about. Just as he reach'd forth
his Hand to take up one of the Papers, *Hippolito* started up

so on the suddain, as surpriz'd *Aurelian* and made him leap
back; *Hippolito*, on the other hand, not supposing that any
810 Body had been near him, was so disordered with the
Appearance of a Man at his Elbow, (whom his
Amazement did not permit him to distinguish) that he
leap'd hastily to his Sword, and in turning him about,
overthrew the Stand and Candles. Here were they both
815 left in the Dark, *Hippolito* groping about with his Sword,
and thrusting at every Chair that he felt oppose him.
Aurelian was scarce come to himself, when thinking to
step back toward the Door that he might inform his
Friend of his Mistake, without exposing himself to his
820 blind Fury; *Hippolito* heard him stir, and made a full
thrust with such Violence, that the Hilt of the Sword
meeting with *Aurelian*'s Breast beat him down, and
Hippolito a top of him, as a Servant alarm'd with the
noise, came into the Chamber with a Light. The Fellow
825 trembled, and thought they were both Dead, till *Hippolito*
raising himself, to see whom he had got under him,
swoon'd away upon the discovery of his Friend. But such
was the extraordinary Care of Providence in directing the
Sword, that it only past under his Arm, giving no Wound
830 to *Aurelian*, but a little Bruise between his Shoulder and
Breast with the Hilt. He got up, scarce recovered of his
Fright, and by the help of the Servant laid *Hippolito* upon
the Bed; who when he was come to himself could hardly be
perswaded, that his Friend was before him and alive, till he
835 shew'd him his Breast, where was nothing of a Wound.
Hippolito begg'd his Pardon a Thousand Times, and curs'd
himself as often, who was so near to committing the most
Execrable Act of Amicide.

They dismiss'd the Fellow, and with many Embraces,
840 congratulated their fortunate Delivery from the Mischief
which came so near them, each blaming himself as the
Occasion: *Aurelian* accusing his own unadvisedness in
stealing upon *Hippolito*; *Hippolito* blaming his own
temerity and weakness, in being so easily frighted to
845 Disorder; and last of all, his blindness, in not knowing his
dearest Friend. But there he gave a Sigh, and passionately

taking *Aurelian* by the Hand, cry'd, Ah! my Friend, Love is
indeed blind, when it would not suffer me to see you—
There arose another Sigh; a Sympathy seiz'd *Aurelian*
immediately: (For, by the Way, sighing is as catching   850
among Lovers, as yawning among the Vulgar.) Beside
hearing the Name of Love, made him fetch such a Sigh,
that *Hippolito*'s were but Fly-blows in Comparison, that
was answered with all the Might *Hippolito* had, *Aurelian*
ply'd him close till they were both out of Breath.   855

   Thus not a Word pass'd, though each wondred why the
t'other sigh'd, at last concluded it to be only Complaisance
to one another.

Aurelian broke the Silence, by telling him the
Misfortune of his Governour. *Hippolito* rejoic'd as at the   860
luckiest Accident which could have befall'n him. *Aurelian*
wondred at his unseasonable Mirth, and demanded the
Cause of it; he answer'd, It would necessitate his longer
Stay in *Florence*, and for ought he knew be the Means of
bringing a happy Period to his Amour.   865

   His Friend thought him to be little better than a Mad-
man, when he perceiv'd him of a suddain snatch out of his
Bosom a Handkerchief, which having kiss'd with a great
deal of Ardour, he took *Aurelian* by the Hand, and smiling
at the Surprize he saw him in;   870

   'Your *Florentine* Cupid is certainly' (said he) 'the most
Expert in the World. I have since I saw you beheld the most
Beautiful of Women. I am faln desperately in Love with
her, and those Papers which you see so blotted and
scattered, are but so many Essays which I have made to   875
the Declaration of my Passion. And this Handkerchief
which I so zealously Caress, is the Inestimable Token
which I have to make my self known to her. O *Leonora!*
(continued he) 'how hast thou stamp'd thine Image on my
Soul! How much dearer am I to my self, since I have had   880
thy Heavenly Form in keeping! Now, my *Aurelian*, I am
worthy thee; my exalted Love has Dignified me, and rais'd
me far above thy poor former Despicable *Hippolito*.'

Aurelian seeing the Rapture he was in, thought it in vain
to expect a settled Relation of the Adventure, so was   885

reaching to the Table for some of the Papers, but *Hippolito*
told him, If he would have a little patience he would
acquaint him with the whole Matter; and thereupon told
him Word for Word how he was mistaken for *Lorenzo*, and
890   his Management of himself. *Aurelian* commended his
Prudence, in not discovering himself; and told him, If he
could spare so much time from the Contemplation of his
Mistress, he would inform him of an Adventure, though
not so Accidental, yet of as great Concern to his own future
895   Happiness. So related all that had happened to him with his
Beautiful *Incognita*.

    Having ended the Story, they began to consider of the
Means they were to use toward a Review of their
Mistresses. *Aurelian* was Confounded at the Difficulty he
900   conceived on his Part. He understood from *Hippolito*'s
Adventure, that his Father knew of his being in Town,
whom he must unavoidably Disoblige if he yet concealed
himself, and Disobey if he came into his Sight; for he
had already entertain'd an Aversion for *Juliana*, in
905   apprehension of her being Imposed on him. His *Incognita*
was rooted in his Heart, yet could he not Comfort himself
with any Hopes when he should see her: He knew not
where she lived, and she had made him no Promise of a
second Conference. Then did he repent his inconsiderate
910   Choice, in preferring the momentary Vision of her Face, to
a certain Intelligence of her Person. Every thought that
succeeded distracted him, and all the Hopes he could
presume upon, were within compass of the Two Days
Merriment yet to come; for which Space he hop'd he
915   might excuse his remaining conceal'd to his Father.

    Hippolito on the other side (though *Aurelian* thought him
in a much better Way) was no less afflicted for himself. The
Difficulties which he saw in his Friend's Circumstances,
put him upon finding out a great many more in his own,
920   than really there were. But what terrified him most of
all, was his being an utter Stranger to *Leonora*; she had
not the least knowledge of him but through mistake,
and consequently could form no Idea of him to his
Advantage. He look'd upon it as an unlucky thought

in *Aurelian* to take upon him his Name, since possibly   925
the Two Ladies were acquainted, and should they
communicate to each other their Adventures, they might
both reasonably suffer in their Opinions, and be thought
guilty of Falshood, since it would appear to them as One
Person pretending to Two. *Aurelian* told him, there was   930
but one Remedy for that, which was for *Hippolito*, in the
same Manner that he had done, to make use of his Name,
when he writ to *Leonora*, and use what Arguments he could
to perswade her to Secrecy, least his Father should know of
the Reason which kept him concealed in Town. And it was   935
likely, though perhaps she might not immediately entertain
his Passion; yet she would out of Generosity conceal, what
was hidden only for her sake.

Well this was concluded on, after a great many other
Reasons used on either Side, in favour of the Contrivance;   940
they at last argued themselves into a Belief, that Fortune
had befriended them with a better Plot, than their regular
Thinking could have contriv'd. So soon had they convinc'd
themselves, in what they were willing to believe.

Aurelian laid himself down to rest, that is, upon the Bed;   945
for he was a better Lover than to pretend to sleep that
Night, while *Hippolito* set himself again to frame his Letter
design'd for *Leonora*. He writ several, at last pitched upon
one, and very probably the worst, as you may guess when
you read it in its proper Place.   950

It was break of Day when the Servant, who had
been employed all the foregoing Day in procuring
Accoutrements for the Two Cavaliers, to appear in at the
Tilting, came into the Room, and told them all the Young
Gentlemen in the Town were trying their Equipage, and   955
preparing to be early in the Lists. They made themselves
ready with all Expedition at the Alarm. And *Hippolito*
having made a Visit to his Governour, dispatch'd a
Messenger with the Letter and Directions to *Leonora*. At
the Signal agreed upon the Casement was opened and a   960
String let down, to which the Bearer having fastned the
Letter, saw it drawn up, and returned. It were a vain
attempt to describe *Leonora*'s Surprize, when she read the

Superscription—*The Unfortunate* Aurelian, *to the Beautiful*
965 Leonora—After she was a little recovered from her Amaze,
she recollected to her self all the Passages between her and
her supposed Cousin, and immediately concluded him to
be *Aurelian.* Then several little Circumstances which she
thought might have been sufficient to have convinced her,
970 represented themselves to her; and she was in a strange
Uneasiness to think of her free Carriage to a Stranger.

   She was once in a Mind to have burn'd the Letter, or to
have stay'd for an Opportunity to send it again. But she was
a Woman, and her Curiosity opposed it self to all thoughts
975 of that Nature: at length with a firm Resolution, she opened
it, and found Word for Word, what is under-written.

The Letter.

MADAM,

   *I*F *your fair Eyes, upon the breaking up of this, meet with*
980 *somewhat too quick a Surprize, make thence, I beseech you,*
some reflection upon the Condition I must needs have been in, at
the suddain Appearance of that Sun of Beauty, which at once
shone so full upon my Soul. I could not immediately disengage
my self from that Maze of Charms, to let you know how
985 *unworthy a Captive your Eyes had made through mistake.*
Sure, Madam, you cannot but remember my Disorder, of
which your Innocent (Innocent, though perhaps to me Fatal)
Error made a Charitable (but wide) Construction. Your
Tongue pursued the Victory of your Eyes, and you did not
990 *give me time to rally my poor Disordered Senses, so as to make*
a tolerable Retreat. Pardon, Madam, the Continuation of the
Deceipt, and call it not so, that I appear'd to be other than my
self; for Heaven knows I was not then my self, nor am I now
my own. You told me something that concern'd me nearly, as to
995 *a Marriage my Father design'd me, and much more nearly in*
being told by you. For Heaven's sake, disclose not to any Body
your Knowledge of me, that I may not be forced to an

immediate Act of Disobedience; for if my future Services and
inviolate Love, cannot recommend me to your Favour, I shall
find more comfort in the cold Embraces of a Grave, than in the 1000
Arms of the never so much admired (but by me dreaded)
Juliana. *Think, Madam, of those severe Circumstances I lie*
under; and withal I beg you, think it is in your Power, and only
in your Power, to make them happy as my Wishes, or much
more miserable than I am able to imagine. That dear, 1005
inestimable (though undesign'd) Favour which I receiv'd
from you, shall this Day distinguish me from the Crowd of
your Admirers; that which I really applied to my inward
bleeding Wound, the welcom Wound which you have made,
and which, unless from you, does wish no Cure; then pardon 1010
and have pity on, O Adored Leonora, *him, who is your's by*
Creation as he is Heaven's, though never so unworthy. Have
pity on

Your
Aurelian. 1015

She read the Letter over and over, then flung it by, then
read it again; the Novelty of the Adventure made her repeat
her Curiosity, and take more than ordinary Pains to
understand it. At last her Familiarity with the Expressions
grew to an Intimacy, and what she at first permitted she now 1020
began to like. She thought there was something in it a little
more serious, than to be barely Gallantry. She wondred at
her own Blindness, and fancy'd she could remember
something of a more becoming Air in the Stranger than
was usual to *Lorenzo.* This thought was parent to another 1025
of the same kind, till a long Chain successively had Birth,
and every one somewhat more than other, in Favour of the
supposed *Aurelian.* She reflected upon his Discretion, in
deferring the Discovery of himself, till a little time had, as
it were, weaned her from her perswasion, and by removing 1030
her farther from her Mistake, had prepared her for a full and
determinate Convincement. She thought his Behaviour, in
personating a Sick Man so readily, upon the first hint was

not amiss, and smil'd to think of his Excuse to procure her
Handkerchief; and last of all, his sifting out the Means to
write to her, which he had done with that Modesty and
Respect, she could not tell how to find fault with it.

She had proceeded thus far in a maze of Thought, when
she started to find her self so lost to her Reason, and would
have trod back again that path of deluding Fancy; accusing
her self of Fondness, and inconsiderate Easiness, in giving
Credit to the Letter of a Person whose Face she never saw,
and whose first Acquaintance with her was a Treachery,
and he who could so readily deliver his Tongue of a Lye
upon a Surprize, was scarce to be trusted when he had
sufficient Time allow'd him to beget a Fiction, and Means
to perfect the Birth.

How did she know this to be *Aurelian*, if he were? Nay
farther, put it to the Extremity, What if she should upon
farther Conversation with him proceed to Love him? What
Hopes were there for her? Or how could she consent to
Marry a Man already Destined for another Woman? nay, a
Woman that was her Friend, whose Marrying with him was
to compleat the happy Reconciliation of Two Noble
Families, and which might prevent the Effusion of much
Blood likely to be shed in that Quarrel: Besides, she should
incurr share of the Guilt, which he would draw upon him
by Disobedience to his Father, whom she was sure would
not be consenting to it.

'Tis strange now, but all Accounts agree, that just here
Leonora, who had run like a violent Stream against *Aurelian*
hitherto, now retorted with as much precipitation in his
Favour. I could never get any Body to give me a satisfactory
Reason, for her suddain and dextrous Change of Opinion
just at that stop, which made me conclude she could not
help it; and that Nature boil'd over in her at that time when
it had so fair an Opportunity to show it self: For *Leonora* it
seems was a Woman Beautiful, and otherwise of an
excellent Disposition; but in the Bottom a very Woman.
This last Objection, this Opportunity of perswading
Man to Disobedience, determined the Matter in Favour
of *Aurelian*, more than all his Excellencies and

Qualifications, take him as *Aurelian*, or *Hippolito*, or both together.

Well, the Spirit of Contradiction and of *Eve* was strong 1075 in her; and she was in a fair Way to Love *Aurelian*, for she lik'd him already; that it was *Aurelian* she no longer doubted, for had it been a Villain, who had only taken his Name upon him for any ill Designs, he would never have slip'd so favourable an Opportunity as when they were 1080 alone, and in the Night coming through the Garden and broad Space before the Piazza. In short, thus much she resolv'd, at least to conceal the Knowledge she had of him, as he had entreated her in his Letter, and to make particular Remarks of his Behaviour that Day in the Lists, which 1085 should it happen to Charm her with an absolute liking of his Person, she resolv'd to dress her self to the best Advantage, and mustering up all her Graces, out of pure Revenge to kill him down right.

I would not have the Reader now be impertinent, and 1090 look upon this to be force, or a whim of the Author's, that a Woman should proceed so far in her Approbation of a Man whom she never saw, that it is impossible, therefore ridiculous to suppose it. Let me tell such a Critick, that he knows nothing of the Sex, if he does not know that a 1095 Woman may be taken with the Character and Description of a Man, when general and extraordinary, that she may be prepossess'd with an agreeable Idea of his Person and Conversation; and though she cannot imagine his real Features, or manner of Wit, yet she has a general Notion 1100 of what is call'd a fine Gentleman, and is prepar'd to like such a one who does not disagree with that Character. *Aurelian*, as he bore a very fair Character, so was he extreamly deserving to make it good, which otherways might have been to his prejudice; for oftentimes, through 1105 an imprudent Indulgence to our Friends merit, we give so large a Description of his excellencies, that People make more room in their Expectation, than the Intrinsick worth of the Man will fill, which renders him so much the more despicable as there is emptyness to spare. 'Tis certain, 1110 though the Women seldom find that out; for though they do not see so much in a Man as was promised, yet they will be so kind to imagine he has some hidden excellencies which time may discover to them, so are content to allow him a considerable share of their esteem, and take him into Favour upon Tick. *Aurelian* as he had good Credit, so he had a good Stock to support it, and his Person was a good promising Security for the payment of any Obligation he could lie under to the Fair Sex. *Hippolito*, who at this time was our *Aurelian*, did not at all lessen him in appearing for him: So that although *Leonora* was indeed mistaken, she could not be said to be much in the wrong. I could find in my Heart to beg the Reader's pardon for this Digression, if I thought he would be sensible of the Civility; for I promise him, I do not intend to do it again throughout the Story, though I make never so many, and though he take them never so ill. But because I began this upon a bare Supposition of his Impertinence, which might be somewhat impertinent in me to suppose, I do, and hope to make him amends by telling him, that by the time *Leonora* was dress'd, several Ladies of her acquaintance came to accompany her to the place designed for the Tilting, where we will leave them drinking Chocholate till 'tis time for them to go.

Our Cavaliers had by good Fortune provided themselves of two curious Suits of light Armour, finely enammelled and gilt. *Hippolito* had sent to *Poggio Imperiale* for a couple of fine led Horses which he had left there with the rest of his Train at his entrance into *Florence*. Mounted on these and every way well Equipt, they took their way, attended only by two Lacqueys, toward the Church *di Santa Croce*, before which they were to perform their Exercises of Chivalry. *Hippolito* wore upon his Helm a large Plume of Crimson Feathers, in the midst of which was artificially placed *Leonora*'s Handkerchief. His Armour was gilt, and enammell'd with Green and Crimson. *Aurelian* was not so happy as to wear any token to recommend him to the notice of his Mistress, so had only a Plume of Sky-colour and White Feathers, suitable to his Armour, which was Silver enammelled with Azure. I shall not describe the Habits of

any other Cavaliers, or of the Ladies; let it suffice to tell the
Reader they were all very Fine and very Glorious, and let
him dress them in what is most agreeable to his own Fancy.

Our Gallants entred the Lists, and having made their
Obeysance to his Highness, turned round to salute and   1155
view the Company. The Scaffold was circular, so that
there was no end of the Delightful Prospect. It seem'd a
Glory of Beauty which shone around the admiring
Beholders. Our Lovers soon perceived the Stars which
were to Rule their Destiny, which sparkled a lustre   1160
beyond all the inferiour Constellations, and seem'd like
two Suns to distribute Light to all the Planets in that
Heavenly Sphere. *Leonora* knew her Slave by his Badge
and blushed till the Lilies and Roses in her Cheeks had
resemblance to the Plume of Crimson and White   1165
Handkerchief in *Hippolito*'s Crest. He made her a low
bow, and reined his Horse back with an extraordinary
Grace, into a respectful retreat. *Aurelian* saw his Angel,
his beautiful *Incognita*, and had no other way to make
himself known to her, but by saluting and bowing to her   1170
after the *Spanish* mode; she guess'd him by it to be her new
Servant *Hippolito*, and signified her apprehension, by
making him a more particular and obliging return, than
to any of the Cavaliers who had saluted her before.

The Exercise that was to be perform'd was in general a   1175
running at the Ring; and afterwards two Cavaliers
undertook to defend the Beauty of *Donna Catharina*,
against all who would not allow her preheminence of their
Mistresses. This thing was only designed for show and
form, none presuming that any body would put so great   1180
an affront upon the Bride and Duke's Kinswoman, as to
dispute her pretentions to the first place in the Court of
Venus. But here our Cavaliers were under a mistake; for
seeing a large Shield carry'd before two Knights, with a
Lady painted upon it, not knowing who, but reading the   1185
Inscription which was (in large Gold Letters) *Above the
Insolence of Competition*, they thought themselves obliged,
especially in the presence of their Mistresses, to vindicate
their Beauty; and were just spurring on to engage the

1190 Champions, when a Gentleman stopping them, told them
their mistake, that it was the Picture of *Donna Catharina*,
and a particular Honour done to her by his Highness's
Commands, and not to be disputed. Upon this they
would have returned to their Post, much concerned for
1195 their mistake; but notice being taken by *Don Ferdinand* of
some Show of Opposition that was made, he would have
begged leave of the Duke, to have maintained his Lady's
Honour against the Insolence of those Cavaliers; but the
Duke would by no means permit it. They were arguing
1200 about it when one of them came up, before whom the
Shield   was   born,   and   demanded   his   Highness's
Permission, to inform those Gentlemen better of their
mistake, by giving them the Foyl. By the Intercession
of *Don Ferdinand*, leave was given them; whereupon a
1205 Civil Challenge was sent to the two Strangers, informing
them of their Error, and withal telling them they
must either maintain it by force of Arms, or make a
publick acknowledgment by riding bare headed before the
Picture once round the Lists. The Stranger-Cavaliers
1210 remonstrated to the Duke how sensible they were of their
Error, and though they would not justifie it, yet they could
not decline the Combate, being pressed to it beyond an
honourable refusal. To the Bride they sent a Complement,
wherein, having first begg'd her pardon for not knowing
1215 her Picture, they gave her to understand, that now they
were not about to dispute her undoubted right to the
Crown   of   Beauty,   but   the   honour   of   being   her
Champions was the Prize they sought for, which they
thought themselves as able to maintain as any other
1220 Pretenders. Wherefore they pray'd her, that if fortune so
far befriended their endeavours as to make them Victors,
that they might receive no other Reward, but to be crown'd
with the Titles of their Adversaries, and be ever after
esteem'd as her most humble Servants. The excuse was
1225 so handsomely designed, and much better express'd than it
is here, that it took effect. The Duke, *Don Ferdinand* and
his Lady were so well satisfied with it as to grant their
Request.

While the running at the Ring lasted, our Cavaliers alternately bore away great share of the Honour. That 1230 Sport ended, Marshals were appointed for the Field, and every thing in great form settled for the Combat. The Cavaliers were all in good earnest, but orders were given to bring 'em blunted Lances, and to forbid the drawing of a Sword upon pain of his Highness's Displeasure. The 1235 Trumpets sounded and they began their Course: The Ladies Hearts, particularly the *Incognita* and *Leonora*'s, beat time to the Horses Hoofs, and hope and fear made a mock Fight within their tender Breasts, each wishing and doubting success where she lik'd: But as the 1240 generality of their Prayers were for the graceful Strangers, they accordingly succeeded. *Aurelian*'s Adversary was unhorsed in the first Encounter, and *Hippolito*'s lost both his Stirrups and dropt his Lance to save himself. The Honour of the Field was immediately granted to them, 1245 and *Donna Catharina* sent them both Favours, which she pray'd them to wear as her Knights. The Crowd breaking up, our Cavaliers made a shift to steal off unmarked, save by the watchful *Leonora* and *Incognita*, whose Eyes were never off from their respective Servants. There was 1250 enquiry made for them, but to no purpose; for they to prevent their being discovered had prepared another House, distant from their Lodging, where a Servant attended to disarm them, and another carried back their Horses to the *Villa*, while they walked unsuspected to their 1255 Lodging; but *Incognita* had given command to a Page to dog 'em till the Evening, at a distance, and bring her word where they were latest housed.

While several Conjectures pass'd among the Company, who were all gone to Dinner at the Palace, who those 1260 Cavaliers should be, *Don Fabio* thought himself the only Man able to guess; for he knew for certain that his Son and *Hippolito* were both in Town, and was well enough pleased with his humour of remaining *Incognito* till the Diversions should be over, believing then that the surprize of his 1265 Discovery would add much to the Gallantry he had shown in Masquerade; but hearing the extraordinary

liking that every body express'd, and in a particular
manner, the great Duke himself, to the Persons and
1270 Behaviour of the unknown Cavaliers, the Old Gentleman
could not forbear the Vanity to tell his Highness, that he
believed he had an interest in one of the Gentlemen, whom
he was pleased to honour with so favourable a Character;
and told him what reason he had to believe the one to be his
1275 Son, and the other a *Spanish* Nobleman, his Friend.

   This discovery having thus got vent, was diffused like
Air; every body suck'd it in, and let it out again with their
Breath to the next they met withal; and in half an hours
time it was talked of in the House where our Adventurers
1280 were lodged. *Aurelian* was stark mad at the News, and knew
what search would be immediately made for him. *Hippolito*,
had he not been desperately in Love, would certainly have
taken Horse and rid out of Town just then; for he could
make no longer doubt of being discovered, and he was
1285 afraid of the just Exceptions *Leonora* might make to a
Person who had now deceived her twice. Well, we will
leave them both fretting and contriving to no purpose, to
look about and see what was done at the Palace, where their
doom was determined much quicker than they imagined.

1290   Dinner ended, the Duke retired with some chosen
Friends to a Glass of Wine; among whom were the
Marquess of *Viterbo* and *Don Fabio*. His Highness was
no Stranger to the long Fewd that had been between the
two Families, and also understood what Overtures of
1295 Reconciliation had been lately made, with the Proposals
of Marriage between *Aurelian* and the Marquess's
Daughter. Having waited till the Wine had taken the
effect proposed, and the Company were raised to an
uncommon pitch of Chearfulness, which he also
1300 encouraged by an Example of Freedom and Good
Humour, he took an opportunity of rallying the two grave
Signiors into an Accommodation: That was seconded with
the praises of the young Couple, and the whole Company
joined in a large Encomium upon the Graces of *Aurelian*
1305 and the Beauties of *Juliana*. The old Fellows were tickled
with Delight to hear their Darlings so admired, which the

Duke perceiving, out of a Principle of Generosity and
Friendship, urged the present Consummation of the
Marriage; telling them there was yet one day of publick
Rejoycing to come, and how glad he should be to have it 1310
improved by so acceptable an Alliance; and what an honour
it would be to have his Cousin's Marriage attended by the
Conjunction of so extraordinary a Pair, the performance of
which Ceremony would crown the Joy that was then in
Agitation, and make the last day vie for equal Glory and 1315
Happiness with the first. In short, by the Complaisant and
Perswasive Authority of the Duke, the *Dons* were wrought
into a Compliance, and accordingly embraced and shook
Hands upon the Matter. This News was dispersed like the
former, and *Don Fabio* gave orders for the enquiring out his 1320
Son's Lodging, that the Marquess and he might make him
a Visit, as soon as he had acquainted *Juliana* with his
purpose, that she might prepare her self. He found her
very chearful with *Donna Catharina* and several other
Ladies; whereupon the old Gentleman, pretty well 1325
warmed with the Duke's Good-fellowship, told her aloud
he was come to crown their Mirth with another Wedding;
that his Highness had been pleased to provide a Husband
for his Daughter, and he would have her provide her self to
receive him to morrow. All the Company at first, as well as 1330
Juliana her self, thought he had rally'd, till the Duke
coming in confirmed the serious part of his Discourse.
Juliana was confounded at the haste that was imposed on
her, and desired a little time to consider what she was
about. But the Marquess told her, she should have all the 1335
rest of her Life to consider in; that *Aurelian* should come
and consider with her in the Morning, if she pleased; but in
the mean time, he advised her to go home and call her
Maids to Counsel.

    Juliana took her leave of the Company very gravely, as if 1340
not much delighted with her Father's Rallery. *Leonora*
happened to be by, and heard all that passed; she was
ready to swoon, and found her self seized with a more
violent Passion than ever for *Aurelian*: Now upon her
apprehensions of losing him, her active fancy had brought 1345

him before her with all the advantages imaginable, and
though she had before found great tenderness in her
Inclination toward him, yet was she somewhat surprized
to find she really lov'd him. She was so uneasie at what she
1350   had heard, that she thought it convenient to steal out of the
presence and retire to her Closet, to bemoan her unhappy
helpless Condition.

Our Two Cavalier-Lovers had rack'd their Invention till
it was quite disabled, and could not make discovery of one
1355   Contrivance more for their Relief. Both sat silent, each
depending upon his Friend, and still expecting when
t'other should speak. Night came upon them while they
sate thus thoughtless, or rather drowned in Thought; but a
Servant bringing Lights into the Room awakened them:
1360   And *Hippolito*'s Speech, usher'd by a profound Sigh, broke
Silence.

'Well! (said he) what must we do, *Aurelian*?' 'We must
suffer,' replied *Aurelian* faintly. When immediately raising
his Voice, he cry'd out, 'Oh ye unequal Powers, why do ye
1365   urge us to desire what ye doom us to forbear; give us a Will
to chuse, then curb us with a Duty to restrain that Choice!
Cruel Father, Will nothing else suffice! Am I to be the
Sacrifice to expiate your Offences past; past ere I was born?
Were I to lose my Life, I'd gladly Seal your Reconcilement
1370   with my Blood. But Oh my Soul is free, you have no Title
to my Immortal Being, that has Existence independent of
your Power; and must I lose my Love, the Extract of that
Being, the Joy, Light, Life, and Darling of my Soul? No,
I'll own my Flame, and plead my Title too—But hold,
1375   wretched *Aurelian*, hold, whither does thy Passion hurry
thee? Alas! the cruel fair *Incognita* Loves thee not! She
knows not of thy Love! If she did, what Merit hast thou
to pretend?—Only Love—Excess of Love. And all the
World has that. All that have seen her. Yet I had only
1380   seen her once, and in that once I lov'd above the World;
nay, lov'd beyond my self, such vigorous Flame, so strong,
so quick she darted at my Breast; it must rebound, and by
Reflection, warm her self. Ah! welcome Thought, lovely

deluding Fancy, hang still upon my Soul, let me but think, that once she Loves and perish my Despair.' 1385

Here a suddain stop gave a Period also to *Hippolito*'s Expectation, and he hoped now that his Friend had given his Passion so free a vent, he might recollect and bethink himself of what was convenient to be done; but *Aurelian*, as if he had mustered up all his Spirits purely to acquit 1390 himself of that passionate Harangue, stood mute and insensible like an Alarum Clock, that had spent all its force in one violent Emotion. *Hippolito* shook him by the Arm to rouze him from his Lethargy, when his Lacquey coming into the Room, out of Breath, told him there was a 1395 Coach just stopp'd at the Door, but he did not take time to see who came in it. *Aurelian* concluded immediately it was his Father in quest of him; and without saying any more to *Hippolito*, than that he was Ruined if discovered, took his Sword and slipp'd down a back pair of Stairs into the 1400 Garden, from whence he conveyed himself into the Street. *Hippolito* had not bethought himself what to do, before he perceiv'd a Lady come into the Chamber close veil'd, and make toward him. At the first Appearance of a Woman, his Imagination flattered him with a Thought of 1405 *Leonora*; but that was quickly over upon nearer Approach to the Lady, who had much the Advantage in Stature of his Mistress. He very civilly accosted her, and asked, if he were the Person to whom the Honour of that Visit was intended. She said, her Business was with *Don Hippolito di Saviolina*, 1410 to whom she had Matter of Concern to import, and which required haste. He had like to have told her, That he was the Man, but by good Chance reflecting upon his Friend's Adventure, who had taken his name, he made Answer, that he believed *Don Hippolito* not far off, and if she had a 1415 Moments Patience he would enquire for him.

He went out, leaving the Lady in the Room, and made search all round the House and Garden for *Aurelian*, but to no purpose. The Lady impatient of his long stay took a Pen and Ink and some Paper which she found upon the Table, 1420 and had just made an End of her Letter, when hearing a Noise of more than one coming up Stairs, she concluded his Friend had found him, and that her Letter would be to no purpose, so tore it in pieces, which she repented; when turning about, she found her Mistake, and beheld *Don Fabio* and the Marquess of *Viterbo* just entring at the Door. She gave a Shriek at the Surprize of their Appearance, which much troubled the Old Gentlemen, and made them retire in Confusion for putting a Gentlewoman into such a Fright. The Marquess thinking they had been mis-informed, or had mistaken the Lodgings, came forward again, and made an Apology to the Lady for their Errour; but she making no reply, walk'd directly by him down Stairs and went into her Coach, which hurried her away as speedily as the Horses were able to draw.

The *Dons* were at a loss what to think, when *Hippolito*, coming into the Room to give the Lady an Account of his Errant, was no less astonished to find she was departed, and had left Two Old Signiors in her stead. He knew *Don Fabio*'s Face, for *Aurelian* had shewn him his Father at the Tilting; but being confident he was not known to him, he ventur'd to ask him concerning a Lady whom just now he had left in that Chamber. *Don Fabio* told him, she was just gone down, and doubted they had been Guilty of a Mistake, in coming to enquire for a Couple of Gentlemen whom they were informed were Lodged in that House; he begg'd his Pardon if he had any Relation to that Lady, and desired to know if he could give them any Account of the Persons they sought for. *Hippolito* made answer, He was a Stranger in the Place, and only a Servant to that Lady whom they had disturb'd, and whom he must go and seek out. And in this Perplexity he left them, going again in Search of *Aurelian*, to inform him of what had passed.

The Old Gentlemen at last meeting with a Servant of the House, were directed to Signior *Claudio*'s Chamber, where they were no sooner entered but *Aurelian* came into the House. A Servant who had skulk'd for him by *Hippolito*'s Order, followed him up into the Chamber, and told him who was with *Claudio* then making Enquiry for him. He thought that to be no Place for him, since *Claudio* must

needs discover all the Truth to his Father; wherefore he left
Directions with the Servant, where *Hippolito* should meet
him in the Morning. As he was going out of the Room he
espied the torn Paper, which the Lady had thrown upon   1465
the Floor: The first piece he took up had *Incognita* written
upon it; the sight of which so Alarum'd him, he scarce
knew what he was about; but hearing a Noise of a Door
opening over Head, with as much Care as was consistent
with the haste he was then in, he gathered up the scattered   1470
pieces of Paper, and betook himself to a Ramble.

Coming by a Light which hung at the Corner of a Street,
he join'd the torn Papers and collected thus much, that his
Incognita had Written the Note, and earnestly desired him
(if there were any reality in what he pretended to her) to   1475
meet her at Twelve a Clock that Night at a Convent Gate;
but unluckily the Bit of Paper which should have
mentioned what Convent, was broken off and lost.

Here was a large Subject for *Aurelian*'s Passion, which he
did not spare to pour forth in Abundance of Curses on his   1480
Stars. So earnest was he in the Contemplation of his
Misfortunes, that he walk'd on unwittingly; till at length
a Silence (and such as was only to be found in that part of
the Town, whither his unguided Steps had carried him)
surpriz'd his Attention. I say, a profound Silence rouzed   1485
him from his Thought; and a clap of Thunder could have
done no more.

Now because it is possible this at some time or other may
happen to be read by some Malicious or Ignorant Person,
(no Reflection upon the present Reader) who will not   1490
admit, or does not understand that Silence should make a
Man start; and have the same Effect, in provoking his
Attention, with its opposite Noise; I will illustrate this
Matter, to such a diminutive Critick, by a Parallel
Instance of Light; which though it does chiefly entertain   1495
the Eyes, and is indeed the prime Object of the Sight, yet
should it immediately cease, to have a Man left in the Dark
by a suddain deficiency of it, would make him stare with his
Eyes, and though he could not see, endeavour to look about
him. Why just thus did it fare with our Adventurer; who   1500

seeming to have wandred both into the Dominions of
Silence and of Night, began to have some tender for his
own Safety, and would willingly have groped his Way back
again; when he heard a Voice, as from a Person whose
1505   Breath had been stopp'd by some forcible Oppression,
and just then, by a violent Effort, was broke through the
Restraint—'Yet—Yet—(again reply'd the Voice, still
struggling for Air,) Forbear—and I'll forgive what's
past'—'I have done nothing yet that needs a Pardon,
1510   (says another) and what is to come, will admit of none.'
     Here the Person who seemed to be the Oppressed, made
several Attempts to speak, but they were only inarticulate
Sounds, being all interrupted and choaked in their Passage.
     Aurelian was sufficiently astonish'd, and would have
1515   crept nearer to the Place whence he guessed the Voice to
come; but he was got among the Ruines of an Old
Monastery, and could not stir so silently, but some loose
Stones he met with made a rumbling. The Noise alarm'd
both Parties; and as it gave Comfort to the one, it so
1520   Terrified the t'other, that he could not hinder the
Oppressed from calling for help. *Aurelian* fancy'd it was a
Womans Voice, and immediately drawing his Sword,
demanded what was the Matter; he was answered with
the Appearance of a Man, who had opened a Dark
1525   Lanthorn which he had by him, and came toward him
with a Pistol in his Hand ready cock'd.
     Aurelian seeing the irresistable advantage his Adversary
had over him, would fain have retired; and, by the greatest
Providence in the World, going backwards fell down over
1530   some loose Stones that lay in his Way, just in that Instant of
Time when the Villain fired his Pistol, who seeing him fall,
concluded he had Shot him. The Crys of the afflicted
Person were redoubled at the Tragical Sight, which made
the Murderer, drawing a Poniard, to threaten him, that the
1535   next Murmur should be his last. *Aurelian*, who was scarce
assured that he was unhurt, got softly up; and coming near
enough to perceive the Violence that was used to stop the
Injured Man's Mouth; (for now he saw plainly it was a
Man) cry'd out,—'Turn, Villain, and look upon thy

Death.'—The Fellow amazed at the Voice, turn'd about to   1540
have snatch'd up the Lanthorn from the Ground; either to
have given Light only to himself, or to have put out the
Candle, that he might have made his Escape; but which of
the Two he designed, no Body could tell but himself: And
if the Reader have a Curiosity to know, he must blame   1545
Aurelian; who thinking there could be no foul Play offered
to such a Villain, ran him immediately through the Heart,
so that he drop'd down Dead at his Feet, without speaking
a Word. He would have seen who the Person was he had
thus happily delivered, but the Dead Body had fallen upon   1550
the Lanthorn, which put out the Candle: However, coming
up toward him, he ask'd him how he did, and bid him be of
good Heart; he was answered with nothing but Prayers,
Blessings and Thanks, called a Thousand Deliverers, good
Genius's and Guardian Angels. And the Rescued would   1555
certainly have gone upon his Knees to have worshipped
him, had he not been bound Hand and Foot; which
Aurelian understanding, groped for the Knots, and either
untied them or cut them asunder; but 'tis more probable
the latter, because more expeditious.   1560
     They took little heed what became of the Body which
they left behind them, and *Aurelian* was conducted from
out the Ruins by the Hand of him he had delivered. By a
faint light issuing from the just rising Moon, he could
discern that it was a Youth; but coming into a more   1565
frequented part of the Town, where several Lights were
hung out, he was amaz'd at the extream Beauty which
appeared in his Face, though a little pale and disordered
with his late fright. *Aurelian* longed to hear the Story of so
odd an adventure, and entreated his Charge to tell it him by   1570
the way; but he desired him to forbear till they were come
into some House or other, where he might rest and recover
his tired Spirits, for yet he was so faint he was unable to
look up. *Aurelian* thought these last words were delivered
in a Voice, whose accent was not new to him. That thought   1575
made him look earnestly in the Youth's Face, which he now
was sure he had somewhere seen before, and thereupon
asked him if he had never been at *Siena*? That Question

made the young Gentleman look up, and something of a Joy
appeared in his Countenance, which yet he endeavoured to
smother; so praying *Aurelian* to conduct him to his
Lodging, he promised him that as soon as they should
come thither, he would acquaint him with any thing he
desired to know. *Aurelian* would rather have gone any
where else than to his own Lodging; but being so very
late he was at a loss, and so forced to be contented.

As soon as they were come into his Chamber, and that
Lights were brought them and the Servant dismissed, the
paleness which so visibly before had usurped the sweet
Countenance of the afflicted Youth vanished, and gave
place to a more lively Flood of Crimson, which with a
modest heat glow'd freshly on his Cheeks. *Aurelian*
waited with a pleasing Admiration the discovery
promised him, when the Youth still struggling with his
Resolution, with a timorous haste, pulled off a Peruke
which had concealed the most beautiful abundance of
Hair that ever graced one Female Head; those dishevelled
spreading Tresses, as at first they made a discovery of, so at
last they served for a veil to the modest lovely blushes of
the fair *Incognita*; for she it was and none other. But Oh!
the inexpressible, inconceivable joy and amazement of
Aurelian! As soon as he durst venture to think, he
concluded it to be all Vision, and never doubted so much
of any thing in his Life as of his being then awake. But she
taking him by the Hand, and desiring him to sit down by
her, partly convinced him of the reality of her presence.

'This is the second time, *Don Hippolito*, (said she to him)
that I have been here this Night. What the occasion was of
my seeking you out, and how by miracle you preserved me,
would add too much to the surprize I perceive you to be
already in should I tell you: Nor will I make any further
discovery, till I know what censure you pass upon the
confidence which I have put in you, and the strange
Circumstances in which you find me at this time. I am
sensible they are such, that I shall not blame your severest
Conjectures; but I hope to convince you, when you shall
hear what I have to say in justification of my Vertue.'

'Justification! (cry'd *Aurelian*) what Infidel dares doubt
it!'—Then kneeling down, and taking her Hand, 'Ah
Madam (says he) would Heaven would no other ways   1620
look upon, than I behold your Perfections—Wrong not
your Creature with a Thought, he can be guilty of that
horrid Impiety as once to doubt your Vertue—Heavens!
(cry'd he, starting up) am I so really blessed to see you once
again! May I trust my Sight?—Or does my fancy now only   1625
more strongly work?—For still I did preserve your Image
in my Heart, and you were ever present to my dearest
Thoughts—'
    'Enough *Hippolito*, enough of Rapture (said she) you
cannot much accuse me of Ingratitude; for you see I have   1630
not been unmindful of you; but moderate your Joy till
I have told you my Condition, and if for my sake you are
raised to this Delight, it is not of a long continuance—'
    At that (as *Aurelian* tells the Story) a Sigh diffused a
mournful sweetness through the Air, and liquid grief fell   1635
gently from her Eyes, triumphant sadness sat upon her
Brow, and even sorrow seem'd delighted with the
Conquest he had made. See what a change *Aurelian* felt!
His Heart bled Tears, and trembled in his Breast; Sighs
struggling for a vent had choaked each others passage up: 1640
His Floods of Joys were all supprest; cold doubts and fears
had chill'd 'em with a sudden Frost, and he was troubled to
excess; yet knew not why. Well, the Learned say it was
Sympathy; and I am always of the Opinion with the
Learned, if they speak first.   1645
    After a World of Condoleance had passed between them,
he prevailed with her to tell him her Story. So having put
all her Sighs into one great Sigh, she discharged her self of
'em all at once, and formed the Relation you are just about
to Read.   1650
    'Having been in my Infancy Contracted to a Man I could
never endure, and now by my Parents being likely to be
forced to Marry him, is in short, the great occasion of my
grief. I fansy'd (continued she) something so Generous in
your Countenance, and uncommon in your Behaviour,   1655
while you were diverting your self, and rallying me with

Expressions of Gallantry, at the Ball, as induced me to hold
Conference with you. I now freely confess to you, out of
design, That if things should happen as I then feared, and
1660 as now they are come to pass, I might rely upon your
assistance in a matter of Concern; and in which I would
sooner chuse to depend upon a generous Stranger, than any
Acquaintance I have. What Mirth and Freedom I then put
on, were, I can assure you, far distant from my Heart; but
1665 I did violence to my self out of Complaisance to your
Temper—I knew you at the Tilting, and wished you
might come off as you did; though I do not doubt, but
you would have had as good Success had it been opposite to
my Inclinations—Not to detain you by too tedious a
1670 Relation, every day my Friends urged me to the Match
they had agreed upon for me, before I was capable of
Consenting; at last their importunities grew to that
degree, that I found I must either consent, which would
make me miserable, or be miserable by perpetually
1675 enduring to be baited by my Father, Brother and other
Relations. I resolved yesterday, on a suddain, to give firm
Faith to the Opinion I had conceived of you; and
accordingly came in the Evening to request your
assistance, in delivering me from my Tormentors, by a
1680 safe and private conveyance of me to a Monastery about
four Leagues hence, where I have an Aunt who would
receive me, and is the only Relation I have averse to the
Match. I was surprized at the appearance of some
Company I did not expect at your Lodgings; which made
1685 me in haste tear a Paper which I had written to you with
Directions where to find me, and get speedily away in my
Coach to an old Servant's House, whom I acquainted with
my purpose: By my Order she provided me of this Habit
which I now wear; I ventured to trust my self with her
1690 Brother, and resolved to go under his Conduct to the
Monastery; he proved to be a Villain, and pretending to
take me a short and private way to the place where he was to
take up a Hackney Coach (for that which I came in was
broke some where or other, with the haste it made to carry
1695 me from your Lodging) led me into an old ruined

Monastery, where it pleased Heaven, by what Accident I know not, to direct you. I need not tell you how you saved my Life and my Honour, by revenging me with the Death of my Perfidious Guide. This is the summ of my present Condition, bating the apprehensions I am in of being taken   1700
by some of my Relations, and forced to a thing so quite contrary to my Inclinations.'

Aurelian was confounded at the Relation she had made, and began to fear his own Estate to be more desperate than ever he had imagined. He made her a very Passionate and   1705
Eloquent Speech in behalf of himself (much better than I intend to insert here) and expressed a mighty concern that she should look upon his ardent Affection to be only Rallery or Gallantry. He was very free of his Oaths to confirm the Truth of what he pretended, nor I believe   1710
did she doubt it, or at least was unwilling so to do: For I would Caution the Reader by the bye, not to believe every word which she told him, nor that admirable sorrow which she counterfeited to be accurately true. It was indeed truth so cunningly intermingled with Fiction, that it required no   1715
less Wit and Presence of Mind than she was endowed with so to acquit her self on the suddain. She had entrusted her self indeed with a Fellow who proved a Villain, to conduct her to a Monastery; but one which was in the Town, and where she intended only to lie concealed for his sake; as the   1720
Reader shall understand ere long: For we have another Discovery to make to him, if he have not found it out of himself already.

After *Aurelian* had said what he was able upon the Subject in hand, with a mournful tone and dejected look,   1725
he demanded his Doom. She asked him if he would endeavour to convey her to the Monastery she had told him of? 'Your commands, Madam, (replied he) are Sacred to me; and were they to lay down my Life I would obey them.' With that he would have gone out of the Room, to   1730
have given order for his Horses to be got ready immediately; but with a Countenance so full of sorrow as moved Compassion in the tender hearted *Incognita*. 'Stay a little *Don Hippolito* (said she) I fear I shall not be able to

1735 undergo the Fatigue of a Journey this Night—Stay and
give me your Advice how I shall conceal my self if I
continue to morrow in this Town.' *Aurelian* could have
satisfied her she was not then in a place to avoid discovery:
But he must also have told her then the reason of it, *viz.*
1740 whom he was, and who were in quest of him, which he did
not think convenient to declare till necessity should urge
him; for he feared least her knowledge of those designs
which were in agitation between him and *Juliana*, might
deter her more from giving her consent. At last he resolved
1745 to try his utmost perswasions to gain her, and told her
accordingly, he was afraid she would be disturbed there
in the Morning, and he knew no other way (if she had not
as great an aversion for him as the Man whom she now
endeavour'd to avoid) than by making him happy to make
1750 her self secure. He demonstrated to her, that the
disobligation to her Parents would be greater by going to
a Monastery, since it was only to avoid a choice which they
had made for her, and which she could not have so just a
pretence to do till she had made one for her self.
1755   A World of other Arguments he used, which she
contradicted as long as she was able, or at least willing. At
last she told him, she would consult her Pillow, and in the
Morning conclude what was fit to be done. He thought it
convenient to leave her to her rest, and having lock'd her
1760 up in his Room, went himself to repose upon a Pallat by
Signior *Claudio*.
    In the mean time, it may be convenient to enquire what
became of *Hippolito*. He had wandered much in pursuit of
Aurelian, though *Leonora* equally took up his Thoughts; He
1765 was reflecting upon the oddness and extravagance of his
Circumstances, the Continuation of which had doubtless
created in him a great uneasiness, when it was interrupted
with the noise of opening the Gates of the Convent of St.
Lawrence, whither he was arrived sooner than he thought
1770 for, being the place *Aurelian* had appointed by the Lacquey
to meet him in. He wondered to see the Gates opened at so
unseasonable an hour, and went to enquire the reason of it
from them who were employ'd; but they proved to be

Novices, and made him signs to go in, where he might meet
with some body allow'd to answer him. He found the   1775
Religious Men all up, and Tapers lighting every where: at
last he follow'd a Friar who was going into the Garden, and
asking him the cause of these Preparations, he was
answered, That they were entreated to pray for the Soul
of a Cavalier, who was just departing or departed this Life,   1780
and whom upon farther talk with him, he found to be the
same *Lorenzo* so often mentioned. *Don Mario*, it seems,
Uncle to *Lorenzo* and Father to *Leonora*, had a private Door
out of the Garden belonging to his House into that of the
Convent, which Door this Father was now a going to open,   1785
that he and his Family might come and offer up their
Oraisons for the Soul of their Kinsman. *Hippolito* having
informed himself of as much as he could ask without
suspicion, took his leave of the Friar, not a little joyful at
the Hopes he had by such unexpected Means, of seeing his   1790
Beautiful *Leonora*: As soon as he was got at convenient
Distance from the Friar, (who 'tis like thought he had
return'd into the Convent to his Devotion) he turned
back through a close Walk which led him with a little
Compass, to the same private Door, where just before   1795
he had left the Friar, who now he saw was gone, and the
Door open.

He went into *Don Mario*'s Garden, and walk'd round
with much Caution and Circumspection; for the Moon
was then about to rise, and had already diffused a   1800
glimmering Light, sufficient to distinguish a Man from a
Tree. By Computation now (which is a very remarkable
Circumstance) *Hippolito* entred this Garden near upon the
same Instant, when *Aurelian* wandred into the Old
Monastery and found his *Incognita* in Distress. He was   1805
pretty well acquainted with the Platform, and Sight of the
Garden; for he had formerly surveyed the Outside, and
knew what part to make to if he should be surpriz'd and
driven to a precipitate Escape. He took his Stand behind a
well-grown Bush of Myrtle, which, should the Moon shine   1810
brighter than was required, had the Advantage to be shaded
by the Indulgent Boughs of an ancient Bay-Tree. He was

delighted with the Choice he had made, for he found a
Hollow in the Myrtle, as if purposely contriv'd for the
Reception of one Person, who might undiscovered
perceive all about him. He looked upon it as a good
Omen, that the Tree Consecrated to *Venus* was so
propitious to him in his Amorous Distress. The
Consideration of that, together with the Obligation he lay
under to the Muses, for sheltering him also with so large a
Crown of Bays, had like to have set him a Rhyming.

He was, to tell the Truth, naturally addicted to
Madrigal, and we should undoubtedly have had a small
desert of Numbers to have pick'd and Criticiz'd upon, had
he not been interrupted just upon his Delivery; nay, after
the Preliminary Sigh had made Way for his Utterance. But
so was his Fortune, *Don Mario* was coming towards the
Door at that very nick of Time, where he met with a Priest
just out of Breath, who told him that *Lorenzo* was just
breathing his last, and desired to know if he would come
and take his final Leave before they were to administer the
Extream Unction. *Don Mario*, who had been at some
Difference with his Nephew, now thought it his Duty to
be reconciled to him; so calling to *Leonora*, who was coming
after him, he bid her go to her Devotions in the Chappel,
and told her where he was going.

He went on with the Priest, while *Hippolito* saw *Leonora*
come forward, only accompanied by her Woman. She was
in an undress, and by reason of a Melancholy visible in her
Face, more Careless than usual in her Attire, which he
thought added as much as was possible to the abundance
of her Charms. He had not much Time to Contemplate this
Beauteous Vision, for she soon passed into the Garden of
the Convent, leaving him Confounded with Love,
Admiration, Joy, Hope, Fear, and all the Train of
Passions, which seize upon Men in his Condition, all at
once. He was so teazed with this Variety of Torment, that
he never missed the Two Hours that had slipped away
during his Automachy and Intestine Conflict. *Leonora*'s
Return settled his Spirits, at least united them, and he
had now no other Thought but how he should present

1815

1820

1825

1830

1835

1840

1845

1850

himself before her. When she calling her Woman, bid her
bolt the Garden Door on the Inside, that she might not be
Surpriz'd by her Father, if he returned through the
Convent; which done, she ordered her to bring down her   1855
Lute, and leave her to her self in the Garden.

All this *Hippolito* saw and heard to his inexpressible
Content, yet had he much to do to smother his Joy, and
hinder it from taking a Vent, which would have ruined the
only Opportunity of his Life. *Leonora* withdrew into an   1860
Arbour so near him, that he could distinctly hear her if she
Played or Sung: Having tuned her Lute, with a Voice soft
as the Breath of Angels, she sung to it this following Air:

I.

Ah! Whither, whither shall I fly,   1865
A poor unhappy Maid;
To hopeless Love and Misery
By my own Heart betray'd?
Not by Alexis *Eyes undone,*
Nor by his Charming Faithless Tongue,   1870
Or any Practis'd Art;
Such real Ills may hope a Cure,
But the sad Pains which I endure
Proceed from fansied Smart.

II.   1875

'Twas Fancy gave Alexis *Charms,*
Ere I beheld his Face:
Kind Fancy (then) could fold our Arms,
And form a soft Embrace.
But since I've seen the real Swain,   1880
And try'd to fancy him again,
I'm by my Fancy taught,
Though 'tis a Bliss no Tongue can tell,
To have Alexis, *yet 'tis Hell*
To have him but in Thought.   1885

The Song ended grieved *Hippolito* that it was so soon
ended; and in the Ecstacy he was then rapt, I believe he
would have been satisfied to have expired with it. He could

not help Flattering himself, (though at the same Time he
checked his own Vanity) that he was the Person meant in
the Song. While he was indulging which thought, to his
happy Astonishment, he heard it encouraged by these
Words:

'Unhappy *Leonora* (said she) how is thy poor unwary
Heart misled? Whither am I come? The false deluding
Lights of an imaginary Flame, have led me, a poor
benighted Victim, to a real Fire. I burn and am consumed
with hopeless Love; those Beams in whose soft temperate
warmth I wanton'd heretofore, now flash destruction to my
Soul, my Treacherous greedy Eyes have suck'd the glaring
Light, they have united all its Rays, and, like a burning-
Glass, convey'd the pointed Meteor to my Heart—Ah!
Aurelian, how quickly hast thou Conquer'd, and how
quickly must thou Forsake—Oh Happy (to me
unfortunately Happy) *Juliana!*—I am to be the Subject of
thy Triumph—To thee *Aurelian* comes laden with the
Tribute of my Heart and Glories in the Oblation of his
broken Vows—What then, is *Aurelian* False!—False! alass,
I know not what I say; How can he be False, or True, or any
Thing to me? What Promises did he ere make or I receive?
Sure I dream, or I am mad, and fansie it to be Love; Foolish
Girl, recal thy banish'd Reason—Ah! would it were no
more, would I could rave, sure that would give me Ease,
and rob me of the Sense of Pain; at least, among my
wandring Thoughts, I should at sometime light upon
Aurelian, and fansie him to be mine; kind Madness would
flatter my poor feeble Wishes, and sometimes tell me
Aurelian is not lost—not irrecoverably—not for ever lost.'

Hippolito could hear no more, he had not Room for half
his Transport. When *Leonora* perceived a Man coming
toward her, she fell a trembling, and could not speak.
Hippolito approached with Reverence, as to a Sacred
Shrine; when coming near enough to see her
Consternation, he fell upon his Knees.

'Behold, O Adored *Leonora* (said he) your ravished
Aurelian, behold at your Feet the Happiest of Men, be
not disturb'd at my Appearance, but think that Heaven

conducted me to hear my Bliss pronounced by that dear
Mouth alone, whose breath could fill me with new Life.'

Here he would have come nearer, but *Leonora* (scarce   1930
come to her self) was getting up in haste to have gone away:
he catch'd her Hand, and with all the Endearments of Love
and Transport pressed her stay; she was a long time in great
Confusion. At last, with many Blushes, she entreated him
to let her go where she might hide her Guilty Head, and   1935
not expose her shame before his Eyes, since his Ears had
been sufficient Witnesses of her Crime. He begg'd pardon
for his Treachery in over-hearing, and confessed it to
be a Crime he had now repeated. With a Thousand
Submissions, Entreaties, Prayers, Praises, Blessings, and   1940
passionate Expressions he wrought upon her to stay
and hear him. Here *Hippolito* made use of his Rhetorick,
and it proved prevailing: 'Twere tedious to tell the many
ingenious Arguments he used, with all her Nice Distinctions
and Objections. In short, he convinced her of his Passion,   1945
represented to her the necessity they were under, of being
speedy in their Resolves: That his Father (for still he was
Aurelian) would undoubtedly find him in the Morning, and
then it would be too late to Repent. She on the other Hand,
knew it was in vain to deny a Passion, which he had heard   1950
her so frankly own; (and no doubt was very glad it was past
and done;) besides apprehending the danger of delay, and
having some little Jealousies and Fears of what Effect might
be produced between the Commands of his Father and
the Beauties of *Juliana*; after some decent Denials, she   1955
consented to be Conducted by him through the Garden
into the Convent, where she would prevail with her
Confessor to Marry them. He was a scrupulous Old
Father whom they had to deal withal, insomuch that ere
they had perswaded him, *Don Mario* was returned by the   1960
Way of his own House, where missing his Daughter, and
her Woman not being able to give any farther Account of
her, than that she left her in the Garden; he concluded she
was gone again to her Devotions, and indeed he found her
in the Chappel upon her Knees with *Hippolito* in her Hand,   1965

receiving the Father's Benediction upon Conclusion of the
Ceremony.

It would have asked a very skilful Hand, to have depicted
to the Life the Faces of those Three Persons, at *Don*
Mario's Appearance. He that has seen some admirable
Piece of Transmutation by a Gorgon's Head, may form to
himself the most probable Idea of the Prototype. The Old
Gentleman was himself in a sort of a Wood, to find his
Daughter with a Young Fellow and a Priest, but as yet
he did not know the Worst, till *Hippolito* and *Leonora*
came, and kneeling at his Feet, begg'd his Forgiveness
and Blessing as his Son and Daughter. *Don Mario*,
instead of that, fell into a most violent Passion, and would
undoubtedly have committed some extravagant Action,
had he not been restrained, more by the Sanctity of the
Place, than the Perswasions of all the Religious, who were
now come about him. *Leonora* stirr'd not off her Knees
all this time, but continued begging of him that he would
hear her.

'Ah! Ungrateful and Undutiful Wretch (cry'd he) how
hast thou requited all my Care and Tenderness of thee?
Now when I might have expected some return of Comfort,
to throw thy self away upon an unknown Person, and, for
ought I know, a Villain; to me I'm sure he is a Villain, who
has robb'd me of my Treasure, my Darling Joy, and all
the future Happiness of my Life prevented. Go—go,
thou now-to-be-forgotten *Leonora*, go and enjoy thy
unprosperous Choice; you who wanted not a Father's
Counsel, cannot need, or else will slight his Blessing.'

These last Words were spoken with so much Passion and
feeling Concern, that *Leonora*, moved with Excess of Grief,
fainted at his Feet, just as she had caught hold to Embrace
his Knees. The Old Man would have shook her off, but
Compassion and Fatherly Affection came upon him in the
midst of his Resolve, and melted him into Tears; he
Embraced his Daughter in his Arms, and wept over her,
while they endeavoured to restore her Senses.

Hippolito was in such Concern he could not speak, but
was busily employed in rubbing and chafing her Temples;

when she opening her Eyes laid hold of his Arm, and cry'd 2005
out—*Oh my* Aurelian—*how unhappy have you made me!*
With that she had again like to have fainted away, but he
took her in his Arms, and begg'd *Don Mario* to have some
pity on his Daughter, since by his Severity she was reduced
to that Condition. The Old Man hearing his Daughter 2010
name *Aurelian*, was a little revived, and began to hope
Things were in a pretty good Condition; he was
perswaded to comfort her; and having brought her wholly
to her self, was content to hear her Excuse, and in a little
time was so far wrought upon as to beg *Hippolito*'s Pardon 2015
for the Ill Opinion he had conceived of him, and not long
after gave his Consent.

The Night was spent in this Conflict, and it was now clear
Day, when *Don Mario* Conducting his new Son and
Daughter through the Garden, was met by some Servants 2020
of the Marquess of *Viterbo*, who had been enquiring for
Donna Leonora, to know if *Juliana* had lately been with her;
for that she was missing from her Father's House, and no
conjectures could be made of what might become of her. *Don
Mario* and *Leonora* were surprized at the News, for he knew 2025
well enough of the Match that was design'd for *Juliana*; and
having enquired where the Marquess was, it was told him,
That he was gone with *Don Fabio* and *Fabritio* toward
Aurelian's Lodgings. *Don Mario* having assured the
Servants that *Juliana* had not been there, dismissed them, 2030
and advised with his Son and Daughter how they should
undeceive the Marquess and *Don Fabio* in their Expectations
of *Aurelian*. *Hippolito* could oftentimes scarce forbear smiling
at the old Man's Contrivances who was most deceived
himself; he at length advised them to go all down together 2035
to his Lodging, where he would present himself before his
Father, and ingenuously confess to him the truth, and he did
not question his approving of his Choice.

This was agreed to, and the Coach made ready. While
they were upon their way, *Hippolito* pray'd heartily that his 2040
Friend *Aurelian* might be at the Lodging, to satisfie *Don
Mario* and *Leonora* of his Circumstances and Quality, when
he should be obliged to discover himself. His Petitions

were granted; for *Don Fabio* had beset the House long
before his Son was up or *Incognita* awake.

Upon the arrival of *Don Mario* and *Hippolito*, they heard
a great Noise and Hubbub above Stairs, which *Don Mario*
concluded was occasioned by their not finding *Aurelian*,
whom he thought he could give the best account of: So that
it was not in *Hippolito*'s power to disswade him from going
up before to prepare his Father to receive and forgive him.
While *Hippolito* and *Leonora* were left in the Coach at the
Door, he made himself known to her, and begg'd her
pardon a thousand times for continuing the deceit. She
was under some concern at first to find she was still
mistaken; but his Behaviour, and the Reasons he gave,
soon reconciled him to her; his Person was altogether as
agreeable, his Estate and Quality not at all inferiour to
Aurelian's; in the mean time, the true *Aurelian* who had
seen his Father, begg'd leave of him to withdraw for a
moment; in which time he went into the Chamber where
his *Incognita* was dressing her self, by his design, in
Woman's Apparel; while he was consulting with her how
they should break the matter to his Father, it happened that
Don Mario came up Stairs where the Marquess and *Don
Fabio* were; they undoubtedly concluded him Mad, to hear
him making Apologies and Excuses for *Aurelian*, whom he
told them if they would promise to forgive he would
present before them immediately. The Marquess asked
him if his Daughter had lain with *Leonora* that Night; he
answered him with another question in behalf of *Aurelian*.
In short, they could not understand one another, but each
thought 'tother beside himself. *Don Mario* was so
concern'd that they would not believe him, that he ran
down Stairs and came to the Door out of Breath, desiring
Hippolito that he would come into the House quickly, for
that he could not perswade his Father but that he had
already seen and spoke to him. *Hippolito* by that
understood that *Aurelian* was in the House; so taking
Leonora by the Hand, he followed *Don Mario*, who led
him up into the Dining-Room, where they found
Aurelian upon his Knees, begging his Father to forgive

him, that he could not agree to the Choice he had made for him, since he had already disposed of himself, and that before he understood the designs he had for him, which was the reason that he had hitherto concealed himself. *Don Fabio* knew not how to answer him, but look'd upon the Marquess, and the Marquess upon him, as if the Cement had been cool'd which was to have united their Families.

All was silent, and *Don Mario* for his part took it to be all Conjuration; he was coming forward to present *Hippolito* to them, when *Aurelian* spying his Friend, started from his Knees and ran to embrace him—'My dear *Hippolito* (said he) what happy chance has brought you hither, just at my Necessity?' *Hippolito* pointed to *Don Mario* and *Leonora*, and told him upon what terms he came. *Don Mario* was ready to run mad, hearing him called *Hippolito*, and went again to examine his Daughter. While she was informing him of the truth, the Marquess's Servants returned with the melancholy News that his Daughter was no where to be found. While the Marquess and *Don Fabritio* were wondering at, and lamenting the Misfortune of her loss, *Hippolito* came towards *Don Fabio* and interceded for his Son, since the Lady perhaps had withdrawn her self out of an Aversion to the Match. *Don Fabio*, though very much incens'd, yet forgot not the Respect due to *Hippolito*'s Quality; and by his perswasion spoke to *Aurelian*, though with a stern Look and angry Voice, and asked him where he had disposed the cause of his Disobedience, if he were worthy to see her or no; *Aurelian* made answer, That he desired no more than for him to see her; and he did not doubt a Consequence of his Approbation and Forgiveness—Well (said *Don Fabio*) you are very conceited of your own Discretion, let us see this Rarety. While *Aurelian* was gone in for *Incognita*, the Marquess of *Viterbo* and *Don Fabritio* were taking their leaves in great disorder for their loss and disappointment; but *Don Fabio* entreated their stay a moment longer till the return of his Son. *Aurelian* led *Incognita* into the Room veil'd, who seeing some Company there which he had not told her of, would have gone back again. But *Don Fabio* came bluntly forwards, and ere she was aware, lifted up her Veil and beheld the Fair *Incognita*, differing nothing from *Juliana*, but in her Name. This discovery was so extreamly surprizing and welcome, that either Joy or Amazement had tied up the Tongues of the whole Company. *Aurelian* here was most at a loss, for he knew not of his Happiness; and that which all along prevented *Juliana*'s confessing her self to him, was her knowing *Hippolito* (for whom she took him) to be *Aurelian*'s Friend, and she feared if he had known her, that he would never have consented to have deprived him of her. *Juliana* was the first that spoke, falling upon her Knees to her Father, who was not enough himself to take her up. *Don Fabio* ran to her, and awakened the Marquess, who then embraced her, but could not yet speak. *Fabritio* and *Leonora* strove who should first take her in their Arms; for *Aurelian* he was out of his wits for Joy, and *Juliana* was not much behind him, to see how happily their Loves and Duties were reconciled. *Don Fabio* embraced his Son and forgave him. The Marquess and *Fabritio* gave *Juliana* into his hands, he received the Blessing upon his Knees; all were over-joy'd, and *Don Mario* not a little proud at the discovery of his Son-in-Law, whom *Aurelian* did not fail to set forth with all the ardent Zeal and Eloquence of Friendship. *Juliana* and *Leonora* had pleasant Discourse about their unknown and mistaken Rivalship, and it was the Subject of a great deal of Mirth to hear *Juliana* relate the several Contrivances which she had to avoid *Aurelian* for the sake of *Hippolito*.

Having diverted themselves with many Remarks upon the pleasing surprize, they all thought it proper to attend upon the Great Duke that Morning at the Palace, and to acquaint him with the Novelty of what had pass'd; while, by the way, the two Young Couple entertained the Company with the Relation of several Particulars of their Three Days Adventures.

FINIS.

Mr. Congreve, to *Mr.* Dennis.

Concerning Humour in Comedy.

Dear Sir,

YOU write to me, that you have Entertained your self
two or three days, with reading several Comedies, of
several Authors; and your Observation is, that there is more
of *Humour* in our English Writers, than in any of the other
Comick Poets, Ancient or Modern. You desire to know my   5
Opinion, and at the same time my Thought, of that which
is generally call'd *Humour* in Comedy.

I agree with you, in an Impartial Preference of our
English Writers, in that Particular. But if I tell you my
Thoughts of *Humour*, I must at the same time confess, that   10
what I take for true *Humour*, has not been so often written
even by them, as is generally believed: And some who have
valued themselves, and have been esteem'd by others, for
that kind of Writing, have seldom touch'd upon it. To
make this appear to the World, would require a long and   15
labour'd Discourse, and such as I neither am able nor
willing to undertake. But such little Remarks, as may be
continued within the Compass of a Letter, and such
unpremeditated Thoughts, as may be Communicated
between Friend and Friend, without incurring the   20
Censure of the World, or setting up for a *Dictator*, you
shall have from me, since you have enjoyn'd it.

To Define *Humour*, perhaps, were as difficult, as to
Define *Wit*; for like that, it is of infinite variety. To
Enumerate the several *Humours* of Men, were a Work as   25
endless, as to sum up their several Opinions. And in my
mind the *Quot Homines tot Sententiæ*, might have been more
properly interpreted of *Humour*; since there are many Men,
of the same Opinion in many things, who are yet quite
different in *Humours*. But thô we cannot certainly tell what   30
Wit is, or, what *Humour* is, yet we may go near to shew
something, which is not *Wit* or not *Humour*; and yet often
mistaken for both. And since I have mentioned *Wit* and

Humour together, let me make the first Distinction between
35 them, and observe to you that *Wit is often mistaken for
Humour*.

I have observed, that when a few things have been Wittily
and Pleasantly spoken by any Character in a Comedy; it has
been very usual for those, who make their Remarks on a
40 Play, while it is acting, to say, *Such a thing is very Humorously
spoken: There is a great Deal of Humour in that Part.* Thus the
Character of the Person speaking, may be, Surprizingly
and Pleasantly, is mistaken for a Character of *Humour*;
which indeed is a Character of *Wit*. But there is a great
45 Difference between a Comedy, wherein there are many
things *Humorously*, as they call it, which is *Pleasantly*
spoken; and one, where there are several Characters of
Humour, distinguish'd by the Particular and Different
Humours, appropriated to the several Persons represented,
50 and which naturally arise, from the different Constitutions,
Complexions, and Dispositions of Men. The saying of
Humorous Things, does not distinguish Characters; For
every Person in a Comedy may be allow'd to speak them.
From a Witty Man they are expected; and even a *Fool* may
55 be permitted to stumble on 'em by chance. Thô I make a
Difference betwixt *Wit* and *Humour*; yet I do not think that
Humorous Characters exclude Wit: No, but the Manner of
Wit should be adapted to the *Humour*. As for Instance, a
Character of a Splenetick and Peevish *Humour*, should have
60 a Satyrical Wit. A Jolly and Sanguine *Humour*, should have a
Facetious Wit. The Former should speak Positively; the
Latter, Carelesly: For the former Observes, and shews
things as they are; the latter, rather overlooks Nature, and
speaks things as he would have them; and his *Wit* and
65 *Humour* have both of them a less Alloy of Judgment than
the others.

As *Wit*, so, its opposite, *Folly, is sometimes mistaken for
Humour.*

When a Poet brings a *Character* on the Stage, committing
70 a thousand Absurdities, and talking Impertinencies, roaring
Aloud, and Laughing immoderately, on every, or rather
upon no occasion; this is a Character of Humour.

Is any thing more common, than to have a pretended Comedy, stuff'd with such Grotesques, Figures, and Farce Fools? Things, that either are not in Nature, or if they are, are Monsters, and Births of Mischance; and consequently as such, should be stifled, and huddled out of the way, like *Sooterkins*; that Mankind may not be shock'd with an appearing Possibility of the Degeneration of a God-like *Species*. For my part, I am as willing to Laugh, as any body, and as easily diverted with an Object truly ridiculous: but at the same time, I can never care for seeing things, that force me to entertain low thoughts of my Nature. I dont know how it is with others, but I confess freely to you, I could never look long upon a Monkey, without very Mortifying Reflections; thô I never heard any thing to the Contrary, why that Creature is not Originally of a Distinct *Species*. As I dont think *Humour* exclusive of *Wit*, neither do I think it inconsistent with *Folly*; but I think the Follies should be only such, as Mens *Humours* may incline 'em to; and not Follies intirely abstracted from both Humour and Nature.

Sometimes, *Personal Defects are misrepresented for Humours*.

I mean, sometimes Characters are barbarously exposed on the Stage, ridiculing Natural Deformities, Casual Defects in the Senses, and Infirmities of Age. Sure the Poet must both be very Ill-natur'd himself, and think his Audience so, when he proposes by shewing a Man Deform'd, or Deaf, or Blind, to give them an agreeable Entertainment; and hopes to raise their Mirth by what is truly an object of Compassion. But much need not be said upon this Head to any body, especially to you, who in one of your Letters to me concerning Mr. *Johnson*'s *Fox*, have justly excepted against this Immoral part of *Ridicule* in *Corbaccio*'s Character; and there I must agree with you to blame him, whom otherwise I cannot enough admire, for his great Mastery of true Humour in Comedy.

External Habit of Body is often mistaken for Humour.

By *External Habit*, I do not mean the Ridiculous Dress or Cloathing of a Character, thô that goes a good way in some received Characters. (But undoubtedly a Man's

Humour may incline him to dress differently from other
People.) But I mean a Singularity of Manners, Speech, and
Behaviour, peculiar to all, or most of the same Country,
115 Trade, Profession, or Education. I cannot think, that a
Humour, which is only a Habit, or Disposition contracted
by Use or Custom; for by a Disuse, or Complyance with
other Customs, it may be worn off, or diversify'd.

Affectation is generally mistaken for Humour.

120   These are indeed so much alike, that at a Distance, they
may be mistaken one for the other. For what is *Humour* in
one, may be *Affectation* in another; and nothing is more
common, than for some to affect particular ways of saying,
and doing things, peculiar to others, whom they admire
125 and would imitate. *Humour* is the Life, *Affectation* the
Picture. He that draws a Character of *Affectation*, shews
Humour at the Second Hand; he at best but publishes a
Translation, and his Pictures are but Copies.

But as these two last distinctions are the Nicest, so it may
130 be most proper to Explain them, by Particular Instances
from some Author of Reputation. *Humour* I take, either to
be born with us, and so of a Natural Growth; or else to be
grafted into us, by some accidental change in the
Constitution, or revolution of the Internal Habit of Body;
135 by which it becomes, if I may so call it, Naturaliz'd.

Humour is from Nature, *Habit* from Custom; and
Affectation from Industry.

Humour, shews us as we *are*.

Habit, shews us, as we appear, under a forcible Impression.
140 *Affectation*, shews what we would be, under a Voluntary
Disguise.

Thô here I would observe by the way, that a continued
Affectation, may in time become a Habit.

The Character of *Morose* in the *Silent Woman*, I take to
145 be a Character of Humour. And I choose to Instance this
Character to you, from many others of the same Author,
because I know it has been Condemn'd by many as
Unnatural and Farce: And you have your self hinted
some dislike of it, for the same Reason, in a Letter to me,
150 concerning some of *Johnson's* Plays.

Let us suppose *Morose* to be a Man Naturally Splenetick
and Melancholly; is there any thing more offensive to one of
such a Disposition, than Noise and Clamour? Let any Man
that has the Spleen (and there are enough in *England*) be
Judge. We see common Examples of this Humour in little   155
every day. 'Tis ten to one, but three parts in four of the
Company that you dine with, are Discompos'd and Startled
at the Cutting of a Cork, or Scratching a Plate with a Knife:
It is a Proportion of the same Humour, that makes such or
any other Noise offensive to the Person that hears it; for   160
there are others who will not be disturb'd at all by it. Well;
But *Morose* you will say, is so Extravagant, he cannot bear
any Discourse or Conversation, above a Whisper. Why, It is
his excess of this Humour, that makes him become
Ridiculous, and qualifies his Character for Comedy. If the   165
Poet had given him, but a Moderate proportion of that
Humour, 'tis odds but half the Audience, would have
sided with the Character, and have Condemn'd the
Author, for Exposing a Humour which was neither
Remarkable nor Ridiculous. Besides, the distance of the   170
Stage requires the Figure represented, to be something
larger than the Life; and sure a Picture may have Features
larger in Proportion, and yet be very like the Original. If this
Exactness of Quantity, were to be observed in Wit, as some
would have it in Humour; what would become of those   175
Characters that are design'd for Men of Wit? I believe if a
Poet should steal a Dialogue of any length, from the
Extempore Discourse of the two Wittiest Men upon Earth,
he would find the Scene but coldly receiv'd by the Town.
But to the purpose.   180

The Character of Sir *John Daw* in the same Play, is a
Character of Affection. He every where discovers an
Affectation of Learning; when he is not only Conscious to
himself, but the Audience also plainly perceives that he is
Ignorant. Of this kind are the Characters of *Thraso* in the   185
Eunuch of *Terence*, and *Pyrgopolinices* in the *Miles Gloriosus*
of *Plautus*. They affect to be thought Valiant, when both
themselves and the Audience know they are not. Now such
a boasting of Valour in Men who were really Valiant, would

190 undoubtedly be a *Humour*; for a Fiery Disposition might naturally throw a Man into the same Extravagance, which is only affected in the Characters I have mentioned.

The Character of *Cob* in *Every Man in his Humour*, and most of the under Characters in *Bartholomew-Fair*, discover only a 195 Singularity of Manners, appropriated to the several Educations and Professions of the Persons represented. They are not Humours but Habits contracted by Custom. Under this Head may be ranged all Country-Clowns, Sailers, Tradesmen, Jockeys, Gamesters and such like, who make use 200 of *Cants* or peculiar *Dialects* in their several Arts and Vocations. One may almost give a Receipt for the Composition of such a Character: For the Poet has nothing to do, but to collect a few proper Phrases and terms of Art, and to make the Person apply them by ridiculous Metaphors in 205 his Conversation, with Characters of different Natures. Some late Characters of this kind have been very successful; but in my mind they may be Painted without much Art or Labour; since they require little more, than a good Memory and Superficial Observation. But true *Humour* cannot be shewn, 210 without a Dissection of Nature, and a Narrow Search, to discover the first Seeds, from whence it has its Root and growth.

If I were to write to the World, I should be obliged to dwell longer, upon each of these Distinctions and 215 Examples; for I know that they would not be plain enough to all Readers. But a bare hint is sufficient to inform you of the Notions which I have on this Subject: And I hope by this time you are of my Opinion, that Humour is neither Wit, nor Folly, nor Personal defect; 220 nor Affectation, nor Habit; and yet, that each, and all of these, have been both written and received for Humour.

I should be unwilling to venture even on a bare Description of Humour, much more, to make a Definition of it, but now my hand is in, Ile tell you what 225 serves me instead of either. I take it to be, *A singular and unavoidable manner of doing, or saying any thing, Peculiar and Natural to one Man only; by which his Speech and Actions are distinguish'd from those of other Men.*

Our *Humour* has relation to us, and to what proceeds from us, as the Accidents have to a Substance; it is a Colour, Taste, and Smell, Diffused through all; thô our Actions are never so many, and different in Form, they are all Splinters of the same Wood, and have Naturally one Complexion; which thô it may be disguised by Art, yet cannot be wholly changed: We may Paint it with other Colours, but we cannot change the Grain. So the Natural sound of an Instrument will be distinguish'd, thô the Notes expressed by it, are never so various, and the Divisions never so many. Dissimulation, may by Degrees, become more easy to our practice; but it can never absolutely Transubstantiate us into what we would seem: It will always be in some proportion a Violence upon Nature.

A Man may change his Opinion, but I believe he will find it a Difficulty, to part with his *Humour*, and there is nothing more provoking, than the being made sensible of that difficulty. Sometimes, one shall meet with those, who perhaps, Innocently enough, but at the same time impertinently, will ask the Question; *Why are you not Merry? Why are you not Gay, Pleasant, and Cheerful?* then instead of answering, could I ask such one; *Why are you not handsome? Why have you not Black Eyes, and a better Complexion?* Nature abhors to be forced.

The two Famous Philosophers of *Ephesus* and *Abdera*, have their different Sects at this day. Some Weep, and others Laugh at one and the same thing.

I dont doubt, but you have observed several Men Laugh when they are Angry; others who are Silent; some that are Loud: Yet I cannot suppose that it is the passion of *Anger* which is in it self different, or more or less in one than t'other; but that it is the *Humour* of the Man that is Predominant, and urges him to express it in that manner. Demonstrations of pleasure are as Various; one Man has a Humour of retiring from all Company, when any thing has happen'd to please him beyond expectation; he hugs himself alone, and thinks it an Addition to the pleasure to keep it Secret. Another is upon Thorns till he has made Proclamation of it; and must make other people sensible of

his happiness, before he can be so himself. So it is in Grief,
and other Passions. Demonstrations of Love and the
270 Effects of that Passion upon several Humours, are
infinitely different; but here the Ladies who abound in
Servants are the best Judges. Talking of the Ladies,
methinks something should be observed of the Humour
of the Fair Sex; since they are sometimes so kind as to
275 furnish out a Character for Comedy. But I must confess
I have never made any observation of what I Apprehend to
be true Humour in Women. Perhaps Passions are too
powerful in that Sex, to let Humour have its Course; or
may be by Reason of their Natural Coldness, Humour
280 cannot Exert it self to that extravagant Degree, which it
often does in the Male Sex. For if ever any thing does
appear Comical or Ridiculous in a Woman, I think it is
little more than an acquir'd Folly, or an Affectation. We
may call them the weaker Sex, but I think the true Reason
285 is, because our Follies are Stronger, and our Faults are
more prevailing.

One might think that the Diversity of Humour, which
must be allowed to be diffused throughout Mankind, might
afford endless matter, for the support of Comedies. But
290 when we come closely to consider that point, and nicely to
distinguish the Difference of Humours, I believe we shall
find the contrary. For thô we allow every Man something
of his own, and a peculiar Humour; yet every Man has it
not in quantity, to become Remarkable by it: Or, if many
295 do become Remarkable by their Humours; yet all those
Humours may not be Diverting. Nor is it only requisite to
distinguish what Humour will be diverting, but also how
much of it, what part of it to shew in Light, and what to cast
in Shades; how to set it off by preparatory Scenes, and by
300 opposing other humours to it in the same Scene. Thrô a
wrong Judgment, sometimes, Mens Humours may be
opposed when there is really no specific Difference
between them; only a greater proportion of the same, in
one than t'other; occasion'd by his having more Flegm, or
305 Choller, or whatever the Constitution is, from whence their
Humours derive their Source.

There is infinitely more to be said on this Subject; thô perhaps I have already said too much; but I have said it to a Friend, who I am sure will not expose it, if he does not approve of it. I believe the Subject is intirely new, and was 310 never touch'd upon before; and if I would have any one to see this private Essay, it should be some one, who might be provoked by my Errors in it, to Publish a more Judicious Treatise on the Subject. Indeed I wish it were done, that the World being a little acquainted with the scarcity of true 315 Humour, and the difficulty of finding and shewing it, might look a little more favourably on the Labours of them, who endeavour to search into Nature for it, and lay it open to the Publick View.

I dont say but that very entertaining and useful 320 Characters, and proper for Comedy, may be drawn from Affectations, and those other Qualities, which I have endeavoured to distinguish from Humour: but I would not have such imposed on the World, for Humour, nor esteem'd of Equal value with it. It were perhaps, the Work 325 of a long Life to make one Comedy true in all its Parts, and to give every Character in it a True and Distinct Humour. Therefore, every Poet must be beholding to other helps, to make out his Number of ridiculous Characters. But I think such a One deserves to be broke, who makes all false 330 Musters; who does not shew one true Humour in a Comedy, but entertains his Audience to the end of the Play with every thing out of Nature.

I will make but one Observation to you more, and have done; and that is grounded upon an Observation of your 335 own, and which I mention'd at the beginning of my Letter, *viz*, That there is more of Humour in our English Comick Writers than in any others. I do not at all wonder at it, for I look upon Humour to be almost of English Growth; at least, it does not seem to have found such Encrease on any 340 other Soil. And what appears to me to be the reason of it, is the great Freedom, Privilege, and Liberty which the Common People of *England* enjoy. Any Man that has a Humour, is under no restraint, or fear of giving it Vent; they have a Proverb among them, which, may be, will shew 345

the Bent and Genius of the People, as well as a longer
Discourse: *He that will have a May-pole, shall have a
May-pole.* This is a Maxim with them, and their Practice
is agreeable to it. I believe something Considerable too may
350 be ascribed to their feeding so much on Flesh, and the
Grossness of their Diet in general. But I have done, let the
Physicians agree that. Thus you have my Thoughts of
Humour, to my Power of Expressing them in so little
Time and Compass. You will be kind to shew me
355 wherein I have Err'd; and as you are very Capable of
giving me Instruction, so, I think I have a very Just title
to demand it from you; being without Reserve,

July 10. 1695.

Your real Friend,
360   *and humble Servant,*
W. Congreve.

AMENDMENTS

OF

Mr. COLLIER'*s*

False and Imperfect CITATIONS, &c.

From the
$\begin{cases}\text{OLD BATCHELOUR,} \\ \text{DOUBLE DEALER,} \\ \text{LOVE for LOVE,} \\ \text{MOURNING BRIDE.}\end{cases}$

By the Author of those Plays.

Quem recitas meus est ô Fidentine Libellus,
Sed male dum recitas incipit esse tuus.

Mart.

Graviter, & iniquo animo, maledicta tua paterer, si te scirem
Judicio magis, quam morbo animi, petulantia ista uti. Sed,
quoniam in te neque modum, neque modestiam ullam animad-
verto, respondebo tibi: uti, si quam maledicendo voluptatem
cepisti, eam male-audiendo amittas.

Salust. Decl.

LONDON,

Printed for *J. Tonson* at the *Judge*'s Head in *Fleet-street*,
near the *Inner-Temple-Gate.* 1698.

AMENDMENTS

OF

Mr. COLLIER'*s*

False and Imperfect CITATIONS, &c.

I HAVE been told by some, That they should think me very idle, if I threw away any time in taking notice ev'n of so much of Mr. *Collier*'s late Treatise of the Immorality, *&c.* of the *English* Stage, as related to my self, in respect of some Plays written by me: For that his malicious and strain'd   5
Interpretations of my Words were so gross and palpable, that any indifferent and unprejudic'd Reader would immediately condemn him upon his own Evidence, and acquit me before I could make my Defence.

On the other hand, I have been tax'd of Laziness, and too   10
much Security, in neglecting thus long to do my self a necessary Right, which might be effected with so very little Pains; since very little more is requisite in my Vindication, than to represent truly and at length, those Passages which Mr. *Collier* has shewn imperfectly, and for   15
the most part by halves. I would rather be thought Idle than Lazy; and so the last Advice prevail'd with me.

I have no Intention to examine all the Absurdities and Falshoods in Mr. *Collier*'s Book; to use the Gentleman's own Metaphor in his Preface, *An Inventory of such a Ware-*   20
house would be a large Work. My Detection of his Malice and Ignorance, of his Sophistry and vast Assurance, will lie within a narrow Compass, and only bear a Proportion to so much of his Book as concerns my self.

Least of all, would I undertake to defend the Corruptions   25
of the Stage; indeed if I were so inclin'd, Mr. *Collier* has given me no occasion; for the greater part of those Examples which he has produc'd, are only Demonstrations of his own Impurity, they only savour of his Utterance, and were sweet enough till tainted by his Breath.   30

I will not justifie any of my own Errors; I am sensible of
many; and if Mr. *Collier* has by any Accident stumbled on
one or two, I will freely give them up to him, *Nullum
unquam ingenium placuit sine venia*. But I hope I have
35 done nothing that can deprive me of the Benefit of my
Clergy; and tho' Mr. *Collier* himself were the Ordinary,
I may hope to be acquitted.

My Intention therefore, is to do little else, but to restore
those Passages to their primitive Station, which have
40 suffer'd so much in being transplanted by him: I will
remove 'em from his Dunghil, and replant 'em in the
Field of Nature; and when I have wash'd 'em of that
Filth which they have contracted in passing thro' his very
dirty hands, let their own Innocence protect them.

45 Mr. *Collier*, in the high Vigour of his Obscenity, first
commits a Rape upon my Words, and then arraigns 'em of
Immodesty; he has Barbarity enough to accuse the very
Virgins that he has deflowr'd, and to make sure of their
Condemnation, he has himself made 'em guilty: But he
50 forgets that while he publishes their shame he divulges his
own.

His Artifice to make Words guilty of Profaneness, is of
the same nature; for where the Expression is unblameable
in its own clear and genuine Signification, he enters into it
55 himself like the evil Spirit; he possesses the innocent
Phrase, and makes it bellow forth his own Blasphemies;[1]
so *that one would think the Muse was Legion.*

To reprimand him a little in his own Words,[2] if these
Passages produc'd by Mr. *Collier* are obscene and profane,
60 *Why were they rak'd in and disturb'd, unless it were to conjure
up Vice, and revive Impurities? Indeed Mr.* Collier *has a very
untoward way with him; his Pen has such a Libertine Stroke,
that 'tis a question whether the Practice or the Reproof be the
more licentious.*

65 *He teaches those Vices he would correct, and writes more like
a Pimp than a P——. Since the business must be undertaken, why
was not the Thought blanch'd, the Expression made remote,*

----

[1] *Coll.* p. 81.   [2] p. 70, 71.

and the ill Features cast into Shadows? So far from this, which is his own Instruction in his own words, is Mr. *Collier*'s way of Proceeding, that he has blackned the Thoughts with his own *Smut*; the Expression that was remote, he has brought nearer; and lest by being brought near its native Innocence might be more visible, he has frequently varied it, he has new-molded it, and stamp'd his own Image on it; so that it at length is become Current Deformity, and fit to be paid into the Devil's Exchequer.

I will therefore take the Liberty to exorcise this evil Spirit, and whip him out of my Plays, where-ever I can meet with him. Mr. *Collier* has revers'd the Story which he relates from *Tertullian*;[3] and after his Visitation of the Play-house returns, having left the Devil behind him.

If I do not return his Civilities in calling him Names, it is because I am not very well vers'd in his *Nomenclatures*; therefore for his *Foot pads*, which he calls us in his Preface, and for his *Buffoons* and *Slaves in the Saturnalia*, which he frequently bestows on us in the rest of his Book,[4] I will onely call him Mr. *Collier*, and that I will call him as often as I think he shall deserve it.

Before I proceed, for methods sake, I must premise some few things to the Reader, which if he thinks in his Conscience are too much to be granted me, I desire he would proceed no further in his Perusal of these Animadversions, but return to Mr. *Collier*'s *Short View*, &c.

First, I desire that I may lay down *Aristotle*'s Definition of Comedy; which has been the Compass by which all the Comick Poets, since his time, have steer'd their Course. I mean them whom Mr. *Collier* so very frequently calls *Comedians*; for the Distinction between *Comicus* and *Comædus*, and *Tragicus* and *Tragædus* is what he has not met with in the long Progress of his Reading.

Comedy (says *Aristotle*) is an Imitation of the worse sort of People. Μίμησις φαυλοτέρων, *imitatio pejorum*. He does not mean the worse sort of People in respect to their

---

[3] p. 257.   [4] p. 81, 63, 175.

105 Quality, but in respect to their Manners. This is plain,
from his telling you immediately after, that he does not
mean Κατὰ πᾶσαν κακίαν, relating to all kinds of Vice:
there are Crimes too daring and too horrid for Comedy.
But the Vices most frequent, and which are the common
110 Practice of the looser sort of Livers, are the subject Matter
of Comedy. He tells us farther, that they must be exposed
after a ridiculous manner: For Men are to be laugh'd out of
their Vices in Comedy; the Business of Comedy is to
delight, as well as to instruct: And as vicious People are
115 made asham'd of their Follies or Faults, by seeing them
expos'd in a ridiculous manner, so are good People at once
both warn'd and diverted at their Expence.

Thus much I thought necessary to premise, that by
shewing the Nature and End of Comedy, we may be
120 prepared to expect Characters agreeable to it.

Secondly, Since Comick Poets are oblig'd by the Laws of
Comedy, and to the intent that Comedy may answer its
true end and purpose above-mentioned, to represent
vicious and foolish Characters: In Consideration of this,
125 I desire that it may not be imputed to the Perswasion or
private Sentiments of the Author, if at any time one of
these vicious Characters in any of his Plays shall behave
himself foolishly, or immorally in Word or Deed. I hope
I am not yet unreasonable; it were very hard that a Painter
130 should be believ'd to resemble all the ugly Faces that he
draws.

Thirdly, I must desire the impartial Reader, not to
consider any Expression or Passage cited from any Play,
as it appears in Mr. *Collier*'s Book; nor to pass any Sentence
135 or Censure upon it, out of its proper Scene, or alienated
from the Character by which it is spoken; for in that place
alone, and in his Mouth alone, can it have its proper and
true Signification.

I cannot think it reasonable, because Mr. *Collier* is
140 pleas'd to write one Chapter of *Immodesty*, and another of
Profaneness, that therefore every Expression traduc'd by
him under those Heads, shall be condemn'd as obscene
and profane immediately, and without any further

Enquiry. Perhaps Mr. *Collier* is acquainted with the
deceptio visus, and presents Objects to the View through a   145
stain'd Glass; things may appear seemingly profane, when
in reality they are only seen through a profane *Medium*, and
the true Colour is dissembled by the help of a Sophistical
Varnish: Therefore, I demand the Privilege of the *habeas
Corpus* Act, that the Prisoners may have Liberty to remove,   150
and to appear before a just Judge in an open and an
uncounterfeit light.

Fourthly, Because Mr. *Collier* in his Chapter of the
Profaneness of the Stage, has founded great part of his
Accusation upon the Liberty which Poets take of using   155
some Words in their Plays, which have been sometimes
employed by the Translators of the Holy Scriptures: I
desire that the following Distinction may be admitted, *viz.*
That when Words are apply'd to sacred things, and with a
purpose to treat of sacred things; they ought to be   160
understood accordingly: But when they are otherwise
apply'd, the Diversity of the Subject gives a Diversity of
Signification. And in truth, he might as well except against
the common use of the Alphabet in Poetry, because the same
Letters are necessary to the spelling of Words which are   165
mention'd in sacred Writ.

Tho' I have thought it requisite, and but reasonable to
premise these few things, to which, as to so many *postulata*,
I may when occasion offers, refer my self; yet if the Reader
should have any Objection to the Latitude which at first   170
sight they may seem to comprehend, I dare venture to
assure him that it shall be remov'd by the Caution which
I shall use, and those Limits by which I shall restrain my
self, when I shall judge it proper for me to refer to them.

It may not be impertinent in this place, to remind the   175
Reader of a very common Expedient, which is made use of
to recommend the Instruction of our Plays; which is this.
After the Action of the Play is over, and the Delight of the
Representation at an end; there is generally Care taken, that
the Moral of the whole shall be summ'd up, and deliver'd   180
to the Audience, in the very last and concluding Lines of
the Poem. The Intention of this is, that the Delight of the

Representation may not so strongly possess the Minds of
the Audience, as to make them forget or oversee the
185 Instruction: It is the last thing said, that it may make the
last Impression; and it is always comprehended in a few
Lines, and put into Rhyme, that it may be easy and
engaging to the Memory.

Mr. *Collier* divides his Charge against the Stage into
190 these four heads, Immodesty, Profaneness, Abuse of the
Clergy, and Encouragement of Immorality.

I have yet written but four poor Plays; and this Author,
out of his very particular Favour to me, has found the means
to accuse 'em every one of one or more of these four Crimes.
195 I will examine each in its turn, by his Citations; and begin
with the Plays in the order that they were written.

In his Chapter of the Immodesty of the Stage, he has not
made any Quotation from my Comedies: But in general,
finds fault with the lightness of some Characters. He
200 mentions slightly,[5] and I think without any Accusation,
Belinda in the *Old Batchelor*, and *Miss Prue* in *Love for
Love. Miss Prue,* he says, is represented *silly to screen her
Impudence,* which *amounts to this Confession, that Women
when they have their Understandings about them, ought to
205 Converse otherwise.*[6] I grant it; this is in truth the Moral of
the Character. If Mr. *Collier* would examine still at this
rate, we should agree very well. *Belinda* he produces as a
Character *under Disorders of Liberty;*[7] this last is what I do
not understand, and therefore desire to be excused, if I can
210 make no Answer to it. I only refer those two Characters to
the Judgment of any impartial Reader, to determine
whether they are represented so as to engage any
Spectator to imitate the Impudence of one, or the
Affectation of the other; and whether they are not both
215 ridiculed rather than recommended.

But he proceeds,[8] *the Double-dealer is particularly
remarkable. There are but four Ladies in this Play, and three
of the biggest of them are Whores.* These are very *big* Words;
very much too *big* for the Sense, for to say *three of the biggest,*

[5] p. 10, 12.   [6] p. 11.   [7] p. 12.   [8] p. 12.

when there are but four in Number, is stark Nonsense: 220
Whatever the *Matter* may be in this Gentleman's Book, I
perceive his *Stile* at least is admirable.

Well, suppose he had said—and the three Biggest, *&c.* for
I am sure he cannot part with *biggest*, he has occasion to use it
so often in the rest of his Book. But mark, he gives us an   225
instance of his *big* good Breeding. *A great Complement to
Quality, to tell them, there is not above a quarter of them
honest!* This Computation I suppose he makes by the help
of political Arithmetick. As thus; the Stage is the Image of the
World; by the Men and Women represented there, are   230
signified all the Men and Women in the World; so that if
four Women are shewn upon the Stage, and three of them are
vicious, it is as much as to say, that three parts in four of the
whole Sex are stark naught. He who dares be so hardy as to
gain-say this Argument, let him do it; for my part, I love to   235
meddle with my Match. It was a mercy that all the four
Women were not naught; for that had been maintaining
that there was not one Woman of Quality honest. What has
Virgil to answer for at this rate, in his *Æneis?* Where, for two
of the Fair Sex that do good, *viz. Venus* and the *Sybill*, (for   240
Cybelle and *Andromache* are but Well-wishers) he has the
following Catalogue, who are always engag'd in Mischief,
viz. Juno, Juturna, Dido, her Sister, her Nurse, an old Witch,
Alecto the Fury, all the *Harpies*; to these you are reminded of
Helen the First Incendiary, *Sylvia* is produc'd as a Second,   245
next *Camilla*, then *Amata*, who despised the Decrees of the
Gods; nay, poor *Creusa* and *Lavinia* are made subservient to
unfortunate Events. This is *Bossu*'s Remark,[9] and he says that
Virgil in the Characters of the Sex, has closely observed the
Rule of *Aristotle*, who in his Treatise of Poetry has ventur'd to   250
affirm, That there are more bad than good Women in the
World; and that they do more harm than good.

In an Epick Poem Ladies of Quality may be used as
Aristotle pleases; but Comedy was meant to complement,
and tickle, and flatter, and all that.   255

[9] *Traite du poem, Epiq;* L. 4. Cap. 2.

Here I take the first Liberty to refer the Reader to my first Proposition. Mr. *Collier*, who talks with great Intimacy of Ancient and Modern Criticks,[10] and amongst others, makes familiar mention of *Rapin*, has unluckily overseen a
260 particular Remark that is made by that learned Critick, on the Improvement of Modern Comedy by *Moliere*, in his raising his ridiculous Characters. If he does not know where to find it, I can help him to it.

Les anciens Poetes Comiques n'ont que des Valets pour les
265 *plaisans de leur Theatre, et les plaisans du Theatre de Moliere sont les Marquis et les gens de qualité, les autres n'ont Joüé dans la Comedie, que la vie bourgeoise et commune, et Moliere a Joüé tout Paris et la Cour.*[11]

Well, this may be the *French*, and it may be the *English*
270 Breeding; but Mr. *Collier* assures us—*This was not the Roman Breeding.*[12] They used to complement Vice in Quality, the gentle *Persius* gives us an Instance of it.

> *Vos o Patricius sanguis, quos vivere fas est*
> *Occipiti cæco, posticæ occurrite sannæ.*
275   Sat. 1.

But *Persius* was a Man of Quality, and perhaps might be a little familiar with his Equals. As for *Juvenal*, he kept his distance, and made it as plain as the Sun.

> *Namque ibi fortunæ veniam damus. Alea turpis,*
280 > *Turpe & adulterium mediocribus: Hæc eadem illi*
> *Omnia cum faciant, Hilares nitidique vocantur.*
>   Sat. 11.

I am finely employed, to furnish my Adversary with two such Authorities against my self: But reflecting that Mr. *Collier*
285 has no great Esteem for *Juvenal*, who he says, *writes more like a Pimp than a Poet.*[13] 'Tis likely that he will return me his Authority, to make the best Use that I can of it for my self; therefore I will take the Liberty to state a short Question.

---

[10] *Vid, Coll.* p. 175.   [11] Rap. *Reflex. sur la* Poet. 26.
[12] p. 12.   [13] p. 71.

Juvenal by the help of an *Irony*, has in these three Lines, lash'd the Vices of great Persons with more Severity, than he could have done by the means of a direct and point-blank Invective. Mr. *Collier* is in plain terms,[14] for having Complements pass'd on Persons of Quality, and neither will allow their Follies nor their Vices to be expos'd. Now the Question that I would ask, is onely, which agrees best with the Character of a Pimp, the Satire of *Juvenal*, or the Complaisance of Mr. *Collier*? In the Conclusion of his Preface he is quite of another Opinion; There *he confesses he has no Ceremony for Debauchery, for to complement Vice, is but one remove from worshipping the Devil*; now that Mr. *Collier* complements Vice is plain. *Ergo*, &c.

This is his own Confession, and so I leave him to lick himself whole with one of his own Absolutions.

When Vice shall be allowed as an Indication of Quality and good Breeding, then it may also pass for a piece of good Breeding to complement Vice in Quality: But till then, I humbly conceive, that to expose and ridicule it, will altogether do as well.

The Double-dealer (he says[15]) *runs riot* upon some occasion or other, *and gives Lord* Touchwood *a Mixture of Smut and Pedantry to conclude with*: For Proof of this, he directs the Reader in his Margin to the 79*th* Page, which is the last of the Play. He has made no Quotation, therefore I will do it for him, and transcribe what Lord *Touchwood* says in that place, being the concluding Lines and Moral of the whole Comedy. *Mellefont* and *Cynthia* are to be married, the Villainies of *Maskwell* having been detected; Lord *Touchwood* gives 'em Joy, and then concludes the Play as follows.

Lord *Touch.—be each others Comfort;—let me join your hands.—unwearied nights, and wishing Days attend you both; mutual Love, lasting Health, and circling Joys tread round each happy Year of your long lives.*

Let secret Villany from hence be warn'd;
Howe'er in private, mischiefs are conceiv'd,

[14] p. 12, 173, 175.   [15] p. 27.

325

> *Torture and Shame attend their open Birth:*
> *Like Vipers in the Womb base treachery lies,*
> *Still gnawing that whence first it did arise;*
> *No sooner born but the vile parent dies.*

This in Mr. *Collier*'s polite Phrase, *is running riot upon*
330 *Smut and Pedantry.* I hope this is some reason for my
having laid down my third Proposition; where the Reader
is desired not to rely upon Mr. *Collier*'s bare word, but to
consult the Original, before he passes his Censure on the
Author.

335 Before he finishes his Chapter of Immodesty, he taxes
the *Mourning-Bride* with *Smut* and *Profaneness*; if he can
prove it, I must of necessity give up the Cause. If there be
Immodesty in that Tragedy, I must confess my self
incapable of ever writing any thing with Modesty or
340 Decency.

Had Osmin (says he) *parted with* Almeria *civilly, it had
been much better, that rant of* Smut *and* Profaneness *might
have been spared.*[16] What he means by *civilly* I know not,
unless he means *dully* and *insensibly*; neither Civility nor
345 Incivility have any thing to do with Passion; where a Scene
is wrought to an Excess of Tenderness and Grief, there is
no room for either Rudeness or Complaisance. Mr. *Collier*
is pleas'd to condemn the parting of *Osmin* and *Almeria*, by
comparing it with the meeting of *Menelaus* and *Helen*; but
350 I must take the Liberty to tell him, that meeting and
parting are two things, and especially between two
Lovers. Now for the rant of *Smut* and *Profaneness.*

> —*Osm. O my* Almeria.
> *What do the damn'd endure but to despair,*
355 > *But knowing Heav'n to know it lost for ever.*

I will not here so much as refer my self to my third
Proposition, nor desire the Reader to trouble himself so far,
as to look on these Lines in their proper Scene and Place,
tho' most of the foregoing Incidents in the Poem were

[16] p. 32, 33, 34.

contrived so as to prepare the Violence of this Scene; and   360
all the foregoing part of this Scene was laid as a Gradation
of Passion, to prepare the violence of these Expressions, the
last and most extream of the whole, in *Osmin*'s Part.

For once I will let these Lines remain as they are set by
Mr. *Collier*, with his own filthy Foil beneath, hem'd in and   365
sullied over with his own *Smut*. And still what is there either
of Profaneness or Immodesty in the Expression? Is not the
Reflection rather moral and religious than otherwise? Does
not the Allusion set forth the terrors of Damnation? I dare
affirm that Mr. *Collier* himself, cannot so transpose those   370
words as to make 'em signifie any thing either *smutty* or
profane: What he may be able to do with the Letters if they
were disjointed, I know not; I will not dispute his Skill in
Anagram; and if the truth were known, I believe there lies
the Stress of his Proof. Well, Mr. *Saygrace*, in the *Double-*   375
dealer, is beholding to him for his new Amusement, for the
future he shall renounce Acrosticks and pursue *Anagrams*.

As to what he says after, that these Verses are a
similitude drawn from the Creed; I no more understand
it, than he himself would believe it, tho' he should affirm it.   380

In the rest of his Remarks upon this Scene, his *Zeal* gives
way to his *Criticism*; he had but an ill hold of *Profaneness*,
and was reduc'd to catch at the *Poetry*. The corruption of a
rotten Divine is the Generation of a sowr Critick.

He is very merry, and as he supposes with me; in   385
laughing at *wasting Air*. *Wasting* he thinks is a senseless
Epithet for *Air*, truly I think so too. I will not lose this
occasion of consenting with him, because he will not afford
me many more: But where does he meet with *wasting Air*?
not in the *Mourning-bride*; for in that Play it is printed   390
wafting Air, so that all his awkard Railery about this
word, reflects alone upon himself: To say nothing of his
Honesty in making a false Quotation, or of his becoming
assurance in charging me with his own Nonsense.

He proceeds in his unlucky and satirical Strain, and   395
ridicules half a dozen Epithets, and about as many
Figures, which follow in the same Scene, with much

Delicacy of fine Railery, Excellence of good Manners, and
Elegancy of Expression.

400 *Almeria*, in the Play, oppress'd and sinking beneath her
Grief, adapts her words to her Posture, and says to *Osmin*—

> —*O let us not support,*
> *But sink each other lower yet, down, down,*
> *Where levell'd low,* &c.

405 *One would think* (says Mr. *Collier*) *she was learning a*
Spaniel to set.

Learning a Spaniel to set! *Delectus verborum est Origo*
eloquentiæ, is an Aphorism of *Julius Cæsar*, and Mr.
Collier makes it plain. This poor Man does not so much
410 as understand even his own Dog-language, when he says
learning, I suppose he means *teaching a Spaniel to set*, a
dainty Critick, indeed!

A little before, *Almeria* is cold, faint and tembling in her
Agony, and says,

415 —*I chatter, shake and faint with thrilling fears.*

By the way (says Mr. *Collier*, for now he is Mr. *Collier*
emphatically) *'tis a mighty wonder to hear a Woman chatter!*
but there is no Jesting, &c.

Jesting quotha! What, does he take the letting a Pun to be
420 the breaking of a Jest? a Whip and a Bell, and away with
him to Kennel again immediately.

Ay, now he's in his Element, as you shall hear.

This litter of Epithets makes the Poem look like a Bitch
over-stock'd with Puppies, and sucks the Sence almost to skin
425 *and bone.* The Comparison is handsome, I must needs say;
but I desire the Reader to consider that it is Mr. *Collier* the
Critick, that talks at this odd rate; not Mr. *Collier*
the Divine: I would not, by any means, that he should
mistake one for the other.

430 If it is necessary for me to give any reason in this place,
why I have used Epithets and Figures in this Scene, I will
do it in few words. First I desire the Reader to remove my
Verses from amongst Mr. *Collier*'s Interlineations of sad
Drollery; and reinstate 'em in the Scene of the Play from

whence they were torn. If there is found Passion in those   435
parts of the Scene where those Epithets and Figures are
used, they will stand in need of no Vindication; for every
body knows that Discourses of men in Passion, naturally
abound in Epithets and Figures, in Agravations and
Hyperboles. To this I add, That the Diction of Poetry   440
consists of Figures; by the frequent use of bold and
daring Figures, it is distinguish'd from Prose and
Oratory. Epithets are beautiful in Poetry, but make Prose
languishing and cold; and the frequent use of them in
Prose, makes it pretend too much and approach too near   445
to Poetry.[17] If Figures and Epithets are natural to Passion,
and if they compose the Diction of Poetry, certainly
Tragedy, which is of the sublime and first-rate Poetry,
and which ought every where to abound in *Passion*, may
very well be allow'd to use Epithets and Figures, more   450
especially in a Scene consisting entirely of Passion, and
still more particularly in the most violent part of that
Scene. Thus much, to justifie the use and frequency of
Epithets and Figures in the Scene abovemention'd. Ay, but
Mr. *Collier* says some of the Figures there are *Stiff*: He says   455
so, I confess; but what then? Why in answer, I say they are
not, and so leave it to be determin'd by better Judges.

Having shewn that men in Passion, naturally make use of
violent Figures and Epithets; I will produce no less a Man
than Mr. *Collier* himself for an Example: If you would   460
behold the Gentleman beginning to swell, see him in
Page 80. there he puffs and blows, and deals mightily in
short periods: At first he is scarce able to Breath, but at
length he Opens; and anon finds vent for a very odd
Expression. He is angry with some Play or other, and   465
says—*Nature made the ferment and rising of the Blood, for
such occasions.* I hope he speaks Figuratively, or else I am
sure he speaks at least Prophanely; for we know who is
meant by *Nature in the Language of Christianity, and
especially under the Notion of a* Maker.[18]   470

[17] *Arist. Rhet.* L. 3. C. 3.   [18] v. p. 72.

He discovers in this Expression, that his Religion and his Natural Philosophy are both of a size. He has declared the very Source of Living, and the Spring of Motion in the Mechanical Part of Man, to be no more than the Fountain-
475 Head of Follies and Passions; and intimates very strongly, That *Nature* made it only for that purpose.

But I think nothing that he says, should be consider'd seriously; therefore I will proceed, and produce Mr. *Collier* as he stands advanc'd both in *ferment* and *figure*. In (p. 84.)
480 he has drawn Quotations from Comedies, *that look Reeking as it were from* Pandemonium, *and almost smell of Fire and Brimstone; Eruptions of Hell with a witness! He almost wonders the Smoak of them has not darkned the Sun, and turn'd the Air to Plague and Poison. Provocations enough to*
485 *Arm all Nature in Revenge; to exhaust the Judgments of Heaven,* &c. He goes on with such terrible Stuff for a considerable while together. I give this only as a Sample of some of this Gentleman's Figures.

Methinks I hear him pronounce 'em every time I behold
490 'em, they are almost Noisy and Turbulent, even in the Print. In short, they are Contagious; and I find he that will speak of them, is in great danger to speak like them. But why does Mr. *Collier* use all this Vehemence in a Written Argument? If he were to Preach, I grant it might
495 be necessary for him to make a Noise, that he might be sure to be heard: But why all this Passion upon Paper? Judgment is never Outrageous; and Christianity is ever Meek and Mild.

I have read it somewhere as the Remark of St.
500 *Chrysostom,* That the Prophets of God were as much distinguish'd from the Prophets of the Devil by their Behaviour, as by the Divine Truths which they utter'd. The former gave Oracles with all Mildness and Temper; the other were ever Bellowing with Fury and Madness; no
505 wonder (says he) for the first were inspir'd with the Holy Ghost; and the last were possess'd with the Devil. So the reason is plain.

But I have employ'd too much time in digressing from my purpose, which is chiefly to Vindicate my self; and only

from Casual Observation, to take Notice of Mr. *Colliers* 510
Errors, as they shall appear Blazing up and down in those
Pages where I am concern'd, or others into which I may dip
accidentally, in searching for Expressions cited from my
own Plays.

I have done with him in his Chapter of Immodesty. The 515
Reader has seen his Charge against the *Mourning Bride*, and
is a Judge of the Justness and Strength of it. I confess I have
not much to say in Commendation of any thing that I
have Written: But if a fair-dealing-man, or a candid
Critick had examin'd that Tragedy, I fancy that neither 520
the general Moral contain'd in the two last Lines; nor the
several particular Morals interwoven with the success of
every principal Character, would have been overseen by
him.

The Reward of Matrimonial Constancy in *Almeria*, of 525
the same Virtue, together with filial Piety and Love to his
Country in *Osmin*; the Punishment of Tyranny in *Manuel*,
of Ambition in *Gonzalez*, of violent Passions, and unlawful
Love in *Zara*: These it may be were Parts of the Poem as
worthy to be observed, as one or two erroneous 530
Expressions; and admit they were such, might in some
measure have aton'd for them.

Mr. *Collier* in his second Chapter, Charges the Stage
with Profaneness. Almost all the Quotations which he has
made from my Plays in this Chapter are represented falsly, 535
or by halves; so that I have very little to do in their
Vindication, but to represent 'em as they are in the
Original, fairly and at length; and to fill up the Blanks
which this worthy honest Gentleman has left.

In the Old Batchelour (says he[19]) *Vainlove asks* Bellmour, 540
Could you be content to go to Heav'n?

Bell. *Hum, not immediately, in my Conscience not Heartily*—
Here Mr. *Collier* concludes this Quotation with a dash,
as if both the Sense and the Words of the whole Sentence,
were at an end. But the remainder of it in the Play *Act.* 3. 545

---

[19] Coll. p. 62.

Scene 2. is in these words—*I would do a little more good in my generation first, in order to deserve it.*

I think the meaning of the whole is very different from the meaning of the first half of this Expression. 'Tis one
550 thing for a Man to say positively, he will not go to Heaven; and another to say, that he does not think himself worthy, till he is better prepared. But Mr. *Collier* undoubtedly was in the right, to take just as much as would serve his own turn. The Stile of this Expression is Light, and suitable to
555 Comedy, and the Character of a wild Debauchee of the Town; but there is a Moral meaning contain'd in it, when it is not represented by halves.

From Scene 3. of the 4*th* Act of the same Comedy, he makes the following Quotation. *Fondlewife* a Jealous
560 Puritan is obliged for some time to be absent from his Wife:

Fond. *Have you throughly consider'd how detestable, how heinous, and how Crying a Sin the sin of Adultery is? Have you weigh'd it, I say? for it is a very weighty sin: and although it may lie—yet thy Husband must also bear his part; for thy*
565 *Iniquity will fall upon his Head.* Here is another Dash in this Quotation, I refer the Reader to the Play to see what words Mr. *Collier* has Omitted; and from thence he may guess at the Strength of his Imagination.

For this Quotation, the Reader sees it in the same
570 Condition that Mr. *Collier* thinks fit to shew it: His Notes upon it are as follow.

This fit of Buffoonry and Profaneness, was to settle the Conscience of Young Beginners, and to make the Terrors of Religion insignificant.

575 Indeed I cannot hold Laughing, when I compare his dreadful Comment with such poor silly words as are in the Text: especially when I reflect how *young a beginner*, and how very much a Boy I was when that Comedy was Written; which several know was some years before it was Acted:
580 When I wrote it I had little thoughts of the Stage; but did it to amuse my self in a slow Recovery from a Fit of Sickness. Afterwards through my Indiscretion it was seen; and in some little time more it was Acted: And I through the remainder of my Indiscretion, suffer'd my self to be drawn in, to the

prosecution of a difficult and thankless Study; and to be   585
involved in a perpetual War with Knaves and Fools. Which
reflection makes me return to the Subject in hand.

Bellmour *desires* Lætitia *to give him leave to Swear by her
Eyes and her Lips.* Well, I am very glad Mr. *Collier* has so
much Devotion for the Lips and Eyes of a Pretty Woman,   590
that he thinks it Profanation to Swear by 'em. I'll give him
up this, if he pleases. To the next.

*He kisses the Strumpet, and tells her—Eternity was in that
Moment.*

To say *Eternity is in a Moment*, is neither Profane nor   595
Sacred, nor good nor bad. With Reverence of my Friend
the Author be it spoken, I take it to be stark Nonsense; and
I had not cared if Mr. *Collier* had discover'd it.

Something or other he saw amiss in it, and Writing a
Chapter of Profaneness at that time, like little *Bays*, he popt   600
it down for his own.

Lætitia when her Intrigue was like to be discover'd, says
of her Lover,

*All my Comfort lies in his Impudence, and Heav'n be
prais'd, he has a considerable Portion.*   605

This Mr. *Collier* calls the *Play-house Grace*. It is the
expression of a wanton and a vicious Character, in the
Distress and Confusion of her Guilt. She is discover'd in
her Lewdness, and suffer'd to come no more upon the Stage.

In the end of the last Act *Sharper* says to *Vain-love*:   610

*I have been a kind of Godfather to you yonder:
I have promis'd and vow'd some things in your name, which
    I think you are bound to perform.*

I meant no ill by this Allegory, nor do I perceive any in it
now. Mr. *Collier* says it was meant for Drollery on the   615
Catechism; but he has a way of discovering Drollery where
it never was intended; and of intending Drollery where it can
never be discovered. So much for the *Old Batchelour*.

In the *Double-Dealer* (he says) *Lady Plyant cries out Jesu,
and talks Smut in the same Sentence.* That Exclamation I give   620
him up freely. I had my self long since condemn'd it, and
resolv'd to strike it out in the next Impression. I will not urge
the *folly*, viciousness, or affectation of the Character to

excuse it. Here I think my self oblig'd to make my
625 Acknowledgments for a Letter which I receiv'd after the
Publication of this Play, relating to this very Passage. It came
from an Old Gentlewoman and a Widow, as she said, and
very well to pass: It contain'd very good Advice, and requir'd
an Answer, but the Direction for the Superscription was
630 forgot. If the good Gentlewoman is yet in being, I desire her
to receive my Thanks for her good Counsel, and for her
Approbation of all the Comedy, that Word alone excepted.

That Lady *Plyant* talks *Smut* in the same Sentence, lies
yet upon Mr. *Collier* to prove. His bare Assertion without
635 an Instance, is not sufficient. If he can prove that there is
downright *Smut* in it, why e'en let him take it for his pains:
I am willing to part with it.

His next Objection is, that Sir *Paul*, who he Observes
bears the Character of a Fool, makes mention too often of the
640 word *Providence*; for says Mr. *Collier*,[20] *the meaning must be*
(by the way, that *must* is a little hard upon me) *that
Providence is a ridiculous Supposition; and that none but
Blockheads pretend to Religion.* What will it avail me in this
place to signifie my own meaning, when this modest
645 Gentleman says, I *must* mean quite contrary?

Lady Froth is pleas'd to call Jehu *a Hackney Coachman.*
(ibid.)

Lady *Froth*'s words are as follow—*Our Jehu was a
Hackney Coachman when my Lord took him.* Which is as
650 much as to say, that the Coachman's Name is *Jehu*: And
why might it not be *Jehu* as well as *Jeremy*, or *Abraham*, or
Joseph, or any other Jewish or Christian Name? *Brisk*
desires that this may be put into a Marginal Note in Lady
Froth's Poem.

655 This Mr. *Collier* says, is meant to *burlesque the Text, and
Comment under one.* What Text, or what Comment, or what
other earthly Thing he can mean, I cannot possibly
imagine. These Remarks are very Wise; therefore I shall
not Fool away any time about them.

[20] p. 62.

Sir *Paul* tells his Wife, *he finds Passion coming upon him by*   660
Inspiration.[21]

The poor Man is troubled with the *Flatus*, his Spleen is
pufft up with Wind; and he is likely to grow very angry and
peevish on the suddain; and desires the privilege to Scold
and give it Vent. The word *Inspiration* when it has *Divine*   665
prefix'd to it, bears a particular and known signification:
But otherwise, to *inspire* is no more than to *Breath into*; and
a Man without profaneness may truly say, that a Trumpet,
a Fife, or a Flute, deliver a Musical Sound, by the help of
Inspiration. I refer the Reader to my fourth Proposition, in   670
this Case. For a Dispute about this word, would be very
like the Controversie in *Ben. Johnson*'s *Barthol. Fair*,
between the *Rabbi* and the *Puppet*; it *is* profane, and it *is*
not profane, is all the Argument the thing will admit of on
either side.   675

The Double-dealer is not yet exhausted. ib.

That is, Mr. *Collier* is not yet exhausted; for to give
double Interpretations to single Expressions, with a
design only to lay hold of the worst, is double dealing in a
great degree.   680

Cynthia the top Lady grows thoughtful. Cynthia it seems is
the Top Lady now; not long since, the other Three were
the three *biggest*.[22] Perhaps the Gentleman speaks as to
personal proportion, *Cynthia* is the Tallest, and the other
Three are the Fattest of the Four.   685

Mell. *Cynthia is thoughtful, and upon the question relates*
her Contemplation.

Cyn. *I am thinking, that though Marriage makes Man and*
Wife one Flesh, it leaves them two Fools.

Here he has filch'd out a little word so slily, 'tis hardly to   690
be miss'd; and yet without it, the words bear a very
different signification. The Sentence in the Play is
Printed thus—*Though Marriage makes Man and Wife one*
Flesh, it leaves 'em STILL two Fools. Which by means of
that little word *still*, signifies no more, than that if two   695
People were Fools, before or when they were married,

---

[21] p. 64.   [22] p. 82.

they would continue in all probability to be Fools still, and
after they were married. *Ben. Johnson* is much bolder in the
first Scene of his *Bartholomew Fair*. There he makes
700 Littlewit say to his Wife—*Man and Wife make one Fool*;
and yet I don't think he design'd even that, for a Jest either
upon *Genesis* 2. or St. *Matthew* 19. I have said nothing
comparable to that, and yet Mr. *Collier* in his penetration
has thought fit to accuse me of nothing less.

705   Thus I have summ'd up his Evidence against the *Double-
dealer*. I have not thought it worth while to Cross-examine
his Witnesses very much, because they are generally silly
enough to detect themselves.

     In *Love* for *Love*, *Scandal* tells Mrs. *Foresight*,[23] he will *die
710 a Martyr rather than disclaim his Passion*. The word Martyr is
here used Metaphorically to imply Perseverance. *Martyr* is a
Greek word, and signifies in plain English, no more then a
Witness. A holy Martyr, or a Martyr for Religion is one
thing; a wicked Martyr, or Martyr for the Devil is another:
715 A Man may be a Martyr that is a Witness to Folly, to Error,
or Impiety. *Mr. Collier* is a Martyr to Scandal and Falshood
quite through his Book. This Expression he says, is
dignifying Adultery with the Stile of Martyrdom; as if any
word could dignifie Vice. These are very trifling Cavils,
720 and I think all of this kind may reasonably be referr'd to
my Fourth Proposition.

     *Jeremy who was bred at the University, calls the natural
Inclinations to Eating and Drinking, Whoreson Appetites.*[24]

     Jeremy bred at the University! Who told him so? What
725 *Jeremy* does he mean, *Jeremy Collier*, or *Jeremy Fetch*? The
last does not any where pretend to have been bred there.
And if the t'other would but keep his own Counsel, and not
Print *M.A.* on the Title Page of his Book, he would be no
more suspected of such an Education than his Name-sake.
730 *Jeremy* in the *Play*, banters the Coxcomb *Tattle*, and tells
him he has been at *Cambridge*: Whereupon *Tattle* replies—
     'Tis well enough for a Servant to be bred at an University.

---

[23] p. 74.   [24] Ibid.

Which is said to expose the impudence of illiterate Fops,
who speak with Contempt of Learning and Universities. For
the word *Whoreson*, I had it from *Shakespear* and *Johnson*,   735
who have it very often in their Low Comedies; and
sometimes their Characters of some Rank use it. I have put
it into the Mouth of a Footman. 'Tis not worth speaking of.
But Mr. *Collier* makes a terrible thing of it, and compares it
to the *Language of Manicheans, who made the Creation to be*   740
the Work of the Devil. After which he civilly solves all by
saying, *the Poet was* Jeremy's *Tutor, and so the Mystery is at*
an end. This by a Periphrasis is calling me *Manichean*; well
let him call me what he pleases, he cannot call me *Jeremy*
Collier.   745

His next Quotation is of one line taken out of the middle
of eight more in a Speech of Sir *Sampson* in the second Act
of this Comedy: he represents it as an Aphorism by it self,
and without any regard to what either preceeds or follows
it. I desire to be excused from transcribing the whole Scene   750
or Speech. I refer to my third Proposition, and desire the
Reader to view it in its place. Mr. *Collier's* Citation is—
Nature has been provident only to Bears and Spiders. I beg the
Reader to peruse that Scene, and then to look into the 139
Psalm, because *Mr. Collier* says it is paraphrased by me in   755
this Place. I wonder how such remote Wickedness can
enter into a Man's Head. I dare affirm the Scene has no
more resemblance of the *Psalm*, than Mr. *Collier* has of the
Character of a Christian Priest, which he gives us in page
127, 128. of his own Book. Towards the end of the third   760
Act, *Scandal* has occasion to flatter Old *Foresight*. He talks
to him, and humours him in the Cant of his own Character,
recites Quotations in favour of Astrology, and tells him the
wisest Men have been beholding to that Science—[25]

Solomon (says he) *was Wise, but how? By his Judgment in*   765
Astrology. So says *Pineda* in his third Book and eight Chap.
But the Quotation of the Authority is omitted by Mr. *Collier*,
either because he would represent it as my own Observation

[25] p. 75.

to ridicule the Wisdom of *Solomon*, or else because he was
770 indeed Ignorant that it belong'd to any Body else.

The Words which gave me the Hint are as above cited.
Pin. de rebus Salom.

—*Illum Judiciariam Astrologiam calluisse circa naturalia,
circa inclinationes hominum*, &c.

775   Do's Mr. *Collier* believe in Prognostications from
Judicial Astrology? Do's he think that *Solomon* had his
Wisdom only from thence? If he does not, why will he
not permit the Superstitions growing from that Science to
be expos'd? Why will he not understand that the exposing
780 them in this Place and Manner, does not ridicule the
Wisdom of *Solomon*, but the Folly of *Foresight*?

Scandal he says, continues his Banter, and says, *The Wise
Men of the East ow'd their Instruction to a Star, which is
rightly observ'd by* Gregory *the Great, in favour of Astrology*.

785   *Scandal* indeed Banters *Foresight*, but he does not banter
the Audience, in mentioning *Gregory* the Great: Take his
own Words.

*Deus accommodate ad eorum scientiam docuit, ut qui in
Stellarum Observatione versabantur ex stellis Christum discerent.*

790   The rest of the Banter is what *Scandal* relates from
Albertus Magnus, who makes it the most *valuable Science,
because it teaches us to consider the Causation of Causes in the
Causes of things*.

I am but a bare Translator in this place; for example:
795 —*Nos habemus unam scientiam mathematicam, quæ docet nos
in rerum causis Causationem causarum Considerare.*[26]

Is not all this stuff, and fit to be exposed; yet these and
some other like Sayings, have I sometimes met with as
Authorities in Vindication of Judicial Astrology.

800   In Page 76. Mr. *Collier* is very angry that Sir *Sampson*
has not another Name; because *Sampson* is a Name in the
Old Testament.

He says it is Burlesquing the Sacred History, for Sir
Sampson to boast of his Strength; because *Sampson* in the
805 Testament is said to be very strong. The rest that he quarrels

---

[26] Albert. Mag. Tom. 5. p. 658.

at is a metaphorical expression or two, of less Consideration
if possible, than any of his former Cavils.

I refer the Reader to the Scene, which is the last in the
Play: And for an Answer, to what has before been said on
the word *Martyr*. When I read in this page these words of   810
Mr. Collier—to draw towards an end of this Play, I thought he
had no more to say to it; but his method is so admirable, that
he never knows where to begin, nor when to make an end.
Five or six pages farther I find another of his Remarks.[27]

In *Love for Love, Valentine* says, *I am Truth*.   815

If the Reader pleases to consult the Fourth Act of that
Comedy, he will there find a Scene, wherein *Valentine*
counterfeits madness.

One reason of his Counterfeiting in that manner, is, that
it conduces somewhat to the design and end of the Play.   820
Another reason is, that it makes a Variation of the
Character; and has the same effect in the Dialogue of the
Play, as if a new Character were introduc'd. A third use of
this pretended madness is, that it gives a Liberty to Satire;
and authorises a Bluntness, which would otherwise have   825
been a Breach in the Manners of the Character. Mad-men
have generally some one Expression which they use more
frequently than any other. *Valentine* to prepare his Satire,
fixes on one which may give us to understand, that he will
speak nothing but Truth; and so before and after most of   830
his Observations says—*I am Truth*. For example. *Foresight*
asks him

—*What will be done at Court?*

Val. *Scandal will tell you—I am Truth, I never come there.*

I had at first made him say, *I am Tom-tell-troth*; but the   835
sound and meanness of the Expression displeas'd me: and
I alter'd it for one shorter, that might signifie the same
thing. What a Charitable and Christian-like Construction
my dear Friend *Mr. Collier* has given to this Expression, is
fit only to be seen in his own Book; and thither I refer the   840
Reader: I will only repeat his Remark as it personally aims
at me—*Now a Poet that had not been smitten with the*

---

[27] Coll. p. 83.

pleasure of Blasphemy, would not have furnish'd Frenzy with Inspiration, &c. Now I say, a Priest who was not himself
845 furnish'd with Frenzy instead of Inspiration, would never have mistaken one for the other.

In his next Chapter he Charges the Stage with the Abuse of the Clergy. He quotes me so little in this Chapter, and has so little reason even for that little, that it is hardly worth
850 examining.

The *Old Batchelour* has a *Throw* (as he calls it[28]) at the dissenting Ministers.

Now this *Throw*, in his own Words, amounts to no more than that a Pimp provides the Habit of a dissenting Minister,
855 as the safest Disguise to conceal a Whoremaster: Which is rather a Complement than an Affront to the Habit.

Barnaby calls another of that Character Mr. Prig. Calls him Mr. *Prig?* Why what if his Name were Mr. *Prig?* Or what if it were not? This is furiously simple! *Fondlewife to hook in the*
860 *Church of* England *into the Abuse, tacks a Chaplain to the End of the Description.*

How this pretty little Reasoner has (as he calls it) hook't in the Church of *England?* Can't a Man be a Chaplain unless he is of the Church of *England?*
865 Father *Dominick* the 2*d.* he's for bringing in Heav'n and the Church by hook or crook into his Quarrel. If a *Mufti* had been tack'd to the Description, he would have been equally offended; for *Mufti* in the Language of the Theater, he says, signifies *Bishop.*[29]
870 *Maskwell* in the *Double Dealer*,[30] has a Plot, and is for engaging *Saygrace* in it. He is for *instructing the Levite*, and says, *without one of them have a Finger in't, no Plot, publick or private, can expect to prosper.*

Perhaps that is a Mistake; many damnable Plots have
875 miscarried, wherein Priests have been concern'd.

After this, he has transcrib'd a broken Piece of a Dialogue between *Maskwell* and *Saygrace*, which I leave to shift for it self; having nothing in it worth an Accusation, or needing a Defence.

[28] p. 101.   [29] p. 103.   [30] p. 102.

Mr. *Collier* is very florid in this Chapter; but it is very   880
hard to know what he would be at. He seems to be
apprehensive of being brought upon the Stage, and in
some Places endeavours to prove, that as he is a Priest, he
should be exempted from the Correction of the *Drama*.[31]
In other Places he does not seem to be averse to treading   885
the Stage; but he would do it in Buskins: He would be *all*
Gold, Purple, Scarlet, and Embroidery; and as rich as Nature,
Art, and Rhetorick, can make him.[32]

We will first enquire whether he may be brought on the
Stage or not; and then shew both how he would, and how   890
he should be represented; granting the Representation of
his Character to be lawful.

Here[33] he lays down something with the appearing face
of an Argument, under 3. Heads, to shew that the Clergy
have a *Right to Regard and fair Usage.* I'm sure I will never   895
dispute that with him in the general Terms. But I suppose
he is particular here; and means that they have a Right to be
exempted from the Theater. Whether they have or not
I will not pretend to determin; This I know, that the
Custom of the Theater in all Ages and Countries is   900
against this Opinion; which in this Chapter is sufficiently
prov'd by the Examples which himself has produc'd.

If Mr. *Collier* is in earnest of that Opinion, he has
behav'd himself either very treacherously or very weakly,
in offering to assert it by a false and a sophistical Argument.   905
His Proof begins.

1. Because of their relation to the Deity.

Now (says he) the Credit of the Service always rises in
Proportion to the Quality and Greatness of the Master. Upon
this Position he builds all the argument under this first   910
Head. The Position is sophistical, & his Inferences
consequently false. The trick lies here. It being granted
him that the Credit of the *Service* rises in Proportion, *&c.*
he slily infers, that the Credit of the *Servant* also rises in
proportion to the Credit of the *Service*, which is false: For   915
every body knows that an ill Servant both discredits his

---

[31] p. 124, 127.   [32] p. 118.   [33] p. 127.

Service, and is discredited by it. And by how much the
more honourable the Service is in which he is employ'd, so
much the more is he accounted an ill Man who behaves
920 himself unworthily in that Service.

If an offending Servant is punish'd by the Law, the
honour of the Service is not by that means violated; so far
from that, that it is rather vindicated: Neither on the Stage
is the divine Service ridicul'd, only the ridiculous Servant
925 is expos'd.

2. Because of the Importance of their Office. And,

3. They have Prescription for their Privilege, their
Function has been in Possession of Esteem in all Ages
and Countries.

930 These 2. are but Branches of the first Head: for *their
relation to the Deity* implies the *importance of their Office*;
and bespeaks that Privilege and Esteem which ever ought
to be paid to their Holy Function.

But here again Mr. *Collier* confounds the Function with
935 the Person, the Service with the Servant: He is Father
Dominick still.

I would ask Mr. *Collier* whether a Man, after he has
receiv'd holy Orders, is become incapable of either playing
the Knave, or the Fool?

940 If he is not incapable, it is possible that some time or
other his Capacity may exert it self to Action.

If he is found to play the Knave, he is subject to the
Penalties of the Law, equally with a Lay-man; if he plays
the Fool, he is equally with a Lay-fool, the subject of
945 Laughter and Contempt.

By this Behaviour the *Man* becomes alienated from the
Priest; as such Actions are in their own nature separate and
very far remov'd from his function, and when such a one is
brought on the Stage, the folly is expos'd, not the function;
950 the *Man* is ridicul'd, and not the *Priest*.

Such a Character neither does nor can asperse the sacred
Order of Priesthood, neither does it at all reflect upon the
persons of the pious and good Clergy: For as *Ben. Johnson*
observes on the same occasion from St. *Hierome, Ubi*
955 *generalis est de vitiis disputatio, Ibi nullius esse personæ*

injuriam, where the business is to expose and reprehend
Folly and Vice in general, no particular person ought to
take offence. And such business is properly the business of
Comedy.

That this may not look like a sophistical distinction in   960
me, to say that the *Man* does, by his behaviour, as it were
alienate himself from the *Priest*, and become liable to an ill
Character, apart from his Office: I desire it may be observ'd
that the Church it self makes the same Distinction.

It was foreseen by the Reverend Bishops and Clergy of   965
this Realm, in their Convocations for establishing the 39.
Articles of our Religion in the Years 1562. and 1604. that
evil Men (unperceiv'd to be such) might creep into the
Ministry of the Church. That afterwards they might
become openly profligate, and notoriously Scandalous in   970
their Lives and Conversations; even to that Degree, that
some scrupulous Christians, and of a very tender
Conscience, might probably take such Offence at the
unworthiness of their Minister, as dangerously to avoid
his Administration of the Holy Word and Sacraments: To   975
refrain from publick Worship, and to lose the real Benefit
of the Communion, thro' a misconceiv'd Opinion of the
invalidity of it when Administred by unclean and wicked
Hands.

They might (and not without some reasonable Grounds)   980
doubt whether the same Man who was personally Impious,
could be spiritually Sacred; whether he who by his
Example would seduce 'em to the Devil, could by his
Precepts be conducing to their Salvation. This I say, they
might doubt; and not without some reasonable Grounds;   985
and not without the Opinions of two of the Fathers, *viz*. St.
Cyprian, and St. *Origen* to Authorize their Distrust.

But to remove this Doubt, and to invalidate the
Authorities of those Fathers, the six and twentieth Article
of Religion was thus Established by the Convocations   990
abovementioned.

Article 26.

Although in the visible Church the Evil be ever mingled with
the Good, and sometime the Evil have chief Authority in the
995 *Ministration of the Word and Sacraments: Yet for as much as*
they do not the same in their own Name, but in Christ's, and do
Minister by his Commission and Authority, we may use their
Ministery both in hearing the Word of God, and in receiving
the Sacraments. Neither is the effect of Christ's Ordinance
1000 *taken away by their Wickedness, nor the Grace of God's*
Gifts diminished from such, as by Faith, and rightly do
receive the Sacraments Ministred unto them; which are
effectual, because of Christ's Institution and Promise,
although they be Ministred by evil Men.

1005 *Nevertheless it appertaineth to the Discipline of the Church,*
that enquiry be made of evil Ministers: And that they be
accused by those that have knowledge of their Offences; and
finally being found Guilty by just Judgment be deposed.

Here is a most manifest Distinction made between the
1010 Man and the Priest. Between the regard to his Person, and
the respect to his Function.

I will shew anon, that Mr. *Collier* himself has made this
very Distinction, when he is pleased to approve of the
Characters of *Joida* and *Mathan* in the *Athalia* of *Racine.*

1015 If any Man has in any Play expos'd a Priest, as a Priest,
and with an intimation, that as such, his Character is
ridiculous: I will agree heartily to condemn both the Play
and the Author. I am confident no Man can defend such an
Impiety; and whoever is guilty of it, my Advice to him is,
1020 that he acknowledge his Error, that he repent of it and sin
no more.

I confess I do not remember any such Character, Mr.
Collier, who is more conversant with bad Plays than any
Man that I know, perhaps may.

1025 Mr. *Collier* in this Chapter produces many Instances of
the Characters of Priests in the Poems of Heathen Writers;
he is extreamly delighted with the Distinctions of their
Habits, with the Show and Splendour in which they
appear'd. The Crown and guilt Scepter of *Chryses*, with

the valuable Ransom which he had in his Power, are   1030
Objects that gratifie his vain Imagination extreamly. He is
indeed so rapt with his splendid Ideas of *Chryses*, *Laocoon*,
and *Chloreus*, that to use his own Phrase, he *runs riot* upon
their Description from *page* 112 to 118. He seems to
have quite laid aside the Thoughts of the *twelve poor Men*   1035
who over-bore all the Oppositions of Power and Learning,
in pag. 81.

He now talks of nothing but great Families, great Places,
wealthy and honourable Marriages, fine Cloaths, and in
short, of all the Pomps and Vanities of this wicked   1040
World. To give him his Due, as in some Places of his
Book he criticizes more like a Pedant than a Scholar;
argues more like a Sophister than a right Reasoner, and
rallies more like a Waterman than a Gentleman; so in this
Place he talks more like a Herald–Painter than a Priest, and   1045
insists more upon Pedigrees and Coats of Arms, than on
moral Virtues or a generous Education.

He tells us the *Jewish* and *Egyptian* Priests, the *Persian*
Magi, and *Druids* of *Gaul* were all at the *upper end of the*
Government, p. 131. What then? What is that to us, any   1050
more than if they were used to sit at the upper end of the
Table? No doubt this Gentleman's Affection for such a
Seat, furnish'd him with this florid and Expression.

In p. 132. He says *the Priesthood was for some time confin'd*
to the Patrician Order. Very well: we know the Reason of   1055
that; but with Submission, that is not the same thing as if
the *Patrician* Order had been confin'd to the Priesthood.
However, this Gentleman's Meaning is plain; certainly if
he were Pope, he would renounce the Title of *Servus*
Servorum Dei.   1060

He quotes *Tully*[34] for his Approbation of the same
Person's being set at the Head both of Religion and
Government. What does he mean by this? What Occasion
is there of this Quotation, in our Country? Is not our King
both at the Head of our Religion and Government? When   1065

[34] p. 133.

Mr. *Collier* allows him one, perhaps he will not deny him the other.

But to come to his Meaning (if he has any) thro' all this vain Stuff. I take it, he would give us to understand, that in all Ages the Function of a Priest was held to be a very honourable Function. Did Mr. *Collier* ever meet with any Body Fool enough to engage him to assert that?

He tells us that Men of the first Quality; nay, Kings and Emperors have been employ'd in the sacred Ministry: And I can tell him that Kings and Emperors have been in all Ages expos'd on the Stage; their Ambition, Tyrannies and Cruelties, all the Follies and Vices which were Consequences of their arbitrary Power and ungovern'd Appetites, have been laid open to the Peoples View. They have been punish'd, depos'd, and put to Death on the Stage; yet never any King complain'd of the Theater, or the Poets. On the contrary, all great Princes have cherish'd and supported them so long as they themselves were great; till they have diminish'd in their own Characters, and turn'd to Bigotry and Enthusiasm; and of this a living Instance might be given.

Yet, 1. Kings have a Relation to the Deity.

They are his Deputies and Vicegerents on Earth.

2*ly*. They are possess'd of a very important Office. And,

3*ly*. Their Function has been in Possession of Esteem in all Ages and Countries.

That Men of Quality have always been, and are now employ'd in the sacred Ministry, is evidently true; and I could heartily wish that more were still employ'd in it: So should the most honourable Office be executed by the most honourable Hands. So should we behold Men of Birth, Title, and Heraldry, despising tinsel Shew, Pageantry, and all Mr. *Collier*'s beloved Bells, Bawbles, and Trinkets. And preferring Decency, Humility, Charity, and other Christian Virtues, to shining Ornaments; or even the *upper End of a Government*. How ill such temporal Pride agrees with the Person and Character of a truly pious and exemplary Divine, I will

not pretend to determine. I will only transcribe the Words
of a learn'd and honour'd Minister of the Church, to this   1105
purpose; and that is the reverend Mr. *Hales* of *Eaton*.[35]

'For we have believ'd him that hath told us, *That in Jesus*
Christ there is neither high nor low; and that in giving Honour,
every Man should be ready to prefer another before himself;
which Sayings cut off all Claim most certainly to   1110
Superiority, by Title of Christianity, except Men can
think that these things were spoken only to poor and
private Men. Nature and Religion agree in this, that
neither of them hath a hand in this Heraldry of *secundum*
sub & supra; all this comes from Composition and   1115
Agreement of Men among themselves. Wherefore this
Abuse of Christianity, to make it *Lacquey* to Ambition, is
a Vice for which I have no extraordinary Name of
Ignominy, and an ordinary I will not give it, lest you
should take so transcendent a Vice to be but trivial.'   1120

Here is not one Syllable of *Heraldry Regulated by* Garter,
and Blazon'd by Stones.[36] I would desire the Reader,
immediately after this Paragraph from Mr. *Hales*, to
consult Mr. *Collier* in p. 136. and to observe how he
stickles for Place, and thrusts himself before the   1125
Gentlemen.

The Addition of Clerk is at least equal to that of Gentleman.
How snappish and short his Clerkship is in his Periods;
mark him, *were it otherwise, the Profession would in many*
Cases, be a kind of Punishment. Good Heaven! To profess   1130
the Service of God would be a Punishment, if the Title of
Clerk were not at least equal to that of Gentleman. Well, —
The Heraldry is every Jot as safe in the Church, as 'twas in the
State. When the Laity are taken leave of, not Gentleman but
Clerk is usually Written. And a little after. *The first Addition*   1135
is not lost but covered. Good Reader, return to Mr. *Hales*,
that you may be reminded of the true Respect and
Veneration that is due to his Memory; and to the rest of
the Meek, the Modest, and the Humble Ministers of the

[35] Vid. his Tract concerning Schism. p. 224, 225.   [36] Coll. p. 135.

1140 Church: For while Mr. *Collier* is before you, you will be very apt to forget it.

I know many Reverend Clergymen now living, whose Names I cannot hear without Awe and Reverence: And why is that? Not from their Heraldry, but their Humility, 1145 their Humanity, their exceeding Learning, which is yet exceeded by their Modesty; their exemplary Behaviour in their whole Lives and Conversations; their Charitable Censures, of Youthful Errors and Negligences, their fatherly and tender Admonitions, accompanyed with all 1150 sweetness of Behaviour; and full of mild yet forcible Perswasion.

He were next to a *Manichean* that would not hold such Men's Persons in a degree of Veneration, next to their Profession. But a Mr. *Prig*, a Mr. *Smirk*, and I'm afraid a 1155 Mr. *Collier* are Names implying Characters worthy of Aversion and Contempt.

Now let us take a View of Mr. *Collier*, as he appears upon the Stage; for while he is examining of Plays; I look upon him as one who has *Eloped* from his Pulpit and Strayed 1160 within the inclosures of the Theatre; and I do not see why the Players should not lay hold of him, and pound him till he has given them Absolution. Why does he abandon his Gown and Cassock to come Capering and Frisking, in his Lay-Doublet and Drawers, between the Scenes? Is he 1165 Master of the Revels? Is the Stage under his Discipline? *And is he fit to Correct the Theatre who is not fit to come into it?* [37] He is not fit to come into it. First, Because his Office requires him in another place. And Secondly, Because he makes naughty uses of innocent Plays, and writes Baudy, 1170 and Blasphemous Comments, on the Poets Works.

Well, he has at length discovered a Play which is *an Exception to what he has observed in* France, (Coll. 124.) the Play is the *Athalia* of *Racine*. In this Play are the Characters of two Priests *Joida* and *Mathan*; of both 1175 which Mr. *Collier* is pleased to admit: By enquiring into his Reasons for Licensing this Play, we shall see in what

[37] v. Coll. p. 139.

manner he will allow a Priest to be represented on the Stage; and from thence we may guess how he himself would be contented to appear there also.

Joida (says he) *the High-Priest has a large Part, but then* the Poet does him Justice in his Station; he makes him Honest and Brave, and gives him a shining Character throughout. That's well. *Mathan is another Priest in the same Tragedy, he turns Renegado, and revolts from God to Baal.* That is not altogether so well. But has not the Poet done him Justice too, in giving him the Character that belong'd to him? Whether he has or not, Mr. *Collier* thinks he has made him ample reparation and more than amends, as you shall see. He goes on. *He is a very ill Man But*— ay, now for the *BUT*—He has turn'd Renegado, has revolted from God to *Baal*, is *positively* a very Ill-Man, But, what? O, *BUT makes a considerable Appearance.* There, now 'tis out, and all's well. If he has but *a guilt Crown, and Scepter, Scarlet and Embroidery in abundance*, let him rebel or revolt, he makes a good Figure, and it becomes him very well. Your Servant Mr. *Racine*, 'twas well for you that *Baal* gave good Benefices, and his Priests could afford to make a considerable Appearance: Or *Mathan*'s Revolt had not been so well taken at your Hands. But hold, Mr. *Collier* goes on.

I'm afraid the Reparation enlarges, and the Complement rises. For the sake of Connexion let us repeat—

—*But makes a considerable Appearance.* And,—

Ay now, what can follow this *AND* in the Name of *Climax*?

You shall see—*And is one of the Top of* Athalia's *Faction.*

Nay, then there is no more to be said. If he had fine Cloaths, and was set at the Top, or rather at the *upper End* of a Faction too, he had his hearts Content: A reasonable *Mathan* would have been satisfied with any one of those Blessings. Tho' I would not answer for Mr. *Collier*'s Continence; at this time, especially: he is so transported with Mr. *Racine*'s Bounty to *Mathan*, that he excuses him frankly for shewing him a Renegado.

1215   He goes on—*As for the Blemishes of his Life, they stick all upon his own Honour, and reach no farther than his Person.*

I think I have now kept the Promise that I made not long since, to shew that Mr. *Collier* himself, when he is in the Humour, will allow of the Distinction betwixt the *Man* and
1220   the *Priest*, the Person and the Function.

But to shew that I can be as cross as he; now when he would admit of this distinction, I should rather say when he alledges it, it shall not by any means be granted him. Here is a renegade Priest, that revolts from the true God to
1225   *Baal*: And this Man is only branded with a Blemish on his Person. What, is it no Affront to his Function then? I take it to be no excuse for him that he should afterwards become a Priest of *Baal*. Sure Mr. *Collier* does not mean to make use of Mr. *Dryden*'s Key as he calls it, and say that *Priests of all*
1230   *Religions*, &c. Well, 'tis only a Blemish upon his Person; or if Mr. *Collier* pleases, because he delights in Phrases of Heraldry, 'tis only a Blot in his Scutcheon. Let Mr. *Collier* answer for this, to those who have Authority to examine him further. He is in every Line growing more and more
1235   gracious to Mr. *Racine*. And now he is come to the very *top* or *upper-end* of his Civility; and says with a *bon grace* and *belle air*, that

—*in fine, the Play is a very religious Poem.*

Indeed! why then *in fine* we are tack'd about; then a Play
1240   *in fine*, may be a religious Poem it seems: Why then Sir *Martin* with his, *in fine*, here has quite unravel'd his own Plot. Ay, ay, the Play is a very religious Poem; if Faction and fine Cloaths wont make a religious Poem, it must be made of strange Stuff indeed.

1245   —*'Tis upon the Matter all Sermon and Anthem*—

O Lord! nay, now I protest Mr. *Collier* this must not be; nay now you're so infinitely obliging! fye, this is too much on t'other side: You quite forget the Fathers indeed Sir, and the Bishop of *Arras*.

1250   —*And if it were not design'd for the Theatre*—

Out with it Man—*I have nothing to Object.*

Why that's well, now he's come to himself. O' my Word, I was half afraid he would have play'd the *Mathan*, and

have revolted to the Theatre. The Mischief is, this naughty
Theatre will be interloping; when Sermon and Anthem,   1255
become the Stage as ill, as Faction and fine Cloaths do the
Pulpit: But Men sometimes travel into Foreign Provinces
for Variety.

I cannot forbear enquiring into one Example more,
which this Gentleman offers us in the very next Page.   1260

In the History of Sir John Oldcastle, *Sir* John, *Parson of*
Wrotham, *Swears, Games, Wenches, Pads, Tilts and Drinks;*
this is extremely bad.

Extremely bad? Can any thing be worse? and yet (says
he) *Shakespear's Sir* John, *has some advantage in his*   1265
Character. Now who can forbear enquiring what
advantage a Character can possibly have, consistent with
such abominable Vices? First, *He appears loyal and stout; he*
brings in Sir John, Acton, *and other Rebels, Prisoners.* So! as
'tis in the *Spanish Fryar*, a Manifest Member of the Church   1270
Militant! That he was Stout, was plain before, from his
Padding and Tilting. But this will not do; the advantage
does not yet appear. No! why then.

—He is rewarded by the King, and the Judge uses him
civilly and with Respect.   1275

This Advantage appears still but coldly. Kings reward
Spys and Executioners, and necessary Instruments of
Policy and Punishment. And Judges are generally Men of
Years, Temper and Wisdom, and use all Gentlemen with
Civility. Ay, say you so? why then—*in short*—ay, now for   1280
the Iliads in a Nut-shell. Here is the *But* coming again, I had
a glimpse of him just now. *ex. gr.*

In short he is represented Lewd, but *not* Little.

There is an Advantage for you now; *in short, Lewd* but
not *Little.*   1285

Concise and pretty! the Gentleman had best take it for a
Motto, and have it annex'd to his Coat-Armour, when he can
get *his Heraldry regulated by Garter, and blazon'd by Stones.*

Well, I confess I have been in an Error; I thought a Man
never appear'd so very little, as when he appear'd extremely   1290
lewd. If I have undervalued Lewdness, I ask Mr. *Collier's*
Pardon.

And the Disgrace falls rather on the Person than the Office.
Here again you see, he will allow this Distinction to all
1295 his Favourites. Here is the Person and the Function
separated again; the Priest and the Man: In short, he
answers himself so often, that I will dispute this Point no
more with him.

But you may see what this poor Gentleman in the
1300 wretched Pride of his little Heart, thinks a sufficient
Alloy to make current a most dissolute or impious
Character. Though you expose a Priest revolting from
God to *Baal*, yet if you let him make a considerable
Figure, and place him at the Head of a Faction, all is well
1305 enough; and the Poem may be a *religious Poem*, &c. Shew
another in Comedy, let him Swear, Game, Wench, Pad,
Tilt and Drink, but withal let him keep good Company; let
a Judge, or some Great Man treat him with Respect, that he
may not appear little, though he appear lewd, and you give
1310 *some advantage to his Character*; at least you will shew that
he *understands his Post, and converses with the Freedom of a
Gentleman.*[38]

In Page 122, Our Author has observ'd *how the Heathen
Poets behav'd themselves in the Argument. Priests seldom
1315 appear in their Plays; and when they come, 'tis business of
Credit that brings them. They are treated like Persons of
Condition; they act up to their Relation, neither sneak, nor
prevaricate, nor do any thing unbecoming their Office.*

Indeed when Men neither sneak, nor prevaricate, nor do
1320 any thing unbecoming their Office in the World, they
ought not to be represented otherwise on the Stage: Nay,
they ought not to be expos'd at all in Comedy; for the
Characters expos'd there, should be of those only, who
misbehave themselves.

1325 Let us suppose that the Character of this Author were to
be shewn upon the Stage: he who should represent him
behaving himself as he ought, would be to blame, and that
for these Reasons.

[38] Ibid.

First, To represent him behaving himself as he ought, would be to represent him in the discharge of some part of his Holy Office, which is by no means fit to be shewn on the Stage; especially in Comedy, where Mens Vices and Follies are expos'd: That would be to bring Mr. *Collier*'s Function, not his Person on the Stage, which is not to be permitted.

Secondly, He that should represent Mr. *Collier* behaving himself as he ought, would very much misrepresent Mr. *Collier*, in respect to the Manners of his Character.

Let us take a slight Sketch of him as he presents himself to us in his Book. Let Mr. *Collier* be represented as he is, not as he ought to be; that by seeing what he is, Mr. *Collier* may be asham'd of what he is, and endeavour at what he ought to be.

And that the Instruction of the Representation may not be lost, let us borrow that Distinction which severs the Priest from the Man: If *Mathan*, and Sir *John* of *Wrotham*, have done with it, they may lend it to us; 'tis for the use of an Humble Servant of theirs, and whenever the Humour takes 'em to Revolt, Pad, Tilt, Wench, Drink, and soforth, let 'em give us a Quarter of an Hours Notice, and they shall have it again.

Well, Our Author being thus divided, we will desire the better Part of him, to take his Place in the Pit, and let the other appear to him like his evil Genius on the Stage.

Suppose the Gentleman in the Scene to appear very intent upon the very Obscene Comedies of *Aristophanes*,[39] *quær*. Whether the Person in the Pit, beholding how very ill this becomes him, will not think that he might with much more Decency, betake himself to his *Septuagint*?

Mr. *Collier* on the Stage shall anathematise the Poets, and tell 'em in plain Terms, they should be excommunicated, and that *they are not fit to come into the Church*.[40] *Quær*. whether Mr. *Collier*, in the Pit, will not think it had been more becoming his Character, to have invited and exhorted them to it?

Mr. *Collier* on the Stage shall behave himself with all the Arrogance, and little Pride of a spruce *Pedant*,[41] that the

[39] *Coll.* p. 40, 44.   [40] *Coll.* 139.   [41] p. 136.

Gentlemen in the Pit may be induc'd to practise the
Meekness and Humility of a Christian Divine. The
former, shall pervert and misconstrue every thing that is
said to him, that the latter may learn to use Justice, Candor,
1370 and Sincerity, in his Interpretations.[42]

The Player *Collier* shall call the Gentlemen that he
converses with, Foot-pads, Buffoons, Slaves, &c. that the
Spectator *Collier* may remember they are Christians, and
should be catechis'd by other Names.[43]

1375   Mr. *Collier*, on the Stage, shall rack Bawdery and
Obscenity out of modest and innocent Expressions; and
having extorted it, he shall scourge it, not out of
Chastisement but Wantonness; he shall forget, that
sometimes to report a Fault is to repeat it.[44] The Spectator
1380 in the Pit shall plainly perceive, that he loves to look on
naked Obscenity; and that he only flogs it, as a sinful
Pædagogue sometimes lashes a pretty Boy, that looks
lovely in his Eyes, for Reasons best known to himself.[45]

Castigo te non quod odio habeam, sed quod amem.

1385   Mr. *Collier*, on the Stage, shall ridicule, rail at, and
condemn all Plays whatsoever: He shall tire himself, and
his Audience, with his Inveteracy and Exclamations against
them. Which done, he shall all on the sudden, and, that
there may be something surprizing, and *præter expectatum*
1390 in his Character, from a Persecutor, become a Promoter of
the *Drama*: He shall be as furious a *Critick* as he was a *Bigot*;
and give the best Rules and Instructions of which he is
capable, for the Composure of Comedy. He shall talk in all
the Pedantical Cant of Fable, Intrigue, Discovery, of
1395 Unities of Time, Place, and Action.[46] But lest this
Behaviour in Mr. *Collier*'s Character should appear
inconsistent, and a violation of the Precept of *Horace*.

—*Servetur ad imum,*
Qualis ab incepto processerit; & sibi constet.

1400   His Vanity shall bear proportion with his Dissimulation;
his Ignorance shall be as great as his Malice; and he shall

[42] V. *most part of Mr.* Collier's *Quotations.*   [43] V. *Pref.* 81, 63, 175.
[44] p. 71.   [45] *Coll.* Ch. 1, 2.   [46] V. *from* p. 209. *to* 228. *and forwards.*

not be able to deviate from his inveterate Zeal against Plays;
for he shall not appear to understand one Syllable of the
Rules of Writing, but shall mislead Poetry as much by his
Instructions, as he has perverted it by his Interpretations;   1405
he shall favour his Adversaries without obliging them; the
Zeal of his Character shall be preserv'd even in his own
despite; and his Devotion, in this Particular, shall be the
Child of his Ignorance: For he can make but

    —*Lame Mischief tho' he mean it well.*[47]   1410

And if Plays are pernicious, Mr. *Collier* shall only be
wicked in his Wishes, he shall be acquitted in his
Performances; his Instigations to Poetry shall prove
checks upon it. He shall appear mounted upon a false
Pegasus, like a *Lancashire* Witch upon an imaginary   1415
Horse, the Fantom shall be unbridled, and the
Broomstick made visible.[48]

    At this *Catastrophe*, Mr. *Collier*, in the Pit, shall exclaim
like *Flecknoe*, and with very little variation.

    O why did'st thou on Learning fix a Brand,   1420
    And rail at Arts thou did'st not understand?

    Now, lest the Poet who shall undertake this Character,
should be gravell'd in the imitation of the Stile of this
elaborate Writer, let him take these few Instances of his
allusive and highly metaphorical Expressions, for Patterns;   1425
*viz. running riot upon Smut: A Poem with a Litter of Epithets,
like a Bitch overstock'd with Puppies: Sucking the Sense to
skin and bone: A Fancy slipstocking high: The upper-end of a
Government: A whole Kennel of Beaux after a Woman,* &c.
For his Elegancy, these are Originals: *Learning a Spaniel to*   1430
*set: This belike is the meaning: Three of the biggest of Four:
Big Alliances, Men of the biggest Consideration for sense,* &c.
To marry up a Top-Lady: Cum multis aliis.[49]

    'Tis a strange thing that a Man should write such Stuff
as this, who is capable of making the following   1435
Observation.

Offensive Language, like Offensive Smells, does but

---

[47] p. 104.   [48] p. 230.
[49] *See* p. 12, 27, 34, 92, 131, 132, 225, 233, *&c.*

make a Man's Senses a burthen, and affords him
nothing but loathing and Aversion.
1440 *For these Reasons, 'tis a Maxim in good Breeding never*
to shock the Senses or Imagination.[50]

Indeed there are few things which distinguish the
manner of a Man's Breeding and Conversation, more
visibly, than the Metaphors which he uses in Writing;
1445 I mean in writing from himself, and in his own Name and
Character. A Metaphor is a similitude in a Word, a short
Comparison; and it is used as a similitude, to illustrate and
explain the meaning. The Variety of *Ideas* in the Mind,
furnish it with variety of Matter for Similitudes; and those
1450 *Ideas* are only so many Impressions made on the Memory,
by the force and frequency of external Objects.

Pitiful and mean Comparisons, proceed from pitiful and
mean *Ideas*; and such *Ideas* have their beginning from a
familiarity with such Objects. From this Author's poor and
1455 filthy Metaphors and Similitudes, we may learn the
Filthiness of his Imagination; and from the Uncleanness
of that, we may make a reasonable guess at his rate of
Education, and those Objects with which he has been
most conversant and familiar.

1460   To conclude with him in this Chapter; I will only say
that no Man living has a greater respect for a good Clergy-
man, nor more contempt for an ill one, than my self; the
former I have often been proud to shew, the latter never fell
in my way till now. I never yet introduced the Character of
1465 a Clergy-man in any of my Plays, excepting that little
Apparition of *Say-grace*, in the *Double-Dealer*; and I am
very indifferent whether ever the Gown appear upon the
Stage, or not: If it does, I think it should not be worn by the
Character of a good Man; for such a one ought not to be
1470 made the Companion of foolish Characters. If ever it is
shewn there, it ought to be hung loosely on the shoulders of
such a one as I have lately instanced; but to no other end,
than to demonstrate that even the sacred Habit is abus'd by
some; but by their Characters and Manners the Audience

[50] Ibid.

may observe what manner of Men they are. And no   1475
question but if our Author, in the Pit, did behold his
Counterpart on the Stage, thus egregiously to play the
Fool in his *Pontificalibus, the rebuke would strike stronger
upon his sense*,⁵¹ and prove more effectual to his
Reformation.   1480

I come now to his Chapter of the Immorality of the
Stage.

His Objections here are rather Objections against
Comedy in general, than against mine, or any bodies
Comedies in particular. He says the Sparks that *marry up*   1485
the Top-Ladies,⁵² and are rewarded with Wives and
Fortunes in the last *Acts*, are generally debauch'd
Characters. In answer to this, I refer to my first and
second Proposition. He is a little particular in his
Remarks upon *Valentine*, in *Love for Love*. He says,   1490

*This Spark, the Poet would pass for a Person of Vertue; but
he speaks too late.*⁵³

I know who, and what he is, that always speaks too soon.
Why is he to be pass'd for a Person of Vertue? Or where is
it said that his Character makes extraordinary Pretensions   1495
to it! *Valentine* is in *Debt*, and in *Love*; he has honesty
enough to close with a hard Bargain, rather than not pay
his Debts, in the first *Act*; and he has Generosity and
Sincerity enough, in the last *Act*, to sacrifice every thing
to his Love; and when he is in danger of losing his Mistress,   1500
thinks every thing else of little worth. This, I hope, may be
allow'd a Reason for the Lady to say, *He has Vertues*: They
are such in respect to her; and her once saying so, in the last
Act, is all the notice that is taken of his *Vertue* quite thro'
the Play.   1505

Mr. *Collier* says, he *is Prodigal*. He was prodigal, and is
shewn, in the first *Act* under hard Circumstances, which
are the Effects of his Prodigality. That he is unnatural and
undutiful, I don't understand: He has indeed a very
unnatural Father; and if he does not very passively   1510
submit to his Tyranny and barbarous Usage, I conceive

---

⁵¹ *Coll.* III.   ⁵² p. 142.   ⁵³ Ibid.

there is a Moral to be apply'd from thence to such Fathers.
That he is *profane* and *obscene*, is a false Accusation, and
without any Evidence. In short, the Character is a mix'd
Character; his Faults are fewer than his good Qualities;
and, as the World goes, he may pass well enough for the
best Character in a Comedy; where even the best must be
shewn to have Faults, that the best Spectators may be
warn'd not to think too well of themselves.

He quotes the *Old Batchelor* twice in this Chapter.[54] His
first Quotation is made with his usual assurance and fair
dealing.

*If any one would understand what the Curse of all tender-
hearted Women is,* Bellmour *will inform him. What is it
then? 'Tis the Pox.*

Here he makes a Flourish upon ill Nature's being
recommended as a Guard of Vertue and of Health, *&c.*

The whole Matter of Fact is no more than this.

Lucy to *Belmour, Act* 5. *Scene* 2.

*If you do deceive me, the Curse of all kind tender-hearted
Women light upon you.*

Bell. *That's as much as to say, The Pox take me.*

It is his Interpretation; and it is agreeable to his
Character. He is a Debauchee, and he thinks there is but
one way for Women to be kind and tender-hearted; and,
I think, his threat'ning them with such a Curse as the
consequence of too much easiness, does not seem to
recommend the Vice at all, but rather to forbid it: His
very Leudness, in this place, is made moral and instructive.

I am very glad our Author is in such Circumstances, in
this Chapter, that he can bear the sight of that *Hellish
Syllable, Pox*; and prevail with himself to write it at its
full length. *Non ita pridem.* In Page 82. he loves his Love
with a P— but no naming: That is not like a Cavalier. What
Ermin was ever an Instance of superfine Nicety comparable
to Mr. *Collier?* I will not say, what *Cat?* Tho' if I should,
I can quote a *Spanish* Proverb to justifie the Comparison.

El gato scaldado tiene miedo de agua fria.

[54] p. 171. 172.

He makes one Quotation more, to what purpose indeed I know not; but I will repeat it, in Justice to him, because it is the last that he has made, and the first fair one. *Old Batch.* Act 4. *Belinda* to *Sharp*.[55]

—*Where did you get this excellent Talent of Railing?*

Sharp.—*Madam, the Talent was born with me.*—*I confess I have taken care to improve it, to qualifie me for the Society of Ladies.*

These are the Words just as the Gentleman quotes 'em; but why, or wherefore, he is not pleas'd to discover; for he says not one Syllable, for, nor against 'em: I suppose he thinks the Proof plain, and the Evidence firm without a Coroborator.

I hope the Reader will not forget, that these Instances are produc'd, to prove that I have encourag'd Immorality in my Plays. I thought the Expression, above-mentioned, had been a gentle Reproof to the Ladies that are addicted to railing; and since Mr. *Collier* has not said that it *must* mean the contrary, I don't see why it may not be understood so still?

I have now gone thorough with all Mr. *Collier's* Quotations; I have been as short as I could possibly in their Vindication; I have avoided all Recriminations, and have not so much as made one Citation from any of my Plays in favour of them: Whatever they contain of Morality, or Invectives against Folly and Vice, is no more than what ought to be in them; therefore I do not urge it as a Merit.

My Business was not to paint, but to wash; not to shew Beauties, but to wipe off Stains.

Mr. *Collier* has indeed given me an opportunity of reforming many Errors, by obliging me to a review of my own Plays.

> *Dum relego scripsisse pudet, quia plurima Cerno*
> *Me quoque qui feci, Judice, digna lini.*

---

[55] p. 172.

But I must affirm, that they are only Errors occasion'd
1585 by Inadvertency or Inexperience, and that I am conscious
of nothing that can make me liable to his Censure, or rather
Slander. I am as ready to own the Advantages I have
received from his Book, as to demonstrate the Wrongs; if
I resent the latter, it is because they were intended me; and
1590 if I do not thank him for the other, it is because they were
not: He would have poison'd me, but he overdosed it, and
the Excess of his Malice has been my Security.

To give him his due, he seems every where to write more
from Prejudice, than Opinion; he rails when he should
1595 reason; and for gentle Reproofs, uses scurrilous Reproaches.
He looks upon his Adversaries to be his Enemies; and to
justifie his Opinion in that Particular, before he has done
with them, he makes them so. If there is any Spirit in his
Arguments, it evaporates and flies off unseen, thro' the heat
1600 of his Passion. His Passion does not only make him appear
in many Places to be in the wrong, but it also makes him
appear to be conscious of it. That which shews the Face of
Wit in his Writing, has indeed no more than the Face; for
the Head is wanting. Wit is at the best but the *Sign* to
1605 good understanding; it is hung out to recommend the
Entertainment which may be found within: And it is very
well when the Invitation can be made good. As the outward
Form of Godliness is Hypocrisie, which very often conceals
Irreligion and Immorality; so is Wit also very often an
1610 Hypocrisie, a Superficies glaz'd upon false Judgment, a
good Face set on a bad Understanding.

It is a Mask which Mr. *Collier* sometimes wears, but it
does not fit the Mold of his Face; he presumes too much on
the Security of his Disguise, and very often ventures till he
1615 is discover'd: He does not know himself in his Foreign
Dress, and from thence concludes that no body else can.
His Ancestor of honour'd Memory, recorded in *Æsop*,
miscarried thro' the same Self-sufficiency. Mr. *Collier*,
when he cloathed himself in the Lion's Skin, should have
1620 thought of an Expedient to have conceal'd his Ears: But, it
may be, he is proud of them, and thinks it proper to shew
that he has them *both*, and at their full length.

He has put himself to some pain to shew his Reading;
and his Reading is such, that it puts us to pain to behold it.
He discovers an ill Taste in Books, and a worse Digestion.   1625
He has swallow'd so much of the Scum of Authors, that the
overflowing of his own Gall was superfluous to make it rise
upon his Stomach. But he ought in good Manners to have
stept aside, and not to have been thus nauseous and
offensive to the Noses of the whole Country. But as his   1630
Reading would not stay with him, so his Writing ran away
with him.

Ben Johnson, in his Discoveries,[56] says, *There be some
Men are born only to suck the Poison of Books.* Habent
venenum pro victu imo pro deliciis. *And such are they that*   1635
only relish the obscene and foul things in Poets; which makes
the Profession tax'd: But by whom? Men that watch for it, &c.
Something farther in the same Discoveries, He is speaking
again very much to our purpose; for it is in justification of
presenting vicious and foolish Characters on the Stage in   1640
Comedy. It seems some People were angry at it then; let us
compare his Picture of them, with the Characters of those
who quarrel at it now. *It sufficeth* (says he[57]) *I know what*
kind of Persons I displease, Men bred in the declining and decay
of Vertue, betrothed to their own Vices; that have abandoned,   1645
or prostituted their good Names; hungry and ambitious of
Infamy, invested in all Deformity, enthrall'd to Ignorance
and Malice, of a hidden and conceal'd Malignity, and that
hold a concomitancy with all Evil.

'Tis strange that Mr. *Collier* should oversee these two   1650
Passages, when he was simpling in the same Field where
they both grow. This is pretty plain; because in the 51st
Page of his Book he presents you with a Quotation from the
same *Discoveries*, as one intire Paragraph, tho' severally
collected from the 706 and 717th Pages of the Original; so   1655
that he has read both before, and beyond these Passages.
But a Man that looks in a Glass often, walks away, and
forgets his resemblance.

---

[56] *Johns. Disc.* p. 702.   [57] *Johns. Disc.* p. 714.

Mr. *Collier*'s Vanity in pretending to Criticism, has
extremely betray'd his Ignorance in the Art of Poetry;
this is manifest to all that understand it. And methinks
his Affectation of seeming to have read every thing,
sometimes betrays him to Confessions that are not much
to his Advantage. I wonder he is not asham'd to own, that
he is so well acquainted with the ἐκκλησιαζούσαι of
Aristophanes. The Dialogues of *Aretine*, or *Aloïsia*, are not
more obscene than that Piece. The Author there, as Mr.
Bays says, *does egad name the thing directly*, and that in
above a hundred Places. But perhaps Mr. *Collier* meant to
veil that Play under a *Misnommer* (to use his own Phrase[58]);
and when he call'd it *Concianotores*, thought we could not
discover, that in spite of his Artifice, or his Ignorance, he
must mean no other than the leud *Concionatrices*, or
Parliament-Women of *Aristophanes*. He has indeed rak'd
together a strange number of Authors Names: But as
Gideon's Army of Two and thirty thousand was order'd
to be reduc'd to Three hundred; so his rabble of Citations,
without any loss to him, might be reduc'd to a much less
number: But his Business is not *Discipline*, but *Tumult*. He
appears like Captain *Tom* at the Head of a People that are
shuffled together, neither the World, nor they, nor *He*, can
tell why; but since they are met, Plunder is the Word, and
the Play-house is first to be demolish'd.

He has outdone *Bays* in his grand Dance; nay, the
Heathen Philosophers in their Notions of the grand
Chaos, never imagin'd a greater confusion. All Religions,
all Countries, all Ages, are jumbled together, to explode
what all Religions, all Countries, and all Ages have allow'd.
He is not contented with his *Battalia*, compounded of
Bramins, *Brachmans*, *Mufties*, Councils, Fathers, the
Bishop of *Arras*, &c. But the Philosophers, nay, the very
Poets themselves are press'd to the Service.

Cicero endeavour'd with all his might to get himself a
Name in Poetry; and *Aristotle* preferr'd *Tragedy* even to
Philosophy. But Mr. *Collier* has converted them both; in

[58] *Coll.* p. 44.

short, between him, and the Bishop of *Arras*, they have
been seduc'd and inviegl'd over to the other side.

He pretends to triumph in the heart of *Parnassus*, and
has sown dissention in the bosoms of some of the chief
Proprietors. *Ovid* and the *Plain Dealer* are revolted, and
take Arms against their Brethren, while Mr. *Collier* sings
with *Lucan* and *Hudibras* of—*Civil Fury, &c.*

> —*populumque potentem.*
> *In sua victrici Conversum viscera dextra:*
> *Cognatasque acies*—
> *Bays* against *Bays*—*& Pila minantia pilis.*

I wish his Seeds of Sedition were not scatter'd elsewhere;
for here I think they will hardly thrive. What effect his
Doctrine in private Families will have, I know not, when
the Superiority comes to be disputed between the Country-
Gentlemen, and their Chaplains; or rather, as Mr. *Collier*
has establish'd it,[59] between the Chaplains, and their
Country-Gentleman.

I am not the only one who look on this Pamphlet of his to be
a Gun levell'd at the whole Laity, while the shot only glances
on the Theatre; what he means by the Attack, or what may be
its Consequences, I know not, and I suppose he cares not.
Bellum inchoant inertes, fortes finiunt. But there are those who
will not be displeas'd at an occasion of making
Recriminations. With respect to his Parts, it is no wise thing
to give any body an Example of searching into Books for
negligent and foolish Expressions. Divines have sometimes
forgot themselves in Controversial Writings; Disputes begun,
or pretended to have been begun on Points of Faith, have
ended in scurrilous and personal Reflections; and from Tracts
of Divinity, have degenerated into *Pasquils* and *Lampoons*.
That Mr. *Collier* has laid the Foundation of such a
Controversie, I think is apparent; but I hope his Credit is
not sufficient to engage any body to go on with the Building.

He has assaulted the Town in the Seat of their principal,
and most reasonable Pleasure. Down with the Theatre

1700

1705

1710

1715

1720

1725

1730

[59] p. 139.

right or wrong. *Delenda est Carthago*, let the Consequence
be what it will. That was a very rash Maxim; and if *Cato*
had liv'd to have seen its Effects, he would have repented it.
1735 To persecute an Allie (and that desires no more than to
continue in our Alliance) as an Enemy, is a weak, and
barbarous Piece of Policy.

Persecution makes Men persevere in the right; and
Persecution may make 'em persist in the wrong. Men
1740 may, by ill usage, be irritated sometimes to assert and
maintain, even their very Errors. Perhaps there is a
vicious Pride of triumphing in the worst of the
Argument, which is very prevailing with the Vanity of
Mankind; I cannot help thinking that our Author is not
1745 without his share of this Vanity. I think truly he had a fair
appearance of Right on his side in the Title Page of his
Book; but with reason I think I may also affirm, that by his
mis-management he has very much weak'ned his Title. He
that goes to Law for more than his Right, makes his
1750 Pretensions, even to that which is his Right, suspected; as
a true Story loses its Credit, when related from the Mouth
of a known Liar.

Mr. *Collier*'s many false Citations, make his true
suspected; and his misapplication of his true Citations,
1755 very much arraign both his Judgment and Sincerity. His
Authorities from the Fathers (with all due respect to them)
are certainly no more to the purpose, than if he had cited the
two *Attick* Laws against the Licentiousness of the Old
Comedy; in Truth not so much: For the Invectives of the
1760 Fathers, were levell'd at the Cruelty of the *Gladiators*, and
the Obscenity of the *Pantomimes*. If some of them have
confounded the *Drama* with such spectacles, it was an
oversight of Zeal very allowable in those days; and in the
Infancy of Christianity, when the Religion of the Heathens
1765 was intermingled with their Poetry and Theatral
Representations; therefore Christians, then, might very
well be forbidden to frequent even the best of them. As for
our Theatres, St. *Austin* and *Lactantius* knew no more of
them, than they did of the *Antipodes*; and they might with as
1770 much difficulty have been perswaded, that the former would

in after-times be tolerated in a Christian State, as that the
latter wou'd be receiv'd for a manifest and Common Truth,
and made intelligible to the Capacity of every Child.[60]

To what end has he made such a Bugbear of the Theatre?
Why would he possess the Minds of weak and melancholick   1775
People with such frightful *Ideas* of a poor Play? Unless to
sowre the humours of the People of most leisure, that they
might be more apt to mis-employ their vacant hours. It may
be there is not any where a People, who should less be
debarr'd of innocent Diversions, than the People of   1780
England. I will not argue this Point; but I will strengthen
my Observation with one Parallel to it from *Polybius*; That
excellent Author, who always moralizes in his History, and
instructs as faithfully as he relates; in his 4th Book, attributes
the Ruin of *Cynetha* by the *Ætolians*, in plain Terms, to their   1785
degeneracy from their *Arcadian* Ancestors, in their neglect of
Theatral and Musical Performances. The *Cynethians* (says
my Author) had their Situation the farthest *North* in all
Arcadia; they were subjected to an inclement and uncertain
Air, and for the most part cold and melancholick; and, for   1790
this reason, they of all People should last have parted with
the innocent and wholesome Remedies, which the
Diversions of Musick administred to that sowrness of
Temper, and sullenness of Disposition, which of necessity
they must partake from the Disposition and Influence of   1795
their Climate; "For they no sooner fell to neglect these
wholesome Institutions, when they fell into Dissentions
and Civil Discords, and grew at length into such depravity
of Manners, that their Crimes in number and measure
surpass'd all Nations of the *Greeks* beside."[61]   1800

He gives us to understand, that their *Chorus*'s on the
Theatres, their frequent Assemblies of young People, Men
and Women, mingling in Musical Performances, were not
instituted by their Ancestors out of Wantonness and
Luxury, but out of Wisdom; from a deliberated and   1805
effectual Policy, and for the Reasons above noted. Much

---

[60] Vid. St. *Aust. de Civ. Dei. l.* 16. *c.*9. & *Lact. de fals. Sap.* 23.
[61] Vid. *Transl. by Sir* H. Sheer, *Vol.* 2. *p.* 46.

more might be cited from *Polybius*, who has made a very
considerable digression on this occasion.

The Application of what I have borrow'd, is very plain.
1810 Is there in the World a Climate more uncertain than our
own? And which is a natural Consequence, Is there any
where a People more unsteady, more apt to discontent,
more *saturnine*, *dark*, and *melancholick* than our selves?
Are we not of all People the most unfit to be alone, and
1815 most unsafe to be trusted with our selves? Are there not
more Self-murderers, and melancholick Lunaticks in
England, heard of in one Year, than in a great part of
Europe besides? From whence are all our Sects, Schisms,
and innumerable Subdivisions in Religion? Whence our
1820 Plots, Conspiracies, and Seditions? Who are the Authors
and Contrivers of these things? Not they who frequent the
Theatres and Consorts of Musick. No, if they had, it may
be Mr. *Collier*'s Invective had not been levell'd that way;
his *Gun-Powder-Treason* Plot upon Musick and Plays (for
1825 he says *Musick is as dangerous as Gun-Powder*[62]) had broke
out in another Place, and all his False-Witnesses been
summoned elsewhere.

FINIS.

[62] p. 279.

The TATLER.

By *Isaac Bickerstaff* Esq;

---

*—Quid prodest, Pontice, longo
Sanguine censeri, pictosque ostendere Vultus
Majorum?—*   Juv.

From *Saturday February* 17. to *Tuesday February* 20. 1710.

From my own Apartment in Channel-Row, *Feb.* 19.

IT is observable of Men of Base Extraction and low Education, that when they have any Thing in them of what the World calls good Sense, they turn it wholly to the getting of Money. They have but that one Point in View, and consequently overlook all either difficult or indirect Ways which lead to it.

If they attain their End, and become rich toward their middle Age, before they decline in Years, and decay in Strength, and that their Appetite of getting is not yet turned into an Avarice of hoarding, if they have any Fire remaining, they commonly feel themselves warmed with a Kind of Ambition of being Somebody, as well as Something. They find a Want of that Respect which they observe to be paid to such who are called Gentlemen, and Persons of Condition, though of small Fortunes. They would give any Consideration to be of an honourable Descent, and alter the Spelling of their Names to bring them on as near as possible to some Name or Seat of Antiquity. If that cannot be brought about, they push for a Knighthood, or an Alliance of some Family of Name or Title, whose Follies or Misfortunes have reduced them to match themselves or Children to Money, however basely lodged, or infamously obtained.

I fell into this Reflection after a Visit made me some
25 Days since by one whom I remember to have known a Link Boy, and who has often lighted me formerly from the *Green-Dragon* in *Fleet-street* to my Lodgings in *Sheer-lane*. We used to call him *Foundling*, a Name given him by his Godfather the Parish, and which he has not yet been
30 able to part with, or vary, though he has found the Secret to be worth very near what they call a Plumb, and upon *'Change* has obtained the Appellation of a good Man. He came to me with such Frankness, owning both his past and present Circumstances; but what made me smile, was, the
35 Request he made me to accompany him to a House in our Row, where lives one *Randall* (as he called him) *a Creature Merchant*. This Person is a great Virtuoso, and deals in Birds and Beasts, though not either as a Butcher or Poulterer; for he nourishes nothing that is eatable, nor ever
40 utters any Commodity while it is alive.

As we walked toward this Virtuoso's Habitation, which I may call an Abridgment of the Ark, my Friend *Foundling* told me, 'He had purchased a fair Seat in the Country, That he had a Mind to appear well in the World; and since
45 he had a Gentleman's Estate, he would endeavour to have every Thing suitable to it; That he had bargained already with the Herald's College for a Coat of Arms; and that his present Errand to *Randall's* was, from among his Variety of Animals to fancy himself a Crest, in which he mightily
50 desired my Assistance and Approbation.' I was delighted with the Folly and Frankness of the Man; but it happened that he saw nothing that pleased him. As we returned, I advised him to an honest home-bred Crest out of his own Farmers Yard, which was a Cock's Head untrim'd,
55 with the Gills and Comb entire. This he approved, and took his Leave. I was about to reflect on what had past, when suddenly returning he called to me, and coming nearer, told me, he would let me into all his Project, and desired I would step with him to a Waterman's House hard

by, where he lodged a Set of Ancestors, which were to go 60
up next Tide to his Seat upon the River. He desired my
Judgment of the Choice he had made of Three Generations
to furnish his Parlor. I went with him, not readily compre-
hending what he meant, till we enter'd the House, where
he explained to me, that at *Fleet-Ditch* he had bought 65
the Pictures of three Men and three Women, which were
suited well enough to each other, and were to personate
his Family up to his Great-Grandfather and Great-
Grandmother, which he thought was pretending far
enough for one who was in Truth related to no Body that 70
he knew of in the World. As I was extremely diverted with
the Oddness and Extravagance of the Man's Fancy, I was
no less satisfied with his Judgment in the Choice of the
Pictures; the Habits, and Dispositions of the Figures being
suited to Three different Periods and Fashions of Time, 75
and concluding, or rather beginning, in the Great-Grandfather and Great-Grandmother, with a Pair of Trunk Hose,
a Ruff, and a Farthingale. I pleased him with my Approbation, and took Leave of him, entertaining my self often
since with the Reflections which naturally arise from the 80
Contemplation of Vanity, Wealth, and titular Happiness.
I have since heard there is a Marriage likely to be concluded
betwixt his Daughter Mrs. *Priscilla Foundling* and the
eldest Son of the Lord *Mortgage*.

Dedication of
The Dramatick Works of John Dryden

To His G R A C E the
Duke of N*ewcastle*,
*Lord Chamberlain of His Majesty's
Houshold*, &c.

My L O R D ,

I T is the Fortune of this Edition of the Dramatic Works
of the late Mr. Dryden, to come into the World at a
Time, when Your Grace has just given Order for Erecting,
at Your own Expence, a Noble Monument to his Memory.
5   This is an Act of Generosity, which has something in it
so very Uncommon, that the most unconcern'd and indifferent Persons must be moved with it: How much more,
must all such be affected by it, who had any due Regard for
the personal Merits of the Deceas'd; or are capable of any
10 Taste and Distinction, for the Remains and elegant Labours of one of the greatest Men that our Nation has
produced.
     That, which distinguisheth Actions of pure and elevated
Generosity, from those of a mix'd and inferiour Nature, is
15 nothing else but the absolutely disinterested Views of the
Agent.
     My Lord, this being granted, in how fair a Light does
your Munificence stand? a Munificence to the Memory, to
the Ashes of a Man whom You never saw; whom You never
20 can see: And who, consequently, never could by any personal Obligation, induce You to do this Deed of Bounty;
nor can he ever make You any Acknowledgement for it
when it shall be done.
     It is evident Your Grace can have acted thus from no
25 other Motive but your pure Regard to Merit, from your
intire Love for Learning, and from that accurate Taste and
Discernment, which by Your Studies you have so early
attained to in the Politer Arts.

And these are the Qualities, my Lord, by which You are
more distinguish'd, than by all those other uncommon   30
Advantages with which You are attended. Your great Disposition, Your great Ability to be beneficent to Mankind,
could by no means answer that End, if You were not
possess'd of a Judgment to direct You in the right Application, and just Distribution of Your good Offices.   35

You are now in a Station, by which You necessarily
preside over the liberal Arts, and all the Practicers and
Professors of them. Poetry is more particularly within
Your Province: And with very good Reason may we hope
to see it revive and flourish, under Your Influence and   40
Protection.

What Hopes of Reward may not the living Deserver
entertain, when even the Dead are sought out for; and their
very Urns and Ashes made Partakers of Your Liberality?

As I have the Honour to be known to You, my Lord, and   45
to have been distinguish'd by You, by many Expressions
and Instances of Your Good-will towards me; I take a
singular Pleasure to congratulate You upon an Action so
intirely Worthy of You. And as I had the Happiness to be
very Conversant, and as intimately acquainted, with Mr.   50
Dryden, as the great Disproportion in our Years could allow
me to be; I hope it will not be thought too assuming in me,
if in Love to his Memory, and in Gratitude for the many
friendly Offices, and favourable Instructions, which in my
early Youth I received from him, I take upon me to make   55
this publick Acknowledgment to Your Grace, for so publick a Testimony as You are pleas'd to give the World of
that high Esteem in which You hold the Performances of
that eminent Man.

I can in some Degree justifie my self for so doing, by a   60
Citation of a kind of Right to it, bequeath'd to me by him.
And it is indeed, upon that Pretension that I presume even
to make a Dedication of these his Works to You.

In some very Elegant, tho' very partial Verses which he
did me the Honour to write to me, he recommended it to   65
me to *be kind to his Remains.* I was then, and have been ever
since most sensibly touched with that Expression: and the

more so, because I could not find in my self the Means of
satisfying the Passion which I felt in me, to do something
70 answerable to an Injunction laid upon me in so Pathetick
and so Amicable a Manner.

You, my Lord, have furnish'd me with ample Means of
acquitting my self, both of my Duty and Obligation to my
departed Friend. What kinder Office lyes in me, to do to
75 these, his most valuable and unperishable Remains, than to
commit them to the Protection, and lodge them under the
Roof of a Patron, whose Hospitality has extended it self
even to his Dust?

If I would permit my self to run on in the way which so
80 fairly opens it self before me, I should tire Your Grace with
reiterated Praises and Acknowledgments, and I might possibly (notwithstanding my pretended Right so to do) give
some handle to such who are inclinable to Censure, to tax
me of Affectation and Officiousness; in thanking You, more
85 than comes to my Share, for doing a Thing, which is, in
truth, of a Publick Consideration, as it is doing an Honour
to Your Country. For so unquestionably it is, to do
Honour to him, who was an Honour to it.

I have but one thing to say either to obviate, or to answer
90 such an Objection, if it shall be made to me, which is, that
I loved Mr. *Dryden*.

I have not touch'd upon any other publick Honour, or
Bounty done by You to Your Country: I have industriously
declined entring upon a Theme of so extensive a Nature;
95 and of all Your numerous and continual Largesses to the
Publick, I have only singled out this, as what most particularly affected me. I confess freely to Your Grace, I very
much admire all those other Donations, but I much
more love this; and I cannot help it, if I am naturally
100 more delighted with any thing that is Amiable, than with
any thing that is Wonderful.

Whoever shall Censure me, I dare be confident, You, my
Lord, will Excuse me, for any thing that I shall say with
due Regard to a Gentleman, for whose Person I had as just
105 an Affection as I have an Admiration of his Writings. And
indeed Mr. *Dryden* had Personal Qualities to challenge

both Love and Esteem from All who were truly acquainted with him.

He was of a Nature exceedingly Humane and Compassionate; easily forgiving Injuries, and capable of a prompt 110 and sincere Reconciliation with them who had offended him.

Such a Temperament is the only solid Foundation of all moral Vertues, and sociable Endowments. His Friendship, where he profess'd it, went much beyond his Professions; and I have been told of strong and generous Instances of it, 115 by the Persons themselves who received them: Tho' his Hereditary Income was little more than a bare Competency.

As his Reading had been very extensive, so was he very happy in a Memory tenacious of every thing that he had read. He was not more possess'd of Knowledge, than he 120 was Communicative of it. But then his Communication of it was by no means pedantick, or impos'd upon the Conversation; but just such, and went so far as by the natural Turns of the Discourse in which he was engag'd it was necessarily promoted or required. He was extream ready 125 and gentle in his Correction of the Errors of any Writer, who thought fit to consult him; and full as ready and patient to admit of the Reprehension of others, in respect of his own Oversight or Mistakes. He was of very easie, I may say, of very pleasing Access: But something slow, and 130 as it were diffident in his Advances to others. He had something in his Nature that abhorr'd Intrusion into any Society whatsoever. Indeed it is to be regretted, that he was rather blameable in the other Extream: For by that means, he was Personally less known, and consequently his Char- 135 acter might become liable both to Misapprehensions and Misrepresentations.

To the best of my Knowledge and Observation, he was, of all the Men that ever I knew, one of the most Modest, and the most Easily to be discountenanced, in his Ap- 140 proaches, either to his Superiors, or his Equals.

I have given Your Grace this slight Sketch of his personal Character, as well to vindicate his Memory, as to justifie my self for the Love which I bore to his Person; and I have the rather done it, because I hope it may be 145

acceptable to You to know that he was worthy of the
Distinction You have shewn him, as a Man, as well as an
Author.

As to his Writings, I shall not take upon me to speak of
150 them; for, to say little of them, would not be to do them
right: And to say all that I ought to say, would be, to be very
Voluminous. But, I may venture to say in general Terms,
that no Man hath written in our Language so much, and so
various Matter, and in so various Manners, so well. An-
155 other thing I may say very peculiar to him; which is, that
his Parts did not decline with his Years: But that he was an
improving Writer to his last, even to near seventy Years of
Age; improving even in Fire and Imagination, as well as in
Judgement: Witness his Ode on St. *Cecilia*'s Day, and his
160 Fables, his latest Performances.

He was equally excellent in Verse, and in Prose. His
Prose had all the Clearness imaginable, together with all the
Nobleness of Expression; all the Graces and Ornaments
proper and peculiar to it, without deviating into the Lan-
165 guage or Diction of Poetry. I make this Observation, only
to distinguish his Stile from that of many Poetical Writers,
who meaning to write harmoniously in Prose, do in truth
often write meer Blank Verse.

I have heard him frequently own with Pleasure, that if he
170 had any Talent for *English* Prose, it was owing to his having
often read the Writings of the great Archbishop *Tillotson*.

His Versification and his Numbers he could learn of no
Body: For he first possess'd those Talents in Perfection in
our Tongue. And they who have best succeeded in them
175 since his Time, have been indebted to his Example; and the
more they have been able to imitate him, the better have
they succeeded.

As his Stile in Prose is always specifically different from
his Stile in Poetry; so, on the other hand, in his Poems, his
180 Diction is, where-ever his Subject requires it, so Sub-
limely, and so truly Poetical, that its Essence, like that of
pure Gold, cannot be destroy'd. Take his Verses, and
divest them of their Rhimes, disjoint them in their Numbers, transpose their Expressions, make what Arrangement

and Disposition you please of his Words, yet shall there   185
Eternally be Poetry, and something which will be found
incapable of being resolv'd into absolute Prose: An incon-
testable Characteristick of a truly poetical Genius.

I will say but one Word more in general of his Writings,
which is, that what he has done in any one Species, or   190
distinct Kind, would have been sufficient to have acquir'd
him a great Name. If he had written nothing but his
Prefaces, or nothing but his Songs, or his Prologues, each
of them would have intituled him to the Preference and
Distinction of excelling in his Kind.   195

But I have forgot my self; for nothing can be more
unnecessary than an Attempt to say any thing to Your
Grace in Commendation of the Writings of this great
Poet; since it is only to Your Knowledge, Taste and Approbation of them, that the Monument which You are now   200
about to raise to him is owing. I will therefore, my Lord,
detain You no longer by this Epistle; and only intreat You
to believe, that it is address'd to Your Grace, from no other
Motive, than a sincere Regard to the Memory of Mr.
Dryden, and a very sensible Pleasure which I take in   205
applauding an Action by which You are so justly, and so
singularly entitled to a Dedication of his Labours, tho'
many Years after his Death; and even tho' most of them
were produced by him, many Years before You were born.

I am with the greatest Respect,   210
   My LORD,

            Your GRACE'*s*
            most Obedient and
            most Humble Servant,

William Congreve.   215

The GAME of QUADRILLE.

An ALLEGORY.

THE TRUE
COPY
OF AN
AFFIDAVIT,

Made before one of His Majesty's Justices of the Peace for
the City of *Westminster.*

T HAT *four* LADIES, whom the Deponent does not
care to Name, repair nightly to a certain convenient
Place, near St. *James's,* to meet their GALLANTS of the
first Rank; whom your Deponent will not Name, but so far
5 describe them, that *two* of them are *Sallow,* and *two* of the
ruddy Complexion; and that he verily believes, they were
most abominably painted.

The LADIES when they begin their Gambols, call their
GALLANTS by the fond Nick-names of *Hercules, Cupid,*
10 *Pit,* and the *Gardiner.* After a plentiful Service of the most
costly Fare, they begin their *Tricks* which they play like the
Tumblers in *Bartholomew-Fair* upon a Carpet, *strip is
the Word;* nay, your Deponent has known them strip a
Gentleman who came accidentally into the House. At
15 *first,* they begin pretty courtly, at least in their Expressions,
as, *Madam, by your leave,* or so; which the LADIES are
so good as *seldom to deny.* Afterwards, it is shameful to
describe the *Tricks* that are play'd by this *lewd Pack.* By *an
established Rule,* each *Lady* has the Choice of her *Gallant* in
20 her *Turn,* and some have been known so unreasonable, after
they have had *Three,* to call for a *Fourth.* Your Deponent
has seen a *Lady* on her *Back,* a *Man* o' Top of *her,* and a
Lady o' Top of *him;* and he avers, it has been known, that a

Court Valet has *stript them all.* Sometimes they are thrown on their *Backs*, sometimes on their *Bellies*, now higgledy 25 piggledy, and anon, they are *all* o' Top of *one another*; and if *any one* is call'd upon, they are oblig'd *to show* A L L. Of the same Nature is their Discourse, your Deponent has often over-heard them talking of their *A—es*, with the same Familiarity as their *Faces*; *I have a Black* one, says one, 30 and named the *Thing* directly; *mine is better than yours*, says the other, and Names her *Thing*; *must I be laught at*, says a Third, *because I have a red one.* There is *one monstrous Thing* that your Deponent is almost ashamed to mention; after *Six* Bouts, a *Lady* has asked *if they could do no more*; nay, a 35 certain *Lady* has been known to play all the *Tricks over* by *her self.* Your Deponent likewise avers, that he has full Proof, after the L A D I E S have been tired with their G A L L A N T S, they have called for *fresh ones*: In short the aforesaid L A D I E S, have not only, *spent their Pin-Money*, 40 *but their Husband's Estates*, upon *Hercules*, *Cupid*, *Pit*, and the *Gardiner*, and when they want more Money, they commonly *Pawn* their *Jewels*, &c.

> *Westminster ss.*
> *Jurat. Coram me*, 45
> T. T.

P.S. The above *Information* is a faithful Description of the G A M E of Q U A D R I L L E, not to be *Literally*, but *Allegorically*, understood.

T H O. W O O L S T O N. 50

LETTERS

1 *To Edward Porter*

[21 August 1692]

Sr

I am forced to Borrow Ladies paper but I think it
will contain all that I can tell you from this place which is
5 so much out of the world that nothing but the last great
news Could have reacht it. I have a little tried what
solitude and retirement can afford, which are here in perfection[.] I am now writing to you from before a black
mountain nodding over me and a whole river in cascade
10 falling so near me that even I can distinctly see it. I Can
onely tell you of the situation I am in, which would be
better expressed by Mr: Grace if he were here. I hope all
our friends are well both at Salisbury and windsor—where
I suppose you spent the last week. pray when ever you
15 write to em give em my humble service I think to go the
next week to Mansfield race where I am told I shall see all
the Country[.] if I see any of yr: acquaintance I will do you
right to them I hope Mr: Longuevilles picture has been
well finishd I am dear Sr

20   yr: most humble
                                    Servt
                                        Will: Congreve.

Ilam near Ashbourn
in Derbyshire.
25 between 6 & 7 in the morning
birds singing Jolly breezes whistling &[c.]

Address: To Mr: Edward Porter
          At his house in Surrey Street in the Strand
          London
30 *Postmark:* AV|21

2 *To Jacob Tonson*
>   [Tunbridge] Satturday Aug: 12 (93)

Dr Mr: Tonson

I received yours of Thursday by the post, by which I
understand that you have delivered the things I wrote
about to the Coachman; I expected them yesterday & to   5
day but they are not come which makes me apprehend their
loss thro' the negligence of the fellow, I am concerned
about the letters because I expected some of buisinesse:
pray enquire if they may be recovered. I am sorry for the
trouble this must needs give you; & can onely wish my selfe   10
twice as much to do you service. if you see Mr: Wycherley
pray tell him with my service that I wrote to him to
Shrewsbery[.] I don't know whether he received it or no. I
suppose you received a letter from me by a private hand
wherein I desired you if you had not provided the things to   15
omitt them, but since you have I think it is better, especially If I Cant get them at all. I sent also by the same hand a
letter for you to send to the post office for my father. I hope
you received them I am dr: mr Tonson

>   yr: most affectionate   20
>   ffriend & srnt
>   W: Congreve.

3 *To Jacob Tonson*
>   [Tunbridge] Tuesday [15 August 1693]

Dr Mr: Tonson.

I write this onely to acquaint you that yesterday I receivd
the things which you sent, & for which I thank you; the
reason of their delay was that they have layn a week at   5
Senock. if this comes time enough I would have it prevent
yr: sending me anything else. for I'm afraid my health will
call me from the satisfaction of this place. to the more noisy
pleasures (or rather conveniencys) of Epsom. I have a
continual heat in the palms of my hands, which I believe   10
those waters are better for than Tunbridge; I shall leave this
place with great regrett, having never in my life been better
pleased for the time. if I am necessitated to come away it

will be either the latter end of this week or beginning of the
15   next. you need not take notice of it for I would go to Epsom
without being much seen in town. I should be glad if your
occasions would give you leave to go thither for a day or
two. I am Dr Mr: Tonson yr affectionate Friend

                                        & servt.
20   W: Congreve
I thank you for giving my service to Dr:
Hobbs pray repeat it. & to whom Else you
think it may be acceptable.

Address: To Mr: Tonson att the Judges head
25   in Chancery Lane
               London
Postmark: AV | 17

4 *To Mrs Arabella Hunt*

                                WINDSOR, *July* 26, 1694.
ANGEL,
THERE can be no stronger Motive to bring me to
Epsom, or to the North of *Scotland*, or to Paradise, than
5   your being in any of those Places; for you make every Place
alike Heavenly where-ever you are. And I believe if any
thing could cure me of a natural Infirmity, seeing and
hearing you would be the surest Remedy; at least, I should
forget that I had any thing to complain of, while I had so
10   much more Reason to rejoice. I should certainly (had I been
at my own Disposal) have immediately taken Post for
Epsom, upon Receipt of your Letter: But I have a Nurse
here, who has Dominion over me; a most unmerciful She-
Ass. *Balaam* was allow'd an Angel to his Ass; I'll pray, if
15   that will do any good, for the same Grace. I would have set
out upon my Ass to have waited upon you, but I was afraid
I should have been a tedious while in coming, having great
Experience of the Slowness of that Beast: For you must
know, I am making my Journey towards Health upon that
20   Animal, and I find I make such slow Advances, that I
despair of arriving at you, or any great Blessing, till I am

capable of using some more expeditious means. I could tell
you of a great Inducement to bring you to this Place, but
I am sworn to Secresy; however, if you were here, I would
contrive to make you of the Party. I'll expect you, as a good 25
Christian may every thing that he devoutly prays for. I am

Your everlasting Adorer,

W. CONGREVE.

Headed: To Mrs. HUNT at *Epsom.*

5 *To John Dennis*

Dear Sir,

IT is not more to keep my Word, than to gratifie my
Inclination, that I write to you; and thô I have thus long
deferr'd it, I was never forgetful of you, nor of my Promise.
Indeed I waited in Expectation of something that might 5
enable me to return the Entertainment I received from your
Letters: but you represent the Town so agreeable to me,
that you quite put me out of Conceit with the Country; and
my Designs of making Observations from it.

   Before I came to *Tunbridge*, I proposed to my self the 10
Satisfaction of Communicating the Pleasures of the Place
to you: But if I keep my Resolution, I must transcribe, and
return you your own Letters; since I must own I have met
with nothing else so truly Delightful. When you suppose
the Country agreeable to me, you suppose such Reasons 15
why it should be so, that while I read your Letter, I am of
your Mind; but when I look off, I find I am only Charm'd
with the Landskip which you have drawn. So that if I
would see a fine Prospect of the Country, I must desire
you to send it me from the Town; as if I would eat good 20
Fruit here. Perhaps the best way were, to beg a Basket from
my Friends in *Covent-Garden*. After all this, I must tell
you, there is a great deal of Company at *Tunbridge*; and
some very agreeable; but the greater part, is of that sort,
who at home converse only with their own Relations; and 25
consequently when they come abroad, have few Acquaintance,

but such as they bring with them. But were the Company
better, or worse, I would have you expect no Characters
from me; for I profess my self an Enemy to Detraction; and
30 who is there, that can justly merit Commendation? I have a
mind to write to you, without the pretence of any manner
of News, as I might drink to you without naming a Health;
for I intend only my Service to you. I wish for you very
often, that I might recommend you to some new Acquaint-
35 ance that I have made here, and think very well worth the
keeping; I mean Idleness and a good Stomach. You would
not think how People Eat here; every Body has the Appetite of an *Oastrich*, and as they Drink Steel in the Morning,
so I believe at Noon they could digest Iron. But sure you
40 will laugh at me for calling Idleness a New Acquaintance;
when, to your Knowledge, the greatest part of my Business, is little better. Ay, But here's the Comfort of the
Change; I am Idle now, without taking pains to be so, or
to make other People so; for Poetry is neither in my Head,
45 nor in my Heart. I know not whether these Waters may
have any Communication with *Lethe*, but sure I am, they
have none with the Streams of *Helicon*. I have often wonder'd how those wicked Writers of Lampoons, could crowd
together such quantities of Execrable Verses, tag'd with
50 bad Rhimes, as I have formerly seen sent from this place:
but I am half of Opinion now, that this Well is an *Anti-*
Hypocrene. What if we should get a Quantity of the Water
privately convey'd into the Cistern at *Will*'s Coffee-House,
for an Experiment? But I am Extravagant—Thô I remem-
55 ber *Ben. Johnson* in his Comedy of *Cynthia*'s Revels, makes
a Well, which he there calls the Fountain of Self-Love, to
be the Source of many Entertaining and Ridiculous Humours. I am of Opinion, that something very Comical and
New, might be brought upon the Stage, from a Fiction of
60 the like Nature. But now I talk of the Stage, pray if any
thing New should appear there, let me have an Account of
it: for thô Plays are a kind of Winter-Fruit, yet I know there
are now and then, some Windfalls at this time of Year,
which must be presently served up, lest they should not
65 keep till the proper Season of Entertainment. 'Tis now the

time, when the Sun breeds Insects; and you must expect to
have the Hum and Buz about your Ears, of Summer Flies
and small Poets. Cuckows have this time allow'd 'em to
Sing, thô they are damn'd to Silence all the rest of the Year.
Besides, the approaching Feast of St. *Bartholomew* both 70
creates an Expectation and bespeaks an Allowance of unnatural Productions and Monstrous Births. Methinks the
Days of *Bartholomew-Fair* are like so many Sabbaths, or
Days of Privilege, wherein Criminals and Malefactors in
Poetry, are permitted to Creep abroad. They put me in 75
mind (thô at a different time of Year) of the Roman *Satur-*
nalia, when all the Scum, and Rabble, and Slaves of *Rome*,
by a kind of Annual and limited Manumission, were suffer'd to make Abominable Mirth, and Profane the Days of
Jubilee, with Vile Buffoonry, by Authority. But I forget 80
that I am writing a Post Letter, and run into length like a
Poet in a Dedication, when he forgets his Patron to talk of
himself. But I will take care to make no Apology for it, lest
my Excuse (as Excuses generally do) should add to the
Fault. Besides, I would have no appearance of Formality, 85
when I am to tell you, that

I am,

Your real Friend,
and Humble Servant,
W. Congreve. 90

Tunbridge–Wells,
Aug. 11. 95.

6 *To Jacob Tonson*

Aug: 20 (95)

Dear Mr: Tonson
I thank you for yr: letter & the kind offers in it. but my
Mother dos not intend to come to town till I write her
word, that I am leaving this place. I am very glad you have 5
had so much satisfaction in the country & that Dr: Hobbs
has improved his health Mr: Jekel & I drank yr: Healths; &
were in hopes it was so because you stayd so long. I think
I have already found benefit from these waters. but the

10 present prospect of wett weather disheartens me. I am glad
you approve so much of my picture, if you should see Sr:
Godfrey again before you goe out of town pray give him my
service, & if he has not finish'd the picture give him a Hint:
for I should be glad it were don before my return I thank
15 you for the agreeable news you sent me. I hope to hear
more of the same kind every post I am Dear Mr Tonson yr
faithfull friend &

servant Will: Congreve

Address: To Mr: Tonson
20   att the Judges head near the inner=
             temple gate in Fleet-street.
             London

7 *To Walter Moyle*

Dear Sir,

I Can't but think, that a Letter from me in *London*, to you
in *C[ornwall]*is like some ancient Correspondence between
an Inhabitant of *Rome* and a *Cimmerian*. May be, my way of
5 Writing may not be so modestly compared with *Roman*
Epistles; but the resemblance of the Place will justify the
other part of the Parallel. The Subterraneous Habitations
of the Miners, and the Proximity of the *Bajæ* help a little
and while you are at *B[ake]* let *B[ake]* be *Cumæ*, and do
10 you supply the Place of *Sybilla*. You may look on this as
raillery, but I can assure you, nothing less than Oracles are
expected from you, in the next Parli[a]ment, if you succeed
in your Election, as we are pretty well assured you will. You
wish your self, with us at *Wills Coffee-house*; and all here
15 wish for you, from the president of the Grave Club, to the
most puny Member of the Rabble; they who can think,
think of you, and the rest talk of you. There is no such
Monster in this *Africa*, that is not sensible of your absence;
even the worst natured People, and those of least Wit
20 lament it, I mean, Half Criticks and Quiblers. To tell you
all that want you, I should name all the Creatures of
Covent-Garden, w[h]ich like those of *Eden-garden* would
want some *Adam* to be a Godfather and give them Names.

I can't tell whether I may justly compare our *Covent-garden*,
to that of *Eden*, or no; for tho' I believe we may have variety   25
of Strange Animals equal to *Paradise*, yet I fear we have not
amongst us, the *Tree* of *Knowledge*. It had been much to the
disadvantage of *Pliny*, had the *Coffee-house* been in his days;
for sure he would have described some who frequent it;
which would have given him, the reputation of a more   30
fabulous Writer then he has now. But being in our age it
does him a Service, for we who know it, can give Faith to all
his Monsters. You who took care to go down into the
Country unlike a Poet, I hope will take care not to come
up again like a Politician; for then, you will add a new   35
Monster to the *Coffee-house*, that was never seen there
before. So you may come back again, in your Souldiers
Coat, for in that you will no more be suspected for a
Politician, than a Poet. Pray come upon any terms, for you
are wished for by every body, but most wanted by your   40

Affectionate Friend
and Servant,
W. Congreve.

Wills Coffee-house,
October 13. 95.   45

8 *To Catharine Trotter*

Friday night. [15 March 1697]

I can never enough acknowlege the honour you have don
me; nor enough regret the negligence of those to whom you
deliverd yr valuable letter. 'tis the first thing that ever
happned to me, upon which I should make it my choice   5
to be vain; and yet such is the mortification that attends
even the most allowable vanity, that at the same instant I
am robd of the means, when I am possesd with the inclination. 'tis but this moment that I received yr verses, and
had scarce been transported with the reading em, when   10
they brought me the play from the press printed off. I hope
you will do me the Justice to believe that I was not so
insensible as not to be heartily vexd. & all the satisfaction
that I can take, & all the sacrifice that I can make to you, is

15 onely to stiffle some verses on the same barren subject
which were printed with it; & now, I assure you shall
never appear, whatever apology I am forced to make to
the Authors. & since I am deprived of the recommendation
you designd me, I will be obliged to no other, till I have
20 some future opportunity of preferring yrs: to every bodys
else. in the mean time give me leave to vallue my selfe upon
the favour you have don me; and to assure you it was not
wanting, to make me more ready than I have been in my
inclinations of waiting on all yr: Commands. & if Mr: Bett:
25 buisinesse does not very speedily disengage him. I will not
wait for his being a witnesse of my proffessing my selfe yr
admirer & obliged

humble servt:

W: Congreve

30 I know not what time the Princesse will give me leave to
present her with the play, it being dedicated to her, but as
soon as that form is over I will make bold to send you one.

9 *To Joseph Keally*

London 7br: 28: 97:

Dear Jo:

I thought you were either drownd or a prisoner at St
Malloes, which would have been a worse thing if not for
5 you, at least for yr: acquaintance, for I would not willingly
hear any more of St: Malloes. You must not wonder if the
Peace which affects all Europe should in some measure
influence me; it has indeed put a stop to my intended
pilgrimage for St Patricks I am sorry you are like to have
10 no better an effect of yr: own. Maybe I may stay in England
to as little purpose as you left it; but I am advised to try My
Ld: D: of Ormond whom I waited on yesterday talks of
going for Ireland on Monday next. I would not miss such
an opportunity if it were not thought absolutely necessary
15 for me to stay here: I believe my Lady Duchesse & the
Good Bishop will have their books at that time. I have no
news of any kind to send you. I have not seen bottom since

I receivd yr: letter but Amory I just now parted with who is
yours. Jerry Marsh is here. as for Luther I find him both by
yr: account & his own proceeding unalterable. and I hope 20
Champ & you will come over together. pray give my hearty
service to my Cosen Congreve. Tell the Good Bishop
I must have very good fortune before I am reconciled to
the necessity of my staying in England at a time when
I promised my selfe the Happinesse of seeing him at 25
Kilkenny I would say something very devout to the Dutch-
esse but you are a prophane dog & would spoil it. if the
Bishop would sanctifie my Duty to her I would requite him
in my way. prithee Keally distribute my service in a most
particular manner & make me popular amongst those ac- 30
quaintance whom I have forgott let me hear when I may
expect you & make haste to your

W: Congreve

Pray lett me know if you did not receive some letters from
yr: brother because I sent such a pacquett after you to 35
Ireland I did not write because I concluded you would
know my Seal.

Postmark: SE|28

10 *To Joseph Keally*

London, July 2. 1700.

Dear Keally,

BY your last from Dublin I may guess this will find you at
Kilkenny; where I hope you will settle your affairs, so that
in a little time it may not be inconvenient for you to see 5
your friends here, who very much regret your absence.
I need not tell you that I do; who am not apt to care for
many acquaintance, and never intend to make many friendships. You know I need not be very much alone; but
I choose it, rather than to conform myself to the manners 10
of my court or chocolate-house acquaintance. My neighbours
are very much yours; and, if you drink not their healths daily,
are before hand with you in a kind remembrance. You have
failed in your commission to Holywell; answer it as you can.

15 The inclosed I received a week since; but could not venture
to direct 'em at large to Dublin. The king goes on Thursday
to Holland. Eccles is made master of his music, which was an
employment void by the death of Dr Staggins; it is worth
L. 300 *per annum*. Mein is well, and yours. I am glad to hear
20 from you. Pray don't grow rusty; and remember sometimes
to write to me when you have idle hours. I am yours,

WILL. CONGREVE.

I have not yet seen Dandridge; but will, in my next, give
you an account of that affair.

11 *To Edward Porter*

Calais Aug: 11th: Old: S: 1700

If any letters are left for me before
you receive this pray enclose em
to be left at the post house in Brussels.
5   for any that shall Come after yr: receipt
of this, I will trouble you with some
other direction

Here is Admirable Champagn for twelve pence a Quart as
good Burgundy for 15 pence; & yet I have vertue enough to
10 resolve to leave this place to morrow for St Omers where
the same wine is halfe as dear again & may be not quite so
good. (dear Neighbour) Charles & Jacob & I have never
faild drinking yr: healths since we saw you, nor never will
till we see you again. we had a long passag[e] but delicate
15 weather. we set sail from Dover on Satturday morning 4 a
clock & did not land here till 6 the same evening; nor had
we arrivd even in that time, if a french open boat with Oars
had not been stragling towards us when we were not quite
halfe-seas over, and rowd us hither from thence in 5 hours;
20 for the packet boat came not till this morning; when I come
to Brussells I shall have more to write to you till then I am
most humbly
& heartily yr:
W: Congreve

25 My humble service to my neighbour, yr: Mother, Mrs: Anne:
Mr: Travers not forgetting the Alcayde who <I> hope in my

Absence may be reconcild to Punch. Poor Charles is Just
writing to Mrs. Anne and striving very hard to send something besides the Ballad, to please her much.

Address: To Mr: Porter   30
              At His house in Arundel Street against the
              blew-ball. London.
Postmark: AV|14

12 *To Mrs Frances Porter*

                        Rotterdam 7br: 27: 1700

I leave you to Judge whither Holland can be said to be
wanting in Gallantry, when it is Customary there to enclose
a Billet doux to a Lady, in a letter to her husband[.] I have not
so much as made mention of this, to yours; & if you tell first,   5
let the sin fall upon your head instead of his. for my part I
keep the Commandments, I love my neighbour as my selfe, &
to avoid Coveting my neighbours wife I desire to be coveted
by her; which you know is quite another thing. about 5 weeks
since, I wrote a very passionate letter to you from Antwerp   10
which I believe you never receivd, for Just now it is found
Carefully put up by my Man, who has been drunk ever since.
I understand you have not been in the Country, I am glad of
it; for I should very much have aprehended the effects which
solitude might have produced, joynd with the regrett which I   15
know you feel for my absence. take it for granted that I sigh
extreamly: I would have written to the Alcayd, but that
would make me reflect that I was at a distance from her,
which is pain I cannot bear. I would have written to yr:
Mother but that I have changed my religion twice since I   20
left England, & am at present so unsettled, that I think it fit to
fix before I endeavour to Convert her to my opinion which I
design to do as soon as I know what it is. I have discoursd with
friers & monks of all orders, with Zealots enthusiasts & all
sectaries of the reformd churches. & I had the benefit to travel   25
12 leagues together in Guelderland with a mad Phanatick in a
waggon, who preachd to me all the way things not to be

written. pray take Care that Mr: Ebbub has good wine for I
have much to say to you over a bottle underground: & I hope
30 within 3 weeks to satisfie you that no man upon the face of the
earth nor in the Cellar is more dear neighbour your Faithfull
& affectionate humble
servant than
W: C:

35 *Address:* For Mrs: Porter.

13 *To Joseph Kealy*

London, *Dec.* 10. 1700.

Dear Kealy,

I AM very glad, if you are in earnest, when you find fault
with not hearing from me; for by that you will know how
5 justly I may reproach you for the same neglect. However,
I was about writing to you when I received yours; but Sapho
being in labour, I was forced to hold my hand till her
deliverance. Among other beauties which she has brought
into the world, she has reserved one most like herself for
10 you, if you can give us directions how to send it. I have not
yet called for the Kerry stones; but your directions shall be
observed. I am mighty sorry Amory has been ill. I have
preached as I ought to Mein, and he has edified as he ought.
Our journey was extremely agreeable, though I think I had
15 much the advantage, having seen French Flanders, which
Mein missed for want of time, and yet lay at the Brill almost
as long (as I was making that tour) for a wind. One thing I
must tell you which gave me much pleasure, and you may
tell it to Amory and Robin. Whenever we have seen any
20 thing extremely surprising, chiefly in painting, though the
picture has been the most solemn, the most devout, the
most moving, both in the subject and the expressions of
the passion; as soon as our Charles began to be touched with
it, he always burst out a laughing, which I like mightily; and
25 so he did the first time he heard Abell sing. Robin cannot be
more the same than he is. Abell is here; has a cold at present,
and is always whimsical; so that when he will sing, or whether
he will sing or not upon the stage, are things very disputable;

but he certainly sings beyond all creatures upon earth; and
I have heard him very often both abroad and since he came 30
over. I am very glad to hear you say you shall remember what
you owe yourself. I wish you would think too what you owe
your friends; who, though not able to engage your gratitude,
ought to influence your good nature to think of seeing 'em,
which you seem to give over even in your mind's eye. The 35
family in Arundel-street are very much yours; so is Charles,
and I am Robins. I have no news: It is none that Mr Montague is Lord Halifax, and that I am entirely yours.

W. CONGREVE.

14 *To John Drummond*

Sr

Upon my arrival in England my affairs obliged me to a long
journey into the West. Just at my return to London I met
with your Kind Obliging letter; I beg you to believe, that
tho' that has prevented my writing first; yet nothing Could 5
have made me longer deferr returning you my thanks for
the great Civillitys and Obligations I receivd from you at
Amsterdam. I shall receive a great deal of pleasure if I can
by any means Contribute to yr: entertainment by recom-
mending or writing anything worthy of yr: leisure hours: & 10
I will not fail with the first opportunity to enjoyn Mr:
Tonson to take Care answerable to yr: directions. My
impatience of writing to you at this time is the occasion
that I send you nothing worth yr: Consideration, for I am
so lately Come to town that I am a perfect stranger to the 15
news of it. I have Observed in the Country & by the lists of
the members for the new Parliament, that there will be but
little alteration in it from the last, how the present Juncture
of affairs may vary the proceedings of the same Persons,
onely time can shew. The reception of the Emperors min- 20
ister you may be sure is as well as possible; & I doubt not
will have a good issue. all Persons of sence & integrity in the
love of their Country, are convinced of the necessity of
enabling the King to make a war if he shall Judge it fitt. and

25 I hope the Parliament will see our Condition in a true light
when they shall meet. I will send you a Pamphlet newly
publishd which I think very well & Justly explains the state
of Europe in Generall as well as of England & Holland in
particular at this time. the Author of it is not Certainly
30 Known; but his good understanding is very evident in the
treatise he has set forth—entituld the Duke of Anjous
succession Considerd as to its Legality & Consequences.
Mr: Abell tho' he has receivd 300^{ll} of the money belonging
to the new Play-house has not yet sung & is full of nothing
35 but lies & shifting tricks his character I suppose is not new
to you. Mr: Mein is heartily yr: servant and I can answer
for the rest of my fellow travellers tho' I have not seen 'em
since my last Coming to town. Pray Sr: on any occasion
wherein you think me Capable of serving you lay yr:
40 Commands on me be assurd you Cannot oblige me more
than by giving me opportunitys of shewing how sensible
I am of yr: Kindnesse & that I am with great truth Sr
Yr: very affectionate
humble servant
45 Will: Congreve
when you favour me with
a letter, pray direct for me
next door below the blew ball
in Arundell street in the strand.
50 London Jan: 15th: 1700[-01]

Address: To Mr: John Drummond Mercht: in Amsterdam

15 *To Joseph Keally*
London, Jan. 28. 1700[-1].

THE only letter which I received from you (Dr Keally) I
immediately answered, though I was forced to direct to
Dublin at large for want of better instructions. Whether
5 you have received it or not I know not; for you take care to
justify the character of the Irish seas. Since you have been
so very silent, I am grown in charity with that brute
Luther; have almost forgiven Fitzgerald; and, if I could

ever have been angry with Tom Amory, should have been now reconciled to him. It is reported that you don't think fit to take notice of young Sapho, who is at a boarding-school accomplishing herself every day more and more, that she may one day find favour in your eyes; such as a certain necklace has done in the eyes of the whole town: for it has such a reputation of being right, that the lady is forced to declare very heartily to the contrary, least she should be thought to be wrong; so is forced to preserve her own reputation at the expence of the brilliants. I give you an account of it; because, as a haughty Spaniard, I know you expect it. Twenty-three beads grinding, cutting, polishing, setting, &c. come to four shillings each, and all together to four pound twelve. Talking of money, I must desire you to put Robin in mind, that his forgetfulness has like to have had an ill effect; for Charles has very narrowly escaped being arrested, and that near the custom-house, which might have had worse consequences than the arrest itself any where else. Maybe his modesty hinders him from writing about it; but I know he is forced to go out of town. We have had two new plays, a tragedy called the Ambitious Stepmother, written by Mr Rowe of the Temple, and a very good one; another called the Lady's Visiting-day, written by Mr Burnaby; both acted at the new house. The last is likely to have a run, and has something more in it relating to the title than the trip. Poor Williams the musician is dead. Sansom has sent me a very beautiful mare, which should be at your service if you were here; but I hear you are going another way, and like to be married. Dick Steel is yours; so is Charles; so are our friends in Arundel-street, besides infinite thanks for the jewels, which I will not undertake to write down. I am just as I used to be, and as I always shall be, yours,

W. CONGREVE.

Headed: *To Joseph Keally, Esq; Dublin.*

16 *To Joseph Keally*

London, *March* 26. 1701.

Dear Keally,

I SHOULD sooner have answered yours, and acknowledged the receipt of your bill; but I have been something
5   uneasy and unwell. I heard by a letter from James Hewsly of
your being gone into the country. I hope it is in order to take
some care about an expedition hither. All your friends in
this quarter are ever inquisitive about you, and nobody
thinks your correspondence frequent enough. I wished
10   particularly for you on Friday last, when Eccles his music
for the prize was performed in Dorset Garden, and universally admired. Mr Finger's is to be to-morrow; and Purcel
and Weldon's follow in their turn. The latter two I believe
will not be before Easter. After all have been heard severally,
15   they are all to be heard in one day, in order to a decision; and
if you come at all this spring, you may come time enough to
hear that. Indeed, I don't think any one place in the world
can show such an assembly. The number of performers,
besides the verse-singers, was 85. The front of the stage was
20   all built into a concave with deal boards; all which was faced
with tin, to increase and throw forwards the sound. It was all
hung with sconces of wax-candles, besides the common
branches of lights usual in the play-houses. The boxes and
pit were all thrown into one; so that all sat in common: and
25   the whole was crammed with beauties and beaux, not one
scrub being admitted. The place where formerly the music
used to play, between the pit and stage, was turned into
White's chocolate-house; the whole family being transplanted thither with chocolate, cool'd drinks, ratafia, Pon-
30   tacq, &c. which every body that would called for, the whole
expence of every thing being defrayed by the subscribers.
I think truly the whole thing better worth coming to see
than the jubilee. And so I remain yours,

W . CONGREVE.

35   Our friend Venus performed to a miracle; so did Mrs
Hodgson Juno. Mrs Boman was not quite so well approved
in Pallas. I have spoken to Dandridge; but he does not mind
me; so let him wait.

17 *To John Drummond*

Sr

Nothing but an indisposition, of which I am yet hardly
recoverd, Could have hinderd my answering your letter,
both in respect of the great desire I have to Continue the
pleasure of yr: acquaintance and in regard of giving you the
best account I am able of the state of our affairs, in such a
manner as might be either serviceable or entertaining to
you. but as to the latter, we are in so much uncertainty that
I think no body can pretend to do more than guess what we
shall do, and even that with more presumption than probability. we observe our parliament to make such slow steps
that tho' we Conclude the necessity of affairs will draw us
into a warr; yet we cannot foresee any time when we may
venture to expect a Commencement of it. Our Parliament
are still proceeding to a further inspection into treatys,
what issue it will have further than the ratification of that
of 77. I cannot guesse. I fancy we shall await yr: motions in
Holland and avoid as far as possible to make our selves
principalls; at least this appears to be the sense of this
present session, how much more vigourous their sentiments will be in the next, time will shew. but sure nothing
can prevent a war sooner or later, before we can think our
selves in any prospect of safety. I have not seen Mr: Tonson
of some time but he promisd me faithfully to take Care of
supplying you from time to time with such books as might
be acceptable to you, and accordingly took a Memorandum
of directions. I hear of ill successe in Mr Foules affairs
I hope you are no sufferer by it. if Mr: Vander Heyden is
married I wish him Joy. and all success to you in every
undertaking. I am very sorry I Can write you no letter at
this time more to the purpose which I would answer, being
very willing to appear to my power very much

Yr: humble servt

Will: Congreve

London April: 10th: 1701

Address: To Mr: John Drummond Mercht: in Amsterdam

18 *To Joseph Keally*

London, June 7th: 1701.

Dear Keally,

Yrs: of the 15th: of may last was very wellcome to me,
because it promises yr: presence here. I hope exchange will
5 fall as low as you would have it, but should it continue as
high as it is I hope you will get over it & lend a hand to poor
Robin for his gutts were not naturally made for mounting.
You desire me to send you news & particulars Concerning
the impeached Lords and say 'tis a banter to you; and truly
10 'tis Just so to me: for tho they are impeached I believe they
will never be tryd; for there is neither matter nor proof
against them. Scaffolds are building in westminster hall;
but however I should be sorry you should not Come sooner
than you need to take notes there at their tryall. all arundell
15 street is much yours & hears of yr: designs with pleasure Mr:
Travers in particular since you will have me name him to
you. pray send me word when you are Just Coming & make
haste, Mein may write merrily or gravely, but I take the man
to be moapd[.] I never saw a fellow so alterd[.] I am if you
20 Come this summer. still more yrs.

W: Congreve

Address: To Joseph Keally Esqre:
              At Kilkenny
              in Ireland
25   10d thro
Postmark: IV|7

19 *To Joseph Keally*

[London, late Summer 1702]

Dear Keally,

You are something slow both in your approaches and
your answers; but I am glad to hear from you, and shall
5 be glad to see you after having been so long tantalized. I had
once thoughts of coming for Ireland this summer, but must
defer it till spring. I hope you will keep your word of
Michaelmas. Every body here wishes for you; but we are

at present in great grief for the death of Sapho. She has left
some few orphans; one of which, if it can live, is designed 10
for you. Nich. Bolton lives at Peckham, somewhere beyond
Camberwell, in a farmer's house, and follows the plough,
and reads Homer at the same time; as Baker the actor and
paver used to pave with his part pin'd upon his sleeve, and
hem and rehearse alternately. Tell Robin I thank him for 15
his last kind letter. I am yours,

W. CONGREVE.

20 *To Joseph Keally*

December 4th: 1702

Dear Keally

I had not time to answer yrs: before; but I carryd the
enclosed for yr: brother to the Secretarys office the next
morning & put it into the Portugall Pacquett. I have no 5
great faith in yr: promises yet I am willing to expect yr:
performance & hope you will Celebrate the ensuing festi-
vall in Arundell street great revolutions have been there
since the Death of Sapho. things not to be entrusted to frail
paper and pacquett boats. My service to inhuman Robin 10
whose letters I allways punctually answerd. an exactnesse
I would not have you observe at this time. for—nil mihi
rescri[bas attamen ipse] veni—
Jack: Allen. Epist: 3d:

[Yrs 15

Will: Congreve]

Address: To Joseph Keally Esqr:
to be left at the post office
in Dublin
Postmark: DE|4 20

21 *To Jacob Tonson*

London July 1st: 1703

Dear Mr: Tonson.

My having been at the Bathe prevented my receiving your
letter so soone as I should have don, had I been in town. & I

5   was in hopes you would have been here before, but by your
staying so much longer I hope you will doe your buisinesse
effectually. I shewd your letter to my Lord Halifax & desird
<h>im to do you right to Sr: Harry Furnes. I hope the
weather will continue fair for yr. return since it is Changed
10 so much for the better. I thank you for the care & trouble
you have taken about my linnen I Could wish for halfe a
dozen a degree Courser if yr: time & leisure permits you.
Your Nephew told me of Copies that were dispersed of the
Pastoral & likely to be printed so we have thought fit to
15 prevent 'em & print it our selves. I believe barn-elms wants
you & I long to see it but dont care to satisfie my Curiosity
before you Come. my humble service to Mr: Addison I am
Yrs: most faithfull
& affectionately
20 Willm: Congreve

Address: Amsterdam

22 *To Catharine Trotter*

Madam

I had sooner acknowledg'd the favour of yr: Letter together, wth: the agreable entertainment of the scheme
you were pleased to send with it, if I had not been unavoid-
5 ably engaged in buisinesse. but at this time I can hardly
Complain of a great Cold, which has confind me, & given
me an oppertunity to Obey yr: Commands. I think the
design in general very great & noble; the Conduct of it
very artfull, if not too full of buisinesse, which may either
10 run into length or obscurity; but both those, as you write,
you have skill enough to avoid. You are the best Judge,
whether those of yr: own sex will approve as much of the
Heroick vertue of Constantia & Christina, as if they had
been engaged in some *Belle passion.* for my part I like em
15 better as they are. In the 2nd: Act I would have that noise,
which generaly attends so much fighting on the stage
provided against; for those frequent allarms & excursions

do too much disturb an audience. The difficulty in the 3d: act is as well solved by you as possible; & Certainly you can never be too carefull not to offend probability, in supposing 20 a man not to discover his own wife.

in the 4th act it does not seem to me to be clear enough, how Constantia Comes to be made free & to return to Gust: the 3d Act intimating so strongly, why we might expect to have her Continued in the viceroys power. this act is full of 25 buisinesse; & intricacy, in the fourth act must by all means be avoided.

the Last act will have many harangues in it, which are dangerous in a Catastrophe if long, & not of the last importance. To Conclude I approve extreamly of your 30 Killing Fredage & Beron poetical Justice requires him, & for her you may easily drop a word to intimate her deliver-ing of Gust: to have proceeded from some spark of love, which afterwards she may repent of & her character remain as perfect as nature need require. one thing would have a 35 very beautifull effect in the Catastrophe if it were possible to manage it thro' the play and that is to have the audience kept in ignorance as long as the Husband (which sure they may as well be) who Fredage really is, till her death.

you see madam I am as free as you Command me to be and 40 yet my objections are none but such as you may provide against even while you are writing the dialogue

I wish you the successe, which you can wish & that I think will hardly be so much as you deserve in whatever you undertake. I am with all acknowledgments for yr: too 45 favourable opinion of me

Madam

Yr: most obedient

humble servt

Willm: Congreve. 50

London 9br: 2d: 1703.

Address: To Mrs: Catherine Trotter
At Mr: Inglis's house in
Salisbury
Postmark: NO|2   55

23 *To Joseph Keally*

Dear Keally,

I THINK it a tedious while since I heard from you; and
though, to the best of my remembrance, I answered your
5 last, yet I write again to put you in mind of your old friends,
every one of whom has very narrowly escaped the hurri-
cane on Friday night last. The public papers will be full of
particulars. 'Tis certain, in the memory of man, never was
any thing like it. Most of the tall trees in the Park are blown
10 down; and the four trees that stood distinct before St
James's, between the Mall and the Canal. The garden-
wall of the priory, and the Queen's garden there, are both
laid flat. Some great sash-windows of the banqueting-house
have been torn from the frames, and blown so as they have
15 never been found nor heard of. The leads of churches have
some of them been rolled up as they were before they were
laid on: others have been skimmed clear off, and transported cross the street, where they have been laid on other
houses, breaking the roofs. The news out of the country is
20 equally terrible; the roads being obstructed by the trees
which lie cross. Anwick, Coventry, and most of the towns
that my acquaintance have heard of, are in great measure
destroyed, as Bristol, where they say a church was blown
down. It is endless to tell you all. Our neighbour in
25 Howard's-street 'scaped well, though frighted, only the
ridge of the house being stripped; and a stack of chimneys
in the next house fell luckily into the street. I lost nothing
but a casement in my man's chamber, though the chimneys
of the Blue Ball continued tumbling by piece-meal most
30 part of the night at Mr Porter's. The wind came down the
little court behind the back parlour, and burst open that
door, bolts and all, whirled round the room, and scattered
all the prints; of which, together with the table and chairs,
it mustered into one heap, and made a battery of 'em to
35 break down the other door into the entry, whither it swept
'em; yet broke not one pane of the window which join'd to
the back-court door. It took off the sky-light of the stairs,
and did no more damage there. Many people have been

killed. But the loss at sea is inconceivable, though the particulars are not many yet confirmed; and I am afraid 40 poor Beaumont is lost. Shovel, they say, and Fairborn, are heard of. I hope you have been less sufferers. One should be glad to hear so from your own hands. Pray give my service to all friends. The King's-Bench walk buildings are just as before their roofs were covered. Tell that to Robin. 45 I am, dear Keally, yours,

W. CONGREVE.

24 *To Joseph Keally*

London, Feb. 12. 1703[-4].

Dear Keally,

I FORGOT to thank you for the hint you gave me concerning a commissioner's place in your former letter, which you have repeated in your last. You may imagine 5 I would not omit such an advantage if it were practicable; but I know it is vain, notwithstanding all the fair promises I have had; for I have not obtained a less matter which I ask'd for. I must have patience; and I think I have. Of my philosophy I make some use; but, by God, the greatest trial 10 of it is, that I know not how to have the few people that I love as near me as I want. You will do me the justice to apply this as I intend it. I am yours

W. CONGREVE.

My service to Robin and the rest. 15

25 *To Joseph Keally*

London, *May* 20. 1704.

Dear Keally,

LAST night I had yours of the 13th; and the first thing I do this morning is to answer it. I remember I told you I should soon write again, which was because I had not then seen the 5 Duke of Ormond, and did not imagine but I might have seen him before this time; but it is impossible, he is so often in private, and so often denied. I met him at court; and had an

opportunity of telling him my unhappiness in not waiting of
10 him. Lady Betty and her sisters are very well, and your
servants: so are all our neighbours. The ministry is not so
much altered as I find you have supposed. Mansell in the
room of Sir Edward Seymour, and Harley in place of Lord
Nottingam, is, as they say here, a change without an alter-
15 ation. The timorous disposition of those at the helm occasions this seeming removal; but, in all probability, a little
more time must produce something more barefaced, and it
must either run openly in one or t'other channel. The translation you speak of is not altogether mine; for Vanbrugh and
20 Walsh had a part in it. Each did an act of a French farce.
Mine, and I believe theirs, was done in two mornings; so
there can be no great matter in it. It was a compliment made
to the people of quality at their subscription music, without
any design to have it acted or printed farther. It made people
25 laugh; and somebody thought it worth his while to translate it
again, and print it as it was acted: but if you meet such a thing,
I assure you it was none of ours; which I don't think will
appear again after next week, when our neighbour is to have it
acted for her benefit. Here is no manner of news but what the
30 prints afford, the town being very dull. I am not much
otherwise: but in dullness or mirth, dear Keally, always your
W. C.

26 *To Joseph Keally*

London June 20th: 1704

Dear Kelly,

I had sooner thankd you for yr: dillask which is very good,
had I not then been very lame of the gout when it came.
5 The fit is pretty well over & I am at ease enough to write
thus much to you. I wish you could keep yr: resolution of
seeing the Bath. I should hope then by some means or other
we might meet. all yr: Friends hereabouts are well & at
your service there is no news, the town is extream thin
10 rather thinner than usual at this time of year. good wine
scarcer than ever & Lemons very dear but I hope these

things will mend by the time that I get abroad. pray let me
hear from you if I must not see you for I am ever

yr: W Congreve

Address: To Joseph Kelly Esqr: in Dublin Ireland   15
Postmark: JU|20

27 *To Joseph Keally*

London, Oct. 14. 1704.

Dear Keally,

I WAS in the country when your letter came with the
inclosed to his Grace of Ormond; but Charles did it, and
I suppose has written to you. That which you mention by   5
Mr Howard I never received. This comes to you by a
gentleman desirous of your acquaintance; and Mr Porter
told me he had a mind, in order thereunto, to carry a letter
from me to you. I have a multitude of affairs, being just
come to town after nine weeks absence. I am grown fat; but   10
you know I was born with somewhat a round belly. I find
you are resolved to be a man of this world, which I am sorry
for, because it will deprive me of you. However, think of
me, as I am nothing extenuate. My service to Robin, who
would laugh to see me puzzled to buckle my shoe; but I'll   15
fetch it down again. I am your

W. CONGREVE.

28 *To Joseph Keally*

London, Oct. 28. 1704.

Dear Keally,

I HAVE at length received yours by Mr Howard, who is
one I like much at first sight. I will observe all your
directions; but my father has been so extremely ill, and   5
yet continues ill, that I have had no leisure nor disposition
to do it; but I hope the danger is past. I wrote to you by one
Mr Mahun, whom I am a stranger to, and to whom you
are to be known. I gave your letter to Mein, who has taken
care to forward it for your picture. I am of your mind as to   10

the Tale of a Tub. I am not alone in the opinion, as you are there; but I am pretty near it, having but very few on my side; but those few are worth a million. However, I have never spoke my sentiments, not caring to contradict a
15 multitude. Bottom admires it, and cannot bear my saying, I confess I was diverted with several passages when I read it, but I should not care to read it again. That he thinks not commendation enough. You will let me hear from you sometimes. I am, my dear Keally, yours entirely,
20   W. CONGREVE.

29 *To Joseph Keally*

                                          London, Dec. 9. 1704.
Dear Keally,

I WROTE to you some time since, upon receiving your letter by Mr Howard, and another of a later date by the
5 post. I thank you for his acquaintance. I like him very well. I have sat to him; and they say it will be a good picture. I wish I had yours; for I don't expect to see you much for the future. Here is nothing in town worth your knowledge; only I can tell you in general terms, that affairs begin to
10 look as if they would mend. Rowe writ a foolish farce called the Biter, which was damned. Cibber has produced a play, consisting of fine gentlemen and fine conversation altogether; which the ridiculous town for the most part likes: but there are some that know better. My service to
15 Robin. I have a great cold, which makes writing uneasy to me. I am, dear Keally, yours ever,
                                          W.C.

30 *To Joseph Keally*

                                       London, Feb. 3. 1704[-5].
Dear Keally,

I RECEIVED yours of the 25th of Jan. and am indebted to you one before that. I am glad you have received your
5 picture, though I wish it had called on me by the way. Mine is not yet finished. I have been so employed, and am still

like to be so, that I have no time for any thing. I know not
when the house will open, nor what we shall begin withal;
but I believe with no opera. There is nothing settled yet.
All neighbours are well, and your servants. Mein is now   10
with me; and says, since your picture is come, he believes
he shall never hear from you again; and for his own part, he
knows not now about what to write to you. Some who have
sccn my picture since the third sitting, don't like it so well
as I did after the first. I have not had time to see Mr   15
Howard these six weeks. My service to Robin. Tell him I
shall want a fat box-keeper. I am yours,
W. CONGREVE.

31 *To Joseph Keally*
[October–November 1705?]
I AM very sorry to hear you have been so much out of
order. I wish you may be well enough to come down this
week. I fancy the air would do you good. For Amory, I wish
for him, but don't expect him. I thank you for sending the   5
cargo, which is at last come safe. I sent my man to pay Mr
Boddy four pound, which was all that was due (discounting
the money which I advanced to him) on the last quarter.
His note, which I have for it, is in my escritoir; and if I had
thought of it I would have sent you the key, that you might 10
have given it him. It seems he durst not trust me in such an
occasion, and would not give my man a full acquittance.
I was by agreement to have six weeks warning. My quarter
was up at Michaelmas or thereabouts, and he gave me
warning on Bartholomew-day; which, I believe upon com-   15
putation, comes more short of what I ought to have had
from him than my escritoir has transgressed by lying in his
lodgings over and above the quarter-day. However, I told
him before I left the town, that I would quit his lodgings at
the quarter's end, having taken new, to commence from the 20
same time; and therefore, if my few goods would be any
trouble to him, desired him to let me know, that they might
be removed in time, for I foresaw I should not be in town at
that time myself. His answer was no civiler than barely
became him; that if they remained there a fortnight there   25

could be no damage; and if any new tenant should come that
might have occasion for the room they took, he would send
me timely notice. Notwithstanding all this, he has sent me
word by my man, by word of mouth, that he hopes I will not
30 let him lose a fortnight by me. Pray give yourself the trouble
to let him know what I have writ, and charge him with the
truth of every particular. If he can deny any one, I am sure I
am much to blame. If he cannot, and I am sure he cannot
honestly, I think modestly he has not paid me the civility nor
35 the justice which belongs to me. You may assure him, when
I come to town he shall have his note or notes, for I think I
have two; and I think they are not more acknowledgements
of his debt to me than they are testimonies of my civility to
him. He says I have done him five pounds damage in his
40 quilt. What he can make appear to be the real damage, I will
satisfy him for it; but advise him to say no more than it is, or
at least than the quilt is worth: for as I would not wrong him,
so I will not be belied: of both which truths, when he gives
me the occasion, I will convince him. This is what I think fit
45 to say to Mr Boddy; and I ask your pardon for making you
my proxy in such an affair, and with such a one. I heartily
wish you your health, and here. Pray remember me to my
very good friends and neighbours in Arundel-street. Yours,
WILL. CONGREVE.
50   I live the life of a Carthusian, and am heartily sorry for
Sanford. The snuff you sent is excellent in both kinds.
Northall, Friday morning.

32 *To Joseph Keally*

London, December 15. 1705.

Dear Keally,
I THANK you for your letter of congratulation, and more
for the account it brought me of your safe arrival. Robin talks
5 of going every day. I would have him stay till the weather is a
little settled; for if he should be cast away, you know your
water swells a man; and what a thing were he if he were

swelled? I know he sends you all the news from the Smyrna;
so I have nothing to add but only that I have quitted the
affair of the Hay-market. You may imagine I got nothing by   10
it: but when I was dipt, and asked myself, *Quid agam?* replies
Terence, *Quid, nisi ut te redimas captum, quam queas minimo,
si nequeas paululo, et quanti queas.* I think I cannot end a letter
better than with a smart quotation. I am, dear Recorder and
Judge *in futuro*, already in wisdom, gravity, and understand-   15
ing, yours, and so is all the neighbourhood,

W. CONGREVE.

33 *To Joseph Keally*

London April; 30th: 1706

Dear Kelly

I am allways glad to hear from you whether there be any
news or buisinesse in yr: letters or not. I have heard you
had some thoughts of coming again for England. I wish it   5
were true. I think there is no doubt of yr: Governors
returning to you again: I have been pretty free from the
gout since the fit at Xmas. I have neither too much nor too
little buisinesse & if I have the spleen it is because this town
affords not one drop of wine out of a private house. all yr: 10
friends hereabouts are well & at yr: service. I believe the
Play house Cannot go on another Winter[.] [I] have heard
there is to be a union of the two houses as well as Kingdoms[.] my service to Robin Luther Amory[.] I am

Yours   15

Will: Congreve

34 *To Joseph Keally*

London, June 8. 1706.

Dear Keally,

I RECEIVED yours with great surprise and concern; and
the more because I had some hopes, about that time, of
hearing you designed for England. I am sure you know me   5
enough to know I feel very sensibly and silently for those
whom I love; but the great escape you have had of your life
is a reflection that alleviates the misfortune which you met

withal. I hope this letter will find you perfectly free from
10 pain and weakness; but have a care of stirring too soon. I am
sorry Robin Fitzgerald continues in so ill a state of health.
I must be plain with you on his account: He did not live at a
rate in this town to hope otherwise. Nothing but an absolute and continued regularity, and that with very good
15 prescriptions, can recover so ill a habit of body. I wish he
would take care of himself, or rather that he could. I was
out of town when Ld Halifax undertook his expedition. If
you had been here, and inclined to such a ramble, I should
not have avoided it; though, excepting the Court of Han-
20 over, I have seen all that such a journey can show. The
news is so general every post, that the public letters tell you
all that can be told you. The ladies had all the concern
imaginable at hearing of your ill accident. I have not seen
Mein since I received your letter; but I expect that he
25 should hang or stab himself when I tell him. I think he
ought to do no less who affected to fast upon the news of
Lord Donnegal's death, and got drunk the night following.
All here are your servants. Pray let me hear of your recovery, which cannot be more welcome to you than to your
30   W. CONGREVE.

35 *To Joseph Keally*

London, June 26. 1706.
Dear Keally,
I HAVE really thought it tedious not to have heard from
you. That I have not written has been, as you imagine, from
5 business; but business no more profitable than mine uses to
be—full of vexation, and without any good consequence.
Mein has succeeded better, which I suppose he has told you
of. How my friends, as you call 'em, mean to proceed in
relation to me, I know not yet. They speak as they used to
10 do, and may consequently do as they use to do. I am glad
you give me hopes of seeing you: I wish you may persevere.
Pray wish Lady Betty joy from me of her boy. I am
removed to Mr Porter's in Surry-street, where I shall be
glad to hear from you till I may hope to see you; which,

believe me, is one of the things I wish the most heartily for 15
in the world. Your neighbours enquire after you, though
you don't remember them. Yours,

W. CONGREVE.

36 *To Joseph Keally*

Dear Keally,
I HAVE of late forborne writing to you till I could see your
brother; which having done, *liberavi animam meam*; though I
hope to meet him more than once before he sets forwards for
Ireland. I could have wished his affairs had obliged him to 5
stay here, that you might have been obliged to come hither as
you once hinted; but I think the least you can do is to set him
so far on of his way back again. I hope your leg is so well that it
makes not any unnecessary addition to the gravity of your
walk. The play-houses have undergone another revolution; 10
and Swinny, with Wilks, Mrs Olfield, Pinkethman, Bullock,
and Dicky, are come over to the Hay-Market. Vanbrugh
resigns his authority to Swinny, which occasioned the revolt.
Mr Rich complains and rails like Volpone when counterplot-
ted by Mosca. My Lord Chamberlain approves and ratifies 15
the desertion; and the design is, to have plays only at the Hay-
Market, and operas only at Covent Garden. I think the design
right to restore acting; but the houses are misapplied, which
time may change. I have written an ode which I presented to
the Queen, who received it very graciously. Though you may 20
have seen it, yet I will send you one by your brother. My
service to Robin. I am, dear Keally, your

W. CONGREVE.

London, Sept. 10. 1706.

37 *To Joseph Keally*

London, July 12. 1707.
Dear Keally,
I MUST congratulate you on report, since you have not
been so kind to give me any more agreeable notice, of your

5 changing your condition so much for the better. I, with all
your friends here, have drank your health and prosperity
ever since the news has been confirmed to us. They all give
you their service and good wishes; and though I long to
hear from you, yet I hope you will be so much taken up
10 with joy, that you will not very soon find time to excuse
your neglecting to inform me of an adventure so important
to you. I would give my service to Robin; but this is
intended only to wish you joy, and must not be profaned
with the name of any bachelor. I am, Dear Keally, yours,
15   W. CONGREVE.

38 *To Joseph Keally*

                              London, Jan. 29. 1707[-8].
Dear Keally,

I HAVE yours of the 5th instant; but have not yet heard any
thing of Mr Howard or the picture. If I committed any
5 mistake in relation to it, it was impossible for me to do
otherwise. I remember at one time of his coming for England, I had a letter from you (I think too he brought it), in
which you recommended me to his acquaintance, and told
me he had promised to draw my picture for you. He said
10 something to the same effect himself. He came afterwards
to see me more than once, to remind me of sitting; and at
last appointed a time. He almost finished one picture; and
not liking it, pressed me to sit again for a new one. I was
willing, because I understood he took all that care for you in
15 friendship; and besides, I thought it might be of consequence to him to have my picture seen in his house well
done, as being a face known by most of them whose
approbation might be of use to him. These two considerations apart, sitting for my picture is not a thing very
20 agreeable to me; but most certainly, had I had the least
ground to apprehend that he expected me to have paid him,
I would [not] have done it. Nay, I knew not of his going for
Ireland; nor indeed did I apprehend that the picture was
finished: for, if I do not misremember, I heard him speak
25 yet of another sitting. So that if chance had put it into my

head to have mumelled something to him about being
obliged—and making amends—and pray tell me—nay be
free, &c. I had not the opportunity. The thing of most
consequence is our liking, and the likeness of the pictures.
I have made your compliments to Mr Addison, having seen 30
him once by accident. It is not so familiar a thing to see him
as it was ten years ago. My service to Robin and all friends.
I have written to Luther. I directed it to Dublin, taking it to
be term-time. All here are your servants. I am your
W. CONGREVE. 35

39 *To Joseph Keally*
London. Feb: 7th: 1707[–8]
Dear Kelly,
You are better at Observing the remissnesse than pursuing
the strictnesse of a Correspondence; or else the pacquett boats
are too blame[.] I have written twice since you found fault with 5
my silence. I write now to know how you do for I have nothing
to send you worth knowing. there is a mighty fraction in all
parties whigs & Torys promiscuously Joyning & opposing
each other, when the present Commotions are likely to subside
I'll tell you which I think will go to the bottom. I believe I told 10
you the D: of Richmond had been long before preengaged;
but if he had not I Could have relyed much on any answer
I might have had from him. my service to Robin: I am
yrs: W Congreve
(all here are well & yr servants) 15

Address: To Joseph Kelly Esqr
in Dublin
Postmark: FE|7

40 *To Joseph Keally*
London, March 2. 1707[–8].
Dear Keally,
I THANK you for your letter, and for the usquebaugh,
though not received; for I believe the ship was gone before

5 it came to the port. I have had two letters this and the last
week from Mr Sansom, and he makes no mention of it.
Whenever it comes to him I am sure he will take care of it.
There is nothing of news, but that the pretended Prince of
Wales is arrived at Dunkirk, 'tis thought in order to embark
10 for Scotland. As for domestic affairs, they are yet in very
whimsical circumstances, and I don't care to write my own
conjectures. The ladies here are much your servants; but
some of them think your remembrance of them too general.
I wish you could give me some hopes of seeing you. I am
15 very much concerned Robin has not better health. Our fat
friends have suffered. King of the Royal Oak died last week,
and poor Cornigh the taylor this week; so there is once more
a widow and a well customed house for Robin, if he be in
condition to venture. I hear a paper crying now in the street,
20 of taking six French men of war before Dunkirk, but it
sounds too like Grubstreet to send it you. Besides, this
being general post night, if there is any public news arrived,
you will have it with the packet. I am, Dear Keally, yours,
W. CONGREVE.

41 *To Joseph Keally*

London, May 12. 1708.

Dear Keally,

I HAVE yours this day of the 6th inst. for which I thank
you, and most particularly for your friendly sense of my
5 loss. I know you are no stranger to sentiments of tender and
natural affection, which will make my concern very intelligible to you, though it may seem unaccountable to the
generality, who are of another make. I am pretty well
recovered of a very severe fit, which has lasted a month. I
10 think to go abroad for air to-morrow; and by degrees
depend upon time to cure what reasoning and reflection
seldom effect. I had written to you sooner than any body;
but the fulness and violence of my fit was such, that it
disabled me. I thank you for your usquebaugh, whether
15 ever it arrives or not, but am more pleased that you give me
hopes of seeing you this summer: I hope your resolution

will continue. All here are always inquisitive after you, and desirous to be remembered to you. The legacy you have heard of is in part true, being one thousand pounds. I can write you nothing of news nor politics, but could tell you something if you were here; for the intricacy and variable posture of things is such, that it does not admit of any account which might not be contradicted, or at least altered in the next post. In the main, there is no doubt of a Whig parliament. My service to Robin, Amory, and Luther. I am, Dear Keally, yours,

W. CONGREVE.

42 *To Joseph Keally*

London, Aug. 2. 1708.

Dear Keally,

I HAVE your letter just on my coming from the country, and have time only to answer it before my going to the bath. I will thank you for it at more leisure; but no leisure will ever afford me time enough to acknowledge the goodness of that lady (who has not her equal), in remembering one, only considerable in being her creature. I am sure she means the usquebaugh should do me good; and in order to that, I am sure it will be more a cordial, and consequently more effectual, by coming with her, than if sent by any thing alive. You will not fail to do me right in my service and thanks to her. I am, Dear Keally, yours,

W. CONGREVE.

P.S. Every body is your servant; but the old gentle-woman is gone to God.

43 *To Joseph Keally*

London, Aug. 3. 1708.

Dear Keally,

THIS is the third letter I have written in answer to the last I had from you; and I hear so much of privateers, and the taking of packet-boats, that I imagine neither of the other have come to your hands. I hope the subject of congratulation

will always belong to you, though the contrary has been
too lately a theme for me. I hear you have encreased your
family by two. I wish you joy, both of the fruit of your
10 own planting, and the engrafting of Robin, to whom I wish
much happiness with your sister. You are close husbands of
your pleasures in Ireland; and we old friends must always
know the first news of you from common fame. All here
are your servants, and wish you joy. I am unalterably yours,
15   W. CONGREVE.

44 *To Joseph Kelly*
                              London, October 9. 1708.
Dear Kelly,
I H A D been in the country for six weeks, and at my coming to
town received both your letters at the same time. My last
5 day's journey I rode very hard; which shook me so much, that
disturbed the gout which was in repose. I have been confined
a week; but I hope, as it was a forced fit, it will be a short one. I
can walk about; and this is the first letter I write. I congratulate Robin's gout, but he must practice patience. I am glad
10 you like Mr Howard's picture: many do, though I always
thought it too chuffy; and you may safely make him take it
down, for I shall never be so fat. I am glad to hope for yours. I
think he has a fair occasion either to touch from Sir Godfrey
after you have sat, or to touch from you after he has copied
15 the other. Mein is well, very fat, and yours. I am sorry from
my soul for Sansom. The neighbourhood are in health and
your servants. I thank you cordially for all. I make use of my
philosophy, and love you as ever. Yours,
            W. CONGREVE.

45 *To Joseph Kelly*
                              London, 9br: 9th: 1708
Dear Kelly,
I extreamly Congratulate yr: recovery and thank you for letting
me know it so soon. I am very well after my short fitt, which
5 I hope has prevented any further visitations for this winter.
I thank you for the Latin Ballad I think it is as well as the thing

will bear. & so dos Mein who Continues of all men the
hardest to be pleased with any Modern essays. They talk
warmly of Ld Pembroks being High admirall Ld Wharton
yr Lord Lieut: & Ld Sommers President of the Councill[.]   10
I think it very likely to be as they talk. I am glad Robin has
got rid of his Urchins at any rate. my service to him & all who
Love you. all here are yr: servants & wellwishers. I am intirely
yrs W Congreve

Lady Betty has brought a Cold with her from Ireland that   15
I thing [*sic*] almost dangerous

Address: To Joseph Kelly Esqr in Dublin
Postmark: NO|9

46 *To Joseph Keally*

London, November 29. 1708.

Dear Keally,

I A M very glad to hear of your recovery; I can send you the
same news of myself; I am very well. I fancy you had not
received a letter from me before you writ your last; for in that   5
I told you of the changes that were intended. The hint you
give me is very kind, and need not seem unfeasible to any who
does not know particular persons and circumstances as well
as myself. There is no explaining such and so many particulars in a letter; but my views lie another way, which if I   10
accomplish, they will more answer my purpose than
the other in every respect, but the pleasure of seeing you. Ease
and quiet is what I hunt after. If I have not ambition, I have
other passions more easily gratified. Believe me I find none
more pleasing to me than my friendship for you. I am, yours,   15
W. CONGREVE.

All here are well at your service.

47 *To Joseph Keally*

London May 23 [1709]

Dear Kelly

Your letter Came Just as I was intending to write to you.
I had written long since but I have been troubled with

5 several light indispositions & threatnings of the gout from ill
weather & easterly winds. but I hope I shall rubb on. Tho' I
have more frequent colds than ever. The preliminaries of the
peace were sent over here & are returnd yesterday again
ratified by the Queene. They are not publickly known, but to
10 be sure you will soon have em. I was 6 or 7 times to look for
Mr: Howard before I could find him at last I saw him & your
picture which is like you but too warmly painted as you
hinted. I shall press him to make an end of it. Mr: Addison
surely knows Mr Tonson to well to think he will come for
15 Ireland for having said so, unlesse some considerable subscription may be set afoot to induce him pray give my service
to Mr: Addison & TidComb: not forgetting Robin, whom I
should be glad to see strutt about the hall as great as the
Prince of Conde. Mein is as you hope fatt rich and mellan-
20 cholly very variable when awake & nothing but his sleepy-
nesse makes him tollerable. Amory looks well[.] I drink your
health with him. & wish to see you. I am glad his excellency
pleases so well[.] no body knows better how to do it. You say
nothing of my Lady. I am Dear Keally yr:
25   W Congreve.

Address: To Joseph Kelly Esqr
             in Dublin
Postmark: MA|24

48 *To Joseph Keally*
                                    [London, March–April 1710]
I sent to you by 9 a clock this morning but you were gon
out. I went and made yr. Compliment to Lady Wharton &
she will be glad to see you when you please. I fasted till 3 in
5 hope you might have come this way. pray let me know how
you are disposed tomorrow.
                           Yrs
                                             W Congreve
thursday afternoone.

10 *Address:*   To
              Mr Kelly

49 *To Joseph Keally*

Richmond, June 6. [1710]

Dear Keally,

I AM weary of the town and politics. I tell you truly, I have not cared to inform myself of the probabilities as to change or continuance of the ministry; and nobody who is   5
in the secret can affect to be more ignorant than I really am. If you would have my own private sentiments, I will own I expect nothing that will please me.

I saw Mein last night. We remembered you and all friends. I find the air of this place and Spaw water does me   10
much good. I believe I shall pass most of the summer here. It is impossible any change can be in the court and Mr Addison not able to inform you. All your friends I left very well. My service to Robin and Amory. I am, dear Joe, yours ever,

W. C.   15

50 *To Joseph Keally*

London, August 10. 1710.

Dear Keally,

YOU will have all the news I can send you before this come to your hand; and I am afraid you will think that time enough. No man that I know (without exception of any) is   5
able to make any conjecture of what is intended by the proceedings at court. There are those who yet are of opinion the present parliament will meet again. If that should be, it can only be because the next, in all appearance, will not differ so extremely from it as some have believed. My   10
service to all friends. Yours,   W. C.

  Lord Rivers sets out on Monday for Hanover on some
   errand of importance and dispatch, not hard to guess.

51 *To Joseph Keally*

London, November 9. 1710.

Dear Keally,

Si vales bene est, ego quidem valeo. And what else can a man write in these latter times, when false prophets arise, and so

5 forth. I write to you because I will write to you, and always
must desire to hear from you. I live entirely at home, see
nobody, nor converse in any manner. I would send you my
books, which will be published in a month, if I knew by whom.
If you know any body coming your way send me word. My
10 service to Robin and Luther and all friends. Excuse me to
Luther and yourself for not writing oftener; 'tis very painful
to my eyes. All here are well and your servants. Yours,

W . C O N G R E V E .

52 *To Joseph Keally*

Dear Kelly
Tu, ne cede malis, sed, contra, audentior ito. I told Ld
Castlecomer Mr: Addison & Mr Dopping with whom I
drank your health last night that I would begin my letter to
5 you like a Tatler with a latin sentence. The aplication of
which I would leave to your selfe. I see Mein seldom but if
he would he could write you no news; for things happen
like earthquakes suddain unusual & unforeseen. Mr: Addison, very well applyd a line out of Oedipus yesterday which
10 will shew you how things go here

—one but began
—To wonder, & strait fell a wonder too,

I have sent to Harry Kelly to inform me by whom I may
send you my books and the print done by Smith which is
15 generally liked. I have since I began this letter seen Mein. I
suppose you will hear soon from him. all the neighborhood
are much yrs. My service to Robin, Luther &c

I am Dear Kelly

Yrs: W C

20 London
December 15. 1710.

Address: To Joseph Kelly Esqr.
              in Dublin
Postmark: DE|15

53 *To Joseph Keally*

London, March 10. 1710[–11].

Dear Keally,

I WAS not enough recovered from a very ill fit of the
gout when I received yours to answer it sooner. I wish
you and Robin joy of your olive-branches. I hear nothing   5
of young Mr Harris about your Holland. All here are ready
to serve you; and bid me tell you so. I have books ready
for you, and three prints in a case; one for you and Robin
and Luther, when I can get any body to carry 'em. Ossy
Butler says his brother will go next week, by whom I may   10
send 'em.

The Marquis de Guiscard was examined on Thursday
last by a committee of the cabinet-council about some
treasonable correspondence with France. Mr St John,
after several questions, to which the prisoner answered   15
very readily, at last produced a letter, the contents of
which made him change colour; and on a sudden, with a
penknife, he offered at Mr St John; but he being too far
from him, he stabbed Mr Harley, who sat nearer him. The
penknife broke against his breast-bone or a rib, so that he is   20
in no danger. Guiscard, not knowing it was broke, stabbed
twice or thrice on. Several of them drew their swords and
wounded him, but not mortally. The matter of the information against him is kept very secret. He is in Newgate.
I am, dear Keally, yours,   25

W. C.

54 *To Joseph Keally*

London July 5. 1711

Dear Kelly

Yesterday at Garraways Coffee house I met your Cosin
Mr: Harris who payd me, on yr account ten guinnes for
which I gave him my receipt. I believe by the time you Can   5
send me directions what to do with it. their will Come a
new Cargo of linnen from holland to the person who is
already well supplyd. The inhabitants of these buildings

are redy to receive yr: Commands & all well at yr service.
10 I know no news. My service to Rob: & all friends
Yrs
W Congreve.

I sent you some prints
& books by Mr Buttler.
15 yr: Cos: Harris sayd he
was to take post for Ireland yesterday afternoone

Postmark: IV|5

55 *To Joseph KealAbby*

55 *To Joseph Kealy*
London, November 2. 1711.
Dear Keally,
I A M well recovered of a fit of the gout, which has hindered my writing to you for some time past. It took me the
5 day after my return from the country, and lasted five weeks;
but was more favourable than usual as to the pain of it. Your
brother was so kind to come twice to see me; but I believe his
journey towards you has prevented my returning his visit.
Mrs Porter has sent you by him eleven shirts; a piece of
10 holland ordinarily making ten, but her skill has produced
eleven. Inclosed is her account. She waits for an occasion to
lay out the remainder of the money in something which may
be acceptable. My service to Robin and all friends. I am, dear
Keally, yours faithfully,
15 W . C O N G R E V E .

56 *To Joseph Keally*

December 11. 1711.
Dear Keally,
I H O P E long before this you have had the satisfaction
of seeing your brother. Mrs Porter hopes you are pleased
5 with your linen. She sent several times to inquire after your
brother (who had promised to call again), in order to have
paid him the remainder, or to have sent some odd thing,
as she calls it, an apron or so, to the value of it. She is

mighty scrupulous about it, and I write this by her direction; after which I will follow your direction, and drink 10
your health down with her scruples. You have all public
transactions in the public papers, so I pretend to write you
no news. I generally give you some early conjectures.
I think I see a glimpse, and that's all. My service to Robin
and all friends. All here are faithfully yours, as I am 15
entirely,

W. C.

57 *To Joseph Keally*

May 6. 1712.

Dear Keally,

I H A V E thought it long since I have either written to you
or heard from you; and I write to you now without any
other pretence than to ask you how you do, and to tell you 5
how I am. As to my gout I am pretty well; but shall never
jump one-and-twenty feet at one jump upon North-hall
Common again. I have an old conjuror who has been some
time about my eyes, and I hope will be able to keep 'em
from being worse; and who, if I had met with him seven 10
years ago, could have quite cured me. The commission of
my office is changed; but I am continued. This is all I can
say, except that all here are much your servants. Pray let me
know how it is with you and honest Robin; to whom give
my love and service. I am ever yours, 15

W. C.

58 *To Joseph Keally*

London, October 29. 1712.

Dear Keally,

I this instant received yours of the 22d, and the first
thing I do is to answer it. You do very well to reproach
me for my silence, after having made me expect to see you 5
every day this summer, or at least this autumn. Mrs Porter
went to the Bath almost on purpose to meet you and bring
you up with her. She and all neighbours are very well,

and very much your servants. Mein is well, and thrives
10 prodigiously. We can't sit on the same side of a coach,
though I am no fatter than I use to be. If you design to
come this winter, pray go on board the packet-boat, that
you may not be liable to any uncertainty but that of the
wind. I had not the happiness to see Sir Pierce at all the last
15 time he was in London; so that he may come off well
enough about saying that I could not see him, if he cares
for an evasion; but I fancy he likes his own way of telling a
thing better. News! No, Sir, no news, I thank you; nor no
glimpse. But one thing I'll tell you, whenever it comes, it
20 will be no longer a glimpse, but a glare: and so my service to
Robin and all friends. Ever your

W. C.

59 *To Edward Porter*

[Stowe, Buckinghamshire]
new years day [1714?]

This is to wish you & Mrs: Porter & my friends in Howard
street a happy new year, & next to Condole with you for the
5 damnd weather[.] god knows when the snow will let me
stirr; or if a thaw should Come upon it when the flouds will
be down. I am by a great fire yet my ink freezes so fast
I Cannot write. the Hautboys who playd to us last night
had their breath froze in their instruments till it dropt of
10 the ends of em in icicles by god this is true my service &
sorrow to my friends for not being with em.

I am yr mo<st o>bedient servant
W. Congreve

Address: To
15   Mr: Porter
          at his house in Surry street
          in the Strand London
Frank: R. Temple
Postmark: Buckinham IA|4

60 *To Edward Porter*

[London 1714?]

Sr

if you see Mr Custis to night pray know of him if it be
possible for me to have a picture of Ld Rochester which
was Mrs: Barrys. I think it is a head. I think it is not as a   5
painting any very great matter. however I have a very
particular reason why I would have it at any reasonable
rate, at least the refusal of it. if this can be don. he will very
much oblige his &

Yr: 10

very humble servant

Wm Congreve.

fryday even:

Address: To Mr Porter.

61 *To Mrs Frances Porter?*

Aug: 9th: [1717?]

I am very sorry to hear you are indisposed; tho I believe the
season is a great part of yr distemper. I assure you it still
keeps me back & I have frequently vapours to that excesse,
that if I had not some free intervals, I should think my selfe   5
rather impaird than improved in my health. I dont tell you
this by way of Complaint so much as by way of Consolation
for if good air, moderate exercise, temperate living perfect
ease & plenty cannot resist the influence of this miserable
season; You may imagine what power it must necessarily   10
have over you in town, upon the remainder of yr last years
disorder. your Cough is what I am most Concernd for
because it is most troublesome to you tho I make no
Doubt of that being also vapourish or hysterick. I am
onely glad you have Dr: Robinson, who I make no question   15
will set you quite right. Pray let me hear soon that you are
better. You must amuse yr selfe any way no matter how. I
am just now as hot as the devil in my hands & it is but
between six & seaven in the morning & promises to be a

20 fine day. but I Can never be again imposed on by the
dissimulation of the weather. we live here like good mid-
dling sort of friars in a pretty retirement onely we have no
Nuns. I fancy a good friar would do you no more harm than
a good nun would me as Dr: R— or Dr: Dunny. I should
25 take it for a prodigious favour if you would let me hear from
you & be overjoyd to have you tell me you were better. if I
Could send you anything that would do you as much good
as such a letter would do me; you should have very little
Cause, & very little time longer to Complain.

62 *To the Secretary of the Board of Trade*
Ashley October ye 5th. 1717
Sir
After a Fitt of Illness of two Month's continuance, I am but
just gott into the Country for the recovery of my health, and
5 am altogether unable to waite upon the Lords Comrs: as you
Signify to me they desire I Shou'd doe.
I beg ye favour of you to acquaint them of this from me
with all due respects to the Lps:
And if you please you may also intimate to their Lps: that
10 I have already given Satisfaction to both the Principal Secre-
tarys of State in what relates to me concerning Mr. Page. I am,
Sr
Yr most humble servt:
Wm Congreve

63 *To Edward Porter*
Ashley thursday [November 1718?]
Sr
I am glad Mrs Porter & you are better in health I was two
days (as usual) in hopes that I had been so too, but on
5 Monday was as ill as ever. I am again in hopes; but I can
say little more till two or 3 days more shall be past. 'tis a
subject I am weary of. I am sorry the house is not done
because if either health or buisinesse should Call me to town
I must be sadly inconvenienced. I make no doubt but you

will know as soon as you can what resolution Mrs Draper or 10
the executors will come to, for it is equally uneasy to us all to
be at an uncertainty: in the mean time I hope you will let me
know when so much of the house is don that if any accident
should incline or oblige me to come to town I may have the
satisfaction of knowing where I may be. as to the rest we 15
must look forward as well as we Can. I am with Constant
inclination & sincerity to Mrs Porter & yr selfe a very
                    Faithfull & humble servant.
                                    Wm Congreve

Address: To Mr Porter at his house in Surry street   20

64 *To Giles Jacob?*
                              Surrey-street, July 7, 1719.
Sir,
I much approve the Usefulness of your Work; any
Morning, about Eleven, I shall be very ready to give you
the Account of my own poor Trifles and Self, or any thing 5
else that has fallen within the compass of my Knowledge,
relating to any of my Poetical Friends.
                    I am, Sir,
                    Your Humble Servant,
                              William Congreve. 10

65 *To Thomas Pelham-Holles, Duke of Newcastle*
                              Wotton Aug 9. 1719.
My Lord
I have the honour of yr Graces Letter of the 3d instant, but
Just now; it having missd me by a day in Worcestershire
I take it as a high Obligation that you would lay yr Commands 5
on me in any thing in my power. but the gentleman who has
applyd to yr Grace in this Particular, has been misinformd;
for my Deputy is not the person dead; but one deputed by
him, upon his late return into England, himselfe now preparing, as by letter he informs me, to return speedily to 10
Jamaica. Next to the happynesse it would have been to me

to have been able to have Obeyd y^r Graces Commands; it is
the greatest, to know you had the goodnesse to think of me,
upon any occasion wherein I might possibly have shewne my
15   respect to You: or to any one for whom you are Concerned,
for I am as with the Greatest Justice, so with the greatest
inclination and respect My Good Lord
                        Yr Graces most
                                Obedient & most humble
20   servant.
                                        William Congreve.

66 *To Alexander Pope*
                        Ashley Monday. [Late summer 1719?]
Sr
I had designd to have waited on you to day but have been
out of order since Saturday as I have been most of the
5   Summer. & as the days are now unlesse I am able to rise in a
Morning, it will be hard to go & Come & have any pleasure
between the whiles[.] the next day after I had known from
you where Lady Mary was, I sent to know how she did but
by her answer I perceive she has the goodnesse for me to
10   believe I have been all this summer here, tho' I had been
here a fortnight when you came to see me. Pray give her my
most humble service if I can I will wait on you. I am Yr
                        Most Obedient
                                humble Servt
15   Wm Congreve

67 *To Thomas Pelham-Holles, Duke of Newcastle*
                        [November 1719?]
My Lord
By Yr Graces direction, Mr Southern has don me the
honour to read his tragedy to me. I cannot but think that
5   it has been a wrong to the town, as well as an injury to
the Author, that such a work has been so long witheld
from the Publick. This I say with respect to it as a Play.
    Whatever may have been supposed or suggested against
it on the score of Politicks is in my Opinion absolutely

groundlesse: I Can see no shadow of an Objection to it   10
upon that account; tho I have attended to it very precisely
even in regard to that particular in Justice to Mr Southern
and in Obedience to Yr Graces Commands. I am thus plain
in my thoughts on this Occasion. I am allways with the
greatest respect   15

My Lord
Yr Graces most Obedient
humble servant
Wm Congreve

68 *To Alexander Pope*

Surry street Jan: 20 [1719–20?]

I return you a Thousand thanks for your letter about spaw
water. Dr Arbuthnot has orderd me at present to drinke
bathe water. So I cannot expressly say when I shall want the
spaw but if the person mentiond by you imports any   5
quantity for himself at any time I shall be glad to know of
it. I am sorry you did not keep yr word in letting me see
You a second time. I am

allways Dr Sr Yr Most Obedient
humble sert: 10
Wm Congreve

Address: To Mr Pope at his house in Twit'nam
Postmark: 20|IA Peny Post Payd

69 *To Alexander Pope*

Dear Sr

I am very sorry to hear you have been ill. it has not been my
fault that I have not been to wait on you. I shall think it is
very long till I hear you are better. I am my selfe but upon a
very indiffrent foot. I thank you a thousand times for yr   5
Case of the Spaw water I have sent this morning to the

Custom house about em. I believe I shall not need quite so
many but some friends may be glad of some of them I am
Dear Sr ever yr most Obedient

10   humble servant
                                                Wm Congreve
June 23 [1720?]

Address: To Mr. Pope
              at his house in
15   Twittenham
Postmark: 23|JV

70 *To Jacob Tonson*

Dear Mr Tonson
My Kinsman Coll Congreve desires by me that you would
do him the favour to lend him my picture to have a Copy
taken of it. I am sure there will be great Care taken of it.
5 I am sorry I am not in town now you are to have the
pleasure of seeing you. I hope you are well. I am with
unalterable esteem & friendship Dear Jacob
                                                Ever Yrs
                                                Wm Congreve

10 Aug. 8th: 1723

71 *To Humphry Morice*

Sr
I had the favour of yr. letter, yesterday and have no Objection to Mr Maxwells renewall of his authority. besides
that your recommendation is of great weight with me. I
5 suppose Mr Maxwell would be single in the office. I would
not do a hard thing by Mr Wood tho I never see nor hear
any thing of him. but as he makes no application, I believe
he dos not think of it. However, as you were also his
security I frankly leave the determination of it to you &

shall in this or any thing in my little power be glad to shew 10
you how much I am with great respect sr

yr. most

humble & Obedient

servant

Wm Congreve 15

Address: Surry street
　　　　　　Novbr: 22. 1726.

72 *To Humphry Morice*

Sr

I had the favour of yrs & sent to Mr Walter who has all
along drawn up the writings in this affair. but he is out of
town on the Dorsetshire Election. he is expected to return
by the beginning of next week & then I will not fail to let 5
you know what day the writing may be executed. I heartily
wish you your health and am Sr: with particular respect

Yr most Obedient

humble servant

Wm Congreve 10

Address: Surry street
　　　　　　feb: 7th
　　　　　　1727/6

73 *To Alexander Pope*

[Bath], May 6 [1727].

I Have the pleasure of your very kind letter, I have always
been obliged to you for your friendship and concern for me,
and am more affected with it, than I will take upon me to
express in this letter. I do assure you there is no return 5
wanting on my part, and am very sorry I had not the good
luck to see the Dean before I left town: it is a great pleasure
to me, and not a little vanity to think that he misses me. As
to my health, which you are so kind to enquire after, it is

10 not worse than in London: I am almost afraid yet to say that
it is better, for I cannot reasonably expect much effect from
these waters in so short a time: but in the main they seem to
agree with me. Here is not one creature that I know, which
next to the few I would chuse, contributes very much to my
15 satisfaction. At the same time that I regret the want of your
conversation, I please my self with thinking that you are
where you first ought to be, and engaged where you cannot
do too much. Pray give my humble service, and best wishes
to your good mother. I am sorry you don't tell me how Mr.
20 Gay does in his health; I should have been glad to have
heard he was better. My young Amanuensis, as you call
him, I am afraid will prove but a wooden one: and you
know *ex quovis ligno*, &c. You will pardon Mrs. R—'s
pedantry, and believe me to be
25   Yours, &c.

P.S. By the inclosed you will see I am like to be impress'd,
and enroll'd in the list of Mr. *Curll*'s Authors; but I thank
God I shall have your company. I believe it is high time you
should think of administering another *Emetick*.

COMMENTARY

INCOGNITA

The suggestion in *Biographia Britannica* that Congreve may have written *Incognita* when he was only 17 is based on a false assumption about his date of birth. Yet if it was finished before he began *OB*, and he was only 19 when he wrote his first version of the latter, it remains a remarkably accomplished piece of work for one so young. Congreve's preface claims that it was '*an Essay began and finished in the idler hours of a fortnight's time*'. True or not, the form of the novel itself confirms that he had indeed taken '*some little pains*' in its composition.

As with all Congreve's work, it is virtually impossible to assign a main source. Among precursors he may have read and absorbed Walter Charleton's *The Ephesian Matron* (1659) and *The Cimmerian Matron* (1668); Joseph Kepple's *The Maiden-Head Lost by Moon-light* (1672); and Charles Cotton's *Scarronides: or, Virgile travestie* (1664). Charles C. Mish suggests the influence of Behn and various works of Scarron ('English Short Fiction in the Seventeenth Century : II. Fiction in the Period 1660–1700', *Studies in Short Fiction*, 6 (1969), 299–300). Certainly Congreve at some point acquired several of Scarron's works, including his *Le Roman Comique* (1655), *Les Nouvelles Oeuvres Tragi-comiques* (1665), and *Scarron's City Romance* (1671), actually from Antoine Furetière's *Roman Bourgeois* (see also the note to *OB* IV. vi. 6). There are one or two parallels with the story of 'The History of the Invisible Mistress' as given in Scarron's *The Comical Romance* (1665): the young Don Carlos of Arragon, in Naples for a wedding feast and the associated public games at which he won the prize for tilting, falls in love with an invisible lady whom he eventually discovers to be Princess Porcia and whom he ends up marrying. But its brevity and lack of dialogue and of sophisticated narration leave it far removed from *Incognita*. The same is true of another tale in the same volume, 'The Rival Brothers', where further parallels may be found. Other pertinent works were those of Charles Sorel, of which Congreve owned *Le Berger Extravagant* (1639), an English translation of the same work, *The Extravagant Shepherd: or, The History of the Shepherd Lysis* (1654), and *La Vraie Histoire Comique de Francion* (1668). He also owned copies of Le P. Dominique Bouhours, *Les Entretiens d'Ariste et d'Eugene* (1671), and Jean Pierre Camus, *A True Tragical History of Two Illustrious Italian Families . . . Alcimus and Vannoza* (1677). When Congreve read or acquired such books is unknown.

None, however, could count as a source of the fiction. Aurelia occurs in Madame de Scudéry's *Clélia* (Paris, 1654–61), English translations of which were published as *Clelia: an Excellent New Romance* in successive volumes from 1655 to 1661; and *The Most Excellent History of Antonius and Aurelia: or, The Two Incomparable Lovers* (1682) may also have caught his attention. The plot could have come from Dryden's *The Assignation* (1672). Summers thinks there is a likeness, 'too striking to be accidental', between the masquing ball at court, with its cross-game of Aurelian and Incognita, and the masquerade in *The Assignation*, III. ii. He also notes a correspondence between Dryden's *Marriage a-la-Mode*, IV. iii, and the episode in which Aurelian encounters Incognita in boy's disguise. Drougge, p. 85, discussing the topos of love and duty reconciled, cites Etherege, *The Comical Revenge; or, Love in a Tub* (1664), and Buckingham, *The Rehearsal* (1672), for immediate precedents. See also Michael McKeon, *The Origins of the English Novel* (Baltimore, 1987), 263–5.

E.S. de Beer has however noted several direct verbal debts to John Raymond's *An Itinerary contayning a Voyage Made through Italy in the Yeare 1646 and 1647* (1648), a copy of which (with his signature) was in Congreve's library. As de Beer observed, Congreve appears to have relied upon Raymond for some local colour and accuracy of topographical detail in commenting on Siena's pure air, the quality of Italian spoken in Tuscany, the names of the Duke's villa, and in Florence those of the cathedral, the Convent of St Lawrence, and the family of Rovori: see 'Congreve's *Incognita: The Source of its Setting, with a Note on Wilson's Belphegor*', *RES* 8 (1932), 74–7, and notes below to ll. 33–5, 62, 65, 71, and 106. At the same time, Congreve stops short of identifying any specific historic event.

Incognita was licensed on 22 December 1691 and advertised in *LG* for 18–22 February 1692 and in the Term Catalogue for Hilary 1693 (*TC* ii. 440). It was reprinted in 1700, and again in 1713 when it was issued in both octavo and duodecimo formats. An advertisement for *Incognita* included in the list of books sold by Peter Buck and printed at $H4^r–H4^v$ of Q6 *OB* (1697) still fails to declare Congreve's authorship, but his name does appear in another advertisement of November 1699 (*TC* iii. 154) announcing the inclusion of *Incognita* in the second volume of Wellington's *Collection of Pleasant Modern Novels* (1700).

Title page

The implications of the sub-title, Love and Duty Reconcil'd, are sketched at ll. 1362–85, and the theme again made explicit in the last scene (ll. 2132–5). Congreve lightly sums up a whole tradition of debates expressing the conflicts of love and duty, love and friendship, and love and honour.

Dedication

0.3 Mrs Katharine Leveson] daughter of Robert Leveson of Willenhall in Staffordshire. The Congreves took their family name from the hamlet of Congreve close to Pentridge in the west of Staffordshire. As Hodges suggests, *Biography*, 30–3, Congreve probably visited Stretton Hall, his own family home, on his way from Ireland to London in 1689. He would then have met Katharine Leveson, a woman 'ten years older than Congreve and matured by her contacts in London'.

1 A Clear Wit, sound Judgment and a Merciful Disposition] Here in the opening sentence of his first publication Congreve offers the clearest statement of his own ethical position as a writer. Like his lifelong commitment to neoclassical principles in his practice of composition, it is one from which he never departs.

5 Trifle] a modesty topos that Congreve re-uses in *LL*, Dedication, in Letter 64 to Giles Jacob, and in conversation with Voltaire (see Allusions, p. 446), but applied most finely by Millamant at *WW* IV. iv. 10 (*'That foolish Trifle of a Heart'*). See also 'To Sir George Etherege *Mr. D— Answer*', ll. 64–7:

> ... setting Worldly Pomp aside ...
> You wou'd be pleas'd in humble way,
> To write a trifle call'd a Play.

7 Rencounter] 'an encounter or contest of any kind; in early use, esp. a contest in wit or argument.'

27 *C L E O P H I L*] a lover of good report or praise ($\kappa\lambda\acute{\epsilon}os$): more to bestow it on those 'Honoured and Worthily Esteem'd' like Katharine Leveson than for himself, as the anonymity of the work makes clear.

Preface

11 *elevate and surprize*] Brett-Smith (p. 71) recalls Buckingham, *The Rehearsal* (1672), I. i, and Johnson's comments there on 'the new kind of Wits. . . . your Blade, your frank Persons, your Drolls: fellows that scorn to imitate Nature; but are given altogether to elevate and surprise. . . . 'Tis a phrase they have got among them, to express their no-meaning by. I'l tell you, as well as I can, what it is. Let me see; 'tis Fighting, Loving, Sleeping, Rhyming, Dying, Dancing, Singing, Crying; and every thing, but Thinking and Sence.' Congreve owned a copy of the 1687 edition of *The Rehearsal*. See also note to *DD* II. ii. 57. In one form or another, the word 'surprize' occurs some dozen times in *Incognita*, together with frequent occurrences of 'admiration', 'amazement', 'astonishment', 'rapture', and 'transport'.

32–5 Segnius . . . *Horace*] Horace, *Ars Poetica*, ll. 180–2. In Francis Howes's translation:

> Those [things] which a tale shall through the ear impart
> With fainter characters impress the heart
> Than those which, subject to the eye's broad gaze,
> The pleased spectator to himself conveys.

41 *not observed it before in a Novel*] Congreve's claims to originality are themselves conventional and the tone and function of the Preface are of a piece with the story. Drougge, p. 15, notes that his distinction between the romance and the more realistic novel (*'Novels are of a more familiar nature'*) repeats the views of writers such as Charles Sorel, Sieur de Souvigny, on *vraisemblance* as a distinguishing feature of the novella, and concludes that Congreve's definition of his own position is neither very new nor startling in 1692. Yet despite his claim merely to have *'gratified the Bookseller in pretending an occasion for a Preface'*, the importance Congreve gave to the unities, to realistic detail, and to dramatic form represents his commitment to a serious and consistently applied set of neoclassical principles for his later work. It is specifically of his imitation of the drama so conceived that he says *'I have not observed it before in a Novel'* and this that he sees as marking his original contribution to prose fiction.

51 *The design of the Novel*] As Drougge notes, p. 71, *OED* distinguishes two main senses for '*design*': I. 'a mental plan', defined in I.3 as 'The thing aimed at; the end in view; the final purpose' (as in French *dessein*); and II. 'A plan in art', defined in II.6 as 'the outline ... after which the actual structure or texture is to be completed' (as in French *dessin*). This second sense is implied in the phrase '*design of the Novel*'. In the phrase below, however, '*the main Design*', Congreve seems to be using the word in the first sense (*dessein*). See also his discussion of design in *DD*, epistle dedicatory, ll. 9–26, and the notes to it. Drougge's analysis of the plot and the interrelatedness of events (pp. 47–51) makes it clear that 'Nothing is merely accidental in this tissue of coincidence'.

52–3 Aurelian *and* Hippolito *with* Incognita *and* Leonora] Summers notes that the names Aurelian, Don Mario, Fabio, and Hippolita ('a Lady design'd to be a Nun') all occur in Dryden, *The Assignation: Or, Love in a Nunnery* (1673), which is set in Rome. 'Aurelia' has a dangerous presence in Congreve's 'Of Pleasing. An Epistle to Sir Richard Temple'.

54 *within the compass of two days*] Congreve's commitment to neoclassical principles is early and unwavering. See also his discussion in *DD*, epistle dedicatory, a play in which he hoped for perfection but settled for regularity.

56 *two Couple*] 'The plural after a numeral is often *couple* ...'

58–9 *Obstacle ... subservient*] So Dryden, 'Essay of Dramatick Poesie' in *Works*, xvii. 19, where Crites says, 'As for the third Unity which is that of Action ... the Poet is to aim at one great and compleat action, to the carrying on of which all things in his Play, even the very obstacles, are to be subservient.' Dryden himself is here indebted to Corneille's *Discours des Trois Unités*: 'Il n'y doit avoir qu'une action complète, qui laisse l'esprit de l'auditeur dans le calme, mais elle ne peut le devenir que par plusieurs autres imparfaites, qui lui servent d'acheminement et tiennent cet auditeur dans une agréable suspension' (*Oeuvres complètes*, ed. André Stegmann (Seuil, 1963), 841). See also at *MB* III. iv. 29–31, Osmyn's reflection on all

> Whom Chance, or Fate working by secret Causes,
> Has made perforce subservient to that End
> The Heav'nly Pow'rs allot me ...

65 *the Copy which I imitate*] i.e. 'Dramatick *Writing*', which Congreve has just said he will imitate '*in the Design, Contexture and Result of the Plot*'.

70 *the idler hours of a fortnight's time*] Swift deservedly parodied such nonsense: see *A Tale of a Tub*: 'I here present *Your Highness* with the Fruits of a very few leisure Hours, stollen from the short Intervals of a World of Business, and of an Employment quite alien from such Amusements as this ...' (*Prose*, i. 18). The reality for Congreve is likely to have been quite different: see the introductory note on the composition of *WW*.

Text

5 the Type of himself] For typologies in *Incognita*, see Paul Korshin, *Typologies in England, 1650–1820* (Princeton, 1982), 233 n. 87. Other instances are at

l. 16, 'reviv'd in the Person of his Son'; Incognita as 'one whole and perfect *Venus*' at l. 689; 'the Spirit of...*Eve*' in Leonora at l. 1075; Aurelian as 'the Sacrifice to expiate [his father's] Offences past' at ll. 1367–8; Aurelian as the deliverer of Incognita at l. 1554; and 'the most probable Idea of the Prototype' at l. 1972.

21–2 Educated from Twelve Years old] perhaps reflecting Congreve's own experience: see Biographical Summary under 25 September 1681.

33–5 There...learned] The quality of the Tuscan language, and the mystique of its purity as a standard for modern Italian, were an old theme: for an earlier discussion, see Castiglione, *The Courtier*, Book I. As de Beer has shown, however, the paragraph is directly indebted for several words and phrases to Raymond's *Itinerary*, 49–50, which also notes Siena's hilltop site, the quality of the air, the response of strangers, the purity of the language, and the benefits of learning 'the Vulgar Tongue' there.

62 *Poggio Imperiale:*] It lies just outside the Porta Romana at Florence; the palace there was built for the Grand-Duchess Maddalena of Austria, wife of Cosimo II (1590–1621). Compare Raymond, *Itinerary*, 48: 'Going out of *Florence*, at the *Porta Romana*, one leaves *Poggia Imperiale a Villa* of the great Dukes...'.

65 *Don Ferdinand de Rovori*] As de Beer notes, Congreve probably derived the name from Raymond's *Itinerary*, 47: 'The wife of this present Great Duke, *Ferdinand* the second of that name, comes from the Duke of *Urbin*, of the family of *Rovori.*' I.M. Westcott adds that Congreve may also have known from another source that Ferdinand II's sister Caterina (1593–1629) married Ferdinando Gonzago (1587–1625), and that his sister Claudia (1604–48) married Frederigo Ubaldo della Rovori ('The Role of the Narrator in Congreve's *Incognita*', *Trivium*, 11 (May 1976), 40–8).

71 Church *Di Santa Croce*] the main Franciscan church in Florence. Compare Raymond, *Itinerary*, 44: 'Before [*Santa Croce*] is a faire spatious Court, in which (it being *Carnavall* time while wee were at *Florence*) we saw the play at *Calce*, with *Cavalcades*, shewes, and other assemblies of the Nobility.'

81 alarm'd] excited.

97 loose] freedom.

106 Fachin] 'a literal rendering of the Italian *facchino*, a porter' (Brett-Smith). This word, which is not in *OED*, occurs in the introduction to Raymond's *Itinerary* and again at p. 210 ('a poore *fachin*, or *porter*'). As de Beer points out, p. 76 n. 1, it was also used by Munday, *Zelauto* (1580), 110: 'Take heede *Strabino*, least in your denying to looue some gallant Ladys you be not procured to *fācie* some poore *Fachine* heere in *Verona.*' The passage from Raymond's introduction reads: 'They are so addicted to Musick....Neither is the Rout lesse propense to that though with lesser skill and art; There's no *Fachin* or Cobler but can finger some Instrument; so that when the heats of the Day are tyr'd out to a coole Evening; the Streets resound with confused, yet pleasant Notes.'

110 go] walk.

119 *Theorbo*] 'a large kind of lute with a double neck and two sets of tuning pegs, the lower holding the melody strings and the upper the bass strings; much in vogue in the 17th century.' Summers cites Shadwell, *The Amorous Bigot* (1690), IV. i, p. 30: 'I had provided this Drum to sing to, which is better than a Theorb or Harpsycord.'

157 in the great Dome] probably, as Summers notes, the Duomo, Santa Maria del Fiore, begun in 1296 but not finished until 1461.

179 fuliginous] sooty. The whole passage is highly parodic, here of scientific inference and of the cant used to present it.

184 digress] Although acceptable, the rarer form 'degress' in the 1692 edition was almost obsolete by then (cf. *OED* 'Digression'); in any case the plain sense of the passage and 'Digression' above demand the less ambiguous spelling.

237 striking sail] See Pope's use of the phrase, cited in note to *WW* II. v. 1.

266 humour] Incognita's comments here have much in common with those at ll. 92–107 of Congreve's essay 'Concerning Humour in Comedy' in this volume.

269–70 brisk] See note to *DD* I. ii. 0.2, as well as *WW* III. v. 101.

293 fancies] 'the ornamental tags, etc., appended to the ribbons by which the hose were secured to the doublet.'

341 no greater sign of folly and ill breeding] so Millamant of Mirabell at *WW* II. vi. 41.

378 set Window] 'perhaps a recessed or bay-window' (Jeffares).

579 swinging] swingeing, forcible.

635 a Man free, as Nature made the first] Brett-Smith notes a reminiscence of Almanzor's rant in Dryden, *The Conquest of Granada*, Part I (1672), I. i. 206–9:

> But know, that I alone am King of me.
> I am as free as Nature first made man . . .
> When wild in woods the noble Savage ran.

681–2 Description . . . impossibility] The passage which follows is much indebted, in its set-piece form and detail, to *Antony and Cleopatra*, II. II. 195–215.

683 *Epicurus*] Congreve alludes to the Epicurean belief that natural objects result from the fortuitous collision of atoms. Epicurus (341–270 BC) adopted the atomist theory of Democritus and in turn influenced Lucretius. For the cult of Epicurus in this period, see Thomas F. Mayo, *Epicurus in England, 1650–1725* (Dallas, 1934), esp. 147–63.

685 that curious Painter] Apelles (*fl.* 4th c. BC), painter at the court of Macedon in the time of Alexander the Great. His most famous painting was of Venus rising from the waves.

703 a little Nest of Cupids] Compare 'On Mrs. Arabella Hunt, Singing', ll. 69–71 (vol. ii, p. 302). Belinda's sylphs in Pope's *The Rape of the Lock* may owe something to this passage: see Herbert Koziol, 'Alexander Popes Sylphen und William Congreves *Incognita*', *Anglia*, 70 (1952), 433–5.

708 blubbing] swelling. Otway, *The Atheist*, I. i. 455, gives 'blub Lips'.

711 Pen-feather'd] 'having the feathers undeveloped, or showing the quills or barrels only, without vanes... half-fledged.'

738 Train] 'a line of gunpowder... laid so as to convey fire to a mine or charge for the purpose of exploding it.'

828 Care of Providence] See note to *MB* III. ii. 74, where the phrase recurs.

838 Amicide] friend-murderer. Congreve's neologism.

850 sighing... Vulgar] See also Congreve's 'The Mourning Muse of Alexis', ll. 39–42, where he writes that 'Each vulgar Grief can Sighs and Tears express', and Dorothy Dallas, *Le Roman français de 1660 à 1680* (Paris, 1932), 37–8, where several precedents are give for this 'maladie des soupirs', an affliction 'non seulement chronique: elle devient contagieuse' (cited by Drougge, p. 41).

988–9 *Your Tongue... Eyes*] re-used by Congreve in *DD* IV. ii. 19.

1051–2 Or how could she consent... Woman] Drougge cites the story told in '*The Argument of the Fifth Act*', in Buckingham, *The Rehearsal* (Q3, 1675), V. i. 368–77: '*Cloris* at length, being sensible of Prince *Pretty-man*'s passion, consents to marry him; but, just as they are going to Church, Prince *Pretty-man* meeting, by chance, with old *Joan* the Chandlers widdow, and remembring it was she that first brought him acquainted with *Cloris*: out of a high point of honour, brake off his match with *Cloris*, and marries old *Joan*. Upon which, *Cloris*, in despair, drowns her self...'.

1070–1 perswading Man to Disobedience:] Jeffares notes Milton, *Paradise Lost*, x. 137 ff. The earlier allusions to 'Man free, as Nature made the first', the conventional stress on the nature of women ('she was a Woman', 'a very Woman'), and the phrase 'Disobedience to his Father' playfully invoke parallels of the Fall. The words 'a very Woman' recur in Congreve's song 'Tell me no more I am deceiv'd' in Southerne's *The Maids Last Prayer* (1693).

1133 Tilting] Like the sighing match at ll. 846–55, the tilt was a stock event and an excuse for extended description in romances. For the tradition, see M. Magendie, *Le Roman français au xviie siècle* (1932), 141–2.

1133 where we will leave them drinking Chocholate] This principle of indicating an off-stage action concurrent with the main one is also to be found in Congreve's plays and is one expression of his imitation of 'Dramatick Writing'. See also ll. 1286–7: 'we will leave them both fretting and contriving to no purpose'.

1138 led Horses] spare horses, because 'led by an attendant or groom'.

1144 artificially] 'In accordance with the rules of art... *arch.* or *Obs.*'

1218 sought] The 1692 reading is quite clearly 'sought' (with a long 's'). Brett-Smith, Dobrée, and Jeffares all read 'fought' without noting their emendation, but 'sought for' also occurs quite acceptably at l. 1450 below.

1364 Oh ye unequal Powers...] Drougge compares Buckingham, *The Rehearsal* (1672), III. ii, where Volscius, pulling on his boots, thereby enacts 'a combat betwixt Love and Honour' while (in Q3, 1675) '*Bayes Stands By and over acts the Part as he speaks it*':

> Shall I to Honour or to Love give way?
> Go on, cryes Honour; tender Love says, nay:
> Honour, aloud, commands, pluck both Boots on;
> But softer Love does whisper, put on none.
> What shall I do? what conduct shall I find
> To lead me through this twy-light of my mind?

Unable to resolve the conflict, Volscius (in Q3, 1675) '*Goes out hopping with one Boot on, and the other off* '.

1378–85 And all the World . . . Despair] Brett-Smith, p. xi, notes a tendency for Congreve to write 'a prose which is apt to fall into blank verse' as here.

1394 Lethargy] Drougge, p. 87, compares *MB* III. ii. 31 ff. for Osmyn's similar ineffectual gesturing towards action.

1478 broken off and lost] Williams, *Approach*, p. 184, notes the parallel with the paper Osmyn holds at *MB* III. i and, against his and Aurelian's dejection, the positive actions which follow.

1502 tender] *tendre*. In W1 *errata*, 'Tender' was corrected to read '*Tendre*' at *LL* I. xv. 8.

1768 Convent of St. *Lawrence*] San Lorenzo, the church of the Medici.

1810–17 Myrtle . . . Consecrated to *Venus*] Summers cites Pliny, *Naturalis Historia*, XV. 36: 'In ea quoque arbore [myrto] suffimenti genus habetur, ideo tum electa quoniam coniunctioni et huic arbori Venus præest. . . . Quin et ara vetus fuit Veneri Myrteæ.' 'And a kind of incense for fumigation is also contained in this tree, which was selected for the purpose on the occasion referred to because Venus the guardian spirit of the tree also presides over unions. . . . Moreover there was also an old altar belonging to Venus Myrtea . . . ' (Loeb).

1824 desert] i.e. dessert.

1865 *Ah! Whither, whither shall I fly*] For the musical setting by John Eccles, see vol. ii, p. 523. Though anonymous here in *Incognita*, these would seem to have been Congreve's earliest published verses. The song would not have been out of place in Ww but Congreve either overlooked it or chose not to include it.

1973 in a sort of a Wood] 'in a difficulty, trouble, or perplexity; at a loss'; so Wycherley, *Love in a Wood; or, St James's Park* (1672), and *A Midsummer Night's Dream*, II. i. 192 ('And here am I, and wod within this wood').

2055 she was still mistaken] as she had been earlier in thinking him Lorenzo.

Concerning Humour in Comedy

Congreve's essay, dated 10 July 1695, first appeared in *Letters upon several Occasions. Published by Mr. Dennis* (1696), advertised in *LG* for 12–16 December 1695. Although Congreve several times refers to his letter as a private one to a friend, Dennis presumably had his permission to publish it.

3–4 more of *Humour* in our English Writers] a common notion; see Jonson, *The Alchemist* (1612), prologue, ll. 5–9; and Sir William Temple, 'Of Poetry', in *Miscellanea. The Second Part. In Four Essays* (1690), 331–2. Writing specifically there of dramatic poetry, Temple says: 'Yet I am deceived, if our *English*, has not in some kind excelled both the Modern and the Antient, which has been by Force of a Vein Natural perhaps to our Country, and which with us, is called Humour, a Word peculiar to our Language too, and hard to be Expressed in any other...'. Dryden, 'Essay of Dramatick Poesie', in *Works*, xvii. 45, 59–61, makes similar points. For further dependence on Temple, see also the note to *Amendments*, l. 1813 (p. 208).

18 continued] Spingarn reads 'contained', but this is part of a series of critical letters by Congreve and others.

23–4 *Humour... Wit*] Dennis, *Works*, i. 494–5, surveys contemporary opinion on the relative value of humour and wit as means of effecting the purposes of comedy to instruct and reform. As Congreve says, the distinction was often left obscure. His attempt to extend the meaning of 'Humour' beyond mere 'Affect-ation' to include a bias of the mind and complexity of character gave it an edge that the superficially 'humorous' representation of affected vanities and artificial fopperies might otherwise lack. It also explains his compassion in exculpating those whose physical condition was none of their own fault, his amused and tolerant exposure of others' affectations and follies, and his severity in judging those whose vicious conduct was deeply prejudicial to the social harmony (how-ever precarious) secured by true wit and exemplified in the resolutions of comedy.

27 *Quot homines tot Sententiæ*] Terence, *Phormio*, 454: 'so many men, so many minds'.

50–1 Constitutions, Complexions, and Dispositions] a logical sequence, from the physical body as constituted by the four humours (blood, phlegm, choler, melancholy), to temperament as determined by their particular mixture or 'com-plexion' in an individual, to their expression as a habit of mind or the 'disposition' of a particular person.

51–2 the saying of Humorous Things, does not distinguish Characters] Com-pare the exchange between Incognita and Aurelian at *Incognita*, ll. 253–306. See also Aristotle, *Poetics*, xxiv. 23: 'Too brilliant diction frustrates its own object by diverting attention from the portrayal of character and thought' (Loeb).

61 Positively] directly, confidently.

69–73 When a Poet... Humour.] cited by John Constable, *The Conversation of Gentlemen Considered* (1728), 100.

70 Impertinencies] irrelevancies.

78 *Sooterkins*] 'an imaginary kind of afterbirth formerly attributed to Dutch women.' *OED* cites Cleveland, *Character of a Diurnal Maker* (1677), 103: 'There goes a Report of the Holland Women, that together with their Children, they are delivered of a Sooterkin, not unlike to a Rat, which some imagine to be the Off-spring of the Stoves.'

85 Monkey] The motif of the similarity of man to monkey is common: the relationship is clearly pointed out in, for example, the portrait of Rochester with his monkey, attributed to Jacob Huysmans, which forms the frontispiece to Graham Greene, *Lord Rochester's Monkey* (London, 1974); and in the monument

to Congreve at Stowe, as engraved by George Bickham, *The Beauties of Stow* (1750), 59, reproduced in *Descriptions of Lord Cobham's Gardens at Stowe (1700–1750)*, ed. G.B. Clarke (Buckingham Record Society, 1990), 77. For the monkey atop Congreve's monument, see note on 'Of Pleasing', vol. ii, p. 673. Another example may be found in the headpiece 'Imitatio Sapiens', probably by Aubert Clouwet, in Gio. Pietro Bellori, *Le Vite de' Pittori, Scvltori et Architetti Moderni* (Rome, 1672), 253. See also note on 'Monster in Glass' at *DD* IV. xviii. 29.

92 *Personal Defects*] See *WW*, Dedication, ll. 25–8.

102–3 one of your Letters] that of (? June) 1695, reprinted in Dennis, *Works*, ii. 384–5. The discussion of Jonson's plays may owe less to their recent appearance on stage than to their reprinting in *Works* (1692). Though several were in stock, few performances are recorded at this time and none at all of *Volpone*, *The Alchemist*, or *Bartholomew Fair* (*LS*, pt 1, p. cxxx).

104–5 *Ridicule in Corbaccio's Character*] Dennis, with reference to *Volpone*, III. ix, had written: '*Corbaccio* the Father of *Bonario* is expos'd for his Deafness, a Personal defect; which is contrary to the end of Comedy, Instruction. For Personal Defects cannot be amended; and the exposing such, can never Divert any but half-witted Men' (Dennis, *Works*, ii. 384).

119 *Affectation... Humour*] so Harriet, in Etherege, *The Man of Mode* (1676), III. iii. 31–3:

> *Y. Bell.* I never heard him accus'd of affectation before...
> *Har.* It passes on the easie Town, who are favourably pleas'd in him to
>   call it humour.

129 Nicest] 'Not obvious or readily apprehended; difficult to decide or settle; demanding close consideration or thought.'

135 Naturaliz'd] in the special sense of *OED*, art. Naturalized, 7a: 'To bring into conformity with nature; to free from conventionality'.

144–5 *Morose... Character of Humour*] so Dryden, also emphasizing the naturalness of Morose, *Essay of Dramatick Poesy*: 'we may consider him first to be naturally of a delicate hearing...' (*Works*, xvii. 59).

149 some dislike of it] Dennis had said that '*Ben Johnson* was driven by the Singularity of *Moroses* Character, which is too extravagant for Instruction, and fit... only for Farce' (Dennis, *Works*, ii. 385). Congreve, like Dryden, takes a more charitable view.

179 the Scene] The implicit definition of a 'scene' here is not a place, but a dialogue between 'the two Wittiest Men'. See also note to ll. 299–300 below.

205–6 Some late Characters] Although Ben in *LL*, first performed on 30 April 1695, is a finer character than those Congreve here refers to, there may be a self-reflecting note in his comment that 'Some late Characters of this kind have been very successful': see also the note on early performances of *LL* for the report that Doggett, to prepare for the part, took lodgings in Wapping to learn how sailors acted and talked.

225–8 *A singular... other Men*] Congreve's description may owe more to Dryden's words than to, say, Jonson's preface to *Every Man Out of his Humour*

(1600). (Dryden, 'Essay of Dramatick Poesie' in *Works*, xvii. 60–1, writes: 'by humour is meant some extravagant habit, passion, or affection; particular . . . to some one person: by the oddness of which, he is immediately distinguish'd from the rest of men.') The whole tenor of Congreve's remarks here about language, however, and its relation to character is directly indebted to Jonson: '*Language most shewes a man: speake that I may see thee. It springs out of the most retired, and inmost parts of us, and is the Image of the Parent of it, the mind. No glass renders a mans forme, or likenesse, so true as his speech' (*Discoveries*, viii. 625, ll. 2031–5). Congreve goes further: 'true *Humour*' is not revealed by '*Cants* or peculiar *Dialects*', or 'ridiculous Metaphors in his Conversation'; it demands 'a Dissection of Nature, and a narrow Search, to discover the first Seeds, from whence it has its Root and growth'. Such searching analysis of what men do or say, of their '*Speech and Actions*', has its natural complement in the scenic forms which structure their social relationships and within which their distinctive natures are delineated. See discussion in Textual Introduction, vol. i, pp. xxxi–xxxii.

230 Accidents . . . Substance] In the philosophical senses Congreve is using here, an accident is 'That which is present by chance, and therefore non-essential', an attribute; whereas substance is 'The essential nature, essence', or 'that in which accidents or attributes inhere'.

253 two Famous Philosophers] Heraclitus of Ephesus (*c*.540–475 BC), the 'weeping philosopher'; and Democritus of Abdera (b. *c*.460 BC), the 'laughing philosopher'.

272 Servants] admirers, professed lovers.

279 Natural Coldness] Vanbrugh, among others, shared this view. See *The Provok'd Wife* (1697), II. i, where Constant says of Lady Fanciful, 'she is cold, my Friend, still cold as the Northern Star'; Heartfree replies, 'So are all Women by Nature, which makes 'em so willing to be warm'd' (Vanbrugh, *Works*, i. 127).

299–300 preparatory Scenes . . . same Scene] 'Scenes' and 'Scene' here imply neoclassical scenes as in Ww. See discussion in 'Textual Introduction', vol. i, pp. xxii–xxvi.

325–6 the Work of a long Life] *WW* was his attempt to write such a work.

330 false Musters] military payrolls which contain the names of non-existent men. Any dramatist who creates false characters merely to entertain his audience to the end of the play 'with every thing out of Nature' deserves to be broken on the wheel.

350–1 Flesh, and the Grossness of their Diet] Prior alludes to this passage in his 'Alma: or, The Progress of the Mind', canto III, ll. 248–9:

> And, if I take *Dan* C O N G R E V E right;
> Pudding and Beef make B R I T O N S fight.

Arbuthnot, Congreve's physician, was later to write in his *Essay on the Nature of Aliments* (1731), 'I know of more than one Instance of irascible Passions being subdu'd by a vegetable Diet' (p. 226), and to argue in his *Essay concerning the Effects of Air on Human Bodies* (1733) that food was a major factor in determining temperament (p. 147).

352 agree] Spingarn, iii. 335, suggests that this may be an error for 'argue'.

Amendments of Mr. Collier's False and Imperfect Citations, &c.

Jeremy Collier's *A Short View of the Immorality and Profaneness of the English Stage* was advertised in the *Post Boy* for 16–18 April 1698; its preface is dated 5 March. Congreve's *Amendments* was advertised in the *Post Man* for 9–12 July 1698. For all its personal focus, it also complements several earlier replies to Collier, among them the preface to Gildon's *Phæton* (30 April), *A Defence of Dramatic Poetry* (26 May), probably by Filmer, Dennis's *The Usefulness of the Stage* (6 June), Vanbrugh's *A Short Vindication of The Relapse and The Provok'd Wife, from Immorality and Profaneness* (8 June), and *A Farther Defence* (23 June).

Title page

10 *Quem recitas…*] Martial, *Epigrams*, I. 38: 'That book you recite, O Fidentinus, is mine. But your vile recitation begins to make it your own' (Loeb).

13 *Graviter, & iniquo animo…*] the opening of *An Invective against Marcus Tullius*, attributed to Sallust: 'I should be troubled and angered by your abuse… if I were sure that your impudence was the result of intention rather than of a disordered mind. But since I perceive in you neither moderation nor any modesty, I shall answer you; so that if you have derived any pleasure from reviling, you may lose it by listening to censure' (Loeb).

Text

25–6 Least… Stage] So too Dennis, Gildon, Dryden, Tate, Wright, Oldmixon, Betterton, and others conceded that, where the stage was corrupt, it should, with proper discrimination, be reformed. See Dennis, *Works*, i. 471.

33–4 *Nullum… venia*] slightly adapted from Seneca, *Epistolæ*, cxiv. 12: 'nullum sine venia placuit ingenium': 'no man's ability has ever been approved without something being pardoned' (Loeb).

35 Benefit of my Clergy] See note to *LL* II. vii. 35, as well as *WW* III. xiii. 36 and v. i. 42–3.

36 Ordinary] See note to *WW* III. xiii. 33–4.

66 *Pimp than a P—*] Congreve is applying a medley of Collier's phrases, not quoting them exactly. Here he substitutes '*Mr. Collier*' for '*Juvenal*', '*P[riest]*' for '*Poet*'.

74–5 stamp'd his own Image] See *Incognita*, l. 879 and *OB* I. iv. 39–40.

79–80 Story… Tertullian] from Tertullian, *De Spectaculis*, chapter xxvi. In Collier's retelling: 'A certain Woman went to the *Play-House*, and brought the Devil Home with Her. And when the Unclean Spirit was press'd in the *Exorcism* and ask'd how he durst attack a Christian. I have done nothing (says he) but what I can justify. For I seiz'd her upon my own Ground' (*Short View*, 257).

102 *Aristotle*] *Poetics*, v. 1–2. Though he clearly read Greek, only Latin and French versions of Aristotle's *Poetics* survive in the list of books in Congreve's library.

105 Quality… Manners] See Dennis, *Works*, i. 476, for a survey of critical opinion on this issue. Collier's argument that the nobility should be immune

from stage criticism, though weak in itself, had to be answered seriously, lest attacks on the nobility be construed as attacks on the government. Molière, defensively, had written in the preface to *Tartuffe* (1669): '*Si l'employ de la Comedie est de corriger les vices des Hommes, ie ne voy pas par quelle raison il y en aura de priuilegiez*' (sig. a4ʳ).

120 Characters agreeable to it] Driven by the need to answer the extremity of Collier's argument, Congreve too firmly insists here on comedy's role in correcting the vicious. Elsewhere, as in his essay 'Concerning Humour in Comedy' and in his dedication of *WW*, where the context is not dictated by Collier, his discussion of characters 'agreeable' to comedy is subtler in its distinctions. But even here, following Aristotle (οὐ μέντοι κατὰ πᾶσαν κακίαν), he softens 'vice' to 'Follies and Faults' and foolish or immoral behaviour in word or deed. While comedies 'represent vicious and foolish Characters', in Congreve's scale of vice and folly, as his plays intimate, the truly vicious are incorrigible and deserving only of punishment, where lesser faults may be corrected by ridicule.

135 its proper Scene] Invariably, where he uses the word 'Scene' in *Amendments*, Congreve means a neoclassical scene, one defined by the presence of a character or group of characters, not by their geographical location. See below, notes to ll. 358–60, 545–6, 558, 750–4, 808, 816–17, 1529. See also discussion in Textual Introduction, vol. i, pp. xxii–xxvi.

145 *deceptio visus*] optical illusion, but possibly a drawing-room toy to illustrate a principle in optics or merely to amuse.

180 Moral of the whole…summ'd up] See note to *LL* v. [xii]. 125–6, but also Valentine's threat at *LL* I. i. 73 to teach Jeremy 'to make Couplets, to tag the ends of Acts'.

192 but four poor Plays] In *Animadversions on Mr. Congreve's Late Answer to Mr. Collier* (1698), p. 16, this is picked up as evidence of Congreve's slow rate of composition. See Allusions, p. 326.

201 *Miss Prue*] Collier, *A Short View*, 10: 'Women are sometimes represented *Silly*, and sometimes *Mad*, to enlarge their Liberty, and screen their Impudence from Censure: This Politick Contrivance we have in *Marcella*, *Hoyden*, and *Miss Prue*.' It is this very argument that Congreve uses to justify Valentine's madness: see *Amendments*, ll. 815–46.

207 *Belinda*] Collier, *A Short View*, 9–11, had argued that 'Modesty was design'd by Providence as a Guard to Virtue', and that by denying his women characters modesty and good sense Congreve had left them vulnerable to licence.

248 *Bossu's* Remark] in René le Bossu, *Traité du Poëme Épique*, Book 4 (1675), ii. 13: 'Pour le sexe, Aristote dit en sa Poëtique, qu'il y a moins de bonnes femmes que d'autres, & qu'elles font plus de mal que de bien. Virgile n'a que trop exactement suivi cette pensée.' Congreve owned a copy of this work. See also note to *DD* II. ii. 68. Congreve's concern is to repudiate Collier's claim that comedy depicts more bad women than good.

259 *Rapin*] in René Rapin, *Reflexions sur la Poetique d'Aristote* (1674), 218. See also *DD* II. ii. 69. Congreve owned a copy of this work and of Thomas Rymer's

translation of it, *Reflections on Aristotle's Treatise of Poetry* (1674), where the passage occurs on p. 133. The error in the citation as printed in *Amendments* ('*commun*': properly 'commune', as in Rapin) is here corrected.

272 *Persius*] *Satires*, I. 61–2: 'O ye blue-blooded patricians, you who have to live without eyes in the back of your head, turn round and face the gibing in your rear!' (Loeb).

277 *Juvenal*] *Satires*, XI. 176–8: 'such men we pardon because of their high station. In men of moderate position gaming and adultery are shameful; but when those others do these same things, they are called gay fellows and fine gentlemen' (Loeb).

349 *Menelaus* and *Helen*] For the passage from Collier, see Allusions, pp. 310–11.

358 proper Scene... Violence of this Scene] See note to l. 135 above.

379 Creed] See Allusions, p. 310. Collier simply means that much of the vocabulary of love is identical with that of the Creed and therefore cannot help but seem to allude to it.

386 *wasting Air*] For this and Collier's other criticisms of *MB* below, see Allusions, pp. 310–11. As the present edition does not preserve the long 's', Collier's error in reading the 'st' ligature here for 'ft' appears more gross than in fact it was.

405–6 *learning* a Spaniel to set] Collier's use of 'to learn' in the sense of 'to teach' was still perfectly proper, although usage was changing. Summers aptly cites Farquhar, *The Recruiting Officer* (1706), III. i. 287–9, where Rose, an awkward country girl, says: 'And see here, Sir, a fine *Turky*-shell Snuff-box, and fine *Mangeree*, see here... the Captain learnt me how to take it with an Air.'

407 *Delectus verborum*...] from Cicero, *Brutus*, lxxii. 253: '[Cæsar] quin etiam in maximis occupationibus ad te ipsum... de ratione Latine loquendi accuratissime scripsit primoque in libro dixit verborum dilectum originem esse eloquentiæ...' 'And more than that, in the midst of the most absorbing activities he wrote and dedicated to you... his careful treatise on the principles of correct Latinity, and prefaced his treatment with the statement that the choice of words was the foundation of eloquence' (Loeb).

445–6 too near to Poetry] For Congreve's copies of Aristotle, *Rhetorica*, to which he here alludes, see Congreve's Library.

499 St. *Chrysostom*] In his homily on I Corinthians; see *Patrologia Graeca*, lxi. 240. Summers notes that St Jerome has a similar remark in his commentary on Isaiah: see *Patrologia Latina*, xxiv. 19.

525–7 The Reward... the Punishment] so Hédelin, *Whole Art*, 5: 'One of the chiefest, and indeed the most indispensible Rule of Drammatick Poems, is, that in them Virtues always ought to be rewarded, or at least commended, in spite of all the Injuries of Fortune; and that likewise Vices be always punished, or at least detested with Horrour, though they triumph upon the Stage for that time.' For a discussion of the opinions of English critics on the principle of poetic justice, see Dennis, *Works*, i. 477–8, ii. 436–9. Rymer had put the case most clearly for them in *The Tragedies of the Last Age* (1678).

540 *the Old Batchelour*] For Collier's criticism, see Allusions, pp. 311–12, 314.

545–6 *Act.* 3. *Scene* 2.] not distinguished in Qq, but *OB* III. iii as printed in Ww. See note to l. 135 above.

558 Scene 3. of the *4th* Act] not distinguished in Qq, but *OB* IV. iv as printed in Ww. See note to l. 135 above.

600 little *Bays*] in Buckingham, *The Rehearsal* (1672), I. i: 'I come into a Coffee-house, or some other place where wittie men resort, I make as if I minded nothing; (do you mark?) but as soon as any one speaks, pop I slap it down, and make that, too, my own.' Johnson there calls Bayes 'little *Bayes*'.

619 *Double-Dealer*] See notes to *OB* V. xiii. 13 and *DD* I. iv. 24. For Collier's extended criticisms of *DD*, see Allusions, pp. 310, 313–15, 335–6.

642 *Supposition*] Congreve had originally misquoted Collier by reading '*Super-stition*' and had then, with heavy irony, described what he conceived to be Collier's true meaning. The offending leaf was cancelled: for Congreve's original text, see Variant Readings at *Amendments*, l. 642 (p. 247).

673 the *Rabbi*] Zeal-of-the-Land Busy in Jonson, *Bartholmew Fayre*, V. v.

698 *Ben. Johnson*] For Collier's rejoinder, see note to *DD* II. iii. 2–3.

709 *Love* for *Love*] For Collier's extended criticisms of *LL*, see Allusions, pp. 336–41.

740 *Manicheans*] a syncretic religion founded by the Persian Mani in the latter part of the third century. As Summers notes, 'The Priscillianists, whose heresies were derived from Gnostic-Manichaean doctrines, taught that the world was created by the Devil.'

750–4 the whole Scene or Speech . . . that Scene] not distinguished in Qq, but *LL* II. vii as printed in Ww. Note that, for Congreve here, 'scene' and 'speech' are in effect coterminous. See also note to l. 135 above.

766 *Pineda*] See note to *LL* III. xi. 19.

773–4 —*Illum . . . hominum*, &c.] Pineda, *De Rebus Salom*, Bk III, ch. 18.

788–9 *Deus . . . discerent*] For Gregory the Great, see note to *LL* III. xi. 24.

795–6 —*Nos habemus . . . Considerare*] For Albertus Magnus, see note to *LL* III. xi. 25.

808 the Scene, which is the last] not distinguished in Qq, but *LL* V. [xii] as printed in Ww. See note to l. 135 above.

816–17 the Fourth Act . . . a Scene] not distinguished in Qq, but *LL* IV. vi. as printed in Ww. See note to l. 135 above.

821 a Variation of the Character] See note to *LL* IV. ii. 9.

824 gives a Liberty] See note to *Amendments*, l. 201 above.

865 Father *Dominick* the 2*d*.] In Dryden, *The Spanish Fryar*, IV. i. 150–2, Lorenzo says of Friar Dominic: 'I never knew a Church-man, if he were person-ally offended, but he wou'd bring in Heaven by hook or crook into his Quarrel' (*Works*, xiv. 162).

953 as *Ben. Jonson* observes] in *Discoveries*, ll. 2305–7, translated: 'Where there is a general discussion of faults, there is no wrong to any individual' (Jonson, viii.

639). Spingarn, i. 226, notes that Jonson paraphrases Erasmus and that he derives from the same source the misquotation from St Jerome. The originals are given by Herford and Simpson at xi. 280–1. Congreve himself evidently used the third edition of Jonson's *Works* (1692), a copy of which he owned. See Library List.

1032 *Chryses, Laocoon,* and *Chloreus*] Chryses is the priest of Apollo in Homer, *Iliad*, I. 8–52, who sought to ransom his daughter. When Agamemnon refused to give her up, Apollo sent a plague of arrows. Laocoon is the priest of Neptune, who advised against admitting the wooden horse to Troy: see Virgil, *Aeneid*, II. 40 ff. For Chloreus, 'sacred to Cybelus, and once a priest', see *Aeneid*, XI. 768 ff. It is of him that Collier, following Macrobius, waxes most eloquent.

1061 *Tully*] The passage opens Cicero's *De Domo Sua ad Pontifices Oratio*. In Collier's translation: '*Amongst the many laudable Instances of our Ancestors Prudence, and Capacity, I know of nothing better contrived then their placing your Order at the Helm, and setting the same Persons at the Head both of Religion, and Government*' (p. 133).

1106 Mr. *Hales* of *Eaton*] John Hales (1584–1656), fellow of Eton. Hales's *A Tract Concerning Schisme and Schismatiques* was first published in 1642. Congreve appears to be quoting from the edition of 1677. See Library List for his copy of the third edition of Hales's *Golden Remains* (1688).

1125 stickles for Place] See note to *OB* I. iv. 37.

1229 Mr. *Dryden*'s Key] Collier, *Short View*, 103: 'The Author of *Don Sebastian* strikes at the *Bishops* through the sides of the *Mufti*, and borrows the Name of the *Turk*, to make the *Christian* ridiculous. He knows the transition from one Religion to the other is natural, the Application easy, and the Audience but too well prepar'd. And should they be at a loss he has elsewhere given them a *Key* to understand him. *For Priests of all Religions are the same.*' (The final sentence is from Dryden, *Absalom and Achitophel*, I. 99.)

1240–1 Sir *Martin* with his, *in fine*] In Dryden, *Sir Martin Mar-all*, III. i. 25–34, 77–87. He there pretends to be 'A plain downright Country Gentleman . . . bred up in the old *Elizabeth* way of plainness'. But his constant use of the modish phrase 'in fine' stings Moody into: 'what is this *in fine* he keeps such a coil with too? . . . and a Pox of In fine, for I'le hear no more on't' (*Works*, ix. 238–9).

1249 Bishop of *Arras*] See note to *Amendments*, 1691 below.

1261 *History of Sir* John Oldcastle] *The First Part of the True and Honourable History of the Life of Sir John Oldcastle* (1600). Collier concedes faults in Sir John but argues that 'The Disgrace falls rather on the Person than the Office'.

1384 *Castigo . . . amem*] 'I chastise you, not from hatred, but from love.'

1389 *præter expectatum*] 'beyond what was expected.'

1394–5 Pedantical Cant . . . Action] This criticism is directed at Collier's personal conceit and his mere affectation of terms, not at the principles themselves, which Congreve discussed with urbanity and exemplified with a relaxed fidelity in his own works. For a discussion of the contemporary criticism of Vanbrugh's phrase, 'the too exact observance of what's call'd the Rules of the Stage' (*Short Vindication*), see Hooker in Dennis, *Works*, ii, pp. lxxxi–lxxxii.

1398–9 —*Servetur... constet*] Horace, *Ars Poetica*, ll. 126–7: 'have it kept to the end even as it came forth at the first, and have it self-consistent' (Loeb).

1410 —*Lame Mischief*] Collier had quoted Benducar in Dryden, *Don Sebastian*, II. i. 131–3:

> ... Church-men, though they itch to govern all,
> Are silly, woful, awkard Politicians;
> They make lame mischief, though they mean it well:
>   (*Works*, xv. 106)

1415 *Lancashire* Witch] See note to *DD* IV. i. 4–5.

1420–1 *O why... understand*] Dryden, *MacFlecknoe*, ll. 177–8:

> Where did his wit on learning fix a brand,
> And rail at Arts he did not understand?
>   (*Works*, ii. 59)

1428 *A Fancy slipstocking high*] In *A Defence*, 90, Collier claims that this is 'an allusion to a known Story, in a Book very well known' and cites John Eachard, *Reasons of the Conscience of the Clergy*, actually *The Grounds and Occasions of the Contempt of the Clergy and Religion* (1698), 67–8.

1429 *A whole Kennel of Beaux*] so Vanbrugh, *The Relapse*, IV. i, p. 64.

1529 *Act 5. Scene 2.*] not distinguished in Qq, but *OB* V. iii as printed in Ww. See note to l. 135 above.

1543 *Non ita pridem*] adapted from Horace, *Satires*, II. ii. 46: 'haud ita pridem...': ''Tis not so long ago that by reason of a sturgeon the table of Gallonius the auctioneer won ill repute' (Loeb).

1543–4 he loves his Love with a P—] Summers cites Pepys, *Diary*, 4 March 1669: 'I did find the Duke of York and Duchess with all the great ladies, sitting upon a carpet on the ground, there being no chairs, playing at "I love my love with an A because he is so and so; and I hate him with an A because of this and that;" and some of them, but perticularly the Duchess herself and my Lady Castlemaine, were very witty' (*Diary*, ix. 469).

1548 *El gato... fria*] translated in Wilson, *Proverbs*, p. 703, as: 'The scalded cat fears cold water'.

1558 why, or wherefore] Collier's point is clear enough: Congreve (and Wycherley) have maligned women by implying the malicious nature of their conversation.

1577–8 My Business... Stains] Compare Vanbrugh, *A Short Vindication of 'The Relapse'* (1698): 'The Stage is a Glass for the World to view it self in; People aught therefore to see themselves as they are; if it makes their Faces too fair, they won't know they are Dirty, and by consequence will neglect to wash 'em' (Vanbrugh, *Works*, i. 206).

1582–3 *Dum... lini*] Ovid, *Ex Ponto*, I. v. 15–16. Actually 'cum relego...'. 'When I read it over I am ashamed of my work because I note many a thing that even in my own, the maker's judgment, deserves to be erased' (Loeb).

1597 Opinion] as used here in contradistinction to 'Prejudice', 'a judgment formed or a conclusion ... a systematic or deeply held belief'.

1633 *Ben Johnson* ... his Discoveries] 'Habent venenum pro victu: imò, pro deliciis.' 'They have poison for their food; even for their sweets' (Jonson, viii. 595; the second quotation from *Discoveries* ('It sufficeth ... ') is at viii. 634–5).

1651 simpling] to simple, 'to seek for, or gather, simples or medicinal herbs'.

1665 ἐκκλησιαζούσαι] As Congreve points out below, Collier, *Short View*, 44, refers to it as *Concianotores* and thereby obscures the true nature of his reading of Aristophanes.

1666 *Aretine*] For Congreve's copy of Aretino, see Congreve's Library. Summers cites Leanerd, *The Rambling Justice, or the Jealous Husband* (1678), IV, p. 51: 'What's here, a Study? *Aristotles Problems*, excellent; and here *Leschole de Filles*, a pretty French book; and here *Annotations upon Aretines Postures*, three Excellent Books for a Ladies Chamber.' See also note to *DD* v. xx. 11. In a manuscript fragment, Prior comments on Collier's *A Short View* in terms that suggest a middle way between Collier and the Congreve of the *Amendments*: 'Collier is not so much in the wrong: our plays are too licentious, and the poets affront the town when they Say that they write bawdy because nothing else takes: they may as well say that we like no musick but a Jigg, or that no pictures sell but Aretines postures: let them work up passion with grace and art and We shall be pleased with it: we liked the Mourning Bride thô Alphonso neither cursed like a swine or couched like a god thrô out the whole piece: and there will always be found so good Sence in the Nation that Some famous for having it will like what is truly good and the rest will not dare to contradict it at first, and form their gout Til afterwards: The French would not endure to hear a conquerour and a Princesse speak bawdy, and Yet that nation is as lewd as we can be for the hearts of Us, not from a dislike of the thing but from its being unnatural that such people talk so: our Imagination is so vitiated by such representations that in time it will be impossible for any thing fine to move them, we shall grow Muscovites putt pepper in our brandy; old lechers, be flogged in stead of being tickled. But Collier makes too much work with his Character, for thô the thing be true that Divines should be abused he should only have touch't upon it lightly, and returned the ridicule where [it] is violently in earnest: and that the more because being a Clergy-man himself the Elogies he gives the Clergy are so many panegyricks upon himself, and one is not so much struck with the truths he evinces, that the Clergye have been always respected whilst one reflects that it is upon a principle of Interest that he proves they ought still to be so ... ' (*Works*, ii. 877–8).

1666 *Aloïsia*] *Aloisiæ Sigeæ Toletanæ Satyra Sotadica de Arcanis Amoris et Veneris. Aloisia Hispanicè scripsit. Latinitate donavit Joannes Meursius* (*c*.1649). It was not in fact written by Luisa Sigea and translated into Latin by Mersius, but written in Latin by Nicolas Chorier (1609–92) and attributed by him to Sigea.

1667–8 as Mr. *Bays* says] Buckingham, *The Rehearsal* (1672), I. i. 198–201: 'said she, *Songes a ma vie Mounsieur*; whereupon I presently snapt this upon her; *Non, non, Madam—Songes vous a mon*, by gad, and nam'd the thing directly to her.'

1676 *Gideon's* Army] Judges 7: 6–8.

1680 Captain *Tom*] Tommaso Aniello, or Masaniello, the revolutionary who led a mob in Naples. He was killed on 16 July 1647. See D'Urfey, *The Famous History of the Rise and Fall of Massaniello*, Parts I and II (1700).

1691 the Bishop of *Arras*] Guy de Sève de Rochechouart (1640–1724). Collier, *Short View*, 245–9, cites his 'Mandemant…contre la Comédie', which he describes as 'a sort of *Pastoral Letter*', dated from Arras 14 December 1695, and published in *Trois Lettres Pastorales* (Delft, 1697).

1700 *Ovid* and the *Plain Dealer*] Collier, *Short View*, 238–40, ignoring their irony, cites Ovid's *Remedia Amoris*, ll. 751–6, and *Tristia*, 11. 279–80, where he forbids the seeing of plays and reading of poets, and Wycherley's dedication of *The Plain-dealer* to the 'Eminent *Procuress*' Lady B.

1702 *Lucan* and *Hudibras*] Lucan, *Pharsalia*, 1. 2–4, 7. Congreve truncates the passage, the sense of which is: 'I tell how an imperial people turned their victorious right hands against their own vitals, how kindred fought against kindred…and javelin threatened javelin.' Samuel Butler, *Hudibras*, ed. John Wilders (Oxford, 1967), 1. i. 1–2:

> When *civil* Fury first grew high,
> And men fell out they knew not why;

As Summers notes, Congreve quotes from an edition later than the first (1663), which reads '*civil Dudgeon*'.

1714–16 I am not the only one…Theatre] Dennis had also accused Collier of having selected the theatre only as a means of attacking the whole town. See Dennis, *Works*, i. 147, 471.

1718 *Bellum…finiunt*] Sallust, *Jugurtha*, lxxxiii. 1, has a similar sentiment: 'omne bellum sumi facile, ceterum aegerrume desinere'. 'It was always easy to begin a war, but very difficult to stop one' (Loeb); and Tacitus, *Historia*, iv. 69: 'sumi bellum etiam ab ignavis, strenuissimi cuiusque periculo geri': 'even cowards can begin war, but…it can be prosecuted only at the risk of the bravest' (Loeb).

1732 *Delenda est Carthago*] 'Carthage must be destroyed'—at any cost. Cato, the elder (234–149 BC), regularly concluded his speeches with the phrase after seeing in the prosperity of Carthage a lasting threat to Rome.

1768 St. *Austin*] *De Civitate Dei*, Book XVI, chapter 9, where the rubric reads: 'An inferiorem, partem terræ, quæ nostræ habitationi contraria est, Antipodas habere credendum sit.' and the text begins: 'Quod uero et Antipodas esse fabulantur, id est, homines a contraria parte terræ, ubi sol oritur quando occidit nobis, aduersa pedibus nostris calcare uestigia, nulla ratione credendum sit.' '*Whether it is credible whether there are men foot to foot opposite us in the lower part of the earth, which is opposite our dwelling-place*. But in regard to the story of the *antipodes*, that is, that there are men on the other side of the earth, where the sun rises when it sets for us, who plant their footprints opposite ours, there is no logical ground for believing this' (Loeb). For Congreve's other references to the antipodes, see *LL* 11. v. 35–7 and *WW* 1v. x. 35–9.

1768 *Lactantius] De Falsa Sapientia*, 111. 24: 'Quid illi, qui esse contrarios uestigiis nostris Antipodas putant; num aliquid loquuntur? aut est quisquam tam ineptus, qui credit esse homines, quorum uestigia sint superiora, quam capita?' 'Well, then, those who say the antipodes are placed directly opposite us do not say anything at all, do they? Or is there anyone so foolish as to believe that there are men whose footprints are higher than their heads?' (trans. Sister Mary Frances MacDonald). Congreve owned a copy of the 1685 Cambridge edition of Lactantius.

1782 *Polybius] Historia*, iv. 20. See the translation by Sir Henry Sheeres, *The History of Polybius* (1693), ii. 46, a copy of which Congreve owned. Sheeres contributed some verses to Southerne's *Oroonoko*, 11. iv.

1813 more *saturnine, dark*, and *melancholick*] Congreve repeats Temple's view of the superiority of English comedy and its source in the physical and political environment of the country: see 'Of Poetry', in *Miscellanea. The Second Part* (1690), 331–2; also the note to 'Concerning Humour in Comedy', ll. 3–4 above. In his *Essay concerning the Effects of Air* (London, 1733), Arbuthnot thought it probable that 'the Genius of Nations depends upon that of their Air' (p. 148).

1819–20 Whence our Plots, Conspiracies, and Seditions] Dennis was attacked for stating similar views in *The Usefulness of the Stage*, and on 28 November 1698, absurdly, was even indicted before the grand jury of Middlesex because such views were considered a libel against the Government. See Dennis, *Works*, i. 471–2.

1824 *Gun-Powder-Treason* Plot] See Hooker's note in Dennis, *Works*, i. 475: 'Congreve slyly insinuated that those who frequented the theater were not given to conspiracy and sedition.' Collier's attitudes to Church and State were, by implication, far more dangerous, and his attack on the stage only a means of expressing his more fundamentally dissentious intent.

The Tatler. No. 292

Steele's *Tatler* came to an end with no. 272 of 2 January 1710/11. The present number is one in the extended series of the *Tatler* published with Swift's support by William Harrison. It was attributed to Congreve by Swift, *Journal to Stella*, 13 February 1711: 'I went to visit poor Congreve, who is just getting out of a severe fit of the gout... He gave me a *Tatler* he had written out, as blind as he is, for little Harrison. 'Tis about a scoundrel that was grown rich, and went and bought a Coat of Arms at the Herald's, and a set of ancestors at Fleet-ditch; 'tis well enough, and shall be printed in two or three days...' (*Journal*, i. 191). Congreve's paper is far gentler in tone than Swift's description would have it. As Novak more fairly notes, Congreve 'does not reveal Foundling, a poor man who has succeeded in the world, as a scoundrel; his tone is superior, amused, and pitying; and the tone is very like Congreve in its combination of aloofness, humanity, and scorn of ambition' (p. 39).

60–1 to go up...to his Seat upon the River] a clear sign of his upward mobility: for the movement of London's population from the City to Westminster and the north-west, see Lawrence Stone, 'The Residential Development of the West End of London in the Seventeenth Century', in *After the Reformation: Essays in Honour of J.H. Hexter*, ed. Barbara C. Malament (Manchester, 1980), 167–212.

Dedication of *The Dramatick Works of John Dryden*

Writing specifically of Dryden's *Amboyna*, the editors of the California edition of the *Works* refer to Congreve as 'Dryden's literary executor' and imply that he took an active part in preparing the text of the plays for publication in 1717, noting that he was 'a careful editor, and normally sent first editions for reprinting' (*Works*, xii. 449). The point is of major importance for the text of *Amboyna* where, exceptionally, the 1717 edition prints parts of the last two acts in blank verse. In fact, while Congreve doubtless had the knowledge to restore Dryden's prose to the verse forms in which the play was first written, it is unlikely that in 1716–17 he was called upon (or indeed physically able) to do so. The occasion was almost certainly created by Tonson's remarkable publishing programme (in this one decade—and to take only plays—he produced new multi-volume editions of Shakespeare, Congreve, Beaumont and Fletcher, Otway, Jonson, Dryden, Southerne, Vanbrugh, and Shadwell). Once created, however, it was clearly the moment for Congreve to offer this gracious acknowledgement of his own gratitude to Dryden and his generous estimate of his master's greatness. As noted below, the dedication was probably designed also to promote the cause of a public monument to Dryden. But the manner in which he selected copy texts for his own *Works*, and (*MB* apart) his relative indifference to minor textual variation, make it more likely that his labour was limited to the writing of this Dedication and that Tonson's in-house editors did the rest.

In his account of Dryden, Giles Jacob cites 'the ingenious Mr. *Congreve*', quotes substantial sections of the dedication, and adds: 'Mr. *Congreve*, out of the good nature peculiar to him, has given this shining Character of Mr. *Dryden*'s Talents; which, by all impartial Readers, must be allow'd to be no less just than affectionate' (*Register*, i. 77). Scott would repeat that praise: 'The Epistle is one of the most elegant and apparently heart-felt effusions of friendship that our language boasts; and the progress of literature from the Restoration is described as Dryden alone could describe it' (*The Works of John Dryden*, ed. Walter Scott, rev. and corr. George Saintsbury, 18 vols. (Edinburgh, 1882–93), xi. 56).

0.3–.4 His GRACE the Duke of *Newcastle*] Thomas Pelham-Holles (1693–1768), Duke of Newcastle upon Tyne. On 2 April 1717 he married Lady Henrietta, eldest daughter of Francis Godolphin and his wife Henrietta, later Duchess of Marlborough, a family connection which doubtless made him quite familiar also to Congreve. This marriage, in which Vanbrugh had been a go-between, also allied him with Charles Spencer, Earl of Sunderland, uncle of the young Henrietta Godolphin. See Vanbrugh, *Works*, iv. 91–3, also Letters 65 and 67.

3 Your Grace has just given Order] possibly in his capacity as Lord Chamberlain, an office to which he was appointed on 13 April 1717. In a letter of 14 May [1700], a few days after Dryden's burial, Edward Hinton reported that 'Mr. Mountague had engaged to build him a fine monument' (HMC, Appendix to the Fifth Report, pp. 359–60). Mountagu died in 1709 and in 1717, when Samuel Garth wrote his preface to *Ovid's Metamorphoses* (published 6 June), the monument was still unbuilt. As Garth said, 'The Man who cou'd make Kings immortal, and raise triumphant Arches to Heroes, now wants a poor square Foot of Stone, to show where the Ashes of one of the greatest Poets, that ever was upon Earth, are deposited.' Congreve's compliment may therefore have been a timely admonition,

chiming with Garth's comments and those of Nicholas Amherst, who would write of Rowe's burial in Westminster Abbey as the place,

> Where great N E W C A S T L E, still to Wit a Friend,
> To D R Y D E N bids the stately Pile ascend;
> (Immortal, glorious Deed! which After-times
> Shall celebrate in their exalted Rhimes,)

See *Musarum Lachrymæ: or, Poems to the Memory of Nicholas Rowe, Esq;* (1719), 29. *The Posthumous Works of William Wycherley Esq;* (1728), prints a poem 'On Mr. Dryden's Wanting an Epitaph' (p. 17). John Sheffield, Duke of Buckingham, is also said to have arranged for a monument to be erected in Westminster Abbey in 1720. If so, Newcastle may have helped to pay for it. For recognition of Sheffield's role, see John Dart, *Westminster-Abbey: A Poem* (1721), 42, foreshadowing those still to come, he refers to Homer (p. 64) and concludes:

> Like him his Sons must view th'oblivious State,
> And *Prior, Pope,* and *Congreve* yield at length to Fate.

Thomas Fitzgerald, *Poems on Several Occasions* (1733), 24, also associates Sheffield with Dryden's memorial.

54 friendly Offices, and favourable Instructions] among them certainly his help in preparing *OB* for the stage.

66 *be kind to his Remains*] See Dryden's prologue to *DD*, 'To my Dear Friend Mr. *Congreve*', l. 72. Congreve's consciousness of this obligation is also recorded by Pope. In his letter to Wycherley of 26 December 1704, he notes Congreve's determination one day to vindicate Dryden's personal and poetical qualities against 'the many libelous Misrepresentations of them' (see Pope, *Correspondence*, i. 2; Allusions). There is no evidence, however, that Congreve was in any sense Dryden's literary executor with privileged access to his papers or responsibility for publishing them.

105 Affection . . . Admiration of his Writings] Pope's letter to Wycherley of 26 December 1704 also reports Congreve assuring him that Dryden's 'personal Qualities were as amiable as his Poetical' (Pope, *Correspondence*, i. 2).

126–7 Correction . . . of any Writer, who thought fit to consult him] Congreve's own self-effacing generosity should not be forgotten. He earned Dryden's gratitude and esteem for reviewing his translation of the *Aeneid*: 'this Excellent Young Man, has shew'd me many Faults, which I have endeavour'd to Correct'. Like the Dryden he describes as 'extream ready and gentle in his Correction', he advised Catharine Trotter, he stepped in for Southerne, and the warmth of Pope's dedication of his Homer to Congreve almost certainly expresses his indebtedness to the deeply informed help of Congreve: 'one of the most valuable Men as well as finest Writers, of my Age and Countrey: One who has try'd, and knows by his own Experience, how hard an Undertaking it is to do Justice to *Homer*' (Pope, *Poems*, viii. 578–9). See Letters 22 and 67, and Allusions, pp. 396, 407.

159 Ode on St. *Cecilia*'s Day, and his Fables] Dryden's *Alexander's Feast: or The Power of Musique. An Ode, In Honour of St. Cecilia's Day* was published late in 1697, his *Fables Ancient and Modern* in March 1700, just before his death.

161–5 His Prose...Diction of Poetry] Congreve's distinction clearly transcends prosodic form and seems to contrast an efficient clarity in prose (see Burnet on Tillotson below) with the imaginative force of poetry, most evident in its language and diction because these fully create its subject (which is therefore 'Eternally...Poetry').

171 Archbishop *Tillotson*] John Tillotson (1630–94), Archbishop of Canterbury, 1691–4. At his funeral Bishop Gilbert Burnet praised the quality of his writing: in 'Truth of Language and Stile, in which no Man was happier, and knew better the Art of preserving the Majesty of things under a Simplicity of Words; tempering these so equally together, that neither did his Thoughts sink, nor his Stile swell: keeping always the due Mean between a low Flatness and the Dresses of false Rhetorick....He said what was just necessary to give clear Idea's of things, and no more: He laid aside all long and affected Periods: His Sentences were short and clear; and the whole Thread was of a piece, plain and distinct' (*Sermon Preached at the Funeral of the...Lord Archbishop of Canterbury* [30 November] *1694* (1694), 13). See Congreve's Library for Congreve's own substantial collection of Tillotson's sermons.

192 nothing but his Prefaces] Perhaps because Dryden's prose writings were prefatory and dispersed, his quality as a prose writer had not been adequately acknowledged before Congreve wrote this preface. In this context, it is worth noting that the inclusion in this 1717 edition of Dryden's 'A Defence of the Essay of Dramatick Poesie', which had not been reprinted since its original suppression, and his 'Defence of the Epilogue: or, An Essay on the Dramatick Poetry of the last Age', was evidently an afterthought, perhaps to reinforce Congreve's point (see Macdonald, 150–1). The first involved insertion in Volume One of a complete new sheet ([NO]¹²), the cancellation of sig. N7, and redistribution of its text between sigs. [NO]1ʳ and [NO]12ᵛ. So too in Volume Three, the 'Defence of the Epilogue' formed a new section ([HI]⁸) with an instruction to the binder that it be placed immediately before *Marriage A-la Mode* (sig. H5ʳ).

The Game of Quadrille. An Allegory

The earliest extant printing appears to be that in *Mr. Congreve's Last Will and Testament* (London: printed for E. Curll, 1729), 30–4. Unlike the verse letter to Cobham in the same volume, it is not attributed to Congreve. The title page of the 1729 edition refers to it simply as 'The GAME of QUADRILLE. An ALLEGORY'; that of the 1730 edition as 'An ALLEGORICAL COURT-SATIRE.' The version printed by Curll attributes the testimony to 'T.T.' and appends the note attributed to Thomas Woolston.

It is not a political but a 'court-satire', more specifically one involving a legal case. The occasion was a controversy that involved Thomas Woolston: he had been indicted for blasphemy between 2 and 12 November 1725 because his allegorical interpretations of scripture had led him to question the literal truth of the resurrection and of the virgin birth. On William Whiston's intervention the trial was suspended. Woolston, however, continued to propagate his views. In 'The Miracle of The Thundering Legion Examin'd' Walter Moyle had offered a reasoned rejection of testimonies to that miracle by Eusebius and Tertullian. The posthumous publication of his tract in his *Works* (1726) drew forth from Woolston in June *A Defence of the Miracle of the 'Thundering Legion', against a Dissertation of Walter Moyle, Esq.* Moyle being dead was in no position to reply, but one of his friends (who included Congreve) did so in the form of 'The Game of Quadrille. An Allegory'. In a letter to Swift of 22 October 1726 Gay noted the current popularity of Quadrille: 'I . . . still can find amusement enough without Quadrille, which here [at court] is the Universal Employment of Life' (Gay, *Letters*, 59).

It must have been composed some time between late June 1726, when Woolston's attack appeared, and 5 November 1726, when Arbuthnot described it in a letter to Swift: 'Ther has been a comical paper about Quadrille describing it in the terms of a Lewd debauch among four Lady's, meeting four Gallants two of a Ruddy & two of a swarthy complexion talk of their A—es &c. The Ridle is carried on in pretty strong terms! it was not found out a long time, the Ladys imagining it to be [a] reall thing begann to guess who were of the party. A great Minister was for Hanging the Author. in short it has made very good sport' (L: Add. MS 4805, f. 128; Swift, *Correspondence*, iii. 44–5). On 16 November he mentioned it to the Earl of Oxford: 'I have just transcribed the substance of the paper of Quadrille' (Pope, *Correspondence*, ii. 411). See also *The Autobiography and Correspondence of Mary Granville, Mrs. Deloney*, ed. Lady Llanover, 3 vols. (1861), i. 125–6, where she notes the enclosure with a letter to Anne Granville dated 27 November 1726, of 'a riddle, but lest you should take it in the wrong sense, I must expound it to you: it is the game of quadrille; the four young ladies are the queens, the gallants the kings; if you have a notion of the game you will easily find out the rest, it does not differ much from Ombre.'

Curll had reason to promote Moyle. He published *An Apology for the Writings of Walter Moyle* and was part-publisher of Moyle's *Whole Works* which appeared in 1727 and contained a succinct verse summary of the controversy:

On the revived Controversy of the *Thundering Legion*

Since *Whiston* and *Woolston* their Shafts have let fly,
To *Catechise* Truth and *Confirm* an old Lye;
Would make *Thunder, Hail, Light'ning* for *Miracles* pass,
And whoe'er disbelieves,—is accounted an Ass,
The *Church-Cant* let's reverse then, and own the true *Foyle*,
Of *Religion*, is *Reason*; and found in a M O Y L E.

(*Works*, i. 286)

Woolston could not keep quiet and so his trial was resumed on 4 March 1729. The account of it published later that month makes clear the charges against him: his claim that 'the Miracles of our Saviour were to be understood in a Metaphorical Sense, and not as they were Literally Written', and that in his writings the Holy Gospel was 'turn'd into Ridicule and Ludicrous Banter, the Literal Scope and Meaning wrested, and the Whole represented as idle Romance and Fiction'. 'The Game of Quadrille' had a renewed topicality that Curll quickly exploited. Its inclusion in *Mr. Congreve's Last Will and Testament*, published in April 1729, is given a contextual propriety by Woolston's name, the Moyle associations, and Curll's own role as Moyle's publisher. Its affadavit form and *reductio ad absurdum* technique also have a wit appropriate to the occasion of a trial.

The joke of course lies in the fact that the language, albeit heightened, literally is that of the card game quadrille: only an imagination like Woolston's, uncontrolled by knowledge and reason, would try to interpret it allegorically. Disingenuous though such an assumption might be, a court of Kings, Queens, and Knaves, red and black, face-up and face-down, will at times lie together higgledy-piggledy on the cloth of a card-table. Hercules, Cupid, Pit, and Gardiner (as club, heart, diamond, spade), fish (that is, gambling chips), pack, hand, trick, A—es (read reasonably as Aces), and even the obligation to show all, are innocent terms and to be taken literally. For the precise rules of the game at this date, see *The Game of Quadrille; or Ombre by Four, with Its Establish'd Laws and Rules, As It Is Play'd at the French Court* ([1720?]; 2nd edn. 1728), the preface to which notes that the game '*has been about two Years, and is at present, the favourite Game at the* French Court'. See also notes to the poem 'A Ballad on Quadrille', vol. ii, pp. 688–9.

Curll caps the joke on the next page by advertising among his new books, not only *The Ladies Preservative*, by Susanna Gray, but Richard Seymour's *The Court Gamester. Being Full Instructions for Playing at Ombre, Quadrille, Picquet, &c.*

The joke does not end with Woolston. 'T.T.' probably refers to Thomas Tickell and adds a further irony. In his letter to Congreve, prefixed to his edition of *The Drummer* (1722), Steele had attacked Tickell for his imperfect editing of Addison's *Works* (1720) and in particular for his omission of *The Drummer*. All this is recited in Wilson, *Memoirs*, possibly first published by Curll in August 1729: its preface is dated 'Bath, July 14, 1729' and it was advertised as '*now in the Press*' at p. 34 of *Mr. Congreve's Last Will and Testament* (1729). Referring to Steele's criticism, *Memoirs* declares: 'Mr. *Congreve*'s Opinion, in this Case, was undoubtedly on Mr. *Addison*'s side, and Mr. *Tickell*'s Error is sufficiently manifested by his Silence' (p. 128). The very idea that Tickell could tell the truth was of course a further joke. Had he signed an affadavit, no reasonable person would have believed him.

Woolston was for Swift a Yahoo, for Pope a Dunce and 'Scourge to Scripture'. The evidence for Congreve's authorship is at best circumstantial. John Almon, who attributed the piece to him in *The New Foundling Hospital for Wit. Part the Fourth* (1771), 93, may have derived his version from a manuscript which happened to have Congreve's name on it, but it is much inferior to Curll's. (See also the introductory note to Attributions, p. 256.)

LETTERS

1 *To Edward Porter*

Edward Porter (d. 1731) was a member of the Inner Temple. His friendship with Congreve may have come about through the law, but they were already close neighbours by the early 1690s, and they also had a mutual interest in Anne Bracegirdle, whose sister Frances was Porter's wife. Porter was a witness to Henry Playford's will, made on 22 July 1690, and a beneficiary under it. Lynch, *Gallery*, 145, cites a note on his own will (NA, PROB11/643 (2 March 1731)) in which Porter is said to have been 'formerly of the Inner Temple, London but late of the parish of Saint Clement Danes'. He was buried on 9 February 1731.

1 [21 August 1692]] The postmark gives the day and the month. Before Porter moved back there in 1702–3, the only year in which he lived in Surrey Street appears to have been 1692–3, and then only briefly ('1/2 y^r gon.': City of Westminster Rate Books). He may then have moved to 'Arundel Street against the blew-ball' (Letter 11), where he was rated for the years 1694–5 to 1701–2 (part only). Surrey Street (on the west) and Arundel Street (on the east) both ran south from the Strand to the river and were linked, as they are still, by Howard Street. But see note to Letter 23, l. 24.

3 Ladies paper] The paper measures 14.5 × 20.4 cm.

5 the last great news] Almost certainly William's defeat at Steinkirk (3 August 1692 n.s.): see note to *OB* II. ii. 56–7 and *LL* I. xiv. 107.

9 river in cascade] the Manifold River, at Ilam in Dovedale, north of Ashbourne, Derbyshire.

10 even I can distinctly see it] Congreve comes back to this theme in Letters 51 ('painful to my eyes') and 57 ('I have an old conjuror who has been some time about my eyes'). On 26 October 1710 Swift described him as 'almost blind with cataracts growing on his eyes; and his case is, that he must wait two or three years, until the cataracts are riper, and till he is quite blind, and then he must have them couched'. On 13 February 1711 Swift again wrote of Congreve: 'He gave me a *Tatler* he had written out, as blind as he is ...'; on 2 July 1711 he recorded that 'Will Congreve, who lives much by himself, is forced to read for amusement, and cannot do it without a magnifying-glass'; and on 5 January 1712 he visited 'poor Will. Congreve, who had a French fellow tampering with one of his eyes; he is almost blind of both': see *Journal*, 69, 191, 305–6, 455. When Congreve was staying at Ashley, Lord Shannon wrote to Pope on his behalf: 'By Candle light Mr Congreve wants a Scribe', the implication being that Congreve could not then see to write: see Hodges, *Documents*, 229, who tentatively dates Lord Shannon's letter to early 1719, when *Works* (1719–20) would have been preparing. It was not until the mid-eighteenth century that cataracts could be wholly removed. Congreve's would have been pierced with a needle and the clouded lens worked down or broken up to settle into the bottom of the eye, still leaving him with only partial vision. The degree of occlusion could vary from day to day,

according to the light and the sufferer's general state of health, but Congreve's poor eyesight may in part explain the large hand and erratic punctuation in his autograph letters.

12 Mr: Grace] probably the painter A. Grace, but known only from the inscription below John Smith's mezzotint portrait of Christopher Rawlinson: '*Christopher Rawlinson of Clark Hall in Lancashire Esq. Anno Christi 1701. Ætatis 24. A Grace pinx: J. Smith fec:*'. See John Chaloner Smith, *British Mezzotint Portraits*, Part III (1880), 1212, no. 210; and E. Bénézit, *Dictionnaire des Peintres, Sculpteurs, Dessinateurs, et Graveurs* (Paris: Librairie Grund, 1976), v. 151, who notes an A. Grace, painter of portraits *c.*1700, and successor of Kneller and Michael Dahl.

16 Mansfield] Mansfield lies some 25 miles east of Ilam.

18 Mr. Longuevilles picture] William Longueville (1639–1721), a member of the Inner Temple, lived in Bow Street, Covent Garden.

2 *To Jacob Tonson*

Jacob Tonson (1656?–1736) was the most remarkable bookseller of his day, instrumental in creating a highly efficient market in belles-lettres. He established a canon of classical English authors with Milton, Dryden, and, in Rowe's edition, Shakespeare, at the head. He successfully developed publishing by subscription. By his essentially sympathetic service of his authors' interests he astutely furthered his own, both economic and social. After 1706–7 he owned a printing house, and was then better able to control the design and standard of the books he printed. His early intimacy with Congreve, succeeded by a lifelong friendship, guaranteed the closest collaboration between them in the editing and printing of Congreve's *Works* (1710).

11 Wycherley] See note to *OB*, Southerne's prologue, l. 26.

17 Cant] Hodges emends to 'can' but the sense is simply 'if I can't [myself] get them at all'.

18 my father] Colonel William Congreve (1637–1708); see note to *OB*, dedication, l. 7.

3 *To Jacob Tonson*

1 [15 August 1693]] This letter is directly related to the preceding one, dated 'Satturday Aug: 12'. As it was postmarked 'AV | 17', the only intervening Tuesday was that of 15 August.

6 Senock] Sevenoaks, Kent.

9 Epsom] about 15 miles south-west of London and much visited then for its mineral springs.

11 Tunbridge] Tunbridge; see Thomas Benge Burr, *A History of Tunbridge-Wells* (1766), 76–86. Among medical properties claimed for the waters was 'cooling the blood when too hot and fluxile'.

22 Hobbs] Dr Thomas Hobbs (1648–98), a member of the Royal College of Physicians. He presented Congreve with a copy of Diemerbroeck's *Anatome Corporis Humani* (1672).

24–5 the Judges Head in Chancery lane] Tonson had probably only just moved to this address. By 16 July 1695 Congreve was lodging there with him: see J.M. Treadwell, 'Congreve, Tonson, and Rowe's "Reconcilement"', *N&Q* ccxx (June 1975), 265–9.

4 *To Mrs Arabella Hunt*

For Arabella Hunt see the note to Congreve's poem, 'On Mrs. Arabella Hunt, Singing', vol. ii, p. 633.

14 *Balaam*] See Numbers 22: 21–33, where the story is told of the prophet Balaam who defied the Lord by saddling his ass and riding off with the princes of Moab; but when the ass saw the angel of the Lord she fell down under Balaam. See also Crowne, *The Married Beau* (1694), v. i. 266.

5 *To John Dennis*

John Dennis (1657–1734), the critic. The civilized literary-critical debates which, probably under Dryden's aegis, marked these earlier years of the 1690s were soon to turn sour and collapse from the effects of Collier's attacks on the stage.

38 Drink Steel] a reference to the iron content of the waters at Tunbridge Wells; so Rochester, 'Tunbridge Wells, A Satyr', ll. 147–8:

> . . . Steele-Waters, let alone,
> A Back of Steele, will bring 'em better downe.

P. Madan, *A Phylosophical, and Medicinal Essay of the Waters of Tunbridge* (1687), 5, quotes the saying: '*That Steel is the worst Instrument of Death, and the best of Life.*' In an undated reply to Congreve printed in *Letters upon Several Occasions* (1696), sigs. *i7$6^r$–i7^r, Dennis picks up the reference to steel: 'While you drink Steel for your Spleen at *Tunbridge*, I partake of the benefit of the Course. For the gaiety of your Letters relieves me considerably. Then what must your Conversation do? Come up and make the Experiment; and impart that Vigour to me which *Tunbridge* has restor'd to you' (*i7^r).

53 *Will*'s Coffee-House] See note to *LL* i. i. 83.

70 Feast of St. *Bartholomew*] 24 August.

81–2 like a Poet in a Dedication] The reflection explains in part the revision of his own dedication of *DD*.

6 *To Jacob Tonson*

4 Mother] Mary Congreve, née Browning, was a granddaughter of Dr Timothy Bright. She was at this time living at Lismore, but Hodges cites a letter of 18 July 1695 from the Marquis of Carmarthen inviting her and Lady Mary Boyle to accompany him to England, probably to Plymouth and thence to Bath. Mary and her husband probably retired to London sometime after 1702 when he ceased

employment with the Earl of Burlington (Hodges, *Documents*, 34, 98). Mary was buried in the parish of St Clement Danes on 22 April 1715: see J.M. Treadwell, 'Congreve Bereaved', *American Notes & Queries*, xiii (1975), 67–8.

5 this place] i.e. Tunbridge Wells, as in Letter 5.

7 Jekel] possibly Joseph Jekel (1663–1738), a Whig and Member of Parliament who had, like Congreve, been a member of the Middle Temple.

12 Sr: Godfrey] Sir Godfrey Kneller; see note to Congreve's poem, 'To Sir Godfrey Kneller, Occasion'd by *L—y —s* Picture', vol. iii, p. 651.

7 *To Walter Moyle*

Walter Moyle (1672–1721), born at Bake, Cornwall, entered the Middle Temple on 26 January 1691, some two months before Congreve. He was a Whig who was elected in late 1695 Member of Parliament for Saltash, Cornwall, serving until 1698. Dryden held a very high opinion of him as 'a most ingenious young Gentleman, conversant in all the Studies of Humanity, much above his years' and one in 'Learning and Judgment above his Age' (Dryden, *Works*, xx. 61, 223). See also the notes to 'The Game of Quadrille. An Allegory', pp. 211–13 above.

Despite an error in the date as first printed (Dennis gave 'August'), the present letter is clearly in answer to one from Moyle of 7 October 1695 which is valuable on at least two counts. First, we can recover from it something of an earlier Congreve letter to Moyle (now lost, probably in the fire that destroyed Moyle's library and manuscripts in 1808), for Moyle refers to Congreve's 'humerous Description of *John Abassus*; since the dubbing of *Don Quixote*, and the Coronation of *Petrarch* in the *Capitol*, there has not been so great a Solemnity as the Consecration of *John Abassus*. In all the Pagan Ritual, I never met with the Form of Poetical Orders; but I believe the Ceremony of Consecrating a Man to *Apollo*, is the same with devoting a Man to the *Dii Manes*, for both are Martyrs to Fame. I believe not a Man of the *Grave-Club* durst assist at this ridiculous Scene, for fear of laughing out-right' (Dennis, sig. ⁕i1ʳ). When Moyle's letter was reprinted in *The Whole Works of Walter Moyle* (1727), 224–6, '*John Abassus*' was annotated as 'A Nickname given to a stupid *Sussex* Squire, fond of Plays and Poems, who came up to Town, as he said, *to see the Poets of the Age*, and was by some of them introduced among the *Wits* of *Will*'s Coffee-House in *Covent-Garden* among whom they admitted him, under the form of a Poetical *Consecration*, as a Member of their Society.' Second, Moyle's letter ends by asking Congreve 'what Progress you have made in your Tragedy', implying that *MB* was already well under way by mid-1695 although not performed until late February or early March 1697. Regrettably, Congreve fails to tell him.

15–16 Grave Club ... Rabble] Their exact character is now unknown, although an unnamed correspondent writing to Dennis remarks: 'While you are happy in the Politicks of the Grave Club,⁕ and the Puns of the Rabble, you have no regard to the forlorn State of your poor Friend', which he footnotes: '*Two* Covent-Garden *Clubs*.' And Dennis, writing in 1693 to Thomas Cheek in the country, notes that a friend of theirs 'has a hundred times, since he came to this Place, regretted the *Rabble*, nay he has regretted the *Grave Club*; nay, has wish'd himself even in the *Witty Club*, which he believes is by this time erected' (*The Select Works of Mr. John Dennis*, 2 vols. (1718), ii. 537–8, 542).

45 October 13. *95*] This date, following Dobrée, makes the reference above to the forthcoming election more fitting. Luttrell, 2 November 1695, notes Moyle's election to Parliament (Luttrell, iii. 546).

8 *To Catharine Trotter*

Catharine Trotter (1679–1749) appears to have been almost as precocious as Congreve himself. When she was only 14 years old her short epistolary novel, *Olinda's Adventures*, opened anonymously the first volume of *Letters of Love and Gallantry* (1693). By the date of this letter, when she was still only 18, she had herself written one tragedy, *Agnes de Castro* (1696), based on the novel by Aphra Behn. It was performed at DL in December 1695, and like Congreve's *LL* dedicated to Charles, Earl of Dorset. It was followed soon after by *The Fatal Friendship*, performed in May 1698, this time at LIF, and like Congreve's *MB* dedicated to Princess Anne. She was to write three more plays, the comedy *Love at a Loss, or Most Votes Carry It* (1701), and two tragedies, *The Unhappy Penitent. A Tragedy* (1701) and *The Revolution of Sweden* (1706). Dedicating *The Unhappy Penitent* to Congreve's principal patron, Charles Montagu, Lord Halifax, she writes of him as 'Patron and Encourager' of all who aspire to perfection, and sees proof of his 'strictest Justice' in his patronage of 'a *Congreve*' as distinct from others like herself who must appeal rather to his goodness. *The Revolution of Sweden*, in which she was indebted to Congreve for advice, is dedicated to his close friend, Henrietta Godolphin. For his comments on the latter play, see Letter 22. In 1708 she married a clergyman, Patrick Cockburn. Her collected *Works*, edited by Thomas Birch, were published in 1751. Congreve may have met her first through his friend Bevil Higgons, on whose recovery from the smallpox she wrote a poem while she was still only 14.

9 yr verses] See Allusions, pp. 302–3, where they are reprinted.

11 printed off] a tactful excuse, implying that the preliminaries had been typeset and printed. His intention 'to stifle some verses … which were printed with it' may be another polite fiction; there is no bibliographical evidence in Q1 *MB* of the suppression of leaves bearing prefatory verses by other authors. In any event his dedication of the play to Princess Anne would have precluded any such tribute to himself.

24 Mr: Bett:] Thomas Betterton, who had played Osmyn. The allusion suggests a meeting of Betterton, Congreve, and Trotter, probably to discuss the staging of *The Fatal Friendship* which took place the following May.

9 *To Joseph Keally*

Joseph Keally (1672?–1713), son of John Keally, High Sheriff of County Kilkenny, was a fellow student with Congreve at Kilkenny College in 1685–6. He matriculated from Pembroke College, Oxford, 30 May 1686 and was admitted to the Middle Temple on 6 February 1689. By the autumn of 1697, as this letter shows, Keally had returned to Ireland where he was called to the Irish Bar in Trinity Term 1700. He died on 21 May 1713 (Lynch, *Gallery*, 25–8). For Keally's marriage to Elizabeth Monck, and their children, see notes to Letter 37 below.

3 St Malloes] English shipping was subject to attack and capture by raids out of the French port of St Malo.

7 the Peace] Following the Treaty of Ryswick. Presumably Congreve's intended visit to Ireland was delayed by his obligation to write *The Birth of the Muse*, his poem celebrating the peace and advertised in *LG* 18–22 November 1697.

12 D: of Ormond] James Butler (1665–1745), who was then about to resume his duties as Lord Lieutenant of Ireland.

16 Good Bishop] John Hartstonge (1654–1717), Bishop of Ossary. He had been chaplain to the first Duke of Ormond when Congreve was at Kilkenny School.

17 bottom] Hodges tentatively identifies him with a Joseph Bottom who died in the Barbadoes on 23 November 1732. See also Letter 28.

18 Amory] Thomas Amory (d. 1728), a graduate of Trinity College, Dublin, who had left Ireland for London in 1688.

19 Marsh] Jeremiah Marsh; see the note to his prologue to *OB*.

19 Luther] Henry Luther, son of John Luther, merchant and mayor of Youghal. He took his BA degree from Trinity College Dublin in 1688 and was the same year entered at the Middle Temple. He presented Congreve with a copy of Eustachius, *Summa Philosophiæ Quadripartita* (1640).

22 Congreve] possibly, as Hodges suggests, Congreve's cousin, Colonel William Congreve (1671–1746), of Highgate. See also Letter 70.

35 brother] John Keally, then living in Portugal; see Letters 20, 36, 55.

10 *To Joseph Keally*

11 neighbours] principally Edward Porter and his wife Frances, who then lived in Arundel Street. At this date Frances's sister, Anne Bracegirdle, and her mother, may also have been living with them at their Howard Street/Arundel Street address, but this cannot be confirmed until 1702–3 (see Letter 23).

17–18 Eccles … Staggins] John Eccles (*c*.1668–1735), the composer, was appointed Master of the King's Music on 30 June 1700. Nicholas Staggins (1650?–1700) had died at Windsor on 13 June 1700.

19 Mein] 'In Berkeley, followed by Summers and Dobrée, this name appears as "Keir", evidently a misreading of "Mein"' (Hodges, *Documents*, 13). Charles Mein was originally from Dublin and, according to Hodges, employed in the Custom-house in London (*Documents*, 13). Swift was later (8 October 1710) to describe him as 'an honest goodnatured fellow, a thorough hearty laugher, mightily beloved by the men of wit' (*Journal*, 49), and Gay refers to him as 'wondring *Maine*, so fat with laughing eyes' ('Mr. Pope's Welcome from Greece', l. 132).

23 Dandridge] possibly the 'Herr Dandridge' whom Uffenbach visited on 28 October 1710. He saw Dandridge's 'collection of insects, over 1500 varieties and all native to England', birds' nests, eggs, and 'a remarkable book in octavo, in which he

had depicted from life most excellently and delicately, with a short description in English, all manner of English spiders' (*London in 1710*, 166–7); see also Letter 16.

11 *To Edward Porter*

1 Calais] Congreve's journey abroad probably extended from 10 August until mid-October: see Letter 12.

12 Charles] Charles Mein.

12 Jacob] Jacob Tonson, the purpose of whose visit would certainly have been bookselling, and perhaps also the ordering of type and equipment for the printing house he was later to establish.

25 Mother] mother-in-law, Mrs Bracegirdle.

25 Anne] Anne Bracegirdle.

26 Travers] possibly Samuel Travers (?1655–1725), a Whig Member of Parliament and bencher (1693) of the Middle Temple; see also Letter 18.

26–7 Alcayde...Punch] See also Letter 12. 'The Alcayde', possibly Anne Bracegirdle, is perhaps from *alcaide* (from the Arabic *al-quaid*), a general, governor of a fortress, here figuratively the one who commands Congreve. 'Punch' is presumably a dog.

12 *To Mrs Frances Porter*

Frances Porter was the wife of Edward Porter and sister of Anne Bracegirdle. Congreve left her £50 in the will he drafted on 26 February 1725, but she predeceased him. Lynch, *Gallery*, 145, notes that Frances was buried on 27 November 1727.

1 Rotterdam] The Earl of Jersey, writing to Prior from Loo on 27 September 1700, n.s., remarks: 'Your friend Congreve is here' (HMC: Calendar of Manuscripts of the Marquis of Bath, [London, 1908], iii. 419).

17 the Alcayd] See Letter 11.

19 yr: Mother] Mrs Bracegirdle.

13 *To Joseph Kealy*

6 Sapho] Congreve's dog; see Letters 15, 19, 20, and note to DD III. xi. 11.

19 Robin] Robert Fitzgerald (1671–1725). He had studied at Trinity College Dublin, and in London at the Inner Temple. About 1700 he was called to the Irish Bar in Dublin (Lynch, *Gallery*, 37–58). See also Letter 43 for his marriage to Kealy's younger sister. He died of a fall from his horse, 21 January 1725.

25 Abell] John Abell (1660?–1716?), lutenist and singer; but see the character Congreve gives him in Letter 14. On 27 January 1682 Evelyn noted that Abell had 'newly return'd from *Italy*, & indeede I never heard a more excellent voice, one would have sworne it had ben a Womans it was so high, & so well & skillfully manag'd' (*Diary*, iv. 270).

37 Montague] Charles Montague; see notes to the dedication to *DD*, the 'Epistle to ... Charles, Lord Halifax', and Letter 34. He was created Baron Halifax in December 1700, and Earl of Halifax in October 1714.

14 *To John Drummond*

John Drummond was a Scottish merchant in Amsterdam; there is a letter from him, dated from Amsterdam 30 August 1692, in the National Library of Scotland (MS 6141, f. 74) the tenor of which suggests that he was long accustomed to acting as an agent and facilitator of visitors.

3 journey ... West] Hodges notes that it was probably to Poole, the port for which Congreve had been appointed collector of customs the year before.

17 the new Parliament] On 4 February 1701 Luttrell had noted that there were some 150 new members (Luttrell, v. 14).

20 Emperors minister] Count Wratislaw, who arrived in England on 28 December and was received by William III at Hampton Court on 30 December (Luttrell, iv. 723).

25 Parliament ... in a true light] On 14 February 1701 Parliament resolved to stand by and support the King in the controversy with France (Luttrell, v. 18).

31 the Duke of Anjous succession] *The Duke of Anjou's Succession Considered* went through four editions in 1701; a second part was published the same year. Charles II had died on 1 November 1700 n.s. and bequeathed his dominions to Philip, duke of Anjou (1683–1746), who then assumed the Spanish crown as Philip V. Louis XIV's attempt to claim guardianship of Philip as his grandson gave, in Evelyn's words, 'more and more umbrage to the rest of Europe'. On 4 April 1701 a solemn fast was indicted for the whole nation to avert the consequences of Philip's succession (Evelyn, *Diary*, v. 453).

33 Abell] See Letter 13. The 'new Play-house' is the Lincoln's Inn Fields Theatre (LIF) which was opened in 1695 and in which Congreve was a sharer. A year earlier, probably on 20 January 1700, Alice Hatton had noted: 'Mr Abel is to have a fine musicke meeting to morrow, and ye tickets are guineas a piece, wch is a little to much for me to throw away; so I shall not be there, and I find so many y^t can afford it better of my mind, y^t I fancy, if he had had lower rates, he would have got more' (*LS*, pt I, pp. 522–3, citing Hatton Correspondence, Camden Society, xxiii (1878), 245). Abell's *A Collction [sic] of Songs, in Several Languages* was advertised in the *Post Boy* for 8–10 April 1701, and his *A Collction [sic] of Songs, in English* also in the *Post Boy* for 22–4 May 1701. D. & M. 192 and 191.

49 Arundell street] Congreve's own address at this date is unknown. On his return from the Continent he might well have stayed with the Porters for a time before finding other lodgings, but the first firm date for his residence with them is 26 June 1706 (Letter 35), by which time they had long been settled in Surrey Street.

15 *To Joseph Keally*

24–5 Charles ... arrested] presumably because Charles Mein had agreed to cover a loan which Robin (Robert Fitzgerald) had failed to pay.

29 the Ambitious Stepmother] by Nicholas Rowe. It was performed at LIF in December 1700.

31 the Lady's Visiting-day] by William Burnaby; it was performed at LIF in January 1701.

33–4 run... the trip] Summers sees an allusion to George Farquhar's *The Constant Couple; or, A Trip to the Jubilee*. It was first performed at Drury Lane on 28 November 1699 and had a long run.

34 Williams] possibly the William Williams who, according to Grove, was one of the king's musicians 1695–9.

35 Sansom] John Sansom, at Charterhouse with Joseph Addison and Richard Steele. Addison records a loan of £600 by Sansom to Steele in January 1702 (Addison, *Letters*, 5 n. 2). Sansom had been appointed comptroller of customs at Bristol in August 1698, but he was to lose that office in August 1708 (Luttrell, entries for 4 August 1698 and 12 August 1708).

16 *To Joseph Keally*

5 James Hewsly] unidentified.

10 Eccles] For Eccles, Finger, Purcell, and Weldon, the four composers who each set Congreve's *JP*, see notes on Early Performances, vol. ii, pp. 603–5.

12 to-morrow] Finger's setting was performed on Friday, 28 March, two days after the date of this letter.

21 throw forwards the sound] Price, *Restoration Theatre*, 85–6, comments: 'Since Congreve writes that the musicians were removed from their usual position between the stage and the pit, one must assume that they were placed somewhere on the stage and that the acoustical reflector was erected upstage, the orchestra being in front of it.'

28 White's] opened in 1699 in St James's Street, next to the Chapel Royal; see Pope, *The Dunciad*, 1. 319–22. Summers cites Swift, *The Intelligencer*, ix, 1728, where its later reputation as a gaming house is noted (see Swift, *Prose*, xii. 50). It is also represented in Hogarth, *The Rake's Progress*, plate 4 (second state).

29 Pontacq] so Hodges, emending Berkeley's reading 'portico'. He explains Pontacq as 'A white or red wine, from the Basses Pyrénées in southern France, that was frequently advertized in the contemporary *Daily Courant* as "perfectly neat, strong, deep, bright, and of the right delicious Flavour"' (*Documents*, 22).

33 jubilee] See note to *WW* IV. xii. 3–4.

35 Our friend Venus] Anne Bracegirdle. The epigraph to *JP* ('—*Vincis utramque Venus*': 'Venus, you surpass the other two.') was doubtless meant personally for her too.

35 Mrs Hodgson] See note to *WW* III. xii. 4.

36 Mrs Boman] See Early Performers, vol. i.

37 Dandridge] See note to Letter 10, l. 23.

17 *To John Drummond*

15 treatys] In February 1701 both the Lords and the Commons had asked the King to lay before them all treaties and alliances with any prince or state since the war (Luttrell, entries for 15 and 19 February 1701).

16 that of 77] i.e. that made with the States General on 3 March 1677 to supply 10,000 soldiers and 20 men of war in the event of an attack (see Luttrell, entries for 20 February and 3 April 1701).

22 a war] The War of the Spanish Succession did in fact break out later in 1701.

27 Foules . . . Vander Heyden] unidentified.

18 *To Joseph Keally*

9 Lords] Halifax, Oxford, Portland, and Somers. The House of Commons was seeking to impeach them for their part in a treaty to divide Spain 'to the prejudice of our antient ally the emperor'. A trial was set for 9 June and scaffolds ordered to be erected at Westminster Hall, but, as Congreve suspected, it proved abortive. On 24 June the Lords acquitted all four, the King prorogued Parliament, and on 28 June the scaffolds were ordered to be torn down (see Luttrell for successive entries from 27 March to 28 June 1701).

16 Travers] Hodges suggests Samuel Travers, MP (*Documents*, 23 n. 3).

25 10d thro] As Hodges notes, 'ten pence "thro" postage had been paid, sixpence from London to Dublin and four pence from Dublin to Kilkenny' (*Documents*, 24).

19 *To Joseph Keally*

1 [London, late Summer 1702]] Letter 20, dated 4 December 1702, also refers to the death of Congreve's dog, Sapho. The reference in this letter to 'this Summer' therefore suggests a date of about August or September 1702.

11 Nich. Bolton] unidentified. Peckham lay some four miles south-east of Congreve's lodgings.

13 Baker] the actor Francis Baker (*fl.* 1670–90), who played at the Smock Alley Theatre, Dublin, before coming to London in 1685. He was also a master paver and rehearsed his parts as he supervised his men. Summers explains the pun in 'hem': 'The hem is the technical term for the outer edge of a millstone or a paving-stone, and to hem is to fit neatly paving-stones together to join them' (i. 237).

20 *To Joseph Keally*

This letter was sold as lot 326 in Sotheby's sale of 14 March 1979 when it was bought by Quaritch for its present owners, the Pierpont Morgan Library, New York. In the manuscript the signature, two words, and part of a third word have been cut away and supplied in facsimile, and a small tear affects a fourth word. The missing text is here restored within square brackets. A detached address panel, reading 'ffor Mr. Joseph Keally | att Kilkenny | in Ireland | 10^d thro', was part of the same lot but must relate to a different letter since the relevant address label for No. 20, confirmed by its postmark, is in the Berg Collection, New York Public Library.

4 brother] John Keally; see Letter 9.

7 festivall] Christmas.

12–13 nil mihi . . . veni] Ovid, *Heroides*, 1. 2 ('Penelope Ulixi'): 'yet write nothing back to me; come yourself'.

14 Jack: Allen] possibly a joke at the expense of Tonson's apprentice, John Allen, bound to him on 2 December 1689 and made free on 3 May 1697. Congreve would have known him well from about 1695 when they lodged together with Tonson: see Treadwell, 'Congreve, Tonson, and Rowe's "Reconcilement" ', 267.

21 *To Jacob Tonson*

8 Furnes] Sir Harry Furnes (1658?–1712), described by Luttrell as a sheriff of London and director of the Bank of England (entries for 4 July and 21 November 1700).

13 Nephew] Jacob Tonson II, son of Richard Tonson, Jacob's brother. He probably began working with his uncle about Michaelmas 1698 when Jacob I moved to his late brother Richard's shop in Gray's Inn Gate. He was made free by patrimony on 6 September 1708.

14 Pastoral] Congreve's *The Tears of Amaryllis for Amyntas*; see Variants, vol. ii, pp. 816–18.

15 barn-elms] This Barn Elms was in Surrey on the south side of the Thames, between Mortlake and Putney. The manor house was rebuilt in 1694. A second house on the estate was leased by Jacob Tonson in 1703 and remained his home until his death in 1736. Congreve's sentiments echo those of Vanbrugh in his letter to Tonson of 15 June 1703: 'the Kit-Cat wants you, much more than you ever can do them. Those who remaine in towne, are in great desire of waiting on you at Barn-Elmes' (*Works*, iv. 7). Their curiosity relates to Tonson's plan, then almost finished with Vanbrugh's help, to make a banqueting room in his new house for meetings of the Kit-Cat Club. Kneller's portraits of its members, the first of which was commissioned by the Duke of Somerset in 1703, were designed specifically for that room. The paintings are now in the National Portrait Gallery, London. See also *LL* 11. ix. 24.

21 Amsterdam] When Vanbrugh wrote to him, on 15 June and 13 and 30 July 1703, Tonson was lodging with a Mr Vatck near the Stadt House Amsterdam (*Works*, iv. 8–11).

22 *To Catharine Trotter*

3 the scheme] The play that accompanied the letter was *The Revolution of Sweden*, based on the abbé de Vertot, *L'Histoire des Révolutions de Suède* (1695), a copy of which Congreve owned. Her play was first performed at the Haymarket on 11 February 1706. Congreve's influence may have extended to its dedication to Henrietta Godolphin. Trotter acknowledges the honour that 'was publickly done me by the Dutchess of *Marlborough*, and all her beauteous Family', and writes in particular of the prudence of Henrietta's conduct, the delicacy of her judgement, and the affability and obligingness of her temper. Curiously, in the light of

Congreve's advice, Downes recorded: 'she kept close to the History, but wanting the just Decorum of Plays, [it] expir'd the Sixth Day' (p. 49).

31 poetical Justice requires him] See Drake, *The Ancient and Modern Stages Surveyed* (1699), 226: 'Poetic Justice has become the Principle Article of the Drama.' The phrase appears to have been used first by Thomas Rymer, *The Tragedians of the Last Age* (1677) but more precisely in Congreve's sense by Dryden, 'The Grounds of Criticism in Tragedy', prefacing his *Troilus and Cressida* (1679): 'we lament not, but detest a wicked man; we are glad when we behold his crimes are punished, and that poetical justice is done upon him.' See M.A. Quinlan, *Poetic Justice in the Drama: The History of an Ethical Principle in Literary Criticism* (Notre Dame, 1912), and Richard Tyre, 'Versions of Poetic Justice in the Early Eighteenth Century', *SP* 54 (1957), 29–44. See also Dennis, *Works*, i. 477, to the effect that poetic justice was generally accepted; and Eric Rothenstein, *Restoration Tragedy* (Madison, 1967), 158 n.: 'poetic justice... remained a dead issue'.

53 Mr: Inglis's house] that of her brother-in-law, Dr Inglis, a physician.

23 *To Joseph Keally*

6 hurricane] The storm occurred on 27 November 1703. In *Mr. Collier's Dissuasive from the Play-house... Occasion'd By the late Calamity of the Tempest* (1703), 15, Collier notes that at a performance of *Macbeth* immediately after the storm, 'at mention of the *Chimnies being blown down*, ... the Audience were pleas'd to *Clap*, at an unusual Length of Pleasure and Approbation. And is not the meaning of all this all too intelligible? Does it not look as if they had a Mind to out-brave the Judgment?'

12 priory] Summers emends to 'Privy' and cites Pepys, 30 August 1668: 'Walked to St. James's and Pell Mell... So I to the Park, and there walk an hour or two; and in the King's garden, and saw the Queen and ladies walk; and I did steal some apples off the trees... Coming into the Park, and the door kept strictly, I had opportunity of handing in the little, pretty, squinting girl of the Duke of York's house' (*Diary*, ix. 295).

24 Our neighbour] Anne Bracegirdle, by now settled with her mother in Howard Street. She is in fact rated as living in Arundel Street from 1702–3 until the 1740s (Howard Street is not distinguished as such), and Edward Porter, no longer in Arundel Street, is rated as in Surrey Street from 1702–3 (part year) until his death in 1731. Despite those suggestively congruent dates, as Congreve here distinguishes between the Howard Street house and Porter's (former?) house in Arundel Street next to the Blue Ball, the two cannot have been identical.

29–30 Blue Ball... at Mr Porter's] See the address to Letter 11: 'To Mr: Porter At His house in Arundel Street against the blew-ball.' As Porter had ceased to pay rates on his Arundel Street house in 1702, Congreve may here mean 'at Mr Porter's former house'.

41 Beaumont... Shovel... Fairborn] Rear-Admiral Basil Beaumont (1669–1703), Sir Cloudesley Shovel (1650–1707), and Admiral Stafford Fairborne (d. 1742). Beaumont was drowned when his ship, *The Mary*, was wrecked on the Goodwin Sands in this storm. Shovel (by then admiral and commander-in-chief

of the fleet) was wrecked off the Scilly Islands on 22 October 1707. Summers tells how Shovel was still alive when cast on shore at Porthellick Cove but, for the sake of an emerald ring he wore, was then dispatched and despoiled by a woman who found him there.

45 Robin] The buildings in King's-Bench Walk were part of the Inner Temple where he had been a student.

24 *To Joseph Keally*

10 philosophy] See *Julius Cæsar*, IV. ii. 199–200:

> Of your philosophy you make no use,
> If you give place to accidental evils.

25 *To Joseph Keally*

6 Duke of Ormond] See note to Letter 9, l. 12.

10 Lady Betty] Hodges, *Documents*, 29–30, identifies her with Elizabeth Cromwell, daughter of Vere-Essex, Baron Cromwell and Earl of Ardglass, Ireland. Since she was apparently an only daughter (Lynch, *Tonson*, 194), the 'sisters' here were probably her sisters-in-law. In October 1703, as 'an heiress of 2,000*l*. a year' (Luttrell, v. 346), she married Edward Southwell (1671–1730) who had become Secretary of State for Ireland in 1702. There were three sons of the marriage, of whom the second, Robert, and the third, Thomas, died young. She herself died in childbed on 31 March 1709 (Luttrell, v. 425). See also Letters 35 and 45, and notes to 'A Hymn to Harmony' and 'The Oath of the Tost'.

18 translation] from Molière's *Monsieur de Pourceaugnac*; see Attributions, pp. 264–8.

28 neighbour] Anne Bracegirdle.

26 *To Joseph Keally*

3 dillask] Hodges (*Documents*, 31) explains that '*Dillask*, or *dillisk*, is a variant form for *dulse* or *dulce* (from the Gaelic *duileasg*), a seaweed used as food'. See *OED* art. Dulse.

4 very lame of the gout] On 11 November 1699 Dryden had reported Congreve, then only 29, ill of the gout. The present letter is the first allusion Congreve himself makes to this recurrent problem and its disabling effects, painful to the point of precluding even the writing of letters. See also Letters 33 (30 April 1706, but alluding to a fit at Christmas 1705), 44 (9 October 1708), 47 (23 May 1709), 53 (10 March 1711), 55 (2 November 1711), 57 (6 May 1712), and Allusions (Gay to Swift, 3 February 1723). Pat Rogers, 'The Rise and Fall of Gout', *TLS* (20 March 1981), 315–16, offers an informative summary of the condition. The fullest account is that by Roy Porter and G.S. Rousseau, *Gout: The Patrician Malady* (New Haven, 1998), where it is described as a condition 'brought on by an abnormally high concentration of uric acid in the blood (hyperuricaemia), which provokes deposition of sodium urate in the joints' (p. 4). In Congreve's

day the term was imprecise and may have been applied to such equally crippling conditions as rheumatoid arthritis. Gout being a heredity disorder, it is pertinent to note that Congreve's father also suffered from it (see Biographical Summary, 10 March 1693). Congreve's gout caused some of his less sympathetic biographers to find in it a fitting punishment for their imputation of his misspent youth. Such a notion informs even Swift's letter to Pope of 13 February 1729, where he claims that Congreve had in youth shown too little care for his health. For discussion of the metaphoric heritage and literary exploitation of that common but fallacious idea of gout as 'the condition of the fallen', its cause debauchery, see Porter and Rousseau, *Gout*, 229–47.

27 *To Joseph Keally*

4 Charles] Charles Mein, who did indeed open Keally's letter to Congreve and deliver the enclosure to the Duke of Ormond (Hodges, *Documents*, 31).

6 Howard] Hugh Howard (1675–1737), a Dubliner who had gone to England in 1688. He eventually settled in London as a portrait painter. See also Letters 44 and 47.

7 a gentleman] presumably the 'Mr Mahun' mentioned in Letter 28 but not otherwise identified.

11–12 born . . . world] an allusion to *2 Henry IV*, I. ii. 187–9 and V. iii. 98–9: 'I was born about three of the clock in the afternoon with a white head, and something a round belly' and 'I pray thee now, deliver them like a man of this world.'

14 nothing extenuate] quoting *Othello*, V. ii. 351.

28 *To Joseph Keally*

5 father] By this date Congreve's parents were evidently settled in London, possibly in the parish of St Clement Danes. They were certainly there by July 1706: see notes to Letter 6 and Hodges, *Documents*, 34, 98. For the father's death in 1708, see Letter 41.

11 the Tale of a Tub] Swift's *Tale of a Tub* was first published in the Easter term, 1704 (*TC* III. 401, 418).

29 *To Joseph Keally*

11 the Biter] Nicholas Rowe's one comedy, *The Biter*, was performed at LIF on 4 December 1704. Summers cites Pope's epigram on Ozell, ll. 10–11:

> How great, how just, the Judgment of that Writer!
> Who the *Plain-dealer* damns, and prints the *Biter*.

11 Cibber] Colley Cibber's *The Careless Husband* was performed at DL on 7 December 1704. Cibber recalls Congreve's comparable judgment on *Love's Last Shift*, performed in January 1696, which 'had only in it, a great many things, that were *like* Wit, that in reality were *not* Wit'. See Allusions, p. 462.

30 *To Joseph Keally*

8 the house] the Queen's Theatre, Haymarket. It was opened on 9 April 1705: see the commentary to *Semele*, vol. ii, pp. 609–17.

9 no opera] The first production was in fact *The Loves of Ergasto*, described as a *pastorale* and sung in Italian, with music by Jakob Greber.

17 box-keeper] i.e. for the new Queen's Theatre.

31 *To Joseph Keally*

1 [October–November 1705?]] Hodges argues that this letter must have been written before 26 June 1706, when Congreve moved to Edward Porter's house in Surrey Street; and, whatever the year, it must also have been written shortly after 29 September, that being Michaelmas. Those references do not fix the year, but 1705 is most likely.

7 Boddy] possibly Richard Boddy, a householder in Norfolk Street, 1698–1700 (Hodges, *Documents*, 38).

51 Sanford] probably Samuel Sanford (*fl.* 1661–99), the actor who played Foresight in *LL* and Gonsalez in *MB*. Cibber implies that he died about 1704–5, probably in 1705 if the date suggested for this letter is right (*Apology*, i. 327).

32 *To Joseph Keally*

3 letter of congratulation] As Hodges suggests, Keally must have congratulated Congreve on his appointment at £200 a year as one of the five commissioners for licensing wine, an office which he continued to hold until 21 December 1714. The Letters Patent are dated 26 December 1705 but Congreve might well have known earlier. See Hodges, *Biography*, 84.

7 water swells a man] Craik notes an allusion to *The Merry Wives of Windsor*, III. v. 11–16: 'I have a kind of alacrity in sinking . . . the water swells a man, and what a thing should I have been when I had been swelled?'

8 Smyrna] a coffee-house in Pall Mall near St James's Square. Summers cites Addison, *Spectator*, 457 (14 August 1712): 'I have known *Peter* publishing the Whisper of the Day by eight a Clock in the Morning at *Garraway*'s, by twelve at *Will*'s, and before two at the *Smyrna*' (*Spectator*, iv. 113).

10 Hay-market] This confirms and dates Congreve's attempt to withdraw from any concern whatever in the management of the Queen's Theatre, Haymarket, although Letter 36 of 10 September 1706 suggests that he remained troubled by it for some months after. For the background, see the commentary on *Semele*.

11 dipt] involved in debt: see *OED* art. Dip, *v.* 7b. See also note on 'pretty deep' at *WW* III. v. 28–9.

12 Terence] *Eunuchus*, I. i. 29–30:

> Quid agas? nisi ut te redimas captum quam queas
> Minumo; si nequeas paululo, at quanti queas;

' . . . Ransom yourself from captivity as cheaply as you can. If you can't do it for a small sum, make the best bargain you can' (Loeb).

14 Recorder] Keally was appointed Recorder of Kilkenny on 2 June 1705 (Lynch, *Gallery*, 29).

33 *To Joseph Keally*

6 Governors] the Duke of Ormond, reappointed Lord Lieutenant for Ireland.

12 Play house] the Queen's Theatre, Haymarket.

13 two houses...Kingdoms] the Queen's Theatre, Haymarket, and Drury Lane, Covent Garden; see Cibber, *Apology*, i. 301, 327–9 where he too reflects on the parallel with the union of England and Scotland, not accomplished until 1707 but then being negotiated. A reunion of the companies was spoken of intermittently throughout this period, although the first production by the re-united companies did not take place until 15 January 1708.

34 *To Joseph Keally*

10 stirring too soon] Keally had broken his leg (Lynch, *Gallery*, 30); see also Letter 36.

17 Ld Halifax] Halifax had been sent to the Court of Hanover in April 1706 and was to return to London on 18 August (Luttrell, entries for 6 and 13 April and 20 August 1706).

27 Lord Donnegal's death] Arthur Chichester (1666–1706), third earl of Don-egal, was killed in battle at Montjoui on 10 April 1706.

35 *To Joseph Keally*

5 business] For some sense of the problems Congreve must also have been grappling with at this time, see Judith Milhous and Robert D. Hume, 'Heidegger and the Management of the Haymarket Opera, 1713–17', *Early Music*, 27 (February 1999), 65–84. The technical problems, inadequate scenery and costumes, inordinate expenses, and poor receipts doubtless had their precedents in 1705–6.

12 Lady Betty] See notes to Letter 25 above. The boy referred to may have been her second son, Robert.

13 Mr Porter's in Surry-street] Congreve lodged with them there until his death. See notes to Letters 1 and 23.

36 *To Joseph Keally*

10 another revolution] Vanbrugh had surrendered the management of the Queen's Theatre to Owen Swiney by 14 August 1706 (Downes, *Vanbrugh*, 322, and Cibber, *Apology*, i. 329–37). The actors listed by Congreve were formerly at Drury Lane, Covent Garden. Cibber gives them as '*Wilks, Estcourt, Mills, Keen, Johnson, Bullock*, Mrs. *Oldfield*, Mrs. *Rogers*, and some few others of less note' (i. 332). Since, as Lowe notes, Cibber was probably wrong to include Estcourt, Congreve's 'Dicky' must refer to Henry Norris, nicknamed 'Jubilee Dicky' from his success in Farquhar's *The Constant Couple* (so Summers, i. 239).

14 Rich] Christopher Rich, manager of the Drury Lane Theatre. See Cibber, *Apology*, i. 328–9, and also the complaint of 5 December 1705 made by Rich against Congreve and Vanbrugh (Hodges, *Documents*, 111–12).

14–15 Volpone . . . Mosca] in Jonson, *Volpone*, v. xi. According to Cibber, Rich had colluded with Swiney and agreed that 'both Companies should be under one and the same Interest'. Believing he would share the profits, Rich allowed most of his actors to go over to the Queen's Theatre only to find Swiney determined to stand alone (*Apology*, i. 334–6).

15 Lord Chamberlain] Henry Gray (1664?–1740), Duke of Kent, held the office 1704–10.

18 misapplied] because the acoustics of the Queen's Theatre were better for music.

19 an ode] 'A Pindarique Ode, Humbly Offer'd to the Queen.'

37 *To Joseph Keally*

7 the news] Keally 'of the parish of St. Mary in the City of Kilkenny, Esq.' married 'Elizabeth Moncke, of the parish of St. Peter in the City of Dublin, Spinster' on 5 June 1707 (Lynch, *Gallery*, 30). They had two children, Elizabeth (1708–83) and Joseph (1711–49).

38 *To Joseph Keally*

21 expected me to have paid him] Cf. Swift, *Journal*, i. 114 (December 1710): 'Congreve and Delaval have at last prevailed on Sir Godfrey Kneller to intreat me to let him draw my picture for nothing'.

22 [not]] The sense demands the emendation: see Congreve's continuing sensitivity on the point in Letter 44 with its pun on 'touch'.

26 mumelled] an obsolete form of 'mumbled'.

39 *To Joseph Keally*

11 D: of Richmond] Charles Lennon (1672–1723), first Duke of Richmond.

40 *To Joseph Keally*

3 usquebaugh] Irish whisky; see also Letters 41 and 42.

8 Prince of Wales] Luttrell reports news of the French embarking at Dunkirk 'with 200 English, Scotch, and Irish officers, and great store of arms, where the pretended prince of Wales, with some Scotch peers, were arrived, and designed to be ready to sail by next Saturday . . . for Scotland' (entry for Thursday 4 March 1708).

41 *To Joseph Keally*

4 my loss] Congreve's father, William, 'from St Giles in the Fields', was buried in Congreve's own parish of St Clement Danes on 10 April 1708; see J.M. Treadwell, 'Congreve Bereaved', 67.

18 legacy] Robert Leake, third earl of Scarsdale, had died on 27 December 1707. In his will, proved on 2 January 1708, he left £1,000 to Anne Bracegirdle. See Hodges, *Documents*, 49, and *Biography*, 87.

42 *To Joseph Keally*

7 that lady] Hodges suggests Lady Elizabeth Cromwell (*Documents*, 49 n. 1).

16 is gone to God] In this context, a sympathetic note quite without irony written to a close friend, the phrase may intimate Congreve's own beliefs. See his citation from John Hales in *Amendments*, p. 1106. The identity of the old gentlewoman is unknown. Hodges suggests the mother of Anne Bracegirdle and Frances Porter (*Documents*, 49 n. 3; but see also p. 69 n. 2 where he implies that she is still alive in 1714).

43 *To Joseph Keally*

5 neither of the other] presumably Letters 41 and 42, which Keally had received but still not answered.

10 Robin] Robert Fitzgerald married Keally's younger sister, Ellen, on 10 July 1708 (Lynch, *Gallery*, 56).

44 *To Joseph Keally*

9 congratulate Robin's gout] probably in the now obsolete transitive use: 'to express sympathetic joy . . . pleasure, or satisfaction at' its brief intermission.

10 Mr Howard's picture] See Letter 38.

13 touch from Sir Godfrey] presumably to copy from a painting of Keally by Kneller, and then to touch Keally for payment as he had Congreve (see Letter 38).

16 Sansom] See Letter 15; in August 1708 he lost his office as comptroller of customs at Bristol.

45 *To Joseph Keally*

6 Latin Ballad] Keally's translation into Latin of Congreve's ballad, 'Jack Frenchman's Defeat'. Keally's version was published together with Congreve's in *Poetical Miscellanies. The Sixth Part* (1709).

9–10 Pembroks . . . Wharton . . . Sommers] Luttrell noted on 16 November 1708 that Pembroke had the previous day succeeded Prince George as Lord High Admiral (the prince having died on 28 October), that Thomas Wharton had become Lord Lieutenant for Ireland, and that John Somers had been made Lord President of the Council. As Hodges notes, Wharton (1648–1715) and Somers (1651–1716) were, like Congreve, members of the Kit-Cat Club.

15 Lady Betty . . . dangerous] She was some months pregnant and would die in giving birth the following March: see notes to Letter 25.

47 *To Joseph Keally*

1 May 23 [1709]] Hodges gives the year as 1709 because of its reference to the peace preliminaries, and quotes Luttrell's entry for Tuesday 24 May 1709 to

the effect that Walpole had arrived from Holland on the previous Saturday bearing the preliminaries for a general peace, that these had been read to the Queen on Sunday, and that on Monday Walpole had returned with them to the Hague.

17 TidComb] Lieutenant General John Tidcomb (1642–1713) was then stationed in Ireland. He was another member of the Kit-Cat Club.

19 Prince of Conde] a by-word for haughtiness; he had died in March 1709.

22–4 excellency...my Lady] Thomas Wharton, who had been appointed Lord Lieutenant for Ireland on 16 November 1708 (Letter 45), and Lady Wharton.

48 *To Joseph Keally*

1 [London, March–April 1710]] Hodges dates this letter by reference to another from Addison to Keally of 13 April 1710. In it Addison writes of Wharton making Keally Commissioner of Appeals, an appointment confirmed on 23 June 1710. See also Lynch, *Gallery*, 30.

49 *To Joseph Keally*

1 June 6. [1710]] The year 1710 is suggested by the likelihood that Addison was then in Ireland and able to see Keally. In the letter to Keally of 13 April 1710 he had intimated his intention of going there: see Hodges, *Documents*, 56.

50 *To Joseph Keally*

12 Lord Rivers] Richard Savage (1662–1712), fourth earl of Rivers. The errand to Hanover was, as Luttrell reported, 'to offer the command of our army in Flanders to that prince'. In September Rivers himself was made 'general of the English horse in Flanders' (Luttrell, 10 August and 26 September 1710).

51 *To Joseph Keally*

3 Si vales...valeo] a Ciceronian tag common at the beginning of letters and often abbreviated to SVBE and EQV. Here, 'If you are well, that's fine. I too am well.' So too Addison to Congreve in his letter of December 1699 (Hodges, *Documents*, 204).

52 *To Joseph Keally*

2 Tu...ito] a Stoic maxim from Virgil, *Aeneid*, v i. 95: 'yield not to ills, but go forth more bravely.'

2 Ld Castlecomer] Christopher Wandesford, second Viscount Castlecomber, Member of Parliament 1710–12 and Member of the Privy Council in Ireland.

3 Mr Dopping] Samuel Dopping, son of Bishop Anthony Dopping. Hodges cites letters of 1710 by Addison reporting Dopping's involvement in the Irish Parliament.

12 To wonder...a wonder too] Dryden and Lee, *Oedipus*, i. i. 25–6:

> one but began
> To wonder, and straight fell a wonder too.

14 Smith] John Smith (1652–1742), engraver. See Letter 53 and the note to 'Epigram, Written After the Decease of Mrs. Arabella Hunt', vol. ii, p. 638. Writing to his nephew in 1729 about a new edition of Congreve's works, Jacob Tonson said: 'I think the head should be done by Virtue, from ye Kit-Cat Picture. Smith did the messotinto print from that, but I think there is a stifness about thee mouth wch is not in ye painting …' (O: MS English Letters c.129). Congreve comments here that Smith's prints were 'generally liked'. In smaller format such a mezzotint might have served as a frontispiece to *Works* (1710) but none is known to have been done. The omission may suggest another act of personal retreat by Congreve, leaving his works to stand alone as the public definition of his achievement and identity.

21 December 15] The transcript of this letter in *The Carl H. Pforzheimer Library*, 3 vols. (New York, 1940), i. 208–9, gives the date as December 17, but the postmark confirms that December 15 is the correct reading.

53 *To Joseph Keally*

6 Harris] Keally's cousin. Letters 54, 55, and 56 make it clear that Harris was buying linen in Holland for Mrs Porter to make into shirts for Keally.

9 Ossy Butler] possibly James Butler, second Duke of Ormond, formerly styled earl of Ossory; see also Letter 54.

12 Marquis de Guiscard] Guiscard was in custody and being examined on a charge of high treason. As Congreve records, Guiscard was himself wounded and taken to Newgate. A week after Congreve's letter, Guiscard 'died in Newgate of a mortification in his shoulder' (Luttrell, 17 March 1711). See also *The Examiner* 32 (15 March 1711), cited by Summers.

14 Mr St John] Henry St John (1678–1751), Secretary of State in the new Tory government of 1710, created Viscount Bolingbroke in 1712.

19 Mr Harley] Robert Harley (1661–1724), Chancellor of the Exchequer 1710–14, created earl of Oxford in 1711.

54 *To Joseph Keally*

3 Garraways Coffee house] in Exchange Alley, and so a suitable place for those whose business was commercial. See also Letter 32.

8 inhabitants] in particular, Frances Porter; see Letter 53.

14 Buttler] brother of the Ossy Butler mentioned in Letter 53. There is no record of Keally's response to Congreve's gift of his *Works* (1710) or the prints.

57 *To Joseph Keally*

9 my eyes] See notes to Letter 1.

11 commission … continued] As Hodges notes, with the change of government Congreve had reason to fear the loss of his office as Commissioner of Wine Licences. Swift had interceded with Harley the previous year. Montagu had pressed Congreve's case early in 1712 and on 25 April 1712 thanked Harley for his favourable decision. On 13 May 1714 Montagu again wrote to

Harley to recommend Congreve's reappointment. See Hodges, *Documents*, 117–19, 121.

58 *To Joseph Keally*

20 no longer a glimpse] probably an optimistic allusion to his hopes of better sight following treatment for cataracts; see Letter 57 and notes to Letter 1.

59 *To Edward Porter*

2 [1714?]] The weather caused some delay, for the letter was not postmarked until 4 January. The year is quite uncertain. T.J. Brown suggested 1 January 1709 as the most likely date, 'for the winter of 1708–9 was exceptionally severe, with hard frost and heavy snow from December to March' (*The Book Collector*, 6 (1957), 61). In support of that suggestion, it may be worth noting that Congreve's 'Of Pleasing; An Epistle to Richard Temple', first published in *Works* (1710), might well have been written a year or two earlier during a stay at Stowe. Hodges, however, claims that 'The date 1714 is indicated by the small postmark, which was just coming into use at that time' (*Documents*, 51 n. 1); and as both he and Brown point out, it cannot have been written later than 1 January 1714, as Richard Temple became Baron Cobham later that year.

3 Howard street] Anne Bracegirdle among them.

60 *To Edward Porter*

1 [London 1714?]] The year is that following Elizabeth Barry's death, 'after Mr. Custis had inherited the picture of Lord Rochester and was in a position to sell it' (Hodges, *Documents*, 70). For Elizabeth Barry, see discussion in Early Performers.

3 Mr Custis] 'John Custis, Gent., formerly Page to the Prince', a beneficiary of Elizabeth Barry's estate: see R.G. Ham, *Otway and Lee: Biography from a Baroque Age* (1931), 181, 239.

4 Ld Rochester] John Wilmot (1647–80), second earl of Rochester, had been influential in establishing Elizabeth Barry as an actress.

5 Mrs: Barrys] Elizabeth Barry, the actress.

61 *To Mrs Frances Porter?*

1 Addressee and date] The addressee and date of this letter are unknown. Because it is preserved with other letters to the Porters, Hodges tentatively suggests Mrs Porter and, on the maturity of the handwriting, but as 'only a very wild guess', a date of 1717. His other suggestion of Lady Elizabeth Cromwell and a date between 9 November 1708 (Letter 45) and her death on 31 March 1709 is not impossible: perhaps only the reference to friars and nuns tells against it (see Letter 12 to Frances Porter).

15 Dr: Robinson] Hodges suggests Dr Tancred Robinson (1657/8–1748), physician in ordinary to George I and knighted by him in 1714. Having mentioned him once, Congreve then abbreviates to Dr:—.

24 Dr: Dunny] unidentified.

62 *To the Secretary of the Board of Trade*

1 Ashley] Ashley, Walton-on-Thames, was the country estate of Richard Boyle, Viscount Shannon, and not far distant from Pope's house at Twickenham. Letter 63 was written from there about a year later, and Congreve seems also to have spent some time there in 1719: see Letter 66 and notes to it below.

5 Lords Comrs:] the Lords Commissioners of Trade and Plantations, constituting the Board of Trade.

11 Mr. Page] Samuel Page, Congreve's deputy as Secretary of Jamaica; see Hodges, *Documents*, 130–1.

63 *To Edward Porter*

1 [November 1718?]] Mrs Jean Haynes has kindly supplied details of the will of William Draper, drawn up on 15 May 1718 and proved on 16 October 1718. Draper asks that his executors continue the lease of his house in Surrey Street and also the adjoining one in the possession of Edward Porter, held on lease from the Duke of Norfolk. Since Congreve intimates that Mrs Draper or the executors have still to come to a resolution, leaving in doubt the Porters' continued occupancy of the Surrey Street house, the present letter was probably written soon after the date on which Draper's will was proved.

64 *To Giles Jacob?*

0.1 Giles Jacob] As published in Wilson, *Memoirs*, the addressee of this letter is said to be Edmund Curll, but it is difficult to believe that the discreet and loyal Congreve would have had anything so friendly to say to him. Its true recipient was undoubtedly Giles Jacob (1686–1744) who actually edited *The Poetical Register*, 2 vols. (1719), as distinct from Curll who published it. The matter is of some importance because, if genuine and addressed to Jacob, the letter implies Congreve's endorsement of the account given of his own life and works. Jacob's prefatory remarks single out Congreve in warm tribute for his help and the title page of each volume bears, as epigraph, ll. 43–4 of Congreve's 'Epistle to Halifax'. Unlike most of Curll's, Jacob's own work is serious, tactful, and laudable.

There is some other evidence that Jacob was responsive to Congreve's opinion. It would seem that Dennis had written a letter dedicating the second volume of *The Poetical Register* to the Duke of Buckingham but that, having shown it to Congreve, Jacob suppressed it and wrote another himself. In a letter to Prior of 11 April 1721 Dennis noted that he had just been visited by 'a scribbler who told me that you and Mr. Congreve were mortally affronted at a letter writ to the late Duke of Buckingham and printed in the book about to be published'. On 18 May 1721 Jacob wrote to Prior: 'I have lately fallen out with Mr. Dennis, on account of inserting among his Letters a dedication to the Duke of Buckingham, designed for my *Lives of the Poets*, reflecting on the memory of Cowley, which you and Mr. Congreve both disapproved; but he says, they are all fools as pretend to find fault with it' (HMC: Calendar of the Manuscripts of the Marquis of Bath, [London, 1908], iii. 502–3). For Jacob's prefatory remarks and the account of Congreve, see Allusions, pp. 403–6.

65 *To Thomas Pelham-Holles, Duke of Newcastle*

For Newcastle see the note on Congreve's dedication to him of *The Dramatick Works of John Dryden*.

8 my Deputy] Samuel Page; see Letter 62.

8 one deputed by him] Hodges identifies him from a letter written by Governor Nicholas Lawes of Jamaica dated 28 April 1719: 'Some days agoe Mr. Daniel who acted as Secretary of this Island, died' (*Documents*, 133, citing NA: CO 138/16, p. 218).

66 *To Alexander Pope*

1 [Late summer 1719?]] The date is suggested by Sherburn (Pope, *Correspondence*, ii. 12–13). There is another undated letter from Ashley at L: Add. MS 4808, also printed by Sherburn (Pope, *Correspondence*, ii. 12; also in Hodges, *Documents*, 229). Although not strictly from Congreve himself, it was in effect written on his behalf by Richard Boyle, Viscount Shannon, probably some weeks before or after the present letter. It reads:

Ashley Thursday

Sir

By Candle light Mr Congreve wants a Scribe. He has not been well indeed, but will take the air your way to morrow morning. Don't let this be any restraint on you, for he is not Qualified for long visits. Since you were so kind to mention me in your letter, I hope you'll keep your promiss, and let me have the pleasure of seeing you here what day is most Convenient for you next weeke, and it will be a very great Satisfaction to Sir

your most humble
servant Shannon

8 Lady Mary] Lady Mary Wortley Montagu was at Twickenham during the summer of 1719 (Pope, *Correspondence*, ii. 12).

67 *To Thomas Pelham-Knowles, Duke of Newcastle*

1 [November 1719?]] The date suggested assumes that the performance of Southerne's play followed shortly after the writing of this letter. Newcastle was acting here in his capacity as Lord Chamberlain.

4 tragedy] Thomas Southerne's *The Spartan Dame* (1719), the preface to which records that '*This Tragedy was begun a Year before the Revolution, and near four Acts written*', but then laid by. He claims that nearly 400 lines were cut and in the printed text he marks those omitted when it was performed at Drury Lane on 11 December 1719.

68 *To Alexander Pope*

1 [1719–20?]] As Sherburn notes (Pope, *Correspondence*, ii. 27), Pope was completing his translation of the *Iliad* early in 1720 and used the verso of Congreve's letter for lines translated from Book XXIV.

2 spaw water] See Letter 69.

3 Dr Arbuthnot] John Arbuthnot (1667–1735), Congreve's physician. In September 1726 he wrote to Swift: 'I have been for near three weeks together every day at the Duchess of Malborrow's, w[ith] Mr Congreve who has been like to dye with a fever, & the gout in his stomach; but he is better, & like to do well' (Swift, *Correspondence*, iii. 28).

69 *To Alexander Pope*

13 [1720?]] The year is suggested by the probable date of Letter 68 and the reference therein to Pope's letter about spaw water.

70 *To Jacob Tonson*

2 Coll Congreve] Colonel William Congreve of Highgate, Congreve's cousin; see also Letter 9.

3 picture] by Sir Godfrey Kneller for the Kit-Cat collection made by Tonson; it is now in the National Portrait Gallery, London. For the 1723 copy, see Hodges, *Documents*, 136 n. 2.

71 *To Humphry Morice*

Humphry Morice (1671?–1731) was deputy governor of the Bank of England, 1725–6, and governor, 1727–8.

73 *To Alexander Pope*

1 [1727]] Sherburn (Pope, *Correspondence*, ii. 433) considers 1727 the most probable year. Hodges cites Pope's letter to Motte of 30 June [1727] which mentions books for 'Mr. Congreve at Bath', probably the first of the *Miscellanies in Prose and Verse* of 1727, a copy of which Congreve owned. See Pope, *Correspondence*, ii. 439.

21 My young Amanuensis] unidentified.

23 *ex quovis ligno*, &c] Sherburn (Pope, *Correspondence*, ii. 434) expands to '*Ex quovis ligno Mercurius non fingitur.*'

23 Mrs. R—'s] possibly Deborah Rooke, to whom Congreve bequeathed £100, his linen and apparel (see Hodges, *Documents*, 244, 254).

29 *Emetick*] Curll had evidently arranged through James Roberts the publication of *Court Poems*, Luttrell's copy of which is dated 26 March 1716, and implied Pope's, Gay's, or Lady Mary Wortley Montagu's authorship of them. Two days later Pope, troubled on his own or Lady Mary's behalf, met and drank with Curll. As Curll himself recalled it in *The Curliad. A Hypercritic upon the Dunciad Variorum* (1729), Lintot drank hock, Pope sack, and Curll himself 'an *Emetic* potion', after which he 'went home and *vomited* heartily'. Pope's own account is given in *A Full and True Account of a Horrid and Barbarous Revenge by Poison, on the Body of Mr. Edm. Curll* (1716). See Pope, *Correspondence*, i. 326; Ralph Straus, *The Unspeakable Curll* (1927), 51–3; and Maynard Mack, *Alexander Pope: A Life* (New Haven, 1985), 295–7.

EARLY EDITIONS AND
VARIANT READINGS

The order of the entries below follows that of the items as given in the present volume.

INCOGNITA

Editions collated: 92, 00, 13^1, 13^2

92 [Within double rules] *INCOGNITA:* | OR, | LOVE | AND | DUTY | RECONCIL'D. | A | NOVEL. | [rule] | *Licens'd* Decemb. 22. 1691. | [rule] | *LONDON,* | Printed for *Peter Buck*, at the Sign | of the *Temple*, near *Temple Bar* | in *Fleet-ſtreet*, 1692.
    12°: A^8 B–F^{12} G^4

Copy collated: CH: 102356 (copy text). Other copies examined: L: Ashley 449; O: 8° T.114.(3.) Art.; MH: *E C 65.C7605.692.

NB. Advertised in *L G* of 18–22 Feb. 1692, and again a year later in *T C* ii. 440 (Feb. 1693).

00 A COLLECTION | Of Pleaſant Modern | NOVELS. | [rule] | Vol. II. | [rule] | VIZ. | *Heroine Muſqueteer: Or Female Warrier,* | *in oſur* [*sic* for *four*] *Parts.* | *Incognito:* [*sic*] *Or Love and Duty Reconciled.* | By Mr. *Congrave.* | *The Pilgrim, in two Parts.* | [rule] | *LONDON,* | Printed for *Jacob Tonſon*, at *Grays-Inn-Gate*, and | *Richard Wellington*, at the *Dolphin* and *Crown* | at the Weſt-end of *St. Pauls* Church-yard: E. | *Rumbole*, at the *Poſt-houſe*, *Covent-Garden*, and | *J. Wild, at the Elephant*, at *Charing-Croſs.* | MDCC.

Copy collated: L: 12511.bb.8.(2.) (lacks general title; that above from copy at O). Other copies examined: LW: 2018.c.2; O: Vet.A3.e.1787.(2.); WF: C5149.

NB. Wellington published in 1699 *A Collection of Novels*, promising a second volume if the first was well received. Volume II, as above, appeared and was followed the same year by a third volume, the whole making *A Collection of Pleasant Novels* (3 vols., 1699–1700). Advertised in *TC* iii. 154 as 'By Mr. Congreve.' *Incognita* in this edition forms part (sigs. 2A1^r–2E7^v) of the second volume; leaf 2E8 carries the title to the succeeding novel, *The Pilgrim*. None of the copies seen of this edition includes the dedication or preface to *Incognita*. The half-title at sig. 2A1 reads:

INCOGNITA: | OR, | LOVE | AND | DUTY | RECONCIL'D. | [rule] | A | NOVEL. | [double rule] | *LONDON,* | Printed for *R. Wellington*, at the *Lute* in | St. Paul's Church-yard, 1700.

13¹ [Within double rules] *I N C O G N I T A :* | OR, | LOVE | AND | DUTY | RECONCIL'D. | A | NOVEL. | By Mr. CONGREVE. | *L O N D O N ,* | Printed for *R. Wellington* at the *Dolphin* and | *Crown* in St. *Paul's* Church-yard, 1713. | [Below rules at foot:] [fist] The Adventures of *Lindamira,* a Lady of | Quality, Written with her own Hand to her Friend | in the Country in 24 Letters, being a very enter- | taining Hiftory. Price 2*s*.
  12°: A⁸ B–F¹² G⁴

Copy collated: LVA: Dyce 2435 (16.E.10). Other copies examined: C: Williams 546 (lacks sigs. A2–A8); CLC: *PR3364/I31; WTu: REng/Congreve/Incog1713.

13² [As for 13¹ except:] . . . [fist] The Lovers Secretary: Or, The Adventures of *Lindamira,* | . . . written . . . entertaining Hiftory. | Price 2*s*.
  8°: A⁶(-A6) B–F⁸ G⁴ (-G4)

Copy collated: LVA: Dyce 2435 (16.E.11). Other copies examined: MH: *EC65/ C7605/692ic (lacks sigs. A2–A5); TxU: PFORZ/199/HRC; PR3364/I5/1713/ HRC; Y: Ik/C760/692c (G2 precedes G1).

NB. 13² might more accurately be described as collating: 8°: A⁸(-A6, 7, 8 = G², *H*1) B–F⁸ G² *H*1. A3ʳ is unsigned, but A3ᵛ is signed A3. The Dyce copy contains as frontispiece an engraved portrait of Congreve taken from Kneller's Kit-Cat Club painting. It is identical with that engraved much later for the *Universal Magazine* for J. Hinton and was clearly tipped in when the volume was rebound.
  The two 1713 printings (12° and 8°) are from the same setting of type with the exception of some headings, including headlines, and advertisements. Errors retained and corrected indicate that the 12° was printed first. The standing type, respaced, realigned, and rejustified to the longer measure, was then reimposed in 8° (hence the 12° misprint 'gene- | nerally' becomes 8° misprint 'genenerally' on A4ʳ). Following the dedication in the 12° issue is a full page (A4ᵛ) of advertisements; these are not present in the 8° reissue (reimpression). Likewise G4ᵛ in the 12° issue contains several advertisements different from those that follow the text of the 8° reissue. The latter may represent an informal intention to provide a companion volume to W1. There was a further printing of *Incognita* in Wilson, *Memoirs,* Part II, pp. 65–124. One of Curll's catalogues of about 1730–1, p. 4, describes it as '*The Adventures of Three Days*' (O: Harding C105).

Variants

Dedication
27 *C L E O P H I L*] *C L E O P H I I* 13.

Preface
  2 *tho'*] *though* 13.
  7 *generally*] *gene-* | *nerally* 13¹; *genenerally* 13².
  49 **forcing*] 13; *force-* | *ing* 92, 00.

Text

  0.3 &] and oo, 13.
  0.4 RECONCIL'D.] ∼∧ 13¹.
  7 Splendour] Splendor oo.
  10 Memory] Momory oo.
  18 sometimes . . . sometimes] somtimes . . . somtimes oo.
  70 proclaimed] proclaim'd 13.
  71 before] beforr 13¹.
  71 *Santa*] *Sante* oo.
  74 work∧] ∼, oo.
  94 early∧] ∼, oo.
  107 for,] ∼∧ oo.
  115 *who∧] 13; ∼, 92, oo.
  121 the] a 13.
  128 Lodging∧] ∼, oo.
  128 returned,] retuned∧ oo.
  140 Complementing] Complimenting 13.
  143 Controversie] Controversy 13.
  144 *Gentleman] Gentlemen 92.
  151 profit∧] ∼, oo.
  151 so] and so 13.
  157 performed] preformed 13.
  169 *darkness, about] Brett-Smith; ∼. About 92, oo, 13.
  184 *digress] 13; degress 92, oo.
  185 self,] ∼∧ oo; ∼; 13.
  190 entering] entring oo.
  192 turn.] ∼! oo.
  194 Cavaliers] Caviliers oo.
  210 fansy'd] fancy'd 13.
  215 *them, they] Brett-Smith; ∼. They 92, oo; ∼: ∼ 13.
  235 recovered] recover'd 13.
  236 and,] ∼∧ 13.
  256 him,] hrm, oo; ∼∧ 13.
  266 ye∧] ∼, oo.
  267 Person∧] ∼, oo
  288 Signior] Siginor oo.
  296 observe,] ∼∧ oo.
  299 you∧] ∼, oo.
  302 own] *om.* oo.
  302 all∧] ∼, oo.
  305 Lady,] ∼∧ W2 oo.
  313 How?] ∼! oo.
  317 readily:] ∼; oo.
  318 Room∧] ∼, oo.
  321 wit∧] ∼, oo.
  334 judgment.] ∼: oo, 13.

369 afterward] aftewards oo.
370–1 He∧ ... rest∧] ~, ... ~, oo.
371 workmanship∧] ~, 13.
372 him∧] ~, oo.
375 *Florence*∧] ~, oo.
387 *Atalanta*] *Atalante* oo.
405 *Leonora's] oo; *Leonara*'s 92.
431 defeated:] ~; 13.
435 *Fabio*] *Fabian* oo.
441–2 Friend, ... believ'd,] ~, ... ~∧ oo; ~; ... ~, 13.
449 chillness] chilness 13.
456 eagerly] eargerly oo.
459 handsomely] handsomly oo.
469 consent∧] ~, oo.
520 violently∧] ~, oo.
526 rest∧] ~, oo.
531 a shift] shift 13.
542 throughly] thoroughly 13¹; tho-/rowly 13².
545 *Wound] oo; would 92.
554 *Leonora*∧] ~, oo, 13.
555 that∧] ~, oo.
555 power∧] ~, oo.
559 *Hippolito*∧] ~, 13.
565 *Aurelian*∧] ~, oo.
569 orders] order oo, 13.
572 Gameing] Gaming 13.
578 *Lorenzo*∧] ~, oo.
578 surviv'd, or∧ ... death∧] ~; or, ... ~, oo.
595 Net∧] ~, oo.
596 worse∧] ~, oo.
597 Body:] ~; oo.
602 rendred] render'd oo.
604 unforced] unforc'd oo.
613 Commendation;] ~: oo.
616 Complement] Compliment 13.
628 rareties] rarities 13.
656 extreamity] extremity oo.
661 heartily,] ~∧ oo.
668 *Face.] oo; ~∧ 92.
684 Atome] Attome oo.
696 untill] until oo, 13.
700 which,] ~∧ oo.
709 pains;] ~: oo.
737 Charms∧] ~, oo.
742 enjoin] enjoyn oo.
743 *Incredulity.] oo; ~∧ 92.

767 stoop'd] stop'd oo.
781 him,] ~∧ 13.
792 *Pallace] 13¹; Ballace 92, oo; Palace 13².
796 Surgeons∧] ~, oo.
823 Servant∧] ~, oo.
841 them,] ~∧ oo.
847 *Aurelian*] *Aurelean* 13.
847 Friend,] ~; oo.
851 Vulgar] Vulger oo.
870 in;] ~: oo.
871 *Cupid] *italic in* 92.
882 worthy] worth oo.
882 thee;] ~: 13.
916 though] tho' 13.
922 mistake,] ~; oo.
926 acquainted,] ~; oo.
927 *Adventures,] oo; ~; 92, 13.
955 Equipage] Equiqage 13.
957 Alarm.] ~: oo, 13.
964 *Superscription∧] ~. 92, oo, 13.
995 *design'd*] *designed* 13.
1009 *welcom*] *welcome* 13.
1012 *Heaven's*] oo; *Heavens* 92, 13.
1029 deferring] defer-/ing 13¹.
1035 Handkerchief] Handkercheif 13.
1049 Extremity] Extreamity oo.
1052 Destined] Destin'd oo.
1064 suddain] sudden oo.
1064 dextrous] dexterous 13.
1097 Man,] ~∧ 13.
1129 *suppose,] Brett-Smith; ~∧ 92, oo, 13.
1150 Habits] Habit 13.
1163 Badge∧] ~, oo, 13.
1164 Lilies] Lillies 13.
1166 Crest] Chrest oo.
1175 that] which 13.
1184 carry'd] carried oo.
1185 *it,] Jeffares; ~; 92, oo, 13.
1187 *Competition*, they] Jeffares; ~. They 92, oo, 13.
1197 begged] begg'd 13.
1198 the Insolence of] *om.* oo.
1206 Error,] ~; oo.
1208 bare] bear 13.
1208 bare∧headed] ~-~ oo.
1212 Combate] Combat oo.
1218 sought] fought oo, Brett-Smith, Dobrée, Jeffares.

1225 handsomely] handsomly oo, 13.
1225 it is] 'tis oo.
1226 *Duke,] oo; ~ₐ 92, 13.
1227 Ladyₐ] ~, oo.
1236 soundedₐ] ~, oo.
1236 Course:] ~. oo.
1244 Stirrups] Stirrops oo.
1246 *Catharina*] *Catherina* oo.
1251–2 theyₐ ... discoveredₐ] ~, ... ~, oo.
1302 Signiors] Signior's 13.
1304 *Aurelian*ₐ] ~, oo.
1324 *Catharina*ₐ ... Ladies;] *Catherina*, ... ~: oo.
1326 Duke's ... aloudₐ] Dukes ... ~, oo.
1332 confirmed] confirm'd oo.
1341 Rallery] Raillery oo.
1347 though] tho' 13.
1351 presenceₐ] ~, oo.
1374 *tooₐ] ~. 92, oo, 13.
1378 *Loveₐ] ~. 92, oo, 13.
1385 Lovesₐ] ~, oo.
1394 *Lethargy] Brett-Smith; Lithargy 92, oo, 13.
1397 *Aurelian*ₐ] ~, oo.
1416 Moments] Moment's oo.
1419 Ladyₐ ... stayₐ] ~, ... ~, oo.
1424 pieces] peices 13.
1426 *Fabio*] *Fobio* oo.
1437 *whenₐ *Hippolito*,] ~, ~ₐ 92, oo, 13.
1443 a] the 13.
1453 them,] ~ₐ oo.
1467 Alarum'd] Alarm'd 13.
1507 *Restraintₐ] ~. 92, oo, 13.
1522 Sword,] ~ₐ oo.
1541 Ground;] ~ₐ oo.
1547 Villain] Villian 13.
1563 delivered.] ~, 13.
1578 *Siena?*] ~! oo.
1580 endeavoured] endeavour'd 13.
1586 lateₐ] ~, oo.
1588 themₐ] ~, oo.
1604 of] if oo.
1605 sit] set 13.
1623 *Vertueₐ] ~. 92, oo; Virtue. 13.
1628 *Thoughtsₐ] ~. 92, oo, 13.
1633 *continuanceₐ—] ~.—92, oo; ~.ₐ 13.
1640 choaked] choacked oo.
1646 Condoleance] Condolance 13.

1654 grief.] ∼, 13.
1654 fansy'd] fancy'd 13.
1657 Ball,] ∼∧ 00.
1658 confess] confess'd 00.
1666 *Temper∧] ∼. 92, 00, 13.
1669 *Inclinations∧] ∼. 92, 00, 13.
1675 Brother∧] ∼, 00.
1680 *Monastery] 00; Monastry 92, 13.
1691 Monastery] Monastry 13.
1694 with] whit 13¹.
1696 Monastery] Monastry 13.
1698 Honour,] ∼∧ 00.
1712 not] nor 00.
1713 nor] not 00.
1719 Monastery] Monastry 13.
1727 Monastery] Monastry 13.
1728 of?] ∼; 00.
1735 *Night∧] ∼. 92, 00, 13.
1749 happy] hapyy 13.
1752 Monastery] Monastry 13.
1753 her,] ∼; 13.
1763 wandered] wandred 13.
1779 answered] answer'd 13.
1782 *seems,] 13; ∼∧ 92, 00.
1783 *Lorenzo∧] ∼, 13.
1784 Garden∧] ∼, 00.
1793 return'd] returned 13.
1805 Monastery] Monastry 13.
1810 well-grown] ∼∧∼ 13.
1812 Boughs∧] ∼, 13.
1814 *Hollow] Brett-Smith; Hallow 92, 00, 13.
1848 slipped] sliped 13¹.
1895 misled] mis-led 00.
1896 Flame,] ∼∧ 00.
1898 Beams∧] ∼, 00.
1904 *Forsake∧] ∼. 92, 00, 13.
1907 Heart∧] ∼, 00, 13.
1908 *Vows∧] ∼. 29, 00, 13.
1909 say;] ∼: 00.
1910 ere] e're 00.
1911–12 Love; ... recal] ∼: ... recall 00.
1912 banish'd] banished 13.
1912 *Reason∧—] ∼.—92, 13; ∼.∧ 00.
1926 Men,] ∼; 00.
1927 disturb'd] disturbed 13.
1934 *Confusion. At] ∼, at 92, 00, 13.

1943 proved prevailing:] ∼ ∼. oo; prov'd ∼: 13.
1959 withal] withall oo.
1963 Garden;] ∼, oo, 13.
1969 Life∧ ... those] ∼, ... these oo.
1974 Daughter∧] ∼, 13.
1983 continued] continu'd oo.
1988 *unknown] 13; unknow 92, oo.
1992 now-to-be-forgotten] ∼∧∼∧∼∧∼ 13.
1996 feeling] fatal oo.
2008 *took] Brett-Smith; shook 92, oo, 13.
2012 *Condition;] Brett-Smith; ∼, 92, oo, 13.
2028 toward] towards 13.
2034 deceived] deceiv'd 13.
2037 ingenuously] ingeniously 13.
2045 up∧] ∼, 13.
2063 *Apparel;] ∼, 92, oo, 13.
2064 *Father,] ∼; 92, oo, 13.
2068 forgive∧] ∼, 13.
2094 happy] happpy oo.
2112 Rarety] Rarity 13.
2128 deprived] depriv'd 13.
2131 awakened] awakend oo; awaken'd 13.
2135 reconciled] Reconcil'd 13.
2138 over-joy'd] overjoy'd oo.

Concerning Humour in Comedy

96 *Letters upon several Occasions. Published by Mr. Dennis.* For Sam. Briscoe, 1696. Sigs. F8ᵛ–G8ᵛ. Copy text: C: Syn.7.69.125.

NB. Letters upon several Occasions was advertised in *LG* of 12–16 December 1695. Congreve's letter was reprinted in *Familiar and Courtly Letters to Persons of Honour and Quality,* by Mons. Voiture, 3rd edn., 2 vols. (1701), i. 69–85 (Part III, Letters of Friendship); in *Familiar Letters of Love, Gallantry, and Several Occasions, by the Wits of the Last and Present Age,* 2 vols. (1718), i. 152–63; in *The Select Works of Mr. John Dennis,* 2 vols. (1718), ii. 514–25; in *A Treatise upon the Usefulness of Eloquence,* by the late Archbishop of Cambray [i.e. Fénelon, François de Salignac de la Motte] (1722), i. 69–85; and in Wilson, *Memoirs,* Part II, pp. 41–57. It was further reprinted by Corbyn Morris in *An Essay towards fixing the true Standards of Wit, Humour, Raillery, and Ridicule* (1744), 66–75.

Variants

 19 *unpremeditated] unpremediated 96.
 31 *Humour∧ is,] ∼, ∼∧ 96.
 78 *with] with 96 [turned 't' in 96].
113 *People.] ∼∧ 96.

221 *written] writte 96.
285 *Stronger] Sronger 96.
301 *Judgment] Judg-|men 96.
308 *too] to 96.

Amendments of Mr. Collier's False and Imperfect Citations

98 [Within double rules] A M E N D M E N T S | O F | *Mr.* C O L L I E R'*s* | *Falſe and Imperfect* C I T A T I O N S , &c.

From the { OLD BATCHELOUR, | DOUBLE DEALER, | LOVE for LOVE, | MOURNING BRIDE.

[rule] | [in black letter:] By the Author of thoſe Plays. | [rule] | *Quem recitas meus est ô Fidentine Libellus,* | *Sed male dum recitas incipit eſſe tuus.* | Mart. | *Graviter, &* *iniquo animo, maledicta tua pate-* | *rer, ſi te ſcirem Judicio magis, quam morbo animi,* | *petulantia iſta uti. Sed, quoniam in te neque mo-* | *dum, neque modeſtiam ullam* *animadverto, reſpon-* | *debo tibi: uti, ſi quam maledicendo voluptatem* | *cepiſti, eam* *male-audiendo amittas.* | Saluft. Decl. | [rule] | *L O N D O N ,* | Printed for *J. Tonſon* at the *Judge's Head* in *Fleet-ſtreet,* | near the *Inner-Temple-Gate,* 1698.

8°: A^2 B–C^8 D^8(± D6) E–H^8 I^4.

Copy text: WTu (2nd state). Other copies examined: (1st state) W F : C5844; C N : Case V.18.180715; (2nd state) DFM (copy 1); L: 641.e.6; Ashley 450 (has cancellans and cancellandum at D6); MH: *EC65.C7605.698a (lacks A1); C H : 120488 (lacks A1); CLC: *PR3364/A51; (3rd state) DFM (copy 2); L: Ashley 451; C: Y.9.46; C H : 120487 (lacks A1); C L C : *P R 3364/A51/1698b (lacks A1); W F : C5844a.

NB. As the C N copy came from the library of the Duke of Leeds, it may be that listed in the catalogue of Congreve's library and therefore his own copy. Unfortunately it bears no inscriptions to confirm the inference.

There are two settings of the title page: the first has a simple brace and reads '*o* *Fidentine*' and '*quem morbo*' (sometimes corrected in MS); the second has a hollow brace, reads '*ô Fidentine*', and has been corrected to read '*quam morbo*'. The first is found in both first- and second-state copies. Otherwise the states may be readily but not conclusively grouped as follows:

1st state: A1^v blank; title page with simple brace; no errata on A2^v; D6 uncancelled.

2nd state: A1^v blank; either title page; two errata on A2^v; cancel at D6.

3rd state: A1^v advertisement accounting for the cancellation of D6; title page with hollow brace; three errata on A2^v; cancel at D6.

Page numbers 71–80 are repeated and appear not to have been corrected, but apart from the cancel at D6 the signature sequence is undisturbed. When reprinted in Charles Wilson's *Memoirs of the Life, Writings, and Amours of William Congreve, Esq.* (1730), the text was presented as a series of eight separate letters described as written to Walter Moyle. The first such letter is dated 'Jul. 14, 1697' but no others are dated. As Collier's preface to *A Short View* is dated '*March 5th*. 1697/8.', and as the *Memoirs* itself carries a prefatory date of '*Bath, July* 14, 1729' the letter-form and any datings are certain to be equally spurious. *Amendments* was next reprinted, together with Congreve's letter to Dennis 'Concerning Humour in Comedy', in *The Dramatic Works of William Congreve Esq; 2* vols. (1773)

Variants

**om.*] ADVERTISEMENT. | AN Oversight in reading *Superstition* for supposition in Mr. *Collier*'s Book, *p.* 64. occasion'd a Mistake in a small Number of these Amendments, which were first Printed off; but in the remainder of the Impression, the Remark grounded on that Mistake is omitted, Care being taken to have that Leaf re-printed. 98 (3rd state).

Title page

10   *ô Fidentine] *o* ∼ 98 (lst setting).
14   *quam] *quem* 98 (1st setting).

Text

**om.*]   ERRATA. | Page 7. line 23. for *worst* read *worse*; p. 105. | l.13. read *Pantomimes*. 98 (2nd state); *so also* 98 (3rd state) *except* '*Pantomimes*, p. 107. l. 3. r. *Cynetha*.'.
52   *Profaneness] Profaness 98.
104   *worse] 98 *errata*; worst 98.
248   **Bossu's*] *Bossus's* 98.
267   *commune] *commun* 98.
336   *Profaneness] *Profaness* 98.
342   *Profaneness] Profaness 98.
352   *Profaneness] *Profaness* 98.
367   Profaneness] Profaness 98.
382   *Profaneness*] *Profaness* 98.
534   Profaneness] Profaness 98.
565   *Iniquity] *Iuiquity* 98.
642   *Supposition*] 98 (2nd state); *Superstiti-|on* 98 (1st state).
645   contrary?] 98 (second state); ∼? I am Civiller to him; I take his Sense as he would have it understood; Though his Expression is exquisite Nonsense: and I humbly conceive he may mean, that *a Belief in Providence is a ridiculous Superstition*, when he says that *Providence is a ridiculous Superstition* 98 (1st state).
686   **Mell.*] Well. 98.
696.1 n. *64] 62 98.
696.1 n. *82] 12 98.

754 *then] than 98.
766 *says *Pineda . . .* Chap.] *roman and italic reversed in* 98.
805.1 n. *658] Summers; 659 98.
855 *conceal] co conceal 98.
881 *be] be | be 98.
1031 *He] he 98.
1190 *BUT$_\wedge$] ~. 98.
1202 *repeat$_\wedge$] ~. 98.
1206 *see$_\wedge$] ~. 98.
1215 *on$_\wedge$] ~. 98.
1217 *kept] kep't 98.
1251 *Man$_\wedge$] ~. 98.
1433 *Top-Lady] ~=~ 98.
1466 *Say-grace] ~=~ 98.
1486 *Top-Ladies] ~=~ 98.
1530 *tender-hearted] ~=~ 98.
1564 *above-mentioned] ~=~ 98.
1618 *Self-sufficiency] ~=~ 98.
1683 *Play-house] ~=~ 98.
1761 *Pantomimes] 98 errata; Partomimes 98.
1764 *Infancy] Infaney 98.
1785 *the Ruin] the the Ruin 98.
1785 *Cynetha] 98 errata; Cy- | nethia 98.
1797 *Institutions] Summers; Institution 98.
1824 *Gun-Powder-Tresason] ~=~-~ 98.
1825 *Gun-Powder] ~=~ 98.
1826 *False-Witnesses] ~=~ 98.

The Tatler. No. 292

10 [Black letter:] Numb. 292 | The Tatler. | [rule] | By *Ifaac Bickerftaff* Efq;. . . . From *Saturday February* 17. to *Tuefday February* 20. 1710. Copy text: L: Burney 147.b. (No variants.)

Dedication of *The Dramatick Works of John Dryden*

17 *The Dramatick Works of John Dryden, Esq.* 6 vols. For J. Tonson, sold by R. Knaplock, W. Taylor, W. Mears, J. Browne, W. Churchill, E. Symon, J. Brotherton, 1717. Vol. I, sigs. a1^r–a12^r. Copy text: DFM; Other copies collated: L: 643.b.2; 11771.aaa.4. (No variants.) Macdonald 109 a i.

NB. Evidently printed late 1717 and published early 1718. It was advertised in the *Daily Courant* for 27 January 1718 ('This Day is published, a neat Elziver Edit. in 12mo'), and again on 29 January and 10 February (as 'Just published'). Reissued (with cancel title leaf) as printed for J. Tonson, and sold by J. Brotherton and W. Meadows, 1718. Copy at O: Don.f.110. Macdonald 109 a ii. Unrevised reprints were published in 1725 and 1735.

The Game of Quadrille. An Allegory

Editions collated:

29 *Mr. Congreve's Last Will and Testament, With Characters of his Writings. . . . To which are added. Two Pieces, viz. I. Of rightly Improving the present Time. An Epistle from Mr. Congreve to the Right Honourable Richard Lord Viscount Cobham. II. The Game of Quadrille. An Allegory.* For E. Curll, 1729. Sigs. E3^v–F1^v. L: 1416.e.47 (copy text).

30 *Mr. Congreve's Last Will and Testament.* 2nd edn. For E. Curll, 1730. Sigs. A8^v–B1^v. L: 275.g.15.(2.).

NB. The copy of the second edition cited at L: 275.g.15.(2) also contains another copy of the first edition; both are bound with *Memoirs of the Life, Writings, and Amours of Mr. William Congreve, Esq.* By Charles Wilson, 1730.

The bibliography is slightly complicated. Congreve died on 19 January 1729. Some few weeks afterwards, Curll published the first edition of *Mr. Congreve's Last Will and Testament* with a title leaf (29 above). He advertised it in the *Monthly Chronicle*, ii. 95 (listed at 16 April 1729), and also in the *Monthly Catalogue*, no. lxxii (April 1729), p. 41. It includes on F1^v the following advertisement:

> *There is now in the Press,*
> MISCELLANEOUS ESSAYS and Familiar Letters. By
> *William Congreve,* Esq; To which will be prefix'd, Memoirs
> of his Life, Writings, and Amours. By *Charles Wilson,* Esq;

This announcement provoked the following comment in the *Daily Post* of 29 April:

> Whereas it has been advertised by E. Curl, that there is now in the Press, Miscellaneous Essays, and familiar Letters; by William Congreve, Esq; To which will be prefix'd, Memoirs of his Life, Writings and Amours, by Charles Wilson, Esq:
> This is therefore to inform the Publick, that Mr. Congreve's Life &c. will be publish'd with all possible Speed from Authentick Papers, by a good Hand sufficiently authorised. To which will be added, an Account of his Works already printed, as well as of his Posthumous Writings, of which no other Person can have any Memoirs relating thereto.

The next day Curll inserted in the same paper (repeating it on 5 and 16 May) the following postscript to his advertisement of books he had published (including *Mr. Congreve's Last Will and Testament*):

> The anonymous Advertiser in the *Daily Post* of Yesterday, who modestly stiles himself, *a good Hand, sufficiently authorized to write* Mr Congreve's Life; is hereby desir'd to take Notice, that Familiar Letters and Essays, written by that

Gentleman, (of which the originals are in Mr Curll's Custody, to satisfy any Person who has a sufficient Authority to inquire) arc in great Forwardness at the Press, and will be publish'd in about a month.

CHA. WILSON

Great-Russel-street, Bloomsbury, 29th April, 1729.

No copy of the *Memoirs* dated 1729 is known to survive, yet a first edition (first issue) was evidently published by 11 August when the following notice appeared in the *Daily Journal*:

> This Day is published, (In Opposition to all ridiculous Messages and Threatenings)…[*Memoirs*, &c.]…P.S. I hope (in the Preface to these Memoirs) I have given a just and full Answer to the Messages of a certain Physician, and the Inquiries of a certain Lady concerning them.
>
> *Honi soit qui Mal y pense.*

CHARLES WILSON.

Wilson's preface makes it clear that the physician was Arbuthnot ('*one Dr.* A*** *a* Scot') and probable that the lady ('*to whom Mr.* Congreve *bequeath'd a handsome Legacy*' and for whom the publication of intimate details of her relationship with Congreve would have been most embarrassing) was Henrietta, Duchess of Marlborough, although a copy at O: G.P.339(5) extensively annotated in a contemporary hand implausibly identifies her as 'Probably Mrs Bracegirdle'. Davies also assumed that she was Anne Bracegirdle, who 'interested herself so far in his reputation as to demand a sight of the book in MS. This was refused. She then asked by what authority his life was written, and what pieces contained in it were genuine? Upon being told, there would be several of his essays, letters, &c. she answered, "Not one single sheet of paper, I dare say"' (iii. 340).

Wilson's statement of 11 August was repeated in the *Daily Journal* four times during that month and in a shortened form again on 5 November. Publication of the *Memoirs* is also noted in the *Monthly Chronicle*, ii. 185 (listed at 11 August 1729), and also in the *Monthly Catalogue*, no. lxxvi (August 1729), 90–1. Further confirmation of a 1729 edition of the *Memoirs* may be found in the annotated copy at O: G.P.339(5), in which a manuscript note on the title page reads: 'Pub$^{d.}$ in August, 1729, with Curl's name in the title-page.' It must have been available before 23 August 1729 when Mrs Pendarves advised her sister 'not to buy Congreve's life; only hire it, for it is very indifferently done' (*The Autobiography and Correspondence of Mary Granville, Mrs. Delany*, ed. Lady Llanover (London, 1861), i. 212). Since publication had been delayed until mid-August 1729, Curll must have decided to date the first edition (first issue) 1730.

A new issue of *Memoirs* in which sheets B–E were reset was advertised on 13 January 1730. This resetting can be quickly identified by the addition of the following note on B1^r: '*While at School, he gave several Instances of his Genius for Poetry; but the most peculiar one was, a very pretty Copy of Verses which he made upon the Death of his Master's* Magpye.' The first edition of *Mr. Congreve's Last Will and Testament* (dated 1729 and collating: 8°: *A*1 B–E⁴ F⁴(-F4)), was reissued with the first edition (first issue) of *Memoirs*. A completely reset second edition of

Mr. Congreve's Last Will and Testament (collating: 8°: A^8–B^4 and with some redisposition of the contents) was published in 1730 together with the second issue of the *Memoirs*. C H : 120486, for example, is a copy of the *Memoirs* with the first setting of sheets B–E and first edition of *Mr. Congreve's Last Will and Testament* (1729); whereas sheets B–E are reset in C H : 120485, a reissue of the *Memoirs* containing also a copy of the second edition of *Mr. Congreve's Last Will and Testament* (1730).

Several of the above details are reported and considered by J.P.W. Rogers, 'Congreve's First Biographer: The Identity of "Charles Wilson"', *Modern Language Quarterly*, 31 (1970), 330–40.

John Almon published a version of 'The Game of Quadrille' in *The New Foundling Hospital of Wit. Part the Fourth* (1771), p. 93. It is misdated 1716 (for 1726), it is attributed to Congreve with misplaced confidence, and its text is grossly corrupt.

Variants

    0.1–.2 The . . . A L L E G O R Y.] *from the title page of* 29.
    6 believes,] ~$_\wedge$ 30.
    25 *Bellies,] 30; ~$_\wedge$ 29.
    27 call'd] called 30.
    27 oblig'd] obliged 30.
    28 Discourse,] ~; 30.
    35 *Bouts] 30 ('bouts'); *om.* 29.
    45 *Jurat. Coram*] ~$_\wedge$ *coram* 30.
    48 *Literally] 30; *Litterally* 29.
    49 *Allegorically*,] ~$_\wedge$ 30.

LETTERS

Where possible the letters have been edited from the autograph manuscripts and their exact spelling, punctuation, capitalization, and abbreviated forms (but not their lineation nor superior letters) reproduced. Where a manuscript has not been seen or is not known to survive, the text has been given from the printed version considered to be closest in form to that of the autograph. Later unauthoritative versions are not recorded; and apart from Letter 2, where the manuscript forms are directly in question, other editors' readings are not noted unless a variant has some claim to explain or correct error.

A document dated 2 October 1716 but recorded as a letter by M.P. Alexeyev, 'British Manuscripts in Russia', *TLS* (21 September 1946), 456, is in fact a warrant to pay over dividends on South Sea stock. Only the signature is autograph. It is in the collection of Count G.V. Orlov, now housed in the State Historical Museum, Moscow: fond N166 (Orlov), delo 19, doc. N125.

By far the greater number of the letters given below were written to Joseph Keally. George-Monck Berkeley notes that these, and perhaps other manuscripts, 'were addressed to a very near relation of mine; at the death of whose only daughter, which happened lately, they came into the possession of my relation Mr Mason, from whom I received, and to whom I now inscribe them . . .'

(Berkeley, p. xi). As Lynch explains (*Gallery*, 24), the only daughter was Elizabeth, who died unmarried on 8 January 1783, and the 'Mr Mason' was John Monck Mason (1726–1809), grandson of her maternal uncle, George Monck, and one of the executors of her estate. Berkeley was the great-grandson of Rebecca Monck Forster, a sister of Keally's wife. For Keally's marriage to Elizabeth Monck, see Letter 37.

Addresses and dates are discussed in the notes to the text. Printed sources and earlier editions are cited as follows:

Berkeley: George-Monck Berkeley, *Literary Relics*. London, 1789.

Dennis: *Letters upon Several Occasions* [by Dryden, Congreve, *et al.*], ed. John Dennis. London, 1696.

Dobrée: William Congreve, *The Mourning Bride, Poems, & Miscellanies*, ed. Bonamy Dobrée. London: Oxford University Press, 1928.

Familiar Letters: *Familiar Letters of Love, Gallantry, and Several Occasions*, vol. 1. London: Printed for Sam. Briscoe, 1718.

Hodges, *Documents*: *William Congreve: Letters & Documents*, collected and ed. John C. Hodges. London: Macmillan, 1964.

Memoirs: *Memoirs of the Life, Writings, and Amours of William Congreve, Esq.*, comp. Charles Wilson. London: printed for E. Curll, 1730.

Pope: *The Works of Alexander Pope, Esq.*, vol. v: *Containing an Authentic Edition of his Letters*. 2nd edn. London: printed for T. Cooper, 1737.

Summers: *The Complete Works of William Congreve*, ed. Montague Summers. 4 vols. London: Nonesuch Press, 1923.

Copy texts

1 Autograph MS. L: Add. MS 4293, f. 56.
2 Autograph MS. Y: Osborn Collection. 8.365.
3 Autograph MS. NYPL: Berg Collection.
4 *Familiar Letters*, i. 82–3.
5 Dennis, 99–103.
6 Autograph MS. NYPL: Berg Collection.
7 Dennis, sigs. *i2^v–*i3^v.
8 Autograph MS. L: Add. MS 4264, f. 335.
9 Autograph MS. NYPL: Berg Collection. Facsimile in Lynch, *Gallery*, 32–3.
10 Berkeley, 320–1.
11 Autograph MS. L: Add. MS 4293, ff. 61–2.
12 Autograph MS. L: Add. MS 4293, ff. 59–60.
13 Berkeley, 322–4.
14 Autograph MS. The Earl of Home, The Hirsel, Coldstream, Berwickshire. Copy held by Scottish Record Office: RH 1/2/490(1).
15 Berkeley, 317–19.
16 Berkeley, 324–7.
17 Autograph MS. The Earl of Home, The Hirsel, Coldstream, Berwickshire. Copy held by Scottish Record Office: RH 1/2/490(2).
18 Autograph MS. Library of the Historical Society of Pennsylvania.

19 Berkeley, 328–9.
20 Autograph MS. Pierpont Morgan Library: MS MA3388. Purchased at Sotheby's 14 March 1979 (lot 326). Facsimile in *British Literary Manuscripts. Series I from 800 to 1800*, ed. Verlyn Klinkenborg, Herbert Cahoon, and Charles Ryskamp (New York: Pierpont Morgan Library in association with Dover Publications, 1981), no. 68. The letter sold by Sotheby's 28 May 1934 (lot 188, described as 'A.L. 1 p. 4 to, *Decr. 14th* 1702' with '*signature and three words cut away*') is almost certainly the same, despite the date. The address and postmark are from that part of the autograph manuscript in NYPL: Berg Collection.
21 Autograph MS. Library of the Historical Society of Pennsylvania. Facsimile in Hodges, *Documents*, 109.
22 Autograph MS. L: Add. MS 4265, f. 19.
23 Berkeley, 332–4.
24 Berkeley, 331.
25 Berkeley, 336–8.
26 Autograph MS. The Earl of Home, The Hirsel, Coldstream, Berwickshire. Copy held by Scottish Record Office: RH 1/2/490(3).
27 Berkeley, 339–40.
28 Berkeley, 340–1.
29 Berkeley, 342–3.
30 Berkeley, 335–6.
31 Berkeley, 380–3.
32 Berkeley, 366–7.
33 Autograph MS. L: Add. MS 70,949, f. 43. Facsimile in Sotheby Sale Catalogue (Lot 479 in sale of 16 March 1937).
34 Berkeley, 344–6.
35 Berkeley, 346–7.
36 Berkeley, 347–8.
37 Berkeley, 354–5.
38 Berkeley, 349–51.
39 Autograph MS. The Earl of Home.
40 Berkeley, 355–7.
41 Berkeley, 358–9.
42 Berkeley, 360.
43 Berkeley, 361.
44 Berkeley, 362–3.
45 Autograph MS. The Earl of Home.
46 Berkeley, 364–5.
47 Autograph MS. NYPL: Berg Collection.
48 Autograph MS. Pierpont Morgan Library: R–V Autogrs. Misc. English. Facsimile in *British Literary Manuscripts. Series I from 800 to 1800*, no. 68.
49 Berkeley, 371–2.
50 Berkeley, 372–3.
51 Berkeley, 373–4.
52 Autograph MS. Humanities Research Center, Austin, Texas.

53 Berkeley, 370–1.
54 Autograph MS. L: Add. MS 39,311, ff. 5–6.
55 Berkeley, 376.
56 Berkeley, 377.
57 Berkeley, 378.
58 Berkeley, 379–80.
59 Autograph MS. L: Add. MS 4293, ff. 57–8. Facsimile in T.J. Brown, 'English Literary Autographs XXI: William Congreve, 1670–1729', *The Book Collector*, 6 (1957), facing p. 61.
60 Autograph MS. L: Add. MS 4293, f. 64.
61 Autograph MS. L: Add. MS 4293, f. 63.
62 Autograph MS. NA: C.O. 137/12, no. 72.
63 Autograph MS. L: Add. MS 4293, ff. 54–5.
64 *Memoirs*, pp. xv–xvi.
65 Autograph MS. L: Add. MS 32,685, ff. 47–8.
66 Autograph MS. L: Add. MS 4808, f. 191^v.
67 Autograph MS. L: Add. MS 32,685, f. 49.
68 Autograph MS. L: Add. MS 4808, ff. 192^v, 193^v.
69 Autograph MS. MH: bMSEng870(29).
70 Autograph MS. WF: MS C.c.1.(6.).
71 Autograph MS. Bank of England.
72 Autograph MS. Bank of England.
73 Pope v. 239–40. From copy at O: 12.Theta.1279.

Variants and emendations

2.2 Dr Mr:] *Dr. Mr.* Summers.
2.9 if] If Summers.
2.15 *provided] Dobrée, Hodges; printed Summers.
2.17 Cant] Summers, Dobrée; can Hodges.
2.19 dr:] dr. Summers.
2.20 yr:] Yr. Summers.
2.21 ffriend] friend Summers.
2.21 snt] srnt Summers.
5.21 *here.] ~, Dennis.
7.45 *October] Dobrée, Hodges; August Dennis; *om.* Summers.
15.30 *Rowe] Summers, Dobrée, Hodges; Love Berkeley.
15.32 *Burnaby] Summers, Dobrée, Hodges; Burnaly Berkeley.
16.12 *Purcel] Hodges ('Purcell'); Russel Berkeley, Summers, Dobrée.
16.29 *Pontacq] Hodges; portico Berkeley, Summers, Dobrée.
17.6 a manner] manner Hodges.
18.16 Travers] Fraser Berkeley, Summers, Dobrée.
20.13 *rescri[bas attamen ipse]] Berkeley; re< ... > MS.
20.15 *[Yrs: | Will: Congreve]] Berkeley ('Yours, | WILL.CONGREVE.'); *om.* MS. 23 priory] Privy Summers.
23.17 *clear] Dobrée, Hodges; clever Berkeley, Summers.
23.41 *Fairborn] Hodges; Fairholm Berkeley, Summers, Dobrée.

26.3 dillask] flask Berkeley, Summers, Dobrée.

32.1 *1705] Hodges; 1708 Berkeley, Summers, Dobrée.

33.4 heard] learned Berkeley, Summers, Dobrée.

34.17 *Ld] Hodges; Dr Berkeley, Summers, Dobrée.

36.15 *Mosca] Mosea Berkeley.

38.22 *[not] *om.* Berkeley, Summers, Dobrée, Hodges.

38.26 mumelled] mumbled Summers.

39.1 Feb: 7th:] *Feb.* 9 Berkeley, Summers, Dobrée.

47.17 TidComb] Aidcomb Berkeley, Summers, Dobrée.

53.9 *Ossy] Summers, Hodges; Offy Berkeley, Dobrée.

63.5 Monday] Monday I Dobrée.

ATTRIBUTIONS

In a letter to Horace Walpole of c.10 May 1762, George Montagu wrote: 'for your pains I have sent you two little songs and a very raw [sc. rare] piece of Congreve that I picked up in Dublin. They were wrote by his own hand, and were amongst many verses that he used to send over to a friend of his there, and a vast collection of his letters I had not time to read, but am to have if ever I go over again' (Walpole, *Letters*, x. 28). The friend was presumably Joseph Keally.

Montagu's distinction between 'two little songs' and 'a very raw piece' might be taken to imply that the latter was a prose squib, possibly 'The Game of Quadrille. An Allegory', which was to resurface a few years later in John Almon's *The New Foundling Hospital for Wit. Part the Fourth* (1771). While the letters were in due course printed by George-Monck Berkeley, the extreme rarity of any autograph manuscripts of Congreve's poems suggests that these must have been destroyed. Even the 'two little songs' sent to Walpole seem not to have survived. What they were like may be inferred from Walpole's reply to Montagu of 25 May 1762, in which he reported an exchange over breakfast between Charles Townshend and his wife Lady Dalkeith: 'Well, my dear, I am going out of town for a day or two; this is a busy time, be upon your guard, let nothing come out here (pointing to his mouth) and nothing go in here (pointing between his thighs).' Walpole then adds: 'By the verses you have sent me, I think, Congreve would have done very well to rhyme Charles's conjugal apostrophes' (*Letters*, x. 33).

Verses on the Death of his Master's Magpye

In the variant state (2nd setting) of Wilson, *Memoirs*, sig. B1^r, a note to the word *Kilkenny* reads: '*While at School, he gave several Instances of his Genius for Poetry; but the most peculiar one was, a very pretty Copy of Verses which he made upon the Death of his Master's* Magpye.' Copy at O: G.P.339(5). The story is repeated by Theophilus Cibber, *Lives of the Poets* (1753), iv. 84. The verses are not known to survive.

Verses written at Tunbridge Wells, on Miss Temple

The following poem is printed and attributed to Congreve in John Almon's *The New Foundling Hospital for Wit. Part the Fourth* (1771), 91–2. It is followed by an inferior version of 'The Game of Quadrille. An Allegory' (93–4) and by Congreve's 'Letter to Cobham' (95–8), which is attributed to Pope. The same poem (with slightly variant text) is also attributed, perhaps more reliably, to Thomas D'Urfey on a song sheet of c.1710–12: 'The Three Goddesses or the Glory of Tunbridge Wells. The Words by Mr Durfey, Made to a Tune of M^r [John] Barretts'; copy at O: Harding Mus. G.41 (6).

WRITTEN AT TUNBRIDGE WELLS, ON
MISS TEMPLE,
AFTERWARDS LADY OF THE LATE
SIR THOMAS LYTTELTON.
BY MR. CONGREVE.
NOT IN THE WORKS OF THAT POET.

L E A V E, leave the drawing-room,
Where flow'rs of beauty us'd to bloom;
The nymph that's fated to o'ercome,
　　Now triumphs at the Wells.
Her shape, and air, and eyes;
Her face, the gay, the grave, the wise,
The beau, in spite of box and dice,
　　Acknowledge, all excels.

Cease, cease, to ask her name,
The crowned muse's noblest theme,
Whose glory by immortal fame,
　　Shall only sounded be.
But if you long to know,
Then look round yonder dazzling row,
Who most does like an angel show,
　　You may be sure 'tis she.

See near those sacred springs,
Which cure to fell diseases brings,
(As ancient fame of Ida sings)
　　Three goddesses appear!
Wealth, Glory, two possest;
The third with charming beauty blest,
So fair, that heav'n and earth confest
　　She conquer'd ev'ry where.

Like her, this charmer now
Makes ev'ry love-sick gazer bow;
Nay, e'en old age her pow'r allow,
　　And banish'd flames recal.
Wealth can no trophy rear,
Nor glory now the garland wear:
To beauty ev'ry Paris here
　　Devotes the golden ball.

Prologue by Sir John Falstaff

On 8 January 1700 Prior wrote to Abraham Stanyan to say that 'To-morrow night
Batterton [*sic*] acts Falstaff, to encourage the poor house the Kit Katters have taken

one side-box, and the Knights of the Toast have taken the other. We have made up a Prologue for Sir John in favour of eating and drinking, and to rally your toasts, and I have on this occasion four lines upon Jacob. We will send you the whole Prologue when we have it together' (cited from Historical Manuscripts Commission: *Calendar of the Manuscripts of the Marquis of Bath*, iii [1908], 394). Prior's allusion to 'Kit Katters' seems to be the earliest that names them.

Henry IV. With the Humours of Sir John Falstaff. A Tragi-Comedy, advertised in *LG* for 13–16 May 1700 as 'Revived, with Alterations', had been adapted by Betterton. Villiers Bathurst, writing to Arthur Charlett, 28 January 1700, noted that it had 'drawn all the town, more than any new play that has bin produced of late; which shews that Shakespeare's wit will always last: and the criticks allow that Mr Betterton has hitt the humour of Falstaff better than any that have aimed at it before' (*LS*, pt I, pp. 522–3, citing G. Thorn-Drury, *More Seventeenth Century Allusions to Shakespeare*, [London, 1924], 48).

Prior's letter to Stanyan makes it possible, though by no means certain, that Congreve as one of the Kit Cats contributed some lines to the prologue. It was indeed Prior who, in *Alma*, later referred to Dan Congreve's view that 'Pudding and Beef make Britons fight'. In his essay 'Concerning Humour in Comedy' Congreve had noted their addiction to flesh 'and the Grossness of their Diet in general', and the recurrence here of Sir Sampson's phrase 'Body o' me', a possible echo of Congreve's then imminent *WW* IV. xiv. 3 ('what a washy Rogue art thou'), and his skill at writing toasts, might perhaps suggest his hand in ll. 5–25 of the prologue. See Lynch, *Tonson*, 195, and the note to ll. 350–1 of 'Concerning Humour in Comedy'. The text, not published in the quarto of 1700, is given here from *Wit and Mirth: or, Pills to Purge Melancholy. The Second Part* (1700), 313–14. It was reprinted in *Songs Compleat, Pleasant and Divertive* (1719–20), iii. 337–8.

PROLOGUE, *By Sir* John Falstaff.

SEE *Britains*, see, one half before your Eyes,
Of the Old *Falstaff*, lab'ring to arise:
Curse on the strait-lac'd Traps, and *French* Machines,
None but a Genius can ascend these Scenes.
5   Once more my *English* Air I breath again,
And smooth my double Ruff and double Chin.
Now let me see what Beauties gild the Sphere;
Body o' me, the Ladies still are Fair;
The Boxes shine, and Galleries are full.
10   Such were our *Bona Roba's* at the *Bull*:
But Supream *Jove*! what washy Rogues are here!
Are these the Sons of Beef and *English* Beer?
Old *Pharaoh* never dream'd of Kine so Lean;
This comes of meagre Soop, and sowre Champeign.
15   Degenerate Race, let your old Sire advise, ⎫
If you desire to fill the Fair one's Eyes, ⎬
Drink Unctuous Sack, and emulate my Size. ⎭

Your half-flown Strains aspire to humble Bliss,
And proudly aim no lower than a Kiss;
Till quite worn out with acting Beau's and Wits,   20
Your all sent crawling to the Gravel-pits;
Pretending Claps, there languishing you lie,
And like the Maids, of the Greensickness die:
The Case was other when we rul'd the Roast,
We Robb'd and Ravish'd, but you Sigh and Toast.   25
    But here I see a side-Box better lin'd,   ⎫
Where old plump *Jack* in Miniature I find,   ⎬
Tho they're but Turnspits of the Mastiff kind.   ⎭
Half-bred they seem, mark'd with the Mungrel Curse,
Oons, which amongst you dare attempt a Purse?   30
If you'd appear my Sons, defend my Cause,
And let my Wit and Humour, meet Applause:
Shew you disdain those nauseous Scenes to taste,   ⎫
Where *French* Buffoon's like honest *Switzer* drest, ⎬
Turns all good Fellowship to Farce and Jest.   ⎭   35
Banish such Apes, and save the sinking Stage,
Let Mimicks and squeaking Eunuchs feel your Rage;
On such let your descending Scourge be try'd;
Preserve plump *Jack*, and banish all beside.

Verses to Charles Montagu, Lord Halifax

Below the title of the following verses at L: Add. MS 69,968, ff. 102^r–102^v, are the
words, in a different hand, 'made by Congreve'. This attribution, the only
evidence for Congreve's authorship, is implausible and may result from a later
confusion of these verses with Congreve's genuine epistle dedicating his poems to
Halifax. As Montagu was created Baron on 13 December 1700 and William died
on 8 March 1702, the poem was probably written in 1701, either before the
charges calling for his impeachment in April or in his defence against them.

'To ye R^t honourable Charles Mountague Ld Hallifax'

Sound Fame! Soar aloft and Proclaime
The Glories of Mountagues Name
        The Muses and Graces agree
                This is he
        The fittest Theme for Harmony
        Within ye verge of Poetry
Why then should not Mellodious Sound
Send soe much worth the World around?
        Apollo now [holds *del.*] takes up his Lire
        To join the humble earthly Choire
For what can better please the God
        Then soe much Greatness

> Soe much Goodness
>   Told abroad.
> Then lett the soft Flute
> All harsh Musick confute
> Bring the Harpsicord too
>   Join the trebles and base
> That Musick may shew
>   To what heights she can [rise *del.*] raise
>   When desert she would [prize *del.*] praise
> Lett the Trumpett and Voice
> In Loud Triumph rejoice
>   And in Extasie Sing
>   This is he
> That the best could deserve
> And the truest can Serve
>   Both the State and the King
> Then why Should not Merritt & Honour appear
>   Join'd by One
> Who never knew wrong, as he never knew Fear
> Lett Hallifax then with his Master agree
> To disapoint France & Sett Europe Free

Toasting Verses

While Tonson's attribution to Congreve of four toasting verses published in *The Fifth Part of Miscellany Poems* (1716) justifies their inclusion with the main body of his poetry, three others may also be his. As printed, there are several pairs of toasts in which the name of the author is given for the first but not the second. The typography implies that both are to be so attributed and that Congreve, to whom Tonson attributed the first of the two toasts addressed to each of Mrs Brudenell, Mrs Digby, and Mrs Kirk, may have also written the second. They probably date from sometime before November–December 1701. Exceptionally for such doubtful works, full details of their early publication and variants are here given below each set of verses.

Mrs. BRUDENELL.

> Imperial *Juno* gave her matchless Grace,
> And *Hebe*'s youthful Bloom adorns her Face;
> Bright as the Star that leads her Heav'nly Host,
> *Brudenell* precedes the Glory of the Toast.

Editions collated: L: Add. MS 40,060, f. 37^r. 04^1. *The Toasters Compleat. With the last Additions.* Printed in the Year, 1704. Sig. B2^r. O: Firth c. 2 (8). 04^2 *Poems on Affairs of State, From the Year 1640. to the Year 1704.* Vol. III. Printed in the Year, 1704. Sig. 2D2^r. O: Douce P. 466. 16 *The Fifth Part of Miscellany Poems.*

For Jacob Tonson, 1716. Sig. D7^v. O: 2805.f.554. Case 172(5)(b). (Copy text.)
The carelessness of the manuscript version is evident in the reading 'Phoebus' for
'*Hebe*'s' in l. 2, Hebe not only being female but the daughter of Juno. So too in l. 4
MS 'proceeds' is less apposite than 'precedes' to the parallel with Venus, who
habitually appears before the other stars and planets.

Variants:
0.1 B R U D E N E L L] B—ll 04^1; *Brudenel* 04^2.
2 *Hebe*'s] Phoebus MS *Hebes* 04.
2 Face;] ~: 04^1.
3 the Star . . . her] the Stars that lead the MS. a Star . . . her 04^1; the Star . . . the 04^2.
3 Heav'nly] Heavenly 04^1. 4 *Brudenell*] B—ll 04^1; *Brudenel* 04^2.
4 precedes] proceeds MS, 04^1.

Mrs. D I G B Y.

> No wonder Ladies that at Court appear,
> And in Front-Boxes sparkle all the Year,
> Are chosen Toasts; 'twas *Digby*'s matchless Frame
> That, *Cæsar*-like, but saw and overcame.

Editions collated: MS L: Add. MS 40,060, f. 39^r. 04^1 *The Toasters Compleat.
With the last Additions.* Printed in the Year, 1704. Sig. B1^v. O: Firth c. 2 (8). 04^2
Poems on Affairs of State, From the Year 1640. to the Year 1704. Vol. III. Printed
in the Year, 1704. Sig. 2D1^r. O: Douce P. 466. 16 *The Fifth Part of Miscellany
Poems.* For Jacob Tonson, 1716. Sig. D8^v. O: 2805.f.554. Case 172(5)(b).
(Copy text.)

Variants:
0.1 D I G B Y] D—y 04^1.
3 Toasts;] ~, 04^1.
3 *Digby*'s . . . Frame$_\wedge$] *D—y*'s . . . frame, 04^1.
4 That, *Cæsar*-like,] ~, ~$_\wedge$ 04^1; ~$_\wedge$ ~$_\wedge$ 04^2.

Mrs. D I. K I R K.

> So many Charms *Di. Kirk* surround,
> 'Tis pity she's unkind;
> Her conqu'ring Eyes, not seeing, Wound,
> As Love darts home, tho' blind.

Editions collated: MS L: Add. MS 40,060, f. 37^r. 04^1 *The Toasters Compleat. With
the last Additions.* Printed in the Year, 1704. Sig. B2^r. O: Firth c. 2 (8). 04^2 *Poems
on Affairs of State, From the Year 1640. to the Year 1704.* Vol. III. Printed in the
Year, 1704. Sig. 2D1^v. O: Douce P. 466. *The Fifth Part of Miscellany Poems.* For
Jacob Tonson, 1716. Sig. D10^r. O: 2805.f.554. Case 172(5)(b). (Copy text.)

Variants:
0.1 D I. K I R K] D. K—k 04^1; *Di- Kirk* 04^2.
1 *Di. Kirk*] Di. K—k 04^1; *Di- Kirk* 04^2.
2 pity] pitty 04^1.

3 Eyes,... seeing,] ∼∧ ... ∼∧ 04¹, 04².
4 home, tho'] ∼∧ tho' 04¹; ∼, tho∧ 04².

A Satyr Against Love, 1703

The attribution of this poem to Congreve rests solely on L: MS Sloane 3996, ff. 46ʳ–46ᵛ, which consists of the first 47 lines and is endorsed 'b. Congreve.', and on the published text of the complete poem of 350 lines:

[Within double rules] A | S A T Y R | A G A I N S T | L O V E. | [rule] | *Revis'd and Corrected* | By Mr. C O N G R E V E. | [rule] | *Invicta gerit tela Cupido.* Sen. Trag. | [rule] | *L O N D O N :* | Printed in the Year, 1703. 2⁰: *A*² B–D².

Foxon S43. Luttrell's copy (CLC: *fPR3364.S21) bears the date '26. June.' The only other evidence worth considering is Congreve's explicit assurance that '*he never saw or heard of any such Verses before they were so Printed*'. This occurs in his prefatory note to *The Tears of Amaryllis*, which was written soon after the death of the Marquess of Blandford on 20 February 1703 but not published until 2 July, the date entered in Luttrell's copy (CLC: *fPR3364.T21). His reasons for having it printed at all are given in his prefatory note to the reader and in a letter to Tonson of 1 July: Tonson's nephew had told Congreve 'of Copies that were dispersed of the Pastoral & likely to be printed so we have thought fit to prevent 'em and print it our selves' (Letter 21). As his prefatory note makes clear, he was the more anxious to do so because of the publication a few days before of *A Satyr Against Love* and the use of his name on it.

The above facts are judiciously presented by John Barnard in 'Did Congreve Write *A Satyr Against Love?*', *Bulletin of the New York Public Library*, lxviii (1964), 308–22. His conclusion is that '*A Satyr Against Love* ought to be relegated to poems ascribed to Congreve on doubtful authority.' His account includes an edition of the version printed in 1703, the first 47 lines of which are collated with the manuscript.

Prologues to *Love for Love*

Two prologues were printed in Q1 *LL*: the first 'For the Opening of the new Play-House, propos'd to be Spoken by Mrs. *Bracegirdle* in Man's Cloaths' and 'Sent from an unknown Hand'; the second by Congreve and spoken by Betterton 'at the opening of the New House'. But there were at least one and possibly three others.

(a) When Betterton's company played *LL* in the tennis-court at Oxford on 5 July 1703, Joseph Trapp wrote *A Prologue to the University of Oxford. Spoke by Mr. Betterton* specially for the occasion. Copy at O: Don. b. 15 (18). It was reprinted a fortnight later in *The Players turn'd Academicks* (1703). Written just when Vanbrugh was acquiring the site for the Queen's Theatre, some lines are not without their point for his and Congreve's aspirations:

> Now to our wish, we have an Audience found,
> Which will be pleas'd with Sence as well as Sound:
> You only can Reform th'unthinking Age,
> Redeem our credit lost, and dignify the Stage...

Then rise! *Athenians!* in the just defence
Of Poetry Opprest, and long neglected Sence;
The Reputation of our Art advance,
Suppress the exorbitance of Song and Dance,
And in one powerful party Conquer France;
Nor have we Vicious entertainment brought,
You safely may Approve, and Smile without a fault. ...

(b) *LL* was acted for the benefit of Mrs Bowman at Lincoln's Inn Fields on 1 June 1704 'With a new Prologue' and 'Several new Songs by Mrs. Hodgson. A New Song by way of Ballad, perform'd by Mr. Bo[w]man, call'd *The Misses' Lamen tation for want of their Vizard Masks in the Play-house*' (*LS*, pt 2, p. 67). The author of this prologue is unknown and no copy of it has been located.

(c) *LL* was acted for the benefit of Thomas Betterton on 7 April 1709. Wilson, *Memoirs*, 11, says: 'There was a Prologue suitable to the Occasion wrote by Mr. *Congreve*, and spoken by Mrs. *Bracegirdle*, and an Epilogue by Mr. *Rowe*, spoken by Mrs. *Barry*. The former was never printed, but the latter, being the justest Compliment that could be paid to Mr. *Betterton*, was publish'd at the Time ... '. *The History of the English Stage* (1741) observes that 'a *Prologue* written by Mr. *Congreve* was, on this Occasion, spoken by Mrs. *Bracegirdle*; and an *Epilogue*, written by Mr. *Rowe*, was spoken by Mrs. *Barry*. The *former* the Public were not obliged with but the latter was printed and dispersed in the House the very Night it was spoken' (pp. 119–20). *A Compleat List of all the English Dramatic Poets*, appended to Thomas Whincop's *Scanderbeg*, says that 'Mr. *Congreve* wrote a Prologue for Mr. *Betterton*'s Night, which was spoke by Mrs. *Bracegirdle*, but never printed' (p. 176). The occasion is described in *Tatler* 1, 12 April 1709, but the prologue is not mentioned. No more is known of Congreve's new prologue.

Rowe's epilogue was printed in 1709 together with the 1695 prologue to *LL* sent 'from an unknown Hand' and printed in Qq but not in Ww. They appear side by side on a single broadsheet, 'for *J. Smith* near Fleetstreet. 1709.' Foxon C377. Copy at MH. Rowe's epilogue was also printed alone as an octavo half-sheet: *Epilogue Spoken by Mrs. Barry, April the 7th, 1709. At a Representation of Love for Love: For The Benefit of Mr. Betterton At His leaving the Stage* (For E. Sanger and E. Curll, 1709). Price 2*d*. Advertised in the *Daily Courant* of 13 April. Foxon R287. Copies at L: 11634.bbb.13 (1); CT: H.7.85(18); MB: Defoe 28.52 no. 11; MH: TS 107.14.50. It was reprinted in *Poetical Miscellanies: The Sixth Part* (1709), 570–2, as 'By Mr. Rowe'. Copy at O: 85 b.20. It was also included in Rowe's *Poems on Several Occasions* (1714), 32–5. Copy at L: 11643.bbb.20 (1).

The History and Fall of the Conformity Bill, 1704

Bills for preventing occasional conformity passed the House of Commons on 7 December 1703 and 14 December 1704, but neither was enacted. As noted by Ellis, *POAS* vii. 3, the present poem was written not only to oppose proposals to prevent occasional conformity by dissenters but to support the low church bishops in the Lords whose votes defeated such proposals. A manuscript copy, 'The History and fall of the Conformity Bill being an excellent New Song to the tune of the Ladys fall &c', is at L: Add. MS 40,060, ff. 41^r–45^r, where it is attributed to a Robert Wisdom and a date suggested of January 1704. The only evidence for Congreve's authorship is Pope's copy of *A New Collection of Poems relating to State Affairs* (1705), iii. 425, which bears his annotation, 'Certainly written by Mr. Congreve' (L: C.28.e.15). Lynch, *Tonson*, 56, accepts Pope's word for the attribution. For the numerous other manuscript copies, see *POAS* vii. 627–8. Foxon M32 records a printed copy, undated but inferred to be 1704 (it is at MH: *EBB7). Like other items from Add. MS 40,060, it was also printed in *Poems on Affairs of State, From 1640. to this present Year 1704.* Vol. III (1704), 425–31. The tune is variously given as 'the Ladys fall' or 'Chivy-Chase', different titles for the same popular setting. The poem was partially reprinted as Mainwaring's in Oldmixon's *The Life and Posthumous Work of Arthur Mainwaring* (1715). Ellis, *POAS* vi. 5, cites Oldmixon's comment at p. 40 that 'Mr. Mainwaring was the Author of it.' The Robert (or Robin) Wisdom to whom five manuscripts and two printed editions attribute it may have been a pseudonym for Mainwaring.

Monsieur de Pourceaugnac, Or, Squire Trelooby, 1704

Congreve, Vanbrugh, and Walsh together made a free translation of Molière's *Monsieur de Pourceaugnac* which was advertised in the *Daily Courant*, 30 March 1704 and performed that day at LIF. Writing to Keally on 20 May 1704, Congreve confirms that Vanbrugh and Walsh also 'had a part in it. Each did an act of a French farce. Mine, and I believe theirs, was done in two mornings; so there can be no great matter in it. It was a compliment made to the people of quality at their subscription music, without any design to have it acted or printed farther' (Letter 25). In the same letter he notes that Anne Bracegirdle was to have it acted again the following week for her benefit. *Roscius Anglicanus*, 49, referring perhaps to the revival there on 28 January 1706, enters it among plays performed a year later at the new theatre in the Haymarket: '*Trelooby a Farce*, Wrote by Captain *Vantbrugg*: *Mr. Congreve* and *Mr. Walsh*, *Mr. Dogget* Acting *Trelooby* so well, the whole was highly Applauded.' James Ralph, in his preface to *The Cornish Squire* (1734), also attributes it to the same three writers, adding 'so great were the Expectations from it, that the Pit and Boxes were laid together at Half a Guinea, and the Gallery at a Crown'. A few weeks after the first performance a distinct translation of the same play was published (the preface is dated 19 April and the quarto was advertised in the *Daily Courant* for 21 April):

Monſieur de Pourceaugnac, | OR, | Squire Trelooby. | Acted at the | Subſcription Muſick at the *Theatre Royal* | IN | *Lincoln's-Inn-Fields. March* 30. 1704. | By Select COMEDIANS from both Houſes. | [rule] | Done into Engliſh from a Comedy of *Moliere*'s, which | was made and perform'd at *Chambord* for the Diverſion | of the *French* King, in the Year 1679. | [rule] | *Lector faſtidioſus ſibi moleſtus.* | [rule] | *LONDON*, | Printed for *William Davis*, at the *Black Bull* againſt the | *Royal Exchange*, and *Bernard Lintott*, at the *Middle-* | *Temple* Gate in *Fleetſtreet*. 1704. | Price 1s.6d. (Copies at L: 841.c.7.(10); CLC: *PQ1838/ M72E/1704.)

As Hodges has shown, 'The Authorship of *Squire Trelooby*', *RES* iv (1928), 404–10, the translator of this version was Ozell, who acknowledged his identity and reprinted the 1704 text in *The Works of Monsieur de Molière*. 6 vols. For Bernard Lintott, 1714. Lintott was Ozell's regular publisher; and as Hodges also notes, Nichols, *Literary Anecdotes of the Eighteenth Century* (London, 1812–15), viii. 299, lists *Squire Trelooby* among plays sold to Lintott by Ozell. In his preface to the 1704 edition Ozell admits his dependence on the stage version, a point confirmed by Congreve in his letter to Keally, but maintains that the text itself is new—and a more complete translation: 'The Author of the following Sheets has to acquaint the Reader that they contain an entire Translation . . . and design'd for the English Stage, had he not been prevented by a Translation of the same Play, done by other Hands, and presented at the New Play-House the 30*th* of last Month.' The claim that he had been forestalled is disingenuous: in fact Ozell almost certainly made his own translation simply to capitalize on the success of the stage version. As Congreve told Keally, 'somebody thought it worth his while to translate it again, and print it as it was acted: but if you meet such a thing I assure you it was none of ours . . .'. Ozell was indebted to the acting version for his title, characters' names (in particular, Trelooby), a contemporary allusion in III. vii (*'On my Conscience I believe he has whipt her'*), a prologue by Garth, and an epilogue, unascribed but 'Spoken by Mrs. *Bracegirdle*'. He even printed the cast-list which, besides Anne Bracegirdle, included Mrs Prince, Doggett, Johnson, Betterton, Cibber, Pinkeman, and Pack.

'When I was told the great Names concern'd in the exhibiting of it to so glorious an Assembly,' Ozell writes, 'and saw what Choice was made of the Comedians . . . I presently resolv'd upon the Publication of it.' He felt further justified in doing so because the stage version 'omitted the long Debate of the two Doctors in the eighth Scene of the first Act entirely; and also the eleventh Scene of the second Act, between *Trelooby* and the Lawyers; which being noted, I think I have justify'd the Title Page of this Play, wherein I say, acted at the Playhouse in *Lincoln's-Inn* Fields, *&c.* . . . '. He tactfully added that he had been 'assured (after due Inquiry made) that their Translation was not likely to be printed, tho' there have been great Demands made for it, by the whole Town, who have taken up with wrong Conceptions of it as it was acted; some thinking it was a Party-Play made on Purpose to ridicule the whole Body of *West-Country* Gentlemen, others averring that it was wrote to expose some eminent Doctors of Physick in this Town.'

Some support for the suggestion that the version performed was indeed topically satirical is found in one further comment by Ozell: 'at the end of the last Act, where *Tradewell* is wondring how his Daughter comes to be so fond of *Trelooby*; in the Original he says, *C'est un Sortilege qu'il lui ait donné*, Sure he has giv'n her a Philtre or Love-Potion; whereas in that Translation which was play'd on our Stage, *Tradewell* is made to say, *On my Conscience I believe he has whipt her*; alluding to a certain whipping Story now in every Body's Mouth, whether true or no I sha'n't examine, nor what the Resentments of the Audience were upon it, but the Expression *mov'd* 'em sufficiently.'

In his letter to Keally of 20 May 1704 (Letter 25) Congreve also notes that the piece would be staged again the following week as a benefit for Anne Bracegirdle.

This performance took place on 23 May, and there was another for Mrs Lee on 6 June with music as performed for Her Majesty on her birthday (*LS*, pt 2, pp. 67–8). The play was given further performances at the Queen's Theatre, Haymarket, on 28, 29, and 31 January and 1, 4, and 18 February 1706, with yet another announced (but deferred) for 22 April. When advertised on its revival in 1706 it was said to have an 'entirely new' last act, probably by Vanbrugh (*LS*, pt 2, p. 115).

Who wrote which act? *The Tryal of Skill: or, A New Session of the Poets* (8 August 1704) gives the first act to Congreve. Walsh is said to have chosen 'the best *Act* of the Play', though 'He knew not which *Act* was the best of the Three' (see Allusions, p. 370).

The play was revived again in January 1734 as *The Cornish Squire* and given another six performances. The text, edited by James Ralph, was published as:

THE | CORNISH *SQUIRE* | A | COMEDY. | As it is Acted at the | THEATRE-ROYAL in *Drury-Lane*, | By His MAJESTY's Servants. | [rule] | Done from the *French* by the late | Sir *JOHN VANBRUGH*. | [rule] | [orn.] | *LONDON:* | Printed by J. WATTS at the Printing-Office in | *Wild Court* near *Lincoln's-Inn Fields*. | [rule] | MDCCXXXIV. | [Price One Shilling and Six Pence.]

Copy at L: 641.d.6. On 1 January 1733–4 Ralph had received twelve guineas from John Watts 'for the whole, and sole Right of the Copy of a Comedy call'd the Cornish Squire' (L: Add. MS 38,728, f. 181).

Despite the claim on its title page that *The Cornish Squire* was wholly by Vanbrugh, Ralph concedes in his preface that Vanbrugh was believed to have written it 'in conjunction with Mr. *Walsh* and Mr. *Congreve:* Each of them being suppos'd to have done an Act a piece.' He adds that 'Tradition says the Book, was taken from the Play-house, after the Run was over . . . I have heard likewise there are other copies in other Hands . . . This was sent to me by a Gentleman, who has had it in his Library several Years . . . 'Tis true it had the Disadvantage of being imperfect in some Places; but these Omissions I have endeavoured to supply in the best manner I could, and have, over and above, taken the Liberty to set aside some incidental Jokes . . . Some Inelegancies at the end of the First Act are likewise alter'd, as being judg'd an Offence to Decorum, and the present delicate Taste of the Age.'

John B. Shipley, 'The Authorship of *The Cornish Squire*', *Philological Quarterly*, 47 (1968), 145–56, has argued that Ralph's *The Cornish Squire* 'would seem to represent the state of the Walsh–Congreve–Vanbrugh manuscript following Vanbrugh's revision of the play in 1706' (156). This view has, however, been persuasively contested by Graham D. Harley, '*Squire Trelooby* and *The Cornish Squire*: A Reconsideration', *PQ* 49 (1970), 520–9, who demonstrates Ralph's dependence not only upon Ozell's version but upon *Squire Lubberly* as published in *Select Comedies of Mr. de Molière* (1732). Although on the face of it Ralph's edition takes us closer than any other to the version first performed, there is no way of knowing whether the manuscript referred to by Ralph (and avowedly defective) was one of the original 1704 version or that of 1706, as revised by Vanbrugh and therefore possibly also influenced by Ozell's published version. If the first version of the first act was in fact by Congreve, Ralph makes it clear that he has further altered it by removing 'Some Inelegancies at the end of the First Act'. On the evidence we have,

Congreve's contribution is irrecoverable; indeed, as Hodges concludes, 'It is doubtful whether any extant play represents the work of Congreve, Vanbrugh, and Walsh.'
    There is, however, one possibility that a text by Congreve survives in the 1704 quarto
of Ozell's translation, namely the unattributed epilogue 'Spoken by Mrs. *Bracegirdle*'. In
his preface Ozell refers to 'two Lines I remember in their Prologue, *viz.*

> *But if to Day some Scandal shou'd appear,*
> *Let those precise Tartuff's bind o're* Moliere.'

As these lines appear in the prologue by Garth which, together with the epilogue,
Ozell prints, and as neither prologue nor epilogue has a source in Molière, they
must derive directly from the version performed on 30 March. Gosse thought the
epilogue in its present form 'evidently from the hand of Congreve' (*Life of
Congreve* (1888), 150). The evidence is wholly circumstantial, although ll. 5–6
do echo the concluding lines of *OB*. It might also be recalled that Garth wrote the
prologue and Congreve the epilogue for *The Loves of Ergasto*, performed as the
opening production at the new theatre in Haymarket a year later. As printed in
1704 the epilogue reads:

EPILOGUE.
Spoken by Mrs. *Bracegirdle*.

> H *A S T Y as Plants in* China, *was this Play,*
> *Which set at Night, are at full growth next Day;*
> *The World by this important Project sees,*
> *Confederates can dispatch if once they please;*
> *They shew you here what ills attend on Life,*
> *And all for that vexatious Whim a Wife.*
> *What World of Woes a wretched Wight surround,*
> *By* Bantlings *baited, and by* Duns *dragoon'd;*
> *By* Bullies *bastinado'd; teaz'd by* Cracks;
> *Wheadled by* Rooks, *and masacred by* Quacks:
> *Such Myriads of new Mischiefs still in Store*
> *That his successful Rival scarce has more.*
> *Beauty it seems in those blest Days cou'd warm;*
> *At least an Heiress never fails to charm.*
> *Lay-men make Love, as Church-men Zeal commend,*
> *Heaven's their Pretence, but Bishopricks their End;*
> *Thus you our Persons study to purloin,*
> *And worship not the Image but the Coin.*
> *But know, vain Men, your Passion we return,*
> *Not for large Wigs, but large Estates we burn.*
> *Your ways we find, but ours you'll ne'r foresee,*
> *Decypher if you can, we keep the Key.*
> *Let* Asian *Wives their blind Obedience own,*
> *And twenty share what's scarce enough for one.*
> *In different Climes, we different Customs see,*

Incest with us is Indian *Charity.*
Grace at Geneva *Heresie at* Rome;
And Plots in France *fine Politicks at home.*
Our English *Beauties shall their Right maintain,*
No Salick *Laws in Love's Dominions Reign;*
In vain to Sovereignty you aim to rise,
You'll ne'er depose the Tyrants in our Eyes.

On Charles Sackville, sixth earl of Dorset

V. Sackville-West, *Knole and the Sackvilles* (1923), 141, reports Congreve as having visited Dorset during his final illness in 1706 and as later saying: 'Faith, he slabbers more wit dying than other people do in their best health.' N.W. Wraxall, *The Historical and Posthumous Memoirs of Sir Nathaniel William Wraxall, 1772–1784*, ed. H.B. Wheatley, 5 vols. (1884), iii. 137, attributes a similar comment to Prior: 'Lord Dorset is certainly greatly declined in his understanding, but he drivels so much better sense now than any other man can talk, that you must not call me into court as a witness to prove him an idiot.'

Unio; On the Union, 1707

In Latin and English. Attributed to Congreve in University of Leeds, Brotherton Collection, MS Lt. 87, f. 82: 'On the Union. By Mr Congreve. 1707'. Although definitely by Nicholas Rowe (see Foxon R304) and included in his *Poems* (1714), the notion that Congreve might have written such politically topical verses accords with his better attested authorship of, for example, 'Jack French-Man's Defeat'.

The Tatler. No. 42, (16 July 1709)

Wilson, *Memoirs*, 20, wrote of Congreve: 'The Publick are likewise oblig'd to him for several ingenious Pieces in Prose, among the Papers of the *Tatler*, *Spectator*, and *Guardian*.' Summers printed the Aspasia section of this *Tatler* as Congreve's (iv. 189–90), perhaps following Caulfield (*Memoirs of the Celebrated Persons composing the Kit-Cat Club* (1821), 220) or Swinburne (see G.A. Aitken, *The Life of Richard Steele*, 2 vols. (1894), i. 250–1 n. 1). There is no evidence for this attribution. Aitken comments: 'whether or no Congreve wrote the paper in no. 42 is at least doubtful', and attributes it to Steele and Addison (*Tatler*, i. 395). R.P. Bond includes among suggestions that 'do not seem to warrant positive attributions' that of Congreve's share in no. 42 and in his edition says that Congreve's authorship of this portrait is 'very unlikely' (*Tatler*, i. 301). Dobrée omits it but substitutes no. 292 as printed in William Harrison's extended series. There is one association with Congreve, however, in that the 'divine *Aspasia*', Lady Elizabeth Hastings (1682–1739), daughter of the seventh earl of Huntingdon, was Congreve's cousin (Hodges, *Biography*, 125).

Squire Bickerstaff Detected, 1710

Addison wrote to Thomas Warton on 24 August 1710: 'Among the prints which I sent you by this Post, the "Essay upon Credit" is said to be written by Mr. Harley, and that of "Bickerstaff detected", by Mr. Congreve' (*Letters*, p. 232). This small prose pamphlet is an ironic defence, as if written by Partridge himself against his detractors, principally Swift:

[H T :] Squire Bickerstaff Detected; | O R , T H E | *Aſtrological Impoſter* Con-victed, | B Y | *J O H N P A R T R I D G E ,* | Student in Phyſick and Aſtrology. 8°: A°. Teerink 1025. Copy at L: C.175.b.24.

G.E. Graves, *DNB* article on Partridge, suggests that it was mainly the work of Thomas Yalden, yet allows that 'Many of the happiest touches, however, were added by Congreve, while Swift himself was in all probability consulted about it.' W.A. Eddy embroiders: 'Written by Swift with the help of Congreve, this essay was given by Thomas Yalden to Partridge, who published it in good faith as a "defence" against his tormentors!' (*Satires and Personal Writings by Jonathan Swift* (1932), 176 n. 1). Graham's gloss on Addison's letter says as much as is known: 'It was included in the *Miscellanies*, 1727, but not as a work of Swift. Faulkner's edition of Swift's *Works*, 1735, ascribed it, in a note, to Rowe . . . Addison, who was repeating gossip of the day, knew little of it.'

Verses on the Princess of Wales, 1715–16

See Allusions, p. 396, for the passage cited from *An Epistle to Sir Samuel Garth. Occasion'd by the Landing of the Pretender, And the Report of His Royal Highness the Prince of Wales's Going to Scotland* (1716), Luttrell's copy of which is dated 2 February. References to 'Fair C A R O L I N A' and 'the Bright P R I N C E S S that Restor'd our Race' immediately precede the line: 'C O N G R E V E for this the Lyre neglected strings'. Nothing further is known to support the implication that Congreve had recently written verses on or addressed to the Princess of Wales, or that he wrote anything relating to the Jacobite rebellion in 1715. It seems too late and imprecise to refer back to Congreve's 'Jack French-Man's Defeat' with its allusion to 'The Young *Hannover* Brave', but see the notes on that poem for Lady Cowper's reference to Congreve and the Prince of Wales (vol. ii, pp. 686–7).

AN ICONOGRAPHICAL CHECKLIST

WRITING to Keally on 29 January 1708 (Letter 38), Congreve remarked that 'sitting for my portrait is not a thing very agreeable to me', yet there are perhaps a dozen well-authenticated paintings of him between the ages of 12 and 45, some of which are alluded to in his letters. That by Godfrey Kneller, completed in 1709 for Tonson's Kit-Cat collection, is the most famous and the most often reproduced, either from Kneller's original or from John Smith's mezzotint of it. Those dated *c*.1710 below were probably studio copies made within the following decade. The finest is that by Richard van Bleeck of 1715, now in the Stedelijk Museum Vanderkelen-Mertens, Leuven.

Pending more thorough enquiry, the following list offers only a tentative record of the known portraits and such evidence as there is for any others not so far located. It almost certainly includes some ghosts (a painting by Van Loo is improbable; none by Maubert is known to be extant); in several, neither the artist nor date is firmly known; and in one or two cases it may even be doubted that Congreve is the sitter. In the library of the National Portrait Gallery, London, are photographs of three portraits not listed below but dubiously identified as paintings of Congreve. One, an oval bust, facing left, is said to be in the G.A. Plimpton Collection, New York. Another, three-quarter-length, facing forward, left arm across waist, and attributed to Kneller, was offered to the National Portrait Gallery in November 1953 by Miss Kirsten Høm of Copenhagen but not bought. A third, half-length, facing left, right hand across waist, is said to be signed in monogram by Kneller, but the sitter's identity is doubtful. There seemed little point here in extending the list beyond 1820 when Thurston's drawing, '*From an original Picture in the possession of the Publisher*' and engraved by Fittler, might imply a portrait from the life not otherwise known. That by Richard Cooper, half-length (171 × 110 mm.), in *Memoirs of the Celebrated Persons Composing the Kit-Cat Club* (1821), is yet again after Kneller.

P&D = Paintings or Drawings   Mezz = Mezzotints
Eng = Line engravings   S&M = Sculptures and Medallions

PAINTINGS AND DRAWINGS

P&D I W.P. Claret (*fl.* 1670–1706). Portrait of 'William Congreve (Poet) as a boy' (so stated on frame), *c*.1682; 730 × 625 mm., excluding frame. Dated 'Æt: 12 | Ja: 24. 1670' lower left corner; signed 'W.P. Claret' lower right. Reproduced by Hodges, *Biography*, facing p. 18 (but misreading the signature as 'W.D. Clarea'). Privately owned. This may have been the 'Picture of Mr. Congreve the Poet, when very young' in the Great Drawing Room at Aldermaston House in 1828: see J.P. Neale, *Views of the Seats of Noblemen and Gentlemen*, 2nd ser., 5 vols. (1824–9), iv. 1–4, 'Aldermanston [*sic*] House', 4.

William Claret, a student of Sir Peter Lely, was active as an English portrait painter *c.*1670–1706. He is credited with a fine portrait of John Egerton, earl of Bridgewater, painted in 1680 (it is simply signed 'Claret'). In 1690 he received £40 each for full-length portraits of William and Mary for the Northampton Court House, the first of which is clearly signed 'W.P. Claret pinxit': see C.A. Markham, *History of the County Buildings of Northamptonshire* (1885), 43–4. A portrait of Anne Rainsford, later Mrs Griffin, is also clearly signed 'W.P. Claret pinx'. A miniature by him of the Duchess of Portsmouth and Aubigny signed in monogram as 'VVC' is reproduced in Daphne Foskett, *A Dictionary of British Miniature Painters*, 2 vols. (1972), ii, plate 46, no. 139; see also i. 204–5. For a brief account of him, see C.H. Collins Baker, *Lely and the Stuart Portrait Painters*, 2 vols. (1912), ii. 72–4; and for his membership of 'The Virtuosi of St Luke', Ilaria Bignamini, 'George Vertue, Art Historians, and Art Institutes in London', *Walpole Society*, 54 (1991 for 1988), 46. What is claimed to be his will, dated 17 August 1706 and proved 5 September the same year, is printed by G.C. Williamson, *Burlington Magazine*, 35 (1919), 87–8, but it is in the name of Wolfgang William Claret, gentleman, of the parish of St Giles in the Fields. Bequests include rings for members of a society of gentlemen meeting two evenings a week at the Vine in Long Acre. Others named include his father Marke Claret (deceased), a brother Anthony Claret (deceased), another brother Charles Francis Claret, a niece Anna Maria Claret, daughter of Charles, and a brother-in-law Anthony Le Dieu. It offers no explanation of his second initial as 'P' nor of the absence of 'Wolfgang' in other contexts.

P&D II   Godfrey Kneller (1646–1723). Oval portrait of 'W I L L I A M   C O N-G R E V E ' (so stated on frame) *c.*1685; 724 × 597 mm. He is shown at perhaps age 14 or 15. The painting is so identified and attributed by the National Portrait Gallery, London, where a photograph is held (negative no. 5892). It is not known to have been reproduced. Such an oval portrait was sold at Christie's on 22 July 1871, lot 54; and again at Christie's on 5 May 1950, lot 108, there described as: 'P O R T R A I T   O F   W I L L I A M   C O N G R E V E ,   E S Q ., in classical dress and red scarf—*oval*'. As it was paired with a second oval painting, of a lady in a blue dress holding a rose, by J. Verstel, and sold as part of the same lot, the dimensions given probably refer to both portraits. Both were sold to Omell Galleries for seven guineas, but their present location is unknown.

P&D III   Henry Tilson (1659–95). Half-length portrait of 'W I L L ^M. C O N-G R A V E Poet' (so painted at the lower left), signed 'T I L S O N ' at the lower right, *c.*1694–5. Reproduced in *Alumni Dubliensis*, ed. G.D. Burtcheall and T.U. Sadleir (1924), facing p. 175, and by Hodges, *Documents* (frontispiece), who notes that it was then (1964) in the possession of Sir Ivone Kirkpatrick, Donaghcomper, County Kildare, Ireland.

Tilson, born in Yorkshire, was a student of Lely, and studied with Michael Dahl in Italy. Disappointed in love, he shot himself and was buried in London on 25 November 1695. Though undated, the painting must therefore have been finished well before November 1695, perhaps soon after the success of *OB*, and may show Congreve at about age 23.

P&D IV   Godfrey Kneller. Half-length portrait, *c*.1695–6. Oil on canvas; 895 × 715 mm. Congreve is shown turned to his right but facing forward, dressed as in V below, his right arm across his waist, his left elbow resting on a book which is in turn lying on part of a sheet bearing the words 'Love for L . . .'. It was presented to Trinity College Dublin in 1926 by Cecil Bisshopp Harmsworth and is reproduced by Anne Crookshank and David Webb, *Paintings and Sculptures in Trinity College Dublin* (1990), 40.

This may be the painting Congreve refers to in Letter 6, to Jacob Tonson, 20 August 1695, not long after the great success of *L L*: 'I am glad you approve so much of my picture, if you should see Sr: Godfrey again before you goe out of town pray give him my service, & if he has not finish'd the picture give him a Hint: for I should be glad it were don before my return.'

P&D V   Godfrey Kneller. Half-length portrait, *c*.1695–6; 762 × 622 mm. It shows Congreve in a painted oval, turned to his left but facing slightly forward, with large wig, velvet coat with three buttons showing, and a Steinkirk. Reproduced by Lionel Cust, *National Portrait Gallery* (1901–2), i. 217, as frontispiece in John Palmer, *Comedy of Manners* (1913) and D. Crane Taylor, *William Congreve* (1931), and in F.M. Kelly, 'Costume at the National Portrait Gallery', *The Connoisseur*, 85 (April 1930), 214–24, plate V.

David Piper says of it: 'Formerly catalogued as by Kneller, it seems rather to be studio work, though possibly related to the same sittings as the Kit-cat Club portrait [of 1709]; it is certainly of almost the same date' (*Catalogue*, no. 67, p. 81). Notwithstanding Piper's conjectural dating of *c*.1709, it may be much earlier. The Steinkirk in particular was highly fashionable in 1695 whereas the portrait of 1709 shows no cravat of any kind. Piper notes that the back of the lining canvas of this portrait is inscribed: '*Mr. Congreve | by Godfrey Kneller | from Lord Bessborough's collection*'. It may therefore have been acquired originally by Brabazon Ponsonby (d. 1758), first earl of Bessborough in County Kilkenny and a contemporary of Congreve. It was acquired by the National Portrait Gallery in February 1859.

P&D VI   Anon. Oval miniature portrait on vellum, *c*.1700; 87 × 68 mm. Royal Library, Windsor Castle. Congreve is shown looking left, with powdered periwig, grey cloak (no buttons), white loose Steinkirk; brown background. The suggested date is from Piper, *Catalogue*, 81: 'Another miniature of him aged twenty-five to thirty is at Windsor Castle.' Reproduced in Richard Garnett and Edmund Gosse, *English Literature: An Illustrated Record*, 4 vols. (1903), iii, plate facing p. 158. Graham Reynolds, *Miniatures in the Collection of Her Majesty the Queen: The Sixteenth and Seventeenth Centuries* (1998), no. 169, notes that it is 'an excellent contemporary miniature, painted in a manner reminiscent of the work of Christian Richter (1678–1732)', though Richter himself was most active in England from 1702 until his death. There is a Richter miniature said to be of Richard Congreve in the Rosenbach Foundation, Philadelphia.

The present painting is probably the one in the Strawberry Hill sale of 1842 when 'A miniature Portrait of Congreve the poet' was sold to P. and D. Colnaghi for £1. 10s. (*A Catalogue of the Classic Contents of Strawberry Hill Collected by*

Horace Walpole (25 April 1842), p. 85, day 18 (14 May), lot 142). It was bought for the Royal Collection in 1852.

P&D VII   Anon. Miniature portrait. It is noted in *A Catalogue of Pictures belonging to the Earl of Ilchester at Holland House* (privately printed, 1904), 190: Miniature, Case VI, no. 6. No artist or date is cited.

P&D VIII   Hugh Howard (1676–1738)? Three-quarter-length portrait of 'William Congreve—Poet. 1669–1728' (so stated on frame), *c*.1704–5; 1245 × 994 mm. Private collection. Congreve is shown standing with his right hand on a table, his left hand open across his stomach. He is dressed in a Romney blue coat with two sets of double buttons on the coat front, white cravat and cuffs, and with the ends of a tie hanging slightly out. Reproduced by Hodges, *Biography*, facing p. 82, as Congreve 'The Government Official . . . in his early thirties'.

   No painter or date is cited, but family tradition has assigned it to Kneller. Piper, *Catalogue*, 81, following Hodges, cites it as a 'three-quarter length by Kneller' and dates it *c*.1703–4. However, both the attribution and dating are uncertain. J. Douglas Stewart's *Sir Godfrey Kneller and the English Baroque Portrait* (Oxford, 1983) says nothing of it, and Congreve's letters make no mention of him sitting for Kneller in 1704–5 (if such be the date). If the painting dates from 1703, Kneller is even less likely to have been involved: a letter of 15 June 1703 from Vanbrugh to Tonson suggests that Kneller was then distracted by a new country house he had recently bought ('there is no getting him to work') and that the Kit-Cat Club pictures destined for Barn-Elms were still unfinished (*Works*, iv. 7).

   There is by contrast frequent mention in 1704–5 of Hugh Howard, for whom he *was* then about to sit. Letter 28, to Joseph Keally, 28 October 1704, records Congreve's meeting with 'Mr Howard, who is one I like much at first sight'. Letter 29, again to Keally, 9 December 1704, further refers to Howard and notes: 'I have sat to him; and they say it will be a good picture.' In Letter 30, to Keally, 3 February 1705, he probably refers to the same portrait and notes that 'it is not yet finished. . . . Some who have seen my picture since the third sitting, don't like it so well as I did after the first. I have not had time to see Mr Howard these six weeks.'

   Howard was born in Dublin, went to Holland in 1697 and thence to Rome, and returned to work as a portrait painter in London *c*.1701–14. He drew the frontispiece for Prior's *Poems on Several Occasions* (1709), which also includes Prior's 'To Mr. Howard. An Ode' and 'Venus Mistaken', alluding to Howard's portrait of Anne Durham ('Chloe'), Prior's mistress. In 1714 he married a wealthy Thomasine Langston and painted little thereafter. The catalogue of his collection, dispersed in 1873, includes a drawing of Jupiter and Semele but its relation, if any, to Congreve's *Semele* (which he was writing 1703–5) and its present location are unknown. See Michael Wynne, 'Hugh Howard, Irish Portrait Painter', *Apollo*, 90 (October 1969), 314–17; and for Howard's friendship with Kneller, see Stewart, *Sir Godfrey Kneller*, 173.

P&D IX   Hugh Howard? Oval miniature portrait of 'William Congreve Esqr. 1708' (so engraved on the reverse); 70 × 54 mm. (frame). He is shown turned right but facing forward, with a blond wig and wearing a bright blue coat with gold buttons and a white lace cravat lying flat, not twirled. Reproduced by Hodges, *Biography*, facing p. 96. It was then in the possession of Sir Geoffrey Congreve, Chartley Hall, Staffordshire.

No artist's name is given. Congreve's Letter 38 to Keally, 29 January 1708, notes that he had 'not yet heard any thing of Mr Howard or the picture' which he understood Howard to be painting of him as a gift for Keally. Congreve had not expected to be asked to pay Howard for it. He notes that Howard had 'almost finished one picture; and not liking it, pressed me to sit again for a new one. I was willing, because I understood he took all that care for you in friendship; and besides, I thought it might be of consequence to him to have my picture seen in his house well done, as being a face known by most of them whose approbation might be of use to him.' But Howard had apparently left for Ireland and taken the picture with him, though Congreve had thought it still unfinished: 'nor indeed did I apprehend that the picture was finished: for, if I do not misremember, I heard him speak yet of another sitting.'

Letter 44, to Keally, 9 October 1708, seems especially apt for this miniature in which Congreve does indeed look 'chuffy' (i.e. plump-cheeked): 'I am glad you like Mr Howard's picture: many do, though I always thought it too chuffy; and you may safely make him take it down, for I shall never be so fat.'

There is another oval miniature bust of about this date in the family's possession. It is gold-cased, 37 × 30 mm., showing an early eighteenth-century man facing slightly left, with large wig, in armour and with lace collar, but neither sitter nor painter is identified.

P&D X   Godfrey Kneller. Sketch of Congreve's head *c*.1708; 380 × 254 mm. Black and white chalks on brown paper. The Witt Collection (no. 1399; neg. no. 287/21 (14)), Courtauld Institute. Reproduced by J. Douglas Stewart, 'Some Drawings by Sir Godfrey Kneller', *The Connoisseur*, 156 (July 1964), 192–8.

P&D XI   Godfrey Kneller. Sketch of Congreve's head *c*.1708; 370 × 270 mm. Black and white chalks on blue paper. The Witt Collection, Courtauld Institute.

P&D XII   Godfrey Kneller. Sketch of Congreve's head *c*.1708; 372 × 286 mm. Black and white chalks on blue paper. The Witt Collection, Courtauld Institute.

P&D XIII   Godfrey Kneller. Half-length portrait, 1709; 915 × 711 mm. Signed and dated bottom left 'G | Kneller | 1709'. The Kit-Cat Club portrait now in the National Portrait Gallery (no. 3199), London. Piper gives the most extensive account of the collection and its history. He notes this particular portrait as 'Half-length, standing almost in profile to right, his head turned threequarters to look at the spectator; his right hand held up in front' (*Catalogue*, 79). It was much copied in Congreve's lifetime and has been often reproduced since; it appears in colour in *The Kit-Cat Club Portraits* (National Portrait Gallery, 1971), p. ix.

P&D XIV   Anon. Copy after Kneller, *c*.1710?; 750 × 635 mm. It was made for Charles Montagu (1661–1715), first earl of Halifax, and noted by Vertue as among 'pictures sold in Ld Halifax sale . . . Congreve. by Sr. G. Kneller. the same as printed' (*Vertue Note Books Volume IV*, Walpole Society, 24 (1936), 165). The

Halifax sale was on 6–10 March 1740, lot 14 (Congreve) being sold on the first day. It was bought, together with Montagu's other literary portraits, by Philip Dormer Stanhope, fourth earl of Chesterfield, and remained in Chesterfield House in Mayfair until about 1870 when the portraits were transferred to Bretby. They were acquired about 1918 by the sixth earl of Harewood and restored to Chesterfield House. In 1951 they were sold by Christie's and bought for Sir Louis Sterling who gave them in 1961 to the University of London where they are now installed in the Sterling Library. See David Piper, 'The Chesterfield House Library Portraits', in *Evidence in Literary Scholarship: Essays in Memory of James Marshall Osborn*, ed. René Wellek and Alvaro Ribeiro (Oxford, 1979), 179–95.

P&D XV Anon. Copy after Kneller, *c*.1710?; 900 × 690 mm. National Gallery of Ireland (catalogue no. 4336), presented by Mr John F. Chambers, 1980. Reproduced by Michael Wynne, *National Gallery of Ireland: Recent Acquisitions 1980–1981* (1981), 10, noting that 'The painting is of good quality, and is probably by the hand of Kneller himself, or at least by a member of his studio.' Its earlier provenance is uncertain.

P&D XVI Anon. Copy after Kneller, *c*.1710?; oval, 902 × 711 mm. The Bristol collection, Ickworth (Piper, *Catalogue*, 80). See Edmund Ferrar, *Portraits in Suffolk Houses (West)* (1908), i. 202, no. 20: 'H.L. Full face, body turned to the sinister, the right hand held out. *Dress:* gray velvet. S. In oval.' No artist, dimensions, or reproduction. Probably first acquired by John Hervey, first earl of Bristol (1665–1751), created Baron Hervey of Ickworth 1703, and earl of Bristol 1714, but not explicitly noted among his expenses for having pictures copied: see *The Diary of John Hervey, First Earl of Bristol, With Extracts from his Book of Expenses, 1688–1742* (1894), 159–64. It is first recorded at Ickworth by John Gage [Rokewode], *The History and Antiquities of Suffolk: Thingoe Hundred* (1838), 308.

P&D XVII Anon. Copy after Kneller, *c*.1710?; 890 × 711 mm. The Sackville collection, Knole (Piper, *Catalogue*, 80). It has been photographed for the Courtauld Institute's Photographic Survey (B60/758). Charles Sackville (1638–1706), sixth earl of Dorset, Lord Chamberlain (1689–97), was the dedicatee of Congreve's *LL*, a friend of Dryden, and an early member of the Kit-Cat Club. Since the present copy must have been made after his death, it may have been commissioned by Charles Sackville's son, Lionel Cranfield Sackville (1688–1765), later first duke of Dorset. Charles J. Phillips, *History of the Sackville Family (Earls and Dukes of Dorset)*, 2 vols. (1930), catalogues it as hanging in the dining room between those of Dryden and Wychlerley, and notes that 'This picture is said to have been copied from that painted for the Kit-Cat Club' (ii. 409, 439).

P&D XVIII Anon. Copy after Kneller, *c*.1710?; 902 × 660 mm. Reproduced in Colnaghis, *English Ancestors: A Survey of British Portraiture 1650–1850*, ed. Clovis Whitfield (1983), p. 55, item 33, and there described as 'a very lively variant' of the original in the National Portrait Gallery.

P&D XIX Anon. Copy after Kneller, 1723; 805 × 655 mm. Private collection. It was made for Colonel William Congreve, the poet's cousin, in 1723. See Letter

70, to Jacob Tonson, 8 August 1723: 'My Kinsman Coll Congreve desires by me that you would do him the favour to lend him my picture to have a Copy taken of it. I am sure there will be great Care taken of it.' Hodges, *Documents*, 136, notes its descent to General Sir Walter Norris Congreve (1862–1927), and thence to Major A.J.C. Congreve. Sold Phillips, 13 December 1994, lot 9, where Congreve is described as 'standing half length wearing a green velvet coat, a landscape beyond'.

This portrait may be seen hanging in Philip Reinagle's painting, dated 1782, of 'Lady Congreve and Children' in their London house, now in the National Portrait Gallery of Ireland, Dublin. See Hugh Belsey, 'A Family Portrait by Philip Reinagle', *Apollo*, 113 (February 1981), 97–9; also reproduced by James Chambers, *The English House* (1985), 158–9. This is probably the Kneller also listed as hanging in the Great Drawing Room at Aldermaston House in 1828: see Neale, *Views of the Seats of Noblemen and Gentlemen*, 2nd ser., iv. 4, where immediately following the entry for a portrait of Mrs Curtis, John Congreve's sister, attributed to Kneller, is another for 'Mr. Congreve the Poet.—Ditto'.

P&D XX   Anon. Dubiously, a copy after Kneller, *c.*1710? This portrait is shown bottom left in Charles Robert Leslie's 1839 painting of 'Lord and Lady Holland, Dr Allen and William Dogget in the Library at Holland House', reproduced by John Russell, *London* (1994), 43. G. Scharf was not alone in noting that it was 'strikingly like Congreve', in particular the Kit-Cat portrait of him (in J.R. Bloxam, *A Register of the Presidents, Fellows, Demies... of Magdalen College: The Demies*, Vol. III (1859), 95). But the only Congreve recorded in *A Catalogue of Pictures belonging to the Earl of Ilchester at Holland House* is the miniature noted as **P&D VII** above. The present portrait was first identified as one of Addison (and so praised by Macaulay in his essay on Addison), and then later argued to be of Sir Andrew Fountaine (see *Joseph Addison and Sir Andrew Fountaine; or the Romance of a Portrait* (1858) and The Earl of Ilchester, *The House of the Hollands* (1937), 29–30, 365–6). It seems most unlikely to be one of Congreve (the almost vertical angle of the right hand clearly distinguishes it from the Kit-Cat painting).

P&D XXI   Edward Byng (*c.*1676–1753). Drawing on blue-grey paper after Kneller, *c.*1710; 286 × 220 mm. British Museum: Sketchbook 5, f. 8^r: 897–8–13–6(7). It is described in Edward Croft-Murray and Paul Hulton, *Catalogue of British Drawings*, Volume I: XVI & XVII Centuries, I: Text (1950), 224: 'Nearly T.Q.L., standing, with body in profile to r., head half-r. and eyes to the front, his r. hand pointing. Wearing a light-coloured coat. Behind him a rock, and in the distance r., a wooded prospect. Pen and brown ink, with grey wash, heightened with white. Inscr.: At the foot, in the centre, *M^r. Congreve*, and in the lower l.-hand corner, 6.' Byng, a portrait and drapery painter, was an assistant to Kneller.

P&D XXII   Anon. Ink wash drawing after Kneller, n.d.; 124 × 105 mm. Present in an extra-illustrated copy of H.B. Wheatley, *London Past and Present: Its History Associations and Traditions*, 3 vols. in 9 (1891), in the library, National Portrait Gallery, London, Volume I, part 3, facing p. 532. From the style in which the frame is painted it is probably a late eighteenth-century copy.

P&D XXIII   Richard van Bleeck (1670–1733). Three-quarter-length portrait of 'Guillaum (Willem) Congreve' (so stated on present frame), 1715; 1219 × 1003 mm. Stedelijk Museum Vanderkelen-Mertens, Leuven (inventory number S/36/B). First reproduced by Arthur Laes, 'Richard van Bleeck (1670 vers 1733): un petit maître hollandais du XVIIIe siècle', *La Revue de l'art ancien et moderne*, 60 (1931), 155–68 (p. 157). It shows Congreve seated, holding a manuscript open at Vanbrugh's *The Provoked Wife*, with a table on the sitter's right on which are a watch and three books, the topmost with a spine label reading BERKELEY. It was sold by Christie's on behalf of the estate of Henry Fowler Broadwood on 25 March 1899, lot 25, when it was described as a 'Portrait of R [*sic*]. Congreve, poet and playwright, in grey and blue gown, grey wig, seated reading the play of "The Provoked Wife," books and watch on a table by his side *Signed, and dated*, 1717 [*sic*] 48 *in*. by 39 1/2 *in*.'. It was bought by or for Mr J. Willems and donated to the Stedelijk Museum Vanderkelen-Mertens in 1900.

From the mid-1690s until his death there in 1733, van Bleeck spent much, perhaps most, of his time working in London. The present portrait fully bears out Vertue's description of him as 'an Excellent portrait painter. his manner strong neat & well finish his colouring natural as by some paintings is apparent' (*Vertue Note Books Volume III, Walpole Society*, 22 (1934), 19). For a full account of van Bleeck, a detailed reading of this portrait, and a suggested provenance for it, see D.F. McKenzie, 'Richard van Bleeck's Painting of William Congreve as Contemplative (1715)', *RES* NS 51 (2000), 41–61. It is reproduced in colour as fig. 1.

P&D XXIV   James or Jacques Maubert (*fl.* 1690–1746). Portrait? Vertue has a note: 'Mr. Maubert portrait painter... some of the Poets, of his Time, he has painted from the life. as Dryden Congreve Pope Wicherly and others' (*Vertue Note Books Volume III, Walpole Society*, 22 (1934), 28). Noting elsewhere that Maubert had done various heads 'all copied from pictures he has met with', Vertue lists as one of them 'Sr Philip Sydney. don from a picture on bord given to Mr. Congreve by the late Eral [*sic*] of Leicester' (*Vertue Notebooks Volume II, Walpole Society*, 20 (1932), 9). Maubert's painting of Dryden is well known, but none of Congreve has been located.

P&D XXV   Jean-Baptiste Van Loo (1684–1745). Oil on canvas, n.d.; 368 × 254 mm. A typed note by J.C. Hodges in the National Portrait Gallery, London, citing a letter of 3 May 1919 from W.R. Bone to General Walter Norris Congreve, reports a portrait (bust) of Congreve by Van Loo. It is said to measure 14 1/2 × 10 in. within a frame 18 3/4 × 14 3/4 in. The inscription on the frame, clearly much later, reads: 'W. Congreve. Dramatist B. 1676–D. 1729. | By V. Baptiste Vanloo | B. 1684–D. 1746 | (French School)'. 'V' is presumably an error for 'J'.

Van Loo is not known to have been active in London until the late 1730s when he became a member of 'The Rose and Crown Club' of artists: see Bignamini, 'George Vertue', 55. His excellent portrait of Congreve's friend, Richard Temple, Viscount Cobham, reproduced by J.M. Robinson, *Temples of Delight: Stowe Landscape Gardens* (1990), 30, would seem to date from this later period. It is not impossible that he painted Congreve from the life on an earlier visit, but the present location of the painting reported by Bone is not known.

P&D XXVI   James Barry (1741–1806). Head only, an image almost certainly derived from Kneller, in 'Elisium and Tartarus or the State of final Retribution', 1777–1801; 3600 × 13080 mm. Royal Society of Arts, London. See William W. Pressly, *James Barry: The Artist as Hero* (1983), 84–5. As Pressly notes, the painting contains 125 'identifiable portraits of men of genius selected by Barry to populate Elysium or heaven.... Poets, writers, and artists dominate the upper regions, and at their apex sits Homer, who, though sightless, is the only figure in the mural to look up as if in a moment of inspiration.' Congreve is shown in the company of Otway, Corneille, Ben Jonson, Terence, Molière, Racine, and Menander.

MEZZOTINTS

Mezz I   John Smith (1652?–1742). Mezzotint after Kneller, 1710; 318 × 251 mm. Inscribed '*J. Smith fec. et ex. 1710.*' British Museum C.S.54 (four impressions). There is another copy in the extra-illustrated Wheatley, *London*, National Portrait Gallery, Volume II, part 3, facing p. 440. A close association between Congreve, Kneller, and the engraver John Smith is evident at other points in Congreve's work: see notes to 'The Mourning Muse of Alexis', 'The Birth of the Muse', 'Epigram, Written After the Decease of Mrs. Arabella Hunt', 'A Hymn to Harmony' in vol. ii, and Letter 52.

Mezz II   John Smith. Mezzotint after Kneller, 1728. H. Bromley, *A Catalogue of British Portraits* (1793), 290, notes another mezzotint print of Congreve by Smith, dated 1728. According to John Chaloner Smith, *British Mezzotint Portraits*, 4 vols. (1878–84), iii. 1153, this is unlikely to have been an after-state of the 1710 mezzotint, but none of 1728 has been located.

Mezz III   John Faber (?1695–1756). Mezzotint after Kneller, 1733; 318 × 248 mm. Inscribed '*I. Faber fecit 1733.*', plate 40 in *The Kit-Cat Club. Done from the original paintings of Sr. Godfrey Kneller.* For J. Tonson and J. Faber (1735). British Museum C.S.208 (four impressions). For Faber, see George S. Hellman, 'The Kit-Cat Club', *The Print-Collector's Quarterly*, 7 (February 1917), 1–23.

Mezz IV   Francis Kyte (*fl.* 1710–45) and J. Bowles (1701–79). Mezzotint after Kneller, half-length, within an oval, n.d.; 136 × 110 mm.; below, '*William Congreve Esq*ʳ', and '*I. Faber Fec*ᵗ *I. Bowles Exc:*'. Congreve's portrait is bottom left in a plate 352 × 250 mm., which also includes portraits of Addison, Steele, and Rowe, and the imprint: '*London Sold by Iohn Bowles at the Black Horse in Cornhill.*'. John Chaloner Smith, *British Mezzotint Portraits*, ii. 794–5. British Museum C.S.13 (2 copies: 2896–7). One of a series of 'Worthies of Britain', the first plate of which is inscribed '*F. Kyte Fecit J. Bowles Ex.*', and includes verses beginning '*See here* Britannia'*s Sons!*—*Justly admir'd*' and ends '*And all those other* Worthies *who are* Shaddow'd *here*' (cited in full by Smith, ii. 794). See also Freeman O'Donaghue, *Catalogue of Engraved British Portraits Preserved in the Department of Prints and Drawings in the British Museum*, 6 vols. (1908–25), v. 80.

Mezz V   John Bowles. Reverse mezzotint after Kneller, n.d.; 192 × 143 mm. Inscribed '*William Congreve Esq'. I. Bowles Exc.*' There is a copy (Hope 30810) in the Ashmolean Museum, Oxford.

Mezz VI   John Simon (1675?–1751). Mezzotint after Kneller, n.d. but before 1751; 343×254 mm. Chaloner Smith, *British Mezzotint Portraits*, iii. 1085, describes it as 'Directed to left, looking to front, wig. Under, *Mr William Congreve*. At bottom, *G Kneller Barot pinx. I Simon Fecit.*' (British Museum: C.S.55). One of a set of six plates showing 'Poets and Philosophers of England', each containing four oval portraits, with title, etc., on scrolls below. The fourth plate shows Addison, Prior, Pope, and Congreve. His plates were sold in 1761. See also O'Donaghue, *Catalogue of Engraved British Portraits*, v. 80–1.

ENGRAVINGS

Eng I   Michael van der Gucht (1660–1725). Bust after Kneller, 1718; 106 × 74 mm. Inscribed '*S'. G. Kneller Pin. M. V^{dr}. Gucht Sculp.*', as frontispiece to *Familiar Letters of Love, Gallantry, and Several Occasions*, 2 vols. (1718) and again to *Familiar Letters* (1724). It is also to be found as frontispiece to *The Works of Mr. Congreve*, 2 vols. (1774) and to a further edition of 1788.

Eng II   Michael Van der Gucht. Bust after Kneller, 1719; 98 × 74 mm. As above but showing less waist and hip and inscribed only '*M. V^{der}. Gucht Sculp. | Mr William Congreve*' (omitting Kneller's name). It appears in Giles Jacob, *The Poetical Register* (1719–20), facing i. 41; and as frontispiece to Charles Wilson, *Memoirs* (1730), and to two 1733 collections of Congreve's plays, one printed for J. & R. Tonson and one for William Feales. It recurs as an insert in *Letters of Mr. Pope, and Several Eminent Persons*, 2 vols. (For the Booksellers of London and Westminster, 1735), facing ii. 88, and in *Mr. Pope's Literary Correspondence*, 2 vols. (For E. Curll, 1735), facing ii. 86.

Eng III   Peter Foudrinier (*fl.* 1720–1750). Bust after Kneller, 1735; oval, 38 × 33 mm., inscribed below within frame 'M^R C O N G R E V E.' Full plate 152 × 95 mm., inscribed bottom right '*P. Foudrinier Sculp.*' Congreve is one of seven medallion portraits, the others being of Cromwell, Wycherley, Pope, Addison, Steele, Gay. Frontispiece to *Letters of Mr. Pope, and Several Eminent Persons, from the Year 1705, to 1735* (For T. Cooper, 1735). It is a very coarse copy of the Kneller.

Eng IV   Peter Foudrinier. Bust after Kneller, n.d.; oval, full plate 200 × 155 mm., inscribed '*P. Foudrinier Sculp.*' Congreve is one of seven oval portraits, the others being Lord Lansdowne, Addison, Prior, Pope, Betterton, and Rowe. See O'Donaghue, *Catalogue of Engraved British Portraits*, v. 80.

Eng V   Thomas Chambars (*fl.* 1761). Bust after Kneller, 1761; 154 × 99 mm. Inscribed '*G. Kneller Bar'. pinx'. T. Chambars sculp.*' Frontispiece to John Baskerville's edition of *The Works of Mr. William Congreve*, 3 vols. (1761).

Eng VI 'P.H.' (*fl.* 1773). Engraved bust, oval, 1773; 41 × 35 mm. Within a frame of leaves, facing forward, loose shirt, jacket, no buttons, in *The Works of William Congreve*, 3 vols., published by Thomas Ewing (Dublin, 1773). Printed on i. 1, immediately above the opening of *OB* 1. i, and inscribed below, '*P.H. Sculp^t.*' It is not from Kneller and gives the impression of being engraved from a good-quality miniature.

Eng VII Thomas Cook (1744?–1818). Bust after Kneller but facing left, 1778; 102 × 66 mm. Part frontispiece to *Bell's The Poets of Great Britain* (1778), inscribed '*From a Picture painted by S^r. Peter Lely* [*sic*], *in the Collection of the late Lord Chesterfield. Cook Scu.*'. It is dated below in letterpress 1 April 1778. Though reversed, the print clearly derives from the Kneller portrait then owned by Chesterfield. The facing engraved title, '*Mortimer delin. Grignion Scul.*', dated below in letterpress 18 May 1778, depicts Amaryllis mourning beside the grave of Amyntas and cites lines 124–5.

The same plates are used in *The Poetical Works of William Congreve* (Edinburgh: Apollo Press, 1778), and in the further Edinburgh edition of 1784 by the Apollo Press (as 'Bell's *second edition*'). They are also to be found in *The Poets of Great Britain*, vol. 60: *The Poetical Works of William Congreve* (London, 1807), though lacking, below the portrait and facing engraving, Bell's letterpress imprints.

Eng VIII —— Birrell (*fl.* 1794). Oval bust after Kneller, 1794; 48 × 37 mm. Letterpress account of Congreve below. Plate to *The Biographical Magazine* (1794), folio 33. Inscribed '*Sir G. Kneller pinx. Birrell sculp. Published by Harrison & Co. Nov. 1, 1794.*'

Eng IX W. Ridley (*fl.* 1796). Bust after Kneller, 1796; 76 × 58 mm. Facing A1^r in *Congreve's Works. Forming part of Cooke's Pocket Edition of the Original and Complete Works of Select British Poets*. Inscribed '*Engraved by W. Ridley, from an Original Picture. CONGREVE. Printed for C. Cooke, 17, Paternoster Row. June 11. 1796.*' An engraved title page by Richard Corbould (1757–1831) depicts three women at the grave of Amyntas, inscribed '*R. Corbould del^. J. Chapman sculp^t.*', and dated 14 May 1796. Other engravings (by T. Kirk, facing p. 45, and by Corbould, facing p. 66) illustrate 'The Tears of Amaryllis for Amyntas', lines 166–9, and 'The Petition', lines 5–6.

Eng X Peltro William Tomkins (1760–1840). Half-length engraving after Kneller, 1803; 72 × 54 mm. Above draped tablet labelled 'C O N G R E V E'. Inscribed '*Painted by S^r. G. Kneller Engraved by P.W. Tomkins | Published 19th. Feby. 1803, by John Sharpe: | Piccadilly*'.

Eng XI Samuel Freeman (1773–1857). Bust after Kneller, above panel, 1807; 90 × 73 mm. Inscribed below 'ENGRAVED BY FREEMAN. FROM AN ORIGINAL PICTURE | PUBLISHED BY LONGMAN & CO | 1807'.

Eng XII James Hopwood (*fl.* 1800–1850). Stipple engraving of bust after Kneller, 1808; 92 × 69 mm. Published by Matthews & Leigh (London, 1808).

Eng XIII   Anon. Bust after Kneller, n.d.; 74 × 61 mm. Above brief biographical note. Inscribed '*London: William Darton; 58 Holborn Hill.*' Darton was at that address 1817–23. Copy at F.W. Hope Collection, Sackler Library, Oxford, 30816.

Eng XIV   John Thurston (1774–1822) and James Fittler (1758–1835). Half-length, to right (99 × 79 mm.), seated with left hand on book, plate to *Effigies Poeticae* (1820). Fittler's engraving is from a drawing by John Thurston said to be '*From an original Picture in the Possession of the Publisher*', W. Walker. The print is dated 1 November 1820. The painting owned by Walker shows a quite different pose from the known portraits but is otherwise unattested.

SCULPTURES AND MEDALLIONS

S&M I   Anon. Oval portrait cut in pear wood, *c.*1700; 208 × 173 mm. Sold to Paul Mellon in 1975 by David Peel and Co. as 'Circa 1700' and now in the Center for British Art, New Haven (Neg. no. B1977.14.10). The sitter appears to be closer to 30 than 40, but an accompanying note of 10 February 1961 by Kingsley Adams, then Director of the National Portrait Gallery, London, says that he feels the carving is based on Kneller's portrait of Congreve in the Kit-Cat Club series and that the carver may not have seen the portrait himself but one of the many engravings of it.

S&M II   Francis Bird (1667–1731). Relief portrait as memorial plaque, bust after Kneller, with open playbook and masks to right below, Westminster Abbey, 1729. Commissioned by Henrietta, second Duchess of Marlborough, for whose father-in-law, the first earl of Godolphin (d. 1712), Bird had also made the monument in Westminster Abbey. For the inscription, see *Allusions*, p. 425. It is reproduced by K.A. Esdaile, *English Church Monuments 1510–1840* (1946), plate 22; and by Lord Killanin, *Sir Godfrey Kneller and his Times, 1646–1723* (1948), plate 76.

S&M III   William Kent (1684–1748). Stone relief portraits, 1736. On the memorial to Congreve in the garden at Stowe, 1736, designed by Kent for Richard Temple, Viscount Cobham, are several portrait heads of which at least two appear to represent Congreve. The monument incorporates an urn surmounted by a monkey holding and looking into a mirror. On the side of the urn are three portraits (presumably, from left to right, youth, manhood, and age), the central one of which appears to be of Congreve. At the top of the mirror's decorative frame is another portrait facing the monkey. Vertue has a note of it: 'an urn Congreves Monument on top a Monkey beholding a Mirrour—comedy is the Imitation of Life and the Mirrour of Fashion—erected 1736' (*Vertue Note Books Volume III, Walpole Society*, 22 (1934), 133). There is an excellent reproduction of it in Robinson, *Temples of Delight*, 24, but in its present condition it differs in some respects from the engraving by George Bickham, *The Beauties of Stowe* (1750), 58. At the base of the urn Bickham shows, to the left, a head and, to the right, an inscribed tablet, neither of which is now present. For the original inscription, see *Allusions*, p. 459.

S&M IV   Peter Vanina (*fl.* 1758–70). R. Gunnis, *Dictionary of British Sculptors 1660–1851*, rev. edn. (1964), 408, notes that there were sales of Vanina's stock-in-trade on 3 and 4 April 1770 and that 'Among the lots sold were busts of Prior, Congreve, Milton . . . '. None by Vanina of Congreve has been located.

S&M V   John Cheere (d. 1787). Bronze bust, stamped 'C O N G R E V E ', in the Castle Museum, York. Cheere was first in partnership with his brother, Sir Henry Cheere, but took over John Nost's yard with his moulds etc. *c.*1739 (R. Gunnis, *Dictionary of British Sculptors 1660–1851* (1953), 97–8). There is little likelihood that he ever saw Congreve.

S&M VI   Charles Harris (*fl.* 1775–1795). *A Catalogue of the Statues, Bass Reliefs, Bustos, &c. of Charles Harris, Statuary, Opposite to the New Church in the Strand* (London, n.d. but *c.*1780), lists two busts of Congreve, one of 16 to 18 inches (407–457 mm.) at 16*s.* (p. 14), and another of 11 in. (280 mm.) at 7*s.* 6*d.* Neither has been located. Gunnis, *Dictionary*, 188–9, notes of Charles Harris (d. 1795?) that 'The monuments have great charm . . . with a lavish use of coloured marbles and reliefs.'

S&M VII   Josiah Wedgwood (1730–95). Sculptured bust, black basalt, *c.*1775. The Royal Scottish Museum, Edinburgh. See *Gazette des Beaux-Arts* (February 1974), lxxxiii, p. 177 (La Chronique des Arts, p. 177, item 593).

S&M VIII   Josiah Wedgwood. Mould of head, facing slightly right. Manchester City Art Galleries. Listed in the 1779 catalogue: see Robin Reilly and George Savage, *Wedgwood: The Portrait Medallions* (1973), 110.

S&M IX   Amédée-Pierre Durand (1789–1873). Bronze Medallion, 1819; diam. 41 mm. Portrait bust, full profile, facing right, open collar. Face, within perimeter: 'GULIELMUS CONGREVE'. Obverse: 'NATUS | AN. M.DC.LXXII. [*sic*] | BANDSAE [*sic*] | IN COMITATU EBORACENSI | APUD ANGLOS | OBIIT | AN. M.DCC.XXIX. | [swollen rule] | SERIES NUMISMATICA | UNIVERSALIS VIRORUM ILLUSTRIUM. | [swollen rule] | M.DCCC.XIX. | DURAND EDIDIT'. Handel House Museum. Donated by Mrs Dororothy Fraser 1997. For Durand, see L. Forrer, *Biographical Dictionary of Medallists*, 8 vols. (1902–39), i. 468.

ALLUSIONS

WHEREVER it has seemed more useful and economical to do so, allusions to Congreve or his works have been recorded in the annotations or in the Biographical Summary. More extensive comments, including some longer documents of business and biographical interest, and those less immediately pertinent to specific passages in the text, are given here in chronological order. They are necessarily selective and are limited to the period of Congreve's own lifetime and soon after his death. Minor errors in the originals have been silently corrected. Entries are arranged in chronological order.

[Peter Motteux] *The Gentleman's Journal: Or the Monthly Miscellany* (February 1693), 61.

The success of Mr. *Congreve*'s *Old Batchelor* has been so extraordinary, that I can tell you nothing new of that Comedy; you have doubtless read it before this, since it has been already printed thrice. And indeed the Wit which is diffus'd through it, makes it lose but few of those Charms in the Perusal, which yield such pleasure in the Representation. Mr. *Congreve* will in some time give us another Play; you may judge by this how acceptable it will be.

Henry Higden, *The Wary Widdow: Or, Sir Noisy Parrat* (London, 1693), preface, sigs. A3^r–A3^v. Probably acted March 1693; advt. *LG*. 29 May–1 June 1693.

Had our unlucky Authour been worthy to have known they were absolutly bent to damn his Play, unsight [*sic*] unseen, his caution would have withdrawn him from the Thunder of their displeasure. But now we are convinc'd by the surprising success of the Baudy Batchelour, that the nicest Ladies may be brought (by good mannagment) to stand the fire of a smutty Jest, and never flinch for the matter. They are the sensible Judges that family duties can not proceed without the creature comfort: Nor Nature be well instructed without the help of a feskue.... The Authours are now convinc'd the Batchelour has touch'd upon the true string, to please and tickle: They are now grown more generous then to deny their sentiments and Inclinations, and scorn any such bashfull pretence, but openly avow and countenance that Poet, that seasons his Scenes with salt and good humour, to please the haut-gousts of their fancies: and make their Eares glow with licentious Farce, which they are resolv'd to stand by and justify: What though the Plots are old, and stale, they are so prettily jumbled and blended together they can never fail of being well receiv'd. Tho some nicer Ladies are of an opinion, that an impure Idea, that is obscene in the first conception (though never so cleanly wrapt up) can no way be made passable: But these are squeamish pallats that strain at a gnat in publick, and after make no bones of a Camel on occasion. What does it import if *Parson Spintext* have a wicked design on the Alderman's wife? What harm was it if his agreable Impudence revenged the City cheats upon the Aldermans head, and exalted his horns above the rest of his Brethren? There cannot be a taking Play without some Limberham or fumbling Alderman, or keeper to expose.

John Dryden, *Examen Poeticum: Being the Third Part of Miscellany Poems* (London, 1693), dedication, sigs. B4^r, B5^r.

(i) Notwithstanding my haste, I cannot forbear to tell your Lordship, that there are two fragments of *Homer* Translated in this *Miscellany*; one by Mr. *Congreve* (whom I cannot mention without the Honour which is due to his Excellent Parts, and that entire Affection which I bear him;) and the other by my self. Both the Subjects are pathetical; and I am sure my Friend has added to the Tenderness which he found in the Original; and, without Flattery, surpass'd his Author.

(ii) I wish Mr. *Congreve* had the leisure to Translate him, and the World the good Nature and Justice, to Encourage him in that Noble Design, of which he is more capable than any Man I know.

Thomas Yalden, 'To Mr. Congreve. An Epistolary Ode. Occasion'd by his late Play', ibid. 343–8.

TO
Mr. *CONGREVE*.
AN
EPISTOLARY *ODE*.
Occasion'd by his late Play.
From Mr. *YALDEN*.

I.

FAm'd *Wits* and *Beauties*, share this common fate,
    To stand expos'd to publick Love and Hate,
    In ev'ry *Breast* They diff'rent Passions raise,
    At once provoke our Envy, and our Praise.
For when, like you, some noble Youth appears,
For Wit and Humour fam'd above his Years:
Each emulous Muse, that views the Laurel won,
Must praise the worth so much transcends their own,

And, while his Fame they envy, add to his renown.
        But sure like you, no youth, cou'd please,
    Nor at his first attempt boast such success:
Where all Mankind have fail'd, you glories won:
        Triumphant are in this alone,
    In this, have all the *Bards* of old outdone.

II.

    Then may'st thou rule our Stage in triumph long,
        May'st Thou it's injur'd Fame revive,
    And matchless proofs of Wit, and Humour, give,
Reforming with thy Scenes, and Charming with thy Song.
    And tho' a Curse ill-fated Wit persues,
    And waits the Fatal Dowry of a Muse:
        Yet may thy rising Fortunes be
    Secure from all the blasts of Poetry;
    As thy own Laurels flourishing appear,
Unsully'd still with Cares, nor clog'd with Hope and Fear.
    As from its want's be from its Vices free,
        From nauseous servil Flattery:
    Nor to a Patron prostitute thy Mind,
Tho' like *Augustus* Great, as Fam'd *Mæcenas* kind.

III.

    Tho' great in Fame! believe me generous Youth,
        Believe this oft experienc'd Truth,
From him that knows thy Virtues, and admires their worth.
    Tho' Thou'rt above what vulgar Poets fear,
        Trust not the ungrateful World too far;
    Trust not the Smiles of the inconstant Town:
    Trust not the Plaudits of a Theater,
    (Which *D—fy* shall, with *Thee*, and *Dryden* share)
Nor to a Stages int'rest Sacrifice thy own.
    Thy *Genius*, that's for Nobler things design'd,
        May at loose Hours oblige Mankind:
    Then great as is thy Fame, thy Fortunes raise,
    Joyn thriving int'rest to thy barren *Bays*,
And teach the World to envy, as thou do'st to praise.
    The *World*, that does like *common Whores* embrace,
    Injurious still to those it does caress:
    Injurious as the *tainted Breath* of Fame,
That *blasts* a Poet's *Fortunes*, while it *sounds* his *Name*.

IV.

When first a *Muse* inflames some Youthful *Breast*,
Like an unpractis'd Virgin, still she's kind:
Adorn'd with Graces then, and *Beauties* blest,
She *charms* the *Ear* with *Fame*, with *Raptures* fills the *Mind*.
Then from all *Cares* the *happy Youth* is free,
But those of Love and Poetry:
Cares, still allay'd with pleasing Charms,
That *Crown* the Head with *Bays*, with *Beauty* fill the *Arms*.
But all a Woman's Frailties soon she shows,
Too soon a stale domestick Creature grows:
Then wedded to a Muse that's nauseous grown,
We loath what we enjoy, druge when the Pleasure's gon.
For tempted with imaginary *Bays*,
Fed with immortal Hopes, and empty Praise:
He Fame pursues, that fair, but treacherous, bait,
Grows wise, when he's undone, repents when 'tis too late.

V.

Small are the Trophies of his boasted *Bays*,
The Great Man's promise, for his flattering Toyl,
Fame in reversion, and the publick smile,
All vainer than his Hopes, uncertain as his Praise.
'Twas thus in Mournful Numbers heretofore,
Neglected *Spencer* did his Fate deplore:
Long did his injur'd Muse complain,
Admir'd in midst of *Wants*, and *Charming* still in vain.
Long did the Generous *Cowley* Mourn,
And long oblig'd the *Age* without return:
Deny'd what every Wretch obtains of Fate,
An humble Roof, and an obscure retreat,
Condemn'd to *needy Fame*, and to be *miserably* great.
Thus did the World thy great Fore-Fathers use,
Thus all the inspir'd *Bards* before,
Did their hereditary Ills deplore:
From tuneful *Chaucer*'s, down to thy own *Dryden*'s Muse.

VI.

Yet pleas'd with gaudy ruin Youth will on,
As proud by publick Fame to be undone:
Pleas'd tho' he does the worst of Labours chuse,
To serve a *Barb'rous Age*, and an ungrateful *Muse*.
Since *Dryden*'s self, to Wit's great Empire born,

Whose Genius and exalted Name,
Triumph with all the *Spoils* of *Wit* and *Fame*;
Must midst the loud *Applause* his barren *Laurels* mourn.
Even that Fam'd *Man* whom all the *World* admires,
Whom every Grace adorns, and Muse inspires:
Like the great injur'd *Tasso* shows,
Triumphant in the midst of Woes;
In all his Wants Majestick still appears,
Charming the *Age* to which he ows his Cares,
And cherishing that *Muse* whose *fatal Curse* he bears.
                    From Mag. Col. Oxon.

William Dove, 'To Mr. *Congreve*'. *The Gentleman's Journal: Or The Monthly Miscellany* (November 1693), 374. The preliminary comments are probably by Peter Motteux.

I need not say any thing of Mr. *Congreve*'s *Double-Dealer*, (the only new Play since my last) after the Character which Mr. *Dryden* has given of it: Yet my Respect for its Author will not suffer me to omit the following Lines.

          To Mr. *Congreve:* by Mr. *William Dove.*

S*Ince Inspiration's ceas'd, I fain would know*
To whom thy wond'rous store of Wit we owe?
'Tis more than e're Philosophy could teach,
How Imperfection should Perfection reach;
Yet while thy Works with native Glory shine,
And sprightly Phrazes render them divine, }
We think thou'rt sprung from the Prophetic Line.
How smooth the Current of thy Fancy glides!
It never ebbs, and knows no boist'rous Tides;
No lofty nonsense in thy Play appears,
With show of Wit to please unskilfull Ears.
Thus we with pleasure, and with wonder view,
That charming Landskip which thy Fancy drew.
There, there, thy Genius revels in each Part,
And lavish Nature is improv'd by Art.
There's in thy Satire, as in Music, found
Something that's pleasing in the sharpest Sound.
Sure thy Soul acts in a divided State,
Free from the Body, and exempt from Fate!
Go on, great Youth, but as thou hast begun,
The Prize thou'lt merit e're the Race is run.
Thus fledg'd with honour, let thy Muse expand

Her infant Wings, and her swift Flight extend,
So far, till at the Last she may come nigh
Wycherly's *Fame, and with his Glory vye.*

Jonathan Swift, 'To Mr. Congreve'. *Miscellaneous Pieces, In Prose and Verse. By the Rev. Dr. Jonathan Swift.* [Edited by John Nichols.] (1789), 225–33.

TO MR. CONGREVE.
Written November 1693.

THRICE, with a prophet's voice and prophet's pow'r,
The Muse was call'd in a poetic hour,
And insolently thrice, the slighted Maid
Dar'd to suspend her unregarded aid;
Then with that grief we form in spirits divine,
Pleads for her own neglect, and thus reproaches mine:
    Once highly honour'd! False is the pretence
You make to truth, retreat, and innocence;
Who, to pollute my shades, bring'st with thee down
The most ungen'rous vices of the town;
Ne'er sprung a youth from out this isle before
I once esteem'd, and lov'd, and favour'd more,
Nor ever maid endur'd such court-like scorn,
So much in mode, so very city-born;
'Tis with a foul design the muse you send,
Like a cast mistress to your wicked friend;
But find some new address, some fresh deceit,
Nor practise such an antiquated cheat;
These are the beaten methods of the stews,
Stale forms of course, all mean deceivers use,
Who barbarously think to 'scape reproach,
By prostituting her they first debauch.
    Thus did the Muse severe unkindly blame
This off'ring long design'd to CONGREVE's fame;
First chid the zeal as unpoetic fire,
Which soon his merit forc'd her to inspire;
Then call this verse, that speaks her largest aid,
The greatest compliment she ever made,
And wisely judge, no pow'r beneath divine
Could leap the bounds which part your world and mine;
For, youth, believe, to you unseen, is fix'd
A mighty gulph unpassable betwixt.

Nor tax the goddess of a mean design
To praise your parts by publishing of mine;
That be my thought when some large bulky writ
Shews in the front the ambition of my wit;
There to surmount what bears me up, and sing
Like the victorious wren perch'd on the eagle's wing;
This could I do, and proudly o'er him tow'r,
Were my desires but heighten'd to my pow'r.
    Godlike the force of my young C O N G R E V E's bays,
Soft'ning the muse's thunder into praise;
Sent to assist an old unvanquish'd pride
That looks with scorn on half mankind beside;
A pride that well suspends poor mortals fate,
Gets between them and my resentment's weight,
Stands in the gap 'twixt me and wretched men,
T'avert th'impending judgments of my pen.
    Thus I look down with mercy on the age,
By hopes my C O N G R E V E will reform the stage;
For never did poetic mine before
Produce a richer vein or cleaner ore;
The bullion stampt in your refining mind
Serves by retail to furnish half mankind.
With indignation I behold your wit
Forc'd on me, crack'd, and clipp'd, and counterfeit,
By vile pretenders, who a stock maintain
From broken scraps and filings of your brain.
Through native dross your share is hardly known,
And by short views mistook for all their own;
So small the gain those from your wit do reap,
Who blend it into folly's larger heap,
Like the sun's scatter'd beams which loosely pass,
When some rough hand breaks the assembling-glass.
    Yet want your critics no just cause to rail,
Since knaves are ne'er oblig'd for what they steal.
These pad on wit's high road, and suits maintain
With those they rob, by what their trade does gain.
Thus censure seems that fiery froth which breeds
O'er the sun's face, and from his heat proceeds,
Crusts o'er the day, shadowing its parent beam
As antient nature's modern masters dream;
This bids some curious praters here below
Call Titan sick, because their sight is so;

And well, methinks, does this allusion fit
To scribblers, and the god of light and wit;
Those who by wild delusions entertain
A lust of rhiming for a poet's vein,
Raise envy's clouds to leave themselves in night,
But can no more obscure my C O N G R E V E 's light
Than swarms of gnats, that wanton in a ray
Which gave them birth, can rob the world of day.
    What northern hive pour'd out these foes to wit?
Whence came these Goths to overrun the pit?
How would you blush the shameful birth to hear
Of those you so ignobly stoop to fear;
For, ill to them, long have I travell'd since
Round all the circles of impertinence,
Search'd in the nest where every worm did lie
Before it grew a city butterfly;
I'm sure I found them other kind of things
Than those with backs of silk and golden wings;
A search, no doubt, as curious and as wise
As virtuosoes' in dissecting flies;
For, could you think? the fiercest foes you dread,
And court in prologues, all are country-bred;
Bred in my scene, and for the poet's sins
Adjourn'd from tops and grammar to the inns;
Those beds of dung, where schoolboys sprout up beaus
Far sooner than the nobler mushroom grows:
These are the lords of the poetic schools,
Who preach the saucy pedantry of rules;
Those pow'rs the criticks, who may boast the odds
O'er Nile, with all its wilderness of gods;
Nor could the nations kneel to viler shapes,
Which worship'd cats, and sacrific'd to apes;
And can you think the wise forbear to laugh
At the warm zeal that breeds this golden calf?
    Haply you judge these lines severely writ
Against the proud usurpers of the pit;
Stay while I tell my story, short, and true;
To draw conclusions shall be left to you;
Nor need I ramble far to force a rule,
But lay the scene just here at Farnham school.
    Last year, a lad hence by his parents sent
With other cattle to the city went;

Where having cast his coat, and well pursu'd
The methods most in fashion to be lewd,
Return'd a finish'd spark this summer down,
Stock'd with the freshest gibberish of the town;
A jargon form'd from the lost language, wit,
Confounded in that Babel of the pit;
Form'd by diseas'd conceptions, weak, and wild,
Sick lust of souls, and an abortive child;
Born between whores and fops, by lewd compacts,
Before the play, or else between the acts:
Nor wonder, if from such polluted minds
Should spring such short and transitory kinds,
Or crazy rules to make us wits by rote
Last just as long as ev'ry cuckow's note:
What bungling, rusty tools, are us'd by fate!
'Twas in an evil hour to urge my hate,
My hate, whose lash just heaven has long decreed
Shall on a day make sin and folly bleed;
When man's ill genius to my presence sent
This wretch, to rouse my wrath, for ruin meant;
Who in his idiom vile, with Gray's-inn grace,
Squander'd his noisy talents to my face;
Nam'd ev'ry player on his fingers ends,
Swore all the wits were his peculiar friends;
Talk'd with that saucy and familiar ease
Of Wycherly, and you, and Mr. Bays;
Said, how a late report your friends had vex'd,
Who heard you meant to write heroics next;
For, tragedy, he knew, would lose you quite,
And told you so at Will's but t'other night.
    Thus are the lives of fools a sort of dreams,
Rend'ring shades, things, and substances of names;
Such high companions may delusion keep,
Lords are a footboy's cronies in his sleep.
As a fresh miss, by fancy, face, and gown,
Render'd the topping beauty of the town,
Draws ev'ry rhyming, prating, dressing sot,
To boast of favours that he never got;
Of which, whoe'er lacks confidence to prate,
Brings his good parts and breeding in debate;
And not the meanest coxcomb you can find,
But thanks his stars, that Phyllis has been kind;

Thus prostitute my C O N G R E V E 's name is grown
To ev'ry lew'd pretender of the town.
'Troth I could pity you; but this is it,
You find, to be the fashionable wit;
These are the slaves whom reputation chains,
Whose maintenance requires no help from brains.
For, should the vilest scribbler to the pit,
Whom sin and want e'er furnish'd out a wit;
Whose name must not within my lines be shewn,
Lest here it live, when perish'd with his own;
Should such a wretch usurp my C O N G R E V E 's place,
And chuse out wits who ne'er have seen his face;
I'll be[t] my life but the dull cheat would pass,
Nor need the lion's skin conceal the ass;
Yes, that beau's look, that voice, those critic ears,
Must needs be right, so well resembling theirs.

    Perish the Muse's hour, thus vainly spent
In satire, to my C O N G R E V E 's praises meant;
In how ill season her resentments rule,
What's that to her if mankind be a fool?
Happy beyond a private muse's fate,
In pleasing *all that's good among the great*,
Where tho' her elder sisters crowding throng,
She still is welcome with her inn'cent song;
Whom were my C O N G R E V E blest to see and know,
What poor regards would merit all below!
How proudly would he haste the joy to meet,
And drop his laurel at *Apollo*'s feet.

    Here by a mountain's side, a reverend cave
Gives murmuring passage to a lasting wave;
'Tis the world's wat'ry hour-glass streaming fast,
Time is no more when th'utmost drop is past;
Here, on a better day, some druid dwelt,
And the young Muse's early favour felt;
Druid, a name she does with pride repeat,
Confessing Albion once her darling seat;
Far in this primitive cell might we pursue
Our predecessors foot-steps, still in view;
Here would we sing—But, ah! you think I dream,
And the bad world may well believe the same;
Yes; you are all malicious standers-by,
While two fond lovers prate, the Muse, and I.

Since thus I wander from my first intent,
Nor am that grave adviser which I meant;
Take this short lesson from the god of bayes,
And let my friend apply it as he please:

Beat not the dirty paths where vulgar feet have trod,
  But give the vigorous fancy room.
  For when like stupid alchymists you try
    To fix this nimble god,
    This volatile mercury,
  The subtil spirit all flies up in fume;
  Nor shall the bubbl'd virtuoso find
More than a fade insipid mixture left behind.

  Whilst thus I write, vast shoals of critics come,
And on my verse pronounce their saucy doom;
The Muse, like some bright country virgin, shows,
Fall'n by mishap amongst a knot of beaux;
They, in their lewd and fashionable prate,
Rally her dress, her language, and her gait;
Spend their base coin before the bashful maid,
Current like copper, and as often paid:
She, who on shady banks has joy'd to sleep
Near better animals, her father's sheep;
Sham'd and amaz'd, beholds the chatt'ring throng,
To think what cattle she has got among;
But with the odious smell and sight annoy'd,
In haste she does th'offensive herd avoid.

  'Tis time to bid my friend a long farewell,
The muse retreats far in yon chrystal cell;
Faint inspiration sickens as she flies,
Like distant echo spent, the spirit dies.

  In this descending sheet you'll haply find
Some short refreshment for your weary mind,
Nought it contains is common or unclean,
And once drawn up, is ne'er let down again.

      *Out of an Ode I writ, inscribed The Poet.
      The rest of it is lost.

Jonathan Swift, Letter to Thomas Swift, 6 December 1693, *Correspondence*, i. 118.

I desire You would inform Y^r self what You mean by bidding Me keep my Verses for Will Congreves next Play, for I tell You they were calculated for any of his, and if it were but acted when you say, it is as early as ever I intended, since I onely design they should be printed before it; So I desire You will send me word immediatly, how it succeeded, whether well, ill or indifferently, because my sending them to Mr Congreve depends upon knowing the Issue

John Dryden, Letter to William Walsh, 12 December [1693], *Letters*, 62–3.

I have rememberd you to all your friends; and in particular to Congreve; who sends you his play, as a present from him selfe, by this conveyance; & much desires the honour of being better known to you. His Double Dealer is much censurd by the greater prt of the Town: and is defended onely by the best Judges, who, you know, are commonly the fewest. Yet it gets ground daily, and has already been acted Eight times. The women thinke he has exposd their Bitchery too much; & the Gentlemen, are offended with him; for the discovery of their follyes: & the way of their Intrigues, under the notion of Friendship to their Ladyes Husbands. My verses, which you will find before it, were written before the play was acted. but I neither alterd them nor do I alter my opinion of the play.

Anon., 'On the late Sickness of Madam Mohun, and Mr. Congreve', in *Chorus Poetarum: Or, Poems on Several Occasions* (London, 1694), 21. The epigram was sometimes later attributed to Congreve himself and included with his poems (e.g. in *A Complete Edition of the Poets of Great Britain*, vol. 7 (1793), 568).

> O N E fatal Day, a Sympathetic Fire
> Seiz'd him, that writ, and her that did inspire.
> *Mohun*, the Muses Theme, their Master *Congreve*,
> Beauty and Wit, had like to've lain in *one Grave*.

A[nthony] H[ammond], 'A Letter to Walter Moyle, Esq;', ibid. 45.

> ... dost some honest, some delightful Friend,
> With easie Conversation, recommend
> The sparkling Wine, while Wit and Mirth attend? }

C O N G R E V E, the matchless rising Son of Fame,
Whom all Men envy, tho' they dare not blame:
H O P K I N S, whose Mind and Muse, both without Art,
Gives him a well-fixt Title in your Heart.

Charles Hopkins, 'To *Walter Moyle*, Esq.', in *Epistolary Poems; On Several Occasions* (London, 1694), 7.

> Late, very late, may the Great *Dryden* dye,
> But when deceas'd, may *Congreve* rise as high.
> To him, my Service, and my Love commend,
> The greatest Wit, and yet the truest Friend.

Charles Hopkins, 'To *Anthony Hammond*, Esq.', ibid. 10, 11.

(i)   When you, and *Southern, Moyle*, and *Congreve* meet,
               The best, good Men, with the best-natur'd Wit,
               Good Wine, good Company, the better Feast,
               And whene're *Wycherly* is present, best.

(ii)   Take the best Wishes of a grateful Soul;
               Congreve, and *Moyle*, and you, possess it whole.

John Dryden, *Love Triumphant; Or, Nature will Prevail* (London, 1694), dedication, sigs. A3^v–A4^r. Probably acted Jan. 1694; advt. *LG* 12–15 March 1694.

As for the Mechanick Unities, that of Time is much within the compass of an Astrological Day, which begins at Twelve, and ends at the same hour the Day following. That of Place is not observ'd so justly by me, as by the Ancients; for their Scene was always one, and almost constantly some Publick Place. Some of the late French *Poets, and amongst the* English, *my most Ingenious Friend, Mr.* Congreve, *have observ'd this Rule strictly; though the Place was not altogether so publick as a Street.*

William Wycherley, Letter to John Dennis, 4 February 1694, in *Memoirs of the Life of William Wycherley, Esq; With a Character of his Writings by . . . George, Lord Lansdowne* (1718), 32.

I would not have my Rivals in your Friendship[,] the *Congreves*, the *Drydens*, the *Walshes*, and the rest of your Tavern Friends enjoy your Conversation while I cannot . . .

Anon., Letter communicating news 'chiefly of the new plays which have been the entertainment of the town', viz. *The Double Dealer*, Dryden's *Love Triumphant*, Southerne's *The Fatal Marriage*, and Settle's *The Ambitious Slave*, 22 March 1694. Reprinted by Edmund Malone, *Historical Account of the Rise and Progress of the English Stage* (Basil, 1800), 179–80, note. According to Malone that part of the letter bearing the writer's signature had been torn away.

(i) The first that was acted was Mr. Congreve's, called *The Double Dealer*. It has fared with that play, as it generally does with beauties officiously cried up; the mighty expectation that was raised of it made it sink, even beneath its own merit. The character of *The Double Dealer* is artfully writt, but the action being but single, and confined within the rules of true comedy, it could not please the generality of our audience, who relish nothing but variety, and think any thing dull and heavy which does not border upon farce.—The criticks were severe upon this play, which gave the author occasion to lash 'em in his Epistle Dedicatory, in so defying or hectoring a style, that it was counted rude even by his best friends; so that 'tis generally thought he has done his business, and lost himself: a thing he owes to Mr. Dryden's treacherous friendship, who, being jealous of the applause he had gott by his *Old Batchelour*, deluded him into a foolish imitation of his own way of writing angry prefaces.

(ii) [Referring to Southerne's *The Fatal Marriage*, the writer notes:] Never was poet better rewarded or incouraged by the town; for besides an extraordinary full house, which brought him about 140 l. 50 noblemen, among whom my lord Winchelsea was one, gave him guineas apiece, and the printer 36 l. for his copy.

This kind usage will encourage desponding minor poets, and vex huffing Dryden and Congreve to madness.

Joseph Addison, 'An Account Of The Greatest English Poets To Mr. H.S. *Ap. 3d.* 1694', in *The Annual Miscellany: For the Year 1694. Being The Fourth Part of Miscellany Poems* (London, 1694), 325–6. Addison alludes first to Dryden:

> How might we fear our *English* Poetry,
> That long has flourish'd, shou'd decay with Thee;
> Did not the Muses other Hope appear,
> *Harmonious Congreve*, and forbid our Fear.
> *Congreve*! who's Fancies unexhausted Store
> Has given already much, and promis'd more.
> *Congreve* shall still preserve thy Fame alive,
> And *Dryden*'s Muse shall in his Friend survive.

Charles Gildon, 'An Essay at a Vindication of the Love-Verses of Cowley and Waller, &c. . . . Directed to Mr. *Congreve*', *Miscellaneous Letters and Essays, On several Subjects* (London, 1694), 209–31. The text itself has no direct allusions to Congreve.

Anon., *The Mourning Poets: Or, An Account of the Poems on the Death of the Queen* (London, 1695), 4–5. Queen Mary died 28 December 1694.

> Ev'n *Dryden* mourns; tho yet he does refuse
> To mourn in public, and exert his Muse;
> Nor can we well his Want of Love suspect,
> Who kindly could an absent Muse correct.
>   In *Congreve Dryden*'s ours, to Him we owe
> The tuneful Notes which from *Alexis* flow:
> He chose out *Congreve*, and inspir'd his Flame;
> *Congreve*, his best belov'd, and next in Fame:
> Whose Beams the unexpecting World surprise,
> As when unseen the Sun in Clouds does rise,
> Then breaking through, at once attracts our Eyes.
> Unlike in this, no Night succeeds his Day,
> But still he shines with one continued Ray.
> When in full Glory *Congreve* first appear'd,
> We saw, we wonder'd, and confest the Bard:
> *Dryden* by Thee All own these Wonders done,
> Thou taught'st this Eagle to approach the Sun.
>   He to the Swains *Pastor*'s Fate bemoans,
> Sighs to the Winds, and fills the Vales with Groans.
> The Vales return his Groans, the Winds his Sighs;
> And ev'ry Swain repeats the tuneful Crys.
> Not so lamented *Græcian Bion* fell,
> Nor *Venus* mourn'd the lovely Boy so well;
> Poets unborn shall make his Lays their Theme,
> And future *Rapins* take their Rules from him.

Anon., *Urania's Temple: Or, A Satyr upon the Silent Poets* (London, 1695), 3–4.

> Nor was this Royal *Hymn* to *Light* all bound
> T'*Urania*'s Walls alone: Th'ascending Sound
> Was hear'd above; hear'd and repeated too,
> Up to her own *Third Heav'n* the Muses *highest Region* flew;
> Both *Quires* united Song. Nay, and to fill

> The *Sacred Chantry* with more Voices still;
> Ev'n the most humble poorest Shepherd Breed
> Taught by the soft *Alexis* well-tun'd Reed,
> Their Great *P A S T O R A* sung; on every Tree
> A *Chorus*, the whole Grove one Rapsodie.
> The mournful *Philomel* sat warbling there,
> Nor wants a *Thorn* to wake to such an *Ayre.*

Edward Howard, Earl of Suffolk, *An Essay Upon Pastoral* (London, 1695), proem, sig. A3ᵛ.

... I often make mention of Virgil *in this following* Essay, *as an Ornament to my Discourse. I say, it is not with any Design to detract from his just Worth, that makes me here thus to Speak of him, (for undoubtedly he was a Celebrated Wit amongst the* Romans, *and may pass for a considerable Poet now-a-days) but only with an intention that Men should not talk so unbecomingly fond of the Shadow and Image of a dead Poet, and to make* Virgil *the Standard of Wit, when we have two such Favourites of the* Muses *continually before our eyes; I mean, a* Dryden *and a* Congreve: *And how much soever some People may be enamour'd with this* Mantuan Poet, *I will here be bold to affirm, that that Great Youngman* (Mr. Congreve) *has in his Pastoral* Alexis *upon the Death of the Late* Queen, *evidenced himself to the World, to have a sufficient degree and quantity of unmingled Fire and pure Rapture of the Poet (as well as a Correctness of Thought and Felicity of Expression) to constitute Ten* Virgils, *nay, and enough to spare to furnish out a* Theocritus.

Thomas Burnett to Leibniz, from Amsterdam, 3/13 June 1695, of Congreve's *The Mourning Muse of Alexis.* In *Gottfried Wilhelm Leibniz: Sämtliche Schriften und Briefe, Erste Reihe: Allgemeiner politischer und historischer Briefwechsel: Elfter Band* (Berlin, 1923–), xi. 503–4.

Mais dans la poesie Engloise rien peu egalér même, la compositione de M. Congrave un jeun Ecoliér etudiant en droit dans le college de Grays-Inn [*sic*] à Londres, c'êt fait en pastorale sous les noms faints de Menalcas, Alexis, et Pastora qui deux premiers en formes de dialogue come deux pasteurs lamentent l'un al autre la mort d'une bergere; rien êt plus pathetique, aisé pourtant naturelle, et y n'entre pas une pensé, ni même une parole ou terme qui n'êt pas propre, de telle maniere que du comencement jusque alla fin on ne quite jamais le champ pastoral. Il a eu recompence du Roy 1000 [*sic*] ginés d'or c'ét ... 6000 Ecus ou 18 000 francs de monoye de France. ... [Burnet also notes the translation into French and Flemish of Gilbert Burnet's *Essay on the Memory of the late Queen* (1695), adding:] depuis deux ou 3 jours une translatione flamande se trouve ici, on y ajoute aussi la poeme de Monsʳ

Congrave en vers flamcnds. Je vous laisse à divinér della boté de cette rime et sa rapporte al origenal.

Thomas Burnett to Leibniz, from London, 17/27 November 1695, of Congreve's *To the King on the taking of Namur*. In *Leibniz*, loc. cit. xii. 163.

Mr Congrave qui a fait la fameuse pastorale sur la mort della Reyne a fait une congratulatione au roy sur la prise de Namour et son retour victorieuse[.] Il y a des belles choses la dedans: mais je trouve la poesie sans aucun dessein[,] je veux dire nullement bien ajousté al occasione, ny du raport juste au dessein qui se proposa dans cet louange.

William Pittis, *An Epistolary Poem to N. Tate... Occasioned by the taking of Namur* (London, 1696), sig. A2^v, pp. 1–2.

(i) *As for my taking notice of Mr. C—'s Ode, I have this to say for my self, that as every Man is Master of his own Sentiments, so he may vent 'em when they are agreeable to truth and good-manners. And I can't see why Mr. C—should take it amiss, that he is not counted the best Pindarick Writer, when he has so large a share of Reputation in Pastoral. A standerby often see's things a Gamester himself does not perceive, and I may tell him his faults, when perhaps I am so fond of my self as not to discern my own. I am so far from using a Gentleman of his Character ungenteely, that tho I can't say of his Ode, as Mr.* Norris *said of Mr.* Lock's Humane Understanding, *(viz.) that he would not after all its faults part with it for a* Vatican; *yet I can't but tell the World I have an extraordinary value for it. I can't see why the same liberty may not be taken with a Gentleman of* Will's, *as those Gentlemen took with Dr.* Blackmore, *and that they who would have Christned a certain poem* Arthur of Bradly, *should have their own examin'd by the Friends of* Prince Arthur. *If I have misinterpreted any of his Beauties, I beg his pardon, but if I have found out his faults I think I may have the liberty to show them.*

(ii)   Lo! C—'s *Dairy-Muse* forgets her charge,
        Tricks up her self, and roams about at large,
        And thinks in Flights and Raptures to excell
        Because she tun'd the *lowly reed* so well!
        As at some Wake, where *Joan* or *Nell* appear,
        And represent the Queen in Sunday's Gear,
        With hobbling steps the Rabble Rout advance,
        And trample round, and form a kind of Dance:
        Susan admidst the rest, with awkward Mien
        Capers, and shows her feet, and will be seen,
        Thinks what she does, deserves the most esteem,

Because she makes good Cheese, and skims the better Cream.
On *Pindar*'s Wings she takes her aery Course,
But *Pindar*'s judgment's wanting to his Force.
Up to the head of Fame she boldly flies,
(And [1]Fames a mischief, or the Poet lies.)
    O Youth take heed, let *Virgill*'s hallow'd Page
Escape thy fury, and avoid thy rage,
With holy dread approach the Reverend Bard,
Nor play with Wit, when Sense should be prefer'd,
A fine digression, and with Judgment wrote,
Is more esteem'd a Beauty than a Fau't
But when a Muse impatient of delay,
Leaps o're the bounds, and frollicks all the way,
Forces through *oppositions self*, and climbs
With all the tinckling chimme of Pack-horse Rhimes;
We damn the Muse, and justly blame her skill,
Who leaves good beaten ways, and chuses ill,
And sweats and drudges upward with her load,
When she might go beneath, and keep the Road.
But above all (for he that Verse endites
Shou'd know his Sense and meaning as he writes)
Thy Verse shou'd speak Thee Loyal, not compare
The Siege of *Namure* to the *Gyants War*:
Nor make *Mars tumble* from the *Empyreal-skie*.
Those whom their [2]Author never brought so high:
Thy *Pow'r unseen*, and boundless force restrain,
Nor make those *Rebells* who deserve to Reign.

[1] *Fama malum-* Virg. Aen.   [2] *Ovid.*

Anon., *Reflections on the Poems Made Upon The Siege and Taking of Namur* (London, 1696). The text is dated 24 December 1695.

(i) ...Mr. *Congreve* immediately gave us a *Pindarique Ode*, the first, in the kind, it seems, he ever made: And I heartily wish, for his Encouragement, he had been as amply rewarded as (they say) he was for his *Pastoral* on the Death of the Queen; For, truly, I think the *Pindarique* not inferior to the *Pastoral*, with Submission to Mr. *Pittis*. And, perhaps, a Judicious Reader will take as much Pleasure in the Variety and Strength of M[r]. *Congreve*'s Numbers, as in the flowing Sweetness of Mr *Pittis*'s: Who, in my Opinion, seems all-a-long to affect the same Turn of Thought and Verse, and so, by ill Management makes a good Figure become Flat and Insipid. This is a Fault not chargeable on

Mr. *Congreve's Ode*; which, however, is justly Censur'd by Men of Learning, as a flashy rutilant Composure, very unworthy a Man of his Character in the World. I could indeed hardly have believ'd any Production of his would have betray'd him so much as this and his Pastoral have done. (p. 5)

(ii) But I would not here be suppos'd to rob Mr. *Congreve* of his just Commendations, since he has really perform'd many things to Admiration for a Man of his Years: And if he does not always write with the same Success, it is no other Misfortune than has attended the best Poets before him. Therefore he has no Reason to suspect that all his Works should be thought absolutely perfect, that being a pretension beyond Human Reach. I have so much Respect for his Worth, that I think him not to be numbred with any of these other Gentlemen. And I heartily wish he would spend less Time in serving a Senseless debauch'd Stage, and undertake some Noble *Epick Poem*, or the Translation of *Homer* (as Mr. *Dryden* has done that of *Virgil*) for such Labours as these would honour his Country and improve its Language.

(pp. 8–9)

Robert Shirley, lines from a poem sent to Thomas Coke, 21 January 1696 (*Historical Manuscripts Commission*, 12th Report, Appendix, pt 2, p. 359).

> Would Congreve or would Blackmoor now engage,
> They might with manly thoughts reform the stage:
> Recall us Muses, and redeem the name
> Of Poets, prostitute to abject fame.

Anon., *The Female Wits: Or, The Triumvirate of Poets at Rehearsal* (1709), 4. First acted *c*. October 1696.

Mar. I hope, Mrs. *Wellfed*, the Lines will bear the being heard twice and twice; else 'twou'd be bad for the Sparks who are never absent from the Play-house, and must hear 'em Seventeen or Eighteen Nights together.

Mrs. *Wellf.* How Madam! that's Three or Four more than the *Old Batchelour* held out.

George Smalridge to Thomas Gough, from Oxford, 29 November [1696], in Nichols, *Illustrations*, iii. 257.

I have read 'The Birth of the Muse,' and am extremely well pleased with the number and majesty of some of the verses. The model I should like better if it were not a little too intricate and perplexed. I should think it had been better that men, finding themselves mortal, should have begged of the Gods some method of rescuing the good and great from the common fate of the rest, than that the Gods should at the same time predestine them to be mortal, and be forced to provide against their own act by forming a Muse that should hinder its taking effect in some special instances. I find Time is appointed Lord of all Futurity in one verse, and in the next the womb of this Lord is mentioned; which seem to be very shocking, incompatible ideas. I do not rightly comprehend how the deeds of future ages are expressed in the bulky volume, whether in words, or pictures, or hieroglyphics, or sometimes in one, and sometimes in another way. I could wish, for good King Charles the First's sake, all the Reigns since Queen Elizabeth had not been so liberally condemned: it seems but an ill compliment to his Majesty to reflect on the Race he is descended from so generally. In the speech of Jove to the Muse, methinks, Homer should have had a place as well as Virgil, Spenser, and Congreve, especially since he was the first, if not the best, of those that the Muse employed in giving immortality.

Thomas Burnett to Leibniz, from London, 6/16 December 1696. In *Leibniz*, loc. cit. xiii. 383.

Quand je vous aye dit qu'on a fait un noveau recuil des pieces choisies des nos poetes d'aujourdhui dont il ny a pas une qui n'êt excellente et que Monsr Congrave done l'esperance baucoup de heritier della lirique de Mr Dreyden dans l'oppinione de lui même qui apelle Mr Congrave son fils ainé dans la poesie.

Catharine Trotter, 'To Mr. *Congreve*, on his Tragedy, the *Mourning Bride*', [March 1697], in *The Works of Mrs. Catharine Cockburn, Theological, Moral, Dramatic, and Poetical*. Revised and published by Thomas Birch. 2 vols. (1751), ii. 564–5.

> *To Mr.* Congreve, *on his Tragedy, the* Mourning Bride.
>
> H A D heav'n bestow'd on me half *Sappho's* flame,
> This noble theme had gain'd me larger fame;
> For none can think great *Congreve's* to extend,
> Or praising thee, ought but their own intend.
> Boundless thy fame does as thy genius flow,
> Which spread thus far, can now no limits know:
> This only part was wanting to thy name,
> That wit's whole empire thou mightst justly claim:
> On which so many vain attempts were made,
> Numbers pretending right their strength assay'd,
> But all alike unfit for the command,
> Only defac'd and spoil'd the sacred land;
> Which thou, as its undoubted native lord,

Has to its ancient beauty thus restor'd;
Where with amazement we at once may see
Nature preserv'd pure, unconstrain'd, and free,
And yet throughout, each beauty, ev'ry part,
Drest to the strictest forms of gracing art:
Thus perfected, on such a finish'd piece,
Where can my praise begin, or admiration cease!
Sublime thy thoughts, easy thy numbers flow,
Yet to comport with them, majestic too!
But to express how thou our souls do'st move,
How at thy will, we rage, we grieve, we love,
Requires a lofty, almost equal flight,
Nor dare I aim at such a dang'rous height,
A task, which well might *Dryden's* muse engage,
Worthy the first, best poet of the age;
Whose long retreat that we might less bemoan, ⎫
He left us thee, his greatest darling son, ⎬
Possessor of the stage, once his alone. ⎭
Tho' even he gain'd not thy height so soon,
And but the young great *Macedonian*, none;
Alike in youth you both sought early fame,
Both sure to vanquish too where'er you came;
But he by others aid his conquests gain'd,
By others too the fame of them remain'd;
Thou sov'reign o'er the vast poetic land,
Unaided, as unrival'd, do'st command,
And not oblig'd for fame, which records give,
In thy own works thou shalt for ever live.

Richard Blackmore, *King Arthur. An Heroick Poem. In Twelve Books*
(London, 1697), preface, pp. vii–viii. Advt. *LG* 18–22 March 1697.

This Poem [*The Mourning Bride*] *has receiv'd, and in my Opinion very justly,
Universal Applause; being look'd on as the most perfect* Tragedy *that has been wrote
in this Age. The* Fable, *as far as I can judge at first sight, is a very Artful and
Masterly Contrivance. The* Characters *are well chosen, and well delineated. That of*
Zara *is admirable. The* Passions *are well touch'd, and skillfully wrought up. The*
Diction *is Proper, Clear, Beautiful, Noble, and diversify'd agreeably to the Variety
of the Subject. Vice, as it ought to be, is punish'd, and Opprest Innocence at last
Rewarded. Nature appears very happily imitated, excepting one or two doubtful
Instances, thro' the whole Piece, in all which there are no immodest Images or
Expressions, no wild, unnatural Rants, but some few Exceptions being allow'd, all*

things are Chast, Just, and Decent. This Tragedy, as I said before, has mightily obtain'd; and that without the unnatural and foolish mixture of Farce and Buffoonry, without so much as a Song, or Dance to make it more agreeable. By this it appears, that as a sufficient Genius can recommend it self, and furnish out abundant matter of Pleasure and Admiration without the paultry helps above nam'd, so likewise that the Tast of the Nation is not so far deprav'd, but that a Regular and Chast Play will not only be forgiven, but highly Applauded.

[William Pittis *et al.*]. 'The Oxford Laureate', in *Miscellanies Over Claret, Or, The Friends to the Tavern The Best Friends to Poetry. Being a Collection of Poems, Translations, &c. to be continued Monthly from the Rose-Tavern without Temple-Bar*. Numb. 1 (1697), 17–18. Probably published May (*TC* iii. 15), the poem is a satire on the recent creation of the Professorship of Poetry at Oxford. The last line of stanza LXIII should perhaps read: '*beside 'em.*'

LX.

Tom Y—n was next, and a combing his Hair,
    When the Court was just going to rise,
And in, Sirs, he steps it, and enters his Prayer,
    To be try'd at this Gen'ral Assize.

LXI.

His crime was for being a Felon in Verse,
    And presenting his Theft to the King,
Tho the first was a trick not uncommon or scarce,
    Yet the last was an impudent Thing.

LXII.

What indeed he had stole was so little worth stealing,
    They forgave him the Damage and Cost,
Had he took the *whole Ode, as he took it peice mealing,
    He had fin'd for't, but Ten-pence at most.

LXIII.

Then he begg'd their excuse for his coming so late;
    But Dryden *and* Congreve *so ply'd Him*
With Letters and Praises, that he thought 'twas his Fate
    To run one day or other beside Him.

LXIV.

Alas! Sir, he said, did these Gentlemen know
    What a Temper I'm of, they not do it;
I have Wit, 'tis true—but they pester me so,
    That I'm quite tyr'd with being a Poet.

[marginal note] *Mr. Congreve*'s Ode to the King upon the Reduction of *Namur*.

Thomas D'Urfey, Epistle Dedicatory, *The Intrigues at Versailles: Or, A Jilt in all Humours. A Comedy* (London, 1697), sig. A2^r. Advt. the *Post Man*, 24 June 1697.

This New *Comedy* which I beg leave to Dedicate to ye, when it was first shewn to some Persons of Principal Quality and Judgment, and afterwards Read to Mr. *Congreve* and Mr. *Betterton*, had, from all, the good Fortune, to be esteem'd as one of the Best I have Written: And 'tis from this undisputed Authority that I hope it will, in the Perusal, have the same Value from you; and appear worthy the Honour of your Patronage.

John Dryden, *The Works of Virgil: Containing his Pastorals, Georgics and Æneis* (London, 1697), dedication, sig. (f)3^r.

... Mr. *Congreve* has done me the Favour to review the *Æneis*; and compare my Version with the Original. I shall never be asham'd to own, that this Excellent Young Man, has shew'd me many Faults, which I have endeavour'd to Correct. 'Tis true, he might have easily found more, and then my Translation had been more Perfect.

Joseph Addison, 'Pax Gulielmi Auspiciis Europae reddita 1697', in *Musarum Anglicanarum Analecta* (Oxford, 1691–9), dedication to Charles Montague, ii. 2.

Quod si Congrevius *ille Tuus divino, quo solet, furore correptus materiam hanc non exornasset, vix tanti esset Ipsa Pax, ut illa laetaremur tot perditissimis Poetis tam misere decantata.* [Davies, *Dramatic Miscellanies*, iii. 376, translates: 'Had not your Congreve, seiz'd with his usual fit of divine madness, condescended to celebrate the subject, the peace itself would not have been of such importance to us, nor could we, indeed, have rejoiced in it, considering how vilely it has been debased by the pens of despicable scribblers.']

Anon., *The Justice of Peace: Or a Vindication of Peace from Several Late Pamphlets, written by Mr. Congreve, Dennis, &c.* (London, 1697), 2–4.

> And *Thou*, First-Cousin to the *Nine*,
> In whom both Wit and Beauty shine,
> *Bright Nymph*, my kind Inspiring Guide,
> Oh, sit down gently by my Side;
> Make tuneful *Crambo* thy Pastime,
> And help thy Slave to pump for Rhyme;
> That in lewd Doggrel I may fall at

Making of Peace, so quaint a Ballad,
That may, as Simple as my Pen is,
Congreve out-Rhyme, and out-Rage *Dennis*.
　　Instead of saying what we want,
One Banters us with rumbling Cant;　　　*Dennis.*
Talks of deep *Pindar*'s sounding Lyre,
Of *Rapture, Fury, Flame* and *Fire*:
As if no Peace cou'd e'er be had,
But Hairbrain'd Poet must run Mad.
Another writes such soothing Number,　　　*Congreve.*
'Twoud almost lull one to a Slumber;
In Frontispiece stands *Birth of Muse*,
A *Porch* too big for such a *House*:
In gentle Strains he tells a Tale
Of *Heavenly Orb*, and *Earthly Ball*;
By dint of Rhyme he proves it clear,
That the *World hangs in Ambient Air*;
Sings of *Creation*, and rehearses
Good Prose of *Moses* in bad Verses.
But sure Transported Bard forgot,
Peace was the thing he shou'd be at;
For what is *Genesis* pray to it,
More than Religion to a Poet?
But I shan't *Moses* filch, nor *Pindar*;
Since nought my honest Heart can hinder,
But in a plain unborrow'd Dress,
I'll treat of nothing but *meer Peace*.

Charles Hopkins, Dedication to *Boadicea, Queen of Britain. A Tragedy*
(London, 1697), sigs. A2^r–A3^r. Probably first acted at LIF,
November 1697.

TO
Mr. Congreve.

LET other Poets other Patrons Chuse,
Get their best Price, and prostitute their Muse:
With flattering hopes, and fruitless labour wait,
And Court the slippery Friendship of the Great:
Some trifling Present by my Lord is made,
And then the Patron thinks the Poet paid.
On you, my surer, nobler Hopes depend,
For you are all I wish; you are a Friend.

From you, my Muse her Inspiration drew,
All she performs, I Consecrate to you.
You taught me first my Genius and my Power,
Taught me to know my own, but gave me more,
Others may sparingly their Wealth impart,
But he gives Noblest, who bestows an Art.
Nature, and you alone, can that confer,
And I owe you, what you your self owe her.
O! *Congreve*, could I write in Verse like thine, ⎫
Then in each Page, in every Charming Line, ⎬
Should Gratitude, and Sacred Friendship shine. ⎭
Your Lines run all on easie, even Feet;
Clear is your Sense, and your Expression sweet.
Rich is your Fancy, and your Numbers go
Serene and smooth, as Crystal Waters flow.
Smooth as a peaceful Sea, which never rolls,
And soft, as kind, consenting Virgins Souls.
Nor does your Verse alone our Passions move,
Beyond the Poet, we the Person Love.
In you, and almost only you; we find
Sublimity of Wit, and Candour of the Mind.
Both have their Charms, and both give that delight,
'Tis pity that you should, or should not Write;
But your strong Genius Fortune's power defies,
And in despight of Poetry, you rise.
To you the Favour of the World is shown,
Enough for any Merit, but your own.
Your Fortune rises equal with your Fame,
The Best of Poets, but above the Name.
O! may you never miss deserv'd success,
But raise your Fortunes 'till I wish them less.
     Here should I, not to tire your patience, end,
But who can part so soon, with such a Friend?
You know my Soul, like yours, without design,
You know me yours, and I too know you mine.
I owe you all I am, and needs must mourn,
My want of Power to make you some return.
Since you gave all, do not a part refuse,
But take this slender Offering of the Muse.
Friendship, from servile Interest free, secures
My Love, sincerely, and entirely, yours,

                    CHARLES HOPKINS

John Hopkins, *The Victory of Death; Or, The Fall of Beauty. A Visionary Pindarick-Poem* (1698), sig. A6ʳ–A6ᵛ. The poem, occasioned by the death of Lady Cutts on 23 November 1697, is addressed to Lord Cutts.

As to my former Poem call'd The Triumphs of Peace, *I know nothing that has offer'd which requires my Defence . . . I content my self, and with reason enough, that Mr. Congreve, Mr. Tate, and Mr. Dennis were pleas'd to like it . . . As to the present Poem . . . long as it is, Mr. Congreve, belov'd for his Candour, as much as for his Wit admir'd, was pleas'd not only to approve, but greatly to commend it, in having read it thrice.*

Anon., *Poems on Affairs of State: From Oliver Cromwell, To this present time. Part III. With other Miscellany Poems; And a new Session of the present Poets* (London, 1698), 307–8.

> The next Thought without pleading the Laurel to get
> Since by most he'd been told he was *the best Wit.*
> *The greatest Young Man*, rising Sun of the Age,
> But *Apollo* the Gentleman's heat to asswage,
> Proclaim'd if his Writing the Laurel shou'd wear,
> Of the Garland he'd have but a very small share.
> Since by his Plays, he most plainly descry'd,
> He did not much in his own Noddle confide;
> But yet him, for one of the Tribe he wou'd own, ⎫
> If in his next play for his Thefts to attone,   ⎬
> He'd Write a whole Leafe that was truly his own: ⎭
> But to show he cou'd Write, and recover his Cause,
> An Elegy out of his Pocket he draws,
> Where he hop'd he shou'd purchase the Bays for this Flight,
> > *Lost is the Day which had from her its Light,*
> > *For ever lost with her in endless Night:*
> > *In endless Night and Arms of Death she lies,*
> > *Death in eternal Shades has shut* Pastoras *Eyes.*
> Concern so Passionate who ever read,
> That Dictates nothing, but she's Dead, Dead, Dead!
> But still of all that fell upon the Queen,
> He's least injurious to her Ashes been.
> For what he has of Dread *Pastora* Sung,
> To *Cloris, Cynthia, Cisly* may belong.

George Powell, *The Fatal Discovery; Or, Love in Ruines* (London, 1698), preface, sig. A3^r. Probably first acted at *D L* , February 1698. Powell's comments were provoked by Dryden's prefatory verses to George Granville's *Heroick Love* in which he wrote 'those Lawrels I resign . . . revive on thine'.

. . . this great Wit [Dryden], with his Treacherous Memory, forgets, that he had given away his Lawrels upon Record, no less then twice before, *viz.* once to Mr. *Congreve*, and another time to Mr. *Southern*. Prithee old *Oedipus*, expound this Mystery: Dost thou set up thy own *Transubstantiation* Miracle in the Donation of thy Idol Bays, that thou hast 'em Fresh, New, and whole, to give 'em three times over? Or rather though three times given already, they are so little worth Acceptance, that thou hast 'em still to dispose threescore times more upon a Civil occasion.

Anon., in John Hughes, *Poems on Several Occasions*, 2 vols. (1735), i, p. vi. A Note is there given on Hughes's poem *The Triumph of Peace* written on the Peace of Ryswick and printed in 1697. It was praised by a 'learned Gentleman at *Cambridge*, in a Letter to a Friend of Mr. *Hughes*, dated the 28 of *February* 1697–8'.

I think I have never heard of a Poem read with so much Admiration, as *The Triumph of Peace* was by our best Criticks here; nor a greater Character given to a young a Poet, at his first appearing; no, not even to Mr. *Congreve* himself.

John Crowne, Epistle to the Reader, *Caligula. A Tragedy* (London, 1698), sigs. A3^v–A4^r. Advt. the *Flying Post*, 29–31 March 1698.

I cannot but take notice of some lines I have read in the Preface to the Poem call'd King Arthur, *where the World is told, that all who have written before the Author of the* Mourning-Bride, *may be asham'd, since for want of a Genius, they have depended on bawdy for their success on Stage. I much commend that Gentleman's [i.e. Blackmore's] design of Reforming the Stage from Obscenity, Immorality, and Profaneness; But I wish he had taken more care of his Pen: I mean not in his Poem.*

Jeremy Collier, *A Short View of the Immorality, and Profaneness of the English Stage* (London, 1698). Preface dated 5 March; advt. the *Flying Post*, 19–21 April 1698.

(i) *Jacinta, Elvira, Dalinda*, and *Lady Plyant*, in the *Mock Astrologer, Spanish Friar, Love Triumphant* and *Double Dealer*, forget themselves extreamly: And almost all the *Characters* in the *Old Batchelour*, are foul and nauseous. *Love* for

Love, and the *Relapse*, strike sometimes upon this *Sand*, and so likewise does *Don Sebastian*.   (p. 4)

(ii) They Represent their single Ladys, and Persons of Condition, under these Disorders of Liberty, This makes the Irregularity still more Monstrous and a greater Contradiction to Nature, and Probability: But rather than not be Vitious, they will venture to spoil a Character. This mismanagement we have partly seen already. *Jacinta*, and *Belinda* are farther proof. And the *Double Dealer* is particularly remarkable. There are but *Four* Ladys in this *Play*, and *Three* of the biggest of them are Whores. A Great Compliment to Quality to tell them there is not above a quarter of them Honest!   (p. 12)

(iii) And before we part with these *Comedians* we may take notice that there are no Smutty Songs in their *Plays*; in which the English [citing *Love for Love* and *Love Triumphant*] are extreamly Scandalous. Now to work up their Lewdness with Verse, and Musick, doubles the Force of the Mischief. It makes it more portable and at Hand, and drives it Stronger upon Fancy and Practice.   (p. 25)

(iv) *Achilles* at the first Sight of *Clytemnestra*, lets her understand he was as much taken with the Sobriety of her Air, as with the rest of her fine Face and Person. She receives the Complement kindly, and commends him for commending Modesty. *Menelaus* and *Helen* after a long Absence manage the surprize of their good Fortune handsomly. The Most tender Expression stands clear of ill Meaning. Had *Osmin* parted with *Almeria* as civilly as these Two met, it had been much better. That Rant of smut and profainness might have been spared. The *Reader* shall have some of it.

> *O my* Almeria;
> *What do the Damn'd endure but to despair,*
> *But knowing Heaven, to know it lost for ever.*

Were it not for the *Creed*, these *Poets* would be crampt in their Courtship, and Mightily at a loss for a Simile! But *Osmin* is in a wonderful Passion. And truly I think his Wits, are in some danger, as well as his Patience. You shall hear.

> *What are all Wracks, and Whips, and Wheels to this;*
> *Are they not soothing softness, sinking Ease,*
> *And wasting Air to this?*

Sinking Ease, and Wasting Air, I confess are strange comforts; This Comparison is somewhat oddly equip'd, but Lovers like sick People may say what they please! *Almeria* takes this Speech for a Pattern, and suits it exactly in her return.

> *O I am struck, thy words are Bolts of Ice?*
> *Which shot into my Breast now melt and chill me.*

Bolts of Ice? Yes most certainly! For the Cold is struck up into her Head, as you may perceive by what follows.

I chatter, shake, and faint with thrilling Fears.

By the way 'tis a mighty wonder to hear a Woman Chatter! But there is no jesting, for the Lady is very bad. She won't be held up by any Means, but Crys out.

—lower yet, down down;

One would think she was learning a Spanel to *Sett*. But there's something behind.

—no more we'll lift our Eyes,
But prone and dumb, Rot the firm Face of Earth,
With Rivers of incessant scalding Rain.

These Figures are some of them as stiff as Statues, and put me in mind of *Sylvesters Dubartas.*

Now when the Winters keener breath began
To Crystallize, the Baltick Ocean,
To glaze the Lakes, to bridle up the Floods,
And periwig with Snow the bald pate woods.

I take it, the other Verses are somewhat of Kin to These, and shall leave them to Mr. *Dryden's* Reflection. But then as for *Soothing Softness, Sinking Ease, Wasting Air, thrilling Fears, and incessant scalding Rain*; It puts me to another stand. For to talk a little in the way of the *Stage*. This Litter of *Epithetes* makes the *Poem* look like a Bitch overstock'd with Puppies, and sucks the Sence almost to skin and Bone. But all this may pass in a *Playhouse*: False Rhetorick and False Jewells, do well together.   (pp. 32–4)

(v) In the *Old Batchelour, Vain-love* asks *Belmour, could you be content to go to Heaven?*

Bell. Hum, *not immediatly in my Conscience, not heartily.*—This is playing I take it with Edge-Tools. To go to Heaven in jeast, is the way to go to Hell in earnest. In the Fourth *Act*, Lewdness is represented with that Gaity, as if the Crime was purely imaginary, and lay only in ignorance and preciseness. *Have you throughly consider'd (says Fondlewife) how detestable, how Heinous, and how crying a Sin the Sin of Adultery is? have you weighed I say? For it is a very weighty Sin: and altho' it may lie—yet thy Husband must also bear his part; For thy iniquity will fall on his Head.* I suppose this fit of Buffoonry and profaness, was to settle the Conscience of young Beginners, and to make the Terrors of Religion insignificant. *Bellmour* desires *Lætitia to give him leave to swear by her Eyes and her Lips*: He kisses the Strumpet, and tells her, *Eternity was in that Moment. Lætitia* is horibly profane in her Apology to her Husband; but having the *Stage-Protection* of Smut for her Guard, we must let her alone. *Fondlewife* stalks under the same shelter, and abuses a plain Text of Scripture to an impudent Meaning. A little before, *Lætitia* when her Intrigue with

Bellmour was almost discover'd, supports her self with this Consideration. *All my comfort lies in his impudence, and Heaven be prais'd, he has a Considerable Portion.* This is the *Play-house* Grace, and thus Lewdness is made a part of Devotion! Ther's another Instance still behind: 'Tis that of *Sharper* to *Vain-Love*, and lies thus.

I have been a kind of God Father to you, yonder: I have promis'd and vow'd something in your Name, which I think you are bound to Perform. For Christians to droll upon their Baptism is somewhat extraordinary; But since the *Bible* can't escape, 'tis the less wonder to make bold with the *Catechisme*.

In the *Double Dealer*, Lady *Plyant* cries out *Jesu* and talks Smut in the same Sentence. Sr. *Paul Plyant* whom the Poet dub'd a Fool when he made him a Knight, talks very Piously! *Blessed be Providence, a Poor unworthy Sinner, I am mightily beholden to Providence*: And the same word is thrice repeated upon an odd occasion. The meaning must be that *Providence* is a ridiculous supposition, and that none but Blockheads pretend to Religion. But the Poet can discover himself farther if need be. Lady *Froth* is pleas'd to call *Jehu a Hackney Coachman*. Upon this, *Brisk* replies, *If Jehu was a Hackney Coachman, I am answer'd—you may put that into the Marginal Notes tho', to prevent Criticisms—only mark it with a small Asterisme and say,—Jehu was formerly a Hackney Coachman.* This for a heavy Piece of Profaness, is no doubt thought a lucky one, because it burlesques the Text, and the Comment, all under one. I could go on with the *Double Dealer* but he'll come in my way afterwards, and so I shall part with him at present. (pp. 62–4)

(vi) *Scandal* solicits Mrs. *Foresight*; She threatens to tell her Husband. He replys, *He will die a Martyr rather then disclaim his Passion.* Here we have Adultery dignified with the stile of Martyrdom: As if 'twas as Honourable to perish in Defence of Whoring, as to dye for the Faith of Christianity. But these *Martyrs* will be a great while in burning, And therefore let no body strive to grace the Adventure, or encrease the Number. And now I am in this *Play* the Reader shall have more. *Jeremy* who was bred at the University, calls the Natural Inclinations to Eating and Drinking, *Whoreson Appetites.* This is strange Language! The *Manicheans* who made Creation the work of the Devil, could scarcely have been thus Coarse. But the *Poet* was *Jeremy's* Tutor, and so that Mystery is at an end. Sr. *Samson* carries on the Expostulation, rails at the Structure of Human Bodies, and says, *Nature has been Provident only to Bears, and Spiders*; This is the Authors Paraphrase on the 139 *Psalm*; And thus he gives God thanks for the Advantage of his Being! The *Play* advances from one wickedness to another, from the *Works* of God, to the Abuse of his Word. Foresight *Confesses 'tis Natural for Men to mistake.* Scandal *replies, You say true, Man will err, meer Man will err—but you are something more—There have been wise Men; but they were such as you—Men who consulted the Stars, and were observers of Omens—Solomon was wise but how?—by his Judgement in*

Astrology. 'Tis very well! *Solomon* and *Foresight* had their Understandings qualified alike. And pray what was *Foresight*? Why an *Illiterate Fellow*. *A pretender to Dreams, Astrology, Palmistry* &c. This is the *Poets* account of *Solomon's* Supernatural Knowledge! Thus the wisest Prince is dwindled into a Gypsie! And the Glorious Miracle resolved into Dotage, and Figure-flinging! *Scandal* continues his Banter, and says, the *wise Men of the East owed their Instruction to a Star; which is rightly observ'd by* Gregory *the Great in favour of Astrology*. This was the Star which shone at our Saviour's Birth. Now who could imagine by the Levity of the occasion, that the Author thought it any better than an *Ignis Fatuus*, or *Sydrophel's* Kite in *Hudibras*? Sr. *Sampson* and the fine *Angelica*, after some lewd raillery continue the Allegory, and drive it up into Profaness. For this reason the Citation must be imperfect.

Sr. Samps. Sampson's *a very good Name for—your* Sampsons *were strong Dogs from the Beginning.*

Angel. *Have a care—If you remember the strongest* Sampson *of your Name, pull'd an old House over his Head at last.* Here you have the Sacred History burlesqu'd, and *Sampson* once more brought into the House of *Dagon*, to make sport for the *Philistines*! To draw towards an end of this *Play*. Tattle would have carried off *Valentine's* Mistress. This later, expresses his Resentment in a most Divine manner! Tattle *I thank you, you would have interposed between me and Heaven, but Providence has laid Purgatory in your way*. Thus Heaven is debas'd into an Amour, and Providence brought in to direct the Paultry concerns of the *Stage*! *Angelica* concludes much in the same strain. *Men are generally Hypocrites and Infidels, they pretend to Worship, but have neither Zeal, nor Faith; How few like* Valentine *would persevere unto Martyrdom? &c.* Here you have the Language of the *Scriptures*, and the most solemn Instances of Religion, prostituted to Courtship and Romance! Here you have a Mistress made God Almighty, Ador'd with Zeal and Faith, and Worship'd up to Martyrdom! This if 'twere only for the Modesty, is strange stuff for a Lady to say of her self. And had it not been for the profane Allusion, would have been cold enough in all Conscience. (pp. 74–7)

(vii) The *Double Dealer* to say the least of him, follows his Master in this Road, *Passibus æquis*. Sr. *Paul Plyant* one would think had done his part: But the ridiculing *Providence* won't satisfie all People: And therefore the next attempt is somewhat bolder.

Sr. Paul. *Hold your self contented my Lady* Plyant,—*I find Passion coming upon me by Inspiration....* The *Double Dealer* is not yet exhausted. *Cynthia the Top Lady grows Thoughtful*. Upon the question she relates her Contemplation.

Cynth. *I am thinking (says she) that tho' Marriage makes Man and Wife one Flesh, it leaves them two Fools.* This Jest is made upon a Text in *Genesis*, and afterwards applyed by our Saviour to the case of *Divorse*. *Love for Love* will give us a farther account of this Authors Proficiency in the *Scriptures*. Our

Blessed Saviour affirms himself *to be the Way, the Truth, and the Light, that he came to bear witness to the Truth, and that his Word is Truth.* These expressions were remembred to good purpose. For *Valentine* in his pretended Madness tells *Buckram* the Lawyer: *I am Truth,—I am Truth.—Who's that, that's out of his way, I am Truth, and can set him right.* Now a *Poet* that had not been smitten with the pleasure of Blasphemy, would never have furnish'd Frensy with Inspiration; nor put our Saviours Words in the Mouth of a Madman. (pp. 82–3)

(viii) The *Old Batchelour* has a Throw at the *Dissenting Ministers.* The *Pimp Setter* provides their Habit for *Bellmour* to Debauch *Lætitia.* The Dialogue runs thus.

Bell. *And hast thou Provided Necessaries?*

Setter. *All, all Sir, the large Sanctified Hat, and the little precise Band, with a Swingeing long Spiritual Cloak, to cover Carnal Knavery,—not forgetting the black Patch which Tribulation* Spintext *wears as I'm inform'd upon one Eye, as a penal Mourning for the—Offences of his Youth* &c.

Barnaby calls another of that Character Mr. *Prig,* and *Fondlewife* carrys on the Humour lewdly in *Play-House Cant;* And to hook the *Church of England* into the Abuse, he tacks a *Chaplain* to the End of the Description.

Lucy gives an other Proof of the *Poets* good Will, but all little Scurilities are not worth repeating.

In the *Double Dealer* the discourse between *Maskwell* and *Saygrace* is very notable. *Maskwell* had a design to cheat *Mellifont* of his Mistress, and engages the Chaplain in the Intrigue: There must be a *Levite* in the cafe; *For without one of them have a finger in't, no Plot publick, or private, can expect to prosper.*

To go on in the order of the *Play.*

Maskwell calls out at *Saygraces door,* Mr. *Saygrace* Mr. *Saygrace.*

The other answers, *Sweet sir I will but pen the last line of an Acrostick, and be with you in the twinkling of an Ejaculation, in the pronouncing of an* Amen. *&c.*

Mask. *Nay good Mr.* Saygrace *do not prolong the time,* &c.

Saygrace. *You shall prevail, I would break off in the middle of a Sermon to do you Pleasure.*

Mask. *You could not do me a greater—except—the business in hand—have you provided a Habit for Mellifont?*

Saygr. *I have,* &c.

Mask. *have you stich'd the Gownsleeve, that he may be puzled and wast time in putting it on?*

Saygr. *I have; the Gown will not be indued without Perplexity.* There is a little more profane, and abusive stuff behind, but let that pass. (pp. 101–3)

(ix) *Bellmour* is Lewd and Profane, And *Mellefont* puts *Careless* in the best way he can to debauch *Lady Plyant.* These *Sparks* generally Marry up the

Top Ladys, and those that do not, are brought to no Pennance, but go off with the Character of Fine Gentlemen: ... *Valentine* in *Love for Love* is (if I may so call him) the Hero of the *Play*; This Spark the *Poet* would pass for a Person of Virtue, but he speaks to late. 'Tis true, He was hearty in his Affection to *Angelica*. Now without question, to be in Love with a fine Lady of 30000 Pounds is a great Virtue! But then abating this single Commendation, *Valentine* is altogether compounded of Vice. He is a prodigal Debauchee, unnatural, and Profane, Obscene, Sawcy, and undutiful, And yet this Libertine is crown'd for the Man of Merit, has his Wishes thrown into his Lap, and makes the Happy *Exit*. I perceive we should have a rare set of *Virtues* if these *Poets* had the making of them! How they hug a Vitious Character, and how profuse are they in their Liberalities to Lewdness?   (pp. 142–3)

(x) If any one would understand what the *Curse of all tender hearted Women is*, *Belmour* will inform him. What is it then? 'Tis the *Pox*. If this be true, the Women had need lay in a stock of ill Nature betimes. It seems 'tis their only preservative. It guards their Virtue, and their Health, and is all they have to trust to. *Sharper* another Man of Sense in this *Play*, talks much at the same rate.   (pp. 172–3)

Robert Gould, 'The Play-House. A Satyr', in *Collected Works*, 2 vols. (1709), ii. 258–9. Except that it must be after March 1697, and probably after Collier's *A Short View*, the date of this passage in Gould's revision of his poem is not known. Claiming that Rich's wealth was based on others' labours, he continues:

> How can our Suffering Tribe but chuse to be
> The Sons of Hardship and Necessity?
> When, let our Plays be acted half an Age,
> W'ave but a third Days Gleaning of the Stage?
> The rest is yours:—and hence your Sharers rise,
> And once above us, all our Aid despise:
> Hence has your *Osmin* drawn his Wealthy Lot,
> And hence has *Zara* all her Thousands got:
> *Zara!* that Proud, Opprobrious, Shameless Jilt,
> Who like a Devil justifies her Guilt,
> And feels no least Remorse for all the Blood sh'has spilt.

[Charles Gildon], Preface to *Phaeton: Or, The Fatal Divorce. A Tragedy. As it is Acted... in Imitation of the Ancients. With some Reflections on a Book call'd, a Short View of the Immorality and Profaneness of the English Stage* (London, 1698), sig. c1ᵛ. Advt. the *Post Boy*, 28–30 April 1698.

[Collier] is full of Indignation to hear Jeremy, in *Love for Love, Call the Natural Inclinations to Eating and Drinking*, Whoreson Appetites. *This is strange Language*, pursues he, the *Manichaeans, who made the Creation the work of the Devil, cou'd scarcely have been thus Coarse. Risem Teneatis?* They are our Authors own words I assure you.... Mr. *Collier* [is] at last as guilty in this particular as Mr. *Congreve*, for he himself calls our Natural Inclinations to Generation *brutal*, and which are fully as Natural as that to *Eating* and *Drinking*; to say nothing of Divine Injunction in *Genesis*. Now I can't help thinking that *brutal*, is to the full as infamous, and impious an Epithete for our *Inclinations*, as *Whoreson*. Again he will have Mr. *Congreve* guilty of no less than Blasphemy, for making *Valentine* in *Love for Love* say that he is *Truth*, because there is an Expression something like it in the *holy Scriptures*. At this way of arguing he may deny us the Use of the Whole *Alphabet*, because the Words of the *Bible* are composed out of it; or evidently cut out three parts of all *the Languages, the Bible is translated into.*

Here he is angry with Mr. *Congreve* for hitting by chance on two words which stood together in the *New Testament?* anon he is more angry with Mr. *Vanbrook* for altering the words of the Text in the *Provok'd Wife.*

Presentmt. of the Grand Jury May Sessions 1698 [Middlesex County, England]. agt Poetts. & Plays. MH: bMS Thr 32. See Luttrell, iv. 379 (12 May 1698).

Wee the Grand Jury for the County of Middx being made sensible of his Ma[ies]ties proue[n] intentions for suppressing profaneness & immorality by his late gratious Proclamac[i]on in that behalfe openli read in Court at the begining of this Seu[er]all Quarter Sessions as the tenour thereof required And Wee observing that such Vices are much incresed by the more then Ordinary licentiousness vsed by the Poets that supply the Playhouses in the County with very profane & Lewd Comedies where the same are Acted & vttered on the Publick Stages thereof, Doe pr[es]ent William Congreve gent the Author of the Comedy called the Duble Dealer acted at the Playhouse in the County called the Theatre Royall, for that amongst other profane and immorall expressions, one of the Dramatick persons in the said Comedy as is extant in print, with his name thereto Fol: 34 profanely and in breach of the Law cryes out, *Jesu:* And Fol 18. Another of them profanely and immorally sayes these words, I am thinking that tho Marriage makes man and wife one flesh it leaues them still two fooles.

Wee also present Thomas Durfey gent the Author of the first part of the Comicall History of Don Quixote acted at the Playhouse in the said County then called the Queens Theatre in Dorsett Garden for that in the said Comicall History as it is printed with his name thereto, amongst other profane and immorall expressions there are these profane words Fol: 61 in allusion to the faln Angells and the torments of Hell,

> You that always in Lucifers Kitchin reside
> Mongst seacoal and Kettles and greace newly tryed
> That pampered each day with a Garbidge of Souls
> Broyle Rashers of fools for a Breakfast on Coals.

Wee being alsoe satisfied in our consciences that the printing and vending of the said Comedy and Comicall History and of a Comedy called the Relapse acted at the Theatre Royall in Drury Lane whereto no Authors name is sett doe further increase the said Vices by reason of the profane and immoral words herein recited as aforesaid and by Reason that in the Said Relaps amongst other profane and immorall expressions are these profane words as tis printed Fol 97 Good Gods, *what slippery stuffe are men composed of sure the account of their creation's false. And twas the womans Rib that they are formed of*

Wee like p[re]sent Jacob Tonson Bookseller for causeing the first part of the said Comicall History to bee printed whereby it hath been exposed to sale,

Wee also p[re]sent Samuel Briscoe Bookeseller for causeing the two severall Comedies called the Duble Dealer and the Relaps to be printed whereby they have been severally exposed to sale.

Wee p[re]sent further that the frequenting of the Theaters by women in Masks is a com[m]on Nusance and tends very much to debauchery & imorality. [Nineteen names are appended.]

[Anon.], '*On Mr.* Congreve *and Mr.* Dennis *his late Poems concerning the* Peace. *The one Entitled,* The Birth of the Muse, *the other,* The Nuptials of Britains Genius with Fame', in *Miscellanies over Claret.* 1698. Edited by William Pittis *et al.* Numb. III, p. 62. The first number was published May 1698 (*TC.* iii. 15).

> T W O Men of Wit desirous of esteem,
> Took Pen in hand, and made the Peace their Theme:
> The same their Subject, both set out for Praise,
> But *different* as in *Age,* in *different ways*:
> The *First* was young, and eager to be doing,
> Nor would He stay the tedious form of *Wooing,*

But fell to work, and unadvis'dly wild,
Made *Father Time*, the *Mother* of a Child,
And in a Trice begat the Muse, to Sing
Her *Father*'s Praises, whilst She Prais'd the *King*.
  The *Last* Confirm'd in Judgment and in Age,
Ask'd Counsel of His *Years* to guide his *Rage*;
Not that *He* wholly did *His* warmth disdain,
For what his *Youth* could Act, His *Age* could feign:
But to be thought sedate, and 'th out offence,
The *Man* of *Wit* put on the *Man* of *Sense*,
  And to prevent the danger of Miscarriage,
Fairly Sate up for *Honourable Marriage*:
Nor would Loves Joyes at *Forty Nine* receive,
Without the Venerable *Parsons* leave.
The Bargain made, the Nuptial Knot was ty'd,
And *Mother* Peace was *Father* to the Bride.
What sort of *Love* is this, when *Man* conceives?
What *Marriage*, when the Bride the *Woman* gives?
Both had done well, and wrote without a Crime,
Had *Father Peace* been chang'd with *Mother Time*:
Well, had the *First* been Parent to *HIS Muse*,
The *Last* assisted at *His Bridal Noose*.

Elkanah Settle, *A Defence of Dramatick Poetry* (London, 1698), 88–9.

Nay, I dare be so bold, as to tell this angry Gentleman, as highly as he Resents the Cuckolding of Aldermen and Quality in our Comedies, that I could find him Matter of very good Instruction, from a Character of this kind, in a very Ingenious Author, though not much in Mr. *Colliers* Favour. For Example, If the Reverend Gentlemen of the Fur would be but half as kind to a *Play-house* as a *Pin-makers-Hall*, and step for Edification, but so far towards *Westminster*, as to see the *Old Batchelor*; I doubt not but an *Isaac Fondlewife* would be a very seasonable Monitor to Reverend City Sixty, to warn against the Marrying to Sixteen. Nor can I think it such a scandalous part of the Dramatick Poet; but rather a true Poetick Justice, to expose the unreasonableness of such Superannuated Dotage, that can blindly think or hope, that a bare Chain of Gold has Magick enough in the Circle to bind the Fidelity of so unequal a Match, a Match so contrary to the Holy Ordinance of Matrimony; and an Itch at those Years that deserves the severest Lash of the Stage. And if an Author would pick out such a Character for a little Stage Satyr, where can he meet with it but amongst the City or Court Quality? Such Inequality of Marriages are rarely to be found, but under the Roofs of Honour, for so Antiquated a Lover, (the least he can do) must bring a Coach and Six, to carry off such a Young Bride.

One thing mightily offends this Divine Author, *viz.* That our Modern Plays make our Libertines of both Sexes, Persons of Figure and Quality, Fine Gentlemen and Ladies of Fashion, a fault utterly unpractis'd by the Ancient Poets: *For* Terence *and* Plautus *his Strumpets are little People.*

Now this is so far from a fault in our Comedies, that there's a necessity of those Characters, and a Vertue in that Choice. For as the greatest and best part of our Audience are Quality, if we would make our Comedies Instructive in the exposing of Vice, we must not lash the Vices at *Wapping* to mend the Faults at *Westminster.*

Anon., *Letter to A.H. Esq; Concerning the Stage* (London, 1698), 18–19. Presumably addressed to Anthony Hammond, possibly by Charles Hopkins.

If the Theatre was down, the Churches wou'd not be the fuller for't. Or if they shou'd, Religion is not always the design of them who come there; so that I cannot see that any thing can be allow'd for the publick Diversion with so much Innocence and so much Advantage. I'm only afraid that such a Regularity wou'd be too Vertuous for the Age; and I don't doubt but the Beaux and Poetasters wou'd be full of Exclamation; For it wou'd be a dreadful Time if the Ladies should regard the Play more than their Beaux Airs; and how wou'd *Vanbroug* be able to pass a Comedy on them, if they shou'd once be so nice in their Taste as to disgust Obscenity; this indeed wou'd be a Vexation, and such a Delicacy which Mr. *Congreve* cou'd not be pleased with: And if the Town shou'd be so refin'd to admit of nothing but what is Natural, we can't expect that ever he will gratifie us with another Tragedy.

[Charles Gildon], *A Letter to Mr. Congreve, Occasion'd by the Death of the Countess Dowager of Manchester, Late Wife to his Excellency the Right Honourable Charles Montague* (London, 1698), 2, 9, 10. Attributed to Gildon in O: MS Rawl. poet. 99, f. 1[r] (undated).

(i)   O *Congreve!* sound again your tuneful Reed,
    To which you sung the great *Pastora* dead.
    How, on thy Verse the Mourning Shepherds hung!
    How blest the Poet! how ador'd his Song!
    Not the *Sicilian,* or the *Mantuan* Bard,

With juster Wonder, and Delight was heard.
Thy charming Voice, O *Congreve!* once more raise,
Another *M A R Y* challenges thy Lays.
Again thro' Woods and Vales thy sorrow spread,
Another *Hero* mourns, another *Heroine* dead.

(ii)   O *Congreve!* here, draw o'er an awful Veil, ⎫
No Art can Paint, no mighty Poet tell   ⎬
The *Hero*'s Pangs, and Tortures when she fell.   ⎭
From hateful Throngs, and ev'n from Friends he flies,
To lonely Shades, and there, a living Death he dies!
Miser in only this, he hugs his Care,
And with strange Avarice of Woe, denys his Friends a share.

(iii)   O *Congreve!*—
Now raise thy Voice, now tow'r above the height
Of the *Meonian*, or the *Mantuan* Flight.
Like *Milton* Soar, like *Milton* too declare   ⎫
Amazing things, that Man's unus'd to hear,   ⎬
That Ecstasie the ravish'd Soul, through the glad listning Ear. ⎭

[Anon.] *A Vindication of the Stage . . . In Answer to Mr. Collier's late Book . . . In a Letter to a Friend* (London, 1698), 14. Advt. the *Post Man*, 17 May 1698.

Words may be wrested to a quite contrary Sense of their Author, and that made to appear ill in a Quotation, which is not so of it self. How can he [Collier] be sure that Mr. *Congreve* intended to ridicule Religion, when he made *Valentine* in his Madness say *he was Truth?* 'Tis very probable Mr. *Congreve* intended no such matter; and if he did not, Mr. *Collier* is guilt of Falshood and Slander.

P. Harman, 'To the Author', in Catharine Trotter, *Fatal Friendship. A Tragedy* (London, 1698), sig. A3ᵛ. Performed May 1698. Advt. *LG*, 4–7 July 1698.

> *'Tis thus you may support the sinking Stage,*
> *Thus learn the Scriblers that infect this Age;*
> *To Mourn how Nature stinted their poor lot*
> *And leave for humble arts their Plays and Plot:*
> *Let* Congreve, Granvile, *and the few who yet,*
> *Support the credit of our Poets Wit;*
> *With you the Empire of the Stage maintain . . .*

Thomas D'Urfey, Preface to *The Campaigners: Or, The Pleasant Adventures at Brussels* (London, 1698). Advt. the *Post Man*, 7–9 July 1698.

(i) ... where he can find no other Name or Character for two Gentlemen of Honour and Merit, *viz.* Mr. *Congreve* and Captain *Vanbrooke*, who have written several excellent Plays, and who are only scandalous to our Critick, by being good Poets, yet these he can give no other Names or Characters, but what are Abusive and Ridiculous. The first, for only making *Jeremy*, in *Love for Love*, call the Natural inclinations to eating and drinking, *Whorson Appetites*, he tells, That the *Manicheans, who made Creation the Work of the Devil, scarcely spoke any thing so course.* And then very modestly proceeding onwards, says, *The Poet was* Jeremy*'s Tutor.*   (p. 5)

(ii) [Charging Collier with hypocrisy, D'Urfey notes a] Remark upon Mr. *Congreve*'s Comedy the *Old Batchelor*, which shews his contradiction of himself, and his fallacy undeniable, for there he seems to roar at young *Belmour* for his forgetfulness of Religion, at a minute where he is desiring *Laetitia to give him leave to swear by her Lips and Eyes,* when he is kissing and telling her, *Eternity was in that moment.* In short, when he has got her fast in his Arms, and intends to go through stitch with the matter; for which he calls the Lady Strumpet, and raves at the smuttiness of the Action; and yet, a little while after, in another page, rallies, jokes upon, and banters young *Worthy* in the *Relapse*, for letting his Lady slip through his fingers, and calls him a *Town-Spark*, and a *Platonick Fool* for't.   (p. 12)

Gabriel Ballam, letter to Anthony Smith who had noted that '*Collier*'s Book is greedily swallow'd', in *A Pacquet from Will's: Or a New Collection of Original Letters* (1701), sig. 2D7ʳ. The letter is undated but must have been written shortly after 9–12 July 1698 when Congreve's *Amendments* was advertised.

Mr. Congreve*'s Answer is come out, wherein he proves Mr.* Collier *to be a very honest Man, by his false and imperfect Citations, and his becoming Assurance, in charging him with his own Nonsense: All this is very plain, and fully proved, with mild, yet forceable Arguments.*

Anon., *A Letter to Mr. Congreve On His Pretended Amendments &c.* (London, 1698). Advt. the *Post Man*, 30 August–1 September 1698.

(i) I must tell you, there is a great deal of difference, between using the same common *Alphabet*, with that in Scripture; and the borrowing of some peculiar Words, or Phrases, from it, that are *Spelt out of that Alphabet.* For Example,

our Saviour has this peculiar Expression of himself, I am the Truth; which
is so emphatical, and remarkable, in relation to his Person, that the whole
tenor of the Gospel depends upon it: When this Expression therefore is put
familiarly into the Mouth of a Mad-man upon the stage, and made as it were,
the distinguishing Catch, and Bob of his Frenzy; this I think, is something
more, than spelling out of the *Alphabet*. I do assure you, it had that ill effect,
that I never met with any one, who came from that Play, but confest, it gave
them Offence; and minded them from whom the expression was taken. Wou'd
you had been contented with your first thought, I am *Tom tell troth*! for that
had been harmless, and foolish enough, and fit for a Mad-man. (pp. 12–13).

(ii) I see no great occasion of moderating distinctly, between you both, in
relation to all the particular matters in dispute, from your Plays: Your
Tragedy is a very good one, and Answers Sir *Rich. Blackmores* Character of
it, who recommends it, for an admirable one; but still with this reserve, *some
few things only excepted*: for instance; when you make King *Manuel*, in the fury
of his resentment, say, of *Osmyns pleading audacious Love* to his Mistress;

[*MB* 11. x. 16–19 is cited here.]

Thats a bold stroke indeed! I protest, if I had been the Author of it, I should
have trembled at the *Gigantick* insolence of my fancy: afterward, the attempt
is likened to *Ixions Embracing Divinity*: Bless me! you Poets do frequently
make so bold with God Almighty, and his Divinity; that if he had not
declared himself, from his own mouth, to be a God of Patience and long
suffering; I should wonder how he does bear it of you.

Then again, you make this blustering King pay his, and your respects, to
the Character, and Office of a Clergyman, very handsomely.

[*MB* 1. iv. 76–8 is cited here.]

But when you make so very bold with God's honour, his Priests may
contentedly take any thing, in the same Play: *The Disciple is not above his
Master, nor the Servant above his Lord, &c.* vid. Matt. 10.24, 25, 26.

I would fain bestow one note more upon the *Mourning Bride*, tho' I am sure to
incur the Censure of ill nature, and the *Splene* for it: This I know is your Darling
Off-Spring, and therefore I would be very tender of it; you have been at the
expence of more Education than ordinary upon it, and therefore you say, p. 23,
If Smut, and Prophaneness, can be prov'd against this, you must give up the Cause.
I am not now upon charging it with *Smut*; but when I have dropt this one remark
more to the two former, I will leave it to your self to judge, whether it is not now
and then a little *Prophane*: Methinks you seem somewhat Conscious of it
already, when immediately after, in that same Paragraph, you silently let fall
the word *Prophaneness*; and cry out, *if there be immodesty in that Tragedy, I must
confess my self incapable of ever writing any thing with modesty, or decency.*

But to convince you farther (if you are not yet convinc't) that there is
Prophaneness in that Play, let me prevail with you to weigh that violent rapture
of *Osmyn* to his *Bride* over again. *Mourn. Bride*, p. 35.

> *My all of bliss, my everlasting Life,*
> *Soul of my Soul, and end of all my wishes.*

Osmyn, or *Alphonso*, is your *Hero*; and design'd for the Character of a very
good, and brave Person; and therefore, when it comes to his turn to speak, we
expect a great deal of the *Poets* mind, and Principles from him; for the
Honourable Mr. *Granville*, makes it *a pretty true observation of Poets, that in
the frame of their Heroes, they commonly draw their own Pictures*: But now,
when *your All of bliss, Your everlasting life, Your very Soul*, and *the end of all
your wishes*, are all wrapt up together, and consummated in the enjoyment of
one Woman; What is become of your *Heaven*? Or what farther business, or
interest can you have depending in that *eternal* state, where *they neither
Marry, nor are given in Marriage*? I am clearly for your encouraging Men to
Love their Wives; but there is no necessity of representing a Good Husband
so very *uxorious*, as to make him declare himself possest of *Heaven*, and the
eternal rewards of Religion, when he has his *Spouse* in his Arms.—But some
grains of allowance must be made here, since

> *This was an Off'ring to the sex design'd.* Epil.

(pp. 14–17)

Anon., *Animadversions on Mr. Congreve's Late Answer to Mr. Collier*
(London, 1698). Advt. the *Flying Post*, 3–6 September 1698. The
title-page epigraph is from *OB* (1694), p. 47: 'A-Gad there are good
Morals to be pick'd out of *Æsop's Fables* . . . Damn your Morals: I must
avenge th'Affront done to my Honour.'

(i) *Being very Idle, I made bold to seize the Reins of your Friend* Will's *Prose*
Pegasus, (*and yet his most fiery Poetick Steed is no better*) *to make my Remarks a
little how he foam'd, and champ'd upon his Bit; and tho' he was a* Guift Horse to
the World *this bout (for I think no body bought him) I presum'd to* look him in
the Mouth. *He had many Faults, I found as I View'd him; very Headstrong;
when Spurr'd, apt neither to run, nor Pace, but Kick and Fling, or at best, fall into
a hard uncouth, unsufferable Trot. I observ'd him from Head to Tail, he was both
Crop'd and Bob'd. He was so untoward, he had given his Rider (while he
pretended to shew him) several Falls, and so I thought fit to take hold of him.*
*This is all the Account I think necessary to be given of my Pebble-stone attempt
upon the very Front of this* Goliah; *one, who braves Heaven as much as the former
did, even in his most Modest and Innocent Play as he calls it. I'll give you an
Instance or two.—*

> *Alm.*—How I have Mourn'd and Pray'd,
> For I have Pray'd to thee as to a Saint;

A Roman-Catholick *no doubt, but on*—

> And thou hast hear'd my Prayer, for thou art come
> To my Distress, to my Despair, which Heav'n
> Without thee cannot Cure.

This is Superfine, for certain; But I find here was a Cure to be perform'd in the business, and Heaven we must suppose, could not have apply'd it to the Wounded part, till the Poet *had spread out* Ozmyn *as a Plaister to be laid upon her—even so, for here again he says*—

> *Ozmyn.* Thou art my Wife—nay, thou art yet my Bride!
> The sacred Union of Connubial Love
> Yet unaccomplish'd; his Mysterious Rites
> Delay'd—
> Is this dark Cell, a Temple for the God?
> Or this vile Earth an Altar for such Offerings?

'Tis pretty plain, he wanted to be doing: And, since Mr. Congreve *left them in the Dark, no doubt, but they grop'd out one anothers Meaning, and he found an Altar for his Offerings.*

Now, If you can be as Grave as a Bishop, when he hears Venereal Causes in the Spiritual Court, you shall have more on't in the next Page—

> *Ozmyn.* Then *Garcia* shall ly Panting on thy Bosom,
> Luxurious, Revelling amidst thy Charms,
> And thou perforce must yield and Aid his Transports.

This is luxuriously *Modest, on my Word. I wonder who* yielded *to* Aid *Mr.* Congreve's Transports *when [he] writ this: He must certainly have beheld several beautiful* Idea's *of Lust, to draw this Picture of Obscenity by, as well as the other Painter had, who drew his* Luscious Venus.

Now for another touch of Prophaneness—

> *Alm.* 'Tis more than Recompence to see thy Face;
> If Heaven is greater Joy, it is no Happiness,
> For 'tis not to be born.—

If that be Mr. Congreve's *Opinion, he need not covet to go to Heaven at all, but to stay and Ogle his Dear* Bracilla, *with sneaking looks under his Hat, in the little side Box. One more, and then I have done; tis a most rampant one.*

> *King.* Better for him to tempt the Rage of Heaven,
> And wrench the Bolt red hissing from the hand

Of him that Thunders, than but think that Insolence.
'Tis daring for a God—

Now, he might have made something of this with a little Paraphrase, and
avoided the Prophanity too, as thus—

Better for him to tempt the Tavern's Fury,
In the full Face of a *Presenting Jury.*
Snatch the brisk Glass red sparkling from the hand
Of him that draws it—
  Comment. (Drawer understand.
Than but to think to thrust out Snout like Hog,
Or Bark, or so—'tis daring for a Dog.

Pray now, was not our Poet a very insolent Capaneus, *to Brave a true* Jove,
and real Thunder? But 'tis my Opinion, that he who [shews] no Morality to Men,
can't shew any Religion to a God.

As an Instance of his unGentile Principles; One Mr. P— *shew'd him his Play,*
he approv'd on't, and tho' perhaps it deserv'd its Fate, yet 'tis very well known who
it was, that by his Interest of Voices, caus'd it to be damn'd. I instance this
Gentleman particularly, because, his false Friend fail'd in all his other attempts
of the like good Office.

However, this Gentleman's Countrymen are not much oblig'd to him; for he is
pleas'd (where he confesses his Demerits) to say he hopes the Faults are to be
Excus'd in a young Writer, and especially a Man of Ireland. *None I think, but*
the Author of such a Play, would have writ such a thing; I resent it, for perhaps
I have the misfortune to have been born in Ireland, *and to own it too. However,*
I think Mr. Congreve *would have done well to have made the like Excuse (in*
spight of Staffordshire) *for his Poetry.* (sigs. $a1^v$–$a6^v$)

(ii) *Others perhaps may fancy that I have been too Severe upon Mr.* Congreve; *but*
I shall only desire these Gentlemen to take a slight View of his Book, and I dare
engage they'll soon be of another Opinion. They'll find his Pages fuller of Malice than
right Reasoning, and instead of being stor'd with Sense, blacken'd with Gall and
Spleen. His way of Answering Mr. Collier, *is with Satyr and Reflection; and since he*
has set the Copy *he can't take it ill if he is Imitated, especially when he sees we have*
observ'd our Distance, and not presum'd to cope with him in his Master-piece.
For we are all assur'd his Prophetick Truth's now fulfil'd, viz.

Not But the Man has Malice, wou'd he show it;
But on my Conscience, he's a bashful Poet:
You think that strange,—no matter—he'll out-grow it.
  (sigs. $a7^v$–$a8^r$)

(iii) In short, those Plays *are little Compounds of the whole Body of Scriblers*:
Nay, even *Tom. Du—y* has not been proof against his Stealths, and I would
have him reflect Mr. *Congreve*'s Motto upon him, *viz.*

> *Those pretty things Friend* Congreve *you rehearse,*
> *Were once my Words, tho' they are now your Verse.*

(p. 7)

(iv) *Smith.* But if he has still the itch to steal and publish on, and scan other
Men's Prose on his own Unpoetical Fingers, he does it so roughly, they must
needs break out to Soreness.

> *Et vivos roderet ungues*, &c.

For Example, I'll repeat you one or two of his smooth Lines.

> *For Love's Island: I for the Golden Coast.*

Now if you can get a Shore on that Island without being plaguily out of
Breath, I'll be bound to find out the Golden Coast for Mr. *Congreve*.

> *Let's have a fair Trial, and a clear Sea.*

There's a Line for you, that has sayl'd it self into a clear Sea of Prose.

(pp. 12–13)

(v) *Smith.* . . . In his 13th. page, he says, he has written but four poor Plays,
here indeed the Man were modest, had he not said *Written*. Well, four Plays;
in how many Years? About eight; doe she not hammer out his *Minerva*'s?

Johns. Why; 'tis necessary a good Play should be a twelve Month or two a
Writing . . .   (p. 16)

(vi) *Epithets make Prose languishing, and cold; and the frequent use of them in*
Prose, makes it pretend too much, and approach too near to Poetry. Sure the
Gentleman forgot himself here, the Ague of inervate coldness, not the Feaver
of Passion has seiz'd him now, but he has been kneading up his Prose so long,
that in spite of all his shaking, it will stick upon his hands; for that the same
thing *should make Prose languishing and cold, and yet approach too near to any*
Poetry, (but Mr. *Congreve*'s) is as strange to me, as that the same acquaintance
between Mr. *Charles Hopkins* and him, should make the former, through too
much good Nature, and willingness to raise his *Friend* as he *thought him*,
Dedicate, and Ascribe to him, what he really owes to Nature only; and the
latter very impudently, in publick; to say he was very angry with him for the
presumption. A very pretty Fellow truly this.   (pp. 26–7)

(vii) *Johns.* Prethee mind the Book, and read that, not the Man, don't make
him worse than he is, or you'll run into as bad a distinction as you say he does,
when he divides Mr. *Collier* the Divine, and Mr. *Collier* the Critick, for here
you make a difference between the *Poet*, and Mr. *Congreve*.

Smith. O there's a great deal of difference, but perhaps I don't pretend to make them the *same person*. Besides, he takes Mr. *Collier*'s person to task, and why should not I inspect him a little, 'tis not his snarling at the Town in a fulsom Dedication to a damn'd Play, when he should Address to his Patron all the while, that shall make me spare him, neither am I bound to believe him when he says in the same Dedication—*If I really wish it might have had a more popular reception; it is not at all in consideration of my self; but because I wish well, and would gladly contribute to the benefit of the Stage, and diversion of the Town.* There's your *Double Dealer* for you, never was Poets Character better drawn by himself, *since the Ignorance and Malice of the greater part of the Audience grew such, that they would make a Man turn Herald to his own Play, and blazon every Character.* I'll no more believe his late Declaration to the World and his Patron, than I believ'd him, when he said he'd go as far as *New-Market* to see a Play which a Friend of mine writ; but perhaps Mr. *Congreve* thought himself particularly concern'd, which made him mention *New-Market*, when the Horse-Races were run there, this Gentleman, he said (as he had heard) declar'd to *set up in opposition to him* in the other House, so, 'tis likely, Mr. *Congreve* thought his Poetry in danger: But, *set up, what?* Not himself, in opposition to Mr. *Congreve*. I dare excuse my Friend from that Grand Presumption, or the open profession of it at least; he only, as being a Poet, design'd indeed to set up his *Pegasus* at the other House, pray, what was that to Mr. *Congreve*: O, but when he talk'd of opposition to his House, perhaps 'twas something to the Beast he rides on. Now in my opinion, it would be well if he could bridle his Tongue, and not spur himself, as well as his *Rosinante*, out of breath; nor would I have him think others, (who may have better Coursers) must be rid out o' the stirrups, because he has got so much the start of them; and I know not how it might have gone, if my Friend had given him the Challenge, (tho' he never design'd more than an ayring) but I dare Swear he would have Sweated Least, and yet I'll allow too what *Hartwell* says,

> *All Coursers the first heat with vigour run,*
> *But 'tis with Whip and Spur the Race is won.*

the Gentleman too thought Mr. *Congreve* not his Enemy at least, because when he was first recommended to him by a Friends Letter, the mighty Man of Wit was pleas'd to say he'd give him what assistance possibly he could in his Art, (as he was pleas'd to call it) when in the end, at the Representation of this Play of my Friend's, he was seen very gravely with his Hat over his Eyes among his chief Actors, and Actresses, together with the two She Things, call'd *Poetesses*, which Write for his House, as 'tis nobly call'd; thus seated in State among those and some other of his Ingenious critical Friends, they fell all together upon a full cry of Damnation, but when they found the malicious

Hiss would not take, this very generous, obliging Mr. *Congreve* was heard to say, *We'll find out a New way for this Spark, take my word there is a way of clapping of a Play down.*—This was heard by very creditable Persons, but his Malice could no way prevail, for spite of him, and all other disadvantages the Play surviv'd with Applause, and overcame his Envy. (pp. 30–5)

(viii) Well, see this same High-born Babe, with not one of his Father's Rays about him, or any thing else of the God, but the fiery Rage, when he's at a loss how to Guide.

Inspiration signifies no more than Breathing into; Now, if if [sic] it be so, I believe when Mr. *Congreve* was *Inspir'd* with Poetry, he was only *Breath'd into*; but whether it might be the back way or no, I leave to the Opinion of the World. He has got a Dog-trick of turning round sometimes before he lyes down, as referring, (when all his other *Breathing into* is gone) to some of his fine Propositions.

Well, after his reference to his *Postulatum*, sure you would think he were lay'd; Ay, but he gets up again to Bark a little; he renews the Discourse, meerly to shew his knowledge of a *Puppet-show*, where he owns he can only argue as the *Puppet* did with the *Rabbi; It is Prophane, and it is not Prophane.* This is *pro* and *con*, that's the Truth on't, but if he would do as Mr. *Brisk* desires, that is, give us *Marginal Notes*; it might be some Satisfaction. (pp. 50–1)

(ix) ... while Mr. *Collier* is thus planted Piecemeal, where do'st think Mr. *Congreve* will take his Post? Why with his Dear *Bracilla*, in the little Box over the Stage, with his Hat held before his Face, to shew his Modesty; or his Hatstring. (p. 61)

(x) *Mr.* Congreve*'s Vanity in pretending to Criticism, has extreamly betray'd his Ignorance in the Art of Poetry: This is manifest to all that understand it, and I am not the only One who look on this Pamphlet of his to be a Gun levell'd at the whole Clergy, while the Shot only glances on Mr.* Collier. ... he has follow'd Capt. *Vanbrook* most servilely in every thing—but his Wit, and Gentleman-like stile ... (pp. 67–8)

Jeremy Collier, *A Defence of the Short View of the Profaneness and Immorality of the English Stage, &c. Being a reply to Mr. Congreve's Amendments* (London, 1699). Advt. the *Post Man*, 3–6 December 1698.

(i) [Congreve's] Latitude of *Comedy* upon *Aristotle*'s Definition; as he Explains it, wont pass without Limitation. For

1st. His Construction of Μίμησις Φαυλοτέρων is very questionable. These Words may as properly be Translated the *Common*, as *the worst Sort of People*. And thus *Hesychius* interprets Φαῦλος by εὐτελής.

2*ly*. *Comedy* is distinguish'd from *Tragedy* by the Quality of the Persons, as well as by other Circumstances. *Aristotle* informs us that the Appearance, Characters, or Persons are greater in *Tragedy*, than in *Comedy* (Lib. de *Poet* cap. 4.). Τὰ σχήματά μείζω καὶ ἐντιμότερα. And to this Sense *Petitus* interprets the Words Βελτίονας ἢ χείρονας, affirming they ought to relate to Quality, as well as Manners (In not. ad. Lib. *Arist.* de Poet. cap. 2.).

Now as the Business of *Tragedy* is to represent Princes and Persons of Quality; so by the Laws of Distinction, *Comedy* ought to be confin'd to the ordinary Rank of Mankind (Scalig. Poet. Lib. 1. c. 6.). And that *Aristotle* ought to be thus interpreted appears from the Form of *New Comedy*, set up in the Time of this Philosopher. And tho' we have none of these *Comedies* extant, 'tis agreed by the Criticks that they did not meddle with Government and Great People; The *Old Comedy* being put down upon this Score. And tho' *Menander* and the rest of that Set are lost, we may guess at their Conduct from the Plays of *Plautus* and *Terence*, in all which there is not so much as one Person of Quality represented, excepting *Plautus*'s *Amphitryon*, which he calls a *Tragecomedy*.

Farther, Mr. *Congreve*'s Reason why *Aristotle* should be interpreted by *Manners*, and not *Quality* is inconclusive. His remark on κατὰ πᾶσαν κακίαν will serve as well the other way. Lets try it a little: *Aristotle* shall say then that *Comedy* is an imitation of the ordinary, and middle sort of People, but not κατὰ πᾶσαν κακίαν, *in every branch and aggravation of Vice*; for as Mr. *Congreve* observes, *there are no Crimes too daring and too horrid for Comedy*. Now I desire to know, if this Sense is not clear and unembarrass'd, if it does not distinguish *Comedy* from *Tragedy*, and bring down the Definition to Matter of Fact?

But granting Mr. *Congreve* his Definition; all Blemishes and Incidents of Scandal are not fit to make sport with. Covetousness, and Profusion; Cowardize, Spleen, and Singularity, well managed, might possibly do. But some Vices Mr. *Congreve* confesses *are too daring for Comedy*. Yes and for *Tragedy* too. And among these I'll venture to say Prophaneness is one. This Liberty even *Aristotle* durst not allow: He knew the Government of *Athens* would not endure it. And that some of the *Poets* had been call'd to account upon this Score (Vit. Eurip. Ed. Cant.).

3*ly*. Immodesty and lewd Talking, is another part of Vice which ought not to appear in *Comedy*. *Aristotle* blames the *Old Comedians* for this sort of Mismanagement; and adds, that intemperate Rallying ought to lie under publick Restraint. And therefore Mr. *Congreve* is mistaken in his Consequence if he makes it general. For *the looser sort of Livers*, as to the Foulness of Conversation, are no proper *Subject of Comedy*. . . .

Before I part with him on this Head, I can't but take notice of his saying, that *the Business of Comedy is to delight, as well as instruct*: If he means as much, by *as well*, he is mistaken. For Delight is but the secondary End of *Comedy*, as I have prov'd at large. And to satisfy him farther, I'll give him one Testimony more of Mr. *Dryden*'s. 'Tis in his *Preface* to *Fresnoy*'s *Art of Painting* (P. XX.). Here he informs us that as to Delight *the parallel of the* (two) *Arts holds true; with this difference; That the principal End of Painting is to please, and the chief design of Poetry is to instruct.* . . .

Pleasure, especially the Pleasure of *Libertines*, is not the Supreme *Law of Comedy*. Vice must be under Discipline and Discountenance, and Folly shown with great Caution and Reserve. Lussious Descriptions, and Common Places of Lewdness are unpardonable. They affront the virtuous, and debauch the unwary, and are a scandal to the Country where they are suffer'd. The pretence of *Nature*, and *Imitation*, is a lamentable Plea. Without doubt there's a great deal of *Nature* in the most brutal Practices. The infamous *Stews* 'tis likely talk in their own way, and keep up their Character. But what Person of probity would visit them for the Propriety, or take Poyson because 'tis true in its kind? All Characters of Immodesty (if there must be any such) should only be hinted in remote Language, and thrown off in Generals.

If there must be Strumpets, let *Bridewell* be the *Scene*. Let them come not to Prate, but to be Punish'd. To give Success, and Reputation to a *Stage Libertine*, is a sign either of Ignorance, of Lewdness, or Atheism, or altogether. Even those Instances which will bear the relating ought to be punish'd. But as for Smut and Prophaneness, 'tis every way Criminal and Infectious, and no Discipline can atone for the Representation: When a *Poet* will venture on these Liberties, his *Perswasion* must suffer, and his *private Sentiments* fall under Censure. For as Mr. *Dryden* rightly observes, *vita proba est*, is no excuse: For *'twill scarcely be admitted that either a* Poet *or a* Painter *can be chast, who give us the contrary Examples in their Writings, and their Pictures* (Pref. to *Fresnoy*. p. XXI.). I agree with Mr. *Congreve it would be very hard a Painter should be believ'd to resemble all the ugly Faces he draws*. But if he suffers his Pencil to grow Licentious, if he gives us Obscenities, the Merits of *Raphael* won't excuse him: No, To do an ill Thing well, doubles the Fault. The Mischief rises with the Art, and the Man ought to smart in proportion to his Excellency: 'Tis one of the Rules in Painting according to Mr. *Dryden* and *Fresnoy*; To *avoid every Thing that's immoral and filthy, unseemly, impudent, and obscene* (Pref. p. XX. Book. p. 56.). And Mr. *Dryden* continues, that a Poet is bound up to the same Restraint, and ought neither to *Design*, or *Colour* an offensive Piece (Ibid. p. XXI.).

[In respect of the holy scriptures] he endeavours to Fence against the Censure of Profaneness. He desires the following Distinction *may be admitted*, viz. *when Words are applied to sacred Things, they ought to be understood accordingly: But when they are otherwise applied, the Diversity of the Subject gives a Diversity of Signification*. By his favour this Distinction is loose, and nothing to the Purpose.

The inspired Text is appropriated to *Sacred Things*, and never to be used but upon serious Occasions. The Weight of the Matter, and the Dignity of the Author, challenge our utmost regard. 'Tis only for the Service of the *Sanctuary*, and Privileged from common Use. But Mr. *Congreve* says *when they* (the Words of Scripture) *are otherwise applied, the Diversity of the Subject gives a Diversity of Signification.* This is strange Stuff! Has Application so transforming a Quality, and does bare use enter so far into the Nature of Things? If a Man applies his Money to an ill Purpose, does this transmute the Metal, and make it none of the King's Coin? To wrest an Author, and turn his Words into Jest, is it seems to have nothing to do with him. The meer Ridicule destroys the Quotation; and makes it belong to another Person. Thus 'tis impossible to Travestie a Book, and *Virgil* was never burlesqu'd by *Ausonius* or Mr. *Cotton*! Not at all! They only made use of the 24 Letters, and happen'd to chop exactly upon *Virgil*'s Subject, his Words and his Versification. But 'tis plain they never intended to quote him: For *Virgil* is always grave, and serious, but these Gentlemen apply, or translate the Words in the most different manner imaginable: And run always upon Buffoonry and Drolling. This is Mr. *Congreve*'s Logick, and to abuse an Author is to have nothing to do with him. The Injury it seems destroys the Relation, and makes the Action perfectly foreign. And by this Reasoning one would think my Book had never been cited by Mr. *Congreve.* . . .

He *desires the impartial Reader, not to consider any Expression or Passage, cited from any Play, as it appears in* my Book; *nor to pass any Sentence upon it out of its proper Scene*, &c. For it must not be medled with *when 'tis alienated from its Character.* Well! Let the *Reader* compare his *Plays* with the *View*, &c. as much as he pleases. However, there's no necessity of passing through all his Forms, and Methods of prescribing. For if the Passage be truly cited, if the Sentence be full, and determin'd, why mayn't we understand it where'ere 'tis met with? Why must we read a Page for a Period? Can't a Plant be known without the History of the Garden? Besides, He may remember I have frequently hinted his *Characters*, touch'd upon their Quality and Fortune, and made them an Aggravation of his Fault.

But to silence this Plea, I had told him before that no pretence of Character, or Punishment, could justify Profaneness on the *Stage*. I gave him my Reasons for't too, which he is not pleas'd to take notice of. (pp. 6–15)

(ii) Mr. *Congreve* proceeds to acquaint us how careful the *Stage* is for the *Instruction* of the *Audience*. That *The Moral of the whole is generally summ'd up in the concluding Lines of the Poem, and put into Rhyme that it may be easy and engaging to the Memory.* To this I answer,

1*st*. That this *Expedient* is not always made use of. And not to trouble the *Reader* with *many* Instances, we have nothing of it in *love in a Nunnery*, and the *Relapse*, both which *Plays* are in my Opinion not a little dangerous.

2*ly*. Sometimes these Comprehensive Lines do more harm than good: They do so in *the Souldiers Fortune*: They do so likewise in the *Old Batchelour*, which instructs us to admirable purpose in these Words;

> *But oh—*
> *What rugged ways attend the Noon of Life?*
> *(Our sun declines) and with what anxious strife,*
> *What pain we tug that galling Load a Wife?*

This Moral is uncourtly, and vitious, it encourages Lewdness, and agrees extreamly well with the *Fable*. *Love for Love* may have somewhat a better Farewel, but would do a Man little Service should he remember it to his dying Day. Here *Angelica* after a fit of Prophane Vanity in *Prose*, takes her Leave as follows;

> *The Miracle to Day is that we find*
> *A Lover true: Not that a Woman's kind.*

This last word is somewhat ambiguous, and with a little help may strike off into a light Sense. But take it at the best, 'tis not overloaded with Weight and Apothegme. A *Ballad* is every jot as sententious.

3*dly*. Supposing the Moral grave, and unexceptionable, it amounts to little in the present Case.... A Moral Sentence at the Close of a Lewd Play, is much like a Pious Expression in the Mouth of a dying Man, who has been Wicked all his Life time. This some ignorant People call making a good End, as if one wise Word would attone for an Age of Folly.... This Expedient of Mr. *Congreve*'s as 'tis insignificant to the purpose 'tis brought, so it looks very like a piece of formal Hypocricy: And seems to be made use of to conceal the Immorality of the *Play*, and cover the *Poet* from Censure.

Mr. *Congreve* in the *Double Dealer* makes three of his Ladies Strumpets; This, I thought an odd Compliment to *Quality*. But my Reflection it seems is over severe. However, by his favour, the Characters in a *Play* ought to be drawn by Nature: To write otherwise is to make a Farce. The *Stage* therefore must be suppos'd an Image of the World, and Quality in Fiction resemble Quality in Life.... Thus in *Plautus* and *Terence*, the *Slaves* are generally represented false, and the Old Men easy and over credulous. Now if the Majority of these Divisions should not answer to the *World*; If the *Drama* should cross upon *Conversation*, the *Poets* would be to blame, as I believe they are in the later Instance. Thus when the greatest part of *Quality* are debauched on the *Stage*, 'tis a broad *Innuendo* they are no better in the *Boxes*.... The Representation in his *Play* turns more upon Condition than Sex. 'Tis the *Quality* which makes the Appearance, marks the *Character*, and points out the Comparison Abroad. (pp. 19–23)

(iii) We are now come to the *Mourning-Bride*, and Mr. *Congreve* seems so well assur'd of the Decency of this *Play*, that he casts the whole Cause upon it. *If there be Immodesty in this Tragedy* (says he) *I must confess my self incapable of ever writing any thing with Modesty.* It may be so:...I still charge Mr. *Congreve* with Immodesty; 'tis in *Osmin*'s last Speech in the *Page* above-mentioned ['Then *Garcia* shall lie panting on thy Bosom']....

This Gentleman quarrels with me because I would have had *Almeria* and *Osmin* parted *Civilly*; as if it was not proper for Lovers to do so; But *Civility*, and *Incivility have nothing to do with Passion.* I deny that, *Incivility* and *Passion*, are often concern'd together; And I suppose his *Amendments* may make an Instance.

By *Civilly*, I meant only decently, as any one might easily imagine. And as for *Tenderness*, when it grows Rank, and Nauseous, 'tis Rudeness, I take it.

Mr. *Congreve* would excuse *Osmin*'s Rant, by saying, *That most of the Incidents of the Poem of this Scene and the former, were laid to prepare for the Violence of these Expressions.* If it be so, I think the Play was not worth the Candle. 'Tis much as Wise as it would be for a Man to make a long Preparation to get out of his Wits, and qualifie himself for *Bedlam.* For nothing can be more distracted than *Osmin.* He is for *riving his clotted Hair, Smearing the Walls with his Blood, and dashing his disfigured Face against* something....Was it worth *Osmin*'s while to be thus Crazy, and are all Lovers to take a Pattern from this *Hero?* I am sorry Mr. *Congreve* was at all this trouble for a Prophane Allusion; but he is positive there's nothing *either of Prophaneness or Immodesty in the Expression.* With *Immodesty* I did not Charge it: But is there nothing of *Prophaneness* in bringing the most solemn Things in Religion upon the *Stage*; In making a Mad-man Rave about *Heaven*, and in comparing the disappointments of Love, with *Damnation?* The Lines shall appear once again.

> *O my* Almeria;
> *What do the Damn'd endure but to despair;*
> *But knowing Heaven to know it lost for ever!*

Mr. *Congreve* does not know how *these Verses are a Similitude drawn from the Creed:* I can't help it. I thought the Eternal Punishment of the Damned had been part of the *Creed.* I shan't untie such knots as these are for the future. He tells me *I had but an ill hold of Profaneness in his Play, and was reduced to catch at the Poetry*; And then makes a miserable jest about *Corruption* and *Generation. I had but ill hold of Profaneness!* As ill as 'twas, he has not yet wrested it from me. 'Twas in my Power besides to have taken better, and since he complains of gentle usage, I shall do it.

In the first place, here's frequent Swearing *by Heaven*; I suppose the *Poets* think this nothing, their *Plays* are so much larded with it. But our *Saviour* has given us an other Notion of this Liberty; He charges us *not to Swear at all.*

And tells us expressly, that *He that swears by Heaven, swears by the Throne of God, and by him that sits thereon* (St. Mat. 5.34. xxiii. 22).

To go on to another Branch of his *Irreligion*. The Scene of this *Play* lies in Christendom, as is evident from the History, or Fable; and to mention nothing more from *Osmin*'s Rant: Let us see then how *Osmin* accosts *Almeria*, when he found her safe on Shore: Truly I think their *Meeting* is as extravagant, as their *Parting*, tho Mr. *Congreve* won't allow it should be so. The Ceremony runs thus.

> *Thou Excellence, thou Joy, thou Heaven of Love.*

Thus the little successes of a pair of Lovers, are equall'd with the Glories of Heaven; And a Paultry Passion strain'd up to the Beatifick Vision. I say Paltry, for so 'tis upon the Comparison. To go on. *Almeria* having somewhat of the *Play-House* Breeding, is resolved not to be wanting in the return of these Civilities. She therefore makes him a Glorified Saint for the first piece of Gratitude, and then gives him a sort of Power Paramount to *Omnipotence*, and tells him that God Almighty could not make her happy without him.

> I *pray'd* to *thee* as to *a Saint*.
> And *thou* hast *heard* my *Prayer*, for *thou* art *come*
> To my *Distress*, to my *Despair; which Heaven*
> *Without thee could not Cure.*

Almeria has another Flight, and shows the Rankness of her Wing every jot as much as in the former.

> *'Tis more than Recompence to see thy Face,*
> *If Heaven is greater Joy, it is no Happiness.*

This is Mrs. *Brides* Complement, which both for the Religion and Decency is somewhat Extraordinary.

Manuel, a Christian Prince, upon the news of a Rival, Swaggers at a most Impious rate, *Paganism* was never bolder with *Idols*, nor *Jupiter* more brav'd by the Gyants. It runs thus.

> *Better for him to tempt the Rage of Heaven,*
> *And wrench the Bolt red hissing from the Hand*
> *Of him that Thunders, than but to think such Insolence,*
> *'Tis daring for a God.*

And to make matters worse, Mr. *Congreve* does not seem to think this Atheistical Sally a fault in *Manuel*. He lets us know he has punish'd him for his Tyranny, but not a Word of his Profaneness.

Once more and I have done. *Osmin*'s Caresses of *Almeria* are an Original in their kind.

My all of Bliss, my everlasting Life,
Soul of my Soul, and End of all my Wishes.

Here's Ceremony to Adoration; He makes her his Supreme Happiness, and gives her Sovereign Worship: In short, This Respect is the Prerogative of Heaven. 'Tis flaming Wickedness to speak it to any thing less than God Almighty: And to set the Prophaneness in the better Light, it runs all in devout Language, and Christian Transport.

I come now to the Vindication of his Poetry: Where in the first place, he Complains extreamly; because I Misquoted *Wasting Air*, for *Wafting Air*. Now to my Mind, the restoring of the Text is a very poor relief. For this later *Epithete* is perfectly expletive and foreign to the matter in hand; there's neither Antithesis nor Perspicuity in't. It neither clears the Sense, nor gives Spirit to the Expression: Besides, the word is almost worn out of use, and were it otherwise, 'twould rather belong to the *Water*; For to *waft* a *Fleet* of *Merchants* is to Convoy them, but not, I suppose, through the Air: So that the *Poet* at best, seems to have mistaken his Element. However, I ask his Pardon for Transcribing an *s*, for an *f*, and expect he should ask mine; for putting *Superstition* upon me, and commenting upon his own Blunder, when 'twas Printed *Supposition* in all the three *Editions* of my Book.

Mr. *Congreve* is now Cruizing for Reprisals, and bears down boldly upon a whole *Period. This litter of Epithets*, &c. He says *this Comparison* of mine is *handsome*. Why, so it may be for all his Disproof: Unless the standing of it in his Book is enough to make it ridiculous....

Mr. *Congreve* in defence of some Lines of his Cited by me, Answers, that the *Diction of Poetry consists of Figures, and the frequent use of Epithets.* I agree with him, but then the *Figures* should be unforc'd, drawn with Proportion, and allyed to the matter in hand. The *Epithets* likewise must be Smooth, Natural and Significant. But when they are lean, and remote from the business, when they look hard and stiff, when they clog and incumber the Sense, they are no great Ornaments. Whether Mr. *Congreve*'s are of this later kind, I shall leave it to the *Reader* to determine!   (pp. 31–8)

(iv) To return to Sir *Paul* [in *The Double-Dealer*]. *I find Passion* (says he) *coming upon me by Inspiration, and I cannot submit as formerly.*

You see what an admirable reason he urges in Defence of his Folly, from the extraordinary Circumstances of it! No *Prophet* could have justified his Resentments from a higher pretence.

The fine Lady *Cynthia* out of her pious Education acquaints us, That *though Marriage makes Man and Wife one Flesh, it leaves them still two Fools.* But the little word S T I L L is left out in the Quotation; which like the Fly on the *Coach-Wheel*, raises a mighty Dust. I grant I have by Chance omitted the word S T I L L ; and if he had done so too, the Sense had been perfectly the same, only better expressed. For

Still is plainly useless, and comprehended in the Verb *Leaves*. *For if Marriage leaves 'em two Fools,* they are Fools after Marriage, and then they are Fools *Still,* I think; Nothing can be clearer than this. But besides, *Cynthia* her self won't allow of Mr. *Congreve*'s excuse. For after she has deliver'd that remarkable Sentence of *leaving 'em two Fools,* &c. *Mellifont* answers, *That's only when two Fools meet,* which is exactly Mr. *Congreve* in his *Amendments.* This *Cynthia* denies to be her meaning. *Cynth. Nay* (says she) *I have known two Wits meet, and by the opposition of their Wits render themselves as ridiculous as Fools.* And therefore after she has given Matrimony an odd Name, she advises him to Court no farther, to *draw Stakes, and give over in time.* So that besides Burlesquing the Bible, the Satyr is pointed against Marriage. And the Folly is made to lye in the State, as well as in the Persons. Upon the whole, we see the *Double Dealer,* and the *Amendments* can't agree; and thus two Blemishes, as well as two Beauties, are sometimes unlike to each other. Mr. *Congreve* says, *Ben. Johnson is much bolder in the first Scene of his Bartholomew Fair.* Suppose all that. Is it an excuse to follow an ill Example, and continue an Atheistical practice? I thought Mr. *Congreve in his penetration* might have seen through this Question. *Ben. Johnson* (as he goes on) *makes Littlewit say, Man and Wife make one Fool. I have said nothing comparable to that.* Nothing comparable! Truly in the usual sense of that Phrase, Mr. *Congreve,* 'tis possible, has said nothing comparable to *Ben. Johnson,* nor it may be never will: But in his new Propriety he has said something more than comparable, that is a great deal worse. For though *Littlewit*'s Allusion is profane, the words of the *Bible* are spared. He does not Droll directly upon *Genesis,* or St. *Matthew*; Upon God the Son, or God the Holy Ghost: Whereas Mr. *Congreve* has done that which amounts to both. And since he endeavours to excuse himself upon the Authority of *Ben. Johnson,* I shall just mention what Thoughts this Poet had of his profane Liberties, at a time when we have reason to believe him most in earnest. Now Mr. *Wood* reports from the Testimony of a great Prelate then present. 'That when *Ben. Johnson* was in his last Sickness, he was often heard to repent of his profaning the Scriptures in his Plays, and that with Horrour.' (Athen. Oxoniens. Vol. 1. p. 519).

Now as far as I can perceive, the Smut and Profaneness of Mr. *Congreve*'s Four Plays out-swell the Bulk of *Ben. Johnson*'s Folio. I heartily wish this Relation may be serviceable to Mr. *Congreve,* and that as his Faults are greater, his Repentance may come sooner....

The *Double Dealer* is now done with, and Mr. *Congreve* concludes his Vindication in the usual Strain of Triumph and Assurance.

Love for Love comes at last upon the Board. In this *Play* I blamed him for making a *Martyr* of a Whoremaster: Upon this, he flies immediately for Succour to *Scapula,* and the *Greek Grammar.* He very learnedly tells us, that Martyr is a Greek *word, and signifies in plain English no more than a Witness.* Right! These two Words are the same; and when a Cause comes on in

Westminster-Hall, the *Martyrs* are call'd immediately! But *Martyr* is but bare *Witness* in the Greek. Not always: Christian Writers often use it in a sense appropriated. And were it otherwise, there's no arguing from one Language to another. *Tyrant* was once an Honourable Name in *Greek*, but always a Reproach in *English*. But to dilate upon these Cavils, is throwing away time. If the Reader desires more, he may please to look back on my Answer to his Objection about *Inspiration....*

I had said that this Libertine Application of his, was dignifying Adultery with the Stile of Martyrdom: As if (says Mr. *Congreve*) *any Word could dignify Vice.* And pray why not? Does not the Varnish hide the Coarseness underneath, and the Pill go down the better for the Guilding? Whether he knows it or not, there's a great deal of Charm and Imposture in *Words*; and an ill practice is often comply'd with upon the Strength of a Fashionable Name.

He asks, who told me Jeremy Fetch was bred at the University? Why *Jeremy* says so himself pretty plainly, and *Tattle* says so, and I suppose Mr. *Congreve* says as much as that comes to in his Reflection immediately following. But this notable question was put to introduce another Business of greater Consequence. For upon this occasion, out of *his excellence* of *good Manners,* he is pleased to observe, That *I should not have been suspected of an University Education any more than his Jeremy in the Play, if I had not printed* M.A. *on the Title Page.* Here the poor Man has shewn his Will, and his Weakness sufficiently! I'm almost sorry 'tis so low with him. When a Poet is so extreamly well inclin'd to be Witty, 'tis pity he has no more in his power. Mr. *Congreve* goes on Manfully in his Defence and says, *For the Word Whoreson, I had it from* Shakespear *and* Johnson. Not unlikely. People are apt to learn what they should not. Mr. *Congreve*'s Memory, or his Invention, is very considerable this way. Indeed one would almost think by his Writings, that he had digested ill Language into a Common Place. But it was not only *Whoreson*, but *Jeremy*'s saying he was born with *Whoreson Appetites*, which I complain'd of; and which I take to be Blaspheming the Creation.

He pretends I have wrong'd him strangely in a Rant of Sir *Sampson*'s: And would make the Reader believe I charge him literally with Paraphrasing the 139*th* Psalm. I'm sorry I'm forced to explain my self in so clear a case.

We may observe then, that the Psalmist in Contemplation of the astonishing Beauty and Serviceableness of Humane Bodies, breaks out in a Rapture of Gratitude, *I will give thanks unto thee, for I am fearfully and wonderfully made, marvellous are thy works, and that my Soul knows right well.* Let us now hear Sir *Sampson*. This Gentleman having railed a Lecture over *Jeremy*'s Body, for being born with Necessities too big for his Condition; he crys, *These things are unacountable, and unreasonable; Why was not I a Bear?—Nature has been provident only to Bears and Spiders*: Thus we see what a Harmony of Thought there is between *David* and our Author. The one

Adores while the other Reproaches. The one Admires, the other Burlesques the wonders of Providence. And this was all the *Paraphrasing* I meant, as any one might easily Imagine.

The Dialogue of *Scandal* and *Foresight* lies next in our way, I shall once more Transcribe it from *Love for Love*.

Fore. Alas Mr. *Scandal*, Humanum est errare.

Scand. You say true, Man *will err; meer* Man *will err—but you are something more—There have been wise Men, but they were such as you—Men who consulted the Stars, and were Observers of Omens*—Solomon *was wise, but how? By his Judgment in Astrology,—So says Pineda* in his Third Book and eighth Chap. But (says Mr. *Congreve*) the *Quotation* of the *Authority* is *omitted* by Mr. Collier, *either because he would* represent *it as my own Observation to ridicule the Wisdom* of Solomon *or else because he was indeed Ignorant that it belong'd to any body else.* To this I answer.

1. That Mr. *Congreve* yields *Solomon*'s Wisdom ridiculed by *this Observation*, therefore by his own confession, if 'tis none of his Authors, he must Answer for't himself. Now *Pineda* gives us a quite different account of the Cause of *Solomon*'s Wisdom, and which is perfectly inconsistent with Mr. *Congreve*'s Banter. '*Pineda* affirms that *Solomon*'s Wisdom was given him by God in a supernatural Dream, mentioned in Scripture (1 Kings 3. 5, 12.). And that after the Dream, he found an unusual Light in his Understanding; his Ideas were brighten'd, and the extent of his Knowledge strangely enlarged (Pined. Lib. 3. Cap. 8. P. 142, 147. Ed. Mogunt.) 'Tis true, *Pineda* believed that *Solomon* understood *Astronomy* in Perfection, and that he had skill in *Prognosticks* which he calls *Astronomia judiciaria* (Lib. 3. C. 18). He continues, that he could in a great measure reach the Inclinations and Reasonings of Men, where they did not depend purely upon choice, and the turn of the *Will*. But then he does not say that *Solomon*'s Skill in *Prognosticks* was that which made him *wise*. No: This Tallent was only a Branch, but not the Cause of his Wisdom. For as *Pineda* speaks elsewhere, *Solomon* had a Universal Knowledge of Nature, but then this Excellency was no result of Natural Parts, or Humane Industry; 'Twas an immediate Bounty from Heaven; And both the Thing, and the Conveyance, were extraordinary.'

Mr. *Congreve* agrees with *Pineda* at least in a jesting way, *Solomon* was *wise, but how? By his Judgment in Astrology*. That is, his distinguishing Attainments were gained this way. There was nothing in the case, but that he had looked into a Star somewhat farther than other people: He Learned his Wisdom it seems from the *Caldeans*, or *Ægyptians*, or from some such Book as *Lillies Almanack*. This is *Scandal*'s Solution of the Mystery; and the best that I can make on it. For 'tis one thing to say that a Man is *wise* by *Astrology*, and another that *Astrology* or *Astronomy* was only a part of his Wisdom. The one Implies the Cause, and the other but a Branch of the Effect. The one excludes the Miracle, and the other affirms it. Upon the whole matter, Mr. *Congreve*, and *Pineda*, are not to be reconciled, so that by his own confession he has *ridiculed the Wisdom of Solomon*, and falsifyed his Author into the Bargain.

2ly. Supposing *Pineda* had been fairly reported by Mr. *Congreve*, the *Poet* had been much to blame; For then the Case had stood thus; *Pineda* as Mr. *Congreve* observes had ridiculed *Solomon*, and himself had done no less, by Citing him without Censure, and upon a Drolling Occasion. For this reason I waved the consulting of *Pineda*, as well knowing that should the Testimony have been right, the *Play* was certainly in the wrong. Besides, 'tis somewhat to be suspected Mr. *Congreve* never saw *Pineda*; My Reason is, because he falls twice into the same Mistake, he Quotes the *Eighteenth* Chapter for the *Eighth*, and to make it appear the more gross, 'tis done in words of Length, and not in Figures. I hope for the future Mr. *Congreve* wont bring in *Solomon* to divert the *Play-House*, nor compare him with Fools and Fortunetellers.

Scandal's telling *Foresight* he was *more than meer Man*, and secure from Mistake upon that Score, is likewise a profane expression. To affirm this of any person, is as much as to say, he is either our *Saviour*, or a *Prophet*, or under some Miraculous Influence.

Scandal goes on with *Foresight*, 'and sayes the Wise Men of the East ow'd their Instruction to a Star, which is rightly observed by *Gregory* the Great in favour of *Astrology*.'

Mr. *Congreve* vindicates this passage by saying, that *Scandal Banters Foresight*, but *not the Audience*. Not Banter the Audience! He affronts the Audience I'm sure, if they have any Christianity in them, by drolling upon a Miracle at our Saviour's Birth: He banters St. *Matthew* too, who has recorded the Miracle, and *Gregory* the Great, who discourses upon it.

Mr. *Congreve* is pleased to say that *I am very angry that Sir Sampson has not another Name*, because *Sampson is a Name in the Old Testament*. This is false in every syllable, as the Reader may see by consulting my Book. But this I say, that Mr. *Congreve* has burlesqu'd the History of *Sampson*, and wrested the *Scripture* into Smut.

There are two other profane Passages Censur'd by me in the same Page: These he leaves as it were to shift for themselves, and has not yet, made them worse by defending them: Excepting that he comes up with his old Cavil about the Word *Martyr*, which I have answer'd already.

The next Place Mr. *Congreve* leads us is to *Bedlam*: And here he gives us three Reasons for *Valentine*'s pretended Madness. The two later are somewhat extraordinary. He makes him Mad it seems *for a variation of the Character*. A shrewd Contrivance, to put a Man out of his Wits for the sake of Variety? For without doubt, Raving and Incoherence are wonderfully taking. I suppose Mr. *Congreve* made *Bellmour* talk Nonsense for this wise reason. For 'tis a dull thing for a Man to be always tyed up to Sense, and confin'd to his Understanding. His third reason for taking away Reason, is *because Madness gives a liberty to Satyr, and authorises a Bluntness, &c. which would otherwise have been a Breach of Manners in the Character*. That is, it gives *Valentine* a Commission to talk Smut, and abuse his Father. But Mr. *Congreve* needed not to have given himself this trouble about *Valentine*; For *Valentine* when he was in his Wits, and under the Character of a fine Gentleman, had Breeding enough to be Smutty, and Undutiful. Mr. *Congreve* would perswade the Reader that I interpret him with too much Rigour, for making *Valentine* in his Lunacy say, *I am Truth*, &c. If this Point needs any farther Disputing, we may take notice that our Blessed Saviour mentions the word *Truth* in a solemn and peculiar manner. He sometimes applies it to Himself, sometimes to the Holy Ghost, and sometimes to the Revelation of the Gospel. In short, 'tis as it were appropriated to the greatest Persons, and Things, mark'd as the Prerogative of God; and used in a sense of Emphasis and Distinction. Let us compare St. *John*, and Mr. *Congreve* a little, and then we may easily judge where the Fault lies.

St. *Thomas* answers our Blessed Saviour, *Lord we know now not whither thou goest, and how can we know the way? Jesus saith unto him, I am the Way, and the Truth, and the Life* (Joh. 14.6.). Sir *Sampson* is at a loss, Swears, and cries out, *I know not which way to go*. Valentine enquires, *Who's that, that's out of his Way? I am Truth, and can set him right*.

Our Saviour assures his Disciples, That he will send them the *Comforter*. And that *when he the Spirit of Truth is come, he will guide you into all Truth, and he will shew you things to come* (Joh. 16.13.).

The execrable *Valentine* says, *Interrupt me not—I'll whisper Prediction to thee, and thou shalt Prophesie. I am Truth, and can teach thy Tongue a new Trick: I am Truth, and come to give the World the Lie.*

And is not this horrible Stuff? What can be more intolerable Boldness, than thus to usurp the Regal Stile, to prostitute the Language of Heaven, and apply it to Drollery and Distraction?

Mr. *Congreve* is advanced to my 3*d* Chapter, concerning the Abuse of the Clergy. As for the Dissenting *Ministers*, he says I charge him with nothing more than *Setter*'s, procuring their Habit for *Bellmour*. Under Favour, this is a great Mistake. The Pimp reads a Lecture of Abuse upon the Habit, exposes *Spintext* from Head to Foot, makes him both a Knave and a Libertine, and his Wife a Whore into the bargain. The *View*, &c. has remark'd, *that Barnaby calls another of the Character Mr. Prig*. He does so. And *Fondlewife* represents him lewd in a luscious Description. Mr. *Congreve* replies, *What if his Name were Mr.* Prig, *or what if it were not?* Now 'tis possible he'll not like it, if I don't consider these weighty Questions. I say then, If his Name was so, he has misbehaved himself by putting him in his *Play*. If 'twere not so, He has used the Dissenting Ministers ill, by representing one of their Order in a contemptuous Manner. For as he himself confesses, a Mr. *Prig, and a Mr. Smirk, are Names implying Characters worthy of Aversion and Contempt*. Now for a Man not to understand his own ill Language, and contradict himself in a few Pages, is, in my own decent expression, *furiously simple*.

Mr. *Congreve* pretends that a Reflection on a *Lord's Chaplain* is no reflection upon a Parson of the Church of *England*. That's somewhat strange. The *Roman* Catholick Lords have no *Chaplains*; the Law does not allow it. And as for the Dissenters, there are very few Lords of their Perswasion. I desire therefore to know upon what Party the Abuse must stick? In earnest, I'm almost tired with answering these things. To strike the Air, does but make a Man's Arm ake. (pp. 51–66)

(v) Now though I have examined Mr. *Congreve*'s Writings but loosely upon this Head, yet in return to his Civilities, I shall present the Reader with some Proprieties of His in Phraseology and Sense. In his Amendments we have, To *Savour of Utterance*, &c. And in the *Mourning Bride*, we have all the Delicacies of Language and Rhetorick, and the very Spring it self upon Paper. Here's *Respiring Lips, ample Roof, and ample Knowledge, the Noon of Night, fear'd*, for frighted, the *pageantry of Souls, Eyes rain Blood*, and what not. To go on a little with the *Mourning Bride*, with reference to Sense and Character.

King *Manuell* asks his Daughter *Almeria*, why she wears Mourning at his Triumph. She tells him, *She mourns for her deliverance from a Wreck*. This was a wise Answer, and a very natural way of expressing her Gratitude for coming safe on Shore.

Gonsalez relates *Manuall*'s Victorious Entry after his Success against the Moors. The Cavalcade is wonderfully Splendid and Pompous: But the Story goes off somewhat unluckily.

> The swarming Populace spread every Wall,
> And cling as if with Claws they did enforce
> Their Hold through clifted Stones stretching and staring.

Here he Struts to purpose in *Sophocles*'s Buskins! *Cling* and *Claws* are extreamly magnificent in solemn Description, and strangely proper for Tragedy and Triumph. To give him his due, I think these two Lines are the best Image of a parcel of Cats running up a Wall, that I have met with. That which follows is worth the remembring.

> As they were all of Eyes, and every Limb,
> Would feed his Faculty of Admiration.

A Limb of an Eye, I confess, is a great Curiosity; And one would think if the *Poet* had any of these Limbs in his Head, he might have discover'd it. We must not forget *Osmin*'s Talent in Arithmetick, who let us understand that

> Heaven can continue to bestow,
> When scanty Numbers shall be spent in telling.

As Scanty as they are, I *fancy Telling* will be spent much sooner than *Numbers*: But Sense in a Tragedy is cold and unaffecting. To go on. *Zarah* makes *Osmin* a high Compliment upon his Air and Complexion: She tells him when she first saw him,

> *Pale and expiring, drenched in briny Waves,*

That he was

> *God-like even then.*

Death and Paleness are strong Resemblances of a Deity! But I perceive, to some People, a Seraphim, and a drown'd Rat, are just alike. King *Manuell* is giving Sentence upon the Rebels: Let us see how he supports his Character:

> *Bear to the Dungeon those Rebellious Slaves,*
> *The ignoble Curs that Yelp to fill the Cry,*
> *And spend their Mouths in barking Tyranny.*

And a little after, he calls the Noble *Osmin, that foreign Dog*. Here's Majestick Passion, Royal Vengeance, and magnificent Railing for ye! A Common Hunt could not have done it better! This, as Mr. *Congreve* has it, is *Dog-Language* with a Witness; and never made for a Monarch's Mouth.

Zara has another Flight very remarkable, and with that I shall conclude. This Princess, we must know, was strangely smitten with *Osmin*, and finding her Amour cross'd, was resolv'd, out of stark Love and Kindness, to Poison him: 'Tis true, she intended to be so just, as to dispose of her self the same way. Now coming to the Prison she spies a Body without a Head, and imagining it *Osmin*'s, grows distracted upon't. And why so? Was it because she was prevented, and had not the satisfaction of dispatching her Spark her self? Or was it because she had a mind to convince *Osmin* of the strength of her Affection by murthering him? That's somewhat odd. Was it then to shew how willing she was to dye with him? She says so; but presently rejects this reason as frivolous and unnecessary. For if you'll believe her, *Osmin* was capable of knowing her Passion, without so barbarous an Expedient.

> *His Soul still sees, and knows each purpose,*
> *And fixt event of my persisting Faith.*

Well, Let the reason of her Disorder be what it will, for we can't agree about it, she falls into a most terrible Fit of Fustian, upon the sight of the Body.

> *Ha! prostrate! bloody! headless! O,—start Eyes,*
> *Split heart, burst every Vein at this dire object;*
> *At once dissolve and flow; meet Blood with Blood,*
> *Dash your encountring Streams with mutual Violence,*
> *Till Surges roll, and foaming Billows rise,*
> *And curle their Crimson Heads to kiss the Clouds!*

One would think by this Rant, that *Zara* had Bloud enough in her Veins to fill the *Bay* of *Biscay*, or the Gulph of *Lions*. At this rate a Man may let the *Thames* out of his little Finger! This is monstrous Impropriety of Thought! Never were

Things and Words, joyn'd more unluckily. Call you this Poetry! The Figures and Flights of Poetry are Bold; but then the Fancy should be Natural, the Figures Just, and the Effects hold some Proportion with the Cause. *Zara* rises in her Rumbling, if 'tis possible, rails bitterly on the King, in *Astronomy*; And, as far as I can discover, she goes somewhat upon the System of *Copernicus*.

> *Rain, rain, ye Stars spout from your burning Orbs,*
> *Precipitated Fires, and pour in Sheets,*
> *The blazing Torrent on the Tyrant's Head.*

Well. 'Tho this Lady has not much Wit in her Anger, she has a great deal of Learning: I must own, this is a very Scholar-like piece of Distraction. If Mr. *Congreve* replies, the Occasion was extraordinary; and that the sight of *Osmin*'s Murther must mightily affect her. Granting all this, the old saying will hold good against him: *Curæ leves loqunter, ingentes stupent*: Here *Almeria*'s Fit of Fainting, and a good Swoon at the end on't, would have look'd like Business, and been very Natural upon the occasion.   (pp. 91–5)

Anon., *Some Remarks upon Mr. Collier's Defence of his Short View of the English Stage, &c. In Vindication of Mr.* Congreve, *&c.* (London, 1698). Advt. the *Post Man*, 3–6 December 1698.

(i) I am inform'd, for all his [Collier's] mighty boasting, and the wondrous Progress he has made, the *Mourning Bride*, against which he rais'd his chief Battery, brought the greatest Audience they have this Winter had . . . (pp. 2–3)

(ii) Mr. *Collier*'s Reproofs to me seem inveterate; he writes with Animosity, as if he had an Aversion to the Man as well as his Faults, and appears only pleas'd when he has found a Miscarriage. Who, but Mr. *Collier*, wou'd have ransack'd the *Mourning Bride*, to charge it with Smut and Prophaneness, when he might have sate down with so many Scenes wherein even his malicious Chymistry cou'd have extracted neither? But against this Play, as if the Spirit of Contradiction were his delight, he musters all his Forces; and having passed Sentence as the Divine, commences Critick, and brings the Poetry to his severe Scrutiny, transcribes half Speeches, puts the beginning and end together, as in *Page 92*.

> *Drenched in briny Waves, pale and expiring,*
> *Yet God like even then.*

His own charming Simile comes next, of a Seraphim and a drown'd Rat: So on the other Leaf he is got to the Image of Cats running up a Wall: Truly (*Frank*) I cannot but impute these abject Thoughts to his own reptile Mind; for I have read the *Mourning Bride* often, and it always inspired me with the noblest Ideas: Then he cavils at *Almeria*'s Answer, That she mourns for a Deliverance from the Wreck:

This too is a Line taken out of a very probable and modest Reply. And here I
conceive Mr. *Collier*, as indeed he has sometimes done before, seems to change his
own Opinion; for I shou'd have thought he wou'd have liked *Almeria* better for
commemorating her Deliverance in Mourning and Humiliation, than if she had
enjoined Mirth and Revelling, nay, perhaps Plays. Well, since Mr. *Collier* by his
good-will shows nothing but what he thinks bad in the Play, pray give me leave to
transcribe one Speech amongst many, which sure will stand Mr. *Collier*'s Test.

[*MB* III. iii. 1–14 is cited here.]

Now I can pick Instruction and Delight out of this, and rest satisfied, if in a
Tragedy the Passions rise either Love, Anger or Madness; I can behold them
without one Thought of Imitation.... So several Characters in Comedy, which
Mr. *Collier* has fell foul upon, I dare venture to affirm, the Poet never design'd
for Examples; the fulsome *Belinda* in the *Old Batchellor* (as the cleanly-mouth'd
Mr. *Collier* is pleas'd to call her) is shown full of Affectation; but I find it no
where in the Play commended; and I always thought the Vanity was design'd to
be exposed, not promoted; and if at last she's married to a Libertine she likes,
where's the mighty Happiness?   (pp. 6–9)

(iii) ... if that Tragedy [*MB*] is not allowable for its Decency, Morals and
Poetry, I despair of ever seeing any thing of the Dramatick kind
unexceptionable.   (p. 14)

(iv) All my Acquaintance that discourse this Matter, are convinced
Mr. *Collier* has a particular Pique against Mr. *Congreve*; nay, some will go
farther, and guess the Cause; perhaps there may be Lines of that Author's
that vex the *Non-Juror* more than all the smutty Jests he has pickt up; Lines
that Mourn the Royal *Pastora*; Heroick Lines, that sound the Glory of our
Monarch. From this sweet Poetry they judge his Gall is raised; which being
gorged and full, overflows, nor spares the dead or living, Friends and Foes,
the bitter Deluge reaches and bespatters all.   (p. 17)

[George Farquhar], *The Adventures of Covent-Garden* (London, 1699),
Farquhar, ii. 269. Apparently published 15 December 1698.

Peregrine ... goes next Evening to the Play; where meeting some of his
ingenious acquaintance, *viz.* Mr. *W*— Mr *H*— Mr. *M*— with others of that
Club, there arose a discourse concerning the Battle between the Church and the
Stage, with relation to the Champions that maintained the parties; the result
upon the matter was this, that Mr. *Collier* showed too much Malice and rancour
for a Church-man, and his Adversaries too little wit, for the Character of Poets;
that their faults transversed would show much better; Dulness being more
familiar with those of Mr. *Collier*'s Function, as Malice and ill nature is more
adapted to the Professors of wit. That the best way of answering Mr. *Collier*, was
not to have replyed at all; for there was so much Fire in his Book, had not his

345

Adversaries thrown in Fuel, it would have fed upon it self, and so have gone out in a Blaze. As to his respondents, that Captain *Va*— wrote too like a Gentleman to be esteemed a good Casuist; that Mr. *C*—'s passion in this business had blinded his reason, which had shone so fair in his other Writings; that Mr. *S*— *le* wanted the wit of Captain *Va*— as much as he did Mr. *Settle*'s gravity; That the two Answers to Mr. *C*— have done his Book too much honour, but themselves too great an Injury: In short, upon the whole matter, that whoever gained the Victory, the Stage must lose by it, being so long the seat of the War; And unless Mr. *Dryden*, or Mr. *Wicherly* remove the combustion into the Enemies Country, the *Theatre* must down. And the rest of this War will be attended by cashiering the Poets, as the last Peace was by disbanding the Army.

[Joseph Addison], 'The Play House', ll. 38–41. First printed as '*The Play-House. A Satyr. By* T.G. *Gent.*' in *A Pacquet from Parnassus*, vol. 1, no. 2 (1702), but reading '*F——r*' for '*Congreve*' at l. 38. It is given here from an earlier version at O: MSS Eng. poet. f. 12, p. 109, headed 'On the Playhouse.' and attributed to 'Io Addison e Coll. Magd: Oxon.'. Another copy at O: MSS Eng. poet. e. 50, p. 127, dates it, being headed 'The Play House. 1699'. See Foxon D236 and *RES* NS 34 (1983), 21–7.

> The Comic Tone, inspir'd by Congreve draws
> At eve'ry Word, loud Laughter & Applause;
> The mincing Dame continues as before,
> Her Character unchang'd, & acts a Whore…

Abel Boyer, 'Dialogue. To go to see a Play', in *The Compleat French-Master For Ladies and Gentlemen*. 2nd edn. (1699), 84–7.

They say there's a New Play acted to day.
Is it a Comedy, a Tragedy, an Opera, or a Farce?
'Tis a Tragedy.
What's its Name?
The Mourning Bride.
Who is the Author of it?
Mr. Congreve.
Is this the first time it is acted?
No, Sir: this is the third time: This is the Poet's day.
How did it take the first and second time it was presented or acted?
It was Acted with a universal Applause.
Mr. Congreve *was already famous by his Comedies.*
And this last Play gains him the Reputation of a great Tragick Poet.
Shall we go and see it?

With all my Heart. I'll go and bid the Coach Man get the Coach ready, and we
will go immediately.

Shall we go into a Box?

I'll do what you please, but I had rather go into the Pit.

Why?

Because we may pass away the time in talking with the Masks, before the
Curtain is drawn up.

What do you say to that Symphony?

How do you like that Musick?

Methinks 'tis very fine.

Don't you take notice of that Hautboy and Trumpet?

They sound very well among the Violins and Harpsecords.

The Galleries are full already.

And as you see we are very much crowded in the Pit.

And the Boxes are as full of Ladies as they can hold.

I never saw the House so full.

There is abundance of fine People.

I love almost as much as the Play, the sight of those fine Ladies who grace the Boxes.

They are very fine or very finely drest.

They joyn the Beauties and the Charms of the Body to the richness of the Attire,
and the brightness of their Jewels.

Do you take Notice of that Lady who sits in the King's Box?

Yes, I see her: She's pretty.

How, pretty! You should say that she's as handsom as an Angel.

She's perfectly handsom.

She's a perfect beauty.

Do you know her?

I have that honour.

She has a fine easie shape.

Have you took notice of her Complexion?

'Tis the finest Complexion in this World.

She has Teeth as white as Snow.

Wherever she casts her Eyes, they are the Center of the amorous Ogles of all the
Beaux.

I think she has a great deal of Wit.

Beauty indeed may be seen, but not Wit.

Had she as much Wit as Beauty, she might be said to be an Abridgment of all
the Perfections.

But the Curtain is drawing, let's hear.

The Play is done.

The Curtain is let down.

Let's return home.

John Dryden, Letter to Mrs Elizabeth Steward, 4 March 1699 (Dryden, *Letters*, 112–13).

This Day was playd a reviv'd Comedy of Mr Congreve's calld the Double Dealer, which was never very takeing; in the play bill was printed,—Written by Mr Congreve; with Severall Expressions omitted: What kind of Expressions those were you may easily ghess; if you have seen the Monday's Gazette, wherein is the Kings Order, for the reformation of the Stage: but the printing an Authours name, in a Play bill, is a new manner of proceeding, at least in England.

[James Drake], *The Ancient and Modern Stages Survey'd* (London, 1699), 108–9, 214–19. Advt. the *Flying Post*, 7 March 1699.

... so far is Revenge from being encourag'd, or countenanc'd by the *Stage*, that to desire and prosecute it, is almost always the mark of a *Tyrant*, or a *Villain*, in *Tragedy*, and *Poetick Justice* is done upon 'em for it; it is generally turn'd upon their own heads, becomes the snare in which they are taken, and the immediate Instrument of their miserable *Catastrophe*. Thus in the *Mourning Bride*, *Don Manuel*, to glut his lust of Revenge, puts himself into the Place and Habit of his unhappy Prisoner, in order to surprize, betray, and insult his own pious, afflicted Daughter, over the suppos'd Body of her Murther'd Husband. In this posture Poetick Justice overtakes him, and he is himself surpriz'd, mistaken for him whom he represented, and stabb'd by a Creature of his own, the villanous Minister of his Tyranny, and his chief Favourite.

...

The next and last Tragedy I shall instance in is the *Mourning Bride*. I have had occasion already to say something of the Observation of Poetick Justice in this Play, but this being the proper place, I shall take it a little more particularly into consideration.

The Fable of this Play is one of the most just, and regular that the Stage, either Antient or Modern, can boast of. I mean, for the distribution of Rewards, and Punishments. For no virtuous person misses his Recompence, and no vitious one escapes Vengeance. *Manuel* in the prosecution and exercise of his Cruelty and Tyranny, is taken in a Trap of his own laying, and falls himself a Sacrifice in the room of him, whom he in his rage had devoted. *Gonsalez* villanous cunning returns upon his own head, and makes him by mistake kill the King his Master, and in that cut off, not only all his hopes, but his only Prop and Support, and make sure of his own Destruction. *Alonzo*, his Creature and Instrument, acts by his instructions, and shares his Fate. *Zara*'s furious Temper and impetuous ungovernable Passion, urge her to frequent violences, and conclude at last in a fatal mistake. Thus every one's own Wickedness or

Miscarriage determines his Fate, without shedding any Malignity upon the Persons and Fortunes of others. *Alphonso* in reward of his Virtue receives the Crowns of *Valentia* and *Granada*, and is happy in his Love; all which he acknowledges to be the Gift of Providence, which protects the Innocent, and rewards the Virtuous. *Almeria*, whose Virtues are much of the same kind, and who Sympathiz'd with him in his afflictions, becomes a joynt Partner of his Happiness. And *Garcia*, tho a Servant of the Tyrant, and Son of the treacherous, ambitious Statesman, yet executing only his Soveraigns lawful Commands, and being untainted with his Fathers guilt, and his Principles undebauch'd, is receiv'd into *Alphonso*'s favour.

All this as well as the *Moral* is summ'd up so fully, and so concisely in *Alphonso*'s last speech, that 'twere injustice not to give it in the Poets own words.

[Drake here cites *MB* v. xii. 29–46.]

...I shall only take notice of two or three things which are apparently the indisputable advantage of the *Moderns* over the *Antients*, in respect of the General *Moral* of their Fables.

1st, That they never are at the expence of a Machine to bring about a wicked Design, and by consequence don't interest Providence in promoting Villany....

2dly, That they never engage Providence to afflict and oppress Virtue, by distressing it by supernatural means, as the Antients have manifestly done, by making their Gods the immediate Actors in or directors of the misfortunes of virtuous persons....

3dly, That their *Malefactors* are generally punished, which those of the Antients seldom were; but if they escape, the Moderns don't provide 'em with a miraculous delivery, or have recourse to such extraordinary Methods as exceed the reach of Humane Force or Cunning, so as to entitle Providence to the Protection of 'em....

From this short review of the different conduct of the Antient and Modern Tragedians, we may see with how much more respect to Providence, and the Divine administration, our Poets have behaved themselves, than they; and how far the Ballance of Religion inclines to our side. I suppose no one can be so silly, as to think, that I argue here for the truth of their Faith, but the measure of it in their respective perswasions, in which the advantage is infinitely on the side of the *English* Stage.

John Oldmixon, *Reflections on the Stage* (London, 1699), 177. Advt. the *Post Man*, 4 May 1699.

Otway's *Venice Preserv'd*, and *Orphan*, part of Lee's *Brutus*, some scenes of Mr *Southern*'s *Fatal Marriage*, and part of the *Mourning Bride*, are examples of as penetrating tenderness as any we can find in . . . the best of *Racine*'s pieces, who is most excellent when he is touching that passion.

Samuel Garth, *The Dispensary. A Poem* (London, 1699), 56 (canto IV, ll. 220–4). *POAS* iv. 103. The 1709 Key to *The Dispensary* describes Congreve as 'a Poet principally famous for his *Pastorals* and Dramatic *Writings*'.

> As tuneful C—*greve* trys his rural Strains,
> *Pan* quits the Woods, the list'ning Fawns the Plains;
> And *Philomel*, in Notes like his, complains.
> And *Britain*, since *Pausanias* was writ,
> Knows *Spartan* Virtue, and *Athenian* Wit.

Charles Hopkins, 'An Epistle . . . to Mr. Yalden in Oxon.', dated from London-Derry, 3 August 1699, in *Poetical Miscellanies: The Fifth Part* (London, 1704), 185–6.

> Methinks I see the tuneful Sisters ride,
> Mounted like Sea-Nymphs on the swelling Tide,
> The Silver Swans are silent while they play,
> *Augusta* hears their Notes, and puts to Sea,
> *Dryden* and *Congreve* meet them half the way.
> . . .
> Hark yonder where the *Mourning Bride* complains,
> And melt with Pity at the moving Strains:
> Wait the Conclusion, then allay your Grief,
> Vice meets with Ruin, Virtue with Relief.

[Charles Gildon], in Langbaine, *Lives and Characters*, sig. A6^r, 21–5.

(i) *I have lately read Mr.* Congreve's Love for Love *over, and am of Opinion, that the Contrivance of the Marriage of* Tattle *and Mrs.* Frail *is highly probable, tho' the Reflections on that Play do seem not to admit it as absolutely so.*

(ii) *William Congreve.*

A Gentleman now living, who derives himself from an Ancient Family in *Staffordshire* of that Name. His Politer Knowledge he owes to *Dublin* Colledge, from whence being returned to *England*, his first Applications were to the *Law*. But Mr. *Congreve* was of too delicate a Taste, had a Wit of too fine a turn, to be long pleas'd with that crabbed, unpalatable Study; in which the laborious dull plodding Fellow, generally excells the more sprightly and vivacious Wit; for the Law is something like Preferment at Court, won by Assurance and Assiduity; this concurring with his Natural Inclinations to Poetry, diverted him from the Bar to the declining Stage, which then stood in need of such a Support; and from whence the Town justly receiv'd him as *Rome's other Hope.*

Rochfoucault truly observes, that Merit alone will never make a Heroe, without the friendly Assistance of Fortune; and therefore Mr. *Congreve* must be said to be as much oblig'd to her for his *Success*, as to Nature for his *Wit*, which truly deserv'd it, and of which all those that read his Plays, must allow him a more than ordinary Share. And indeed he took the most certain way to make sure of *Fortune*, by the Intimacy he contracted with the most active part of the *establish'd* and *receiv'd* Wits and Poets of the Age, before he ventur'd his Reputation to the Publick. For as a celebrated French Writer has observ'd, an Author should never expect to raise his Fame in the World, from an unknown State, by the Single Force of his own Genius, and without the Help and Concurrence of the Men of Wit, that have an Influence over the Opinion of the World in things of that Nature. But then on the other side, it must be confess'd, that his Merit was certainly of more than ordinary Power, to oblige them to forget their habitual *Ill-Nature*; and criminal Emulation or Jealousy (to give it no worse Name) of all those, whom they have any Cause to fear, will once prove any considerable Rivals in their Fickle Mistress, *Fame*. Mr. *Congreve* has already given us Four Plays, of which in their Alphabetical Order.

The Double Dealer, a Comedy, Acted at the Theatre Royal by their Majesties Servants, 1694. 4*to.* and Dedicated to the Right Honourable *Charles Montague*, Esq. one of the Lords of the Treasury. This Play not meeting with that Success as was expected, the Author, as Poets are generally apt to do, engages a little too violently in a Defence of his Comedy. The Character of *Maskwell* I take to be an Image of *Vernish* in *The Plain Dealer.*

Love for Love, a Comedy, Acted at the Theatre in *Little Lincolns-Inn-Fields*, by his Majesty's Servants, 1695. 4*to.* and Dedicated to the Right Honourable *Charles*, Earl of *Dorset* and *Middlesex*. This Play, tho' a very good Comedy in it self, had this Advantage, that it was Acted at the Opening of the New House, when the Town was so prepossess'd in Favour of the very Actors, that before a Word was spoke, each Actor was Clapt for a considerable Time. And yet all this got it not more Applause than it really deserv'd: For there is abundance of Wit in it, and a great deal of diverting Humour. The Characters are justly distinguish'd, and the Manners well marked. Yet in the Plot he has not given himself the Pains of avoiding that so often repeated Improbability of Marrying in Masques and Disguises, which Mr. *Tattle*, nor Mrs. *Frail* had Sense enough to avoid, if we may judge by the rest of their Characters; yet it must be own'd, that he has much better prepar'd this Incident to gain it, at least some shew of Probability, than in the *Old Batchelor*, or than I have generally met with in other Plays. I leave the nicer Criticks to decide whether the unravelling of the Plot, and the Conduct of *Angelica* in it, be extreamly just or no: I shall only say it pleas'd, and that is a considerable Defence, whatever some may think to the contrary.

The Mourning Bride, a Tragedy, Acted at the Theatre in *Little Lincolns-Inn-Fields*, by His Majesty's Servants, and Dedicated to her Royal Highness the Princess *A N N* of *Denmark*, 1697. *4to*. This Play had the greatest Success, not only of all Mr. *Congreve*'s, but indeed of all the Plays that ever I can remember on the English Stage, excepting none of the incomparable *Otway*'s; and if what Dr. *Blackmore* says of it be true, it deserved even greater than it met with; for the learned Doctor in the Seventh Page of his Preface to *King Arthyr*, says thus: [The critique by Blackmore is cited above at pp. 303-4.]

Thus far the Learned Doctor, of whom I will not say, as the *Plain Dealer* says of my Lord *Plausible*, That *rather than not Flatter, he will Flatter the Poets of the Age*, &c. Yet I must needs say, so very great a Commendation, will make some of the Censorious Criticks imagine what it was that oblig'd him to take such particular Notice of this Play; which, tho' I should be never so willing to allow a Place in the first Form, yet I can never prefer it to the *All for Love* of Mr. *Dryden*, *The Orphan*, and *Venice Preserv'd* of Mr. *Otway*, or the *Lucius Junius Brutus* of Mr. *Lee*, either in true Art in the Contrivance and Conduct of the Plot; or the Choice and Delineation of the Characters for the true End of Tragedy, *Pitty* and *Terror*; or the *true* and *natural Movement* of the Passions, in which Particular, none of the Ancients (I was going to say equal'd, but I will boldly say) surpass'd our English dead Bards in those Plays, and our living Poet in this of his that I have mention'd. Or the *Diction*, either in regard to its *Propriety*, *Clearness*, *Beauty*, *Nobleness*, or *Variety*. Let any impartial Judge read but *All for Love*, and tell me if there is or can be a Style more Pure, or more Sublime, more adapted to the Subject in all its Parts: And I believe, notwithstanding all that some Gentlemen have urg'd against the Language in *Otway*'s Plays, it seldom wants any of those Qualities that are necessary to the Perfection of the Piece he has undertaken; he has seldom given us any Persons of Kings or Princes, and if his Stile swell not so much in the Mouths of those of a Lower Degree, whom he has chosen, it was because he had too much regard to the Nature of the Person he introduces. And in *Lee* (with the *Critick's* permission let me speak it) you find always something Wildly Noble, and Irregularly Great; and I am unwilling, with some, to think his Stile puffie or tumid; I'm sure in his Play of *Lucius Junius Brutus* he is generally Just, both in his Thoughts and his Expressions; and it is rather for want of a true Taste of him, than his want of Merit, that he is condemn'd in that Play, I mean, if there be any that do not exempt that from the Faults of his other Plays.

I urge not this as any Reflection on Mr. *Congreve*'s Performance, for which I have all the just Value the Merit of the Play commands; but to do justice to his great Predecessors on the Stage, at the depressing whose Praise, the Doctor, both in this and his former Preface, seems rather to aim, than at the raising that of Mr. *Congreve*. No, had I a mind to exert the *Critick*, I might, like many other of that Denomination, urge those Defects that either the Malice, or too nice Palate of others have discover'd in the Play itself. But I think 'tis a very ungenerous Office (and not to be excus'd by any thing but some extraordinary Provocation) to dissect the Works of a Man of Mr. *Congreve*'s undoubted Merit, when he has done his Endeavour to please the Town, and so notoriously obtain'd his End; and when the Faults that may perhaps be found in 'em, are of a Nature that makes them very disputable, and in which both his Predecessors and Contemporaries have offended; and I suppose he does not pretend to infallibility in Poetry. But tho' I purposely omit all Critical Reflections, yet the Duty of this Undertaking, and the Foundation I build on, obliges me to examine what he may have borrowed from others; which indeed is not much, tho' the Incident of the Tomb, seems to be taken from the Meeting of *Artaban* and *Eliza*, at the Tombe of *Tyridates*, in the Romance of *Cleopatra*. And *Zara* has many Features resembling *Nourmahal* in *Aurenge Zebe*, and *Almeria* in the *Indian Emperor*; I know some will have the whole Play a kind of Copy of that; but I confess I cannot discover likeness enough to justify their Opinion: unless it be *Zara*'s coming to the Prison to *Osmin*, as *Almeria* does to *Cortez*. I believe our Poet had the *Bajazet* of *Racine* in view, when he formed his Design, at least there is as much Ground for this as the former Opinion. *Perez* resenting the Blow the King gave him, is like an Incident in *Cæsar Borgia*; but the *Spaniard*'s Revenge is more generous, and less cruel than that of the *Italian*.

Thus much for the *Mourning Bride*, of which, if I may be allow'd to speak my impartial Sense, I must needs say, that in spite of its *Excellence*, it discovers Mr. *Congreve*'s *Genius* more inclin'd and turn'd to Comedy, than Tragedy, tho' he has gain'd an uncommon Praise for both; however, it being his first Poem of that Kind, it promises more perfect Products hereafter; and for which all Lovers of Poetry long with Impatience.

Old Batchelor, a Comedy, Acted at the Theatre Royal by their Majesties Servants, and Dedicated to the Right Honourable *Charles* Lord *Clifford*, of *Lanesborough*, 1693. 4*to*. This Comedy was Acted with so general an Applause, that it gave both Fame and Fortune to our Author; at once made him known to the Town, and to an Honourable *Mecænas*; who, to the Satisfaction of all Lovers of Learning, Wit, and Poetry, has ever since prov'd a generous Friend to our Poet. The *Old Batchelor* was usher'd into the World with several Copies of Verses of his Friends, and which the Merit of the Play abundantly justifies: For there's a genteel and sprightly Wit in the Dialogue, where it ought to be; and the humorous Characters are generally within the Compass of Nature, which can scarce be truly said of those of several Poets, who have met with Success enough on the Stage. *Bluff* seems an Imitation of the *Miles Gloriosus* of *Plautus*; of *Bounce* in *Greenwich Park*; and *Hackum* in the *Squire of Alsatia*, &c. The Incident of Sir *Joseph Wittoll*'s Marrying *Sylvia*, and Captain *Bluff*, *Lucy*, in Masques, has been too often an Incident on the Stage, since I'm confident it was scarce ever done in reality. Some other Characters are not entirely new, but that is very excusable in a Young Poet, especially in a Play, which I have been assur'd was writ, when our Author was but Nineteen Years Old, and in nothing alter'd, but in the Length, which being consider'd, I believe few Men that have writ, can shew one half so good at so unripe an Age.

Sir Richard Blackmore, *A Satyr Against Wit* (London, 1700), 9–10, 11.

(i)   Set forth your Edict, let it be enjoyn'd
             That all defective Species be recoyn'd.
             St. E—m—t and *R—r* both are fit
             To oversee the Coining of our Wit.
             Let these be made the Masters of Essay,
             They'll every Piece of Metal touch and weigh,
             And tell which is too light, which has too much Allay.
             'Tis true, that when the course and worthless Dross
             Is purg'd away, there will be mighty Loss.
             Ev'n *C——e*, *S——n*, *Manly W——ly*,
             When thus refin'd will grievous Suff'rers be.
             Into the melting Pot when *D——n* comes,
             What horrid Stench will rise, what noisome Fumes?
             How will he shrink, when all his leud Allay,
             And wicked Mixture shall be purg'd away?

(ii)   *V——e* and *C——e* both are Wealthy, they ⎫
             Have Funds of Standard-Sense, need no Allay, ⎬
             And yet mix'd Metal oft they pass away. ⎭
             The Bank may safely their Subscriptions take, ⎫
             But let 'em for their Reputation's sake, ⎬
             Take care their Payments they in Sterling make. ⎭

[Dr Thomas Smith], 'To the Indefatigable Rhimer', in *Commendatory Verses, On the Author Of The Two Arthurs, And The Satyr against Wit* (London, 1700), 6. Advt. the *Post Boy*, 12–14 March 1700.

             D——n, shall Numbers, *C——ve* Wit inspire,
             Dr—ke nicest Rules, but *B——le* and *Codron* Fire.

[Thomas Brown], 'An Epitome of a Poem, truly call'd *A Satyr against Wit*', ibid. 28.

> Then all our Friends the Actions shall cry up,   *l. 6. p. 12.*
> And all the railing Mouths of Envy stop.
> *Wou'd we cou'd Padlock thine, Eternal Fop.*
> The Project then will *T—tts* Test abide,   *l. 11. p. 16.*
> And with his Mark please all the World beside.
> *But dare thy Arthurs by this Test be tried?*
> Then what will *Dr—d—n, G—h*, or *C—ng—ve* say   *l. 27. p. 9.*
> When all their wicked Mixture's purg'd away?
> *Thy Metal's baser than their worst Allay.*

[Daniel Defoe], *The Pacificator. A Poem* (London, 1700), 6, 8–9, 13–14. *POAS* vi. 168–73, 179.

(i)   *C——e* and *D——n, H——s* and *M——x,*
> *D——y*, and everlasting Fops, and Beaus,
> Led up the Battel Fifty thousand strong,
> Arm'd with *Burlesque, Bombast*, and *Bawdy-Song*;
> Flesh'd with Great *C——*'s Slaughter they led on,
> Shouting *Victoria*, the Day's their own.
> No Bounds to their Licentious Arms they know,
> But Plunder all the Country as they go,
> Kill, Ravish, Burn, Destroy, do what they please!
> The *French* at *Swamerdam* were Fools to these.
> The Cruelties they Exercis'd were such,
> *Amboyna*'s nothing, they've out-done the *Dutch*;
> Never such Devastation sure was known,
> A Man of Sense cou'd not be seen in Town.
> *T——n*, even Hackney *T——n*, wou'd not Print,
> A Book without Wits *Imprimatur* in't;

(ii)   Among the Foot the Battel was severe,
> For Wits best Troops were wisely planted there,
> Led up by old Experienc'd Commanders,
> As *D——n, C——e, A——n* and *S——s*.

(iii)   Between these mighty Wings was rang'd in sight,
> A solid Phalanx of Compounded Wit:
> Ten thousand *Lyrick Foot*, all Gallant Beaus,
> Arm'd with *soft Sighs*, with *Songs*, and *Billet-Doux*.
> There was Eight thousand *Elegiack* Foot,

By *Briny Tears* and *Sullen Grief* made stout;
Five Pastoral Bands, lately bred up in Arms,
By Chanting *Gloriana*'s Mighty Charms,
And Thund'ring out King *W I L L I A M* 's loud Alarms.
Pindarick Legions, seven I think appear'd
Like *Brandenburghers*, with Enchanted Beard,
For Lions Skins, and Whisker's late so Fear'd.
These were led up by able old Commanders,
As *C——e*, *H——s*, Soldiers Bred in *Flanders*,
With *D——s*, *D——y*, *T——n*, Dull *M——x*,
B——r, *W——y*, *P——s*, Fops and *Beaus*,
Dull *T——e*, and Pious *B——y*, old *T——e*,
G——n, *Tom B——n*, and many a Subaltern;

(iv)   Let *Prior* Flatter Kings in Panegyrick,
R——ff Burlesque, and *W——y* be Lyrick:
Let *C——e* write the Comick, *F——e* Lampoon,
W——y the Banter, *M——n* the Buffoon,
And the Transgressing Muse receive the Fate
Of Contumacy, Excommunicate.

Samuel Wesley, *An Epistle to a Friend Concerning Poetry* (London, 1700), 19.

  CONGREVE from *Ireland* wond'ring we receive,
Would he the *Town's loose way* of Writing leave,
More Worth than all their Forfeit Lands will give:
Justness of *Thought*, a *Courtly Style*, and clear,
And well-wrought Passions in his *Works* appear:
None knows with *finer Strokes* our Souls to move,
And as he please we *smile*, or *weep*, or *love*.
When *Dryden* goes, 'tis he must fill the *Chair*,
With Congreve *only* Congreve *can compare*.
Yet, tho' he *natural* is as untaught Loves,
His *Style* as smooth as *Cytherea*'s Doves,
When e'er unbyass'd *Judges* read him o'er,
He sometimes *nodds*, as *Homer* did before:
Some Lines his most *Admirers* scarce would please,
Nor *B*—'s Verse alone could *raise Disease*.*

[marginal note] *Vide Collier's *Reflexions on* Mourning Bride, *and* Garth's *Dispensary.*

Pierre Motteux, 'The Translator's Preface', in *The History Of the Renown'd Don Quixote De la Mancha*. Translated from the Original by several Hands. 4 vols. (1700–3), i, sig. A6ᵛ. Motteux there cites his debt to:

> ... *some other Gentlemen, who are not only Masters of the Spanish, but of the Delicacies of our Tongue. I have also Acknowledgements to pay to Mr.* Wycherly, *Mr.* Congreve, *Dr.* Garth ... *and some other ingenious Friends* ...

John Oldmixon, Epilogue to Charles Gildon's adaptation, *Measure for Measure, Or Beauty the Best Advocate* (1700), ll. 23–8. Performed at LIF April–May 1700?

> *So, late may* Betterton *forsake the* Stage,
> *And long may* Barry *Live to Charm the* Age.
> *May a New* Otway *Rise, and learn to Move*
> *The* Men *with Terror, and the* Fair *with Love!*
> *Again, may* Congreve, *try the Commic Strain*;
> *And* Wycherly *Revive his Ancient* Vein ...

A.M., 'On the Memory of the Great D R Y D E N', in *Luctus Britannici: Or The Tears of the British Muses; For the Death of John Dryden, Esq.* (London, 1700), 10–11. The poem is dated 28 May 1700.

> But Stay, Methinks I see Great *Congreve* Frown,
> And *Southern* look's with Indignation down,
> To see an Unlearn'd Pen, unknown to Fame,
> In tuneless Lines Prophane their *Father*'s Name:
> My Muse, at sight of Theirs, is Aw'd and gone,
> As twinkling Stars expire before the *Sun*.

B.K., '*On the Death of Mr.* John Dryden', ibid. 12.

> What thô Impartial Fate ha's taken *Him* away,
> Reduc'd *His* Body to its Native Clay?
> Yet in *His* Works he will for ever live,
> In *Congreve* too his Glory will survive;
> *Congreve* the Lawful Heir of all his Sense,
> His Language, Fancy, and his Eloquence;
> To which Estate none else can make Pretence.

S.F., '*An Ode, On the Death of* John Dryden, *Esq; By a Young LADY*', ibid. 30. The poem is dated 7 May 1700. The author was Sarah Fyge, later Egerton. A revised version is included in her *Poems on Several Occasions* (1703).

> Our best Encomiums but Prophane Thy Name,
> Unless a *Congreve* would a Piece design,
> Whose Numbers, as they're dear to Fame,
>   Can Justice do to Thine.

Digby Cotes, 'Upon the Death of Mr. D R Y D E N', ibid. 32.

> Since Charming *Dryden* has so late confest
> Your base returns, and prov'd your barb'rous tast,
> Still may your long successive Dulness reign,
> Still may your Sons the War with Wit maintain;
> Let *C——e* still the Ladies Pity raise,
> And Torture one poor Maid a thousand ways,
> While pleas'd or Griev'd, she still the *Mourning Bride* betrays.
> Let *Ways o'th' World* in three dull years be writ,
> And want of time, excuse his want of Wit.

Anon., 'To the Memory of John Dryden, Esq.', ibid. 35.

> 'Tis true thou long hadst left th' ungrateful Stage,
> Where only *Congreve* now can please this Age.
> *Congreve* the Darling of the Sacred Nine!
> Whose Charming Numbers only yield to Thine.

Robert Gould, '*On the Death of* John Dryden, *Esq.*', ibid. 38.

> His Loss we all did with Impatience bear,
> And every Muse bemoan'd Him with a Tear.
> So they again wou'd Sigh, shou'd *Congreve* be,
> An Early Instance of Mortalitie;
> And the Expecting World (so seldom kind)
> Lose all the Wonders that are yet behind,
> In the unbounded Treasures of the Mind.

John Froud, '*Upon the Death of* John Dryden, *Esq*; A PINDARIQUE', ibid. 43.

> But whither, whither wouldst Thou fly
> My feeble Muse? The Quarry's much too high.

To some great Genius leave his praise,
Which may survive to After-days:
Let *Congreve* then in Deathless Song,
    His Father's Loss deplore;
Congreve must his Fame prolong,
In such soft rural Strains, as once he Sung before.
Whilst generous *Montague*, both Great and Just,
In some rich Urn preserves his Sacred Dust,
And or'e his Grave a *Mausolæum* rears,
To be the Envy'd Wonder of succeeding Years.

R. Key, '*An* E L E G Y *on the much Lamented Death of* John Dryden, *Esq; the famous* English *Poet*', ibid. 46.

Cease then to Weep till I have gain'd the Sky,
Least Grief shou'd to the World my Beams deny;
In Garth, *or* Congreve, *shall his Genius shine,*
Then cease thy Tears, nor at harsh Fate repine:
He said; the Promise cheer'd his drooping Breast;
And Light, the present Deity confest.

Anon., '*To Dr.* Samuel Garth, *occasioned by the much Lamented Death of* John Dryden, *Esq.*', ibid. 52.

And who shall make us known, and stamp Esteem,
On what we Write, since He's the Writer's Theme,
Though 'midst our Verse no Fav'rite *Congreve* shines,
Nor *Urwin* sends Auxilliary Lines.
Though Title Page no swelling *Kitcat* Grace,
And *Playford*'s Name, takes *Jacob Tonson*'s place.

Anon., 'Gallus', ibid. 2 (sig. 2Al[v]).

        solus tantis *Congrevius* ausis
Par erit: O quàm tunc tua mollitèr ossa quiescant,
Ista tuas olim si dicat fistula laudes!

[Congreve alone will be equal to such bold deeds: O how quietly then shall thy bones rest, if only *that* pipe once sings your praises!]

Thomas Wroughton, '*In obitum* Drydeni', ibid. 12 (sig. 2C2[v]).

At fœti properant cineres turgescere; dignus
Hæres *Congrevius*, Geniiq; Monarcha Paterni,

Instaurat lauros, & Famæ remigat alas.
Orbis ab integro volvetur, & aurea surget
Ætas; dum sacrâ sedanti voce minaces
Drydeno superûm nimbos, & ferrea monstra,
Congrevioq; ferum vulgus, Pacisq; procellas,
Aspirent æterna Deique, & sceptra Wilhelmi.

[But the pregnant ashes hasten to swell. Congreve, worthy heir and absolute ruler of his father's genius, renews the laurels and waves the wings of Fame. The wheel turns afresh, and a Golden Age arises, while the eternal things of God, and William's royal rule, waft away from Dryden, with calming, holy voice, the threatening clouds and hard-hearted omens, and towards Congreve the wild mob and the violent winds of Peace.]

Joseph Wyvill, '*In Obitum* Johannis Dryden *Armigeri, Poetæ omnibus numeris absoluti*', ibid. 24 (sig. [2]F2^v).

Sed levius damnum ut fiat, Congreve resurgas,
    Et felix pergat carmine Musa novo.
Ipse Poeta locum possis supplere Poetæ
    Fulgebitque suo funere, vita tua.
Cum moritur Phænix hoc quod compenset habemus,
    Ex summo est Phænix altera nata rogo.

[But may thou, O Congreve, arise, that the loss may be made the less; and may the fortunate Muse continue on her way with a new song. Thou art that poet who is able to take the place of the Poet and thy life shall shine in his death. Although the Phoenix is dead, we have that which compensates: I ask that a second Phoenix be born from on high.]

Alexander Oldys, *An Ode By way of Elegy, on the Universally lamented Death Of... Mr Dryden* (London, 1700), sig. C2^r.

For *Dorset* what a Pallace did I see!
For *Montague*! And what for *Normanby*!
    What Glorys wait for *Wycherly*!
For *Congreve, Southern, Tate, Garth, Addison*?
For *Stepney, Prior* and for *Dennis* too;
What Thrones are void, what Joys prepar'd and due?

[Daniel Kenrick] in *A New Session of the Poets, Occasion'd by the Death of Mr. Dryden* (London, 1700), 6–7.

> Stiff, as his Works, th'elab'rate *Cong—ve* came,
> Who could so soon Preferment get, and Fame.
> And with him brought the Product of his Pen,
> Miss *Prue* before, behind his Back stood *Ben*:
> Who quickly found the *Foible* of the Town,
> When ev'ry thing that *Dogget* did went down.
> His *Double Dealer* at a distance stood,
> At once extreamly regular, and lew'd.
> While in Procession by their Parent's Side
> March't the *Old Batchelour* and *Mourning Bride*.
> Then, at *Apollo*'s Feet his Labours laid,
> Thus to his Sire with good assurance said:
> If, bright *Apollo*, Young to gain renown,
> And please each Palate in this Ticklish Town,
> Has been my Talent still, and mine alone;
> Your Godship must the Laurel needs allow
> Of all your Sons, the best to suit my Brow:
> This Truth the Under-Graduates all Confess
> Of both the Famous Universities.
> And who so fit to be great *Dryden*'s Heir,
> As he, who living did his Empire share?
> This said, he bow'd, and bluffishly sate down;
> Whilst thus the God harangu'd his hopeful Son.
> How can you from those Bards expect the Bays,
> Who him that wore 'em, could so sadly praise?

Anon., *An Epistle to Sr. Richard Blackmore, Occasion'd by The New Session of the Poets* (London, 1700), 7, 8.

(i)
> His mighty *Dr—n* to the Shades is gone,
> And *Con—ve* leaves Successor of his Throne:
> Tho long before his final *Exit* hence
> He was himself an abdicated Prince,
> Disrob'd of all Regalities of State,
> Drawn by a *Hind* and *Panther* from his Seat:
> Heir to his Plays, his Fables and his Tales,
> *Con——* is the *Poetick Prince of Wales*;
> Not at *St. Germains*, but at *Will*'s his Court,
> Whither the Subjects of his Dad resort;
> Where Plots are hatch'd, and Councils yet unknown,

How young *Ascanius* may ascend the Throne,
That in despite of all the *Muses* Laws
He may revenge his injur'd Father's Cause.

(ii)   Tho *Con*—— may in time, when he has merit,
The Prophet's Throne in peaceful sway inherit,
The Poets all with one consent agree
His Mantle falls to *G*—— by Destiny,
Who did whilst living wear his Livery;
Who never did a Hero form in Verse,
But what he fashion'd still in *Dr*——*n*'s Dress . . .

Anon., *The Court* [November 1700–March 1701]. L: Add. MS.
21,094, ff. 167ᵛ–168ʳ. See *POAS* vi. 251, 761–2.

To diffrent Muses, diffrent Things belong
To Congreve lofty Verse, to Durfy Song.

Anon., 'A Letter to Mr. Congreve', in *A New Miscellany of Original
Poems* (London, 1701), 299–301.

AS Papist when his restiff Saint,
At home denies his Suit to grant
Trudges away to his, or her shrine,
With Nick-Nacks gay to make it more fine,
(For froward Saint above, who'd think it,
T'appease like Children here, with Trinket)
Hoping he never will disgrace
With a denial that dear place.
(For as we love our *Soil natale*,
So they love their *Soil Sepulchrale*)
So often having Sought in vain,
Early and late your Sight to gain.
Waited like Dun, or Court depender,
On Nobleman, or Fortune Mender.
At the great Mid-Wife of the Muses,
Who Judges Head for Cradle uses:
Whom Academic Wits importune,
As Rise of their poetic fortune,
Lo! now on Pilgrimage I am come
From *Brent-ford* Town to Court of Hampton.
Whether this be your dear *Samos*
Or any other Place that's famous.
Among the Gods, let this solicite
To waiting friend a speedy visit.

So may the Neighb'ring Nymphs adore you,
And when you please, fall down before you.
All Wives distress'd invoke your Name,
And distant Husbands dread your Fame:
Or if your Worship more delight in
Our vows that do affect your Writing.
May *Critic*'s ne'r disect your Plays,   }
Provok'd by what they want, your Praise,   }
Nor Poet envy you the Bays.   }
May *Hiss* and Catcalls ne'r attaque you
May smiles of Boxes ne'r forsake you.
But when you write may you still find
An Audience pleas'd, and Patron kind.
As you to *Bulloks* Strait repair
To find your humble Servant there.

[John Froud], *The Grove: Or, the Rival Muses* (London, 1701), 12.
Advt. the *Post Man*, 15 March 1701.

Whilst *Garth*, and *Congreve*, Heirs to all the Flame
With which he [Dryden] wrote, and rose to endless Fame:
Charm with soft Harmony the list'ning Age,
Or lash its Vices with a noble Rage.

Anon., *The Town Display'd, In a Letter to Amintor In the Country*
(London, 1701), 15. Luttrell 10 July. Foxon T433.

C—— in Vain, in Tragick *Buskins* try'd
To please the Criticks with his *Mourning Bride*;
For who the Devil knows where all the Sense is,
In the Epistle to our Royal Princess?
Or who is so much a Philosopher,
To tell the meaning of his wafting Air?
Let him forsake the lofty Tragick Scene,
And the Dull Town with Humour Entertain;
For the *Old Batchelor*, without a Plot,
Will Live, when the poor *Mourning-Bride*'s forgot.

[Abel Boyer, ed.], *Letters of Wit, Politicks and Morality* (London,
1701). Boyer's dedication is dated 5 July 1701.

(i) [Among coffee-houses,] *Will*'s Coffee-house in *Covent-Garden*, holds the
first Rank, as being consecrated to the Honour of *Apollo*, by the first-rate Wits
that flourish'd in King *Charles* II's Reign . . . and tho' this Place has lost most of

its illustrious Founders, yet it has ever since been supported by Men of great Worth; but its being accounted the Temple of the *Muses*, where all *Poets* and *Wits* are to be initiated, has given occasion to its being pester'd with abundance of false Pretenders, who rather darken, than heighten its former Splendour.

The Company which now generally meets at *Will*'s, may be divided into two Classes; the first of which contains the *Wits*, justly so call'd, and the other the *Would-be-Wits*.

Among the first are Men of distinguish'd Merit and Abilities, such as Mr. *Wicherley*, Dr. *Garth*, Mr. *Congreve*, the Honourable Mr. *Boyle*, Colonel *Stanhope*, Mr. *Vanbruk*, Mr. *Cheek*, Mr. *Walsh*, Mr. *Burnaby*, Mr. *Rowe*, and some few others whose names at present do not occur to my memory. (p. 216)

(ii) Mr. *Congreve* is a Gentleman, whose Poetry has been in vogue for 6 or 7 years past, but whose late Performances have not met with so favourable a Reception; not so much, as I am told, thro' the defect of his Muse, as the fickleness of the Town, in their Tastes and Opinions. He has writ two Comedies, *viz.* the *Old Batchelour*, and *Love for Love*, and a Tragedy call'd, *The Mourning Bride*, which have been acted with an universal Applause. His Master-piece is an Elegy, by way of Pastoral, on the Death of the late Queen of *England*, which comes up to the best performances of that kind of *Theocritus* and *Virgil*. Mr. *Congreve* is a polite, well-bred Person, but somewhat cold and reserv'd, unless he be among his intimate Friends. He is particularly belov'd by my Lord *Dorset*, and my Lord *Hallifax*, the *Mæcenas's* of the *English* Muses. (p. 218)

(iii) [Among judgements delivered by Would-be-Wits in Will's:] *Shakespear*, with them, has neither Language nor Manners; *Ben. Johnson* is a Pedant; *Dryden* little more than a good Versifier; *Congreve* a laborious unnatural Writer; and *Garth* a Copier. (p. 221)

(iv) [Letter V, signed W.B., is on comedy and tragedy, and is claimed to offer] enough to enable you to make a true Judgment of the *Mourning Bride*, the *Ambitious Step-Mother*, the *Trip to the Jubilee*, and other celebrated Plays ... By this too you may form some Judgment of the *Way of the World*, from my liking of which, I confess, I cannot yet recede, in spite of all the Malice of our brisk, false Criticks. (pp. 236–7)

George Farquhar, 'A Discourse on Comedy', in *Love and Business* (published 22 November 1701), *Works*, ii. 368–9, 378.

(i) [With a restless audience] tho' the Play be as regular as *Aristotle*, and modest as Mr. *Collier* cou'd wish, yet it promotes more Lewdness in the Consequence, and procures more effectually for Intreague than any *Rover*, *Libertine*, or old *Batchelour* whatsoever.

(ii) [As Aesop] would improve Men by the Policy of Beasts, so we endeavour to reform Brutes with the Examples of Men. *Fondlewife* and his young Spouse are no more than the *Eagle* and *Cockle*; he wanted Teeth to break the Shell himself, so somebody else run away with the Meat.

Thomas Parnell, 'A Letter to a friend. On poets Satyr 1st', autograph manuscript, 1700–2? Printed in *Collected Poems of Thomas Parnell*, ed. Claude Rawson and F.P. Lock (Newark: University of Delaware Press, 1989), 345, ll. 30–5.

> Wn C—r taught how plays debaucht ye age
> he left to V—ke to defend ye stage,
> in rufull ballad humbly pleas'd to rage.
> how great & undisturb'd by censuring foes
> might eithers fame beneath thier wreaths repose
> had B—l nere written verse nor C—ve prose.

William Ayloffe, preface to *The Miscellaneous Works of the Honourable Sir Charles Sedley, Bart* (1702), sig. A4ᵛ, A5ʳ.

Our Theaters have done no small Honour to the Tragic Buskins; and *Terence* and *Plautus* wou'd contentedly sit out the *Old Batchelour*: ... Why shou'd we step back to *Beaumont* and *Fletcher*, to *Shakespear* and *Ben. Johnson*? We have later Proofs (tho' not greater) of the *English* Genius: We have the *Utile dulci*, the natural and sublime.

Anon., *A Comparison Between the Two Stages* (London, 1702).

(i) *Ramb.* Don't be too severe *Critick*; you know the New-House opened with an extraordinary good Comedy, the like has scarce been heard of.

Cri. I allow that Play contributed not a little to their Reputation and Profit; it was the Work of a popular Author; but that was not all, the Town was ingag'd in its favour, and in favour of the Actors long before the Play was Acted.

Sull. I've heard as much; and I don't grudge 'em that happy beginning, to compensate some part of their Expence and Toil: But the assistance they receiv'd from some Noble Persons did 'em eminent Credit; and their appearance in the Boxes, gave the House as much Advantage as their Contributions.

Ramb. Faith if their Boxes had not been well crowded, their Galleries wou'd ha' fallen down on their Heads.

Sull. The good Humour those Noble Patrons were in, gave that Comedy such infinite Applause; and what the Quality approve, the lower sort take upon trust. But this like other things of that kind, being only nine Days wonder, and the Audiences, being in a little time sated with the Novelty of the *New-house*, return in Shoals to the Old. (pp. 12–13)

(ii) *Congreve* has a great Character for Comedy, and in my poor Judgement has perform'd well in Tragedy. (p. 57)

(iii) *Sull.* . . . . this I know, that he has publickly Panegyrick'd one Author with the *Old Batchelor*, another with the *Relapse*, and Mr. *Southern* very frequently on all occasions; and yet I have seen him bite his Nails for Vexation that they came so near him.

Crit. Two of those three you've named have oblig'd us with better Comedies than any of his; and tho' Mr. *Congreve*'s Reputation arises from his first, third and fourth Play, yet I must needs say, that according to my taste, his second is the best he ever writ.

Ramb. If you mean the *Double Dealer*, you go against the Opinion of all the Town.

Crit. I can't help that; I'll follow my own Judgment as far as it will carry me, and if I differ from the Voice of the crowd, I shall value my self the more for my Sincerity: But you're mistaken, all the Town was not of that Opinion; some good Judges were of another; but without being byass'd or prejudic'd, I do take the *Double Dealer* to be among the most correct and regular Comedies: Mr *C.* intended it so, and it cost him unusual Labour to do't; but as he says, he has been at a needless Expence, and the Town is to be treated at a cheaper rate: But with all Mr. *Congreve*'s Merit, I don't take his Characters to be always natural; even in the *Double Dealer* some are out of probability, one in his *Old Batchelor*, and several in *Love for Love* obsolete.

Sull. We shall be glad you'll convince us of that; for as yet I have not heard that objected.

Crit. Whenever you please Gentlemen.

Ramb. Why not now?

Crit. My time's expir'd; I have an Appointment at Four in a Ladies Chamber; and I love to be punctual in such a Case.

Sull. Methinks you'll carry but little good Humour with you to the Lady; this discourse has put you into a kind of ferment.

Crit. Then I'll go and work it off there; at six I'll meet you at *Lincolns-Inn-fields* Play-House.

Sull. What Play is't?

Ramb. *The way of the World*, with the new wonder *Madam D'Subligny*.

Crit. There's another Toy now—Gad there's not a Year but some surprizing Monster lands: I wonder they don't first show her at *Fleet-bridge* with an old Drum and a crackt Trumpet—walk in and take your Places—just going to show—by such a Stratagem, and a Monkey or two thrown into the bargain, Mr. *B*. might double his Stake, and come off pretty snug with his *French* Adventure.

 Ramb. Let's meet there; methinks I long to be ogling *Madam*'s Feet.

(pp. 65–7)

(iv) *Sull*. You forget what we propos'd at our first meeting.

 Crit. What's that?

 Sull. To consider some things of the Author's who writ the *Mourning Bride*: How d'ee stand inclin'd to that now?

 Crit. I am tir'd with the Drudgery of my Office: Besides my Forces are so weaken'd already, I have not strength enough left to incounter such a gigantick Author.

 Ramb. What, not *The way o'the World?* as weak as I am, I dare appear against that.

 Sull. 'Tis not so easy a matter as you imagine: That Comedy cost Mr. *Congreve* (as some say) two Years study.

 Ramb. I have known a better writ in a Month; *Ben's Fox* was begun and finish'd in that time: *Shadwel's Libertine* was writ in One and twenty Days; nay, I have seen a very modern Comedy which the Author says he writ in ten Days.

 Crit. Ten Days? sure his Thought ran as fast as his Pen; it will ask that time to Transcribe one. . . .

 Sull. Shall we say nothing then to Mr. *Congreve?*

 Crit. Pray excuse me: I stand very well with that Gentleman at present, and shall be very sorry to incur his displeasure.

 Ramb. Oh fie! this is partial—

 Crit. Besides, he has done with the Stage, and is (in a poetical Sense) in the circumstances of the Dead; so let him sleep in peace.   (pp. 195–7)

Thomas Brown, 'Amusement II: The Court', in *Amusements Serious and Comical*, 2nd edn. (London, 1702), 19.

. . . and as for the *Dirty Acres*, like Sir *Joseph* in Mr. *Congreve's Old Batchelour*, he has *wash'd his Hands of 'em*, but in another manner, for he has sufficiently *daub'd* 'em with fingering what he receiv'd in Exchange for 'em.

Thomas Brown, 'Amusement IV: The Play-house', ibid. 51–2.

. . . that *Poet* there, that shews his Assiduity by following yonder Actress, is the most entertaining sort of Animal imaginable. But 'tis *the way of the World*, to have an Esteem for the fair Sex, and She looks to a Miracle when She is acting a Part in one of his own Plays. Would not any one think it pitty She should not have an Humble Servant, when that Mrs. *Abigal* there, who is one of her Attendants can be brought to Bed of a Living Child without any manner of notice taken of her. Look upon him once more I say, if She goes to her *Shift*, 'tis Ten to One but he follows her, not that I would say for never so much to take up her *Smock*; he Dines with her almost ev'ry day, yet She's a *Maid*, he rides out with her, and visits her in Publick and Private, yet She's a *Maid*; if I had not a particular respect for her, I should go near to say he lies with her, yet She's a *Maid*. Now I leave the World to Judge whether it be His or Her Fault that She has so long kept her *Maidenhead*, since Gentlemen of his Profession have generally *a greater Respect for the Lady's than that comes to*.

Richard Burridge, *A Scourge for the Play-Houses: Or, The Character of the English Stage* (London, 1702), preface.

To make no longer Preambulation, I shall conclude by way of a short Advertisement, to a certain Irish Bard, *which is to Notifie, That if he durst pretend again to defend the School of Hell, he would use more Wit and Sense, than he did in his Answer to Mr.* Collier's *View of that wretched Place; by which Attempt he has made himself so much a May-game to all Men of Sense, that it is now become an Adage to say, when one Reflects on a Blockhead,* he Writes like C——e: *or if any other durst to take up the* Cudgels, *they shall have* Hockly i'th' Hole Play, *A Clean Stage, and no Favour.*

Anon., *The Proceedings and Tryals of the Players in Lincoln's-Inn-Fields, Held at the King's-Bench Bar... 16th of February 1701/2* (1702), 1.

[It charges] particularly that they had used many abominable Expressions in the two Plays, one called *Love for Love*; and the other *The Sham Doctor.*...[A witness gave evidence] That not long since he heard them express in a Play, call'd the *Sham Doctor*, several Insufferable vain Repetitions, and another said, he heard the like in a Play call'd *Love for Love.*...the Defendants made great defence for themselves, but to no purpose; the Plays being brought in against them in Print, the Judge declar'd to the Jury the ill Consequence of such Prophane Wicked Speeches.

Anon., *The Golden Age, from the Fourth* Eclog *of* Virgil, &c. (London, 1703), 5–6. Also in *Poems on Affairs of State, From the Reign of K. James the First, To this Present Year 1703* (London, 1703), ii. 444–5. *POAS* vi. 463. 'C— H—' may refer to Charles Montagu, created Baron Halifax in 1700.

> Oh! that this *Life* of mine so long would last,
> As I might Sing, thy Future Deeds and past...
> Not *C—ve* stock'd with all his Patron's Praise,

Produce a Zeal like mine, or equal Lays;
To *C— H—* his Friend should be,
C—ve, if *H—* were Judg, should yield to me.

Anon., *Religio Poetae: or, a Satyr on the Poets* (1703). Foxon R153.
Cited Milhous & Hume, i. 373, from Yale (Folio Pamphlets 30).

The *Way o'th' World* first shew'd his Muse decay:
We all expected Wonders from that Play...
But after drudging for above two Years,
To our Amazement, out the M O U S E appears.
He spurr'd his Comick Muse at first too fast,
And run the Race of Wit too quick to last.

[— Bryan], *The Temple of Fame. A Poem... Inscrib'd to Mr. Congreve*
(London, 1703), 3. Luttrell's copy 30 January (Foxon B551). Text
here from the 1709 edition (Foxon B552), 3–4.

And now, *O Congreve*, wil't thou slight thy Pen,
To sing the Arms of the Victorious Men?
Not thy own *William*'s was a Nobler Name,
Or more renown'd in *Poetry* and Fame;
Eugene's *Cremona* may with *Namur* joyn,
And *Vigo* be an equal to the *Boyn*:
Th'Illustrious *Ann* her *Poets* will regard,
And *Ormond* well as *Montague* reward.

S[arah] F[ield], *Poems on Several Occasions* (London, 1703).
Born Sarah Fyge, she became Field by her first husband and
Egerton by her second. 'The fond Shepherdess. A Pastoral', which
was probably also issued separately, is included in this volume and
dedicated 'T O T H E Most Learn'd, and Ingenious, Mr. *William
Congreve*'.

E.C., 'To my Ingenious Friend Mrs. S.F. on her Poems', ibid. sig A8^v.

Let the soft Pen, who great *Pastora* Mourn'd,
To more delightful rural Strains be turn'd;
And sing *Clarinda*'s Fame, whose tender Lays,
Next to his own, deserve immortal Praise.

George Granville, Lord Lansdowne, 'A Letter with a Character of
Mr. Wycherly', in *The Genuine Works in Verse and Prose Of The Right
Honourable George Granville, Lord Lansdown.* 2 vols. (1732), ii. 436.
The date is probably *c.*1703–4 (Pope is mentioned as 'not above
Seventeen or Eighteen Years of Age'). The only hint of the
addressee's name is the conclusion 'Dear Harry, Adieu'.

Congreve is your familiar Acquaintance, you may judge of *Wycherly* by
him: They have the same manly way of Thinking and Writing, the
same Candour, Modesty, Humanity, and Integrity of Manners: It is impossible
not to love them for their own sakes, abstracted from the Merit of their Works.

Tom Brown, *The Stage-Beaux Toss'd in a Blanket: or Hypocrisie
Alamode* (1704), 25. There are brief allusions also at pp. 26, 32. Of
Collier's *A Short View* and its supporters, he writes:

Your Party I confess is not without their trifling Evasions to pretend this
Book not Answer'd. If the Author be easie, Genteel and Witty, like the
Vindicators of the Relapse, &c. [by Vanbrugh] then 'tis *Banter.* If it be mixt
with just Repartees, admirable Reflections, like the *Amendments* [by
Congreve], then 'tis Scurrilous. If like others, the Matter be seriously and
plainly handl'd with sound Reasoning, then 'tis Dull.

[William Shippen], *Faction Display'd. A Poem* (London, 1704), 13.
POAS vi. 665. Published before 28 April. Foxon S427. The Whig
'Bathillo' speaks:

> The Poet Tribe are all at my Devoir,
> And write as I Command, as I inspire.
> C—g—ve for me *Pastora*'s Death did Mourn,
> *And her white Name with Sable Verse adorn.*

[Elizabeth Singer], 'A Pastoral, Inscrib'd to The Honorable, Mrs.—',
in *Poetical Miscellanies: The Fifth Part* (London, 1704), 380–1.

> Propitious God of Love, my Breast inspire
> With all thy Charms, with all thy pleasing Fire:
> Propitious God of Love, thy Succour bring,
> While I thy Darling, thy *Alexis* sing;
> *Alexis,* as the op'ning Blossoms, Fair,
> Lovely as Light, Soft as the yielding Air;

For him each Virgin Sighs, and on the Plains
The matchless Youth without a Rival reigns;
With such an Air, with such a graceful Mien,
No Shepherd dances on the flow'ry Green:
Nor to the ecchoing Groves, and whisp'ring Springs,
In sweeter Strains the tuneful *Co—ve* sings.

Anon., *The Tryal of Skill: or, A New Session of the Poets. Calculated for the Meridean of Parnassus, In the Year, MDCCIV* [8 August 1704]. *POAS* vi. 705–6.

When *Congreve* brim full of his Mistresses Charms,
　　Who had likewise made bold with *Molier*,
Came in piping hot from his *Bracegirdle*'s Arms,
　　And would have it his Title was clear.

What he rendred in English, was nothing like *Smut*;
　　For he wisely had taken his Choice;
And though the first Act in this Version might not,
　　Yet his Prudence should give him their Voice.

Said *Apollo*, You did most discreetly to take
　　A Part that was easiest and best;
Though the Rules of Behaviour Distinction should make,
　　And you'd not done amiss to chuse last.

But never pretend to be Modest or Chast,
　　Th'Old Batchelor speaks you Obscene,
And *Love for Love* shews, notwithstanding your hast,
　　That your Thoughts are Impure and Unclean.

That meaning's Lascivious your Dialogues bear,
　　Fit to grace the foul Language of *Stews*,
And though you are said to make a Wife of a Play'r,
　　You in those make a Whore of your Muse.

Anon., *An Elegy On The Much Lamented Death of Sir Roger L'Estrange* (London, 1704). L'Estrange died on 11 December 1704.

　　L'Estrange Departed! And no Mourning Muse
　　To bear about the Melancholy News!

Henry Grey, first Duke of Kent, Lord Chamberlain to the Queen. Printed *London Gazette*, 21–5 December 1704. MS: NA, LC 5// 154, p. 35.

December 14, 1704

A NN E R. License for a New Company of Comedians.

W H E R E A S We have thought fitt for the better reforming the Abuses, and Immorality of the Stage That a New Company of Comedians should be Establish'd for our Service, under stricter Government and Regulations than have been formerly

We therefore reposing especiall trust, and confidence in Our Trusty and Welbeloved John Vanbrugh and Willm. Congreve Esqrs. for the due Execution, and performance of this our Will and Pleasure, do Give and Grant unto them the said John Vanbrugh, and Willm. Congreve full power and Authority to form, constitute, and Establish for Us, a Company of Comedians with full and free License to Act and Represent in any Convenient Place, during Our Pleasure all Comedies, Tragedys Plays, Interludes Operas, and to perform all other Theatricall and Musicall Entertainments whatsoever and to settle such Rules and Orders for the good Government of the said Company, as the Chamberlain of our Household shall from time to time direct and approve of G I V E N at our Court at St. James this 14th. day of December in the third Year of Our Reign.

By her Majesty's Command

Anon., 'A *Prologue* design'd to be Spoke before *Henry* the VIII. by Mr. *Betterton*', *The Diverting Post*, 9–16 December 1704, ll. 1–4. Performed at LIF *c*.16 December 1704.

> *W I T H diff'rent Scenes, we diff'rent Arts have try'd,*
> *To gain that Favour you've so long deny'd;*
> *Still all our Labours unsuccessful prove,*
> *No more can* Congreve *please, or* Otway *move.*

Alexander Pope, Letter to William Wycherley. 26 December 1704. Pope, *Correspondence*, i. 2. Pope here refers to Dryden.

I was not so happy as to know him; *Virgilium tantum vidi*—Had I been born early enough, I must have known and lov'd him: For I have been assur'd, not only by your self, but by Mr. *Congreve* and Sir *William Trumbul*, that his personal Qualities were as amiable as his Poetical, notwithstanding the many libelous Misrepresentations of them (against which the former of these Gentlemen has told me he will one day vindicate him).

Anon., 'Advertisement' [March–April 1705]. This mock advertisement, which refers to the Queen's Theatre as 'The New Hospital in the Hay-Market for the Cure of Folly', lists eight 'Places under the Governours to be dispos'd of'. For the identifications, see *N&Q* 203 (1958), 393–6.

1. Cryer of the Rehearsals—fit for an Herald. [Vanbrugh?]
2. Play Cutter—fit for an Exhausted Poet. [Congreve?]
3. Engrosser of Good Parts—fit for an old proud Actor. [Betterton?]
4. Warden of the Chandlery—fit for a Barren Actress. [Mrs. Bracegirdle?]
5. Midwife to the Women—proper for a Superanuated Actress. [Mrs. Barry]
6. Her Deputy—fit for a Surgeon. [Garth?]
7. Quality tickler in dead times—fit for a Barren Actress. [Mrs. Bracegirdle]
8. Chaplain—fit for an Occasional Conformist.

Owen MacSwinny, Prologue to *The Quacks; or, Love's the Physician* (1705), ll. 7–12. Performed 'after being twice forbid' at DL on 29 March 1705 (*LS* pt 2, i. 90). The '*coupled Bards*' in l. 9 are Vanbrugh and Congreve.

> Maim'd as he is, he Trembles to Engage,
> The slow Productions of yon Rival Stage.
> On deep Designs the coupled Bards have hit,
> And wisely wou'd Engross, all Foreign Wit.
> And think the surest way to gain the Town
> Wou'd be to shew, but little of their own.

[Thomas Birch], 'To Mr Congreve and Vanbrugh upon ye building of ye new play-house in ye Hay-market'. April 1705? From the Portland (Holles) MS Pw V975*, University of Nottingham. It follows other verses by 'Mr Burch' and is said to be 'By ye same'.

> To Mr Congreve and Vanbrugh
> upon ye building of ye new play-house in ye Hay-market.

> Touch'd by Amphion ye attractive Lyre
> Did List'ning stones with living souls inspire;
> The heavy flints obey'd ye magic call,
> Forgat their weight, and nimbly danced into a wall.
> Now witt and harmony again combine
> To raise new Trophys to ye sacred nine;
> Again ye stones in beauteous order place,

And rising building wth rich fancy grace.
The muses view ye work with ravish'd eyes,
And their long lov'd Pierian grove dispise;
To their new Temple with glad haste repair,
And fill'd with pleasure shed their influence there.
Harmonious pair! Well were you pointed out,
To bring with art ye wondrous work about:
No Artist but ye son of mighty Jove,
Can make Apartments fit for th'King above
None but the muses tunefull sons can raise
A worthy Temple to ye muses praise,
Deck't with immortall witt, and never dying bays.

Anon., *A Second Advertisement Concerning the Profaneness of the Playhouse* (Bristol, 1705), 3–15. The page references to *Love for Love* are to the fourth edition of 1704. Except for the examples cited on p. xxx the square brackets are the original author's.

> *Remarks upon the* Comedy *called* Love for Love, *as it was acted on* Monday *the 23d of* July, *according to their publick* Advertisement.

FIrst, This *Play* hath already been censured by Mr. *Collier* in his *View of the Stage*; and the lame defence of it written afterward by the *Author* did only give an Opportunity for Exposing it farther in Mr. *Collier's Reply*. The *Actors* therefore could not but be sensible that this was a *Comedy* publickly known to be *scandalous* and *profane*; but nothing of this Nature could prevail upon them to omit it.

Mr. *Collier* particularly tells us of the *Immodesty* hereof, Pag. 4, and Pag. 10, that *Miss* Prue *is represented silly, the better to enlarge her Liberty, and skreen her Impudence from the publick Censure.* He tells us, pag. 24, that *Heathen* Comedians *had no smutty Songs in their Plays; but for this the* English (*especially* Love for Love) *are extreamly scandalous.* He largely charges this *Comedy*, pag. 74, *&c.* and pag. 83, with *Profaneness*, in *Abusing of Religion, and the Holy Scriptures*; and, pag. 142, with *representing* Valentine *the* Hero *of the* Play as a Person *compounded of Vice, a prodigal Debauchee, unnatural and profane, obscene, sawcy and undutiful; and rewarding him at last, for a Man of Merit, with a Fine Lady, and Thirty Thousand Pounds:* So that since this *Comedy* hath been painted in its proper Colours, the Reader may the better excuse it, if I sometimes borrow the Words of the same Author.

Secondly, The Songs set to Musick in this Play are also remarkable. The first which I shall mention is in pag. 45. The *Words* are intolerably *obscene* and *scandalous*, with a Mixture of *profane Wit*, to please a Country-man's Fancy; and the Notes are plain and easy, according to his Capacity. The Design hereof is that such Verses may be disperst and sung in Country Places for their Diversion, that the Poison of the Play-house may spread farther than many imagine, and such also may be debauch'd by them, who never came to hear them.

The second Song is in pag. 33. The Design of it is to tell the World that all Women are Whores who were ever tempted: or in their own Language—

—*The Nymph may be chast that has never been try'd.*—

This is set for Ladies to learn to sing if they please to complement their own Sex so far; and it is observable that the frequent Repetitions of the Words, as designed by the Composer, do make the Sence the more emphatical.

The Third is in Pag. 61, written in Praise of Whoring and Debauchery. The Musick is indeed too fine for the Words, and the Composer hath shewn his Art, only he wanted to employ it better. The Tune is fit for a Lady to learn, and the Words seem better polished for a nicer Palate than the rest, for which Reason I shall venture to transcribe some of them.

> *Love hates to center in a Point assign'd,*
> *But runs with Joy the Circle of the Mind.*
> *Then never let us chain what should be free.*
> *But for Relief of either Sex agree,*
> *Since Women love to change, and so do we.*

Here we have Lewdness in Verse, though wrapp'd up in cleaner Linnen, and fine Musick to double the Force of the Mischief, and drive it stronger upon Fancy and Practice. And there is no doubt but many a Fine Woman hath been insensibly debauch'd when they learn such Songs for their better Breeding, and which hath proved the Ruin of some Families. Thus Vice and Profaneness corrupts a most noble Science, spreads with Delight, both in City and Country, among Gentle and Simple; and the Original of all lies at the *Play-house* Door.

Fourthly, The Comedy it self is notoriously scandalous, *particularly for profane Swearing.* [As examples, the anonymous author here cites, with page references: "'Slife, *(that is by God's Life)*', 'Faith', 'In Faith', 'Faith and Troth', "Sheart, *(that is by God's heart)*', "'Sdeath *(that is by God's death)*'; and, to show also that '*This Comedy is scandalous for Cursing*', adds: 'Pox on't', 'A Pox confound *etc*', 'Pox take 'em', 'Pox on her', 'Pox on the Time', 'O damn you Toad', 'O hang you', 'Devil take you confounded Toad', 'Oh hang him, old Fox', 'The Devil Take Me'.]

This Comedy exposeth Marriage, and pleads for Whoring.

You are a Woman now, and must think of a new Man every Morning, and forget him every Night. To marry, is to be a Child Again, and play with the same Rattle always. pag. 70, lin. 9. [*Spoken to* Miss Prue *for her Information.*

You have secured your Honour, for you have purchased an Husband which is a perpetual Opportunity for Pleasure; and it is the least I can do to take Care of your Conscience (*that is to lull it asleep*) Pag. 43, lin. 37. [*Note the whole Dialogue is horridly scandalous on this Subject.*

This Comedy exposeth Honour and Conscience.

Honour is a Publick Enemy, and Conscience a Domestick Thief, pag. 43, lin. 32.

This Comedy stinks with lewd and smutty Expressions.

In this respect, *Benjamin* the *Sailor* is such a Monster, that his Words cannot be mentioned at length. His exposing of Marriage, Pag. 35. lin. 39. and pag. 36. lin. 4 is too filthy to be transcribed. He talks Smut, pag. 36, lin. 12: and *Frail* a Woman answers him in the same Language. His Discourse to *Miss Prue*, pag. 37, lin. 14. is of the same Nature, and his Song, pag. 45, intolerable.

The Expression of *Miss Prue*, pag. 71. lin. 25, will better bear to be transcribed, and therefore the Reader shall have some, though not one half of it, lest I should tire his Patience or turn his Stomach. *Now my Mind is set upon a Man, I will have a Man some way or other. Oh! methinks I'm sick when I think of a Man; and if I cannot have one, I would go to sleep all my Life.* I shall only observe that a Father, who puts such Words into the Mouth of his own Daughter, must thank himself, and acknowledge *God*'s Judgements to be just, should he withdraw his Grace and give her up to her own Hearts Lust, and what is spoken for a *Jest*, may prove so in *Earnest*.

This Comedy asperseth the Government.

Pag. 57, lin. 31, *Foresight* asks, *Pray what will be done at Court?* To this *Valentine* answers, *Scandal* will tell you; I am Truth, I never come there.

Lastly, *This Comedy is notoriously scandalous for its profane Ridiculing and Exposing the Holy Scripture.*

First, As to the Morality.

Doth she leave us together out of good Morality? [*To give them an Opportunity for Whoring.*] and to do as she would be done by? Pag. 27, lin. 24. [*This is their Interpretation of* Matth. 7. 12. *and thus they pervert the Words of Christ himself, as if he was the Patron of Sin, and commanded us to practise such Uncleanness.*

Thus *Scandal* an *Actor* sollicits Mrs. *Foresight*, she threatens to tell her Husband; he replies, pag. 42, lin. 3. *I'll die a Martyr rather than disclaim my Passion.* Here we have Adultery dignified with the Style of Martyrdom. As if it were as honourable to perish in the Defence of Whoring, as to die for the Cause of Christianity.

Like to this is that of *Angelica* in the End of the Play; *Men are generally Hypocrites and Infidels, they pretend to worship, but have neither Zeal nor Faith: How few like* Valentine *would persevere unto Martyrdom?* Here we have the Language of the *Scriptures*, and the most solemn Instances of Religion prostituted to Courtship and Romance! Here you have a Mistress made God

Almighty, adored with Zeal and Faith, and worshipped up to Martyrdom! This, if it were only for the Modesty, is strange Stuff for a Lady to say of herself, and had it not been for the profane Exposing of these Graces, would be far from the *Wit* which some Men pretend they hear in the Play-house.

Secondly, As to the Doctrinal Part.

Our Blessed Saviour affirms himself *to be the Way, the Truth, and the Light, that he came to bear Witness of the Truth, and that his Word is Truth.* These Expressions are mentioned in this Play to a fine Purpose: For *Valentine* in his pretended Madness tells *Buckram* the Lawyer, pag. 50, lin. 38. pag. 51, lin. 2, 8. pag. 52, lin. 31. *I am Truth.—I am Truth.—Who is he that is out of his Way? I am Truth, and can set him right.* Now such Persons as are not pleased with Blasphemy, would never have furnished Frensy with Inspiration, and put our Saviour's Words in the Mouth of a Madman, as if they were both alike.

Pag. 77, lin. 37. *Tattle* would have carried off *Valentine*'s Mistress: But *Valentine* expresseth his Resentment in these Words; Tattle, *I thank you, you would have interposed between me and Heaven, but Providence hath laid Purgatory in your Way.* Thus Heaven is debased into an Amour, made like a Turkish Paradise, and Providence brought in to direct the paultry Concerns of the Stage, as if God delighted to see himself mock'd.

Pag. 22, lin. 32. *Jeremy* faith, *I was born with the same Whoreson Appetites too that my Master speaks of.* This is strange Language to such as consider, that *God* was the Author of these Inclinations to Eating and Drinking. The *Manichæans* who believed that Creation was the Work of the Devil, could scarcely have been thus course. And *Julian* the *Apostate* was never (as I think) so blasphemous as to load our Blessed Saviour with such an Epithet. [*From such Expressions, Good Lord deliver us.*]

Pag. 23. lin. 12. *Sir Sampson*, speaking of the Frame of Human Bodies, rails at them saying, *These Things are unreasonable*, and then he proceeds with an Oath; *Why was not I a Bear, that my Cubs might have lived by sucking their Paws? Nature hath been provident only to Bears and Spiders, the one has its Nutriment in his own Hand, and the other spins his Habitation out of his Entrails.* This the Play-house Paraphrase on the 139th *Psalm*; and thus they give God thanks for the Advantage of their Being.

Thirdly, As to the historical Part.

Pag. 65, lin. 32, Sir *Sampson* saith, *I am one of your Patriarchs, I, a Branch of your* Antediluvian *Families, Fellows that the Floud could not wash away.* Here the Scripture-Account of the Floud is exposed as false, and *God* himself made a Lyar to please the Auditors.

Pag. 68, lin. 11. *Sir Sampson* tells the fine *Angelica*, Sampson's *a very good Name for an able Fellow: Your* Sampson's *were strong Dogs from the Beginning.*

To this *Angelica* answers; *Have a care, and don't over-act your Part. If you remember, the strongest* Sampson *of your Name pull'd an old House over his Head*

at last. Here we have again the sacred History burlesqu'd, and *Sampson* once
more brought into the House of *Dagon*, to make Sport for the *Philistins.*

Pag. 40, lin. 25. *There have been wise Men, but they were such as you: Men
who consulted the Stars, and were observers of Omens.* This is a Character of
Astrology, and Heathen Vanities, far different from what we find in
Scripture. But that which follows is more profane. Solomon *was wise, but
how? by his Judgment in* Astrology. This was spoken to *Foresight,* who was, as
the *Drama* tells us, *an illiterate old Fellow, pretending to understand Astrology,
Palmestry, Physiognomy, Omens, Dreams, &c.* Now according to the Language
of the Play-house, *Solomon* and *Foresight* had their Understandings qualified
alike. This is the Players Account of *Solomon*'s supernatural Knowledge!
Thus the wisest Prince is dwindled into a Gypsie, and those glorious Gifts
of God look'd on as nothing but Dotage and Erecting of Schemes.

I am sick of such horrid, blasphemous Language, and shall therefore only
add what follows in the same Page, lin. 31. *The Wise Men of the East owed their
Instructions to a Star; which is rightly observed by* Gregory *the* Great, *in favour
of Astrology.* This was the Star which shone at our Saviour's Birth. Now
according to the Players Language, and the Banter in the forementioned
Page, any one would conclude they take it to be no more than an *Ignis
Fatuus,* to lead People out of the Way. And thus while we observe the Feast
of *Epiphany* they ridicule the Miracle.

There are many scandalous Expressions in this Play which I shall not relate.
But from hence we may observe that the Church and Play-house are as contrary
to each other as *Christ* and *Belial,* Light and Darkness, Heaven and Hell. The
Design of the Church is to make Men serious: the Design of the present
Comedies is chiefly to make Men laugh. The Design of Religion is to awaken
the Conscience; but the Design of the Stage is to *sear it with an hot Iron.*

William Harison, *Woodstock Park. A Poem* (London, 1706), 7–8. Advt.
the *Daily Courant,* 16 March 1706.

> I cannot, must not tempt the wond'rous Height.
> Themes so exalted, with proportion'd Wing,
> Let *Addison,* let *Garth,* let *Congreve* sing;
> Whilst list'ning Nations crowd the vocal Lyre,
> Foretaste their Bliss, and languish with Desire.

[Sir Richard Blackmore], *Advice to the Poets* (London, 1706), 13.
Luttrell's copy 23 July (Foxon B238).

> Then *Prior,* for distinguish'd Lays renown'd,
> And *Congreve* with repeated Laurels crown'd,
> Harmonious *Granville* of superior Name,

Stepny and *Walsh*, both of establish'd Fame,
And in a tuneful Genius happy *Hughes*,
Strike your concordant Lyre, and join your noble Muse.

[Anon.], *A Panegyrick Epistle, (Wherein is given an Impartial Character of the present English Poets)* (1706), 7. Advt. the *Daily Courant*, 10 August 1706.

Congreve and *Southern* too adorn the Stage;
One boasts the labour'd, one the flowing Page.

Jacob Tonson, Letter to Alexander Pope. 20 April 1706, Pope, *Correspondence*, i. 17. Sherburn's note to this letter reads: The MS. of Pope's Pastorals, now in the collection of Arthur A. Houghton, Jr., has the following entry by Pope on the blank page preceding the MS. of 'An Essay on Pastoral': 'Mem: This Copy is that which past thro' the hands of Mr Walsh, Mr Congreve, Mr Mainwaring, Dr. Garth, Mr Granville, Mr Southern, Sir H. Sheers, Sir W. Trumbull, Lord Halifax, Lord Wharton, Marq. of Dorchester D. of Bucks. &c. Only the 3rd Eclog was written since some of these saw the other 3. which were written as they here stand with the Essay, anno 1704.—Ætat. meae, 16./The Alterations from this Copy were upon the Objections of some of these, or my own.'

I have lately seen a pastoral of yours in mr. Walsh's & mr Congreves hands, which is extreamly ffine & is generally approv'd off by the best Judges in poetry. I Remember I have formerly seen you at my shop & am sorry I did not Improve my Accquaintance with you. If you design your Poem for the Press no person shall be more Carefull in the printing of it, nor no one can give a greater Incouragement to it; than Sir Your Most Obedient Humble Servant Jacob Tonson.

John Tutchin, *The Observator*, 13–16 November 1706. Reviewing Bedford's *The Evil and Danger of Stage-Plays*, he cites Bedford on *An Act at Oxford* wherein the author, it is said,

gives fair Warning, (tho' in respectful terms) *that the Regulating of the Play-house, may occasion a Rebellion.*

Country-m. Impudent Fellows! Occasion a Rebellion! Her Majesty has God and all good Men of her side, and they have the Devil and his Imps of theirs; let 'em rebel as soon as they please.

Obs. Roger, her Majesty did not value their Threats; for since that, her Majesty has authoriz'd Mr. *Vanbrugh* and Mr. *Congreve*, to inquire into the Plays, for the better reforming the Abuses and Immorality of the Stage, *&c.*

Country-m. Master, I think those two People are both Play-wrights, and then we can't expect much Reformation.

Obs. That shall be our Task the next time we talk on this Head; we will then inquire how far these Gentlemen have answer'd their Patent, and how they have reform'd the Stage.

Anon., 'The Benefits of a Theatre', in *Poems on Affairs of State, From the Year 1620. to the Year 1707* (London, 1707), iv. 49–50.

> PRithee *Jerry* be quiet, cease railing in vain,
> Nor banter the Stage with Invectives again;
> I find thou art ignorant still of its Merit,
> And rail but as Quakers when warm'd with the Spirit.
> Shall a Place be put down when we see it affords
> Fit Wives for great Poets, and W——s for great Lords?
> Since *Angellica* blest with a singular Grace
> Had by her fine Acting preserv'd all his Plays,
> In an amorous Rapture young *Valentine* said,
> One so fit for his Plays, might be fit for his Bed;
> He warmly pursu'd her, she yielded her Charms,
> And blest the kind Youngster in her kinder Arms:
> But at length the poor Nymph did for Justice implore,
> H'as married her now, tho' he'd — her before. . . .

[Nicholas Rowe], 'The Reconcilement [between Jacob Tonson and Mr. Congreve. In Imitation of Horace, Book III. Ode IX.] *The Muses' Mercury* (March 1707), 75–6. The poem is preceded by John Oldmixon's note disclaiming any satirical intent.

The following Paper of Verses is far from being satyrical, and we respect the Persons of all the Gentlemen mention'd in it too much, to have publish'd it, had it been of that kind. 'Tis a Burlesque Imitation of an Ode of *Horace*, very humerous, and very inoffensive, and what has not at all lessen'd the good Correspondence among the Parties concern'd.

The Reconcilement
Hor. *Lib.* 3. *Ode* 9 Donec gratus eram, *&c.*
By *N.R.* Esq;

> Ton. W*hile at my House in* Fleetstreet *once you lay,*
> *How merrily, dear Sir, Time past away;*
> *While I partook your Wine, your Wit, and Mirth,*
> *I was the happiest Creature on God's* Yearth.

Con. While in your early Days of Reputation,
  You for blew Garters had not such a Passion,
  While yet you did not use (as now your Trade is)
  To drink with noble Lords, and toast their Ladies;
  Thou Jacob Ton— *wert to my conceiving*
  The chearfullest, best, honest Fellow living.
Ton. *I'm in with Capt.* V—g *at the present,*
  A most sweet-hearted *Gentleman, and pleasant;*
  He writes your Comedies, draws Schemes and Models,
  And builds Dukes Houses upon very odd Hills:
  For him, so much I doat on him, that I,
  If I were sure to go to Heaven, wou'd die.
Con. T—le *and* Del—l, *are now my Party.*
  Men that are tam Mercurio, *both* quam Marte;
  And tho for them I shall scarce go to Heaven,
  Yet I can drink with them six Nights in seven.
Ton. *What if from Van's dear Arms I shou'd retire,*
  And once more warm my Bunnians *at your Fire;*
  If I to Bowstreet *shou'd invite you home,*
  And set a Bed up in my dining Room,
  Tell me, dear Mr. Cong— *wou'd you come?*
Con. *Tho the gay Sailor, and the gentle Knight,*
  Were ten times more my Joy and Heart's Delight;
  Tho civil Persons they, you ruder were,
  And had more Humours than a dancing Bear.
  Yet for your sake I'd bid 'em both Adieu,
  And live and die, dear Cob! *with only you.*

Anon., 'To Mrs. B[race]g[ird]le, upon her leaving the Playhouse.' *The Muses' Mercury* (May 1707), 107–9.

The poem is introduced as follows: 'The Author of the following Poem having forbidden us to take any further notice of it, than to publish it, we shall say only that his Modesty is an Injury to his Merit. And the World will excuse such a Fault in one Poet, since 'tis so seldom that those Gentlemen want to be excus'd on this Account.' An erratum on p. 124 alters 'a Man' in l. 15, to 'the Man'.

To Mrs. B—g—le, upon her leaving the
Playhouse.

AT length, O Nymph, forget injurious Rage,
Revive the Town, and raise the sinking Stage;
Enough is giv'n to Honour and to Spleen;

Return, and be a Princess, or a Queen.
Be any thing—You grace your ev'ry Part,
In you 'tis natural to gain the Heart.
And still you act in such a moving Strain,
You make the Audience feel what you but feign.
Return—your num'rous, firm Admirers show,
Their Tongues, their Hands, were never false to you.
When e'er you spoke, if no Applause they paid,
'Twas all for fear of losing what you said.
As grateful Intervals with Time supply'd,
They prais'd with Pleasure, and they clap'd with Pride.
Let not the Man *provoke you to depart,*
Who like a Tyrant rules Apollo's *Art:*
Who, blind to your Superior Merit, durst
Postpone e'en you, and set an—first!
Your Virtue, not her Worth, produc'd this Slight,
He gave a Day *where he might hope a* Night.
Hard! that for this you hasten to be gone,
And unoffending Thousands smart for one!
Think what they were, nor thus from Crowds retire,
Gods! how All throng'd, and sweated with Desire,
Pleas'd to be prest when you requir'd their Sight,
And made your Benefit *their own Delight;*
Think how again they'd fasten on your View,
And be for ever thankful, ever true.
Pity, ah pity the Most Fragrant *P—r,*
Come, and at least content his Eye and Ear,
Those lesser Comforts would restore his Case,
Your Absence was the Cause of his Disease.
Think how distrest Oriana *wants your Aid,*
B—s—w's a Murd'rer to the charming Maid;
Who that's unbrib'd with private Joye can bear
That squeaking, awkward Shaddow of a Play'r?
Granville *implores, the sweetest Rhiming Bard,*
Well he deserves, his Muse can well reward.
But above all, think how the Mourning Bride
To endless Times her weeping Form must hide,
Or dragg'd to Light by some officious Friend,
Move faint Regard, and only not offend,
Unless she wears your Ornaments of Woe,
And from your Eyes her Pearly Sorrows flow;
Your Congreve *begs, with Notes, like* Orpheus *blest,*

> *E'en Rocks the* Thracian'*s Harmony confest.*
> *How* Otway'*s ravish'd Shade would smile to hear*
> *That his* Lavinia *was your latest Care?*
> *You added Softness to the softest Strains,*
> *And made your* Marius *envy'd 'midst his Pains.*
> *To future Ages shall this Wonder last,*
> *That you, just possible! your self surpast.*
> *If no Perswasions urge you back, we'll guess*
> *Your Fame already grown to that Excess,*
> *You seem'd unable to be more compleat,*
> *And so in full Perfection chose Retreat.*
> *Thus Saints remove, but with this Diff'rence shown,*
> *They die to meet, you live to shun Renown.*

[John Oldmixon], *The Muses Mercury* (September 1707), 218.

As for *Comedies*, there's no great Expectation of any thing of that kind, since Mr. *Farquhar*'s Death. The two Gentlemen, who would probably always succeed in the *Comick* Vein, Mr. *Congreve* and Capt. *Steel*, having Affairs of much greater Importance to take up their Time and Thoughts. And unless the *Players* write themselves, the Town must wait for Comedy till another *Genius* appears.

[John Downes], *Roscius Anglicanus* (London, 1708).

(i)   *The Old Bachelor*, wrote by Mr. *Congreve*.
        The Fatal Marriage, or Innocent Adultry; by Mr. *Southern*
        The Double Dealer; by Mr. *Congreve*.
   All 3 good Plays; and by their just Performances; specially, Mr. *Doggets* and Madam *Barry*'s Unparrell'd.   (p. 42)

(ii) *Love for Love*, Wrote by Mr. *Congreve*; this Comedy was Superior in Success, than most of the precedent Plays: *Valentine, Acted* by Mr. *Betterton*; *Scandall*, Mr. *Smith*; *Foresight*, Mr. *Sandford*; *Sampson*, Mr. *Underhill*; *Ben the Saylor*, Mr. *Dogget*; *Jeremy*, Mr. *Bowen*; Mrs. *Frail*, by Madam *Barry*; *Tattle*, Mr. *Boman*; *Angelica*, Mrs. *Bracegirdle*: This Comedy being Extraordinary well Acted, chiefly the Part of *Ben* the Sailor, it took 13 Days Successively. . . .   (p. 44)

(iii) *The Mourning Bride*, a Tragedy, wrote by Mr. *Congreve*: had such Success, that it continu'd Acting Uninterrupted 13 Days together.   (p. 44)

(iv) *The Way of the World*, a Comedy wrote by Mr. *Congreve*, 'twas curiously *Acted*; Madam *Bracegirdle* performing her Part so exactly and just, gain'd the Applause of Court and City; but being too Keen a Satyr, had not the Success the Company Expected.   (p. 45)

Richard Steele, *The Tatler*, no. 1, 12 April 1709. *Tatler*, i. 18–19.

Will's *Coffee-house, April* 8.
On *Thursday* last was acted, for the Benefit of Mr. *Betterton*, the Celebrated Comedy, call'd *Love for Love*. Those Excellent Players, Mrs. *Barry*, Mrs. *Bracegirdle*, and Mr. *Dogget*, tho' not at present concern'd in the House, acted on that Occasion. There has not been known so great a Concourse of Persons of Distinction as at that Time; the Stage it self was cover'd with Gentlemen and Ladies, and when the Curtain was drawn, it discovered even there a very splendid Audience. This unusual Encouragement which was given to a Play for the Advantage of so Great an Actor, gives an undeniable Instance. That the True Relish for Manly Entertainment and Rational Pleasures is not wholly lost. All the Parts were acted to Perfection; the Actors were careful of their Carriage, and no one was guilty of the Affectation to insert Witticisms of his own, but a due Respect was had to the Audience, for encouraging this accomplish'd Player. It is not now doubted but Plays will revive, and take their usual Place in the Opinion of Persons of Wit and Merit, notwithstanding their late Apostacy in Favour of Dress and Sound.

Richard Steele, *The Tatler*, no. 9, 30 April 1709. *Tatler*, i. 79–80.

Will's *Coffee-house, April* 28.
THIS Evening we were entertain'd with *The Old Batchelor*, a Comedy of deserved Reputation. In the Character which gives Name to the Play, there is excellently represented the Reluctance of a Batter'd Debauchee to come into the Trammels of Order and Decency: He neither languishes nor burns, but frets for Love. The Gentlemen of more Regular Behaviour are drawn with much Spirit and Wit, and the *Drama* introduc'd by the Dialogue of the first Scene with uncommon, yet natural Conversation. The Part of *Fondlewife* is a lively Image of the unseasonable Fondness of Age and Impotence. But instead of such agreeable Works as these, the Town has this half Age been tormented with Insects call'd *Easie Writers*, whose Abilities Mr. *Wycherly* one Day describ'd excellently well in one Word. *That*, said he, *among these Fellows is call'd* Easy Writing, *which any one may easily Write*.

Anon., *The Observator*, 17–21 September 1709.

... what the Fathers or ancient Church of *England* Divines wrote against the Stage, does not affect the Play-houses of our Times, which are reform'd by the Order of the State, and the Care of Mr. *Vanbrugg*, and Mr. *Congreve*, who were appointed by the Court to do it.

Alexander Pope, 'Winter. The Fourth Pastoral, Or Daphne. To the Memory of a Fair Young Lady', in *Poetical Miscellanies: The Sixth Part* (London, 1709), 746.

> Behold the *Groves* that shine with silver Frost,
> Their Beauty wither'd, and their Verdure lost.
> Here shall I try the sweet *Alexis*' Strain,
> That call'd the list'ning *Dryads* to the Plain?
> *Thames* heard the Numbers as he flow'd along,
> And bade his Willows learn the moving Song.

Matthew Prior, 'Paulo Purganti and His Wife: An Honest, but a Simple Pair', in *Poems on Several Occasions* (London, 1709), 117.

> Thus, in the Picture of our Mind,
> The Action may be well design'd;
> Guided by Law, and bound by Duty;
> Yet want this *Je ne scay quoy* of Beauty:
> And, tho' its Error may be such,
> As *Knags* and *Burgess* cannot hit,
> It yet may feel the nicer Touch
> Of *Wicherley*'s or *Congreve*'s Wit.

[Mrs Mary Delariviere Manley], *Memoirs of Europe, Towards the Close of the Eighth Century*. Written by Eginardus, Secretary and Favourite to Charlemagne; And done into English by the Translator of The New Atlantis (London, 1710), 285–6. Keys present in copies of the 1716 and 1720 editions identify Julius Sergius with Lord Halifax, Cassius with Wycherly, and Corvino with Congreve.

... the Gallery is adorn'd with modern Pieces of Painting, but the best in the kind, done by the most able Masters, and the Representatives of those that have been famous in the Sciences and Poetry; there are not only such of the Departed who have been admirable, but the happy Living find themselves already secur'd of Immortality (in the Choice *Julius Sergius* has made) of which they are ascertain'd by being plac'd in his Gallery, there you may behold an excellent *Cassius* who in one Comedy has furnish'd out more Wit than cou'd *Plautus* and *Terence* in their whole Compositions. *Corvino* lives in an Age unworthy of him, who in exalting the *Drama* to the Perfection of the Ancients, never consider'd his inimitable Performances were to be judg'd by the undistinguishing Moderns; the Moderns, who have not only lost all good Taste with the very Knowledge of the true Beauties of Writing, but are grown doatingly fond of a Bad, preferring Farce, Noise, Sound and Buffoonery, before the nicest turn'd Wit, the genteelest Dialect, and even (which indeed is wonderful, because a Rustick is Judge of that) before the truest Representations of Nature wherein *Corvino* is admirable, and in spight of their no Learning, no Breeding, and Stupidity, pleases even the degenerate; yet far from suffering himself to be entic'd by the Applause of an ill-judging Audience, he is contented to depart and please no more the Many, who know not why they are pleas'd; he confines all his Excellencies to the few distinguishing, yet a Number suffers by that Partiality, who tho' they can't give an account why he gives 'em Pleasure, but as his Silence gives 'em pain, yet think it hard that so excellent a Muse as *Corvino*'s, shou'd upon any terms, disappear.

[Charles Gildon], *The Life of Thomas Betterton... Wherein The Action and Utterance of the Stage, Bar, and Pulpit are distinctly consider'd* (London, 1710), 173–4.

Mr. *Congreve* in three Plays has merited great Praise, and very well distinguish'd his Characters and hit true Humour.

Thomas Brown, in *Serious and Comical Essays... by a Person of Quality* (London, 1710).

(i) He [a would-be wit] is very often at *Will*'s and takes as much Notice what *Congreve*, *Garth*, or *Wycherly* say, when in dispute about the different Interpretation of an Expression in *Horace*, as a Parcel of Country Church-wardens when the Parson of the Parish laudibly reads the *Gazette* to 'em at a blind Hovel over a black George. (p. 76)

(ii) *Macro*, one of our exactest Dramatick Writers, obliges the Town Once only in Two or Three years; which lets us know that the ignorantest Persons are the most Conceited, while modest men Cautiously and deliberately make themselves Publick. (p. 116)

(iii) The *Mourning Bride*, *Plain Dealer*, *Volpone*, or *Tamerlane*, will hardly fetch us a tolerable Audience, unless we stuff the Bills with long Entertainments of Dances, Songs, Scaramouches, Entries, and what not.
(p. 167)

(iv) EPIGR. XXIV.
On the Marriage of Mr. Congreve *to Mrs.* Bracegirdle.

HEre Wit and Beauty join, and who can say
There is a Couple Prettier, or more Gay?

She with her Charms and Voice ensnares the Pit,
While he's applauded for his Lines and Wit.
They cannot fail most Fortunate to prove
Since as they Pity move they both should Love.

(p. 245)

(v)   EPIGR. XXIII
          To Dr. Garth and *Mr*. Congreve *on the same Occasion*.

WHile Brother *Prior* in his Numbers sings
The Glorious Acts of Princes and of Kings,
Of Conquest writes, and haughty *Gallia*'s Fear,
Glitt'ring in Arms when *Churchill* does appear,
You in a softer Sphere Great Bards may move,
And sing of tender Virgins and of Love;
Of Conquests gain'd among th'unwilling Fair,
Who blushing long for what they seem to fear.
Pastora, if there now be such on Earth,
Tho' dead, from you will have a Second Birth;
The Muses will *Pastora* should survive,
And in your Numbers will for ever live.
Lycoris's Breasts, and Fair *Corinna*'s Eyes,
To *Garth* and *Congreve* fall a Sacrifice:
In them the Authors cannot but delight,
And love the Authors who of Love do write.

(p. 264)

[Bernard Lintott], the *Post Boy*, 1–3 March 1711. Advertisement for
Lintott's *A Collection of Poems, In two Volumes; Being all the
Miscellanies of Mr. William Shakespeare, which were Publish'd by
himself in the Year 1609* [1711]:

This day is publish'd, A Collection of Poems, in 2 vols. being all the
Miscellanies of Mr. Wil. Shakespear, which were publish'd by himself in
1609. and now correctly Printed Literatim from those Editions. The first Vol.
contains. 1 Venus and Adonis. 2. The Rape of Lucreece. 3. The Passional [*sic*]
Pilgrim. 4. Some Sonnets set to sundry Notes of Musick. The 2nd Vol.
contains One hundred fifty and four Sonnets inimitably varying in the Praises
of his Mistress. 2. A Lover's Complaint of his angry Mistress. Some of these
Miscellanies were printed from an Old Edition, which Mr. Congreve oblig'd
me with; others from an ingenious Gentleman of the Middle-Temple, who is
pleas'd to leave his old Copy with me, to shew any Person that has a mind to
gratify this [*sic*] Curiosity therewith. Printed for Bernard Lintott: And sold by

A. Baldwin in Warwick-Lane, W. Taylor at the Ship in Pater-Noster-Row, and O. Lloyd near the Church in the Temple. Price bound 3*s*.

Richard Steele, *The Spectator*, no. 17, Tuesday 20 March 1711. *Spectator*, i. 77.

... a Congratulatory Ode inscrib'd to Mrs. *Touchwood*, upon the loss of her two Fore-teeth.

Joseph Addison, *The Spectator*, no. 40, 16 April 1711. *Spectator*, i. 169–70.

Terrour and Commiseration leave a pleasing Anguish in the Mind; and fix the Audience in such a serious Composure of Thought, as is much more lasting and delightful than any little transient Starts of Joy and Satisfaction. Accordingly we find, that more of our *English* Tragedies have succeeded, in which the Favourites of the Audience sink under their Calamities, than those in which they recover themselves out of them. The best Plays of this Kind are the *Orphan*, *Venice preserv'd*, *Alexander the Great*, *Theodosius*, *All for Love*, *Oedipus*, *Oroonoko*, *Othello*, &c. *King Lear* is an admirable Tragedy of the same Kind, as *Shakespear* wrote it; but as it is reformed according to the chymerical Notion of poetical Justice, in my humble Opinion it has lost half its Beauty. At the same time I must allow, that there are very noble Tragedies which have been framed upon the other Plan, and have ended happily; as indeed most of the good Tragedies, which have been written since the starting of the abovementioned Criticism, have taken this Turn: As the *Mourning Bride*, *Tamerlane*, *Ulysses*, *Phaedra* and *Hyppolitus*, with most of Mr. *Dryden*'s.

Jonathan Swift, *Journal to Stella*, 22 June 1711. Swift, *Journal*, i. 295.

I saw Will. Congreve attending at the treasury, by order, with his brethren, the commissioners of the wine licences. I had often mentioned him with kindness to lord treasurer; and Congreve told me, that after they had answered to what they were sent for, my lord called him privately, and spoke to him with great kindness, promising his protection, &c. The poor man said, he had been used so ill of late years, that he was quite astonished at my lord's goodness, &c. and desired me to tell my lord so; which I did this evening, and recommended him heartily. My lord assured me he esteemed him very much, and would be always kind to him; that what he said was to make Congreve easy, because he knew people talked as if his lordship designed to turn every body out, and particularly Congreve; which indeed was true, for the poor man told me he apprehended it. As I left my lord treasurer, I called on Congreve (knowing where he dined) and told him what had passed between my lord and me: so I have made a worthy man easy, and that is a good day's work.

Joseph Addison, *The Spectator*, no. 189, Saturday 6 October 1711. *Spectator*, ii. 242. *LL* had been presented on 27 September with Escourt as Sir Sampson.

I have exposed this Picture of an unnatural Father with the same Intention, that its Deformity may deter others from its Resemblance. If the Reader has a mind to see a Father of the same Stamp represented in the most exquisite stroaks of Humour, he may meet with it in one of the finest Comedies that ever appeared upon the *English* Stage: I mean the Part of Sir *Sampson* in *Love for Love*.

Jonathan Swift, *Journal to Stella*, 29 October 1711. Swift, *Journal*, ii, 396.

I was all this terible rainy day with my friend Lewis upon business of importance; and I dined with him, and came home about seven, and thought I would amuse myself a little after the pains I had taken. I saw a volume of Congreve's Plays in my room, that Patrick had taken to read; and I looked into it, and in mere loitering read in it till twelve, like an owl and a fool: if ever I do so again; never saw the like.

William Diaper, 'To Mr. Congreve.' *Nereides: Or, Sea-Eclogues* (London, 1712), pp. iv, v–vi. Advt. *The Daily Courant*, 15 March 1712.

> So, would your Smiles protect the fearful Muse,
> The vulgar Praise I would with Scorn refuse.
> By you approv'd, condemn'd by all beside,
> I'd court my Fate, and swell with careless pride.
> . . .
>
> But should the harmless Pen have no Regard,
> Your NAME (like sacred Spells that charm when heard
> From blasting Tongues secures the tender Bard,
> The beauteous Nymphs to your Protection throng,
> And beg, you would not scorn the humble Song:
> As Indian Travellers Wild Beasts affright
> By kindled Fires, and skreen themselves with Light.
> So Critick-wits, like other Brutes of Prey,

From a surrounding Brightness slink away.
Men dare not censure (even when they ought)
If *Virgil* will approve what *Mævius* wrote.

John Gay, 'On a Miscellany of Poems. To Bernard Lintott.'
Miscellaneous Poems and Translations by Several Hands (London,
1712), 171. Gay, *Poetry and Prose*, i. 39.

> If thou wouldst have thy Volume stand the Test,
> And of all others be reputed Best,
> Let *Congreve* teach the list'ning Groves to mourn,
> As when he wept o'er fair *Pastora*'s Urn.

Joseph Addison, *The Spectator*, no. 358, Monday 21 April 1712.
Spectator, iii. 342.

[*Escourt*] gives one some Idea of the antient *Pantomime*, who is said to have
given the Audience, in Dumb-show, an exact Idea of any Character or
Passion, or make an intelligible Relation of any publick Occurrence with no
other Expression than that of his Looks and Gestures. If all who have been
obliged to these Talents in *Estcourt*, will be at *Love for Love* to Morrow Night,
they will but pay him what they owe him, at so easy a Rate as being present at
a Play which no Body would omit seeing that had, or had not ever seen it
before. [The performance for the following day was advertised as 'For the
Benefit of Mr. Estcourt'.]

Charles Montagu, Earl of Halifax, Letter to the Earl of Oxford, 25
April 1712. Hodges, *Documents*, 119.

I can not omit returning Your Lordship my particular thanks for
continuing Mr Congreve in his little Office, for though Mr Congreve
deserves so much Your favour, I flatter my selfe that my solicitation had
some weight with Your Lordship, and shall allways be acknowledged with the
utmost gratitude.... In the great Uncertaintys We are in of News from
abroad I will not importune Your Lordship for an Audience, but when
some matters are a little better known, I hope You will allow me to presse
into Your Presence, for I think I could serve You. I am with great Respect,
My Lord

Richard Steele, *The Spectator*, no. 443, Tuesday 29 July 1712.
Spectator, iv. 56. The ostensible writer of this letter is 'Camilla' or
Mrs Catherine Tofts.

The *Italians* see a thousand Beauties I am sensible I have no Pretence to, and
abundantly make up to me the Injustice I received in my own Country, of
disallowing me what I really had. The Humour of Hissing, which you have
among you, I do not know any thing of; and their Applauses are utter'd in
Sighs, and bearing a Part at the Cadences of Voice with the Persons who are
performing. I am often put in Mind of those complaisant Lines of my own
Countryman, when he is calling all his Faculties together to hear *Arabella*:

> Let all be hush'd, each softest Motion cease,
> Be ev'ry loud tumultuous Thought at Peace;
> And ev'ry ruder Gasp of Breath
> Be calm, as in the Arms of Death:
> And thou, most fickle, most uneasy Part,
> Thou restless Wanderer, my Heart,
> Be still; gently, ah! gently leave,
> Thou busy, idle Thing, to heave.
> Stir not a Pulse; and let my Blood,
> That turbulent, unruly Flood,
>   Be softly staid:
> Let me be all but my Attention Dead.

The whole City of *Venice* is as still when I am singing, as this polite Hearer
was to Mrs. *Hunt*. But when they break that Silence, did you know the
Pleasure I am in, when every Man utters his Applause, by calling me aloud
the *Dear Creature*, the *Angel*, the *Venus*; *What Attitude she moves with!—Hush,
she sings again!* We have no boisterous Wits who dare disturb an Audience,
and break the publick Peace meerly to shew they dare.

[Francis Reynardson], *The Stage: A Poem* (1713), 14–15. A prefatory
advertisement notes that the poem was written in the summer of 1712.
Reprinted in William Egerton, *Faithful Memoirs of The Life, Amours
and Performances, of ... Mrs. Anne Oldfield* (London, 1731), 184–204,
in which the correction of 'Host a-gaze' to 'Hosts aghast' is followed
here. In l. 1 below 'his' refers to Dryden.

> Wrap'd in the Prophet's Robe arose his Friend,
> CONGREVE alone, the Heroe's Bow could bend,
> CONGREVE his second-self, his CONGREVE rose,
> And soars like DRYDEN, and like DRYDEN flows.

THUS did ACHILLES from the Dusty Plain
Laden with Bays and Injuries abstain;
But when PATROCLUS to the Battle went
His Golden Panoply the Hero lent;
And him so well the mighty Arms became,
So like ACHILLES all his graceful Frame,
Both Hosts aghast the raging War suspend,
And none but PHOEBUS knows him from his Friend.
    THY Comic Muse, and trust me, CONGREVE, I
With greater Truth than *Foresight* prophecy,
Far as thy BEN can sail, or Waters flow,
Receiv'd with Praise thy Comick Muse shall go;
Bless her, ye Lovers, for from her the Fair
Have learnt to prize the Constant in despair,
No more your Sighs, no more your Tears are scorn'd,
But *Love for Love* shall ever be return'd.
    Some know the Sock and some the Buskin's Pace,
But CONGREVE treads in both with equal Grace;
When dress'd in widdow'd Weeds his Muse appears,
Who can refuse the *Mourning Bride* his Tears?

Joseph Addison, *The Spectator*, no. 530, Friday 7 November 1712.
Spectator, iv. 389.

> *Sic visum Veneri; cui placet impares*
> *Formas atque animos sub juga ahenea*
> *Sævo mittere cum joco.*
>   Hor.

IT is very usual for those who have been severe upon Marriage, in some
part or other of their Lives to enter into the Fraternity which they have
ridiculed, and to see their Raillery return upon their own Heads. I scarce
ever knew a Woman-hater that did not, sooner or later, pay for it. Marriage,
which is a Blessing to another Man, falls upon such an one as a Judgment.
Mr. *Congreve*'s *Old Batchelor* is set forth to us with much Wit and Humour, as
an Example of this kind. In short those who have most distinguished
themselves by Railing at the Sex in general, very often make an honourable
Amends, by chusing one of the most worthless Persons of it, for a Companion
and Yoke-fellow. *Hymen* takes his Revenge in kind, on those who turn his
Mysteries into Ridicule.

Alexander Pope to John Caryll, 21 December 1712. Pope, *Correspondence*, i. 167.

Hor. *Lib. I. Ode* [9]
Vides ut *alta* stet nive *candidum*
Soracte nec jam sustineant *onus*
Sylvæ *laborantes?*—

We have a fine description wrought up from thence with amplification by Mr Congreve, as follows [ll. 4–15 are cited, evidently from memory, and from a version pre-dating that of 1710]:

Big with the offspring of the north,
The frozen clouds bring forth;
A shower of soft and fleecy rain
Falls to new cloathe the earth again:
    And see, how by degrees
The universal Mantle hides the trees
    In hoary flakes that downward fly
As if it were the autumn of the sky,
    Whose fall of leaf would theirs supply.
Trembling the trees sustain the weight and bow
    Like aged limbs that feebly go
Beneath a venerable head of snow.

Thomas Tickell, *A Poem, To His Excellency the Lord Privy Seal, On the Prospect of Peace* (1713), 19.

In happy Chains our daring Language bound,
Shall sport no more in arbitrary Sound,
But buskin'd Bards henceforth shall wisely rage,
And *Grecian* plans reform *Britannia*'s Stage:
Till *Congreve* bids her smile, *Augusta* stands,
And longs to weep when flowing *Rowe* commands.

Thomas Parnell, 'The Book Worm', autograph manuscript, late 1714? Printed in *Collected Poems of Thomas Parnell*, ed. Claude Rawson and F.P. Lock (Newark: University of Delaware Press, 1989), 519.

Heres Fame to *Pope*, and Wealth to *Steel*,
And all to *Addison* he will,
May *Garth* have a Practice, *Congreve* sight;
May *Row* have many a full third night;
Be Gentle *Gays* & *Tickels* lot
At least as good as *Budgel* got:

Richard Steele, *Poetical Miscellanies, Consisting of Original Poems and Translations. By the best Hands* (1714), dedication to Congreve, sigs. A2^r–A5^v.

S I R,
[M]Y Name, as Publisher of the following Miscellanies, I am sensible, is but a slight Recommendation of them to the Publick; but the Town's Opinion of them will be raised, when it sees them address'd to Mr. *Congreve*. If the Patron is but known to have a Taste for what is presented to him, it gives an hopeful Idea of the Work; how much more, when He is an acknowledg'd Master of the Art He is desired to Favour? Your just Success in the various Parts of Poetry, will make Your Approbation of the following Sheets a Favour to many Ingenious Gentlemen, whose Modesty wants the Sanction of such an Authority. Men of your Talents oblige the World, when they are studious to produce in others the Similitude of their Excellencies. Your great Discerning in distinguishing the Characters of Mankind, which is manifested in Your Comedies, renders Your good Opinion a just Foundation for the Esteem of other Men. I know, indeed, no Argument against these Collections, in Comparison of any other *Tonson* has heretofore Printed; but that there are in it no Verses of Yours: That gentle, free, and easie Faculty, which also in Songs, and short Poems, You possess above all others, distinguishes it self where-ever it appears. I cannot but instance Your inimitable *D O R I S*, which excels, for Politeness, fine Raillery, and courtly Satyr, any Thing we can meet with in any Language.

Give me leave to tell You, that when I consider Your Capacity this Way, I cannot enough Applaud the Goodness of Your Mind, that has given so few Examples of these Severities, under the Temptation of so great Applause, as the ill-natured World bestows on them, tho' addressed without any Mixture of Your Delicacy.

I cannot leave my Favourite *D O R I S*, without taking Notice how much that short Performance discovers a True Knowledge of Life. *D O R I S* is the Character of a Libertine Woman of Condition, and the Satyr is work'd up accordingly: For People of Quality are seldom touched with any Representation of their Vices, but in a Light which makes them Ridiculous.

As much as I Esteem You for Your Excellent Writings, by which You are an Honour to our Nation; I chuse rather, as one that has passed many Happy Hours with You, to celebrate that easie Condescention of Mind, and Command of a pleasant Imagination, which give You the uncommon Praise of a Man of Wit, always to please and never to offend. No one, after a joyful Evening, can reflect upon an Expression of Mr. *Congreve*'s, that dwells upon him with Pain.

In a Man Capable of Exerting himself any Way, this (whatever the Vain and Ill-natured may think of the Matter) is an Excellence above the brightest Sallies of Imagination.

The Reflection upon this most equal, amiable, and correct Behaviour, which can be observed only by your intimate Acquaintance, has quite diverted me from acknowledging your several Excellencies as a Writer; but to dwell particularly on those Subjects, would have no very good Effect upon the following Performances of my Self and Friends: Thus I confess to You, your Modesty is spared only by my Vanity, and yet I Hope You will give me leave to indulge it yet further, in telling all the World, I am, with great Truth,

SIR,

Your most Obedient, and
most Humble Servant,
RICHARD STEELE.

Alexander Pope, Letter to Joseph Addison, 30 January 1714. Pope, *Correspondence*, i. 209. After referring to critics of his Greek, Pope continues:

I have met with as much malignity another way, some calling me a Tory, because the heads of that party have been distinguishingly favourable to me; some a Whig because I have been favour'd with yours, Mr. *Congreve*'s, and Mr. *Craggs* his friendship, and of late with my Lord *Halifax*'s Patronage.

Alexander Pope, Letter to John Caryll, 8 June 1714. Pope, *Correspondence*, i. 229. Pope has just referred to an incident at Button's coffee-house involving Ambrose Philips whose pastorals he had attacked in *Guardian* no. 40.

This is the whole matter; but as to the secret grounds of *Philips*'s malignity, they will make a very pleasant History when we meet. Mr. *Congreve* and some others have been much diverted with it, and most of the Gentlemen of the *Hanover Club* have made it the subject of their ridicule on their Secretary. It is to this management of *Philips*, that the world owes Mr. *Gay*'s *Pastorals*.

Alexander Pope, Letter to John Caryll, 25 July 1714. Pope, *Correspondence*, i. 238–9.

I really wish all men so well, that I am satisfied but few can wish me so; but if those few are such as tell me they do, I am content, for they are the best people I know: While you believe me what I profess as to Religion, I can bear any thing the bigotted may say; while Mr. *Congreve* likes my poetry, I can endure *Dennis* and a thousand more like him; while the most honest and moral of each party think me no ill man, I can easily support it, tho' the most violent and mad of all parties rose up to throw dirt at me.

Joseph Spence, reporting Alexander Pope in 1734 [*c*. October 1714]. Spence, i. 87.

The famous Lord Halifax was rather a pretender to taste than really possessed of it. When I had finished the two or three first books of my translation of the *Iliad*, that Lord 'desired to have the pleasure of hearing them read at his house.' Addison, Congreve, and Garth were there at the reading. In four or five places Lord Halifax stopped me very civilly, and with a speech each time much of the same kind: 'I beg your pardon, Mr. Pope, but there is something in that passage that does not quite please me. Be so good as to mark the place and consider it a little at your leisure. I'm sure you can give it a better turn.'

Mary, Countess Cowper, reporting a conversation with the Prince of Wales, later George II [*c*.27–8 November 1714]. *Diary of Mary Countess Cowper, 1714–1720, Lady of the Bedchamber to The Princess of Wales*, ed. C.S. Cowper. 2nd edn. (London, 1865), 23–4.

I told him that before his coming hither, I and my Children had constantly drunk his Health by the name of *Young Hanover Brave*, which was the Title Mr. *Congreve* had given him in a Ballad. This made him ask who Mr. *Congreve* was, and so gave me an Opportunity of saying all the Good of Mr. *Congreve* which I think he truly deserves.

[William Somervile], *An Imitation of the Ninth Ode of the Fourth Book of Horace* (1715), 3. Allusions to Milton, Addison, and Garth precede that here to Congreve.

> Nymphs yet unborn shall melt with am'rous Flames
> That *Congreve*'s Lays inspire.
> And *Philips* warm the gentle Swains
> To Love and soft Desire.

Alexander Pope, *The Iliad of Homer, Translated by Mr. Pope*. 6 vols. (1715–20), preface, vol. i, sig. F4^r. Pope, *Poems*, vii. 23.

I must also acknowledge with infinite Pleasure the many friendly Offices as well as sincere Criticisms of Mr. *Congreve*, who had led me the way in translating some Parts of *Homer*, as I wish for the sake of the World he had prevented me in the rest.

John Gay, *Trivia* (1716). Advt. the *Daily Courant*, 26 January 1716. Bk ii, 550–1, 561–2.

> Volumes, on shelter'd Stalls, expanded lye,
> And various Science lures the learned Eye...
> Here saunt'ring 'Prentices o'er *Otway* weep,
> O'er *Congreve* smile, or over *D[ennis]* sleep...

Anon., *An Epistle to Sir Samuel Garth. Occasion'd by the Landing of the Pretender, And the Report of His Royal Highness the Prince of Wales's Going to Scotland* (1716), 11–12. Luttrell's copy dated 2 February.

> Their various Notes the Tuneful Tribe imploy,
> To count the Blessings we in G E O R G E enjoy.
>   ...
>
> But others softer Notes of Joy rehearse;
> Fair C A R O L I N A beautifies the Verse.
> How High by Her *Britannia*'s Hopes ascend,
> While thro' Unnumber'd *Kings* Her C H A R M S extend,
> And distant Times shall the Resemblance trace
> Of the Bright P R I N C E S S that Restor'd our Race.
>   C O N G R E V E for this the Lyre neglected strings:
> In A D D I S O N a Second *Virgil* Sings:
> Nor wilt thou, G A R T H, unmindful of the Day,
> Refuse to *Britain*'s Hopes a Solemn Lay:
> Not Unrewarded will descend thy Song,
> That must, with Theirs, the P O E T 's Fame prolong.
> To Bless, like them is First; the Next Degree
> Of Mortal Glory is To Praise like Thee.

Alexander Pope, Letter to Lady Mary Wortley Montagu, 20 August 1716. Pope, *Correspondence*, i. 357.

I communicated your Letter to Mr Congreve: He thinks of you and talks of you as he ought; I mean as I do, (for one always thinks that to be as it ought.) His health and my own are now so good, that we wish with all our Souls you were a witness of it. We never meet but we lament over you; we pay a Sort of Weekly Rite to your Memory, where we strow Flowers of Rhetorick, and offer such Libations to your name as it were a Prophaness to call Toasting.

John Dennis, *Remarks Upon Mr. Pope's Translation of Homer* (London, 1717), 7–8. Dennis, *Works*, ii. 120–1.

There is a Gentleman, the living Ornament of the Comick Scene, who after he had for several Years entertain'd the Town, with that Wit and Humour, and Art and Vivacity, which are so becoming of the Comick Stage, produc'd at last a Play, which besides that it was equal to most of the former in those pleasant Humours which the Laughers so much require, had some certain Scenes in it, which were writ with so much Grace and Delicacy, that they alone were worth an entire Comedy. What was the Event? The Play was hiss'd by Barbarous Fools in the Acting; and an impertinent Trifle was brought on after it, which was acted with vast Applause. Which rais'd so much Indignation in the foresaid Writer, that he quitted the Stage in Disdain, and Comedy left it with him. And those nice great Persons, whose squeamish Palates rejected Quails and Partridges, have pin'd ever since in such a Dearth, that they greedily feed upon Bull-Beef.

Thus have I set before the Readers Eyes, in as short a Method as I could, the cruel Treatment that so many extraordinary Men have received from their Countrymen for these last hundred Years. If I should now shift the Scene, and show all that Penury, and that Avarice chang'd all at once to Riot and Profuseness, and more squander'd away upon one Object, than would have satisfied the greater part of those extraordinary Men, the Reader to whom this one Creature should be altogether unknown, would fancy him a Prodigy of Art and Nature, would believe that all the great Qualities of those extraordinary Persons were centred in him alone; that he had the Capacity and Profoundness of BACON, the fine Painting of SPENSER, the Force and Sublimity, and Elevation of MILTON; the fine Thinking and Elegance, and Versification of DRYDEN; the Fire and Enthusiasm of LEE; the moving melting Tenderness of OTWAY; the Pleasantry of BUTLER; the Wit and Satire of WYCHERLEY; and the Humour and Spirit, and Art and Grace of C——.

[John Durant Bredval], *The Art of Dress* (1717), 10. Advt. February (Foxon B418). The poem is addressed 'To the Toasts of Great-Britain'.

> But Ah! to venture on such lofty Things,
> Beware my Muse, nor trust thy feeble Wings.
> O PRIOR, CONGREVE, LANSDOWN, gentle Peer,
> And ADDISON so strong, and yet so clear;
> Yours be the Task, ye Swans of Silver hue,
> Who Soar so wondrous High, and Sing so true.

[Leonard Welsted], *Palaemon to Caelia, at Bath; or, The Triumvirate* (1717), 7. Advt. 7 March (Foxon W303).

> The Stage, said *Bruce*, yet feels a harder Fate;
> We see and mourn in vain its drooping State:
>
>   . . .
>
> No Heroe wakes our Pity, or our Fears,
> No soft Distress dissolves the Soul to Tears:
> The Comic Muse—here *Wildair*—hides her Head;
> The Comic Muse with *St–le* and *C——ve* fled . . .

Lady Mary Wortley Montagu, Letter to Alexander Pope, 17 June 1717. Montagu, *Letters*, i. 367.

The Reflection on the great Gulph between You and Me cools all News that comes hither. I can neither be sensibly touch'd with Joy or Grief when I consider that possibly the Cause of either is remov'd befor the Letter comes to my hands; but (as I said before) this Indolence does not extend to my few friendships. I am still warmly sensible of Yours and Mr. Congreve's and desire to live in your remembrances, thô dead to all the World beside.

[****], in *The Poetical Works of Samuel Daniel*, 2 vols. (1717–18), i, p. x.

. . . They [our 'great Predecessors in Poetry'] have a Right to the Tribute of our Praise, and we may give it without the Envy that waits on our justest Applauses to the Living; to commend *Cato*, the *Mourning-Bride*, and *Tamerlane*, is to the Criticks Flattery; but we are allowed to adore, if we please, *Gordebourk* [*sic*], *Julius Caesar*, and *Philotas*.

[George Brereton], in *The Critick* no. 1, 6 January 1718.

. . . One Example [of censure] in the Case of Poetry may suffice for all: And that shall be Mr. *Congreve*'s Pastoral on the Death of Queen *Mary*; which, notwithstanding his other masterly Performances, is, with all its Graces of Diction and Numbers, when consider'd in this View, but a mean Performance. Had the Author judiciously weigh'd his Subject, he would have found that it requir'd some Topicks not only peculiar to the Character of a Queen, but of *such* a Queen. In pursuance of which, either the nice Part She bore in the late Revolution, or her ardent Concern in the Cause of Universal Love and Unity, or some such other of her eminently Royal Virtues, might have been finely celebrated. But contrariwise, our Poet is so far from this, that he has not touch'd upon any one princely Quality. Allusions to Groves and Streams, and the Mourning of Flocks and Birds, are nothing at all to the Purpose; and in a word, this Piece might with very little Variation be equally apply'd to a Queen and a Milk-maid. Nay, in one respect, the last had been more proper; since those Images would then be just, which are now absurd and ridiculous.

[George Brereton], in *The Critick* no. 21, 26–8 May 1718. He is writing of those who demean poetry.

. . . what shall We say of Mr. *Congreve* and *Dryden?* Who in their Comedys, so contrary to the Conduct of him [Jonathan Richardson, the painter] and all Mankind, introduce the First of Them a Footman making merry with the Rhyming Talent in the Presence of his Master; and the Last a Poet, who offering an *Epithalamion* at a Marriage . . . is kick'd out by the Servants.

Arthur Bedford, *A Serious Remonstrance In Behalf of the Christian Religion* (London, 1719).

(i) In an old *Play*, but still frequently acted, *Valentine* loves *Angelica*, and is so well rewarded by her, that the *Comedy* takes its Name from them both. He is the *Hero* of the whole Performance, and recommended as a Person of many *Virtues*. 'Tis true, he was hearty in his Affection to *Angelica*. He was indeed Fifteen Hundred Pounds in Debt to one Man, with half a dozen Duns, who came in a Morning, and several others, to the value of Four Thousand pounds. This made him under Confinement; and therefore in his case, to be in love with a Lady of Thirty Thousand Pounds, must need be a great Commendation. But abating this one Character, he is altogether compounded of Vice. He is a *Prodigal*, and unnatural, and spent all his Substance in riotous Living. He was scandalously guilty of whoring, and seems to glory in it. He is undutiful. He curses, and swears. He talks profanely, and applies to himself the words of our *Saviour, I am the Truth*; as if in the midst of his pretended Madness, he was really smitten with the Pleasure of Blasphemy: And yet this Libertine is crown'd for the Man of Merit, he hath his Wishes thrown into his

Lap, and makes the happy *Exit* by obtaining his Mistress, who receives him with profane Raptures on that occasion. (pp. 188–9)

(ii) Besides, the Gratitude of the *Poets* and *Actors* is shewn in Language of the same nature. One reads us this Lesson upon the *Creation: And if this Rogue was anatomiz'd and dissected, he hath his Vessels of Digestion and Concoction, and so forth. These things are unaccountable and unreasonable. Why was I not a Bear, that my Cubs might have liv'd upon sucking their Paws? Nature* (that is, GOD) *hath been provident only to Bears and Spiders; the one hath his Nutriment only in his own hands, and the other spins his Habitation out of his Entrails.* Another in the same *Play* gives GOD thanks for the Advantage of his Being, by calling the Effects of his immortal Soul, even *Reason, Thought, Passions, Inclinations, Affections, Appetites* and *Senses,* an *invincible and a craving Retinue, and so many Devils, that will have Employment.* And it is observable, that this *Actor* was the *Poet's* chief Favourite, and crown'd with the utmost Success. A third, who was bred at the *University,* calls the natural Inclinations to Eating and Drinking *Whoreson Appetites.* All this is strange Language. The *Manicheans,* who affirm'd some part of the *Creation* to have been the Word of the *Devil,* could scarcely have been so coarse in their *Compliments.* And if a Mother cannot but be affronted when such an Epithet is given to her Child, can we imagine that GOD will not be angry, when it is given to such things which he created? (p. 304)

Charles Beckingham, 'To Mr. Congreve.' *Musarum Lachrymæ, Or, Poems to the Memory of Nicholas Rowe, Esq.* (London, 1719), Epistle Dedicatory to Mr. Congreve. The title-page epigraph cites ll. 41–4 of Congreve's epistle to Halifax.

SIR,

[T]HE only Hope I have of obtaining Your Pardon for prefixing Your Name to these Sheets, is, from their being an Attempt to preserve the Memory of a Person, who, when Living, was so nearly allied to You, by the most sincere Endearments of a mutual, extensive, and disinterested Friendship.

THO' I am an absolute Stranger to Your Person, I cannot be so to Your Character, and must be allowed to say, That as You were distinguished for so uncommon a Union in Affections, You were equally celebrated for as extraordinary a Superiority in Genius; and the declining Stage may now justly complain of a Double Loss in their most substantial Entertainments, by the Death of Mr. ROWE, and Your Own voluntary Retirement. But I am afraid I transgress the Bounds I prescribed my self for this short Address, and shall therefore wave any Freedoms of this Nature (however due to Merit) which may prove the least disagreeable to a Person placed so happily above

them. And if the A U T H O R S of the following P O E M S are so fortunate as to
have contributed any thing worthy the Character of the Deceased, and the
Patronage of his Living Friend, it will answer the utmost Wishes of

S I R ,
Your most Obedient,
Humble Servant,
Ch. Beckingham.

Nicholas Amhurst, 'On the Death of Mr. Rowe', ibid. 25–6.

> He judg'd it always an inglorious thing
> To court their Praises who defam'd their K I N G ;
> Enough for him that C O N G R E V E was his Friend,
> That G A R T H and S T E E L E , and A D D I S O N commend...

John Sheffield, 'The Election of a Poet Laureate in 1719', in *The*
Works of John Sheffield, the Earl of Mulgrave, Marquis of Normanby,
and Duke of Buckingham. 2 vols. (1723), i. 196. Laurence Eusden had
been appointed poet laureate in succession to Rowe on 24 December
1718.

> Lame *Congreve* unable such things to endure,
> Of *Apollo* beg'd either a Crown or a Cure?
> To refuse such a Writer *Apollo* was loth,
> And almost inclin'd to have granted him both.

Richardson Pack, *Miscellanies in Verse and Prose* (London, 1719), 95.

C O N G R E V E , of all the Moderns, seems to me, to have the rightest Turn for
Comedy. In all his Plays there is a great deal of Lively and Uncommon
Humour, and such as yet, for the most part, is a Picture of true Life.
Besides, he hath raised the Vein of *Ridicule*, and made the Stage, which had
been too much prostituted to the Mob, *edifying* to Persons of the first
Condition. And as his Fable is Diverting, so is it wrought according to the
strictest Rules.

Thomas Killigrew, *Chit-Chat. A Comedy* [1719], 10. First performed
at DL, 14 February 1719.

> *Town.* As I was a Saying, What was your Thoughts employ'd on?
> *Ala.* Why?—A Criticism on one of Mr. *Congreve*'s Plays, where he exposes
> Men of Quality, by making 'em Fops and Fools.

Bell. I have heard Judges say, he drew exactly after Nature.

Ala. Good, *Bellamar*; very good.—*Townly*, when shall I hear thee say such a Thing? Thy Wit is like a certain Friends of ours, who to be very sharp, bids you kiss his A— ...

Anon., 'An Epilogue [to *Love for Love*]', in Thomas D'Urfey, *Wit and Mirth: Or, Pills to Purge Melancholy.* 6 vols. (London, 1719–20), i. 355–6.

An EPILOGUE.

AMONGST all Characters nearest Divine,
You that are Witty-men, should cry up mine;
And of all Bargains that are daily driven,
Ours is the most ingaging under Heaven:
Whose Souls in a Seraphick station move,
As all must do who Marry, Love for Love.
Sir *Sampson* here, a strange Old sordid Sot,
Meaning by Candle Inch to buy my Lot,
Would settle on me, Oh! the Lord knows what;
He for a Purchase the old way takes Care,
And like a Higler in a Country Fair,
Bawls out aloud, take Money for your Mare:
Or Brother like Stockjobbing cheat would make,
My Friend so much you give, so much you take;
But *Valentine*, whose Person, Wit and Art,
Pleads fairer Title to a tender Heart;
With an endearing Claim, fine Words address,
A Graceful Person, and a taking Face:
A solid Judgment that can stand the test,
Trick humour gay—I fancy'd all the rest;
Compell'd my Love—The Passion strong did grow,
Whither all this, a Woman's Heart should bow,
Your Pardon Ladies, I am sure you know:
Besides by Subtilty I Tryal made,
Found out his Haunts, and Snares each way I laid;
Mark'd, tho' the frolick Widows—City Dames,
Inmates of *Leicester-field, Pall-Mall*, St. *James*:
The Tall, the Short the Freckl'd—Fair and Brown,
The straight-lac'd Maiden, and the Miss o'th' Town;
We're sure to work on in Adversity,
Yet still what Stock he had was kept for me:
And for such Love, if we should Love alow,

Your Pardon Ladies, I am sure you know;
I took Compassion on the Bankrupt Debtor,
He had no Money, But had something better:
Faith like a generous Girl, I paid his worth,
For I had Honour in me from my Birth;
I paid him well—A Wife that's Fair and Young,
Discreet and Kind, and Forty Thousand strong:
Is no bad Consolation sure—In Life,
How would some snigger here, for such a Wife;
Then if this part I Play be rare or no?
Your Pardon Gentlemen—You likewise know:
The Author of the Scenes appear to Day,
Draws every Figure justly through his Play;
Mind, Sence and generous Humour, seems to hit, ⎫
Let Beauty grant him then superior Wit, ⎬
Since by the Boxes it was chose and Writ. ⎭

Giles Jacob, *The Poetical Register*. 2 vols. (London, 1719–20). Jacob also lists, at ii. 248–50, Congreve's poems and translations, and at ii. 325, his 'Two Tales'.

I am in particular oblig'd to Mr. C O N G R E V E for his free and early Communication of what relates to himself, as well as his kind Directions for the Composing of this Work. I have tried to follow his advice, and been very sparing in my Reflections on the Merits of Writers, which is indeed nothing but anticipating the Judgment of the Reader, and who after all will judge for himself. I forbear to mention the Names of other Gentlemen who have transmitted their Accounts to me, hoping a general Acknowledgment will be sufficient.

(i, sigs. A8ʳ–A8ᵛ)

W I L L I A M C O N G R E V E , *Esq*;

T H I S Gentleman is descended from the very ancient Family of the *Congreves*, of *Congreve* in the County of *Stafford*; and he is the only surviving Son of *William Congreve*, Esq; who was second Son to *Richard Congreve*, of *Congreve* and *Stretton* in the said County, Esq; He was born at a Place call'd *Bardsa*, not far from *Leeds* in *Yorkshire*; being a part of the Estate of Sir *John Lewis*, his Great Uncle by his Mother's Side.

His Father being a younger Brother, his Affairs and Command in the Army carried him into *Ireland*, when Mr. *Congreve* was very Young, by which means he had his Education, as to Humane Learning, in the great School or College of *Kilkenny*, and the University of *Dublin*; from whence returning into *England* soon after the Revolution, he was enter'd into the Society of the

Middle Temple, where he began the Study of the Law; but did not make so great a Progress as ever to be call'd to the Bar. 'And, as a certain Author has observ'd, Mr. *Congreve* was of too delicate a Taste, had Wit of too fine a turn to be long pleas'd with a crabbed unpalatable Study; in which the laborious dull plodding Fellow generally excells the more sprightly and vivacious Wit; This concurring with his natural Inclinations to Poetry, diverted him from the Bar to the declining Stage, which then stood in need of such a Support; and from whence the Town justly receiv'd him as *Rome*'s other Hope.

Mr. *Congreve*, notwithstanding he has justly acquir'd the greatest Reputation in Dramatick Writings, is so far from being puff'd up with Vanity (a Failing in most Authors of Excellency) that he abounds with Humility and good Nature. He does not shew so much the Poet as the Gentleman; he is ambitious of few Praises, tho' he deserves numerous Encomiums; he is genteel and regular in Oeconomy, unaffected in Behaviour, pleasing and informing in his Conversation, and respectful to all. And as for his Talents in Dramatick Poetry, I shall omit a Description of the Beauty of his Dialogue, Fineness of his Humour, and other particulars; and confine what I have to say in the smallest Compass of Poetical Expression.

> *As rising Sparkles in each Draught of Wine,*
> *So Force of Wit appears in ev'ry Line.*

Mr. *Congreve* has oblig'd the World with the following Plays.

I. *The Old Batchelor*, a Comedy, acted at the Theatre Royal, in the Year 1693. Dedicated to the Right Honourable *Charles* Lord *Clifford*. This Comedy was acted with a general Applause, and was introduc'd into the World with several Copies of Verses, which it justly merited, tho' the Author was then not above nineteen Years of Age; and it not only made him known to the Town, and a noble *Mecænas*, but was honour'd with the Presence of the beautiful and virtuous Queen *Mary*: And Mr. *Congreve*, in return of Gratitude, wrote one of the finest Pastorals we have in the *English* Language, on the lamented Death of that incomparable Princess. There's a genteel and sprightly Wit in the Dialogue of this Play; and the humorous Characters are agreeable to Nature, which can be said of few other Dramatick Performances; yet the Criticks attack him for the Incidents of Marriages in Masks, as being scarce ever done in reality.

II. *The Double Dealer*; a Comedy, acted at the Theatre Royal, 1694. Dedicated to the Right Honourable *Charles Montague*, Esq; one of the Lords of the Treasury. This Play did not meet with the Encouragement as the former; neither had it equal Success with any of Mr. *Congreve*'s latter Dramatick Pieces; but I never saw any particular Criticism on its Defects; which gives me leave to think its ill Reception proceeded more from a capricious Humour of the Town, than any considerable Errors in the Composure of the Play.

III. *Love for Love*; a Comedy, acted at the Theatre in Little *Lincolns-Inn-Fields*, by his Majesty's Servants, 1695. Dedicated to the Right Honourable *Charles* Earl of *Dorset* and *Middlesex*. This Play was acted with very great Applause, at the opening of the New House. There is abundance of Wit in it, and a great deal of fine and diverting Humour; the Characters are justly distinguish'd, and the Manners well mark'd. Some of the nicer Criticks find fault with the unravelling of the Plot, and the Conduct of *Angelica* in it: But in spite of Envy, this Play must be allow'd to be one of the best of our modern Comedies.

IV. *The Mourning Bride*; a Tragedy, acted at the Theatre in *Little Lincolns-Inn-Fields*, by his Majesty's Servants, 1697. Dedicated to her Royal Highness the Princess *Anne* of *Denmark*. This Play had the greatest Success of all Mr. *Congreve*'s Performances; and indeed met with Encouragement inferior to no Dramatick piece, that has at any time appear'd on the *English* Stage. The Excellency of this Tragedy can in nothing be more particularly describ'd, than in Sir *Richard Blackmore*'s Preface to his Poem, entitled, *King Arthur*; which runs thus: [Jacob here cites the critique by Blackmore reprinted at pp. 303–4 above.] This is the Character given by the learned Doctor of Mr. *Congreve*'s *Mourning Bride*; and I can, by no means, be of Opinion with some pretending Criticks, that Sir *Richard*'s Aim, in this Commendation, was more to depress the Praises of Mr. *Congreve*'s Predecessors, Mr. *Dryden*, Mr. *Otway*, and Mr. *Lee*, than the raising of Mr. *Congreve*; I look upon it to be meerly a Debt due to Merit, and pursu'd without any further protracted Views.

V. *The Way of the World*; a Comedy acted at the Theatre in Little *Lincolns-Inn-Fields*, by his Majesty's Servants, Dedicated to the Right Honourable *Ralph* Earl of *Mountague*. This Play, equal to, if not the best of Mr. *Congreve*'s Comedies, unless it be his *Love for Love*, had not the Success of most of his other Performances; which shews there is still an uncertainty in hitting the Humour of the Town: But tho' at first it seem'd to be rejected, it has been lately reviv'd at the Theatre in *Drury-lane*, and acted several Nights with very great Applause.

VI. S E M E L E ; an Opera. This Performance was never represented on the Theatre.

VII. *The Judgement of* P A R I S ; a Masque.

These Dramatick Performances of Mr. *Congreve*, were publish'd with his other Poetical Writings, in three Volumes *Octavo*, 1710. and the Criticks do him the Justice to confess, that the Faults which may be found in them, are of a Nature that makes them very disputable; and in which both his Predecessors and Contemporaries have offended. Whatever small Errors there may be in Mr. *Congreve*'s Dramatick Pieces, he may be justly excus'd, when 'tis consider'd, that he both began and left off to write when he was very Young; he quitted writing at the Age of seven and twenty: And what might not the World have expected from him, if he had continu'd his Dramatical Studies, when he was capable of writing an *Old Batchelor* at Nineteen? and the great Mr. *Dryden* did not compleat his first Performance till he was above the Age of Thirty.

He is the only Dramatick Poet now living, excellent for both Comedy and Tragedy; the Plays he has written in both ways, being very much applauded: And what Mr. *Dennis* has lately observ'd of Mr. *Congreve*, is esteem'd, by most Persons, very just; That he left the Stage early, and Comedy has quitted it with him.

Tho' I am doubtful I shall trespass upon Mr. *Congreve*'s Modesty, I cannot omit inserting some Verses sent to him by Mr. *Dryden*, upon his writing the *Double Dealer*. [Jacob here cites ll. 20–30, 64–77 of Dryden's prologue to *DD*.] (pp. 41–6)

John Gay, 'Epistle IV. To the Right Honourable Paul Methuen Esq;', *Poems on Several Occasions* (London, 1720), 307. Gay, *Poetry and Prose*, i. 217.

> 'Tis the sublime that hurts the Critic's ease;
> Write nonsense and he reads and sleeps in peace.
> Were *Prior*, *Congreve*, *Swift* and *Pope* unknown,
> Poor slander-selling *Curll* would be undone.
> He who would free from malice pass his days,
> Must live obscure, and never merit praise.

'Sir John Falstaffe', in *The Anti-Theatre*, no. 2 (18 February 1720; repr. 1791), 222.

... when we compare Sir JOHN EDGAR's dissertations with the writings of Dr. SWIFT, Mr. ADDISON, Mr. CONGREVE, and others, who flourish'd in his period, we find the style of that age had quite a different turn and fashion from that of our dissertator.

John Gay, 'Mr Popes Welcome from Greece' [*c*. March–April 1720]. Gay, *Poetry and Prose*, i. 257.

> See generous *Burlington* with goodly *Bruce*
> (But *Bruce* comes wafted in a Soft Sedan)
> Dan *Prior* next belov'd by every Muse,
> And Friendly *Congreve*, unreproachfull man!

Alexander Pope, *The Iliad of Homer, Translated by Mr. Pope* [1 October 1719–25 March 1720]. 6 vols. (London, 1720), vi. 220–1. Pope, *Poems*, viii. 578–9. Pope's decision to dedicate his translation to Congreve is noted on the back of a letter from James Cragg dated 1 October 1719: 'End the notes with a dedication to Mr. Congreve, as a memorial of our friendship occasioned by his translation of this last part of Homer.' See Pope, *Correspondence*, ii. 16.

I must end these Notes by discharging my Duty to two of my Friends, which is the more an indispensable piece of Justice, as the one of them is since dead: The Merit of their Kindness to me will appear infinitely the greater, as the Task they undertook was in its own nature of much more Labour, than either Pleasure or Reputation. The larger part of the Extracts from *Eustathius*, together with several excellent Observations were sent me by Mr. *Broome*: And the whole Essay upon *Homer* was written upon such Memoirs as I had collected, by the late Dr. *Parnell*, Archdeacon of *Clogher* in *Ireland*: How very much that Gentleman's Friendship prevail'd over his Genius, in detaining a Writer of his Spirit in the Drudgery of removing the Rubbish of past Pedants, will soon appear to the World, when they shall see those beautiful Pieces of Poetry the Publication of which he left to my Charge, almost with his dying Breath.

For what remains, I beg to be excus'd from the Ceremonies of taking leave at the End of my Work; and from embarassing myself, or others, with any Defences or Apologies about it. But instead of endeavouring to raise a vain Monument to my self, of the Merits or Difficulties of it (which must be left to the World, to Truth, and to Posterity) let me leave behind me a Memorial of my Friendship, with one of the most valuable Men as well as finest Writers, of my Age and Countrey: One who has try'd, and knows by his own Experience, how hard an Undertaking it is to do Justice to *Homer*: And one, who (I am sure) sincerely rejoices with me at the Period of my Labours. To Him therefore, having brought this long Work to a Conclusion, I desire to *Dedicate* it; and to have the Honour and Satisfaction of placing together, in this manner, the Names of Mr. *C O N G R E V E* , and of

A. P O P E .

March 25.

1720.

Jonathan Swift, Letter to Charles Ford, 4 April 1720. Swift, *Correspondence*, ii. 343. Referring to Edmund Curll's malpractices, Swift comments:

I would go into any Scheam you please with Mr Congreve and Mr Pope and the rest, but cannot imagine a Remedy unless he be sent to Bridewell for Life.

Richard Steele, in *The Theatre*, no. 28 (5 April 1720; repr. 1791), 212.

[Some men] put me in mind of VALENTINE in Mr. CONGREVE'S Comedy, who makes a very humorous lecture upon a doubt, whether his man had not the same organs, for the supply of the appetites of hunger and thirst, with which a Gentleman, of an estate and means to supply himself with food, is furnished.

James Heywood, 'On the Death of the Honourable Joseph Addison, Esq;', in *Original Poems on Several Occasions* (1721), 11.

> Not *Young*'s, not *Pope*'s, nor *Congreve*'s Pen can tell,
> How much our *English Maro* did excell:
> They may in nervous Lines thy Praise rehearse,
> In sublime Numbers, and harmonious Verse;
> But which of our great *British* Bards can show,
> Or paint this Loss, this dismal Scene of Woe?

Jonathan Swift, Letter to Alexander Pope, 10 January 1721. Swift, *Correspondence*, ii. 369–70.

But, whatever opportunities a constant attendance of four years might have given me for endeavouring to do good offices to particular persons, I deserve at least to find tolerable quarter from those of the other Party; for many of which I was a constant advocate with the Earl of Oxford, and for this I appeal to his Lordship: He knows how often I press'd him in favour of Mr. Addison, Mr. Congreve, Mr. Row, and Mr. Steel, although I freely confess that his Lordship's kindness to them was altogether owing to his generous notions, and the esteem he had for their wit and parts, of which I could only pretend to be a remembrancer. For I can never forget the answer he gave to the late Lord Hallifax, who upon the first change of the Ministry interceded with him to spare Mr. Congreve: It was by repeating these two lines of Virgil,

> Non abtusa adeo gestamus pectora Poeni,
> Nec tam aversus equos Tyria Sol jungit ab urbe.

Pursuant to which, he always treated Mr. Congreve with the greatest personal civilities, assured him of his constant favour and protection, adding that he would study to do something better for him.

Richard Steele, 'To Mr. Congreve Occasion'd by Mr. Tickell's
Preface to the Four Volumes of Mr. Addison's Works.' Dedication
to Joseph Addison, *The Drummer* (London, 1722). Published 22
December 1721.

(i) To Mr. Congreve
Occasion'd by Mr. *Tickell*'s Preface to the Four Volumes of Mr. *Addison*'s
Works.

SIR,
    THIS is the second time that I have, without your leave, taken the Liberty
to make a publick Address to you. However uneasy you may be for your own
sake in receiving Compliments of this nature, I depend upon your known
Humanity for Pardon, when I acknowledge, that you have this present
Trouble for mine. When I take my self to be ill treated with regard to my
Behaviour to the Merit of other Men, my Conduct towards you is an
Argument of my Candour that way, as well as that your Name and
Authority will be my Protection in it. You will give me leave therefore, in a
matter that concerns us in the Poetical World, to make you my Judge,
whether I am not injur'd in the highest manner; for with Men of your
Taste and Delicacy, it is a high Crime and Misdemeanour to be guilty of
any thing that is disingenuous...

(ii) Mr. *Dryden*, in his *Virgil*, after having acknowledged, that *a certain
excellent young Man* had shew'd him many Faults in his Translation of
Virgil, which he had endeavour'd to correct, goes on to say, 'Two other
worthy Friends of mine, who desire to have their Names conceal'd, seeing
me straitned in my time, took Pity on me, and gave me the Life of *Virgil*, the
two Prefaces to the *Pastorals*, and the *Georgics*, and all the Arguments in Prose
to the whole Translation.' If Mr. *Addison* is one of the two Friends, and the
Preface to the *Georgics* be what the Editor calls the Essay upon the *Georgics*, as
one may adventure to say they are from their being word for word the same,
he has cast an inhuman Reflection upon Mr. *Dryden*, who, tho' tied down not
to name Mr. *Addison*, pointed at him, so as all Mankind conversant in these
matters knew him, with an Elogium equal to the highest Merit, considering
who it was that bestow'd it. I could not avoid remarking upon this
Circumstance, out of Justice to Mr. *Dryden*, but confess at the same time
I took a great Pleasure in doing it, because I knew, in exposing this Outrage,
I made my court to Mr. *Congreve*.   (sigs. A6ᵛ–A7ʳ)

(iii) These, you know very well, were not the Reasons which made Mr.
Addison turn his thoughts to the civil World: and as you were the
Instrument of his becoming acquainted with my Lord *Hallifax*, I doubt not

but you remember the warm Instances that Noble Lord made to the Head of the College not to insist upon Mr. *Addison's* going into Orders; his Arguments were founded upon the general Pravity and Corruption of Men of Business who wanted liberal Education. And I remember, as if I had read the Letter yesterday, that my Lord ended with a Compliment, that however he might be represented as no Friend to the Church, he never would do it any other Injury than keeping Mr. *Addison* out of it. (sig. A8^r)

(iv) I must conclude without satisfying as strong a Desire as ever Man had of saying something remarkably handsome to the Person to whom I am writing; for you are so good a Judge, that you would find out the Endeavourer to be witty: and therefore as I have tir'd you and my self, I will be contented with assuring you, which I do very honestly, I had rather have you satisfied with me on this Subject, than any other Man living.

You will please to pardon me, that I have, thus, laid this nice Affair before a person who has the acknowledg'd Superiority to all others, not only in the most excellent Talents, but possessing them with an Æquanimity, Candour and Benevolence, which render those Advantages a Pleasure as great to the rest of the World, as they can be to the Owner of them. And since Fame consists in the Opinion of wise and good Men, you must not blame me for taking the readiest way to baffle an attempt upon my Reputation, by an Address to one whom every wise and good Man looks upon with the greatest Affection and Veneration. I am, *S I R*, *Your most oblig'd, most obedient and most humble Servant,*

Richard Steele.

(sig. A11^r)

Daniel Bellamy, Dedication to *Love Triumphant: or, The Rival Goddesses. A Pastoral Opera* (1722), sig. A3^r. This adaptation of *JP* was performed at Mrs Bellamy's School, London, on 26 March 1722 (*LS* pt 2, ii. 669).

My Principal Business on this Occasion, being to find out a *Story* very *Innocent*, strictly *Modest*, and yet truly *Poetical*; I could not, I thought, build on a better Foundation than the Ingenious Mr. *C O N G R E V E*'s justly Admir'd *Musical Interlude*, Entituled, *The Judgment of P A R I S*; Which, I almost blush to own, I have plunder'd without Mercy...

Thus far I think myself oblig'd, in Point of Common Justice, frankly to acknowledge; yet the General Applause and Approbation *This Performance* met with from *Your Friends*, thro' *Your Agreeable*, (and I may say in some Measure) *Just Representation* of It, has encourag'd me to suffer its Appearance in Publick and Publish It as my own.

James Sterling, (i) Epilogue to *The Rival Generals* (1722), ll. 7–12. Performed at the Theatre-Royal, Dublin, on 4 or 5 November 1722. (ii) Verses to the author of *The Rival Generals*, ll. 15–18.

(i)   *The Patriot Youth has taught with gen'rous Rage*
               The Tragick Muse to tread the Irish *Stage; . . .*
               Revive, thou sinking Genius of our Isle,
               On new Roscommons *and new* Congreves *smile!*

(ii)   *You shew us Life, a Bubble fill'd with Air:*
               How fleeting are its Joys, how insincere:
               With such a blooming Muse young Congreve *writ.*
               And charm'd with Wonder the attentive Pit . . .

Benjamin Victor, *An Epistle To Sir Richard Steele, On his Play, call'd The Conscious Lovers* (London, 1722), 27–8. The text is dated 18 November 1722.

. . . I shall take the Freedom to trouble you, Sir, with a very entertaining Passage that pass'd between this Critic [John Dennis], Mr. *Purcell*, and Mr. *Congreve*, which is as follows:

Mr. *Purcell* and Mr. *Congreve* going into a Tavern, by chance met *D—s*, who went in with 'em; after a Glass or two had pass'd, Mr. *Purcell*, having some private Business with Mr. *Congreve*, wanted *D—s* out of the Room, and not knowing a more certain Way than Punning, (for you are to understand, Sir, Mr. *D—s* is as much surpriz'd at Pun as at a Bailiff) he proceeded after the following Manner: He pull'd the Bell, and call'd two or three Times, but no One answering, he put his Hand under the Table, and looking full at *D—s*, he said, I think this Table is like the Tavern; says *D—s*, (with his usual prophane Phrase) God's Death, Sir, How is this Table like the Tavern? Why, says Mr. *Purcell*, because here's ne'er a Drawer in it.

Says *D—s*, (starting up) God's Death, Sir, the Man will make such an execrable Pun as that in my Company, will pick my Pocket, and so left the Room.

[John Sturmy], Prologue to *The Compromise: or, Faults on both Sides* (1723), ll. 22–7. Performed at LIF on 15 December 1722 (*LS* pt. 2, ii. 700).

       'Twas Congreve's M U S E *alone gave full Delight,*
       And gain'd Perfection in her Virgin Flight.
       Your friendly Favour to his B R I D E'*s* D I S T R E S S,
       Made him thus venture in a Comick *Dress:*

> *As then in Pity you inclin'd to grieve,*
> *Now gracious smile, and kindly bid him live.*

John Gay, Letter to Jonathan Swift, 3 February 1723. Swift, *Correspondence*, ii. 446.

Mr Congreve I see often, he always mentions you with the strongest expressions of esteem and friendship, he labours still under the same afflictions as to his Sight and Gout, but in his intervals of Health, he has not lost any thing of his Cheerfull temper; I pass'd all the last Season with him at the Bath, and I have great reason to value myself upon his friendship, for I am sure he sincerely wishes me well. we pleas'd ourselves with the thoughts of seeing you there, but Duke Disney, who knows more intelligence than any body besides, chanc'd to give us a wrong information.

Peter Davall, Dedicatory Letter to William Congreve, in *Memoirs of the Cardinal de Retz.* 4 vols. (London, 1723). Vol. i, sigs. A2^r–A3^v. Dated from the Middle Temple, 1 March 1723.

SIR,

I S H O U L D never have thought of Publishing the following Translation, if I had not been in some measure encourag'd to it, by the Approbation You seem'd to express for some Part of it, when my Father took the Liberty to communicate it to You. If the Stile in which it is written is in any manner tolerable, it is chiefly owing to your kind and useful Instructions. You know, Sir, that I was inclined to have kept this Translation by me, for a longer Time, during which I might possibly have brought it somewhat nearer Perfection: And You likewise know the Reasons which have prevailed upon me to venture it Abroad, sooner than I intended. Such as it is, I hope You will excuse the Freedom which I have taken in Addressing it to You; and the Regard I have had for my Self, in making use of the Name of Mr. *Congreve*, which alone is sufficient to bespeak the good Opinion of the Publick, or to excite, at least, a Curiosity of reading a Book, which has that Name prefixt to it. I am, *SIR,*
> *Your most Humble, and most Obedient Servant,*
> P. Davall.

Jonathan Swift, Letter to Alexander Pope, 20 September 1723. Swift, *Correspondence*, ii. 466.

You must remember me with great Affection to Dr Arburthnet, Mr Congreve, and Gay . . .

[Elizabeth Tollet], *Poems on Several Occasions. With Anne Boleyn to King Henry VIII. An Epistle* (London, 1724), 15–16.

On Mr. C O N G R E V E'*s Plays and Poems.*

C O N G R E V E! the justest Glory of our Age!
The whole *Menander* of the *English* Stage!
Thy Comic Muse, in each complete Design,
Does manly Sense and sprightly Wit combine.
And sure the Theatre was meant a School,
To lash the Vitious and expose the Fool:
The wilful Fool, whose Wit is always shown
To hit another's Fault and miss his own,
Laughs at himself when by thy Skill exprest;
And always in his Neighbour finds the Jest.
A Fame from vulgar Characters to raise
Is ev'ry Poet's Labour, and his Praise:
They, fearful, coast; while you foresake the Shore,
And undiscover'd Worlds of Wit explore,
Enrich the Scene with Characters unknown,
There plant your Colonies, and fix your Throne.
Let *Maskwell*'s Treacheries, and *Touchwood*'s Rage,
Let rugged *Ben*, and *Foresight*'s tim'rous Age,
And *Heartwell*'s sullen Passion grace the Stage:
Then let Half-Criticks veil their idle spite,
For he knows best to rail who worst can write,
Let juster Satire now employ their Pen,
To tax the Vicious on the World's great Scene;
There the Reformer's Praise the Poet shares,
And boldly lashes whom the Zealot spares.
Ye *British* Fair! Cou'd your bright Eyes refuse
A pitying Tear to grace his Tragic Muse?
Can gen'rous *Osmyn* sigh beneath his Chain,
Or the distress'd *Almeria* weep in vain?
A kindly Pity ev'ry Breast must move,
For injur'd Virtue, or for suff'ring Love.
The Nymphs adorn *Pastora*'s sacred Tomb;
And mourn the lov'd *Amyntas* short-liv'd Bloom:
The Learn'd admire the Poet, when he flies
To trace the *Theban* Swan amid the cloudless Skies.
When he translates, still faithful to the Sense,
He copies, and improves each Excellence.
Or when he teaches how the rich and Great,

And all but deathless Wit must yield to Fate:
Or when he sings the Courser's rapid Speed;
Or Virtue's loftier Praise, and more immortal Deed.
Each various Grace conspires t'adorn his Song;
As *Horace* easy, and as *Pindar* strong:
Pindar, who long like Oracles ador'd
In rev'rend Darkness now to Light restor'd
Shall stamp thy current Wit, and seal thy Fame's Record.

Edward Young, Satire I, in *The Universal Passion* (London, 1725), 3.

Congreve, who crown'd with Lawrels fairly won,
Sits smiling at the Goal while Others run,
He will not Write; and (more provoking still!)
Ye Gods! He will not write, and *Mævius* will.

William Congreve, Will. 26 February 1726. NA: PROB11/621. Printed in *Mr. Congreve's Last Will and Testament, with Characters of his Writings* (1729) and reissued with *Memoirs of the Life, Writings, and Amours of William Congreve Esq;* (1730). See also Hodges, *Documents*, 254–8, and for the interlocking will of Henrietta, Duchess of Marlborough, pp. 254–9.

In the Name of God Amen. This is the last Will of mee William Congreve of the parish of St. Clement Danes Westminster in the County of Middlesex Esqr. made the Twenty Sixth day of February Anno Domini 1725[-6]. And first I desire and direct that my Funerall shall bee privately performed without the least Ostentation and the place where, I refer to my Executor to appoint. I give to the Severall persons herein after named the respective Legacyes following (That is to say) To
[First Testamentary Schedule]
My intention is that the following Legacys be given to the respective persons herein named as if they were insert[ed] in the blank Space left in this Will for that purpose. Imprimis I give and bequeath to Ann Jellet twenty pounds a Year during her life. Item to William Congreve Son to Coll: Willm Congreve of Highgate and my Godson three hundred pounds. To Mrs. Ann Congreve Daughter to my late Kinsman Coll: Ralph Congreve of Clarges Street, two hundred pounds. To Mrs. Ann Bracegirdle of Howard Street two hundred pounds. To Mrs. Frances Porter Fifty pounds. Item to Mrs. Deborah Rooke one hundred pounds with all my Linnen and apparel. For other lesse legacys I leave them as Specified in a Codicil enclosed in the duplicate of this Will and left in the Custody of the Dutchess of Marlborough.

All the rest and residue of my Estate the same consisting in personall things only (not having any Lands or other Reall Estate) I give and bequeath to the Dutchess of Marlborough the now Wife of Francis Earl of Godolphin of Godolphin in the County of Cornwall But not soe as to vest in him the said Earl of Godolphin the Equitable right and Interest of such rest and residue But that the same and every part thereof and the Interest produce and benefitt thereof shall and may at all times from and after my Decease bee had and received by her the said Dutchess, Namely Henrietta Dutchess of Marlborough to her Sole and Seperate use and wherewith her said Husband or any after taken Husband of her the said Dutchess of Marlborough shall not intermeddle or have any controuling power over, nor shall the said rest and residue or the Interest and produce thereof bee lyable to the Debts and Incumbrances of the said Earl of Godolphin or of any after taken Husband of her the said Dutchess of Marlborough in any Wise But shall be had and received Issued and payd as Shee the said Dutchess of Marlborough Shall by Writeing under her hand from time to time Direct and appoint and her owne acquittance shall bee a Sufficient discharge for all or any part of the Estate soe given to her as aforesaid and in Confidence of the honesty and Justice of him the said Francis Earl of Godolphin I do hereby Constitute and Appoint him the Sole Executor of this my Will in Trust for his said Wife as aforesaid. In Witness whereof I have hereunto Subscribed my name and Sett my Seale the day and Yeare aforesaid. William Congreve Signed Sealed and Declared by the said William Congreve the Testator to bee his last Will in the presence of us Timo: Kiplin Thos. Swan. [A duplicate will gives as witnesses: William Humpstone, George Thorpe, and Jonathan White.]

[Second Testamentary Schedule]

Legacys intended to be inserted in the Blank Space of this Will and which I desire may be payd tho any thing should prevent my inserting them with my own hand in manner as I have filled up the other Blanks in the same. Imprimis to Ann Jellet twenty pounds a Year for her Life. Item to my Godson William Congreve Son of Coll Wm. Congreve of Highgate three hundred pounds. Item to Ann Congreve daughter of the Late Coll Ralph Congreve of Clarges Street two hundred pounds. Item to Mrs Ann Congreve her Mother and to Coll Willm. Congreve of Highgate each twenty pounds. Item to Mrs Ann Bracegirdle of Howard Street two hundred pounds. Item to Mrs. Deborah Rook one hundred pounds and all my wearing apparel and Linnen of all Sorts. Item to Mrs. Frances Porter fifty pounds. Item to Peter Walter Esqr. of St. Margets Westminster twenty pounds. Item to Richard Lord Viscount Cobham and Richard Lord Viscount Shannon twenty pounds each. Item to Charles Mein Esqr. and Mr. Edward Porter and Mr. Joshua White twelve pounds each. Item to her Grace Henrietta Dutchess of Newcastle I give and bequeath the Dutchess of Marlboroughs picture by Kneller. Item to the Lady

Mary Godolphin Youngest Daughter to the Dutchess of Marlborough I give and bequeath her Mothers picture Ennamelld in Miniature together with my white brilliant Diamond Ring. Item to Coll. Charles Churchill twenty pounds together with my gold headed Cane. Item to all and each of my Domestick Servants a years Wages and proper Mourning. Item to the poor of the parish ten pounds.

Whereas I William Congreve did by my last Will and Testament bearing date the [Twenty-]Sixth day of February 1725[–6] affix a Schedule of Legacys written in my own hand over a blank space left for that purpose in the said Will I do hereby revoke and annul those Legacys excepting such as are bequeath'd to persons related to me and bearing my own name as also what is therein Bequeath'd to Mrs. Ann Jellet and Mrs. Ann Bracegirdle which said Legacys I do hereby Confirm and do hereby revoke and annull all other Legacys therein mention'd or in the Counterpart of the said Will more at large Set down which Counterpart is by me left in the Custody of her Grace Henrietta Dutchess of Marlborough my Sole Executrix as is Specified in the said Will and Counterpart thereof. Be it understood that my intention is by this Writing to revoke those Legacys not herein Confirm'd as above mention'd, in such manner onely as to leave them absolutely in the power and determination of the abovenamed Henrietta Dutchess of Marlborough, my Sole Executrix, either to pay or refuse to pay them, or take from them or add to them as She shall Judge the persons therein named especially my Domestick Servants therein mention'd or not mention'd may have merited of me William Congreve. Signed and Sealed in the presence of Joseph Lee William Humpstone.

29° Januarij 1728[–9]°.

Which day appeared personally Thomas Snow of Saint Clements Danes in the County of Middlesex Goldsmith and John Paltock of the same parish Goldsmith and by virtue of their Oaths Deposed that they Severally knew and were well acquainted with William Congreve late of the parish of St. Clements Danes in the County of Middlesex Esqr. deceased and with his handwriting Character and manner of Writing having Severall times Seen him Write, and having Seen and perused a Codicil annexed to the last Will and Testament of the said deceased beginning thus (my intention is that the following Legacys be given to the respective persons herein named) and ending thus (and left in the Custody of the Dutchess of Marlborough) and having also Seen and perused another Codicil enclos'd in the Duplicate of the said Will beginning thus (Legacys intended to be inserted in Blank Space of this Will) and ending thus (Item to the poor of the parish Ten pounds) these Deponents do beleive that the said Codicills and each of them were totally wrote by and are the proper handwriting of the said William Congreve deceased Tho Snow. John Paltock. Eodem die Dicti Thomas Snow et Johannes Paltock Jurati fuerunt Super veritate premissorum Coram me G Paul Sur. prsen. Tho: Tyllott Notario Publico.

Probatum Londini cum quatuor Codicillis sive schedulis testamentis, annex: tertio Die Mensis Februarij 1728[–9]. Coram venli viro Georgio Paul, legum Doctore surrog: &c. Jurato prenobilis, & honli viri Francisci Comitis: de Godolphin, Extris unici, &c. Cui, &c. De bene & Jurat. Lata prius sententia definitiva pro valore, et valididate dicti testamenti prout, ex actis curiæ liquet.

Linthwaite Farrant,
Registrar: Deputat: Assumpt.

Received this Twenty first day of February 1728[–9] of Mr. Linthwaite Farrant Deputy Registrar assumed of the prerogative Court of Canterbury the Original Will and four Codicills or Testamentory Schedules of the above named William Congreve Esqr. deceased of which the above written is a true copy. I say received the said Originall Will and Codicills or Testamentary Schedules as Proctor and for the Use of the Right Honourable Francis Earl of Godolphin the Sole Executor therin named pursuant to an Order or Decree of the Judge of the said Court bearing date of the Seventeenth day of this Instant February.

Per me
Robert Rous

Witnesses
L. Farrant.
Jo: Taylor
Tho. Lort.

Voltaire, François Marie Arouet de, *An Essay upon the Civil Wars of France . . . And also upon the Epick Poetry of the European Nations, From Homer down to Milton* (1727), 110.

The *Italian* in Point of Tragedy would catch the Flame from the *English*, and all the Rest from the *French*. In Point of Comedy, they would learn from Mr. *Congreve* and some other Authors, to prefer Wit and Humour to Buffoonery.

Alexander Pope, 'Fragment of a Satire', in *Miscellanies. The Last Volume* (1727 [for 1728]), 132, ll. 39–42. Of writers like Charles Johnson, he continues:

> Should modest Satire bid all these *translate*,
> And own that nine such Poets make a *T——te*;
> How would they fume, and stamp, and roar, and chafe!
> How would they swear, not *Congreve*'s self was safe!

[Jonathan Smedley], 'A History of Poetry, in a Letter to a Friend', in *Gulliveriana: Or, A Fourth Volume of Miscellanies* (London, 1728), 60.

Another of them, who was of my old Acquaintance, succeeded well in Comedy, but failed when he began to CON GRAVE Subjects.

Anon., *An Essay against Reading* (1728), 8, 15, 16.

Poor old *Milton*, to get up his *Paradise Lost*; and *Congreve*, his *Love for Love*; they both read themselves blind . . .

Mr. *Congreve* writ his first Play before he was sixteen Years of Age. Do you think, he was a Historian before he had done with his School-Books? No; the Dictates of Nature only refin'd his Judgment, which was surprizing in a Youth: and he would have given Spirit and Life to the Age 'till this Minute; but I am afraid he fell into the other Way, being over-curious of seeing what *Shakespear*, and others had done, which forewarn'd him of great Difficulties; or was afraid, he should not excel those that gave him the Surprize: whereas, otherwise, it would have been almost as easy as writing a common Letter.

I do assure you, I would not read any of *Shakespear*'s or *Congreve*'s Plays for Fifty Pounds, for fear it should puzzle or surprize me with Wonder, that might dispirit me from going on.

Joseph Spence, reporting Alexander Pope, *c*.1728. Spence, i. 56. There is no other evidence of Congreve's membership of the club.

The design of the *Memoirs of Scriblerus* was to have ridiculed all the false tastes in learning, under the character of a man of capacity enough that had dipped in every art and science, but injudiciously in each. It was begun by a club of some of the greatest wits of the age: Lord Bolingbroke, Lord Oxford, the Bishop of Rochester, Mr. Pope, Congreve, Arbuthnot, Swift, and others. Gay often held the pen, and Addison liked it very well and was not disinclined to come into it.

Joseph Spence, reporting Congreve in a lost letter to Alexander Pope, *c*.1728. Spence, i. 106.

Gay [is] a great eater. 'As the French philosopher used to prove his existence by *Cogito ergo sum*, the greatest proof of Gay's existence is *Edit, ergo est*.'

Joseph Spence, reporting comments by Alexander Pope, [January 1728]. Spence, i. 107. The subject is John Gay's *The Beggar's Opera*, first performed at LIF on 29 January 1728.

He began on it, and when first he mentioned it to Swift the Doctor did not much like the project. As he carried it on he showed what he wrote to both of us, and we now and then gave a correction or a word or two of advice, but 'twas wholly of his own writing. When it was done, neither of us thought it would succeed. We showed it to Congreve, who after reading it over, said, 'It would either take greatly, or be damned confoundedly.'

Alexander Pope, Letter to Jonathan Swift [January 1728]. Pope, *Correspondence*, ii. 469.

John Gay's Opera is just on the point of Delivery...Mr Congreve (with whom I have commemorated you) is anxious as to its Success, and so am I; whether it succeeds or not, it will make a great noise, but whether of Claps or Hisses I know not. At worst it is in its own nature a thing which he can *lose* no reputation by, as he lays none upon it.

Henry Fielding, Preface to *Love in Several Masques. A Comedy* (1728), sig. A4^r.

These were Difficulties which seemed rather to require the superior Force of a Wycherly, *or a* Congreve, *than of a raw and unexperienced Pen (for I believe I may boast that none ever appeared so early on the Stage.)*

[Mary Barber], *A Tale Being an Addition to Mr. Gay's Fables* (Dublin, 1728), 4–5.

> *Steel*'s Comedies gave vast Delight,
> And entertain'd them many a Night.
> C—n—s cou'd no Admittance find,
> Forbid as Poisons to the Mind.
> That Authors Wit and Sense, says she,
> But heightens his Impiety.

Jonathan Swift, Letter to John Gay, 28 March 1728. Swift, *Correspondence*, iii. 278. Mary Barber deleted the reference to Congreve when the poem was republished in *Poems on Several Occasions* (London, 1734).

I hope Dr Delany hath Shown you the Tale writ by Mrs Barbar a Citizen's wife here in praise of your Fables There is Something in it hard upon

Mr Congreve, which I Sent to her (for I never Saw her) to change to Dryden, but She absolutely refused.

Alexander Pope, *The Dunciad* (1728). I. 235–40; II. 113–16, III. 303–4, 307–8, 311–14. Published 18 May.

(i)   How, with less reading than makes felons 'scape,
         Less human genius than God gives an ape,
         Small thanks to France and none to Rome or Greece,
         A past, vamp'd, future, old, reviv'd, new piece,
         'Twixt Plautus, Fletcher, Congreve, and Corneille,
         Can make a Cibber, Johnson, or Ozell.
                                                      (I. 235–40)

(ii)   Heav'n rings with laughter: Of the laughter vain,
         Dulness, good Queen, repeats the jest again.
         Three wicked imps of her own Grubstreet Choir
         She deck'd like Congreve, Addison, and Prior...
                                                      (II. 113–16)

[Note to ll. 115–16] These Authors being such whose names will reach posterity, we shall not give any account of them, but proceed to those of whom it is necessary. [See also *Miscellanies in Prose and Verse*, i. 12: 'Nay these Fellows are arriv'd at that Height of Impudence, as when an Author has publickly disown'd a spurious Piece, they have disputed his own Name with him in printed Advertisements, which has been practis'd to Mr. *Congreve* and Mr. *Prior*.']

(iii)   [For Dulness]
         Already, Opera prepares the way,
         The sure fore-runner of her gentle sway...
         Pluto for Cato thou for her shalt join,
         And link the Mourning-Bride to Proserpine...
         Another Æschylus appears! prepare
         For new Abortions, all ye pregnant Fair!
         In flames, like Semeles, be brought to bed,
         While opening Hell spouts wild-fire at your head.
                                     (III. 303–4, 307–8, 311–14)

Alexander Pope, Letter to John Gay [after 19 January 1729]. Pope, *Correspondence*, iii. 3.

I never pass'd so melancholy a time, and now Mr. *Congreve*'s death touches me nearly. It is twenty years that I have known him. Every year carries away something dear with it, till we outlive all tenderness, and become wretched Individuals again as we begun.

The Earl of Oxford, Letter to Alexander Pope, 20 January 1729. Pope, *Correspondence*, iii. 9.

poor honest Gay recovers. but congreve is gone.

Alexander Pope, Letter to the Earl of Oxford, 21 January 1729. Pope, *Correspondence*, iii. 10.

Mr Congreves death was to me sudden, & strook me through. You know the Value I bore him & a long 20 years friendship—

Henrietta, Duchess of Marlborough, Letter to George Berkeley, 22 January [1729]. Hodges, *Documents*, 260, from L: Add. MS 22,628, f. 88.

Sir

I must desire you to be one off the Six next Sunday upon this very melancholley occation I allways used to think you had a respect for him and I woud not have any there that had not. I am your most Humble servant.

Jacob Tonson, Letter to Jacob Tonson II, 27 January 1729. Hodges, *Documents*, 147.

The death of my old acquaintance & freind mr Congreve does really much concern me, tho his long indisposition makes it the less Surprizing. I flatterd my self with my Seeing him at ye Bath this Spring woud have been a sufficient reason for my going there, but my decay of strenth, a consequence of a decay of appetite, makes it necessary & after Easter week I propose ye journy. You shall have a long notice before I goe—pray let me know how Mr Congreves circumstances were at his Death. I beleive they must be considerable, & to whom left & his executors. his collection of books were very genteel & wel chosen. I wish you coud think them worth your buying; I think there are in [his] books several notes of his own or corrections & every thing from him wil be very valuable.—I hope the Dutchess of Marlborough wil order a monument for him. But I think if these monuments are not soon finished they wil lye undertaken longer than any Aldermans.

Henrietta, Duchess of Marlborough, Letter to George Berkeley, 28
January 1728[–9]. Hodges, *Documents*, 261, from L: Add. MS 22,
628, f. 87.

Sir,
    The last letter I writ to you was upon allways having thought that you had a
respect and a kind one, for Mr. Congreve. I dare say you believe I coud sooner
think off doing the most monstrous thing in the world, then Sending any
thing that was his, where I was not perswaded it woud be valued. The number
off them I think So off, are a mighty few indeed. therefore must allways be in
a particular manner your most Humble Servant.
            Marlborough
Jan: ye 28th 1728[–9]

Lady Mary Wortley Montagu, 'To the Memory of Mr Congreve',
[January–February 1729], *Essays and Poems*, 246–7. The following
stanza originally came after line 8 but was struck out:

> How keen his Wit, how pierceing, and how bright,
> The smallest error could not 'scape his sight
> Yet such a gentlenesse his Judgment rein'd
> His verses never were by Malice stain'd.

To the Memory of Mr Congreve

> Farewell the best and loveliest of Mankind
> Where Nature with a happy hand had joyn'd
> The softest temper with the strongest mind,
> In pain could counsel and could charm when blind.

> In this Lewd Age when Honor is a Jest
> He found a refuge in his Congreve's breast,
> Superior there, unsully'd, and entire;
> And only could with the last breath expire.

> His wit was never by his Malice stain'd,
> No rival writer of his Verse complain'd,
> For neither party drew a venal pen
> To praise bad measures or to blast good men.

> A Queen indeed he mourn'd, but such a Queen
> Where Virtue mix'd with royal Blood was seen,
> With equal merit grac'd each Scene of Life
> An Humble Regent and Obedient Wife.

If in a Distant State blest Spirits know
The Scenes of Sorrow of a World below,
This little Tribute to thy Fame approve,
A Triffling Instance of a boundless Love.

Jacob Tonson, Letter to Jacob Tonson II. 3 February 1729. Hodges, *Documents*, 148. MS: University of Texas at Austin.

Congreves works in qto wil most certainly doe but ye Sooner the better, Let a mans worth be nevour so great after Death it gets strangely out of ye minds of his Surviving acquaintance if mr Addisons works were now to bee published there woud not, I beleive, be the same number of Subscribers—What ye Prints say of mr Congreves agee[*sic*] must needs bee a mistake. They say 57, wanting 12 days. Now I wel know yt Juvenal in folio was printed & published 1693. & ye Satyr he translated was done a Yearee[*sic*] before & he coud not bee [have been] less than 20 or rather more. pray let me know how it stands.... Let me know who you design to Supervise mr Congreves works; He took a great deal of care himself in the 8° edition I printed, I beleive that wil be ye best coppy for you to follow.

Jonathan Swift, Letter to Alexander Pope, 13 February 1729. Swift, *Correspondence*, iii. 311.

But this renews the grief for the death of our friend Mr. Congreve, whom I loved from my youth, and who surely besides his other talents, was a very agreeable companion. He had the misfortune to squander away a very good constitution in his younger days; and I think a man of sense and merit like him, is bound in conscience to preserve his health for the sake of his friends, as well as of himself. Upon his own account I could not much desire the continuance of his life, under so much pain, and so many infirmities. Years have not yet hardened me, and I have an addition of weight on my spirits since we lost him, although I saw him so seldom; and possibly if he had lived on should never have seen him more.

William Rose, Poem occasioned by the Death of William Congreve, accompanying a letter of 26 February 1729 from the parsonage, Wootton. L: Evelyn Papers, 1032.

Occasiond by ye Death of Mr Congreve, & inscribed to Her Grace, Hariot Duchess of Marlborough.

O, First of Glorious Marlbro's Race!
How swift ye Course, how short ye Space
Betwixt ye Cradle, & ye Tomb!

Nor Arms, nor Arts, nor Wit avail;
Ev'n Beauty's matchless Pow'r will fail
To arrest th'inevitable Doom.

Death huddles in ye silent Grave
The Prince, ye Beggar, Coward, & ye Brave.
All There, without Distinction lie conceald,
   Save on an Urn; Or he, whose Name
Still blossoms fragrant in ye Breath of Fame,
And stands in Glory's endless Roll reveald.

Great Churchill, who so oft intrepid stood
'Mid Ranks of Fire, & Deluges of Blood;
And Death, in all his Ghastly Forms, defy'd:
   Obedient to His destin'd Hour,
Submitted to ye Universal Conquerour;
   And, full of Years, & Glory, dy'd.

Young Blanford, summond by an hasty Doom,
   Deceasd, a Hero but in Bloom.
   Death cropd so fair, so sweet a Flow'r,
   E'er half his Beauties were displaid;
   And, long e'er ye expected Hour,
      The promisd Fruit decay'd.
   Had Fate relenting heard our Pray'rs,
In him another Marlbrô we had seen;
   In Manly Port, & Godlike Mien:
And, as in Feature, like in Fame, & Years.

O'er Congreve's fragrant Hearse, ye Muses' moan
   Their best belovd, Their Darling Son:
   For Each, in Congreve, claims a Share.
   Whether He laugh, in Comic Strain;
   Or He, in Tragic Scenes, complain;
      The Sock, or Buskin wear:
In Both his Characters are so compleat,
As, for Her Picture, Nature's Self had sate.
His Pen, like Raphael's happy Brush, pourtrays;
And Beauties unobserved paints forth to View,
In Lines as strong, as masterly, as true.
Touchd by his Hand, ye breathing Figure lives.
To perfect Beauty He Perfection gives.
E'en Blemishes, by Him set off, can please.
   If Congreve strike ye warbling Lyre,
Such is ye Turn, & such His Numbers are;

Such Force ye Magic Notes inspire,
    We all Attention seem.
And all consent to Think, with Him;
    Like Him to Think, despair.
Oh, Thou to Congreve, as His Muse, Benign!
Despise not these my far unequal Lays.
Still Thou, like Her, in Native Beauty, shine
Above my Skill, as Needless of my Praise.
    Long may'st Thou live, in lasting Prime!
By Sickness unassaild, unmarkd by Time:
Godolphin, ever Bounteous, crown Thy Daies!
Thy Blanford, & Newcastle bless Thine Eyes!
May Both,* in These, & Your Maria, see
The Sire, & Mothers of a Num'rous Progeny!
Such be Your Bliss: wch:, Bounteous Heav'n, bestow!
    E'er, in Their Turn,
The Muses, & ye Arts their Patroness shall mourn;
    As Thou, Thy Congreve now.

[marginal note]* ie Ld Godolphin & Her Grace

Inscription on the Congreve monument [by Francis Bird] in Westminster Abbey, beneath a portrait medallion sculptured in reproduction of Kneller's Kit-Cat Club portrait of Congreve. Medallion and inscription are reproduced as plate 76 in Lord Killanin, *Sir Godfrey Kneller and his Times, 1646–1723* (London: Batsford, 1948).

M^r. WILLIAM CONGREVE,

Dyed *jan* ye 19th 1728 Aged 56. And was buried near this place,
To whose most Valueable Memory this MONUMENT is Sett up by
HENRIETTA *Dutchess* of MARLBOROUGH as a mark how dearly,
    She remembers the happiness and Honour She enjoyed in
    the Sincere Friendshipp of so worthy and Honest a Man,
    Whose Virtue Candour and Witt gained him the love and
    Esteem of the present Age and whose Writings will be the
        Admiration of the Future.
F. Bird Fecit.

Sarah, Duchess of Marlborough, as reported by Horace Walpole, *Reminiscences Written... in 1788*, ed. Paget Toynbee (Oxford: At the Clarendon Press, 1924), 87.

When the younger Duchess exposed herself by placing a monument & silly epitaph of her own composition & bad spelling to Congreve in Westminster abbey, her Mother, quoting the words, said, 'I know not what pleasure She might have in his company, but I am sure it was no honour.'

Jacob Tonson, Letter to Jacob Tonson II [*c*.March 1729.] Hodges, *Documents*, 149–50. O: Ll. Eng. Letters C. 129.

for ye old Batchelour it was printed for Peter Buck, & I beleive ye entering of it in ye Hall Book wil shew ye time of printing it wch was imediately upon its being Acted. Buck before that printed a litle novel in 12, written by Mr Congreve & wch has been Since reprinted by Wellington. Buck, alsoe about thee same time printed a 12° of miscellany Poems in wch were Several poems of Mr Congreves, wch Poems hee revised & then put them into my 3d. part of M. Poems & that was published in 1693—I think the head should bee done by Virtue, from ye Kitcat Picture. Smith did the messotinto just from that, but I think there is a stifness about thee mouth wch is not in ye painting.

Anon., *The Female Faction: Or, The Gay Subscribers. A Poem* (1729), 4–5. Advt. 25 March (Foxon F92). Manuscript notes in L: 163.n.16 identify Almeria as the 'Young D. of Marlborough' and Alphonso as 'Mr Congreve'.

> First in thy List does great *Almeria* stand,
> And deal her Favours with a lavish Hand?
> Her *bury'd Bard's* Resemblance does she see,
> And think, *Alphonso* still survives in Thee?
> Grateful, the generous Patronage repay,
> And shew, she errs not, when she smiles on G—— ;
> Equal to *His*, thy *Talents* boldly prove,
> Like *Him* that you can *write*, like *Him*, can *love* ...

Jonathan Swift, Letter to Viscount Bolingbroke and Alexander Pope, 5 April 1729. Swift, *Correspondence*, iii. 329.

I have read my friend Congreve's verses to Lord Cobham, which end with a vile and false moral, and I remember is not in Horace to Tibullus, which he imitates, 'that all times are equally virtuous and vicious' wherein he differs from all Poets, Philosophers, and Christians that ever writ. It is more probable that there may be an equal quantity of virtues always in the world, but sometimes there may be a peck of it in Asia, and hardly a thimble-full in Europe.

Alexander Pope, *The Dunciad* (1729). II. 132 n. Published in April. Writing of Curll as praised by Dulness, Pope adds the note:

Nothing is more remarkable than our author's love of praising good writers. He has celebrated Sir *Isaac Newton*, Mr. *Dryden*, Mr. *Congreve*, Mr. *Wycherley*, Dr. *Garth*, Mr. *Walsh*, Duke of *Buckingham*, Mr. *Addison*, Lord *Lansdown*; in a word, almost every man of his time that deserv'd it.

Charles Coffey, Prologue to *The Beggar's Wedding. A New Opera* (2nd edn., 1729), ll. 28–31. Performed at the New Haymarket Theatre 'with the New PROLOGUE and EPILOGUE' on 30 May 1729 (*LS* pt 2, ii. 1036).

> *From* Shakespear, Cheshire-Bard *should bear the Bell,*
> One Writes, *'tis true, but 'tother* Fiddles *well.*
> *Thus* Sing-Song *only can be sure of Praise,*
> *And* Congreve *must to* Johnson *yield the Bays.*
> *In strict Compliance to the* present Taste
> *A Modish* OPERA *is to Night your Feast—*

[David Mallet?], *A Poem to the Memory of Mr. Congreve*. London, 1729. Advt. 9 May (Foxon M56–7).

Advertisement.

THE author of the following Poem, not having had the happiness of a personal acquaintance with Mr. CONGREVE, is sensible that he has drawn his private character very imperfectly. This all his friends will readily discover: and therefore, if any one of them had thought fit to do justice to those amiable qualifications, which made him the love and admiration of all that knew him, these verses had never seen the light.

A

POEM

To the M EMORY of

Mr. *CONGREVE*.

Inscribed to her G RACE,

HENRIETTA,

Dutchess of *Marlborough*.

OF T has the muse, with mean attempt, employ'd
Her heaven-born voice to flatter prosperous guilt,
Or trivial greatness: often stoop'd her song
To sooth ambition in his frantick rage,
The dire destroyer, while a bleeding world
Wept o'er his crimes. Of this pernicious skill
Unknowing I, these voluntary lays
To genuine worth devote; to worth, by all
Confess'd and mourn'd; to C ONGREVE now no more.
　　First of the fairer kind! by heaven adorn'd
With every nobler praise; whose smile can lift
The MUSE unknown to fame, indulgent now
Permit HER strain, ennobled by a name,
To all the better few, and chief to thee,
Bright MARLBRO', ever sacred, ever dear.
　　Lamented Shade! in him the comic Muse,
Parent of gay instruction, lost her lov'd,
Her last remaining hope; and pensive now
Resigns to Folly, and his mimic rout,
Her throne usurp'd: presage of darker times,
And deeper woes to come! with taste declin'd
Fallen vertue droops; and o'er th' ill-omen'd age,
Unseen, unfear'd, impend the thousand ills
That wait on ignorance: no C ONGREVE now
To scourge our crimes, or laugh to scorn our fools,
A new and nameless herd. Nature was his,
Bold, sprightly, various: and superiour Art,
Curious to chuse each better grace, unseen
Of vulgar eyes; with delicacy free,
Tho' labour'd happy, and tho' strong refin'd.
Judgment, severely cool, o'erlook'd his toil,
And patient finish'd all: each fair design
With freedom regular, correctly great,
A Master's skilful daring. Closely wrought
His meaning Fable, with deep art perplex'd,
With striking ease unravel'd: no thin plot

Seen thro' at once and scorn'd; or ill conceal'd
By borrow'd aids of mimickry and farce.
His Characters strong-featur'd, equal, just,
From finer nature drawn: and all the mind
Thro' all her mazes trac'd; each darker vice,
And darling folly, under each disguise,
By either Sex assum'd, of study'd ease,
False friendship, loose severity, vain wit,
Dull briskness, shallow depth, or coward-rage.
Of the whole Muse possess'd, his piercing eye
Discern'd each richer vein of genuine mirth,
Humour or wit; where differing, where agreed;
How counterfeited, or by folly's grin,
Or affectation's air: and what their force
To please, to move, to shake the ravish'd scene
With laughter unreprov'd. To him the Soul,
In all her higher workings, too was known:
What passions tumult there; whence their prompt spring,
Their sudden flood of rage, and gradual fall;
Infinite motion! source supreme of bliss,
Or woe to man; our heaven, or hell, below!
    Such was his public name; nor less allow'd
His private worth: by nature made for praise.
A pleasing form; a soul sincere and clear,
Where all the human graces mix'd their charms,
Pure candour, easy goodness, open truth,
Spontaneous all: where strength and beauty join'd.
With wit indulgent; humble in the height
Of envy'd honours: and, but rarely found,
Th' unjealous friend of every rival-worth.
Adorn'd for social life: each talent his
To win each heart; the charm of happy ease,
Free mirth, gay learning, ever-smiling wit,
To all endear'd, a pleasure without pain:
What HALLIFAX approv'd, and MARLBRO' mourns.
    Not so th' illiberal mind, where knowledge dwells,
Uncouth and harsh, with her attendant, Pride,
Impatient of attention, prone to blame,
Disdaining to be pleas'd; condemning all,
By all condemn'd; for social joys unfit,
In solitude self-curst, the child of spleen.
Oblig'd, ungrateful; unoblig'd, a foe;
Poor, vitious, old: such fierce-ey'd ASPER was.
Now meaner CENUS, trivial with design,
Courts poor applause by levity of face,

And scorn of serious thought; to mischief prompt,
Tho' impotent to wound; profuse of wealth,
Yet friendless and unlov'd; vain, fluttering, false:
A vacant head, and an ungenerous heart.

    But slighting these ignobler names, the Muse
Pursues her favourite S O N, and sees him now,
From this dim spot enlarg'd, triumphant soar
Beyond the walk of Time to better worlds,
Where all is new, all wonderous, and all blest!
What art thou, death! by mankind poorly fear'd,
Yet period of their ills. On thy near shore,
Trembling they stand, and see thro' dreaded mists
Th' eternal port, irresolute to leave
This various misery, these air-fed dreams
Which men call life, and fame. Mistaken minds!
'Tis reason's prime aspiring, greatly just;
'Tis happiness supreme, to venture forth
In quest of nobler worlds; to try the deeps
Of dark futurity, with H E A V E N our guide,
Th' unerring H A N D that led us safe thro' time:
That planted in the soul this powerful hope,
This infinite ambition of new life,
And endless joys, still rising, ever new.

    These C O N G R E V E tastes, safe on th' ethereal coast,
Join'd to the numberless, immortal quire
Of spirits blest. High-seated among these,
He sees the public Fathers of mankind,
The greatly Good, those universal Minds,
Who drew the sword, or plan'd the holy scheme,
For liberty and right; to cheque the rage
Of blood-stain'd tyranny, and save a world.
Such, high-born M A R L B R O ', be thy Sire divine
With wonder nam'd; fair freedom's champion he,
By heaven approv'd, a conqueror without guilt.
And such, on earth his friend, and join'd on high
By deathless love, G O D O L P H I N 's patriot-worth,
Just to his country's fame, yet of her wealth
With honour frugal; above interest great.
Hail men immortal! social V E R T U E S hail!
First heirs of praise!—But I, with weak essay,
Wrong the superiour theme: while heavenly quires,
In strains high-warbled to celestial harps,
Resound your names; and C O N G R E V E 'S added voice
In heaven exalts what he admir'd below.

    With these he mixes, now no more to swerve
From reason's purest law; no more to please,

Borne by the torrent down, a sensual age.
Pardon, lov'd shade, that I with friendly blame
Slight-note thy error; not to wrong thy worth,
Or shade thy memory (far from my soul
Be that base aim) but haply to deter,
From flattering the gross vulgar, future pens,
Powerful like thine in every grace, and skill'd
To win the listening soul with vertuous charms.
    If manly thought and wit refin'd may hope
To please an age, in aimless folly sunk,
And sliding swift into the depth of vice.
Consuming Pleasure leads the gay and young
Thro' their vain round; and venal Faith the old,
Or Avarice, mean of soul: instructive arts
Pursu'd no more: the general taste extinct,
Or all-debas'd: even sacred liberty
The great man's jest, and BRITAIN'S welfare nam'd,
By her degenerate Sons, the Poets dream,
Or fancy's air-built vision, gaily vain.
Such the lost age: yet still the Muse can find,
Superiour and apart, a sacred band,
Heroic vertues, who ne'er bow'd the knee
To sordid Interest: who dare greatly claim
The Priviledge of men, unfearing truth,
And freedom, heaven's first gift; th' ennobling bliss
That renders life of price, and cheaply sav'd
At life's expence; our sum of happiness.
On these the drooping Muses fix their eyes;
From these expect their ancient fame restor'd.
Nor will the hope be vain: the public Weal
With theirs fast-link'd: a generous truth conceal'd
From narrow-thoughted power, and known alone
To souls of highest rank. With these, the Fair
Be join'd in just applause; the brighter few,
Who rais'd above gay folly, and the whirl
Of fond amusements, emulate thy praise,
Illustrious MARLBRO'; pleas'd, like thee, to shine
Propitious on the Muse; whose charms inspire
Her noblest raptures, and whose goodness crowns.

Charles Wilson, *Memoirs of the Life, Writings, and Amours of William Congreve, Esq.* (London, 1730).

(i) [From the dedication to George Ducket:] ... my Offering is a *Memorial* of one of the finest *Genii* this Nation ever produc'd, (if Mr. *Dryden*'s Judgment be of any weight) and one whom all knew to be a hearty Lover of his Country.   (sig. A2ᵛ)

(ii) *A certain Lady, to whom Mr.* Congreve *bequeath'd a handsome Legacy, would be more prudent, if hereafter she would not be so fond of exposing her own Ignorance in the* Republick *of* Letters; *for her Inquisitiveness led her so far, as to* fancy *she had a* Right *to demand a sight of these Papers, while they were under the Press; which being* justly *refus'd her, she then wanted to know by what Authority Mr.* Congreve*'s Life was written, and what pieces were contain'd in it that were genuine? Upon being civilly told, there would be found several Essays, Letters, and Characters of that Gentleman's writing, she with most affected, contradictory, Dramatick-drawl, cry'd out,* Not one single Sheet of Paper I dare to swear.

I know no more Business that any Person whatever has, nor any more Authority, to make any Inquisition after the Printing *Mr.* Congreve*'s Will, than I have to censure Him for* making *it. And therefore as my Sphere of Life is in a tolerable Degree of Situation, I value neither the Messages nor Threats, either of Peer or Peasant, on these occasions; and as such* Drawcansir-*Bullyings proceed only from an* insolent Arrogance, *I here return for* Answer, *the most* abject Contempt, *being the only* suitable Requital. *I employ'd Mr.* Curll *to print these* Memoirs, *and think my* own Authority *sufficient for whatever I am* inclin'd *to* publish. *Therefore if Dr.* A * * * *be dispatch'd with any more Expresses, he may, if he pleases, come to me; who am as easily to be found in* Great-Russel-Street, Bloomsbury, *when in Town, as he is in* Burlington-Gardens.

Charles Wilson.

P.S. *For the Sum of three Shillings and Sixpence, the following* most notable Advertisement *was inserted in the* DAILY-POST *of* April 29, 1729. viz.

'*Whereas it has been advertis'd by* E. Curll, *that there is now in the Press, miscellaneous Essays and familiar Letters, by* William Congreve *Esq; to which will be prefix'd Memoirs of his Life, Writings and Amours, by* Charles Wilson *Esq; This is therefore to inform the Publick, that Mr.* Congreve*'s Life, &c. will be publish'd with all possible speed from authentick Papers, by a good Hand sufficiently authorized. To which will be added, an Account of his Works already printed, as well as of his posthumous Writings, of which no other Person can have any Memoirs relating thereto.*'

Well, Mr. Anonymous, *you now have what Mr.* Curll, *by my Direction, advertised. I have written Mr.* Congreve*'s Life, not from Papers, but from an intimate Acquaintance with him of near thirty Years. I have also given an exact Account of all his Works already printed. As to his posthumous Papers I know nothing; but am pretty well convinc'd that whenever your doughty Performance starts forth, your Authority and Ability will appear equally ridiculous.*

Now to convince our authoriz'd good Hand *that there was a very friendly Correspondence between Mr.* Congreve *and Mr.* Curll, *when he was printing the first Volume of the Lives of the Poets, intitled,* The Poetical Register, *He intimated his Design to Mr.* Congreve *requesting his Account of himself, and Writings, (he having been represented by some Scriblers as an* Irishman*;) upon which Mr.* Congreve *sent the following Letter, viz.* [Letter 64 is here cited].(pp. xi–xvi)

(iii) [Of *The Way of the World*:] The unkind Reception this excellent Comedy met with, was truly the Cause of Mr. *Congreve*'s just Resentment; and upon which, I have often heard him declare, that he had form'd a strong Resolution never more to concern himself with Dramatical Writings.   (p. 11)

(iv) [Of *The Judgement of Paris*:] Every Word in this Masque is Music, and Juno's Song, *Let Ambition fire thy Mind*, &c. renders it Immortal.   (p. 14)

(v) Now, to what more immediately relates to Mr. *Congreve*;—by a scurrilous Piece of *John Dennis*'s just publish'd [*Remarks* upon the D U N C I A D], I am oblig'd, like the *Crab*, to go backward a little. I find Mr. *Congreve* was the universal Peace-Maker among the Poets, for Mr. *Pope* having complain'd to him of *Dennis*'s Billing's-Gate-Attacks upon his Writings, Mr. *Congreve* prescribed a very easy Method of healing all Breaches, by giving *Dennis* a little Money in subscribing for some of his Books, (which to speak the Truth were only re-printed for those Persons of whom he begg'd the small Pittance of a Guinea Subscription, there being no Demand for them by the Publick, nor never will.) This Mr. *Pope* readily came into, and subscrib'd to *Four Volumes* of his Trumpery; two of which were *Plays*, *Poems*, &c. and the other two call'd *Familiar Letters*, tho' most scandalously abusive, as may be seen by several of them being wrote against Mr. *Addison*, and others of them scandalously address'd to Mr. *Booth*, under the Name of *Judas Iscariot*, for which the Scribler is justly intitled to *Argumentum Baculinum.*

However, Mr. *Pope* upon his second Payment, sent *Dennis* the following Letter, *viz.*

S I R ,
I Call'd to receive the two Books of your Letters from Mr. *Congreve*, and have left with him the little Money I am in your Debt. I look upon my self to be much more so, for the Omissions you have been pleas'd to make in those *Letters* in my Favour, and sincerely join with you in the Desire, that not the least Traces may remain of that Difference between us which indeed I am sorry for. You may therefore believe me, without either Ceremony or Falseness,

May 3d 1721.   *S I R ,* Your most obedient
Humble Servant,
A. P O P E .

It was Mr. *Congreve*'s good Fortune never to be attack'd by this vile, mercenary, universal Defamer of Mankind. But this I attribute rather to his great Humanity, who was continually bestowing upon *Dennis* Pecuniary Favours, than to any Esteem for his just Merit. Having often heard him say, *it was of the two Evils, better to have* Dennis's *Flattery than his* Gall.
                                                              (pp. 135–7)

[William Bond], *Cobham and Congreve. An Epistle to Lord Viscount Cobham, In Memory of his Friend, The late Mr. Congreve* (London, 1730). Foxon B315.5. The poem is inscribed '*to the Lord* Cobham, *as an Anniversary Memorial designed in Honour of the Deceased, He being Mr.* Congreve's *best-loved Patron, and the* English Pollio *of him our* English Virgil . . . '.

> *Primâ dicte mihi, summâ dicende Camoenâ.* Hor.

SINCE my weak Voice in *Congreve*'s Praise preferr'd,
Will, thro' a *Virgil*, be by *Pollio* heard;[1]
Low Rhimes made sacred, to his Name I join,   ⎫
Fix'd to such Fame they'll make great Glories mine; ⎬
Such humblest Swains deserve for *saying* Hymns divine.[2] ⎭

    Far from these Lines, all low-Lamentings Be!
His Soul sprung, glad, to Immortality!
That, first from Heav'n commission'd, for our sake,
Men happier, wiser, better, came to make.
This Task long try'd, in each divinest Strain,
Call'd Home, It Heav'nwards took its flight again;
But first his Dirge he makes, and Fun'ral Rites,[3]
And, just at Death, as all thro' Life, Delights:
To Dust gives Dust, his Corps, pale Ashy-Pile!
Then upwards flies the *Phoenix* of our Isle.

    Now what vain Poet, what poor Rhiming Elf,
Shall mend what *Congreve* sung upon himself;
Sung in sweet Notes, o'er dying *Swans*, admir'd,
Which he, like them, just ended, and expir'd,
When they can drop such Tears upon the Dead
As *Amaryllis* for *Amintas* shed,[4]
Or with *Alexis*'[5] mourning Muse can vye,   ⎫
Then, nor till then, let vainest Voices try,   ⎬
To tune in Verse, a *Congreve*'s Elegy—   ⎭
    No, let us rather decent Feasts prepare,   ⎫
And Off'rings on his annual Day, now near,[6]   ⎬
Sing round his Shrine his Songs, and mend the *British* Ear: ⎭
Nor mend their Ear alone, but, thro' that part,
Sound, in good Sense, each Soul, and honest make each Heart.[7]
    Might, 'mong these sweet Memorials so prepar'd
By Nymphs and Heroes, my mean Voice be heard,
While Nymphs to sing his fair *Cecilia* chuse,
Heroes the *Birth* immortal of his *Muse*;
To whom were my Memorial justly due,

But you alone, *O Cobham*, only you?
   Thee early, and thee last his tuneful Breath,
Addrest with grateful Notes—till stopt by Death.
   Your *Art* of *Pleasing*,[8] in his earlier days
He writ and gain'd as you gain'd, all Men's Praise:
That hardest Art he paints with greatest ease,
In Lines so proper, that they'll ever please.
   By Friendship more, tho' vastly much by Wit,
That Art of pleasing, oft I've thought was writ;
From Him *it's* Master You,
By Sympathy[9] the charming Poem grew.
   Your Ways were One; Wits of congenial Parts!
That sure had Consanguinity of Hearts;
Both, of Delighting all Mankind, could boast,
But, knowing best that Art, each other most.
   'Twas fit it should be so—what other Two
Could be by Nature match'd more near than you?
A Bard that Sieges, Battles, Conquests writes,
And a young Hero fam'd at fifty Fights,[10]
That of his *Marlbro*'s Toils had Sharer been,
And War's whole Art as much as *Julius* seen.
   Thus *Horace* lov'd *Augustus*, thus was lov'd,[11]
Wit rais'd War's Glory, Glory Wit improv'd.
In all Heroic Times 'tis Wit's Reward,
That War's chief Champions love the noblest Bard.[12]
That this was, is, and will, nay must be *so*,
Witness the *Bard* your Friend, and your Friend *Marlborough*.[13]

. . .

   Say, *Cobham*, now,[31] where's now thy Hero's Soul?
Can he his Passions for true Fame controul?
Does he not read, rise raptur'd, sit again,
Then read, till fir'd afresh by some new Strain,
He makes, with well-pleas'd Mind, each past Campaign?
So, when his Harp divine[32] *Timotheus* strung,
And play'd, by *Dryden*'s Mouth, what *Phoebus* sung,
Warm'd into Flights of War young *Ammion* flew,
And fought, in Thought, his Battles o'er a-new?
   He read; new Life felt rising, while he read
His Deeds compar'd, with those most mighty Dead,
Whose Names, in Fame's immortal Life, enroll'd,
Their Glories date from Years, by thousands told,
And found in *Congreve*'s like Prophetic Song,

His soar'd as high, and sure to last as long.
But when to those warm well-judg'd Lines he came,
That *Churchill*'s justly fix'd o'er[33] *Cæsar*'s Fame;
Able no longer to contain, he said,
'I own my Toils and Hazards all repaid.
How short the Verse, that so great Truths displays! ⎫
They, like collected[34] Beams thro' Crystals blaze! ⎬
He, with the Lustre, gives the Fire of Praise! ⎭
Matchless as *Pindar*'s is my *Congreve*'s Rage,
That can contract an *Iliad* to a Page;
Yet so judicious, while he sings with Flame,
That where he heightens most, he most secures my Fame,
Cæsar's *Pharsalia* (true!) made Slaves,[35] but I
Fought at *Ramillia*'s Plain for precious Liberty.
Perish that mean-born Pride, that Bastard State,
Which aims to grow, by Men's Misfortunes, Great.
Sooner might I be beat,—myself made Slave,
Than subdue Realms, to ruin, not to save.
More Curses on such Chiefs than Blessings wait,
Those that their Triumphs love, the Traytors hate.
The Laurels *Congreve* brings me, I approve,
Sprung from, and nourish'd by my Country's Love.
My End, Man's Freedom gain'd; to crown the Scene
The Muse applauds me, and the World's best Queen.'

                              . . .

Yet this[51] *Mæonian*, and the *Mantuan* Flame,
And *Congreve*'s Modern Fire are all the same;
All from one Source, in diff'rent Ages came.
'Twas hard, indeed; thus coming last, to climb,
Against their advantageous Hill of Time;
Yet still we find Priority of Days
No Birth-right to Priority of Praise.
Change but each Age, when these three Poets shone,
Their Persons, to impartial Eyes, are O N E.
Congreve had *Homer* been, in *Homer*'s Time;
Homer been *Congreve*, now, and wrote such *British* Rhime.
Both could, with Magic Arts of Verse, alike,
Rouze Souls to Arms, and warlike Passions strike.
    Cobham, if Poesy's persuasive Parts,
Thus move (best Martial[52] Musick!) Heroes Hearts;
'Tis hard to say, we, rather of the two,
To You owe Poets, or to Poets You.

If your brave Acts make their bright Numbers shine,
They fire you to those Acts by Verse divine.
Pleas'd with both Song and Subject, Thus we know, ⎫
Arms and the Man (like *Virgil*'s sung) we owe, ⎬
Alike to *Congreve* and to *Marlborough*.   ⎭
    When his brave *Stilico*[53] bright *Claudian* sung,
Rome with the Poet's Praise and Hero's, rung:
Senates and Emperors, by Statutes wise,
Bad to their *Claudian* Bay-crown'd Statues rise.
Greater our Chief, sublimer was our Bard;
And shall more Merit meet with less Reward?
Shall it in *Britain* be the Poet's Doom,
To fall neglected for excelling *Rome*?
Forbid *That* Monarchs, Senates, Heroes, all,
Whom we can Brave, Great, Wise, and Noble call:
All, whose Deeds claim *that Verse*, which never dies, ⎫
Those Deeds, their Glories to immortalize;   ⎬
Else, may those Poems cease, they cease to prize!   ⎭
    That Pen, O Chief, which a Chief's Mind uprears,
Is to a Nation worth a Grove of Spears.
That Pen's the Spring, which makes War's Movement whole,
The Captain moves his Troops; the Bard their Captain's Soul.
    Think not, Thou Hero, this is strain'd too high,
In praise of *Everlasting* Poetry.
Fight all your Days, fresh Fame get ev'ry Day;
Not sung by *such* as *Congreve* 'twould decay.
                    . . .

Example pleads my Cause, since *Horace* too
Wrote to *Augustus*[58] what I write to you;
Tho', true! he did what I but wish to do.
Virgil's he rais'd, as I would *Congreve*'s Name,
And, where he *hit* the Mark, I'm proud to *aim*,
His Skill's superior, but our Task's the same.
                    . . .

The Argument *And* Design *of this*
EPISTLE.

TH E *main End of this Epistle is the Eulogy and Praise of Mr.* Congreve, *as an Exceller in all the different Branches of Poetry; but principally in that prime, noble One, which the Professors of that ingenious Art term the* Great Poetry; *that is to say, the* Heroic *or* Epic *and* Pindaric *kinds.*
                    . . .

The latter Part of the Epistle is wholly spent in praise of the Great of Heroic Poetry, and Epic Poets in general, and Mr. Congreve, *above all the Poets of that sort in our Time, in particular, in which Judgement of him, I am confirmed by the Authority of Mr.* Dryden, *and the Testimony of Mr.* Pope, *who speaking of their Translations of* Homer, *give him, in this Capacity, a pre-eminence to themselves.*

. . .

NOTES.

[1] INtimating that the same Friendship subsisting between Lord *Cobham*, and Mr. *Congreve*, as there was between the Noble *Pollio* and *Virgil*; any thing in the Praise of such a Poet, must be acceptable to such a Nobleman's Ear.

[2] These Hymns (as they are called by the Ancients) were usually sung, but sometimes only recited; and as I pretend not to write of these sublime Poems in a Style, beyond that, which consists of Rhimes, that are *Sermoni propiora*, I pretend to call it only *saying a Hymn*; to which *Pliny*, in the beginning of his Panegyric to the Emperor *Trahan* gives, methinks, sufficient Commendation for a *less modest Man* than myself, that is but an Epistolary Writer, to be contented with. He represents these bare Reciters as acceptable to the Gods as the sublimest Poets; they were reckoned by many of the Ancients as much inspired as the Poets themselves, whose Works they recited, as *Spondanus* tells us.

[3] Alluding to the last Poem Mr. *Congreve* wrote not long before he died to the Lord *Cobham*, on the Improvement of Time, in which are these Preparatory remarkable Lines on Death, in Imitation of *Horace*'s Epistle to *Alb. Tibullus*.

> — *Still think the present Day the last of Life.*
> *Who thus can think, and who such Thoughts pursues,*
> *Content may keep his Life, or calmly lose.*
> *All Proof 's of this thou mayst thy self receive:*
> *When Leisure from Affairs will give thee leave,*
> *Come see thy Friend,* &c.

[4] [5] These two Verses refer to those two Patterns for *Elegy* Writing, Mr. *Congreve*'s Pastorals on the Death of Q. *Mary*, and the Marquis of *Blandford*.

[6] Alludes to the Custom of the Antients, by Annual Celebrations of their Poets and Heroes.

[7] [8] Alludes to Mr. *Congreve*'s *Art of Pleasing*, and his last Copy of Verses, both address'd to Lord *Cobham*.

[9] The *Sympathy* here mentioned, and in some following Verses, representing the Friendships Great Personages naturally take to one another, makes a fine Chapter in *Gracian*'s Hero, and is delicately handled by several eminent Writers, quoted in the Notes upon that Chapter.

[10] *Fifty Fights*, &c. meaning a great Number, or near the Number, which is true.

[11] [12] [13] This is manifest by many Parts of *Horace*'s Works, particularly from the Esteem *Augustus*, had for him. Herein also the Friendship of Mr. *Congreve*, Lord *Cobham* and the Duke of *Marlborough* are represented.

[31] This Appeal to Lord *Cobham* is to shew the Power of Poetry, and refers still to Mr. *Congreve*'s Ode, on the Success of the Victorious Duke of *Marlborough*'s Arms.

[32] Mr. *Dryden*, in his *Alexander*'s Feast, very finely describes the Power of Music and Poetry over the Passions.

[33] All this Passage shews, that, in this Praise attributed to the Duke by Mr. *Congreve*, the principal Regard is, that the highest Parts of it are carried no farther, than what are truly, exactly, and religiously *just*.

[34] Alluding to Mr. *Congreve*'s Ode, *ut supra*.

[35] Here is given a very just Reason for preferring the Victories of *Marlborough* to those of *Cæsar*.

[51] Refers to the beginning of Mr. *Congreve*'s *Ode*, &c. viz.

> O well-known Sounds! O Melody the same,
> That kindled *Mantuan* Fire, and rais'd *Mæonian* Flame.

[52] *Poesy best Martial Musick*, &c. Many are the fine Descriptions of the *Power* of *Music*; such is that with which Mr. *Congreve* opens his Tragedy of the *Mourning Bride*.

[53] See *Claudian*'s Praise of *Stilico*.

[58] Alluding to *Horace*'s Epistle to *Augustus*, on the same Subject as this to Lord *Cobham*.

Jonathan Swift, *A Libel on D— D—. And a Certain Great Lord* ([Dublin], 1730), ll. 33–48.

> Thus, *Congreve* spent, in writing Plays,
> And one poor Office, half his Days;
> While *Montague*, who claim'd the Station
> To be *Mæcenas* of the Nation,
> For *Poets* open Table kept,
> But ne'er consider'd where they Slept.
> Himself, as rich as fifty *Jews*,
> Was easy, though they wanted Shoes;
> And, crazy *Congreve* scarce cou'd spare
> A Shilling to discharge his Chair,
> Till Prudence taught him to appeal
> From *Pæan*'s Fire to *Party* Zeal;
> Not owing to his happy Vein
> The Fortunes of his latter Scene,
> Took proper *Principles* to thrive;
> And so might ev'ry *Dunce* alive.

Matthew Pilkington, 'Phoibo-Bathros: Or, The Poet's-Well', in *Poems upon Several Occasions* (1730), 147–8. The frontispiece depicts the works of certain authors, including Congreve, being rescued from a well.

> First of the Time-surviving Train,
> Appears th'inimitable *Dean* ...
> Then *Pope*, and wise *Arbuthnot* gain
> Exalted Honours with the *Dean*:
> And soon the *Graces* snatch'd away
> The Strains of *Addison*, and *Gay*:
> And *Congreve*, *Dryden*, *Parnel*, *Prior*,
> Whose Writings boast *Apollo*'s Fire ...

Anon., The following poem is inscribed on a fly-leaf in each volume of Congreve's *Works* (1730) at CLC: *PR3360 D30. Also at O: MS Rawl. poet. 207, p. 156, but headed 'For Mr Congreves Tomb' and reading 'The Comedy . . .'.

Willm.
Congreve.

True Comedy (O, fatal Doom!)
Now lies (once Congreve) in this Tomb:
The Tragic Muse (his Mourning Bride)
Gives up the Ghost with sullen Pride
And lies in Buskin by his Side.

Joseph Spence, reporting Alexander Pope and Jacob Tonson, 28 or 29 November 1730. Spence, i. 50, 206, 208, 331.

Garth, Vanbrugh, and Congreve were the three most honest-hearted, real good men of the poetical members of the Kit-Cat Club.

None of our writers have a freer, easier way for comedy than Etherege and Vanbrugh. 'Now we have named all the best of them,' (after mentioning those two, Wycherley, Congreve, Fletcher, Jonson, and Shakespeare).

Aye, Mr. Tonson, he was Ultimus Romanorum! (with a sigh, speaking of poor Mr. Congreve, who died a year or two before).

Addison was so eager to be the first name that he and his friend, Sir Richard Steele, used to run down even Dryden's character as far as they could. Pope and Congreve used to support it.

William Egerton, Letter II (To Mrs Anne Oldfield), in *Faithful Memoirs of The Life, Amours and Performances, of . . . Mrs. Anne Oldfield* (London, 1731), 88–9.

Mr. C O N G R E V E, one of the greatest Ornaments of the Comic-Scene, after he had for several Years entertained the Town, with that Wit, and Humour, and Art, and Vivacity, which are so becoming of the Comic-Stage, produced at *last* a Play (*The Way of the World*) which, besides that it was equal to most of the *former* in those pleasant Humours which the Laughers so much require, had some certain Scenes in it, that were wrote with so much Grace and Delicacy, that they alone were worth an entire Comedy. What was the Event? the Play was hissed by barbarous Fools in the Acting; and an impertinent Trifle was brought on after it, which was acted with vast

Applause. This Treatment justly raised so much Indignation in Mr. CONGREVE, that he quitted the stage in Disdain, and it may almost be said, that, Comedy left it with him. And You, MADAM, very well know, that it is our Fondness of introducing whimsical Farces upon the Stage, which has so long kept Sir JOHN VANBRUGH's excellent Muse silent.... For, the Present, must be called the *Degenerate Age*. Where is now ... the Spirit, and Art, and Grace of CONGREVE?

Theophilus Cibber, Prologue to *The Lover. A Comedy* (1730), ll. 5–10. Performed at DL on 20 January 1731 (*LS* pt 3, i. 110).

> *Here* Congreve *oft' your gay Attention warms,*
> *Yet, oft' repeated, loses half his Charms.*
> *Still the same Round of Mirth fatigues your View;*
> *Old Pleasures tire, unless reliev'd by New;*
> *Reliev'd by New, again their Forms invite;*
> *And like old Friends, grow welcome to your Sight: ...*

Philo Grubstreet, Letter dated 7 May 1731, *The Grub-street Journal*, 27 May 1731.

... nor need *Grub-street* ever fear an enemy, while there is an Author of the *Contrast* [John Hoadley] to defend it. What honours ought you not to decree to perpetuate his memory, who has made such bold attacks against those formidable enemies, STEEL, CONGREVE, ROWE and the immortal SHAKESPEAR, not in the least fearing their wit, nor paying a decent regard to their Manes, and for the latter gives this reason: that *by G—he hates all Ghosts from the bloody Ghosts in Richard the 3d, to that in Tom Thumb.*

Anon., 'The Modern Poets ... By a young Gentleman of Cambridge', the *Gentleman's Magazine* (November 1731), 493.

> That BAYS to farce, turns his tragic strain,
> And easy CONGREVE imitates in vain ...

Anon., 'Epigram', the *Gentleman's Magazine* (August 1732), 921.

> Charg'd with writing of Bawdy, this was *F—g*'s Reply:
> 'Tis what DRYDEN and CONGREVE have done as well as I.
> 'Tis true—but they did it with this good Pretence,
> With an ounce of rank Bawdy went a Pound of good Sense ...

Anon., 'Apology for writing Bawdy expos'd', the *Gentleman's Magazine* (September 1732), 971.

> ... Thus modern poetaster fain would hit
> The sense of Wycherly, or Congreve's wit;
> But finding soon his labour all in vain,
> He imitates alone their smutty strain ...

Anon., 'A Reformation of Parnassus. A Tale. Serving to explain the Frontispiece', in *The Hive. A Collection of the most Celebrated Songs*. 4th edn. 4 vols. (1732), vol. i, sig. A2ᵛ.

> And to the flames a thousand *Satires* fly;
> But G A R T H , and Y O U N G , and D*ryden*, cou'd not die.
> Unnumber'd *Epic* songs the fires consume;
> Nor does the *Drama* meet a gentler doom:
> But A D D I S O N and C O N G R E V E favour find;
> To O T W A Y , L E E , and V*anbrugh* too, the muse is kind.

Anon., Prologue to *The Intriguing Courtiers; or, The Modish Gallants*. 2nd edn. (1732), ll. 1–4. The play may not have been acted.

> *W H E N Congreve wrote, and Wycherly the sage;*
> *When Betterton in Buskins trod the Stage;*
> *A Play was deem'd the Product of a Year:*
> *But now new Plays like Mushrooms do appear.*

A Miscellany on Taste ... *Mr. Congreve's fine Epistle on Retirement and Taste. Address'd to Lord Cobham*. Sold by G. Lawton [*sic*, for Lawton Gilliver], T. Osborn, and J. Hughes, 1732. Sigs. E1ᵛ–E3ᵛ. At p. 25 an introductory note to Congreve's 'Letter to Cobham' reads in part:

I shall now add Mr. Congreve*'s Epistle to the Lord Viscount* Cobham, *(on a Subject not much different) whereby the World will easily perceive that this Work* [i.e. Pope's] *falls as far short of Mr.* Congreve*'s as his Ode on* Music *did of Mr.* Dryden*'s* ...

Anon., *Memoirs of the Life of Robert Wilks, Esq.* 2nd edn. (1732), 24.

The Dramatick Writings of Mr. *Congreve* are certainly an Honour to the *English* Nation; the Excellence of their Design, the Sprightliness of their Wit, and the Purity and Politeness of their Language, set them justly above any other Performances in the same Way, that have succeeded them; and perhaps

we do not say too much, if we add, that they excell also all them that went
before them. I will not presume to say, that the Parts Mr. *Wilks* played in his
Old Batchelor, and the *Way of the World*, received any Addition from his
Acting, yet I may venture to assert, that he alone was equal to the
Performance, and that *Valentine* in *Love for Love* will hardly ever be so well
done again.

[Gilbert West], *Stowe, The Gardens of the Right Honourable Richard
Viscount Cobham* (London, 1732), 2.

> Here *Congreve*, Welcome Guest, oft chear'd the Days,
> With friendly Converse, or poetick Lays.

[Fettiplace Bellers], Prologue to *Injur'd Innocence* (1732), ll. 5–12.
Performed at DL on 3 February 1732 (*LS* pt 3, i. 187). The
immediately preceding lines refer to Athens and Rome.

> *From these our* stage, *transplanted, took its rise,*
> *The school of* virtue, *and the scourge of* vice:
> *Rude in its youth, till* Shakespear's *master-hand*
> *Taught the strong scene each passion to command;*
> *And* Dryden, Otway, Congreve, Southern, Rowe,
> *With honest heat bad all your bosoms glow.*
> *Establish'd names! who for revolving years,*
> *From every eye have drawn applauding tears.*

Anon., *Phino-Godol. A Poem. In Hudibrastick Verse* (London, 1732), 5,
8–12, 14–16. Foxon P261. The passage which precedes the poem was
originally published on 15 July 1732.

We hear that the Effigies of the late ingenious WILLIAM CONGREVE, Esq;
done in Wax-Work, at the Expence, of 200£. and which was kept at a person
of Quality's in St. James's, was broke to Pieces by the Carelessness of
a Servant in bringing it down Stairs last Monday Night. Daily-Post.
Numb. 3997.

> Thus, to a *single Paragraph*,
> (A simple Thing to make one laugh)
> I' th' DAILY-POST, a while ago,
> The World th' ensuing Word does owe....
> Examine we that Fabrick *dread*,
> The *Noblest* Store-House of the Dead,
> And 'mong the sev'ral Regions,

You'll find a Tomb of Comick *Con's*,
Erected to his Memory
By Great HOTONTA *worthily*;
Not *undeserv'd*—such Excellence
Most *justly* claims that Deference; ...
Pictures and *Prints* she now possesses,
And oft ingenious CONNY blesses;
But long nor this, nor that contents;
She something *more of Substance* wants;
Something that she might, with her Arm,
Stroke o'er, and Finger ev'ry Charm;
Might privately survey the Part,
That made the Conquest of her Heart. ...

   She now, judicious, gives a Plan
To raise in WAX the GOD-LIKE Man,
She shews his *Statue*, how't must be;
Assigns the Limbs their Symmetry.
Make *Face* and *Eyes*, says she, *just so*— ⎫
But let the *Nose* be *long*—you know— ⎬
Somewhat approaching—that below. ⎭

   The Figure form'd, with lively Grace, ⎫
Having for *Niche*, a *curious Case*, ⎬
She visits oft the *dear-lov'd* Place. ⎭
Breaths out her soft Desires, some say,
Full Half a Dozen Times a Day;
And thus, for Years, she has gone—on, ⎫
As if she never meant t' have done ⎬
Lamenting for APOLLO's Son. ⎭

   But, lo! a Judgment singular
Befals the *Wax-Work*, and the *Fair*;
Which, in the Sequel, we propose,
For your Instruction, to disclose. ...

IT happen'd, O! the fatal Day!
That TOM was order'd to convey
The Relick to another Room,
(Perhaps it better wou'd become.)
Poor Tom, being aukward, let it fall, ...
It came with such a Swank to th' Ground,
That scarce a Morsel whole is found.
He strives to patch it up again,
But all his Labour is in vain; ...
'Tis sure HOTONTA, if she cou'd,

Wou'd have exacted Blood for Blood;
At least, his Sight she wou'd not bear,
Who'd been her C O N N Y 's *Murderer.*
 And now sh' indulges wild Dispair,
And frets, and fumes, and rends her Hair.
No Victuals wou'd she eat that Day,
And, tho' she fasted, cou'd not pray.
Her House, a House of Lamentation,
Where every thing's in Fermentation,
No Peace, or Quiet, find you there;
Both High and Low the Sorrow share....
 And is the dear, good Man, then lost?
And am I to be always crost?...
Ye Gods! ye Trees! ye murmuring Brooks!
Be ye my Comfort, with my Books.
Henceforth, H O T O N T A , Man detest,
No longer with thy C O N N Y blest;
Henceforth renounce the worthless Sex,
Nor let 'em more thy Peace perplex;
But use the Slaves, that prostrate fall,
As thou wert wedded to them all.
 O, dearest C O N N Y ! for thy Sake,
This Resolution sad I make.
O Shade immortal! (does she cry)
Twice it was given to Thee to die.
A second Burial thou shalt have;
Nobler shall be thy second Grave;
Encircled with the Muses Nine,
Their darling Friend, as well as *mine.*
 Come, dear C O N N E L I A , come, my Love,
Help me the *Manes* to remove.
Let 'em no longer on the Floor
Be strew'd about, or trampled o'er;
Let us collect them, and bemoan;
For thou must give me Groan for Groan....

Philalethes [i.e. Henry Fielding?], *The Daily Post*, 31 July 1732, replying to Publicus, *Grub-street Journal*, 13 July 1732, notes that more indecencies will be found 'in *Dryden, Congreve, Wycherly, Vanbrugh, Cibber,* and all the best Writers of *Comedy* ... to those of a most *Witty, Learned,* and *Reverend Writer of our own Age* [i.e. Swift]'.

Anon., *Grub-street Journal*, 3 August 1732.

> Charg'd with writing of bawdy, this was F[ielding]'s reply:
> Tis what DRYDEN and CONGREVE have done as well as I.
> Tis true—but they did it with this good pretence,
> With an ounce of rank bawdy went a pound of good sense . . .

Voltaire, François Marie Arouet de, *Letters Concerning the English Nation* (London, 1733), 188–9, 224–5, 235–6. The index, at sig. S1ᵛ, describes Congreve as 'A famous *English* Poet. Author of some excellent Comedies.' Swift's *A Proposal for Correcting, Improving, and Ascertaining the English Tongue* (1712), alluded to in the third extract, makes no mention of Congreve. His membership of Swift's academy is inferred by Voltaire.

Voltaire was in London from 1726 to 1729. While successive English editions (in which he had no hand) repeated the text as given below, Voltaire himself in 1739 clearly came to think his criticism of Congreve ill-conceived. In the first French edition to receive his fully considered correction, *Œuvres de M. de Voltaire*, 4 vols. (Amsterdam: Et. Ledet et Cie, 1738–9), he deleted the passage 'He was infirm . . . Piece of Vanity.' as it had been translated into earlier French editions. See *Lettres Philosophiques*. Édition critique, avec une introduction et commentaire par Gustave Lanson. Nouveau tirage revu et complété par André M. Rousseau. 2 tom. (Paris: Librairie Marcel Didier, 1964), i, pp. xv, xix–xx; ii. 108–9.

THE late Mr. *Congreve* rais'd the Glory of Comedy to a greater Height than any English Writer before or since his Time. He wrote only a few Plays, but they are all excellent in their kind. The Laws of the Drama are strictly observ'd in them; they abound with Characters all which are shadow'd with the utmost Delicacy, and we don't meet with so much as one low, or coarse Jest. The Language is every where that of Men of Honour, but their Actions are those of Knaves; a Proof that he was perfectly well acquainted with human Nature, and frequented what we call polite Company. He was infirm, and come to the Verge of Life when I knew him. Mr. *Congreve* had one Defect, which was, his entertaining too mean an Idea of his first Profession, (that of a Writer) tho' 'twas to this he ow'd his Fame and Fortune. He spoke of his Works as of Trifles that were beneath him; and hinted to me in our first Conversation, that I should visit him upon no other Foot than that of a Gentleman, who led a Life of Plainness and Simplicity. I answer'd, that had he been so unfortunate as to be a mere Gentleman I should never have come to see him; and I was very much disgusted at so unseasonable a Piece of Vanity.

MR. *Congreve*'s Comedies are the most witty and regular, those of Sir *John Vanbrugh* most gay and humourous, and those of Mr. *Wycherley* have the greatest Force and Spirit. It may be proper to observe, that these fine Genius's never spoke disadvantageously of *Moliere*; and that none but the contemptible Writers among the *English* have endeavour'd to lessen the Character of that great comic Poet.

. . .

The *English* have so great a Veneration for exalted Talents, that a Man of Merit in their Country is always sure of making his Fortune.... Mr. *Addison* was rais'd to the Post of Secretary of State in *England*. Sir *Isaac Newton* was made Warden of the Royal Mint. Mr. *Congreve* had a considerable *Employment.
    *Secretary for *Jamaica*.

. . .

THE celebrated Dean *Swift* form'd a Design ... to found an Academy for the *English* Tongue upon the Model of that of the *French*.... Those only wou'd have been chosen Members of it, whose Works will last as long as the *English* Tongue, such as ... Mr. *Congreve* who may be call'd their *Moliere* ...

Anon., *Ingratitude to Mr. Pope* (London, 1733), 8–9. Alleging Pope's envy of Addison, the writer continues:

That Satire writ by *Maevius* brings to my Remembrance what Mr. *Congreve* said *inter alia*, viz. *That he was in great Hopes of working a perfect Cure upon* Mævius; *for the* Violence *of his* peevish *and* sowre Temper *began to abate, nor were his* Malice *and* Ill-nature *so* predominant *as they had been*: But when a Gentleman shew'd him the Satire on the deceas'd Mr. *Addison*, Mr. *Congreve* sighing said, *From this Day forward I number him among the* Incurables.

Anon., *The Court Parrot. A New Miscellany, in Prose and Verse* (London, 1733), 13–22.

THE
SECRET HISTORY
OF
Henrada Maria Teresa.

HENRADA MARIA TERESA, was descended from a very ancient and honourable Family, on her Father's Side, but her Mother was of low Extraction. This Gentleman, having but a small Estate of paternal Inheritance, was obliged to cut out his Fortune with his Sword, which was the Fate of many others; he was a person of great Conduct and Courage, and his gallant Behaviour soon rendered him conspicuous in the Eyes of the World. He had a lively and enterprizing Genius, was tall, well-shaped, and his Complexion was so fair mixed with a due Proportion of red, and there was such a Symmetry of Parts in his Face, that he obtained the Name of *Fair*.

In his younger Years he married *Jenina*, whose Mother had but an indifferent Character; but the Daughter had a plentiful Fortune, was a Woman of a deep Penetration, an aspiring Nature, and always pushed herself forward, hoping that she should thereby be one Day advanced, and her Husband promoted to some considerable Post in the Army: Nor was she deceived in her Expectation, for she had wormed herself into the Affection and good Graces of the Empress's Sister, who gave her not only a Place under her at Court, but made her (as it were) her Companion, and intrusted her with all her Secrets.

She soon gained the Ascendant over this Royal Lady, and nothing was transacted without her Consent and Approbation. She was a Woman of so much Policy that she prevailed with the Emperor to make her Husband a *Count*, and indeed his Conduct and personal Bravery rendered him worthy of that Title. He commanded in Chief the Confederate Forces, when the Empire was threatened with a total Destruction upon an Invasion of their Enemies, whom he frequently routed, and at last forced them to quit the Country, and in the most supplicant Manner to sue for Peace. Having preserved the Empire from the impending Ruin that was over its Head, and compelled the Enemy to retire shamefully into their own Country, having suffered many ignominious Defeats, he had several Places of great Profit and Honour given to him, and was advanced to a higher Degree of Dignity. The Income of the many Posts he enjoy'd, together with the Advantages that accrued from the War, rendered him the most wealthy Person in the Empire. As there is no Man without one Fault or another, so the greatest Imperfection this Nobleman had, was Coveteousness; but in reality he was not so very penurious as People represented him, nor indeed so liberal as his Wealth and Dignity required. He considered that he had several Daughters, and as he did intend to match them with Families of high Rank, so he resolved to give them Portions adequate to his own and their Husbands Qualities.

Henrada was his Eldest Daughter, whose Wit and Beauty attracted the Hearts of many Noblemen, particularly of the young Count *Adolphus*, the Eldest Son of Count *Gustains Adolphus*. This young Nobleman had all the Qualifications necessary to form a complete Gentleman; but above all he was singularly remarkable for the noble Endowments of the Mind, he was strictly Virtuous, and strictly Chaste; Charitable, Even-temper'd, Good-natur'd, and a most kind and indulgent Husband. He esteemed himself extreamly happy in his Marriage with *Henrada*, and she was well pleased with her Felicity of having espoused a young Nobleman, who had so many shining Excellencies, and manifested such conjugal Tenderness, that she was sensible of her being the only Object of his Desire. Thus they lived for many Years; and indeed might have lived many more in the same State had *Henrada* been so prudent to have adhered to virtuous Principles.

As she was a Lady of Wit and Spirit, she took a secret Pleasure in reading Poetry, of which she was a good Judge; but the Words of *Congravino*, gave her the greatest Satisfaction. To give him what is due to his Character, he was one of the best of the Age, and a peculiar Talent in writing Comedies, wherein he never failed of some double *Entendre's*, to raise a becoming Blush in the Fair Sex: And when he made Love his Subject, he writ such Softness, that he made a deep Impression in their Hearts. This was the Fate of *Henrada*, who was captivated with his Poems. If, says she, the bare Reading the Works of this Gentleman, can have such an Effect upon our Minds, what Wonders must he needs be capable of performing, when we hear the Words from his own Mouth? From that Day she studied how there might be an Interview between them; and as Secrecy was a material Point in this Case, it was some time before she could accomplish her Design: At last she determined to write to him, which she did to the following Effect.

Signior Congravino,
IF *you have the Spirit of an* English-man, *you will not refuse a Woman's Challenge; meet me therefore this Evening in the* Inamorate's *Grove at the Back of the Palace.* Adieu.

She sent this Letter by a trusty Servant, with Orders to deliver it into *Congravino's* own Hand, who as soon as he had read it, said, Give my humble Service to the Lady, and let her know that her Commands shall be punctually obey'd.

This was acceptable News to *Henrada*, who, in reading her Favourite's Poems, had let the Time pass away imperceptibly 'till it was almost Six o' Clock. She then began to prepare herself for a Sally, and disguising herself in the best Manner she was able, and yet not to appear as a Person of the inferior Sort, she hasten'd to the Place of Rendezvous, accompanied by the Female Servant whom she intrusted with the Secret.

In a few Minutes after she came thither, she saw *Congravino* coming towards the Grove, upon whose Approach the Servant retired, and play'd the Part of a Centinel to give an Alarm, if any Person approached to interrupt their Conversation. As soon as he had the Honour of comming up to the Lady, whose Face was covered with a Veil, he said, Madam, if you are the Heroine, who sent me a Challenge this Day to meet you at this Place, I desire to know your Commands; but if you are some other Lady, who have made an Assignation here, I will instantly withdraw: For as you have the Right of

Possession, as being the First, it would be indecent, as well as injust, to interrupt you.—Sir, answered *Henrada*, I flatter myself in saying, that the Conversation of so polite a Gentleman as the celebrated *Congravino*, cannot fail of a kind Reception from me, who am the person that sent you the Challenge. They then seated themselves on a Green Bank, and when they had talked half an Hour about one Affair or another, she pulled out of her Pocket a Volume of his Writings, and turning to a particular Page, which treated of Love, told him, that she had read that Piece with an inexpressible Pleasure, but desired she might hear it repeated by him, for then she was sure it would receive an Addition of many Beauties, which she had not Sense enough to discover. He readily complied with her Request, and laying every Emphasis in its proper Place, raised such an Emotion in the young Countess, that she could not refrain from squeezing his Hand, and thereby letting him know what an Extacy she was in. To work up her Imagination to the Height, hoping thereby to gratify his Inclinations, he turned to some other Parts of the Book, which he read with such a Grace, that she had certainly yielded to any thing he would desire, if they had not been interrupted by the sudden Approach of her Servant, who nevertheless hem'd and coughed twenty times before she enter'd the Grove. She went directly to her Lady, and whispering said, Madam, I perceive a Gentleman steering his Course this Way, and by his Stature, Air, and Mien, I am persuaded that he is my Lord the Count. Go back, says the Lady, and bring the best Intelligence you can; then turning to *Congravino*, she said, Sir I have too much Reason to apprehend a Discovery, and therefore must retreat in Time, but as a Signal of the Value I have for you, I request you to wear this for my Sake. She then took a Diamond Ring off her Finger, which she presented to him, and which he received upon his Knees, and begg'd the Favour of kissing her Hand. My Hand, said she! there is but little Satisfaction in such a Trifle: And thereupon she unveiled her Face. By all the Saints above, Madam, said he, if I were to draw the Picture of *Venus* to the utmost Perfection, I wou'd only aim to copy from such a beautiful Original. Upon this he embraced her, kissed her with Extacy, and vow'd eternal Fidelity. The young Countess promised he should hear quickly from her, and upon her Servant's Return, she went out at a private Part of the Grove, and was not detected by her Lord.

Contrary to the practise of most Persons of Quality, *Henrada* performed her Promise, for the very next Day she sent him a Letter, wherein she acquainted him, that she would be at his House in cog that Afternoon. She came punctual to the Time appointed, and was received with all the tender Respect imaginable. They pass'd the Evening in Gallantry, and before they parted, they had the Satisfaction of revelling together for the space of two Hours. The Countess in a short Time perceived the blooming Hopes of their unlawful Pleasures, which prov'd to be a Pregnancy, and thereupon having a Meeting to consult what was proper to be done, they concluded to go to *Aix le Chapele*, where there was not so great a Probability of their being discovered, as there might be if they went to the *Spaw*. However they did not think it convenient to travel together, and therefore concluded that the Countess should set out first, and her Lover follow her the next Day. Henrada travelled by slow Stages on purpose to give *Congravino* an Opportunity of overtaking her, which he did in about two Days Journey from *Aix le Chapele*; they dined together, and in the Afternoon he took his Leave and set forward. When he had arrived at *Aix*, he hired a first Floor consisting of six Rooms, and going to meet the Countess, he seperated her trusty Servant from the rest, and slipt a Letter into her Hand, directed for her Lady, wherein he acquainted her with what Steps he had taken; and advised what Method to pursue. In the Evening *Henrada* arrived at the Lodgings, but was informed that a Gentleman had taken the first Floor: The young Countess seemed surprized, but on a sudden, with a smiling Countenance, she said, If he be a true *Chevaliere*, he will surrender five Rooms to a Lady in my Distress, and thereupon she took Possession of them. *Congravino* being informed by the Mistress of the House of what had passed, and that she could not possibly refuse a Lady of her Quality, to whose Family she was under many Obligations, he said, He would be content with the single Room, and hoped the Countess would permit him to acknowledge the Honour she had done him in accepting the Lodgings. He was introduced immediately, and after mutual Complements, they passed the Time away in discoursing on various Subjects, 'till Supper was laid upon the Table. When the Cloth was removed, *Henrada* told him, That there was a greater Conveniency in the Lodgings, than he was aware of; for a Door opened out of her Bed-chamber upon the Stair-Case, opposite to his, whereby they might have an Opportunity of conversing together without Suspicion.

They continued here the whole Season, to the great Joy and Satisfaction of each other; and tho' they were known by several Persons of Quality, yet they carried on their Intrigue with such Subtlety, that they did not give the least Occasion for Censure. They now prepared to return home, and began their Journey after the same Manner as when they set out.

The Kind, the Tender, and the Affectionate *Adolphus* received his Lady with open Arms; whether he had received any Information of her Behaviour, is what History does not mention; however he was so cautious, that he did not give his Domesticks any Umbrage to suspect his Uneasiness. A little before Bed-time, looking very intently upon the young Countess, he said, Either my Eyes deceive me, or your Ladyship is with Child. Your Lordship is much in the Right, she replied, without shewing any Manner of Concern. Then, Madam, said the young Count, I hope your Ladyship will give me the Satisfaction of knowing the Father's Name. As she would not comply with his Desire, they were seperated by Consent from Bed, and in that State they continued for twelve Years, and kept a constant Correspondance with *Congravino*. At length *Henrada* was delivered of a Daughter, of whom all the Care imaginable was taken; and she was brought up in the House with her Mother. Much about this Time the Countess's Father died, whereby his Titles descended to her, and with them, a large Estate to support the Dignity. Little Miss, encreasing in Years, had the Happiness of pleasing her Mother, who perceived in her the Wit and Sprightliness of the Father, who dying a few Years after, placed such an entire Confidence in *Henrada*, that he made her his sole Heiress and Executrix, not in the least doubting but she would take care of his Daughter. 'Tis true, he did not recommend the Child to her, which he imagined would be fruitless, being persuaded that *Henrada* would always look upon her with an Eye of Tenderness and Affection. She took as much Care of her Education, as if she had been her Legitimate-Daughter, and no Pains or Cost were spared to make her an accomplished young Woman. She would not permit her to be called by any other Name than her Father's, for whom she retained a grateful Remembrance, and, as it is said, shed many Tears, when she looked earnestly upon Miss: She took Care to have her imbibe the most virtuous Principles, and to be instructed in the strictest Rules of Morality, that her Mind might not be formed only with an Idea of what was Good, but cultivated with the practice of it; and also to have an Abhorrance of entertaining a Notion of any thing tending to Vice or Dishonesty, even in the most minute Point. A Mind thus framed in its tender Years, must render the Person the Delight of Mankind, especially when arrived to Maturity.

Whether *Henrada* laid too much to Heart the Death of *Congravino*, I cannot take upon me to determine; she did not survive him above five Years; at last being seized with a lingring Distemper, she was advised to take the Country Air, but relapsing several times, and her Constitution being greatly impaired by her Sickness, she was at last constrained to pay the last Debt to Nature.

When she was sensible of the Approach of Death, she called for Miss, gave her her Blessing, and having made her Will, left her all her Father's Estate, by whom she was impowered to leave it to whom she pleased, and made a very large Addition to it. She died a Penitent, and was sorry she had wronged so good a Husband as *Adolphus*.

Samuel Richardson, *The Apprentice's Vade Mecum* (1734), 12.

Genteel Comedy (even in which sound Morals were seldom enough consider'd) has long left the Stage, as well as the nobler Tragic Muse: And all our late Heroines of the Drama, have been fetch'd from *Newgate* and *Bridewell*. The celebrated *Congreve*'s *Niky*, *Horner*, and others that I might name, were odious and detestable Characters ... but then there was so much Wit mingled with the Immorality, as made it pass when we could get no better.

Alexander Pope, *An Epistle from Mr. Pope, to Dr. Arbuthnot* (London, 1734), 7–8.

> But why then publish? *Granville* the polite,
> And knowing *Walsh*, would tell me I could write;
> Well-natur'd *Garth* inflam'd with early praise,
> And *Congreve* lov'd, and *Swift* endur'd my Lays...

Anon., in *The Prompter*, no. 14, 27 December 1734.

SEVERAL *sober Midwives* have remarked, with Astonishment, that the *Impressions* of *Men*, in this Island, seem of late to be stamp'd in *Little*—Our Massy old-fashioned *Folios* in Calve's Leather, are reduced to neat *Pocket Volumes*; and we can peruse nothing above *Twelves*, or *Octavo*.

. . .

I TAKE this publick Opportunity to beg Pardon of a celebrated *Actress*, who begins the Tragedy of the *Mourning Bride*, with this extraordinary *Encomium* on the Power of *Musick*.

> *Mu–u–sick has Cha–a–a–rms to so–o–o–th a savage Breast,*
> *To so–o–often Rocks, or be–e–end the* Knotted Oak

I MUST confess, I was under the Mistake of supposing this Lady *affected*, when I heard her *whining* out good Verses, in a *Drawl* so unpleasingly extended: Little dreamt I, all the while, that she was *topping* her *Character*, and deriving her Ideas of *Musick*, from the fashionable Present State of the *Art*, as it flourishes under Royal Encouragement.

Lady Mary Wortley Montagu, Letter to John Arbuthnot, 3 January 1735. *Letters*, ii. 100.

I wish you would advise poor Pope to turn to some more honest livelihood than libelling.... Can any thing be more detestable than his abuseing poor Moor scarse cold in his Grave, when it is plain he kept back his Poem while he liv'd for fear he should beat him for it? This is shocking to me thô of a man I never spoke to, and hardly knew by sight; but I am seriously concern'd at the worse scandal he has heap'd on Mr. Congreve, who was my Freind, and whom I am oblig'd to Justify because I can do it on my own knowledge, and which is yet farther, being witness of it from those who were then often with me, that he was so far from loveing Pope's Rhyme, both that and his Conversation were perpetual jokes to him, exceeding despicable in his opinion, and he has often made us laugh in talking of them, being particularly pleasant on that subject.

Anon., in *The Prompter*, no. 34, 7 March 1735.

[In Mrs E. Cooper's *The Fair Libertine*] L A D Y *Bellair*, and *Lady Lurcher*, have a strong Resemblance, in several Places, with Mrs. *Millamant* and Mrs. *Marwood*, in the *Way of the World* . . .

'P.', in *The Prompter*, no. 105, 11 November 1735.

T H E *Double Dealer*, like all *Congreve*'s Plays, abounds in *Wit*: It has, besides, the Advantage of a Plot, which, tho' very *intricate*, is not in the least *confused*, and is conducted in so masterly a Manner, that it *thickens* naturally from the Circumstances in which the Characters of the Drama are placed, and *is unravelled* by the same happy Intervention of *probable* and *expected* Incidents. Each *Light Character* has likewise a pleasing Vein of Humour running through it, strongly *distinguished*, yet theatrically P L A Y I N G into each other.

N E V E R T H E L E S S, with all this Merit, the Play is *fundamentally bad*, because its Fable, like that of *Alexander*, is *ill-chosen*; and a *Play*, where the *Fable* is *ill-chosen*, can never be *good*.

T H E principal Character, that of *Maskwell*, or the *Double Dealer*, is out of the Province of Comedy: No *Vice* can be introduced there, that does not result from some *Passion*—A cold, deliberate, thinking Villain, that *preponderates* every *Stroke*, and *consults* his *Understanding*, how *best* to *perpetrate* it, and laughs at the very Notion of Virtue, is only to be corrected by T Y B U R N.—*Maskwell* is the most consummate Villain that can be painted, without one single Passion that might soften his original Deformity.—'*He is kept by his Patron's Wife, whom he loves not—Not content with receiving, each day, fresh Proofs of his increasing Friendship, and aggravating his Villany by fresh Wrongs, in Proportion as his Patron's Confidence in him administers fresh Occasions to do it, he is under-hand at work to make him disinherit his Nephew, (who is his Bosom-Friend, and by whom he is employed, as a trusty Agent, for very contrary Purposes) and settle his Estate upon him, with his Niece,* whom his Friend is in love with.—*He sticks at nothing, and is so* base-principled, *that the* very Woman *that* maintains him *is not only* deceived *in her Turn, but by him who was privy to her Passion for her Husband's Nephew (a fine Character for Comedy, by the bye, that of a Woman who* wrongs her Husband with *one Man, at the same time that she is* in love with *another,) put upon endeavouring to gratify that Passion, and, in case of Disappointment,* presented with a Dagger to M U R T H E R *him!*' In short, these two Characters are so *deformed* and *diabolical*, and the *Whole* such *a Complication of Villainy*, and the lighter Characters so *obscene*, that Comedy blushes to have received, with a *Stain* not to be *washed out, a mortal Stab* from one of her favourite Sons. To sum up the Contents of the principal Chracters—in a few Words—

I N *Maskwell* we have, (besides his Proneness to *Murther*) *Adultery, Ingratitude* to his Patron, *Treachery* to his Bosom-Friend, *Deceit* to the Woman who (in the Grossness of his Ideas) *keeps him*, and to the young Lady whom he proposes to marry;—with (not a *bare Want*, but) an *argumented Rejection* of all the Principles of common *Honour* and *Honesty,* as well as *Humanity.*

I N Lady *Touchwood,* (but in her Vice is made an Effect of strong Passions) the same *murtherous* Disposition, together with the *actual Commission* of *Adultery* with one Man through *Intemperance*, and a strong Desire to *commit* it with *another*, through (what she calls) *Love.*

O F Four Ladies in the Drama, *Two more* treat the *Audience* with *Adultery*; but their Characters are so drawn, that their *Adultery* seems less than *Simple Fornication* in another, not being of Weight enough to give any of their Actions the Stamp of *Virtue* or *Vice.*—But there may be some Alleviation to their Case, for the Poet claims a Right of *Prescription* in behalf of Cuckoldom, where-ever he introduces a *Coxcomb*, a *Fool*, or an *Old Man, Married.*

W H A T then could justify the Revival of this Comedy? Nothing *critically* or *morally.* What apologize for it? The infinite *Humour* that shoots, like a Porcupine's Quills, from *every Part of every one of the Comick Characters*! Lord and Lady *Froth*, Sir *Paul Plyant* and his Lady, together with Mr. *Brisk*, are Characters (abstracted from their *moral* and *obscene* Failings) such as Comedy derives, with *Beauty* and *Propriety*, its greatest Power of *Pleasing* from. In favour therefore of the T R U L Y C O M I C Genius of the Play, we'll suppose the *Manager* that revived it rather weighing in his Judgment, whether the *Bad* might not be tolerated on account of the *Good*, than ignorant of the *Bad*, and led into the Mistake of *Reviving it*, from the Approbation given too commonly to *loose* and *immoral* Scenes by the Generality of Audiences, when *heightened* by *Wit, Humour*, or *Action.*

T H E *Word* therefore to be *given him*, is, henceforward not to *represent Vicious Characters* because they may be *indulged* by the *Corruption* of the *Times*, but to reform the *Corruption* of the *Times* by Scenes adapted to that Purpose. Now the Stage is not to punish such Vices as are *cognizable* by Course of Law, and *punitively terminable* at *Tyburn*: Poetical Justice extends only to such as the Law cannot lay hold off, such as are to be tried in F O R O C O N S C I E N T I Æ, where the Delinquent, being strongly touched by a Resemblance of Himself, may amend.

'P.', in *The Prompter*, no. 115, 16 December 1735.

To what but to such an *early Notice* of *Genius* and *Merit*, do we owe our present *Pope*, the late Mr. *Congreve*, Dean *Swift*, and many others, that might be named? These did not shine out at once, *Stars of the Magnitude* they appeared afterwards to be. They but GLIMMER'D, and their Influence was FELT. They were taken from their narrow Sphere, and PLACED in that of the *Great*. They were *cherished* by their particular Patrons, *recommended* by them to others, and *honour'd* by all.

Thomas Southerne, 'Memoirs relating to Mr. Congreve written by Mr. Thomas Southerne and communicated to me [Thomas Birch] by the Hands of Dr Thomas Pellet, January 12th 1735/6.' L: Add. MS 4221, f. 341.

Mr Will: Congrave was the Son of a younger brother of a good old family in Staffordshire, who was employd in the Stewardship of part of the great estate of ye Earl of Burlington in Ireland, where he resided many years, his only son the Poet was born in that Country, went to the free school at Kilkenny, and from thence to Trinity College in Dublin, where he had the advantage of being educated under a polite schollar, and ingenious Gentleman Dr St George Ash, who was after Provost of that College, then Bp of Clogh[ar], and then Bp of Derry. This Bp had the great good fortune of haveing the two famousest Witts his pupills the most extraordinary Dr Swift, Dean of St Patricks, and Mr Will: Congreve, tho not at the same time. Mr Congreve was of the Middle Temple, his first performance was an Novel, calld incognita, Then he began his Play the old Batchelor haveing little Acquaintance withe the traders in that way, his Cozens recommended him to a friend of theirs, who was very usefull to him in the whole course of his play, he engagd Mr Dryden in its favour, who upon reading it sayd he never saw such a first play in his life, but the Author not being acquainted with the stage or the town, it woud be pity to have it miscarry for want of a little Assistance: the stuff was rich indeed, it wanted only the fashionable cutt of the town. to help that Mr Dryden, Mr Arthur Manwayring, and Mr Southerne red it with great care, and Mr Dryden putt it in the order it was playd, Mr Southerne obtaind of Mr Tho: Davenant who then governed the Playhouse, that Mr Congreve shoud have the privilege of the Play house half a year before his play was playd, wch I never knew allowd any one before: it was playd with great success that play made him many friends, Mr Montacue, after Ld Hallyfax, was his Patron, putt him into the Commission for hackney coaches, and then into the Pipe Office, and then gave him a Patent place in the Customs of 600 Pds per ann. and Secretary to Jamaica, yt payd him 700 Pounds a year by deputy on the Exchange at Lond

Pierre Bayle, *A General Dictionary, Historical and Critical*, ed. John Peter Bernard, Thomas Birch, John Lockman, George Sale, and others. 10 vols. (1734–41), iv. 427–9. Material in the marginal and foot notes offers no new evidence and is therefore omitted.

CONGREVE (WILLIAM), an eminent English Poet, was the son of Mr. Will. Congreve, a younger brother of an ancient and good family in Staffordshire, who was employed in the Stewardship of part of the great estate of the Earl of Burlington in Ireland, where he resided many years. His only son the Poet was born in that Kingdom in 1672, and educated at the Free-school at Kilkenny, from whence he was sent to Trinity-College in Dublin, where he had the advantage of being under the tuition of a Gentleman well skilled in polite Learning, Dr. St. George Ash, afterwards Provost of that College, and successively Bishop of Clogher and Derry, who had likewise the honour of having Dr. Jonathan Swift, Dean of St. Patrick's, another of his pupils, though not at the same time with Mr. Congreve. Upon Mr. Congreve's coming to England, he was entered in the Middle-Temple, where he began the study of the Law, but was diverted from a vigorous prosecution of it by his inclination to polite Literature and Poetry. His first performance was a Novel intitled, *Incognita, or Love and Duty reconciled*; and he soon after began his Comedy of the *Old Batchelor*. But having little acquaintance with the traders in that way, he was recommended by his cousins to Mr. Thomas Southerne, who was very useful to him in the whole course of the Play, and engaged Mr. Dryden in its favour. That great man upon reading it declared, "that he never saw such a first Play in his life; but that the Author not being acquainted with the stage or the town, it would be a pity to have it miscarry for want of a little assistance. The stuff was rich indeed; it wanted only the fashionable cut of the town." Mr. Dryden, Mr. Arthur Mainwaring, and Mr. Thomas Southerne read it with great care; and Mr. Dryden put it in the order in which it was played; and Mr. Southerne obtained of Mr. Thomas Davenant, who then governed the Theatre Royal in Drury-Lane, that Mr. Congreve should have the privilege of the house half a year before his Comedy was acted; a favour never granted before. It was at last acted in 1693 with universal applause, and ushered into the world with a commendatory by Mr. Southerne, Mr. Marsh, and Mr. Bevil Higgons, tho' when he wrote it he was but nineteen years of age, and but one and twenty, when it was brought upon the stage. The reputation of it gained him a great many considerable friends, and particularly Mr. Montague, afterwards Lord Hallifax, who procured him to be appointed one of the Commissioners of the Hackney-Coaches, and then gave him a place in the Pipe-Office, and afterwards a Patent-place in the Customs of six hundred pounds *per annum*, and the Post of Secretary to Jamaica, which paid him seven hundred and nine pounds a year on the Exchange at London. In 1694 his *Double Dealer* was acted at the Theatre in Drury-Lane, and together with his former Comedy, was honoured with the presence of Queen Mary, upon whose death December the 28th 1694, our Author wrote a beautiful Pastoral intitled, *The Mourning Muse of Alexis; A Pastoral lamenting the Death of Queen Mary*. The year following the State-factions grew so high, that the company divided, and Mr. Betterton being the most injured person, Mr. Congreve gave him the Comedy of *Love for Love* to open the New Theatre, which Mr. Betterton had made out of the Tennis-Court in Portugal-Row in Lincoln's-Inn-Fields. His next performance was the *Mourning Bride*, a Tragedy, which was likewise acted in Lincoln's-Inn-Fields in 1697, and dedicated to the Princess Anne of Denmark, afterwards Queen. In 1698 his four Plays were attacked from the Press by Mr. Collier in his *View of the Immorality and Profaneness of the English Stage*; in an answer to which Mr. Congreve wrote *Amendments of Mr. Collier's false and imperfect Citations &c. from the* Old Batchelor, Double Dealer, Love for Love, Mourning Bride. *By the Author of those Plays*. London 1698 in 8vo. Mr. Collier replied to this piece in his *Defence of the* Short View of the Profaneness and Immorality of the English Stage &c. *Being a Reply to* Mr. Congreve's Amendments, &c. *and to the* Vindication *of the* Author *of the* Relapse. London 1699 in 8vo. The last of his Plays was the *Way of the World*, acted by Mr. Betterton's Company in Lincoln's-Inn-Fields, and dedicated to the Earl of Montague. This excellent Comedy met with very indifferent success the first night of its being exhibited, but afterwards was received in a manner suitable to its merit. He revised Mr. Dryden's Translation of Virgil's *Æneis*. He wrote likewise a *Masque* intitled, *The Judgment of Paris*; and an Opera, intitled *Semele*, which was never performed, but excellently set to music by his friend Mr. John Eccles. In 1710 he published an edition of his Poetical Works, in three volumes in 8vo, containing, besides his performances already mentioned, *A Collection of Poems upon several Occasions*; and all his Poetical Works have been reprinted at London in 1730 in three volumes in 12mo. He wrote also some *Letters*, particularly one *upon Humour in Comedy*, published by Mr. John Dennis in a Collection of Letters written by Mr. Dryden, Congreve, Moyle, &c. and a Dedication of Mr. Dryden's Plays to the Duke of Newcastle. In the latter part of his life his health began extremely to decline, and his sight to fail. He died about five of the clock on Sunday morning, January the 19th 1728/9, at his house in Surrey-street in the Strand, in the fifty seventh year of his age, and on the Sunday following, January the 26th, his corps lay in state in the Jerusalem-Chamber; from whence the same evening it was carried with great decency and solemnity into King Henry VII's chapel in Westminster-Abbey, and interred near the late Earl of Godolphin, and a monument was erected to him there by Henrietta, late Duchess of Marlborough. We shall give the character of him and his Writings in the Note [*I*]. [The latter note merely summarizes comments by Steele.]

Richard Temple, Viscount Cobham. Inscription on the Congreve memorial, designed by William Kent, in the garden at Stowe, 1736.

INGENIO,
ACRI, FACETO, EXPOLITO,
MORIBUSQUE
URBANIS, CANDIDIS, FACILLIMIS
GULIELMI CONGREVE,
HOC
QUALECUNQUE DESIDERII SUI
SOLAMEN SIMUL AC
MONUMENTUM
POSUIT COBHAM.
1736.

The above is translated in George Bickham, *The Beauties of Stow* (1750), 59, as follows:

To the piercing, elegant, polished
Wit,
and civilized, candid, most unaffected
Manners,
of *William Congreve*,
hath *Cobham* erected
this poor Consolation for, as well as
Monument of, his Loss.
1736.

'Æquus', in *The Prompter*, no. 139, 5 March 1736.

...the Probability, that there is no such Dramatick *Genius* now living in *England*, as *Shakespeare*, *Dryden*, or *Congreve*....DRYDEN'S first Play was the *Wild Gallant*, one of the worst in our Language; *Shakespeare* wrote many that are intolerable; nobody has set out with *Congreve*'s Vigour besides himself.

Lady Mary Wortley Montagu, 'Conclusion of a Letter to Lord H— giving an Account of the Death of Mr. Hedges Treasurer to his *R.H.*' [*c*.20 June 1737]. *Letters*, ii. 112–13.

—This is wrote with Tears,
Tears for our loss, it is not his I mourn,
Who past all Care sleeps in his peace-full Urn;

Or crown'd with Roses in Elysian Groves
With bright Ophelia now renews his Loves;
Where Purer Light and happier Feasts they share
With Ovid, Congreve, Sapho, Delawar,
Perhaps with Pity at a distance view
The Paths poor Poets militant persue.

Louis Riccoboni, *An Historical and Critical Account of the Theatres in Europe* (London, 1741), 175. The passage appeared originally in *Réflections Historiques et Critiques sur les Différens Théâtres de l'Europe; avec des pensées sur la déclamation* (Paris, 1738).

Amongst the Crowd of *English* Poets, Mr. *Congreve* is most esteemed for Comedy. He was perfectly acquainted with Nature; and was living in 1727, when I was in *London*; I conversed with him more than once, and found in him Taste joined with great Learning. It is rare to find many Dramatic Poets of his Stamp.

Elizabeth Boyd, *Don Sancho Or, The Students Whim* (1739), 15:

> *Congreve* who with c[a]reless Art,
> Charm'd the Brain and warm'd the Heart...

[James Ralph], *The Champion*, no. 3, Tuesday 20 November 1739. Reprinted here from the collected edition of 1741.

Wycherly, whom I have always esteemed one of the best of our comic Writers, left the *Drama*, where he had acquired so great and so just an Applause, to write some of the worst Poems that any Age hath produced; and *Congreve*, who will always be esteemed by those who have a polite Taste in Comedy, could not forbear attempting Reputation, in a Manner for which he was so disqualified, that he produced a Tragedy (notwithstanding its Success) little Superior to those of our worst Writers.

Colley Cibber, *An Apology for the Life of Colley Cibber* (London, 1740).

(i) Queen *Mary* having commanded the *Double Dealer* to be acted, *Kynaston* happen'd to be so ill, that he could not hope to be able next Day to perform his Part of the Lord *Touchwood*. In this Exigence, the Author, Mr. *Congreve*, advis'd that it might be given to me, if at so short a Warning I could undertake it. The Flattery of being thus distinguish'd by so celebrated an Author, and the Honour to act before a Queen, you may be sure, made me blind to whatever Difficulties might attend it. I accepted the Part, and was ready in it before I slept; next Day the Queen was present at the Play, and was receiv'd with a new Prologue from the Author, spoken by Mrs. *Barry*, humbly acknowledging the great Honour done to the Stage, and to his Play in particular: Two Lines of it, which tho' I have not since read, I still remember.

> *But never were in* Rome, *nor* Athens *seen,*
> *So fair a Circle, or so bright a Queen.*

After the Play, Mr. *Congreve* made me the Compliment of saying, that I had not only answer'd, but had exceeded his Expectations, and that he would shew me he was sincere, by his saying more of me to the Masters—He was as good as his Word, and the next Pay-day, I found my Sallary, of fifteen, was then advanc'd to twenty Shillings a Week. But alas! this favourable Opinion of Mr. *Congreve*, made no farther Impression upon the Judgment of my good Masters; it only serv'd to heighten my own Vanity; but could not recommend me to any new Trials of my Capacity; not a Step farther could I get, 'till the Company was again divided; when the Desertion of the best Actors left a clear Stage, for younger Champions to mount, and shew their best Pretensions to favour. (pp. 150–2)

. . .

(ii) . . . the new Theatre was open'd against us, with a veteran Company, and a new Train of Artillery; or in plainer *English*, the old Actors, in *Lincoln's-Inn-Fields* began, with a new Comedy of Mr. *Congreve*'s, call'd *Love* for *Love*; which ran on with such extraordinary Success, that they had seldom occasion to act any other Play, 'till the End of the Season. This valuable Play had a narrow Escape, from falling into the Hands of the Patentees; for before the Division of the Company, it had been read, and accepted of at the Theatre-Royal: But while the Articles of Agreement for it were preparing, the Rupture, in the Theatrical State, was so far advanced, that the Author took Time to pause, before he sign'd them; when finding that all Hopes of Accommodation were impracticable, he thought it adviseable to let it take its Fortune, with those Actors for whom he had first intended the Parts.

Mr. *Congreve* was then in such high Reputation, as an Author, that besides his Profits, from this Play, they offered him a whole Share with them, which he accepted; in Consideration of which he oblig'd himself, if his Health permitted, to give them one new Play every Year. *Dryden*, in King *Charles*'s Time, had the same Share with the King's Company; but he bound himself to give them two Plays every Season. This you may imagine he could not hold long, and I am apt to think, he might have serv'd them better, with one in a Year, not so hastily written. Mr. *Congreve*, whatever Impediment he met with, was three Years before, in pursuance to his Agreement, he produc'd the

Mourning Bride; and if I mistake not, the Interval had been much the same, when he gave them the *Way of the World*. But it came out the stronger, for the Time it cost him, and to their better Support, when they sorely wanted it: For though they went on with Success for a Year or two, and even, when their Affairs were declining, stood in much higher Estimation of the Publick, than their Opponents . . .   (pp. 160–2)

. . .

(iii) . . . *Love's last Shift*, which (as Mr. *Congreve* justly said of it) had only in it, a great many things, that were *like* Wit, that in reality were *not* Wit. And what is still less pardonable (as I say of it myself) has a great deal of Puerility, and frothy Stage-Language in it, yet by the mere moral Delight receiv'd from its Fable, it has been . . . in a continued, and equal Possession of the Stage, for more than forty Years.   (pp. 179–80)

. . .

(iv) The Authors of the *Old Batchelor*, and of the *Relapse*, were those, whom *Collier* most labour'd to convict of Immorality; to which they severally publish'd their Reply; the first seem'd too much hurt, to be able to defend himself, and the other felt him so little, that his Wit only laugh'd at his Lashes.   (pp. 224–5)

. . .

(v) In the Year 1706, when this House [the Haymarket Theatre] was finish'd, *Betterton*, and his Co-partners dissolved their own Agreement, and threw themselves under the Direction of Sir *John Vanbrugh*, and Mr. *Congreve*; imagining, perhaps, that the Conduct of two such eminent Authors, might give a more prosperous Turn to their Condition; that the Plays, it would, now, be their Interest, to write for them, would soon recover the Town to a true Taste, and be an Advantage, that no other Company could hope for; that in the Interim till such Plays could be written, the Grandeur of their House, as it was a new Spectacle, might allure the Crowd to support them: But if these were their Views, we shall see, that their Dependence upon them, was too sanguine. As to their Prospect of new Plays, I doubt it was not enough consider'd, that good ones were Plants of a slow Growth; and tho', Sir *John Vanbrugh* had a very quick Pen, yet Mr. *Congreve* was too judicious a Writer, to let any thing come hastily out of his Hands.   (p. 258)

Joseph Spence, reporting Lady Mary Wortley Montagu, January–February 1741. Spence, i. 304.

It was my fate to be much with the wits; my father was acquainted with all of them. Addison was the best company in the world. I never knew anybody that had so much wit as Congreve *perhaps his conversation was, like his plays, too full of it*. Sir Richard Steele was a very good-natured man, and Dr. Garth a very worthy one.

Joseph Spence, Letter to his mother. 25 February 1741. Cited in Spence, i. 303–4. It may have been under such circumstances that Congreve had once advised Lady Mary Wortley Montagu, the subject of this account, to hide her temper (Montagu, *Letters*, i. 201 n. 4, citing MS Commonplace Book, f. 22, Fisher Library, University of Sydney).

As she was born with fine Parts enough for twenty Men, she took early to study; & her Infancy was very learn'd. As she read extreamly, somebody put it into her head that 'twas a great Pity she shou'd not understand Latin. Her Governante, who was a very rigid one, she thought wou'd never allow this; so she got a Dictionary & Grammar, wth all the Privacy in the world: & as she had the use of the Library, she hid them in a private corner there; lock'd herself in every morning, from ten to two, & every afternoon from 4 to 8; and set to the study of those two very dull Books. By this means, in two years time, she stole the Latin Language; and at Fifteen, understood it perhaps as well as most men. 'Twas Mr Wortley, (her husband afterwards,) that first gave her this thought; and Mr Congreve was of great use to her, after it came to be known. She now understands, at least, seven Languages; English, French, Italian, Spanish; German, Latin; & the modern Greek.

Joseph Spence, reporting Nathaniel Hooke, 1742. Spence, i. 324. There was a French compositor John Deelle, Dell, Dellee, Dele, or Dilly, at Oxford in 1691. A John Délié, probably his son, was a compositor at Cambridge in 1700–3 and 1708–10.

Congreve's story of his printer, Dell: Deal, Deel, Delle; dele, and be damned to you.

[Anon.], *Memoirs of the Nobility, Gentry, &c. of Thule; or, The Island of Love. Being a Secret History of Their Amours, Artifices, and Intrigues* (1742–44), ii. 220. Copy at L has the MS identifications noted here within square brackets. The account also refers to her provision of the monument to Congreve, the wax effigy, and her burial near him.

The Thaness of BADIN ['Henrietta Churchill Css of Godolphin'] was yet more extravagant in her Passion for TERENTIO ['W^m. Congreve. Esq^"]; his Person was formed for Love, and all his Works breath'd the most amorous Sentiments, *Badin* beheld him and loved, she was not of a Temper to sigh long for what she desired; her Passions were violent, and she was linkt to

a meek humble Helpmate ['Francis Earl of Godolphin'] . . . she made the first
Advances: An Apartment was allotted for *Terentio* even in the House . . .

Joseph Spence, reporting Alexander Pope, 5–7 April 1744. Spence,
i. 170. The asterisks indicate the four writers of familiar dialogues.

In talking over the design for a dictionary that might be authoritative for our
English writers, Mr. Pope rejected Sir Walter Raleigh twice, as too affected.

The list for prose authors (from whose works such a dictionary should be
collected) was talked over several times and quite settled. There were
eighteen of them named by Mr. Pope, but four of that number were only
named as authorities for familiar dialogues, and writings of that kind.

Lord Bacon, Hooker, Hobbes, *Ben Jonson, Lord Clarendon, Barrow,
Tillotson, Dryden, Sir William Temple, *L'Estrange, Locke, Sprat, Atterbury,
*Congreve, Addison, *Vanbrugh, Swift, Lord Bolingbroke.

Anon., *The British Magazine* (July 1747), ii. 311.

How great is the advantage the man enjoys . . . whose kind stars have not
suffered him to be born a poet; when, for his shilling, nay, for his sixpence, he
can take his hard-hearted Cynthia to be courted by all the wit of a Congreve,
or the softness of a Rowe, or an Addison, and that with all the additional
graces of a masterly composer, and employ them only as a client does his
counsel; he pays for their words, and they all go to his account.

Anon., *The British Magazine* (November 1749), iv. 464.

 . . . would it not be a reflection on the generosity, as well as good sense, of our
English ladies, to leave *Shakespear*, *Otway*, *Dryden*, *Congreve* &c. for the
mimickry of a *Harlequin?*

John Campbell, in *Biographia Britannica: Or, The Lives of the Most
Eminent Persons who have flourished in Great Britain and Ireland, from
the Earliest Ages.* 7 vols. (1747–66), iii. 1439–49. Vol. iii is dated 1750.
Marginal and foot notes are included only if they offer new
information.

CONGREVE (WILLIAM) a celebrated English Poet in the last and
present century. There is no sort of question about the descent of this
gentleman, which was from the antient house of Congreve in Staffordshire,
flourishing there with honour and reputation; neither is there any doubt as to
his immediate family, for he was the only surviving son of William Congreve,

Esq; who was the second son of Richard Congreve, Esq; of Congreve and Stratton in the county of Stafford. As to the place, and indeed as to the kingdom, in which he was born, authors differ, and not only so, but are positive on both sides; some are clear that he was a native of Ireland, but it seems more probable, or, to speak more plainly, it is morally certain, that he was a native of England, and drew his first breath in the village of Bardsa, near Leeds in Yorkshire, which was the estate of a near relation of his by the mother's side. The reason of our giving the preference to this sentiment, rather than that which entitles another island to the honour of his birth, will be found at the bottom of the page [*A*]. [The note cites Sir James Ware's *Works*, iii. 249, the *General Dictionary*, iv. 247, and Giles Jacob, *Lives of the English Poets*, i. 41.] The time when it happened can only be collected by circumstances, which place it in 1671 or 1672. His father carried him, when a very child, into Ireland, where at that time he had a command in the army, but afterwards was entrusted with the management of a considerable part of the large estate of the noble family of Burlington, which fixed the residence of himself and family in that kingdom. Our author received the first tincture of letters in the great school of Kilkenny, and gave very early proofs of his pregnant genius; and it is said, that one of the first essays of his poetical talent was a copy of verses upon the death of his master's magpye. He went from the school of Kilkenny to the university of Dublin, then flourishing under the direction of Dr St George Ash, where, in a very short time, Mr Congreve became perfectly acquainted with all the branches of polite literature, and acquired not only a general acquaintance with, but a correct and critical taste in, the Classicks. His father, however, was desirous that his parts should be applied to more profitable studies, and therefore sent him over to England a little after the Revolution, and placed him as a student in the Middle-Temple. But the severe study of the Law had so little relation to the active disposition and sprightly humour of the young Gentleman, that though he continued for three or four years to live in chambers, and pass for a Templar, yet it does not appear that he ever applied himself with diligence to conquer his dislike to a course of life which been chosen for him, with so little respect either to the turn of his natural parts, or the preceding course of his education. But how little soever he answered the expectation of his friends, in the prosecution of that profession to which they had destin'd him, certain it is, that he was not either indolent or inactive in the cultivation of those studies, that were both his early and his latest care. His first performance, when almost a boy, was extraordinary in it's kind, and though no more than a novel, which, under the assumed name of *C L E O P H I L*, he dedicated to Mrs Catherine Leveson, yet it was a proof, not only of the vivacity of his wit, and the fluency of his stile, but also of the strength of his judgment[*B*]. [The note in part reads: 'The title of this first work of our ingenious author's was I N C O G N I T A : or,

Love and Duty reconciled. It has always been considered as a piece very well written, more especially as it was the first production of a youth of seventeen. It has been also asserted, that at the bottom it is a true history, and though the scene is by Mr Congreve laid in Italy, yet the adventures happened here in England. It is not our business to enter into the secret history of this entertaining piece, or to attempt to give the reader a key to what the writer took so much pains to conceal; but what we intend in this note, is to justify the observation in the text, and to prove, that though this was the first essay, and the first essay of a very young man, yet there is in it something very extraordinary, more especially when we add to what has been said before, that it was a very hasty essay likewise. There is nothing more common, and indeed there is nothing more natural, than for young men to pique themselves upon the brightness of their parts, the quickness of their wit, and, in pieces of this nature, the elegancy and flowriness of their language. But this was not Mr Congreve's point; he aimed at perfection from the very beginning, and his design in writing this novel, was to shew how novels ought to be written. Let us hear what he says himself, and from thence we shall entertain a higher opinion of his abilities, than could possibly be raised by the warmest commendations.' The note then cites Congreve's preface.] As he did not then think proper to own this piece to the world, so the reputation resulting from it was confined within the narrow compass of his acquaintance; but, as true genius cannot remain long hid, and as untoward accidents rather provoke than tame high spirits; so, upon a fit of sickness which seized him about three years after his return to England, he amused himself, during a slow recovery, in writing a comedy which he very soon finished, and though he was very modest and diffident of his own abilities, yet he suffered himself to be overcome by the persuasion of his relations and friends, and consented to bring it upon the stage. In order to this he was recommended to Capt. Southerne, who, in conjunction with the great Mr Dryden, and that excellent Critick Arthur Manwairing, Esq; revised the *Old Batchelor*, of which Mr Dryden said, He never saw such a first play in his life, and that the author not being acquainted with the stage or the town, it would be pity to have it miscarry for want of a little assistance. The stuff was rich indeed, only the fashionable cut was wanting, which was soon given it. Mr Thomas Davenant, who had then the direction of the Theatre-Royal in Drury-Lane, was so much struck by the merit of the piece, and the author's conversation, that he granted him what is called the privilege of the house, half a year before his play came upon the Stage, which, according to the maxims of Theatrical Government, was not barely an unusual, but an unprecedented favour. In 1693, *The Old Batchelor* was acted before a numerous and noble audience. The prologue, intended to be spoken, was written by Lord Falkland; the play was admirably performed, and received with such general applause, that

Mr Congreve was thenceforward considered as the prop of the declining Stage, and as the rising genius in Dramatick Poesy. It was this play, and the very singular success that attended it upon the Stage, and after it came from the press, that brought our author to the notice of that great patron of the English Muses, Charles Mountague, Lord Halifax, who being desirous to place so eminent a Wit in a state of ease and tranquillity, made him immediately one of the Commissioners for licensing Hackney-coaches; bestowed upon him soon after a place in the Pipe Office; and gave him likewise a post in the Custom-House of the value of six hundred pounds a year. As these were favours of a very extraordinary nature, so they raised in the breast of Mr Congreve a noble spirit of gratitude and affection, which shewed itself in an unutterable attachment to that Nobleman during his life, and the most profound reverence for his memory after his decease. We need not be surprized, that after such encouragement as the town, and even the Criticks, had given him, our author quickly made his appearance again upon the Stage, as he did the year following, when he brought on the *Double Dealer*. This play was honoured with the presence of Queen Mary, and though it was not so universally applauded as his former performance, yet it had the honour to be very highly commended, as well as generally approved, by the best judges. We need not at all wonder at the fate of this fine performance, for regular Comedy was at that time a new thing. Our author was the very first who attempted it; I will not say he was the last who succeeded in it; but I may safely assert, that he carried it to the highest degree of perfection, and that if we were to wish any of our Comedies translated into French, for the honour of our nation, it should be his, and amongst them there is none that does him greater credit than the *Double Dealer*, notwithstanding some objections that have been made to it[*D*]. [Note *D* cites part of Congreve's dedication and adds that, in it, Congreve 'has fairly unravelled the true source of false criticism, and shewn himself thereby a deep enquirer, as well as an excellent judge of human nature, which, as we shall have frequent occasions to shew hereafter, appears to have been the constant study of his life, as well as the chief fund from whence he drew the many fine and beautiful strokes that distinguish all, but more especially his comic writings.'] It was towards the close of that year Queen Mary died, which melancholy accident, as it afforded a pregnant subject to Orators and Poets, so, amongst all that attempted it, none succeeded better than Mr Congreve, in the Pastoral which he wrote upon that occasion, and which, in point of simplicity, elegance, and correctness, is at least equal to any thing of the kind that has appeared in our language. We have taken notice in another place of the great Revolution that happened in the theatrical world in the succeeding year, and of the justice and generosity with which Mr Congreve espoused the cause of our English Roscius, when he opened his new Theatre in Portgual-Row, Lincoln's-Inn-Fields, by giving him his excellent Comedy of *Love for Love*, so judiciously contrived, and so happily executed, as to unite at once the approbation of the few, and the tumultuous applause of the many, in its favour [*E*]. [Note *E* adds that Congreve's dedication is 'written, as all his dedications are, with great decency and good sense, and without any of that fulsome flattery, which reflects at once upon the patron and the writer, and is, at the same time, such a plague and punishment to a reader, as he has seldom the patience to go through. Some faults have been found with several characters in this play; but if the reflections, proceeding from the severe morals of Mr Collier, can be averted by any tolerable excuses, drawn from the very nature of comedy, which requires the representing the manners of the age as they really are, nothing else can affect it. The sense of succeeding times has fully justified the judgment of those in which it was first acted, and *Love for Love* continues, and is like to continue, an admired comedy, as long as true taste for theatrical entertainments shall prevail.'] The same year he distinguished himself in a new kind of Poetry, by addressing to King William an irregular Ode on the taking of Namur, in which the sublimity of the sentiments, the harmony of the numbers, the happy imitation of the Antients, the graceful turn of his panegyrick, are truly admirable; but perhaps there is nothing in it that deserves higher commendation than the delicate compliment with which it ends, and where, in a single line, he says the finest things possible of his two great patrons Halifax and Dorset. As he had now attained the highest reputation as a Comick Poet, he was inclined to shew that a regular and finished tragedy might succeed upon the English theatre. It was an adventurous task that he set himself, and a very high stake he made, when he hazarded all the reputation he had already acquired upon this new performance, which, though written according to the rules, was altogether destitute of those artificial and irregular helps, frequently relied on by former writers. It seems to have cost him more pains than any of his former pieces, for it was not till 1697 that the *Mourning Bride* was acted at the new Theatre in Lincoln's-Inn-Fields. Very few plays ever excited so great expectations as this did, and fewer still have met, after such expectation raised, with so universal an approbation. In short, it was the best received of all his pieces, and, without doubt, whatever credit he drew from this exquisite tragedy, was in some measure shared by the audience, who fairly entitled themselves to the character of equal and able judges, by the applause they bestowed upon that excellent performance. He was called off from his attention to the theatre to another kind of writing, that to him, of all men living, was the most tedious and tiresome, and that was controversy. His four Plays were attacked with equal fury and celerity by the famous Mr Jeremy Collier, who, without the least pity to his fine parts, or the slightest tenderness for a reputation raised with so much pains, fell upon him, not as a dull or tasteless, but as a dangerous and destructive, writer. An answer was necessary, and therefore an answer was given, under a very plain title, and written with much modesty as well as wit. There are abundance of judicious things in this defence, which was drawn up in the form of letters to that candid Critick, and the author's constant friend, Walter Moyle, Esq; which, though the subject seems to render them now out of date, will make them always well worth a judicious reader's perusal [G]. [Note G, in offering a brief summary of it, commends Congreve's *Amendments* in which he is said to have laid down 'many things which are extreamly well worth the knowing, and without knowing which, it is impossible to form a right notion of the innocence, excellency, or use of plays.' In referring to *Amendments* as a series of letters, the writer refers to the later version in *Memoirs*.] In all probability, this quarrel created in our author some distaste to the Stage; however, he afterwards brought on another Comedy, the last, not the least valuable, of his performances. It was intituled *The Way of the World*, of which it was so just a picture, that the world could not bear it, which compleated the disgust of our author to the theatre, upon which Mr Dennis (though not very famous for either) said a very fine, and a very kind thing, *That Mr Congreve quitted the Stage early, and that Comedy left it with him*. He seems to have foreseen the fate of his play, which is well revenged in his Epilogue, as it is justly exposed in the Dedication prefixed to it when it was published, wherein our author shewed, that he knew how to resent the injuries done to him by little Criticks, but it would have been better if he had stopped there, and not punished the rest of the world for their sakes, by dropping his pen in the prime of life, and when he was most capable of doing honour to himself and to his country. This play has long ago triumphed over it's feeble adversaries, and is now justly esteemed as much as it deserves [H]. [Note H, commenting that the play 'did not meet with so universal an approbation as his former pieces', adds: 'It is very certain, the fault is not in the play but in the audience, who were not as yet arrived at that correct taste, which requires that all kinds of follies, how general or fashionable soever, should be submitted to the chastisement of the stage. In his dedication to Ralph Earl of Mountague, a nobleman justly celebrated both as a competent and candid judge, the author treats this matter with great penetration and perspicuity.'] He amused himself, however, after this, and obliged the world by a great variety of original poems and translations. He had a fine taste for Musick as well as Poetry, which sufficiently appears in his Hymn to Harmony in honour of St Cecilia's day 1701, set by Mr John Eccles, his great friend, and one of the most elegant Composers our nation has produced. To him also our author was obliged, for setting several of his songs, which are very beautiful in their kind, and have all that vivacity of wit which can give life and lustre to such performances. His early acquaintance with the Great, had promised him not an easy only, but a happy station in life, to which it is very rare that either true genius, or any kind of literary merit, recommends any man. This freed him from all obligations of courting any longer publick favour, though it still left him under the tie of gratitude to his illustrious friends. He acted in a manner suitable to his situation, he very seldom risked the character he had obtained for the sake of exalting it: but he never missed any opportunity of paying his complements to his high patrons, in a manner worthy of himself and of them. The death of the Marquis of Blandford, only son to the Duke of Marlborough, which happened Feb. 20, 1705 [*sic* for 1703], afforded him a melancholy occasion of endeavouring to soften, by celebrating, the distress of that illustrious family, which he did in a most beautiful Pastoral, inscribed to the Lord Godolphin, Lord High-Treasurer of England. The glorious successes of the British arms, under the invincible Duke beforementioned, supplied a glorious theme for an Ode to the late Queen Anne, in which he celebrates victories most honourable to this nation, in numbers that fully entitle their author to unfading reputation, as they cannot fail of preserving the memory of those victories, as long as our language shall last, or a true taste in poetry remains. In another pindarick Ode he celebrated that great Statesman, and true Patriot, the Lord High-Treasurer Godolphin, taking occasion from that Nobleman's great delight in horse-racing, to imitate, or rather to emulate, the Greek Poet, in his favourite manner of writing, by a truly elegant and exquisite digression. We owe to him not only these two pieces in a kind of poetry almost before unknown to our language, but also a very learned and judicious Dissertation upon this species of poesy, which contains a solid and just criticism on those sort of irregular pieces, that hitherto have passed, though very undeservedly, for Pindaricks [*I*]. [Note *I* introduces a passage from Congreve's remarks with the comment: 'It has been hinted in the text, that whenever Mr Congreve applied himself to any kind of writing in prose or verse, his constant aim was perfection; to which he had not the vanity to think he might arrive by the strength of his genius, but applied himself first as a critic, to acquire a thorough knowledge of the nature of his task, before he undertook to execute it as a poet. It was this led him to examine the works of Pindar, with the greatest care, before he attempted to imitate him, and at first sight he discovered how little resemblance the odes, pretending to the character of pindarick, in our language, had to the odes of that author in respect to numbers, structure or sentiment. He resolved therefore to restore this ancient and sublime manner of writing, by giving the world a true pindarick in substance as well as show, that it might appear the force and spirit of this kind of poetry, consisted in the strength of the thought, and not in the loosness or irregularity of the numbers. He enquired also into the cause of so general a mistake, and has assigned it with an equal mixture of critical justice, and the candour of a gentleman.' Congreve's remarks on Cowley are then cited. The note ends: 'This shews not only how desirous Mr Congreve was of writing correctly himself, but also how willing to establish so true a taste, as might render correctness necessary to applause.'] The clearness and candour of his criticism, ought to give him as high a character in the Republick of Letters, as even his fine performances in so many different kinds of poetry. His *Birth of the Muse*, and his *Dedication* in verse of his poems when collected, both addressed to his old patron Charles Lord Halifax, are equally grateful and pleasing, though as different in their composition as any two pieces can be; the former is solemn and sublime, the latter easy and familiar. We see in one, how able the Poet was to rise to the greatest heights without the least mixture of bombast or fustian; and on the other, how finely he could unite the becoming liberty of a friend, with that respect which was nevertheless due to his patron's superior rank and dignity. But as, in the earlier part of his life, Mr Congreve had received obligations from persons of less exalted station, so of these he was highly sensible, and never let slip any favourable opportunity of returning. He wrote an Epilogue for his old friend Mr Southerne's fine tragedy of *Oroonoko*, and we learn from Mr Dryden himself, how much he owed to his assistance in the translation of Virgil [K]. [Note *K* adds in part: 'The English translation of Virgil was not published 'till 1697, but Mr Dryden was engaged in it in 1695, and consequently at the time he consulted our author, he was only between twenty three and twenty four years of age. What an honour to have his opinion asked by the greatest poet of his time, upon a subject of such importance to his reputation, what an honour to justify both his friendship and his judgment on so critical an occasion, and what an honour to receive the laurel from his learned brow, only to fix it again upon his tomb, to be the defender of that great man's fame when he was dead, who had loved him so much living, and piously to vindicate the character of him, whose generous, tho' just, praises, had laid the foundation of his own?] He contributed by translating the eleventh Satire to the translation of Juvenal published by that great Poet, and wrote an admirable copy of verses on the version of Persius performed by Mr Dryden alone. He wrote likewise a Prologue for a Play of Mr Charles Dryden's, full of kindness for that young gentleman, and of respect for his father. But the noblest testimony he gave of his filial reverence for that exalted genius, was in that inimitable panegyrick upon his writings, contained in the Dedication of his Plays to his Grace the Duke of Newcastle, a monument that will for ever express, in the most lively colours, the worth of him to whose honour it is consecrated, and the capacity, candour, and critical justice, of the hand that raised it. His translations have done him the greatest honour, in the sentiments of those who were the best judges, and who have taken pains to compare them with their originals. The *Hymn to Venus*, and some of the most moving passages in the *Iliad*, appear with all the spirit and dignity of Homer in the English version, and it is impossible for a learned writer to peruse them without confessing his accuracy, so whoever has a true taste for poetry must feel the effects of that art and force, which with all the emotions naturally rising from the passions of the human mind, are expressed in these nervous pieces. His imitations of Horace have as much the air of that Poet as our times or language will permit, that is, the same strength, vivacity, and delicacy, for which, through a long series of years, they have been admired in the original. The third book of Ovid's *Art of Love* appears in our tongue with all the sweetness and softness peculiar to that author, who was perfectly acquainted with the passion, and who knew how to describe it with all the masterly graces of a great Poet, and what was admired in the Augustan age, becomes excellent in ours, from the skill of Mr Congreve, and the happy union of the most distant excellencies in a translator, ease and exactness. He was the better qualified for an undertaking of this kind, from the natural turn of his own temper, for his Poem to, and his excellent Epigram on, Mrs Arabella Hunt, are entirely in the Ovidian strain, and are as pleasingly pathetick as any Poems in their kind, in our own, or perhaps in any other language. There is a strength and solemnity in his verses to the memory of Lady Gethins, and in his Epitaph on the two Huntingtons, that makes one scarce conceive it possible that he should succeed as well in lighter compositions, and yet the tales that he has told after a celebrated French author, are so unaffected and natural, that if we were not apprised of it we should never have suspected they were translations; but there is one piece of his which ought to be particularly distinguished, as being so truly an original, that though it seems to be written with the utmost facility, yet we may despair of ever seeing it copied; this is his *DORIS*, so highly and so justly commended by Sir Richard Steele, as the sharpest and most delicate satire he had ever met with. We must not omit, in this free catalogue of his works, two pieces of the dramatick kind, which do him equal honour as a Poet, and as a lover of Musick, *viz.* the *Judgment of Paris*, a *Masque*, and the *Opera of Semele*. Of these, the former was acted with great applause, and the latter finely set to musick by Mr Eccles. In respect to both it is but bare justice to say, that they have the same stamp of excellency borne by the rest of Mr Congreve's works, were considered as master-pieces when published, and may serve as models to posterity [*L*]. [Note *L* introduces Congreve's prefatory remarks to *Semele* with the following comment: 'The great art of adapting poetry to musick, tho' studied by many, has been acquired by few. This very plainly appears by the want of a true poetick spirit, in many of the pieces set to fine musick, in which we evidently perceive, that the notes were not accommodated to the words, but the words to the notes. We do not indeed perceive this so plainly, during the performance, when the faculties of the mind are so transported by the sweetness of the sound, that we have not power to discern the defects in the sense. But what escapes us on the Theatre, stares us in the face in the closet, and we cannot help wondering, when we read what it was that transported us so much in the hearing. But the few great masters that have reached the sublime heights of Harmony, instead of receiving from, communicate helps to the most able composer. In this we have the strongest instance in Mr Dryden's celebrated ode on St Cecilia's day, which not only ravishes us when performed, but when read, and thereby convinces the judicious peruser of the real force of numbers. The same thing may with equal justice be said of our author's masque, the songs in which are most admirably adapted to the characters, as well as the musick, and the performance is not only perfect upon the stage, but perfect also when considered only as a poetick entertainment; and though we may see it with more rapture, yet we read it too with the highest delight, and find nothing in it flat or insipid for want of the support of musick. There is an excellency in every kind of writing, and as an author is justly entitled to reputation who reaches this in any; so admiration is the just tribute to that exalted genius that reaches it in all, I need not tell the reader, that this is Mr Congreve's claim to admiration. His opera of Semele was never performed; but, for all that, it has been universally admired. The fable is happily chosen and skillfully managed, the scenes are finely disposed, the sentiments perfectly agreeable to the subject, and the language exactly suitable to the sentiments. There is, however, one thing that deserves peculiar notice, and that is, the manner in which our author has disposed that part of his work which seemed least susceptible of sense and grace at the same time.' There follows an extract from Congreve's own notes on recitative. 'This explains what had never been explained before, that is to say, the nature and meaning of the recitative, how far it approaches, and how far it is removed from prose, what the use of it, and consequently what rules are to be observed in it's composition, so as to keep it from sinking servilely low, and to restrain it from swelling into rant and bombast.'] We have now almost finished the list of his poetical labours, in which we have been the more particular, because it was peculiar to Mr Congreve to have written and excelled, not barely in every kind of dramatick poetry, but almost in every kind of poetry. The last to which he turned his genius was that of familiar epistles, of these that on the *Art of Pleasing*, addressed to Sir Richard Temple, now the Field Marshal Viscount Cobham, is the only one inserted in his works, and is so truly admirable, that the publick has just reason to regret some others that are still said to be preserved in the cabinets of his friends to whom they were addressed, and which it is hoped will one day see the light. Another epistle of his to the same noble person, as it is not to be found in his works, we have, as one of it's brightest ornaments, inserted in ours, from a copy that appeared to be very correct [*M*]. [Preceding the text is the following note: 'This beautiful poem is written with that simple elegance, that force of genius, and that dignity of sentiment, which leaves no room to doubt of it's being justly attributed to Mr Congreve. At what time it was written cannot be said with any pretence to certainty; but as there is a visible allusion in the poem to measures, which the writer thought were too complaisant to the *French*, it is very evident that it must have been penned but a very small time before his death.'] This naturally leads us to mention his prose letters, which are dispersed through the works of other men, but, whenever they have a new edition, would make a very natural and a very valuable addition to his own. His letter upon *Humour* in English Comedy, is without doubt as instructive and entertaining, and as correct a piece of criticism as is any where to be met with. All his other letters are written with infinite wit and spirit, and at the same time with a wonderful facility and a fine flow of language, so happily intermixed with lively and inoffensive raillery, that it is impossible not to be pleased with them at the first reading, or to find any fault with them on the most mature reflection. We may be satisfied from the perusal of them, that his conversation must have been very engaging, and therefore we need not wonder that he lived in such familiarity with the greatest men of his time, or that they courted his friendship by rendering him every good office in their power. It has been observed, that no change of Ministries affected him in the least, nor was he ever removed from any post that was given him except to a better. His place in the Custom-house, and his office of Secretary in Jamaica, are said to have brought him in upwards of twelve hundred pounds a year, and though he lived in a manner suitable to such a fortune, yet he was so far an œconomist, as to raise from thence a competent estate. No man of his parts and learning ever passed through life with more ease or less envy, and as in the dawn of his reputation he was very dear to the greatest wits of his time, so during his whole life he preserved the utmost respect, and received continual marks of esteem from men of genius and letters, without ever being involved in any of their quarrels, or drawing upon himself the least mark of distaste, or even dissatisfaction. On the contrary, they sought his approbation with concern, and received it as the highest sanction of merit. Mr Addison testified his personal regard for him, and his high esteem of his writings, upon many occasions. Sir Richard Steele considered him as his patron on one occasion, and was desirous of submitting to his judgment as an umpire on another. Even the judicious Mr Pope, tho' sufficiently jealous of his poetical character, thought fit to honour him with the highest testimony of deference and esteem [N]. [Pope's postscript to his translation of the *Iliad* is prefaced by these comments: 'Those who were well acquainted with the late Mr Pope know, that there was nothing he despised so much in others, or the imputation of which he could have bore with so little patience himself, as the paying a servile court, and shewing a mean dependance upon any man, how great soever. He knew that virtue was true nobility, and parts the riches of nature; hence his deep reverence for Mr Bethel, and his high regard for Mr Congreve. To them, however, he would have been ashamed to dedicate his works, and yet to them he was proud to inscribe them. He looked upon his performances, as monuments secure from time and accident, and every name they bore as consecrated to immortality. This was his sentiment, nor was it vanity; the most generous possessor of gold knows the properties and value of the metal as well as the meanest miser. Let us hear then what praises one who was so sparing of them has bestowed on Mr Congreve . . . '.] We may add to all this, that Mr John Dennis, who valued himself so much upon criticizing the works of the ablest writers of his time, was so sensible of the superior excellence of Mr Congreve's writings, or at least was so grateful for the repeated marks of affability and beneficence which he received from him, that he always spoke of him, not with decency only but with veneration, which, if not a peculiar felicity, must at least have been a singular satisfaction to a man of Mr Congreve's peaceable disposition, who, as he never gave any offence, was very desirous, if it was possible, to avoid abuse. There is no doubt that Mr Congreve had an appetite to fame, and was not insensible of praise; yet never any man was freer from vanity, or shewed less concern about the fate of his writings; insomuch, that a foreigner of distinction, and without comparison the best Poet his country has to boast, was a little offended at this, and thought him rather too careless as to his literary reputation [*O*]. [Note *O* adds: 'The gentleman mentioned in the text, is the present eminent wit, and justly esteemed poet of France, Mr Voltaire, who, in the short time that he stayed here, acquired indeed a wonderful knowledge of our language, and of our manners; notwithstanding which, however, he was sometimes mistaken, and it is the more necessary to take notice of his mistakes, because no man's authority in the world is likely to pass them upon the present age, or upon posterity, for undoubted truths.' Following the quotation from Voltaire are these further comments: 'It is somewhat strange to hear an author accused of vanity, for under-valuing his own works. We often meet with censures even upon great men, for talking continually of themselves and their writings; but it is a very singular censure that is passed upon Mr Congreve, that he was troubled with an unseasonable vanity, which hindered him from talking of them at all. The truth of the matter seems to have been, that instead of feeling an unseasonable vanity, he had out-lived the season of vanity, if he ever had any, and having no longer any thing of the pride of an author about him, it is not at all wonderful that his conversation was not relished by Mr Voltaire, whose merit, as an author, is superior to every thing—but the sense he has of that merit.'] The best part of the last twenty years of his life were spent in ease and retirement, but towards the end of his days he was very much afflicted with the gout, which at length broke his constitution so much as to bring on a gradual decay. It was for this, that in the summer of the year 1728, he made a tour to the Bath for the benefit of the waters, where he had the misfortune to be overturned in his chariot, from which time he complained of a pain in his side, which was supposed to arise from some inward bruise. However it was, upon his return to London, his health declined more and more, but without making any impression on his spirits or understanding. He had accustomed himself to consider life, and every thing belonging to it, as blessings in which we have a very uncertain tenure, and therefore was not either surprized or disturbed at the prospect of losing it; the only concern he expressed, was for the grief it occasioned to his friends, more especially those for whom he had a tender affection and a most profound esteem. He yielded his last breath about the hour of five on Sunday morning, Jan. 19, 1728–9, at his house in Surrey-street in the Strand, in the fifty-seventh year of his age, and on the Sunday following, Jan. 26, his corps lay in state in the Jerusalem-Chamber, from whence, the same evening, between the hours of nine and ten, it was carried with great decency and solemnity into King Henry the VIIth's chapel, and after the funeral service was performed, was interred in the abbey. The pall was supported by the Duke of Bridgwater, Earl of Godolphin, Lord Cobham, Lord Wilmington, the Honourable George Berkeley, Esq; and Brigadier-General Churchill; and Col. Congreve followed his corps as chief-mourner. Some time after, a neat and elegant monument, with a suitable inscription thereupon, was erected to his memory by Henrietta Duchess of Marlborough.

Lady Mary Wortley Montagu to Lady Bute, 23 July 1754. *Letters*, iii. 67.

Since I was born, no original has appear'd excepting Congreve, and Fielding, who would I beleive have approach'd nearer to his excellencies if not forc'd by necessity to publish without correction ...

Joseph Spence, reporting Edward Young, 1757. Spence, i. 324.

Congreve [was] very well for years with Mrs. Bracegirdle, lived in the same street, his house very near hers, till his acquaintance with the young Duchess of Marlborough. He then quitted that house.

The Duchess showed me a diamond necklace (which Lady Di[ana Spencer] used afterwards to wear) that cost £7,000 and was purchased with the money Congreve left her. How much better would it have been given to poor Mrs. Bracegirdle?

James Boswell, recalling a report by Mrs Douglas. 20 January 1763. *Boswell's London Journal, 1762–1763*, ed. Frederick A. Pottle (London, 1950), 156–7.

Mrs. Douglas, who has a prodigious memory and knows a thousand anecdotes, especially of scandal, told me that Congreve the poet lived in the family of old Lord Godolphin, who is yet alive, and that Lady Godolphin was notoriously fond of him. In so much that her lord having gone abroad upon an embassy for two years, on his return she presented him with a fine girl by the author of *Love For Love*, which he was so indulgent as to accept of; nay, after Congreve's death, he joined with her in grief, and allowed her to have an image of him in wax daily set at table and nightly in her bedchamber, to which she spoke, believing it through heat of fancy, or believing it in appearance, to be Congreve himself. The young lady was most tenderly educated, and it is a certain fact that she was never suffered to see the moon for fear she should cry for it. She is now Duchess of Leeds, and has turned out extremely well.

Owen Ruffhead, reporting Alexander Pope. *Life of Alexander Pope* (London, 1769), 493 n.

Mr. POPE esteemed Congreve for the manners of a gentleman and a man of honour, and the sagest of the poetic tribe. He thought nothing wanting in his Comedies, but the simplicity and truth of nature.

Samuel Johnson, Letter to Mrs Thrale, 25 May 1780, from Southwark where he completed his life of Congreve while attending to Henry Thrale's pre-election business. *The Letters of Samuel Johnson*, ed. Bruce Redford, 5 vols. (Princeton: Princeton University Press, 1992–4), iii. 262.

Congreve, whom I dispatched at the Borough, while I was attending the election, is one of the best of the little lives; but then I had your conversation.

Andrew Kippis, 'William Congreve'. In *Biographia Britannica: Or, The Lives of the Most Eminent Persons who have flourished in Great-Britain and Ireland, from the Earliest Ages.* 2nd edn. 6 vols. (1778–[95]), iv. 79. Vol. iv is dated 1789. Marginal note 23 adds: 'From the information of the late Robert Dingley, Esq; whose account was from Mr. Bevern.' Dingley was brother to Rebecca Dingley, the close friend of Swift's Stella.

In the latter part of his life, he became convinced that his conduct as a writer could not admit of a justification. On a visit to Mr. Bevern the Quaker, in company with Mr. Pope, he said, in the course of the conversation, that he most sincerely wished that it were possible to obliterate all the offensive and impure passages in his works; and that he was fully sensible of the errors into which he had been betrayed, by the liveliness of youth.

CONGREVE'S LIBRARY

'BIBLIOTHECA Gulmi: Congreve, Armigeri', a 44-page manuscript catalogue of Congreve's library as it was constituted at his death, is in the possession of the Yorkshire Archaeological Society, Leeds. It has been admirably edited by John C. Hodges as *The Library of William Congreve* (New York: The New York Public Library, 1955). Its entries as numbered by Hodges amount to 659, but duplication, cross-references, and the inclusion of several titles in a single volume make it difficult to be quite sure of the total number of works in the collection. Noting the presence in the manuscript of three distinct hands, Hodges has indicated that the list must have been compiled in 1726, for the first hand accounts for 587 entries, all for books published before or during 1725. A second hand adds a further 31 entries, but none is for a book published later than 1727. Finally, a third hand has made another 41 entries, 4 of which are for books dated 1727 and 14 for ones dated 1728. At this stage Congreve's books were arranged by theca number on 33 shelves, doubtless in his lodgings in Surrey Street.

As Hodges explains, Congreve had willed the bulk of his estate to Henrietta, Duchess of Marlborough, on the understanding that she would care for his personal possessions, including his library, until on her own death they might pass to Mary Godolphin, the daughter born to Henrietta in 1723 and evidently fathered by Congreve. By her own will, made on 11 July 1732, Henrietta bequeathed to 'my Daughter Mary all Mr Congreve's Personal Estate that he left me and all my own money or which I enjoyed as such ... And the Three thousand pounds which is mine.' This last sum corresponds exactly with that left to Henrietta in Congreve's account at the Bank of England, presumably for transmission in due course to Mary (Hodges, *Library*, 6; *Documents*, 254–9, 264–9).

The list is provided here mainly as a complement to the commentary, but it also gives in a more readily consultable form the titles of books Congreve is known to have owned. Although it adopts the numbers Hodges used to identify each entry and is much indebted to his notes, it has been re-edited from a photocopy of the manuscript and independently annotated. It reduces the 659 entries to standard forms, gives them a more rigorous alphabetical order, and supplies cross-references. Notes are also given of ESTC, STC, or Wing numbers; the number of the entry in the original manuscript list ('List 413'); the number of the entry in the catalogue of books from the library of the Duke of Leeds sold by Sotheby's in London on 2–4 June 1930 ('Leeds 5'); the number of the entry in the catalogue of books remaining at Hornby Castle and auctioned there shortly afterwards by Knight, Frank, and Rutley; the theca number if applicable; and the identification of any copy known to bear Congreve's signature. The manuscript list is occasionally mistaken in the details it gives of formats, dates, and places of publication, although in some cases it may record editions of which copies appear to be no longer extant. Attention is therefore drawn to any major discrepancy between the main entry as given below and the detail as recorded in the original list. Similarly, a note is given of any additional information supplied by the original list or the catalogue of the Leeds sale (e.g. a form of signature or large- or small-paper copies). A shelf list is appended in which the theca numbers are concorded by author or title. As many books were shelved by format, and as many theca numbers were altered and some not entered (mainly the items acquired in 1727–8), it can give only a rough indication of how Congreve's books must have been grouped during the last two or three years of his life.

In a letter to the *Times Literary Supplement* of 2 September 1949, J. Isaacs cited the inscription 'Ex libris Gul: Congreve' in a copy of Virgil's *Opera* (1636), and a similar inscription in a copy of Robert Boyle's *Some motives and incentives to the love of God* (1661). He also observed that Congreve's copy of *Robinson Crusoe*, another work not listed in the catalogue, had 'turned up some time ago'. Only the Robert Boyle work has been located, and is included in this list.

Jacob Tonson Senior, writing to his nephew on 27 January 1729, noted of Congreve's library that 'his collection of books were very genteel & wel chosen. I wish you could think them worth your buying; I think there are in [his] books several notes of his own or corrections & every thing from him will be very valuable' (Allusions, p. 421). However, such books as are known to have been Congreve's are significantly lacking in annotations by him. The completeness of the collection as it stood when catalogued in 1726–8 is also in question: there were almost certainly losses of many books acquired earlier in life. His range of references in, for example, *Amendments of Mr. Collier's False and Imperfect Citations*, implies ready access to texts not included in the catalogue but many of which in 1698 he probably owned, and it is inconceivable that he had read no Molière or Racine before 1697, the date of the earliest editions in his library. Hodges has noted that, as there were in 1700 no fewer than five living members of the family bearing the name William Congreve, some books so inscribed may not have been those of the dramatist, but there may be some, like the copy of *The Poetical Works of John Milton* (1695) now in the William Andrews Clark Library, which were indubitably his but were not catalogued in 1727–8. Another signed 'W Congreve' but absent from the catalogue is Guarini's *Il Pastor Fido* (Venice, 1608). In 1711 he was said to have lent to Bernard Lintott 'an Old Edition' of Shakespeare's poems, probably *Poems: Written by Wil. Shakespeare. Gent.* (1640), possibly even *Shake-speares Sonnets* (1609), which was used in preparing the second volume of Lintott's collection, but these too are missing from the catalogue. Of even greater interest in many ways is the record by William Oldys that 'the famous Dryden, and also Mr. Congreve after him, had collected some volumes of old ballads and penny story books' (*A Literary Antiquary: Memoir of William Oldys, Esq.* (1862), 98). Only one volume of such 'Miscellanies bound together' appears in the catalogue (List 405). But it would be a mistake to think of personal libraries in the period as stable collections. Generous as he was, Congreve undoubtedly lent many of his books to friends who never returned them.

Also uncertain are the dates on which he might have acquired them: while imprints indicate the *terminus a quo* for some books published during Congreve's lifetime, there is no sure way of knowing when he actually obtained any particular item. A high proportion of the books listed here could not have been in his library before 1701, the period of his greatest literary output.

The existing list is nevertheless a valuable record of books he certainly owned. One might note its linguistic range: it includes works in English, Latin, Greek, French, Italian, and Spanish. It is of course rich in classical texts, English poetry, and drama. The authors most often represented and perhaps most important to him are: Cicero, Homer, Virgil, Juvenal, Terence, Montaigne, Ovid, and Shakespeare. As to the ancient classics, as Hodges notes, 'The breadth of his interest is shown by the fact that over sixty Greek and Latin writers are either represented in his library or referred to in his own writings.' Yet the collection is also strong in philosophy, with texts by Hobbes, Descartes, Spinoza, Locke, and Newton, and there are several works on medicine, pharmacology, and mathematics. His library also contained an interesting selection of travel books (some twenty or so), romance narratives, and popular literature. For a consideration of the import of Congreve's library in suggesting the nature of his attitude to Christian belief, see Harold Love, 'Was Congreve a Christian? *An Approach to Congreve* by Aubrey Williams', in *Themes in Drama 5: Drama and Religion* (Cambridge University Press, 1983), 293–309, esp. pp. 305–6. Yet such questions are rarely resolved by book lists. While, by the standards of the day, his library was weak in theology, it still had room for works as diverse as Paolo Sarpi's *The Historie of the Councel of Trent* and Robert Barclay's *An Apology for the True Christian Divinity*; see also his praise of John Hales and of Tillotson, both Christian authors whose works he owned and clearly valued (*Amendments*, p. 105, and dedication, 'Dramatick Works of John Dryden', p. 132).

Ablancourt, Nicolas Perrot d' (1606–64) (tr.), *see* Cæsar [Commentarii. 1650].

—— (tr.), *see* Lucian of Samosata, *Lucien de la traduction de N. Perrot* (1655).

—— (tr.), *see* Tacitus, *Les oeuvres* (1691).

—— (tr.), *see* Thucydides, *L'histoire de Thucydide* (1662).

Addison, Joseph (1672–1719), *The Campaign, a poem to his grace the Duke of Marlborough.* 3rd edn. (London: printed for Jacob Tonson, 1705). ESTC N929; Foxon A30. In: *A Collection of poems, occasionally written upon the victories of Blenheim and Ramillies* (1708).

—— *Remarks on several parts of Italy, &c. in the years 1701, 1702, 1703* (London: printed for Jacob Tonson, 1705), 8°. List 23. Theca 28. ESTC T74545.

—— (ed.), *see Musarum anglicanarum analecta* (1699).

—— (tr.), *see* Ovid [Metamorphoses. 1717].

Ainsworth, Robert (1660–1743) (ed.), *see* Kemp, John, *Monumenta* (1720).

Aléman, Mateo (1547–1614?), *The rogue; or, the life of Guzman de Alfarache* (Oxford: printed by William Turner for Robert Allot, 1630), 2°. List 262. Theca 2. Leeds 9. STC, 290. Translated by James Mabbe. Congreve's copy, signed 'Will: Congreve' on the title page and bearing the Leeds bookplate: Y: Z65/O216.

Alexander ab Alexandro (d. 1523), *Alexandri ab Alexandro iurisperiti neapolitani Genialium dierum libri sex* (Hanoviæ: typis Wechelianis, apud Claudium Marnium & heredes Joan. Aubrii, 1610), 8°. List 17. Theca 7.

L'Amant oisif, see Riflé de Garouville, Savinien.

Amours des dames illustres de nostre siècle (1700), *see* Bussy-Rabutin, Roger, comte de.

Ampelius, Lucius (2nd or 3rd c. AD), *Liber memorialis*. In: Florus, Lucius Annæus [Epitome rerum romanorum].

Amyot, Jacques, Bishop of Auxerre (1513–93) (tr.), *see* Longus, *Les Amours pastorales de Daphnis et Chloé* (1716).

Anacreon (6th c. BC), and **Sappho** (b. mid-7th c. BC), *Les Poesies d'Anacreon et de Sapho, traduites de grec en françois . . . par Madame Dacier* (Amsterdam: chez Paul Marret, 1699), 12°. List 190. Theca 25.

Anghiera, Pietro Martire d' (1457–1526), *The history of trauayle in the West and East Indies, and other countreys lying eyther way, towards the fruitfull and ryche Moluccas . . . done into Englyshe by Richarde Eden . . . augmented, and finished by Richarde Willes* (London: printed by Richarde Jugge, 1577), 4°. List 646. Theca 8. STC 649; ESTC S122069.

Annales galantes, see Desjardins, Marie Catherine Hortense.

Annesley, Arthur (d. 1737), *see* Catullus [Works. 1702].

Anton, Robert (b.1584 or 1585), *The valiant Welshman. Or the true chronicle history of the life . . . of Caradoc the Great . . . Written by R.A. gent.* (London: printed for William Gilbertson, 1663), 4°. List 551 ('Shirley's Plays: And also Caradoc the Great *or the Valiant Welchman.* 4°. 1663'). Theca 8. Wing A3698; ESTC R6872. Bound with James Shirley's *Two Playes* (1657). Sometimes also attributed to Robert Armin or Robert Aylett.

Arbuthnot, John (1667–1735), *Oratio anniversaria harvæana, habita . . . die xviii Octobris, A.D. 1727* (Londini: impensis Jacobi Tonson, 1727), 4°. List 35. ESTC T132532.

—— *Tables of ancient coins, weights and measures, explain'd and exemplify'd in several dissertations* (London: printed for J. Tonson, 1727), 4°. List 34. ESTC N65572.

Aretino, Pietro (1492–1556), *La Prima parte de ragionamenti* ([London: printed by J. Windet], 1584), 8°. List 25 (place of publication and publisher not given). Theca 6. STC 19912; ESTC S4825.

Aristophanes (*c*.457–*c*.385 BC), *Comedies grecques . . . traduites en françois, avec des notes critiques, & un examen de chaque peice selon les regles du theatre, par madame Dacier* (Paris: chez Denys Thierry, et Claude Barbin, 1692), 12°. List 192. Theca 25. Congreve's copy, signed 'W: Congreve' on the title page: Boston Public Library.

Aristotle (384–322 BC) [Poetics. 1542] *Aristotelis Poetica, per Alexandrum Paccium . . . in latinum conuersa* (Paris: prostant apud Jacobus Bogardum, 1542), 16°. List 8 ('24°.'). Theca 5.

—— [Poetics. 1692] *La Poëtique d'Aristote . . . Traduite en françois avec des remarques critiques sur tout l'ouvrage. Par Mr. Dacier* (Paris: chez Claude Barbin, 1692), 12°. List 198. Theca 12.

—— [Rhetoric. 1619] *Aristotelis De rhetorica seu arte dicendi libri tres* (Londini: typis Eduardi Griffini, 1619), 4°. List 7. Theca 22. STC 766; ESTC S100218. Edited by Theodore Goulston.

—— [Rhetoric. 1668] *La Rhétorique d'Aristote en françois* (Paris, 1668?), 4°. List 9 ('4°. Par. 1668.'; this edition not located). Theca 22. Translated by François Cassandre.

—— *see also*, Rapin, René, *Reflections on Aristotle's treatise of poesie* (1674).

Arnauld, Antoine (1612–94), and **Pierre Nicole** (1625–95), *La logique, ou L'Art de penser. Septiéme edition, revuë & de nouveau augmentée* (Amsterdam: chez Henri Wetstein, 1697), 12°. List 11. Theca 24.

Arsinoe, *see* Stanzani, Tomaso.

Astell, Mary (1666–1731), *The Christian religion, as profess'd by a daughter of the Church of England* [i.e. Mary Astell] (London: printed by S.H. for R. Wilkin, 1705), 8°. List 515. Theca 14. ESTC T115540.

Athenæus, of Naucratis (*fl. c.*200) [Deipnosophistæ. 1556] *Athenæi Dipnosophistarum sive coenae sapientium libri XV. natale de Comitibus* (Basiliæ: per Henrichum Petri, 1556), 8°. List 33 ('12°.') Theca 18.

—— [Deipnosophistæ. 1611] *Deipnosophistarum libri xv. Isaacus Casaubonus Græcum textum recensuit ... Addita est Jacobi Dalechampii Latina interpretatio, cum notis* ([Heidelberg]: in bibliopolio Commeliniano, 1611), 2°. List 1. Theca 1.

Atterbury, Francis, Bishop of Rochester (1662–1732), *The rights, powers, and privileges of an English Convocation stated and vindicated.* 2nd edn. (London: printed for Tho. Bennet, 1701), 8°. List 16. Theca 14. ESTC T45106.

Aubignac, François-Hédelin, abbé d' (1604–76), *La pratique du theatre* (Paris: chez Antoine de Sommaville, 1657), 4°. List 469. Theca 14. Congreve's copy, signed 'Will: Congreve' on the title page, is in a private collection in North America. There are no annotations.

—— *The whole art of the stage* (London: printed for the author, and sold by William Cadman, Rich. Bentley, Sam. Smith, & T. Fox, 1684), 4°. List 10. Theca 27. Leeds 298 ('*bound in* 2 vol. *original vellum* ... William Congreve's copy, with his signature in each volume.'). Sold to Tregaskis, but its present location is unknown. Wing A4185; ESTC R16044. Presumably printed for the (anonymous) editor-translator.

Aubrey, John (1626–97), *Miscellanies, viz. I. Day-fatality. II. Local-fatality. III. Ostenta....* (London: printed for Edward Castle, 1696), 8°. List 15. Theca 8. Wing A4188; ESTC R18928.

Aulnoy, Marie Catherine La Mothe, Comtesse (1650?–1705), *Tales of the fairys. Translated from the French* (London: printed for T. Cockerill, 1699?). List 405 (edition not given; bound with 10 other miscellaneous 4° items). Theca 28. Not in Wing, but cf. *TC* iii 123: 'Tales of the Fairys. Translated from the French. Twelves.... printed for T. Cockerill'.

—— *Histoire nouvelle de la cour d'Espagne* (La Haye: chez Jean Alberts, 1692), 12°. List 297. Theca 26.

Balzac, Jean Louis Guez, Sieur de (d. 1654), *Les oeuvres diverses* (Paris: par P. Rocolet, 1644), 4°. List 55. Theca 2. Leeds 33.

—— *Le Prince* (Paris: chez Toussainct du Bray, Pierre Roccolet, et Claude Sonnius, 1631), 4°. List 56. Theca 2.

Barclay, Robert (1648–90), *An apology for the true Christian divinity, as the same is held forth ... by ... Quakers.* 4th edn. (London: printed and sold by T. Sowle,

1701), 8°. List 53 (date of publication not given, but place of publication and format suggest the 4th or 5th edn.). Theca 14. ESTC T2240 (4th edn.); T85687 (5th edn.).

Barker, Ralph (*c*.1648–1708) (ed.), *see* Tillotson, John, *Sermons* (1700–4).

Barnes, Joshua (1654–1712) (ed.), *see* Homer [Works. 1711] *Homerou Ilias kai Odysseia*.

Bate, George (1608–89), *Pharmacopœia Bateana: or, Bate's dispensatory. Translated from the last edition of the Latin copy, publish'd by Mr. James Shipton. . . . By William Salmon*. 4th edn. (London: printed for W. Innys, 1713), 8°. List 215. Theca 4. ESTC T89309.

Baudoin, Jean (1590?–1650) (tr.), *see* Lucian of Samosata, *Les œuvres* [1613].

Baudot de Juilly, Nicolas (1678–1759), *Germaine de Foix, reine d'Espagne* (Amsterdam: chez Hans Henry, MDCCC [i.e. 1700]), 12°. List 275. Theca 26.

—— *Relation historique et galante de l'invasion de l'Espagne par les Maures*. 4 vols. (La Haye: chez Adrian Moetjens, 1699), 12°. List 302, 522. Theca 11.

Bayle, Pierre (1647–1706), *Dictionnaire historique et critique*. 3rd edn. 4 vols. (Rotterdam: chez Michel Bohm, 1720), 2°. List 172. Theca 16. Hornby Castle 1175. Edited by Prosper Marchand.

Beard, Thomas (d. 1632), *Pedantius* (1631), *see* Forsett, Edward.

Beaumont, Francis (1584–1616), and **John Fletcher** (1579–1625), *Fifty comedies and tragedies*. 2nd edn. (London: printed by J. Macock [and H. Hills] for John Martyn, Henry Herringman, Richard Marriot, 1679), 2°. List 42 (large paper). Theca 1. Leeds 40. Wing B1582; ESTC R13766.

—— *Cupids revenge*, 4°. List 407, 490 (edition not given; bound with 5 other miscellaneous 4° items). Theca 28. Cf. STC 1667–9; ESTC S101156–8.

Bentley, Richard (1662–1742), *see* Boyle, Charles, *Dr. Bentley's Dissertations* (1698).

Bentley, Thomas (1693–1742) (ed.), *see* Cicero [De finibus. 1718].

Berneville, Marie Catherine Jumelle de, *see* Aulnoy, Marie Catherine La Mothe, Comtesse.

Bernier, François (1620–88) (ed.), *see* Gassendi, Pierre, *Abregé de la philosophie* (1684).

Betterton, Thomas (1635?–1710), *see* Shakespeare [Henry IV. pt. 2. 1720].

Bible, *The holy Bible, containing the Old and New Testaments*. 2 vols. (Oxford: printed by J. Baskett, 1727, 26), 4°. List 69 ('in four Voloumns'; i.e. 2 vols., possibly interleaved, bound in 4?). Theca 22. Cf. ESTC T81311; *Historical Catalogue of the Printed Editions of Holy Scripture in the Library of the British and Foreign Bible Society*, 2 vols., comp. T.H. Darlow and H.F. Moule (1903–11).

Bignon, abbé (Jean Paul) (1662–1743), *Les avantures d'Abdalla . . . Traduites en françois sur le manuscrit arabe, trouvé à Batavia par Mr. De Sandisson* [i.e. Abbé Jean Paul Bignon] (La Haye: chez Guillaume de Voys, 1713), 12°. List 27 ('24°'). Theca 26.

Blackmore, Richard, Sir (d. 1729), *Creation. A philosophical poem* (London: printed for S. Buckley; and J. Tonson, 1712), 8°. List 48. Theca 28. ESTC T74300; Foxon B242.

——— *Eliza: an epick poem* (London: printed for Awnsham and John Churchill, 1705), 2°. List 47. Theca 1. ESTC T75146; Foxon B249.

——— *Essays upon several subjects* (London: printed for E. Curll, and J. Pemberton, 1716), 8°. List 49. Theca 14. ESTC T74855.

——— *King Arthur. An heroick poem* (London: printed for Awnsham and John Churchil, and Jacob Tonson, 1697), 2°. List 46. Theca 1. Wing B3077.

——— *The nature of man. A poem. In three books* (London: printed for Sam. Buckley; and sold by the booksellers of London and Westminster, 1711), 8°. List 422. Theca 28. ESTC T92961; Foxon B263.

Blasius, Gerardus Leonardus (1626?–1692?) (ed.), *see* Willis, Thomas, *Opera omnia* (1682).

Blenheim, see Lyttelton, George.

Blount, Thomas (1618–79), *A law-dictionary and glossary*. 3rd edn. (In the Savoy: printed by Eliz. Nutt and R. Gosling, assignees of Edw. Sayer, for D. Browne, J. Walthoe, J. Nicholson, G. Sawbridge, B. Tooke, D. Midwinter, B. Cowse, R. Gosling, W. Mears, J. Browne, J. Hooke, and E. Nutt, 1717), 2°. List 50. Theca 1. ESTC T143722 or T149943 (reissue).

Boccaccio, Giovanni (1313–75), [Decameron. 1684] *The novels and tales of John Boccaccio, the first refiner of Italian prose*. 5th edn. (London: printed for Awnsham Churchill, 1684), 2°. List 68 ('Boccac.s' Nouels English'; format and edition not given, but listed with other folios). Theca 33. Wing B3378; ESTC R2136. Translation sometimes attributed to John Florio.

——— [Decameron. 1712] *Contes et nouvelles de Bocace Florentin*. 2nd edn. 2 vols. (Cologne: chez Jacques Gaillard, 1712), 8°. List 123. Theca 23.

——— *Violenta, or the rewards of virtue: turn'd from Boccace into verse, see* Pix, Mary Griffith, *Violenta* (1704).

Boccalini, Traiano (1556–1613), *I ragguagli di Parnasso; or, Advertisements from Parnassus. With the politick touch-stone.... now put into English by the right honourable, Henry Earl of Monmouth* (London: printed for Humphrey Moseley, and Thomas Heath, 1656), 2°. List 43. Theca 2. Wing B3380; ESTC R2352.

Boiardo, Matteo Maria, conte de Scandiano (1440 or 1441–94), *Nouvelle traduction de Roland l'amoureux... ornez de figures*. 2 vols. (Paris: chez Pierre Ribou, 1717), 12°. List 513. Theca 23. Translated by Alain René Le Sage.

Boileau Despréaux, Nicolas (1636–1711), [Works. 1695] *Oeuvres diverses... avec Le Traité du sublime*. Nouvelle édn. 2 vols. (Amsterdam: chez Antoine Schelte, 1695), 12°. List 59. Theca 30.

——— [Works. 1717] *Oeuvres... avec des éclaircissemens historiques, donnez pare lui-même*. Nouvelle édn. 4 vols. (Amsterdam: chez David Mortier, 1717), 12°. List 58. Theca 30. Edited by Claude Brossette.

——— [Works. 1718] *Oeuvres... avec des éclaircissemens historiques, donnez par lui-même*. Nouvelle édn. 2 vols. (Amsterdam, chez David Mortier, 1718), 4°. List 57. Theca 19. Edited by Claude Brossette.

Bonarelli della Rovere, Guido Ubaldo, conte (1563–1608), *Filli di Sciro, favola pastorale* (Amsterdam: nella stamperia del S.D. Elsevier; Paris: si vende appresso Thomaso Jolly, 1678), 32°. List 253 ('24°.'). Theca 5.

Bononcini, Giovanni Battista (1670–1747), *Cantate e duetti dedicati alla Sacra Maèsta di Giorgio Re dei la Gran Bretagna &c.* (Londra: [s.n.], 1721), 2°. List 65. Theca 21. Répertoire International des Sources Musicales A/1, B3601. Engraved musical score, with letterpress subscription list; subscribers include Congreve.

Book of Common Prayer [Greek translation of the Book of Common Prayer of 1662] (Cambridge: printed by John Field, 1665). List 371 ('8°. Cantabr. 1665.'). Theca 14. Wing B3631A; ESTC R172833. Translated into Greek by James Duport. Congreve's copy, signed 'Ex libris Gulielmi: Congreve' on the first page of the text proper (A1^r), is in a private collection in North America.

Bouhours, Dominique (1628–1702), *Les entretiens d'Ariste et d'Eugene.* 2nd edn. (Paris: chez Sebastien Mabre-Cramoisy, 1671), 12°. List 31. Theca 12.

Bourdeille, Pierre de, seigneur de Brantôme (1540–1614), *Memoires... contenant les vies de dames galantes de son temps.* 2 vols. (Leyde: Jean Sambix le jeune, 1699), 12°. List 63. Theca 26.

Boxhorn, Marcus Zuerius (1612–53) (ed.), *see* Sallust [Works. 1634].

Boyer, Abel (1667–1729) (tr.), *see* Hamilton, Anthony, *Memoirs of the life of Count de Grammont* (1714).

Boyle, Charles, 4th Earl of Orrery (1676–1731), *Dr. Bentley's Dissertations on the Epistles of Phalaris and the Fables of Æsop, examin'd by the Hon. Charles Boyle* (London: printed for Tho. Bennet, 1698), 8°. List 60. Theca 33. Wing O469 or O470; ESTC R17620 or R22017.

Boyle, Robert, *Some motives and incentives to the love of God, pathetically discours'd of in a letter to a friend.* 2nd edn. (London: printed for Henry Herringman and are to be sold at his shop, 1661). Wing B4033; ESTC R209935. Not listed in the catalogue of Congreve's library. Congreve's copy, signed 'Ex Lib: Guilm Congreve' on the title page: Thomas Fisher Rare Book Library, Toronto.

Brébeuf, Georges de (1617?–1661) (tr.), *see* Lucan [Pharsalia. 1683].

Brent, Nathaniel, Sir (1573?–1652) (tr.), *see* Sarpi, Paolo, *The historie of the Councel of Trent* (1620).

Broome, William (1689–1745?), *The oak, and the dunghill. A fable* (London: printed: and sold by J. Roberts, 1728), 2°. List 438. ESTC T41690; Foxon B499–B500.

—— (ed.), *see* Homer [Iliad. 1712].

—— (tr.), *see* Homer [Odyssey. 1725–6].

Brossette, Claude (ed.), *see* Boileau Despréaux, Nicolas [Works. 1717, 1718].

Brown, Thomas (1663–1704) (tr.), *see* Scarron, Paul, *The whole comical works* (1712).

Browne, Thomas, Sir (1605–82), *Religio medici.* 4th edn. (London: printed by E. Cotes for Andrew Crook, 1656), 8°. List 519 ('12°.'). Theca 6. Wing B5172; ESTC R22776.

Browne, William, *see* Le Roy, Marin, *The history of Polexander* (1648).

Buckingham, George Villiers, Duke of (1628–87), *The rehearsal.* 5th edn. (London: printed for Thomas Dring, and sold by John Newton, 1687), 4°. List 406. Theca 27. Leeds 209 (Congreve's signature). Wing B5327; ESTC

R28540. Congreve's copy, signed 'Will: Congreve': Robert H. Taylor collection, Princeton University.

Buckingham, John Sheffield, Duke of (1648–1721), *A Collection of poems: viz. The temple of death: by the Marquis of Normanby. An epistle to the Earl of Dorset: by Charles Montague, Lord Halifax. With several original poems . . . by the E. of Roscommon. The E. of Orrery* (London: printed for Daniel Brown; and Benjamin Tooke, 1701), 8°. List 410. Theca 20. Case 151 (e). ESTC T116471.

—— *Essay on poetry.* In: Dillon, Wentworth, *Poems by the Earl of Roscommon* (1717).

Budgell, Eustace (1686–1737) (tr.), *see* Theophrastus, *The moral characters* (1714).

Bulstrode, Whitelocke (1650–1724), *An essay of transmigration, in defence of Pythagoras* (London: printed by E.H. for T. Basset, 1692), 8°. List 52. Theca 8. Wing B5449A; ESTC R16493.

Burgersdijck, Franco Petri (1590–1635), *Fr. Burgersdicii Institutionum logicarum libri duo* (Cantabridgæ: apud Joann. Hayes. 1680. Prostant venales apud Guil. Graves jun.), 8°. List 62 ('Abest titulus.'). Wing B5636; ESTC R29149. Theca 6. This edition, the latest in English, seems likely, but cf. STC 4108, Wing B5631–5, and ESTC.

Burnaby, William (1673?–1706) (tr.), *see* Petronius Arbiter, *The satyr* (1694).

Burnet, Gilbert, Bishop of Salisbury (1643–1715), *Bishop Burnet's History of his own time.* Vol. 1 (London: printed for Thomas Ward, 1724), 2°. List 37. Theca 1. Hornby Castle 1138. ESTC T144689; T144688 (large paper).

—— *Some letters, containing an account of what seemed most remarkable in travelling through Switzerland, Italy, some parts of Germany, &c., in the years 1685. and 1686. Written . . . to R[obert]. B[oyle].* 2nd edn. (Rotterdam: printed for Abraham Acher, 1687), 8°. List 38. Theca 3. Wing B5918; ESTC R25315.

Burnet, Thomas (1635?–1715), *Archæologiæ philosophicæ* (Londini: typis R.N. impensis Gualt. Kettilby, 1692), 4°. List 39. Theca 14. Wing B5943; ESTC R4159.

—— *Telluris theoria sacra.* 3rd edn. (Londini: impensis Benj. Took, 1702), 4°. List 40. Theca 14. ESTC T112057.

—— *The theory of the earth . . . The two first books concerning the deluge, and concerning paradise* (London: printed by R. Norton for Walter Kettilby, 1684), 2°. List 41. Theca 1. Wing B5950; ESTC R10963.

Busbecq, Ogier Ghislain de (1522–92), *A. Gislenii Busbequii Omnia quæ extant* (Lugd. Batavorum [Leiden]: ex officina Elzeviriana, 1633), 24°. List 64. Theca 5.

Busby, Richard (1606–95), *Græcæ grammatices rudimenta in usum scholae westmonastriensis* (Londini: ex officinâ Eliz. Redmayne, 1693), 8°. List 265. Theca 7. Wing B6224; ESTC R4460.

Bussy-Rabutin, Roger, comte de (1618–93), *Amours des dames illustres de nostre siècle* (Cologne: chez Jean Le Blanc, 1700), 12°. List 21. Theca 26. By Roger de Bussy-Rabutin and others.

C., J.D.D., monsieur, *L'Honnête homme et le scelerat . . . Par monsieur J.D.D.C. suivant la copie de Paris* (Brusselles: chez Louis de Wainne, 1710), 12°. List 316. Theca 26.

Cæsar, Julius (102–44 BC) [Works. 1712] *C. Julii Cæsaris quæ extant... Tabulis Æneis ornata.* 2 vols. (Londini: sumptibus & typis Jacobi Tonson, 1712), 2°. List 71. Theca 10. Hornby Castle 1187. ESTC T136730.

—— [Commentarii. 1571] *C. Julii Cæsaris Commentarii, post omnes omnium editiones accurata sedulitate... emendati & studiosissimè recogniti à Joanne Rosseto* (Lausannæ: excudebat Joannes Probus, 1571), 2°. List 72. Theca 1.

—— [Commentarii. 1650] *Les Commentaires de César. De la traduction de N. Perrot D'Ablancourt. Remarques sur la carte de l'ancienne Gaule tirée des Commentaires de César par le Sr Sanson d'Abbeville* (Paris: chez la veuve Jean Camusat et Pierre Le Petit, 1650), 4°. List 73. Theca 13.

—— [Commentarii. 1677] *The commentaries of C. Julius Cæsar, of his wars in Gallia and the civil wars betwixt him and Pompey. Translated into English... By Clement Edmonds* (In the Savoy: by Tho. Newcomb for Jonathan Edwin, 1677), 2°. List 74. Theca 1. Wing C200; ESTC R16632.

Calvi, François de, *Histoire generale des larrons* (Rouen: chez Robert Daré, 1649), 8°. List 295. Theca 3.

Camões, Luiz de (1524?–80), *The Lusiad, or, Portugals historicall poem.... Put into English by Richard Fanshaw* (London: printed [by Thomas Newcombe] for Humphrey Moseley, 1655), 2°. List 152. Theca 2. Leeds 125. Wing C397; ESTC R18836. Congreve's copy, signed 'Wᵐ Congreve' on the title page: Baker Library, Dartmouth College.

Camus, Jean Pierre, Bishop of Belley (1584–1652), *A true tragical history of two illustrious Italian families; couched under the names of Alcimus and Vannoza. Written in French... Done into English by a person of quality* (London: printed for William Jacob, 1677), 8°. List 14. Theca 8. Wing C419; ESTC R12883.

Canter, Willem (1542–75) (tr.), *see* Stobæus, *Ioannis Stobæi Eclogarum libri duo* (1575).

Carey, Henry, 2nd Earl of Monmouth (1596–1661) (tr.), *see* Boccalini, Traiano, *I ragguagli di Parnasso* (1656).

Cartwright, William (1611–43), *Comedies, tragi-comedies, with other poems... The ayres and songs set by Mr. Henry Lawes* (London: printed for [Thomas Robinson and] Humphrey Moseley, 1651), 8°. List 90. Theca 20. Wing C709; ESTC R208874.

Casaubon, Isaac (1559–1614) (ed.), *see* Athenæus of Naucratis [Deipnosophistæ. 1611].

—— *see* Celsus [De medicina. 1713].

—— *see* Strabo, *Strabonis Rerum geographicarum* (1620).

Cassandre, François (d. 1695) (tr.), *see* Aristotle [Rhetoric. 1668].

Cassius Dio Cocceianus (*c.*150–235), *The history of Dion Cassius abridg'd by Xiphilin... Done from the Greek by Mr. Manning.* 2 vols. (London: printed for A. and J. Churchill, 1704), 8°. List 202. Theca 13. ESTC T130908.

Catullus, Gaius Valerius, Tibullus, and **Sextus Propertius** [Works. 1680] *Catullus, Tibullus et Propertius, ex recensione Joannis Georgii Grævii, cum notis integris Jos. Scaligeri* (Trajecti ad Rhenum [Utrecht]: sumptibus Rudolphi a Zyll, 1680), 8°. List 92. Theca 7.

—— [Works. 1686] *Catullus, Tibullus, Propertius, cum C. Galli fragmentis* (Amstelædami: apud Isbrandum Haring, 1686), 24°. List 94. Theca 5.

—— [Works. 1691] *C. Valerii Catulli opera, ex recensione Isaaci Vossii, cum ejusdem notis.* 2nd edn. (Lugduni Batavorum [Leiden]: apud Danielem à Gaesbeeck, Cornelium Boutesteyn, Johannis de Vivie, Petrum van der Aa, 1691), 4°. List 95. Theca 7.

—— [Works. 1702] *Catulli, Tibulli, et Propertii Opera* (Cantabrigiæ: typis academicis, impensis Jacobi Tonson bibliopolæ Londin., 1702), 4°. List 91. Theca 17. ESTC T101568. Edited by Arthur Annesley. Congreve was one of the 'Subscribers for the Encouragement of this Undertaking': see Horace [Works. 1699].

—— [Works. 1715] *Catulli, Tibulli, et Propertii Opera* (Londini: ex officinâ Jacobi Tonson, & Johannis Watts, 1715), 12°. List 93. Theca 24. ESTC T145213; T145212 (large paper). Edited by Michael Maittaire.

Caumont de La Force, Charlotte Rose de (d. 1724), *Gustave Vasa, histoire de Suède.* 2 vols. (Paris: chez Simon Benard, 1697–8), 12°. List 274 ('1697'). Theca 26. Vol. 2 is dated 1697.

—— *Histoire de Marguerite de Valois, reine de Navarre, soeur de François I.* 4 vols. (Paris: chez François Fournier, 1720), 12°. List 303. Theca 23.

Caxton, William (*c.*1422–91) (tr.), *see* Lefèvre, Raoul, *The destruction of Troy.*

Cebes (*fl. c.*405–366 BC), Κέβητος Θηβαίου Πίναξ. *Cebetis Theban Tabula. Novâ versione, in puerorum usus, donata, et selectionioribus criticorum notis illustrata. Accedit...Ludovici Odaxii versio...Operâ Thomæ Johnson* (Londini: impensis authoris, 1720), 8°. List 108. Theca 6. ESTC T144292.

Celimauro, Il, *Istoria Spagnvola* (Naples, 1622), 12°. List 114. Theca 5. Not located.

Celsus, Aulus Cornelius (53 BC–AD 7) [De medicina. 1592] *Aurelii Cornelii Celsi De re medica libri octo* (Lugduni Batavorum [Leiden]: ex officina Plantiniana, apud Franciscum Raphelengium, 1592), 4°. List 158 ('8°. Lug: Bat:'). Theca 4. Hornby Castle 1256.

—— [De medicina. 1713] *Aur. Corn. Celsi De medicina libri octo, brevioribus Rob. Constantini, Is. Casauboni* (Amstelædami: apud Joannem Wolters, 1713), 8°. List 118. Theca 4.

Cervantes Saavedra, Miguel de (1547–1616) [Don Quixote. 1620] *The history of Don-Quichote.* 2 vols. (London: printed [by William Stansby and by Eliot's Court Press] for Ed. Blounte, 1620), 4°. List 209. Theca 3. STC 4916–17; ESTC S107641–2. Translated by Thomas Shelton.

—— [Don Quixote. 1652] *The history of the valorous and witty-knight-errant, Don-Quixote, of the Mancha* (London: printed by Richard Hodkinsonne for Andrew Crooke, 1652), 2°. List 208. Theca 2. Leeds 134. Wing C1776; ESTC R3484. Translated by Thomas Shelton.

—— [Don Quixote. 1662] *Vida y hechos del ingenioso cavallero Don Quixote de la Mancha.* Nueva ed. 2 vols. (Bruselas: de la emprenta de Juan Mommarte, 1662), 8°. List 207 ('Parte 1'). Theca 8. Leeds 179 ('Parte Primera *only (should be two).*').

Cervantes Saavedra, Miguel de [Don Quixote. 1678] *Histoire de l'admirable Don Quixotte de la Manche.* 4 vols. (Paris: chez Claude Barbin, 1678), 12°. List 210 ('Paris 1679'). Theca 23. Probably the translation by Filleau de Saint-Martin.

—— [Don Quixote. 1697] *Vida y hechos del ingenioso Cavallero Don Quixote de la Mancha.* 2 vols. (Amberes: por Henrico y Cornelio Verdussen *or* por Juan Bautista Verdussen, 1697), 8°. List 206. Theca 11.

—— *Il novelliere Castigliano . . . tradotto . . . nell'Italiana dal Sig. Guglielmo Alessandro de Nouilieri,Clauelli* (Venetia: presso il Barezzi, 1626), 8°. List 115. Theca 3.

—— *Nouvelles . . . traduction nouvelle. Seconde édition, augmentée de plusieurs histoires.* 2 vols. (Amsterdam: chez Claude Jordan, 1709), 12°. List 116. Theca 26.

Céspedes y Meneses, Gonzalo de (1585?–1638), *Gerardo the unfortunate Spaniard, or a pattern for lascivious lovers* (London: printed by William Bentley, and are to be sold by William Shears, 1653), 8°. List 268. Theca 20. Wing C1783; ESTC R210432. Translated by Leonard Digges.

Challes, Robert (1659–*c*.1720), *Les illustres Françoises, histoires veritables.* 2 vols. (La Haye: Hondt, 1713), 12°. List 331. Theca 26.

—— *Journal d'un voyage fait aux Indes orientales par une escadre de six vaisseaux commandez par Mr. Du Quesne, depuis le 24 février 1690, jusqu'au 20 août 1691.* 3 vols. (Rouen: chez Jean Batiste Machuel le Jeune, 1721), 12°. List 621. Theca 3.

Chapelain, Jean (1595–1674), *Les Sentimens de l'Académie françoise sur la tragicomédie du Cid* (Londres: chez Daniel du Chemin, 1703), 12°. List 30. Theca 24. ESTC N49868. Chiefly by Jean Chapelain.

Chapman, George (1559?–1634), *The conspiracie, and tragedie of Charles Duke of Byron, marshall of France,* 4°. List 407, 490 (edition not given. Bound with 5 other miscellaneous 4° items). Theca 28. STC 4968, ESTC S107689 (1608) or STC 4969, ESTC S107690 (1625).

—— (tr.), see Homer [Works. 1616].

—— (tr.), see Homer [Iliad. 1598].

Chardin, Sir John (1643–1713), *The travels of Sir John Chardin into Persia and the East-Indies* (London: printed for Moses Pitt, 1686), 2°. List 81. Theca 9. Wing C2043; ESTC R12885.

Charpentier, François (1620–1702) (tr.), see Xenophon, *La Cyropædie* (1717).

—— see Xenophon, *La vie de Socrate* (1699).

Charron, Pierre (1541–1603), *Of wisdom . . . With an account of the author. Made English by George Stanhope.* 2 vols. (London: printed for M. Gillyflower, M. Bentley, H. Bonwick, J. Tonson, W. Freeman, T. Goodwin, M. Wotton, J. Walthoe, S. Manship, and R. Parker, 1697), 8°. List 117, 549. Theca 33. Wing C3720; ESTC R2811.

Chaucer, Geoffrey (1340?–1400) [Works. 1561] *The workes . . . newlie printed* (London: printed by Ihon Kyngston for Ihon Wight, 1561), 2°. List 75 ('Old Edit. Black letter'). Theca 1. STC 5075–6; ESTC S107206–7.

—— [Works. 1687] *Works . . . To which is adjoyn'd, The story of the siege of Thebes, by John Lidgate* (London: printed in the year 1687), 2°. List 76. Theca 1. Leeds 141. Wing C3736; ESTC R3920. Edited by Thomas Speght.

—— [Works. 1721] *Works . . . compared with the former editions, and many valuable MSS . . . by John Urry.* (London: printed for Bernard Lintott, 1721), 2°. List 77 ('Best Edit.'). Theca 10. ESTC T106027, N066255.

—— *Amorum Troili et Creseidæ libri duo priores Anglico-Latini* (Oxoniæ: excudebat Johannes Lichfield, 1635), 4°. List 601. Theca 20. STC 5097; ESTC S107787. Translated by Sir Francis Kinnaston.

Chaumont, Alexandre de (1640–1710), *A relation of the late embassy of Monsr. de Chaumont, Knt. to the court of the king of Siam* (London: printed for Henry Mortlock, 1687), 12°. List 647 ('Chaumonts Voyage to Siam 16° Lon. 1685'; this edition not located). Theca 6. Wing C3737C; ESTC R6683.

Chiflet, Laurent (1598–1658), *Essay d'une parfaite grammaire, de la langue françoise,* 6th edn. (Bruxelles: chez Lambert Marchant, 1680), 12°. List 130 ('Brux. 1688'; this edition not located). Theca 24.

Choisy, abbé de (1644–1724), *Histoire de Charles Cinquième roi de France. Par monsieur l'abbé de Choisy* (Paris: chez Antoine Dezallier, 1689), 4°. List 294. Theca 13.

Chomel, Pierre Jean Baptiste (1671–1740), *Abregé de l'histoire des plantes usuelles* (Paris: chez Charles Osmont, 1712), 12°. List 127 ('8°.'). Theca 4.

Chorier, Nicholas (1612–92), *Joannis Meursii elegantiæ latini sermonis,* 12°. List 398 (edition not given). Possibly the undated edition published about 1658. Theca 24. Wrongly attributed to Johannes van Meurs.

Cicero, Marcus Tullius [Works. 1692] *Marci Tulli Ciceronis Opera quæ extant omnia: . . . studio atque industria Jani Gulielmii & Jani Gruteri . . . nunc denuo ab Jacobo Gronovio,* 11 vols. (Lugduni Batavorum [Leiden]: apud Petrum van der Aa, 1692), 12°. List 137. Theca 33.

—— [Academica. 1725] *M. Tullii Ciceronis Academica. Recensuit . . . Joannes Davisius* (Cantabrigiæ: typis academicis; sumptibus autem Corn. Crownfield. Prostant apud Jacobum Knapton, Robertum Knaplock, & Paulum Vaillant, 1725), 8°. List 148. Theca 31. ESTC T138133.

—— [De divinatione. 1711] *Traité de la divination traduit du Latin . . . par Mr. l'Abbé Regnier Desmarais* (Amsterdam: chez Isaac Trojel, 1711), 8°. List 142. Theca 12.

—— [De divinatione. 1721] *M. Tullii Ciceronis Libri De divinatione . . . emendavit Joannes Davisius* (Cantabrigiæ: typis academicis; sumptibus autem Cornelii Crownfield, prostant apud Jacobum Knapton, Rob. Knaplock, & Paullum Vaillant, 1721), 8°. List 149. Theca 31. ESTC T111294.

—— [De finibus. 1702] *Tully's five books De finibus . . . Done into English by S.P. gent.* [i.e. Samuel Parker]. *Revis'd . . . with a recommendatory preface. By Jeremy Collier. Together, with an apology for the philosophical writings of Cicero . . . By Mr. Henry Dodwell* (London: printed for Jacob Tonson and Robert Gibson, 1702), 8°. List 139. Theca 32. ESTC T138130.

—— [De finibus. 1718] *M.T. Ciceronis De finibus bonorum et malorum . . . Emendavit, notisque illustravit Thomas Bentley* (Cantabrigiæ: typis academicis, 1718), 8°. List 140. Theca 32. ESTC T136978.

—— [De natura deorum. 1718] *M. Tullii Ciceronis De natura deorum . . . Recensuit . . . Joannes Davisius* (Cantabrigiæ: typis academicis; impensis Cornelii

Crownfield, prostant apud Jacobum Knaptum, Robertum Knaplock, & Paulum Vaillant, 1718), 8°. List 146. Theca 31. ESTC T138222.

—— [De officiis. 1677?] *M.T. Ciceronis De officiis libri tres. Item Cato M. vel De senectute. Lælius vel De amicitia. Paradoxa Stoicorū sex. Somnium Scipionis* (Amsterdam: ex officinâ Elzevriana, 1677). 12°. List 141 ('Cato Major, Lælius, et Somnium Scipionis'; edition not given). Theca 24.

—— [De officiis. 1688] *M.Tulii Ciceronis De officiis libri tres, Cato Maior Laellius, paradoxa, somnium Scipionis. Ex recensione Ioannis Georgii Grævii* (Amstelodami: ex typographia P. & I. Blaeu, 1688), 8°. List 134. Theca 31.

—— [De officiis. 1689] *M.Tullii Ciceronis De officiis libri tres . . . ex recensione Joannis Georgii Grævii* (Amstelodami: apud Henricum Wetstenium, 1689), 12°. List 135. Theca 32.

—— [De oratore. 1696] *M. Tullius Cicero De oratore ad Q. fratrem. Ex recensuit Tho. Cockman* (Oxoniæ: e theatro Sheldoniano, 1696), 8°. List 138. Theca 32. Wing C4298; ESTC R24275.

—— [Epistolæ. 1684] *M. Tullii Ciceronis Epistolarum libri XVI ad T. Pomponium Atticum, ex recensione Joannis Georgii Grævii*. 4 vols. (2 vols. text, 2 vols. notes) (Amstelædami: sumptibus Blaviorum, & Henrici Wetstenii, 1684), 8°. List 144. Theca 31.

—— [Epistolæ. 1689] *M. Tullii Ciceronis Epistolarum libri XVI. ad familiares . . . Ex recensione Io. Georgii Grævii* (Amstelædami: apud Henricum Wetstenium, 1689), 12°. List 136. Theca 32.

—— [Epistolæ. 1693] *M. Tullii Ciceronis Epistolarum libri XVI ad familiares . . . ex recensione Joannis Georgii Grævii*. 4 vols. (2 vols. in 4?) (Amstelodami: ex typographia P. & I. Blaeu, prostant apud Wolfgang, Jansonio-Waesbergio, Boom, à Someren, & Goethals, 1693), 8°. List 143. Theca 31.

—— [Orationes. 1695-9] *M. Tullii Ciceronis Orationes, ex recensione Joannis Georgii Grævii*. 14 vols. (6 vols. text, 7 vols. notes, index) (Amstelodami: ex typographia P. & I. Blaeu, prostant apud Jansonio-Waesbergio, Boom, à Someren, & Goethals, 1695-99), 8°. List 145. Theca 31.

—— [Quæstiones Tusculanæ. 1723] *M. Tullii Ciceronis Tusculanarum disputationum libri V. Cum commentario Joannis Davisii*. 2nd edn. (Cantabrigiæ: typis academicis, sumptibus Cornelii Crownfield, prostant apud Jacobum Knapton, Rob. Knaplock, & Paulum Vaillant, 1723), 8°. List 147. Theca 31. ESTC T138923.

Clay, Stephen, *An Epistle from the elector of Bavaria to the French king: after the battel of Ramillies* (London: printed for Jacob Tonson, 1706), 2°. List 413, 485. Theca 15. ESTC T062160; Foxon C233. In: *A Collection of poems, occasionally written upon the victories of Blenheim and Ramillies* (1708).

Clericus, Joannis (ed.), *see* Menander, *Menandri et Philemonis reliquæ* (1709).

Cluverius, Philippus (1580–1622), *Philippi Cluverii Introductionis in universam geographiam tam veterem quam novam libri VI* (Amstelodami: ex officina Elzeviriana, 1659), 24°. List 131 (date of publication not given). Theca 5.

Cobb, Samuel (1675–1713) (tr.), *see* Quillet, Claude, *Callipædia* (1712).

Cockman, Thomas (ed.), *see* Cicero [De oratore. 1696].

Cogan, Henry (tr.), *see* Mendes Pinto, Fernando, *The voyages and adventures* (1663).

A Collection of poems, occasionally written upon the victories of Blenheim and Ramillies. By the most eminent hands. Now publish'd in one volume in folio (London: for Jacob Tonson, 1708), 2°. List 413, 485. Theca 15. ESTC N27926. Leeds 5 ('William Congreve and others. A Collection of Poems… upon the Victories of Blenheim and Ramillies'). Although it lacks his signature and the Leeds book-plate, the Leeds copy was probably that owned by Congreve. It was bought, presumably on 2 June 1930, by Quaritch and bears the note 'Collated and Complete. pp. Bernard Quaritch the 3/6/30', i.e. 3 June 1930. It is now in a private collection in North America.

It includes: [Matthew Prior], *A Letter to Monsieur Boileau Depreaux; occasion'd by the victory at Blenheim* (1704); Joseph Addison, *The Campaign, a poem to his grace the Duke of Marlborough.* 3rd edn. (1705); [Matthew Prior], *An Ode humbly inscrib'd to the queen on the late glorious success of her majesty's arms. Written in imitation of Spencer's stile* (1706); William Congreve, *A Pindarique ode, humbly offer'd to the queen, on the victorious progress of her majesty's arms. To which is prefix'd, a discourse on the pindarique ode* (1706); [William Walsh], *Ode for the thanksgiving day* (1706); [Stephen Clay], *An Epistle from the Elector of Bavaria to the French king: after the battel of Ramillies* (1706); Nicholas Rowe, *A Poem upon the late glorious successes of her majesty's arms &c. Humbly inscrib'd to the right honourable the Earl of Godolphin, and High-Treasurer of England* (1707); [John Conduitt], *A Poem upon the late glorious successes &c. Humbly inscrib'd to his grace the Duke of Marlborough* (1707); John Paris, *Ramillies. A poem humbly inscrib'd to his grace the Duke of Marlborough. Written in imitation of Milton* (1706); [Elijah Fenton], *An Ode to the sun for the new-year* (1707); William Harison, *Woodstock Park. A poem.* 2nd edn. (1706); [Rev. Mr Vernon], *Corona civica. A poem to the right honourable the lord-keeper of the great seal of England* (1706); and [Rev. Mr Vernon], *The Union. A poem, inscrib'd to the right honourable lord Marquis of Granby, one of her majesty's commissioners of the Scotch union* (1707).

A Collection of poems: viz. The temple of death: by the Marquis of Normanby, see Buckingham, John Sheffield, Duke of, *A Collection of poems* (1701).

A Collection of the several statutes, and parts of statutes, now in force, relating to high treason (London: printed by Charles Bill and the executrix of Thomas Newcomb, 1709), 12°. List 106. Theca 6. ESTC T136807.

Collier, Jeremy (1650–1726), *A short view of the immorality, and profaneness of the English stage* (London: printed for S. Keble, R. Sare, and H. Hindmarsh, 1698), 8°. List 100. Theca 8. Wing C5263; ESTC R19806.

—— (ed.), *see* Cicero [De finibus. 1702].

Collins, Anthony (1676–1729), *A discourse of the grounds and reasons of the Christian religion. In two parts: The first containing some considerations on the quotations made from the Old in the New Testament… The second containing an examination of the scheme advanc'd by Mr. Whiston in his Essay towards restoring the true text of the Old Testament* (London, 1724), 8°. List 204, 530. Theca 14. Cf. ESTC N869, T140491, T217216 (variants).

Colsoni, François (*fl.* 1693), *Le Guide de Londres dedié aux voyageurs etrangers.* 3rd edn. (Londres: imprimé pour le German Bookseller-shop, 1710), 8°. List 273 ('12°.'). Theca 6. ESTC T56043.

Colvius, Petrus (d. 1594), *see* Sidonius, *Opera* (1578).

Comines, Philippe de, Seigneur d'Argenton (1445–1509), *The history of Philip de Commines.* 4th edn. (London: printed for Samuel Mearne, John Martyn, and Henry Herringman, 1674), 2°. List 151. Theca 2. Wing C5542; ESTC R1689.

—— *Mémoires... contenans l'histoire des rois Louys XI. & Charles VIII. depuis l'an 1464. jusques en 1498. Augumentez... par feu Mr. Denys Godefroy.* 3 vols. (Brusselle: chez François Foppens, 1706), 8°. List 150. Theca 11.

Comitia Westmonasteriensium, in collegio Sti Petri habita die anniversario fundatricis suæ reginæ Elizabethæ inauguratæ Jan. XV (London: typis Guil. Bowyer, 1728), 2°. List 657. ESTC T145251 or T153318 (variant).

Conduitt, John (1688–1737), *A Poem upon the late glorious successes &c. Humbly inscrib'd to his grace the Duke of Marlborough* (London: for Jacob Tonson, 1707). ESTC T118145; Foxon C334. In: *A Collection of poems, occasionally written upon the victories of Blenheim and Ramillies* (1708).

Congreve, William (1670–1729) [Works. 1710] *Works.* 3 vols. (London: printed for Jacob Tonson, 1710), 8°. List 96 (large paper). Theca 28. Leeds 548? ESTC T052950. A copy of the large-paper issue signed 'The Gift of the Author to A Henley' on the title page is at CLC: *PR 3360 D10.

—— [Works. 1710] *Works.* 3 vols. (London: printed for Jacob Tonson, 1710), 8°. List 97 (small paper). Theca 27. Leeds 548? ESTC T052950.

—— [Works. 1719] *The works... The third edition, revis'd by the author.* 2 vols. (London: printed for Jacob Tonson, 1719), 12°. List 98 ('2d Vol. Fine Papr.'). Theca 27. Leeds 156. ESTC T026066.

—— *Amendments of Mr. Collier's false and imperfect citations* (London: printed for J. Tonson, 1698), 8°. List 99. Theca 8. Wing C5844. Congreve's copy may be that at CN: Case V.18.180715, which was formerly in the library of the Duke of Leeds.

—— *A Pindarique ode, humbly offer'd to the queen, on the victorious progress of her majesty's arms, under the conduct of the Duke of Marlborough. To which is prefix'd, a discourse on the pindarique ode* (London: printed for Jacob Tonson, 1706). ESTC T042300; Foxon C376. In: *A Collection of poems, occasionally written upon the victories of Blenheim and Ramillies* (1708).

—— (ed.), *see* Dryden, *The dramatick works* (1717).

—— (tr.), *see* Ovid [Ars amatoria. 1709].

Constantin, Robert (d. 1605) (ed.), *see* Celsus [De medicina. 1713].

Conti, Natale (1520?–1580?), *Natalis Comitis Mythologiæ, sive explicationis fabularum libri decem* (Genevæ: sumptibus Petri Chouët, 1651), 8°. List 424. Theca 7.

—— (tr.), *see* Athenæus of Naucratis [Deipnosophistæ. 1556].

Cooper, Thomas (1517?–1594), *Thesaurus linguæ Romanæ & Britannicæ* (Impressum Londini: in ædibus Henrici Bynnemani [by Henry Denham], 1584), 2°. List 86. Theca 9. STC 5689; ESTC S121950.

Corneille, Pierre (1606–84) *Le Théâtre de P. Corneille.* 3 vols. (Imprimé à Rouen, et se vend à Paris, chez Augustin Courbé et Guillaume de Luyne, 1660), 8°. List 83. Theca 30.

—— *Le Théâtre de P. Corneille*. 2 vols. (Imprimé à Rouen, et se vend à Paris, chez Thomas Iolly, 1664), 2°. List 82. Theca 1. Each volume signed 'Wm. Congreve the gift of my Friend Mr. Jacob Tonson Senr.' (J. Isaacs, *TLS* 2 September 1949), but their present location is unknown.

Corneille, Thomas (1625–1709), *Poëmes dramatiques de T. Corneille*. 2 vols. (Imprimés à Rouen, et se vendent à Paris, chez Augustin Courbé et Guillaume de Luyne, 1661), 8°. List 84. Theca 30.

Coste, Pierre (1668–1747) (ed.), *see* Horace [Works. 1710].

Cotgrave, Randle (*fl.* 1610, d. 1634), *A French and English dictionary.... this work is exposed to publick*. By *James Howell* (London: printed by William Hunt, 1660), 2°. List 85. Theca 9. Wing C6378; ESTC R23785.

Cotton, Charles (1630–87) (tr.), *see* Montaigne, Michel de [Essays. 1685].

—— (tr.) *see* Pontis, Louis de, *Memoirs* (1694).

Cowley, Abraham (1618–67), *The works*. 9th edn. (London: printed for Henry Herringman; and are to be sold by Jacob Tonson, and Thomas Bennet, 1700), 2°. List 78. Theca 9. Wing C6660; ESTC R2108.

—— *The works*. 10th edn. 2 vols. (London: printed for Jacob Tonson, 1707), 8°. List 79 (large paper). Theca 19. Leeds 361? ESTC T133365.

—— *The works*. 10th edn. 2 vols. (London: printed for Jacob Tonson, 1707), 8°. List 80 (small paper). Theca 27. Leeds 126? ESTC T133365.

Creech, Thomas (1659–1700) (ed., tr.), *see* Manilius, Marcus, *The five books* (1697).

—— (tr.) *see* Lucretius Carus [De rerum natura. 1695].

—— (tr.), *see* Horace, *The odes, satyrs, and epistles* (1688).

Crispin, Daniel (1640–1716) (ed.), *see* Sallust [Works. 1715].

Crotus Rubianus (*c.*1480–1539) and **Ulrich von Hutten** (1498–1523), *Epistolarum obscurorum virorum, ad Dn. M. Ortuinum Gratium volumina II* (Francofurti ad Moenum: [Egenolff Emmel], 1624), 8°. List 237. Theca 6. Attributed mainly to Crotus Rubianus and Ulrich von Hutten.

Culpeper, Nicholas (1616–54) [Pharmacopœia Londinensis. 1654] *Pharmacopœia Londinensis: or the London dispensatory* (London: printed by Peter Cole, and are to be sold at his shop, 1654), 12°. List 128, 218. Theca 4. Wing C7527 or C7526; ESTC R224855 or 32396.

—— [Pharmacopœia Londinensis. 1675] *Pharmacopœia Londinensis; or, the London dispensatory* (London: printed for George Sawbridge, 1675), 8°. List 221 ('Culpepers Dispensatory and English physn'). Theca 4. Wing C7534; ESTC R31670. Probably bound with an edition of Culpeper's *The English physician*.

D., Sieur (pseud.), *see* Boileau-Despréaux, Nicolas.

Dacier, André (1651–1722), *The life of Pythagoras, with his symbols and golden verses... Now done into English. The golden verses translated from the Greek by N. Rowe, Esq.* (London: printed for Jacob Tonson, 1707), 8°. List 365 (large paper), 524. Theca 13. ESTC T67781.

—— *La Vie de Pythagore, ses symboles, ses vers dorez, & la vie d'Hierocles*. 2 vols. (Paris: chez Rigaud, 1706), 12°. List 631. Theca 12.

—— (tr.), *see* Aristotle [Poetics. 1692].

—— *see* Hippocrates, *Les Oeuvres* (1697).

Dacier, André *see* Horace [Works. 1709].

—— *see* Plato, *Les oeuvres* (1699).

—— *see* Sophocles, *Tragedies grecques* (1693).

Dacier, Anne Lefèvre (1654–1720), *Des Causes de la corruption du goust* (Paris: aux dépens de Rigaud, 1714), 12°. List 195. Theca 18.

—— (tr.), *see* Anacreon, *Les Poesies d'Anacreon et de Sapho* (1699).

—— *see* Aristophanes, *Comedies grecques* (1692).

—— *see* Homer [Iliad. 1711, 1712].

—— *see* Homer [Odyssey. 1716].

—— *see* Terence [Comedies. 1706].

Dager, Abraham, Sir, *see* Moretti, Tomaso, *A general treatise of artillery.*

Dale, Samuel (1659?–1739), *Samuelis Dale Pharmacologiæ, seu manductio ad materiam medicam...supplementum* (Londini: impensis Sam. Smith, & Benj. Walford, 1705), 12°. List 201 (format and place of publication not given). ESTC T67770.

—— *Pharmacologia, seu manuductio ad materiam medicam... Iterata editio* (Londini: apud Benj. Walford, 1710), 12°. List 200. Theca 4. ESTC T67775.

Dalechamps, Jacob (ed.), *see* Athenæus of Naucratis [Deipnosophistæ. 1611].

Daniel, Gabriel (1649–1728), *Abregé de l'histoire de France depuis l'etablissement de la monarchie françoise dans les Gaules.* 9 vols. (Paris: chez Denys Mariette, Jean-Baptiste Delespine, Jean-Baptiste Coignard, 1723–4), large 12°. List 528 ('8°.'). Theca 30.

Davall, Peter (tr.), *see* Retz, Jean François Paul de Gondi de, *Memoirs* (1723).

Davenant, Charles (1656–1714), *An essay on the East-India-trade* (London: printed anno, 1696), 8°. List 179. Theca 8. Leeds 181. Wing D307; ESTC R7736.

D'Avenant, William, Sir (1606–68), *The works* (London: printed by T[homas]. N[ewcomb]. for Henry Herringman, 1673), 2°. List 177. Theca 9. Wing D320; ESTC R10223.

—— *A Discourse upon Gondibert* (Paris: chez Matthiev Gvillemot, 1650), 12°. List 178. Theca 5. Leeds 182. Wing D322; ESTC R8934.

Davies, John (1625–93) (tr.), *see* Murtadá ibn al-Khafif, *The Egyptian history* (1672).

—— *see* Olearius, Adam, *The voyages and travells of the ambassadors* (1669).

—— *see* Sorel, Charles, *The extravagant shepherd* (1654).

Davies, John (1679–1732) (ed.), *see* Cicero [Academica. 1725].

—— *see* Cicero [De divinatione. 1721].

—— *see* Cicero [De natura deorum. 1718].

—— *see* Cicero [Quæstiones Tusculanæ. 1723].

de la Vega, Garcilaso (1539–1616), *The royal commentaries of Peru...rendered into English, by Sir Paul Rycaut* (London: printed by Miles Flesher for Jacob Tonson, 1688), 2°. List 500 (publisher not given). Theca 15. Wing G217; ESTC R11046, but possibly one of G214–6 (ESTC R34865, R2511, or R11045). Hornby Castle 1199 or 1223.

Deloney, Thomas (1543?–1600), *The plesant and princely history of the gentle craft,* 4°. List 405 (edition not given; bound with 10 other miscellaneous 4° items). Theca 28. Cf. STC 6554.5–6555.7 and Wing D944–5.

Demosthenes (385?–322 BC), *Several orations of Demosthenes, to encourage the Athenians to oppose the exorbitant power of Philip of Macedon. English'd from the Greek by several hands* (London: printed for Jacob Tonson, 1702), 12°. List 211. Theca 11. ESTC T47999. Edited by John Somers, Baron Somers.

—— *Philippiques . . . avec des remarques* (Paris: chez la veuve de Claude Barbin, 1701), 4°. List 212, 487. Theca 22.

—— *Traduction des Philippiques.* 2 vols. (Amsterdam: chez Pierre Mortier, 1688), 12°. List 223 ('24°').

Dennis, John (1657–1734), *The select works.* 2 vols. (London: printed by John Darby, 1718), 8°. List 186. Theca 28. ESTC T74495.

—— *Original letters familiar, moral and critical.* 2 vols. in 1 (London: printed for W. Mears, 1721), 8°. List 189 ('4°'). Theca 33. ESTC T135783 or N061393.

—— *Remarks on a book entituled, Prince Arthur, an heroick poem* (London: printed for S.Heyrick and R. Sare, 1696), 8°. List 187. Theca 8. Wing D1040; ESTC R35663.

—— *Vice and luxury publick mischiefs: or, remarks on a book intituled, The fable of the bees; or, private vices publick benefits* (London: printed for W. Mears, 1724), 8°. List 188. Theca 33. ESTC T50744.

Descartes, René (1596–1650), *Renatus Des-Cartes excellent compendium of musick* (London: printed by Thomas Harper for Humphrey Moseley, to bee sold at his shop, and by Thomas Heath, 1653), 4°. List 185 ('4°. Lond. 1657.'; but no such edition listed by Wing or ESTC). Theca 3. Wing D1132.

—— *see also* Regis, Pierre Silvain, *Cours entier* (1691).

Desjardins, Marie Catherine Hortense (d. 1683), *Annales galantes. Divisée en huit parties.* 2 vols. (Paris [i.e. Amsterdam?]: chez Claude Barbin, 1677), 12°. List 26 ('5.6.7.8 Parties'). Theca 26.

Des Maizeaux, Pierre (ed.), *see* Saint-Évremond, *Oeuvres meslées* (1705).

Desprez, Louis (ed.), *see* Horace [Works. 1694].

—— (ed.), *see* Juvenal and Persius [Works. 1691].

Diaper, William (1685–1717), *Nereides: or, Sea-eclogues* (London: printed by J.H. for E. Sanger, 1712), 8°. List 423. Theca 20. Leeds 190. ESTC T126092; Foxon D294.

—— (tr.), see Quillet, Claude, *Callipædia* (1712).

Dictionnaire universel François et Latin. 5 vols. (Imprimé à Trevoux, & se vend à Paris, chez Florentin Delaulne, &c., 1721), 2°. List 173. Theca 10.

Diemerbroeck, Isbrandus de (1609–74), *Anatome corporis humani* (Ultrajecti [Utrecht]: sumptibus & typis Meinardi à Dreunen, 1672), 4°. List 184. Theca 4. Leeds 194. Signed 'Willm. Congreve ex dono Dr Hobbs' (J. Isaacs, *TLS* 2 September 1949), but its present location is unknown.

Digges, Leonard (1588–1635) (tr.), *see* Céspedes y Meneses, *Gerardo* (1653).

Dillon, Wentworth, 4th Earl of Roscommon (1633?–1685), **John Sheffield**, Duke of Buckingham (1648–1721), and **Richard Duke** (1658–1711), *Poems by the Earl of Roscommon. To which is added, An essay on poetry, by the Earl of Mulgrave, now Duke of Buckingham. Together with poems by Mr. Richard Duke* (London: printed for J. Tonson, 1717), 8°. List 507. Theca 19. Leeds 548. ESTC T132427.

Dillon, Wentworth, 4th Earl of Roscommon (tr.), *see* Horace [Ars Poetica. 1684].

Dodwell, Henry (1641–1711), *An epistolary discourse, proving, from the scriptures and first fathers that the soul is a principle naturally mortal* (London: printed for R. Smith, 1706), 8°. List 203. Theca 14. ESTC T117511.

—— *see also* Cicero [De finibus. 1702].

Donne, John (1573–1631), *Poems... With elegies on the authors death* (London: printed by M[iles]. F[lesher]. for John Marriot, 1633), 4°. List 182. Theca 20. Leeds 200. STC 7045; ESTC S121864.

—— *Poems... With elegies on the authors death.* 7th edn. (In the Savoy: printed by T[homas]. N[ewcomb]. for Henry Herringman, 1669), 8°. List 183. Theca 20. Leeds 631. Wing D1871; ESTC R32770.

Dousa, Janus (1571–97) (ed.), *see* Plautus [Fables. 1604].

Dryden, John (1631–1700) [Works. 1695] *The third volume of the works. Containing, Duke of guise. Vindication of the Duke of Guise. Albion and Albianus. Don Sebastian. Amphitryon. Cleomenes. King Arthur. Love triumphant* [Plays] (London: printed for Jacob Tonson, 1695), 4°. List 166. Theca 27. Wing D2210; ESTC R228675.

—— [Works. 1695] *The fourth volume of the works. Containing, A poem upon the death of O. Cromwell. Poem on the return of K. Charles II. On the coronation of K. Charles II. A poem on the L. Chancellor Hide. Annus mirabilis. Mack Flecknoe. Absalom and Achitophel. The medal, a poem. Religious laici, a poem. Elegy on the death of K. Charles II. The hind and panther. Poem on the birth of the Prince. Eleonora* [Poems] (London: printed for Jacob Tonson, 1695), 4°. List 167. Theca 27. Wing D2210; ESTC R228675.

—— [Works. 1701] *The comedies, tragedies, and operas... Now first collected together, and corrected from the originals.* 2 vols. (London: printed for Jacob Tonson, Thomas Bennet, and Richard Wellington, 1701), 2°. List 160 ('1721', apparently in error for 1701; large paper). Theca 10. Leeds 210. ESTC T143004.

—— [Works. 1701] *The works... In four volumes. Containing all his comedies, tragedies, and operas; with his original poems and translations: The third volume* (London: printed for Jacob Tonson, 1701), 2°. List 165. Theca 9. ESTC N25881.

—— *The dramatick works.* 6 vols. (London: printed for Jacob Tonson, 1717), 12°. List 170. Theca 27. ESTC N10169 or T1453328. Edited by Congreve.

—— *Fables ancient and modern; translated into verse, from Homer, Ovid, Boccace, & Chaucer. By Mr. Dryden* (London: printed for Jacob Tonson, 1700), 2°. List 164. Theca 9. Wing D2278; ESTC R31983.

—— *Of dramatick poesie an essay,* 2nd edn. (London: printed for Henry Herringman, 1684), 4°. List 171, 406 (another copy). Theca 27. Leeds 209. Wing D2328; ESTC R228550. Bound with Horace's *Art of poetry. Made English by the... Earl of Roscommon* (1684), Buckingham, *The rehearsal* (1687). Congreve's copy, signed 'Will: Congreve': Robert H. Taylor collection, Princeton University.

—— (ed.), *Miscellany poems: the first [-sixth] part.* 3rd edn. 6 vols. (London: printed for Jacob Tonson, 1702–1709), 8°. List 168 ('1702 &c.'). Theca 27. Hornby Castle 1110. ESTC T117015. Case 172 (1) (d)+.

—— *The first [-sixth] part of Miscellany poems.* 4th edn. 6 vols. (London: printed for Jacob Tonson, 1716), 12°. List 169. Theca 27. ESTC N6906. Case 172 (1) (e)+.

—— (tr.), see *Fables ancient and modern; translated into verse* (1700).

—— see Juvenal and Persius [Works. 1693].

—— see Ovid [Ars amatoria. 1709].

—— see Ovid [Heroïdes. 1681].

—— see Ovid [Metamorphoses. 1717].

—— see Polybius, *The history* (1693).

—— see Virgil [Works. 1697].

—— see also Milbourne, Luke, *Notes on Dryden's Virgil* (1698).

Dufresny, Charles Rivière (1654–1724), *Les Puits de la verité, nouvelle gauloise. Suivant la copie imprimé à Paris* (Amsterdam: chez Henry Desbordes, 1699), 12°. List 482. Theca 6.

Duke, Richard (1658–1711), *Poems.* In: Dillon, Wentworth, *Poems by the Earl of Roscommon* (1717).

Du Noyer, Anne Marguerite Petit (1663–1719), *Lettres historiques et galantes.* 7 vols. (Cologne: chez Pierre Marteau, 1707–18), 12°. List 372 ('12°. Colon 1710'; '4 Tom'). Theca 26. Congreve may have had only vols. 3–6 (1710–13).

Dunton, John, mariner, *A true journall of the Sally fleet with the proceedings of the voyage. . . . Whereunto is annexed a list of Sally captives names, and the places where they dwell, and a description of the three townes in a card* (London: printed by John Dawson for Thomas Nicholes, 1637), 4°. List 224, 644 ('Blue pap'). Theca 29. STC 7357; ESTC S111090.

Duport, James (1606–79) (tr.), see *Book of Common Prayer* (1665).

Du Quesne, Abraham, the Younger (*fl.* 1690), see Challes, Robert, *Journal d'un voyage fait aux Indes* (1721).

Du Ryer, Pierre (1605–53) (tr.), see Herodotus, *Les Histoires* (1658).

Dyson, Humphrey (*fl.* 1611–33) (ed.), see Stow, John, *The survey of London* (1633).

Earle, John, Bishop of Salisbury (1601?–65), *Micro-cosmographie.* 5th edn. (London: printed [by T. Cotes] for Robert Allot, 1629), 12°. List 231, 416 ('24°'). Theca 5. STC 7442; ESTC S100208.

Eccles, John (d. 1735), *A collection of songs for one two and three voices together with such symphonys for violins or flutes as were by the author design'd for any of them* (London: printed for J. Walsh, [1704]), 2°. List 232. Theca 21.

Echard, Laurence (1670?–1730), *The history of England. From the first entrance of Julius Cæsar and the Romans, to the end of the reign of King James the First.* Vol. 1 (London: printed for Jacob Tonson, 1707), 2°. List 226 (large paper). Theca 16. ESTC T145502. Vols. 2 and 3 were published in 1718. Congreve appears to have had only vol. 1.

—— *The Roman history, from the building of the city, to the perfect settlement of the empire.* 2nd edn. (London: printed by T. Hodgkin for M. Gillyflower,

J. Tonson, H. Bonwick, and R. Parker, 1696); ...*from the settlement of the empire by Augustus Caesar, to the removal of the imperial seat by Constantine the Great... Vol. II* (London: printed by T.H. for M. Gillyflower, J. Tonson, H. Bonwick, and R. Parker, 1698), 8°. List 227. Theca 13. Wing E152, E155; ESTC R34428, R25571.

—— *The Roman history, from the removal of the imperial seat by Constantine the Great, to the total failure of the Western empire in Augustulus. Vol. III. Being a continuation of Mr. Echard's History* (London: printed for Jacob Tonson, 1704), 8°; ...*from the total failure of the Western empire... to the restitution of the same by Charles the Great... Vol. IV* (London: printed for Jacob Tonson, 1704) 8°; ...*from the restitution of the empire by Charles the Great, to the taking of Constantinople by the Turks.... Vol. V* (London: printed for Jacob Tonson, 1705), 8°. List 228 ('Large Paper'). Theca 13. ESTC T213177; T149534; T169418.

—— (ed., tr.), *see* Plautus [Comedies. 1694].

—— (tr.), *see* Terence [Comedies. 1694].

Eden, Richard (1521?–76) (ed.), *see* Anghiera, Pietro Martire d', *The history of trauayle* (1577).

Edmonds, Clement, Sir (1564?–1622) (tr.), *see* Cæsar [Commentarii. 1677].

Egerton, Sarah Fyge (1670–1723), *A collection of poems on several occasions... To which is added a pastoral, entitled, The fond shepherdess. Dedicated to Mr. Congreve* (London: printed and are to be sold by the booksellers of London and Westminster, 1706), 8°. List 255, 461 ('12°'). Theca 20. ESTC N27927; cf. Foxon i. 213.

English military discipline. Or, The way and method of exercising horse & foot, according to the practice of this present time (London: printed for Robert Harford, 1680), 8°. List 229 ('12°.'). Theca 8. Wing E3105A; ESTC R9992.

Entretiens d'Ariste, see Bouhours, Dominique, *Les entretiens d'Ariste et d'Eugene* (1671).

Erasmus, Desiderius (1466?–1536), *Adagiorum D. Erasmi Roterodami epitome* (Amsterodami: apud Joan. Janssonium, 1649), 12°. List 230. Theca 5.

—— (tr.), *see* Gazes, Theodorus, *Grammaticæ institutionis* (1516).

L'escole parfaite des officiers de bouche, contenant, Le vray maistre-d'hostel. Le grand escuyer-tranchant. Le sommelier royal. Le confiturier royal. Le cuisinier royal. Et le patissier royal. 7th edn. (Paris, 1715), 12°. List 240 ('Par. 1716') and 443 ('8°. Par. 1716'). Theca 32.

Estienne, Charles (1504–64), *Dictionarium historicum, geographicum, poeticum... A Carolo Stephano inchoatum. Ad incudem verò revocatum, innumerisque penè locis auctum & emaculatum per Nicolaum Lloydium.* New edn. (Londini: impensis B. Tooke, T. Passenger, T. Sawbridge, A. Swalle & A. Churchill, 1686), 2°. List 180. Theca 9. Wing E3349; ESTC R2758.

Estienne, Henri (1531–98) (ed.), *Poetæ græci principes heroici carminis, & alii nonnulli* ([Geneva]: excudebat Henricus Stephanus, illustris viri Huldrichi Fuggeri typographus,1566), 2°. List 456. Theca 15.

Estienne, Henri, Sieur des Fossez (*fl.* 1639–52), *L'Art de faire des devises, où il est traicté des hieroglyphiques, symboles, eblemes... Avec un traicté des rencontres ou mots plaisans* (Paris: chez Jean Paslé, 1645), 8°. List 12. Theca 12.

Etherege, George, Sir (1635?–91), *Works... containing his plays and poems* (London: printed for H. H. and sold by J. Tonson; and T. Bennet, 1704), 8°. List 235. Theca 20. ESTC T138423.

Eustachius, a Sancto Paulo (1573–1640), *Summa philosophiæ quadripartita de rebus dialecticis, ethicis, physicis, & metaphysicis* (Cantabrigiæ: ex officina Rogeri Danielis, 1640), 8°. List 236. Theca 7. STC 10578; ESTC S101805. Congreve's copy, inscribed inside the front board 'Gulielmus Congreve est verus Possessor hujus Libri ex Dono Henrici Luther' and with Congreve's signatures ('W: Congreve' on $^\pi6^r$; 'Gulielmus Congreve' on A1^r; 'Ex Libris Gulielmi Congreve' on A2^v and 'Ex Libris Guilemi: Congreve' on 207^v): Y: K8.Eu8/C640.

Exquemelin, Alexandre Olivier (1645?–1707), *Histoire des avanturiers boucaniers qui se sont signalez dans les Indes*. 2 vols. (Paris: chez Jacques Le Febvre, 1688), 12°. List 301. Theca 3.

Fairfax, Edward (d. 1635) (tr.), *see* Tasso, Torquato, *Godfrey of Bulloigne* (1687).

The famous and renowned history of the life and glorious actions of the mighty Hercules of Greece (London: printed for S. Bates, [1720?]), 4°. List 405 (edition not given; bound with 10 other miscellaneous 4° items). Theca 28. ESTC T67469.

Fanshawe, Richard, Sir (1608–66) (tr.), *see* Camões, Luiz de, *The Lusiad* (1655).

Félibien des Avaux, Jean François (*c*.1658–1733), *Les Plans et les descriptions de deux des plus belles maisons de campagne de Pline le Consul. Avec des remarques sur tous ses bâtimens, et une dissertation touchant l'architecture* (Londres: chès David Mortier, 1707), 12°. List 394 ('12° Lond. 1717.'; probably an error for 1707). Theca 12. ESTC T55191.

Fénelon, François de Salignac de la Mot, Archbishop of Cambray (1651–1715), *Les Avantures de Telemaque fils d'Ulysse*. 2 vols. (Paris: chez J. Estienne [de l'imprimerie de F. Delaulne], 1717), 12°. List 578 ('1718'). Theca 18.

—— *Dialogues des morts anciens et modernes, avec quelques fables*. 2 vols. (Paris: chez Florentin Delaulne [or Estienne Jacques], 1718), 12°. List 577 ('8°.'). Theca 18.

—— *Dialogues sur l'eloquence en general, et sur celle de la chaire en particulier* (Paris: chez Jacques Estienne, 1718), 12°. List 576 ('8°'). Theca 18.

—— *Lettres sur divers sujets concernant la religion et la métaphysique* (Paris: chez Jacques Estienne, 1718), 12°. List 575 ('8°'). Theca 18.

Fenton, Elijah (1683–1730), *An ode to the sun for the new-year* (London: printed for Jacob Tonson, 1707). List 413, 485. Theca 15. ESTC T42010; Foxon F110–11. In: *A Collection of poems, occasionally written upon the victories of Blenheim and Ramillies* (1708).

—— (ed.), *Oxford and Cambridge miscellany poems* (London: printed for Bernard Lintott, [1708]), 8°. List 412, 446. Theca 20. ESTC T145730. Case 248.

—— (tr.), *see* Homer [Odyssey. 1725–6].

Filleau de Saint-Martin, François (tr.), *see* Cervantes [Don Quixote. 1678].

Filmer, Edward (b. 1657?), *A defence of plays: or, the stage vindicated, from several passages in Mr. Collier's Short view* (London: printed for Jacob Tonson, 1707), 8°. List 103. Theca 8. ESTC T66128.

Fléchier, Valentine Esprit, Bishop of Lavaur, &c (1632–1710), *Histoire du Cardinal Ximenés*. 2 vols. (Amsterdam e se vend à Anvers: chez la veuve de Barthelemy Foppens, 1700), 12°. List 300. Theca 11.

Fletcher, John (1579–1625), *see* Beaumont, Francis.

Florio, John (1553?–1625), (tr.), *see* Boccaccio, Giovanni [Decameron. 1684].

Florus, Lucius Annæus (*fl.* 2nd c.) [Epitome rerum romanorum. 1715] *Cui subjungitur Lucii Ampelii liber memorialis* (Londini: ex officinâ Jacobi Tonson, & Johannis Watts, 1715), 12°. List 254. Theca 24. ESTC T146535 or T146536 (large paper). Edited by Michael Maittaire.

Fontenelle, M. de (Bernard Le Bovier) (1657–1757), *Entretiens sur la pluralité des mondes*. 4th edn. (Paris: chez Michel Brunet, 1698), 12°. List 243. Theca 25.

—— *Fontenelle's Dialogues of the dead, in three parts* (London: printed for Jacob Tonson, 1708), 8°. List 248. Theca 8. ESTC T139460. Translated by John Hughes.

—— *Histoire des oracles* (Paris: chez Michel Brunet, 1698), 12°. List 242. Theca 25.

—— *Jugement de Pluton, sur les deux parties des Dialogues des morts* (Paris: chez C. Blageart [or 'imprimé à Paris, & se vend à Lyon T. Amaulry'], 1684), 12°. List 245. Theca 25.

—— *Lettres galantes de Monsieur le Chevalier d'Her****. 3rd edn. (Paris: [de l'imprimerie de Jean Moreau] chez Michel Brunet, 1599 [i.e. 1699]), 12°. List 247. Theca 25.

—— *Nouveaux dialogues des morts*. 5th edn. 2 vols. (Paris: chez Michel Brunet, 1700), 12°. List 244. Theca 25.

—— *A Plurality of worlds.... Translated into English by Mr. [John] Glanvill* (London: printed for R. W. and sold by Tho. Osbourne, 1702), 8°. List 249 ('12°.'). Theca 8. ESTC N11587.

—— *Poesies pastorales: avec un traité sur la nature de l'églogue & une digression sur les anciens & les moderns* (Paris: chez Michel Brunet, 1698), 12°. List 246. Theca 25.

Forsett, Edward (*c.*1553–*c.*1630), *Pedantius, Comœdia, olim. Cantabrig. acta in Coll. Trin.* (Londini: excudebat W. S[tansby].; impensis Roberti Mylbourn, 1631), 12°. List 481. Theca 5. STC 19524; ESTC S114425. Variously attributed to Forsett, to Anthony Wingfield, to Walter Hawkesworth, and to Thomas Beard.

Fracastero, Girolamo (1483–1533), *Syphilis: or, a poetical history of the French disease... And now attempted in English by N. Tate* (London: printed for Jacob Tonson, 1686), 8°. List 557. Theca 20. Wing F2049; ESTC R24339.

Frézier, Amédée François (1682–1773), *A voyage to the South-Sea, and along the coasts of Chili and Peru, in the years 1712, 1713, and 1714* (London: printed for Jonah Bowyer, 1717), 4°. List 639. Theca 29. Leeds 250. ESTC T145981.

Fuller, Thomas (1608–61), *Andronicus, or the unfortunate politician* (London: printed by W. Wilson for John Williams, 1646), 8°. List 252 ('12°.'). Theca 6. Wing F2403, 2405, or 2406; ESTC R16036, R202059, or R14475.

Funnell, William, *A voyage round the world. Containing an account of Captain Dampier's expedition into the South-Seas in the ship St George, in the years 1703 and 1704. . . . Together with the author's voyage from Amapalla* (London: printed by W. Botham for James Knapton, 1707), 8°. List 642. Theca 29. ESTC T52634.

Furetière, Antoine (1619–88), *Scarron's City romance, made English* (In the Savoy: printed by T. N[ewcomb] for H. Herringman, 1671), 8°. List 573. Theca 33. Wing F2540; ESTC R40251. A translation of Furetière's *Le roman bourgeois*; not connected with Scarron.

Gabalis, Comte de, *see* Villars, Nicolas-Pierre-Henri de Montfaucon, Abbé de, *Le Comte de Gabalis* (1670).

Gale, Thomas (1635?–1702) (ed.), *see* Iamblichus, *De mysteriis liber* (1678).

Galland, Antoine (1646–1715), *Les mille & une nuit: contes arabes.* 11 vols. (Paris: chez la veuve de Claude Barbin, 1704–17), 12°. List 120 ('12 Tom . . . 1705.'). Theca 23.

Galliard, Johann Ernest (1687?–1749), *Six English cantatas after the Italian manner* (London: printed for J. Walsh, & J. Hare [1716]), 2°. List 256. Theca 21. Contains Galliard's setting of Congreve's song 'The Reconciliation'.

Gallus, Gaius Cornelius (*c.*69 BC–AD 26), *see* Catullus [Works. 1686].

Gand, Louis de, *Sol Britannicus, regi consecratus* (Londini: excudebat J. Beale & S. Buckley, 1641), 8° in 4s. List 564. Theca 4. Wing G194; ESTC R24046.

Garth, Samuel, Sir (1661–1719), *The dispensary, a poem.* 4th edn. (London: printed and sold by John Nutt, 1700), 8°. List 260 (large paper). Theca 19. Wing G276; ESTC R227072.

—— *The dispensary, a poem.* 7th edn. (London: printed for Jacob Tonson, 1714), 12°. List 261. Theca 20. ESTC T34568; Foxon G25.

Gassendi, Pierre (1592–1655), *Abregé de la philosophie de Mr. Gassendi. . . . Par F. Bernier.* 2nd edn. 7 vols. (Lyon: chez Anisson, Pousel, & Rigaud, 1684), 12°. List 272 ('7 Tom 6 voll'), 488. Theca 12.

Gay, John (1685–1732), *Poems on several occasions.* 2 vols. (London: printed for Jacob Tonson, and Bernard Lintot, 1720), 4°. List 257 (large paper). Theca 2. Leeds 257, 258, or 259 (each copy noted as '2 vol. in 1'). ESTC T13893; cf. Foxon i. 295. List of subscribers includes Congreve.

—— *Fables* (London: printed for J. Tonson and J. Watts, 1727), 4°. List 259. ESTC T13818; cf. Foxon i. 295.

—— *Trivia, or, the art of walking* (London: printed for Bernard Lintott, [1716]), 8°. List 258 (large paper). Theca 28. Leeds 256 (this edition). ESTC T13931; Foxon G82.

Gazes, Theodoros (*c.*1400–*c.*1475), *Grammaticæ institutionis liber primus, sic translatus per Erasmum Roterodamum* (Basileæ: apud Joannem Frobenium, 1516), 4°. List 263 ('Antv.'; probably from preface dated 'Antverpiæ' 1516). Theca 14.

Gellius, Aulus (*c.*123–*c.*165), *Noctes atticæ. Editio nova . . .* (Amstelodami: apud Danielem Elzevirium, 1665), 12°. List 6 ('24°.'). Theca 5.

—— *Noctium atticarum libri XX prout supersunt . . . perpetuis notis & emendationibus illustraverunt Johannes Fredericus et Jacobus Gronovii* (Lugduni Batavorum

[Leiden]: apud Cornelium Boutesteyn, & Johannem du Vivié, 1706), 4°. List 5, 278. Theca 22.

Gemelli-Careri, Giovanni Francesco (1651–1725), *Voyage du tour du monde, traduit de l'Italien*. 6 vols. (Paris: chez Etienne Ganeau, 1719), 8°. List 617. Theca 3.

A General collection of treatys, declarations of war, manifestos, and other publick papers... from 1648 to the present time (London: printed by J. Darby for Andrew Bell, and E. Sanger, 1710), 8°. List 105. Theca 14. ESTC T96502.

The gentleman's jockey, and approved farrier, see Halfpenny, John.

Geoffrey of Monmouth, Bishop of St Asaph (1100–54?), *The British history, translated into English from the Latin of Jeffrey of Monmouth... By Aaron Thompson* (London: printed for J. Bowyer, H. Clements, and W. and J. Innys, 1718), 8°. List 327, 610. Theca 13. ESTC T146343.

Gesner, Conrad von (1516–65) (ed.), *see* Stobæus, Johannes, *Sententiæ* (1543).

Gherardi, Evaristo (d. 1700), *Le theatre italien de Gherardi, ou Le recueil general de toutes les comedies & scenes françoises jouées par les comediens italiens du Roy, pendant tout le temps qu'il ont été au service*. 6 vols. (Paris: chez Jean-Bapt. Cusson et Pierre Witte, 1700), 12°. List 270. Theca 25. Hornby Castle 1219.

Giffin, Hubert van (c.1533–1604) (ed.), *see* Lucretius Carus, Titus [De rerum natura. 1659].

Gildon, Charles (1665–1724), *Miscellaneous letters and essays on several subjects. Directed to John Dryden, Esq; the Honourable Geo. Granvill Esq; Walter Moile, Esq; Mr. Dennis, Mr. Congreve, and other eminent men of th' age* (London: printed for Benjamin Bragg, 1694), 8°. List 417. Theca 8. Wing G732; ESTC R14504.

—— (ed.), *see Miscellany poems upon several occasions* (1692).

—— (ed.), *see* Shakespeare, William [Poems. 1709].

Giphanius, Obertus (1534–1604) (ed.), *see* Lucretius Carus, Titus [De rerum natura. 1659].

Glanvill, John (1664?–1735) (tr.), *see* Fontenelle, M. de (Bernard Le Bovier), *A Plurality of worlds* (1702).

Godefroy, Denys (1653–1719) (ed.), *see* Comines, Philippe de, *Mémoires* (1706).

Godfrey of Bulloigne, see Tasso, Torquato, *Godfrey of Bulloigne* (1687).

Goulston, Theodor (c.1575–1632) (ed.), *see* Aristotle [Rhetoric. 1619].

Grævius, Joannes Georgius (1632–1703) (ed.), *see* Catullus [Works. 1680].

—— *see* Cicero [De officiis. 1688, 1689].

—— *see* Cicero [Epistolæ. 1684, 1689, 1693].

—— *see* Cicero [Orationes. 1695–9].

Granville, George *see* Lansdowne, George Granville, Baron.

Greene, Robert (1560?–92), *The pleasant history of Dorastus and Fawnia*, 4°. List 405 (edition not given; bound with 10 other miscellaneous 4° items). Theca 28. Cf. STC 12291.5–12292.5, Wing G1833–G1838, and numerous editions listed in ESTC.

Gronovius, Jacobus (1645–1716), (ed.), *see* Cicero [Works. 1692].

—— *see* Gellius, Aulus, *Noctium atticarum* (1706).

—— *see* Menander, *Menandri et Philemonis reliquæ* (1709).

Gronovius, Joannes Fredericus (1611–71), (ed.), *see* Livy, *Titi Livii Historiarum libri* (1654, 1678).

—— *see* Plautus [Comedies. 1684].

The grove; or, a collection of original poems, translations, &c. by W. Walsh, esq; Dr. J. Donne. Mr. Dryden. Mr. Hall of Hereford. The Lady E— M— Mr. Butler. Mr. Stepney. Sir John Suckling. Dr. Kenrick. And other eminent hands (London: printed for W. Mears, 1721), 8°. List 157, 269. Theca 20. ESTC T35894. Case 319.

Gruterus, Janus (1560–1627), (ed.), *see* Cicero [Works. 1692].

Guarini, Giovanni Battista (1538–1612), *Il Pastor fido, tragicomedia pastorale* (In Amsterdam: nella stamperia del S.D. Elsevier. Et in Parigi si vende appresso Thomaso Jolly, 1678), 32°. List 484 ('24°. Amsterd. 1678.'). Theca 5. A copy of an edition of this work published at Venice in 1608 and bearing the signature 'W Congreve' and price of 6s. on the recto of a preliminary blank leaf, is at MH. It is not listed in the manuscript catalogue of his library and the form of the signature leaves his ownership of it doubtful.

Gueulette, Thomas-Simon (1683–1766), *Les Avantures merveilleuses du mandarin Fum-Hoam, contes chinois.* 2 vols. (Paris: Denis Moughet, 1723), 12°. List 122 ('8°.'). Theca 30.

—— *A Thousand and one quarters of hours; being Tartarian tales* (London: printed for Jacob Tonson, 1716), 12°. List 605. Theca 30. ESTC T115693.

Guide de Londres, *see* Colsoni, François, *Le Guide de Londres* (1710).

Gulielmus, Janus (1555–84), (ed.), *see* Cicero [Works. 1692].

Gustavus I, Vasa, King of Sweden (1496–1560), *see* Caumont de La Force, Charlotte Rose de, *Gustave Vasa* (1697–8).

Hales, John (1584–1656), *Golden remains. The third impression. With additions from the authors own copy, viz. sermons and miscellanies* (London: printed by T. B[raddyll]. for George Pawlet, 1688), 8°. List 284. Theca 14. Wing H272; ESTC R14621.

Halfpenny, John, *The gentleman's jockey, and approved farrier. Instructing in the natures, causes, and cures of all diseases incident to horses.... With divers other curiosities, collected by... J. H. Esq; Matthew Hodson, Mr. Holled, Mr. Willis, Mr. Robinson, Mr. Holden, Thomas Empson, Mr. Roper, Mr. Medcalf, and Nath. Shaw.* 10th edn. (London: printed for J. Phillips, H. Rhodes, R. Sare, J. Taylor, T. Varnam, and J. Osborn, 1717), 8°. List 277. Theca 4. ESTC N18175.

Hamilton, Anthony, Count (1645?–1719), *Memoirs of the life of Count de Grammont... Translated from the French by Mr. Boyer* (London: printed and are to be sold by J. Round, W. Taylor, J. Brown, W. Lewis, and J. Graves, 1714), 8°. List 404. ESTC T113751.

Hardouin, Jean (1646–1729), *Apologie d'Homère, où l'on explique le véritable dessein de son Iliade* (Paris: aux dépens de Rigaud, 1716), 12°. List 293. Theca 18.

Hare, Francis, Bishop of Chichester (1671–1740), *The management of the war. In four letters to a Tory-member* (London: printed for Egbert Sangar, 1711), 8°. List 400 ('Management of the War 2 Parts, with other Pamphlets'). Theca 33. ESTC T100760. Possibly *An examination of The management of the war*, with half-title: *An examination of the two parts of The management of the war* (London: printed, and sold by J. Morphew, 1711), 8°. ESTC T100753.

Harison, William (1685–1713), *Woodstock Park. A poem.* 2nd edn. (London: printed for Jacob Tonson, 1706). List 413, 485. Theca 15. ESTC N25214; Foxon H53. In: *A Collection of poems, occasionally written upon the victories of Blenheim and Ramillies* (1708).

Hawkesworth, Walter (d. 1605), *Pedantius* (1631), *see* Forsett, Edward.

Hawkwood, John de, Sir (d. 1394), *see* Winstanley, William.

Head, Richard (1637?–1686?), *The life and death of the English rogue* (London: printed for Charles Passinger, 1679), 4°. List 405 (edition not given; bound with 10 other miscellaneous 4° items). Theca 28. Wing H1262; ESTC R9762. Possibly one of the undated quarto editions published by Ebenezer Tracy *c*.1700.

—— *The life and death of Mother Shipton* (London: printed for B. Harris, 1677), 4°. List 405 ('Mother Shipton—Tales of'; editions not given; bound with 10 other miscellaneous 4° items). Theca 28. Wing H1257; ESTC R9762; cf. also Wing H2158–61 and S3442+.

Heinsius, Daniel (1580–1655) (ed.), *see* Horace [Works. 1676].

Heinsius, Nicholas (1620–81) (ed.), *see* Virgil [Works. 1704].

Heliodorus (*fl.* 220–50), *The famous historie... Amplified, augmented, and delivered paraphrastically in verse; by... William Lisle* (London: by Iohn Dawson [and John Haviland] for Francis Eglesfield, 1638), 4°. List 407, 490 (edition not given; bound with 5 other miscellaneous items). Theca 28. STC 13048; ESTC S103936.

Her, Chevalier d', *see* Fontenelle, M. de (Bernard Le Bovier), *Lettres galantes* (1699).

Herodotus (5th c. BC), *Herodoti Halicarnassei Historiae libri IX: et De vita Homeri* (Francofurti: apud haeredes Andreae Wecheli, 1584), 8°. List 287. Theca 7.

—— *Les Histoires d'Herodote mises en françois par P. Du-Ryer.* 2nd edn. (Paris: chez Augustin Courbé, 1658), 2°. List 285 (large paper). Theca 16.

—— *The history of Herodotus. Translated from the Greek. By Isaac Littlebury.* 2nd edn. 2 vols. (London: printed for A. Bell, J. Darby, A. Bettesworth, W. and J. Innys, F. Fayram, J. Pemberton, C. Rivington, J. Hooke, F. Clay, J. Battley, and E. Symon, 1720), 8°. List 286, 369. Theca 13. ESTC T129614.

Hind, James, Captain (d. 1652), *see Wee have brought our hogs to a fair market* (1651).

Hippocrates (*fl.* 469–399 BC), *Les Oeuvres d'Hippocrate traduites en françois.* 2 vols. (Paris: par la Compagnie des Libraires, 1697), 12°. List 288 ('8°.'). Theca 4. Translated by André Dacier. Hornby Castle 1182.

Histoire de Marguerite de Valois, see Caumont de la Force, Charlotte Rose de (1720).

Hobbes, Thomas (1588–1679), *Leviathan, or the matter, forme, & power of a common-wealth ecclesiasticall and civill* (London: printed for Andrew Crooke, 1651), 2°. List 281. Theca 9. Leeds 303 or 304. Wing H2246 or H2247; ESTC R17253 or R13936.

—— (tr.), *see* Thucydides, *Eight bookes of the Peloponnesian warre* (1634).

Holyday, Barten (1593–1661) (tr.), *see* Juvenal and Persius [Works. 1673].

Homer [Works. 1606] *Homeri quæ extant omnia Ilias, Odyssea, Batrachomyoma-chia, Hymni, poëmata aliquot cum Latine versione . . . Jo. Spondani . . . commentar-iis* (Basileæ: per Sebastianum Henricpetri, 1606), 2°. List 289. Theca 9. Congreve's copy, signed 'W. Congreve': Pierpont Morgan Library, NY.

—— [Works. 1616] *The whole works of Homer prince of poetts in his Iliads, and Odysses. Translated according to the Greeke, by Geo: Chapman* (London: [printed by Richard Field and William Jaggard] for Nathaniell Butter, [1616?]), 2°. List 292. Theca 21. Leeds 309. STC 13624; ESTC S106768. A reissue of *The Iliads of Homer* (STC 13634; ESTC S119234) and *Homer's Odysses* (STC 13637; ESTC S118235). Evidently bound with *The crowne of all Homers worckes Batrachomyomachia. His hymn's and epigrams* (London: printed by [Eliot's Court Press], for J. Bill, [1624?]). STC 13628; ESTC S119240. Leeds 309, which mentions both, is described as 2 vols. in 1.

—— [Works. 1711] *Homerou Ilias kai Odysseia . . . Operâ, studio, & impensis, Josuæ Barnes.* 2 vols. (Cantabrigiæ: apud Cornelium Crownfield, 1711), 4°. List 290. Theca 22. ESTC T90248.

—— [Iliad. 1591] *Homeri Ilias, id est, De rebus ad Troiam gestis* (Londini: excudebat Georgius Bishop, 1591), 8°. List 291. Theca 7. STC 13629; ESTC S104176.

—— [Iliad. 1598] *Seaven bookes of the Iliades of Homere, prince of poets, translated according to the Greeke . . . by George Chapman* (London: printed by J. Windet, 1598), 4°. List 407, 490 (edition not given; bound with 5 other miscellaneous items). Theca 28. STC 13632; ESTC S106157.

—— [Iliad. 1700] *Le premier livre de l'Iliade en vers françois. Avec une dissertation sur quelques endroits d'Homére. Par m. l'abbé Regnier* (Paris: chez Jean Anisson, 1700), 8°. List 512. Theca 18.

—— [Iliad. 1711] *L'Iliade d'Homere traduite en françois . . . par Madame Dacier.* 3 vols. (Paris: chez Rigaud, 1711), 12°. List 194. Theca 18.

—— [Iliad. 1712] *The Iliad of Homer, with notes. To which are prefix'd, a large preface and The life of Homer, by Madam Dacier. Done from the French by Mr. Ozell.* 5 vols. (London: printed by G. James for Bernard Lintott, 1712), 12°. List 196. Theca 6. ESTC T54873. Translated from the French by John Ozell, William Broome, and William Oldisworth.

—— [Iliad. 1714] *L'Iliade. Poëme. Avec un discours sur Homere. Par Monsieur de la Motte* (Paris: chez Gregoire Depuis, 1714), 8°. List 391. Theca 18.

—— [Iliad. 1715–20] *The Iliad of Homer, translated by Mr. Pope.* 6 vols. (London: printed by W. Bowyer for Bernard Lintott, 1715–20), 4°. List 465 (large paper). Theca 17. Leeds 312 or 313. ESTC T59731. List of subscribers includes Congreve. According to Hodges, citing the *Post Boy* for Tuesday, 31 May 1715, regular subscribers received their copies of the first volume on 6 June 1715 (*Library*, p. 82), whereas Congreve's holograph receipt shows that he received his five days sooner. The receipt is at CH: HM 445 and reads: 'June 1st: 1715 Receivd of Mr Lintott the first volume of Mr Popes translation of Homer by me Wm Congreve.'

Homer [Odyssey. 1716] *L'Odyssée d'Homere traduite en françois...par Madame Dacier*. 3 vols. (Paris: aux dépens de Rigaud, 1716), 12°. List 193. Theca 18.

—— [Odyssey. 1725–6] *The Odyssey*. 5 vols. (London: printed for Bernard Lintott, 1725–6), 4°. List 466 (large paper). Theca 11. Leeds 312 or 313. ESTC T67135. Translated by Alexander Pope, with Elijah Fenton and William Broome. List of subscribers includes Congreve.

—— *see also* Roberti, Antonius, *Clavis homerica* (1655).

The honour of the taylors, *see* Winstanley, William.

Hopkins, Charles (1664?–1700?), *Boadicea Queen of Britain. A tragedy* (London: printed for Jacob Tonson, 1697), 4°. List 51. Theca 27. Wing H2719; ESTC R2285. Dedicated to Congreve.

Horace [Works. 1676] *Q. Horatius Flaccus. Daniel Heinsius ex emendatissimis editionibus expressit* (Amstelodami: apud Danielem Elzevirium, 1676), 16°. List 322 ('24°.'). Theca 5.

—— [Works. 1690] *Q. Horatii Flacci Poemata interpretatione et notis illustravit Petrus Rodellius* (Londini: impensis Abelis Swalle, 1690), 8°. List 319. Theca 7. Wing H2780; ESTC R3778.

—— [Works. 1694] *Q. Horatii Flacci Opera. Interpretatione & notis illustravit Ludovicus Desprez* (Londini: impensis R. Clavel, H. Mortlock, S. Smith & B. Walford, 1694), 8°. List 318. Theca 7. Wing H2763; ESTC R23468.

—— [Works. 1699] *Quinti Horatii Flacci Opera* (Cantabrigiæ: typis academicis, impensis Jacobi Tonson, London, 1699), 4°. List 317. Theca 17. Wing H2764; ESTC R21196. Edited by James Talbot. The 'Proposals for Printing Horace, Virgil, Terence, Catullus, Tibullus and Propertius, In the New Press at Cambridge' (Wing P3734B), printed there in the week ending 3 December 1698, list Congreve as a subscriber to the set.

—— [Works. 1699] *Q. Horatii Flaccus. Accedunt J. Rutgersii lectiones* (Traject. Batav. [Utrecht]: apud Franciscum Halman, Guiljelmum van de Water, 1699), 12°. List 321. Theca 24.

—— [Works. 1709] *Oeuvres d'Horace en latin et en françois, avec des remarques critiques et historiques. Par Monsieur Dacier*. 3rd edn. 10 vols. (Paris: J.-B. Christophe Ballard, 1709), 12°. List 199. Theca 18.

—— [Works. 1710] *Oeuvres d'Horace, traduites en françois par le P. Tarteron. ...Avec des remarques critiques sur la traduction, par Pierre Coste*. 2 vols. (Amsterdam: chez Pierre de Coup, 1710), 12°. List 315 ('8°.'). Theca 3.

—— [Works. 1715] *Quinti Horatii Flacci Opera* (Londini: ex officinâ Jacobi Tonson, & Johannis Watts, 1715), 12°. List 320. Theca 24. ESTC T46224. Edited by Michael Maittaire.

—— [Ars Poetica. 1684] *Horace's Art of poetry. Made English by the Right Honourable the Earl of Roscommon* (London: printed for Henry Herringman, and sold by Joseph Knight and Francis Saunders, 1684), 4°. List 406. Theca 27. Leeds 209. Wing H2769; ESTC R4513. Bound with Dryden, *Of dramatick poesie* (1684), and Buckingham, *The rehearsal* (1687). Congreve's copy, signed 'Will: Congreve': Robert H. Taylor collection, Princeton University.

—— *Odæ in locos communes ad lyricæ poëseos studiosorum utilitatem digestæ. Studio & operâ Josephi Langii* (Hanoviæ: typis Wechelianis, apud Claudium Marnium

& heredes Joannis Aubrii, 1604), 8°. List 323 ('12°. Lugd. 1604.': not found). Theca 5.

—— *The odes, satyrs, and epistles of Horace. Done into English.* 2nd edn. (London: printed for Jacob Tonson, 1688), 8°. List 104. Theca 20. Wing H2776. ESTC R27419. Translated by Thomas Creech.

Howell, James (1594?–1666) (ed.), *see* Cotgrave, Randle, *A French and English dictionary* (1660).

Hughes, John (1677–1720) (tr.), *see* Fontenelle, M. de (Bernard Le Bovier), *Dialogues of the dead* (1708).

—— (ed.), *see* Spenser, Edmund [Works. 1715].

Hurtado de Mendoza, Diego (1503–75), *La vie et avantures de Lazarillo de Tormes. Escrites, par lui meme. Traduction nouvelle* (Brusselles: chez George de Backer, 1698), 12°. List 632. Theca 26. Translation of *La vida de Lazarillo de Tormes* by Diego Hurtado de Mendoza.

Iamblichus of Chalcis (*c*.250–*c*.325), *Iamblichi Chalcidensis ex Coele-Syria, De mysteriis liber. Praemittitur epistola Porphyrii ad Anebonem Ægytium, eodem argumento. Thomas Gale anglus græce nunc primum edidit, Latine vertit, & notas adjecit* (Oxonii: e theatro Sheldoniano, 1678), 2°. List 326. Theca 9. Wing I26; ESTC R13749.

Ides, Evert-Ysbrants (1660?–1700), *Three years travels from Moscow over-land to China . . . Printed in Dutch . . . done into English* (London: printed for W. Freeman, J. Walthoe, T. Newborough, J. Nicholson, and R. Parker, 1706), 4°. List 640 ('1705', so dated on engraved title page). Theca 29. ESTC T55175.

Jacob, Giles (1686–1744), *The poetical register: or, the lives and characters of the English dramatick poets.* 2 vols. (London: printed for Edmund Curll, 1719), 8°. List 367 (large paper). Theca 28. Leeds 414. ESTC T137459.

—— *The student's companion: or, the reason of the laws of England* (In the Savoy: printed by E. and R. Nutt and R. Gosling, (assigns of Edward Sayer, esq;), for T. Corbett, 1725), 8°. List 329. Theca 32. ESTC T137466.

—— *A treatise of laws: or, a general introduction to the common, civil, and canon law* (In the Savoy: printed by Eliz. Nut and R. Gosling, (assigns of Edw. Sayer, esq;) for T. Woodward, 1721), 8°. List 328. Theca 32. ESTC T137996; or N13977 (edition printed for T. Woodward and J. Peele, 1721).

Johnson, Thomas (ed.), *see* Cebes, *Tabula* (1720).

Jonson, Ben (1573?–1637) [Works. 1616] *The workes of Beniamin Jonson* (Imprinted at London by Will Stansby, 1616), 2°. List 44 ('Old Edit.'; date and volume(s) not given). Theca 2. STC 14751; ESTC S111817. A copy bearing the name 'Congreve' on sig. ¶ʳ is in a private collection in France; the form of the name is unlike his normal signature but the copy may have been his and the name a sign of the association.

—— [Works. 1692] *The works of Ben Jonson . . . To which is added a comedy called The new inn.* 3rd edn. (London: printed by Thomas Hodgkin for H. Herringman, E. Brewster, T. Bassett, R. Chiswell, M. Wotton, G. Conyers, 1692), 2°. List 45 ('Best Edit. L. Papr.'), 338. Theca 1. Wing J1006; ESTC R15282.

Justinian I, Emperor of the East (483?–565), *D. Justiniani, sacratissimi principis, institutionum . . . cura & studio Arnoldi Vinnii* (Amstelædami: ex officina Elzeviriana, 1663), 12°. List 332. Theca 5.

Justinus, Marcus Junianus (*fl.* 3rd c.), *Justini Historiarum ex Trogo Pompeio libri XLIV* (Londini: ex officinâ Jacobi Tonson, & Johannis Watts, 1713), 12°. List 336. Theca 24. ESTC T145556. Edited by Michael Maittaire.

Juvenal and **Persius** [Works. 1673] *Decimus Junius Juvenalis and Aulus Persius Flaccus, translated and illustrated, as well with sculptures as notes. By Barten Holyday* (Oxford: printed by W. Downing for F. Oxlad, Senior, J. Adams, and F. Oxlad, Junior, 1673), 2°. List 337. Wing J1276; ESTC R12290.

—— [Works. 1691] *D. Junii Juvenalis et A. Persii Flacci Satyræ. Interpretatione ac notis illustravit Ludovicus Prateus* (Londini: impensis Tho. Dring, & Abel Swalle, 1691), 8°. List 334. Theca 7. Wing J1285; ESTC R21136.

—— [Works. 1693] *The satires of Decimus Junius Juvenalis. Translated into English verse. By Mr. Dryden, and several other eminent hands. Together with the Satires of Aulus Persius Flaccus. Made English by Mr. Dryden* (London: printed for Jacob Tonson, 1693), 2°. List 163. Theca 10. Wing J1288; ESTC R12345. Includes Congreve's poem to Dryden on his translation of Persius and Congreve's own translation of Juvenal's Satire XI.

—— [Works. 1716] *Decii Junii Juvenalis at Auli Persii Flacci Satyræ* (Londini: ex officinâ Jacobi Tonson, & Johannis Watts, 1716), 12°. List 335. Theca 24. ESTC T92179. Edited by Michael Maittaire.

Kemp, John (1665–1717), *Monumenta vetustatis Kempiana* (Londini: typis Danielis Bridge. Veneunt à Paulo Vaillant; G. & J. Innys; & J. Osborn, 1720), 8°. List 339. Theca 6. ESTC T121266. Edited by Robert Ainsworth and John Ward.

Kennett, Basil (1674–1715), *The lives and characters of the ancient Grecian poets* (London: printed for Abel Swall, 1697), 8°. List 340. Theca 11. Wing K297; ESTC R16618.

—— *The lives and characters of the ancient Grecian poets* (London, 1709?), 8°. List 368 ('Lives of the Grecian poets. 8°. Lond. 1709'; no 1709 edition has been located. The 2nd edn. of Kennett's work was not published until 1735.).

—— *Romæ antiquæ notitia: or, The antiquities of Rome. In two parts* (London: printed for A. Swall and T. Child, 1696), 8°. List 341, 523. Theca 11. Wing K298; ESTC R18884.

Killigrew, Thomas, the Elder (1612–83), *Comedies, and tragedies* (London: printed [by John Macock] for Henry Herringman, 1664), 2°. List 342. Theca 9. Leeds 341. Wing K450; ESTC R7715.

Kinnaston, Francis, Sir (1587–1642), *see* Chaucer, Geoffrey, *Amorum Troili et Creseidæ* (1635).

Labottière, Claude (*fl.* 1724), *La vie et les avantures de Zizime, fils de Mahomet II* (Paris: chez Claude Labottière, 1724), 12°. List 629 ('8°.'). Theca 33.

La Bruyère, Jean de (1645–96) (ed.), *see* Theophrastus, *Caracteres* (1693).

La Chapelle, Jean de (1655–1723), *Les Amours de Tibulle.* 3 vols. (Amsterdam: chez Jean Fred. Bernard, 1715), 12°. List 22. Theca 24.

Lactantius (240?–320?), *Lucii Cælii Lactantii Firmiani opera, quæ extant omnia* (Cantabrigiæ: ex officinâ Johan. Hayes, impensis Hen. Dickinson, & Rich. Green, 1685), 8°. List 361. Theca 14. Wing L140; ESTC R2417.

La Fayette, Madame de (Marie-Madeleine Pioche de La Vergne) (1634–93), *Zayde, histoire espagnole. Par M. de Segrais.* 2 vols. (Paris: chez Pierre Aubouyn, 1705), 12°. List 659. Theca 23.

La Fontaine, Jean de (1621–95), *Les Amours de Psiché et de Cupidon* (La Haye: chez Adrian Moetjens, 1700), 12°. List 19. Theca 25.

—— *Contes et nouvelles en vers.* Nouvelle edition. 2 vols. in 1 (Amsterdam: chez Pierre Brunel, 1699), 8°. List 126. Theca 25.

—— *Contes et nouvelles en vers.* Nouvelle edition (Amsterdam: chez N. Etienne Lucas, 1721), 8°. List 125. Theca 30.

—— *Fables choisies. Mises en vers.* 4 pts. in 2 vols. (Anvers: chez la veuve de Barthelemy Foppens, 1699), 8°. List 250. Theca 25.

—— *see also* Maucroix, François de, *Ouvrages de prose et de poësis* (1688).

La Grange-Chancel, Joseph de (1667–1758), *Ino et Mélicerte, tragédie* (Paris: chez Pierre Ribou, 1713), 12°. List 330. Theca 30.

Lamb, Patrick, *Royal cookery or, The complete court-cook. Containing the choicest receipts in all the particular branches of cookery, now in use in the queen's palaces* (London: printed for Abel Roper, and sold by John Morphew, 1710), 8°. List 110. Theca 32. ESTC T91554 or T117552 (another issue, 'printed for Maurice Atkins', 1710).

Lambin, Denys (*c.*1516–72) (ed.), *see* Plautus [Comedies. 1587].

La Motte, M. de (Antoine Houdar) (1672–1731), *Fables nouvelles* (Paris: chez Gregoire Depuis, 1719), 4°. List 389 ('8°.'). Theca 30.

—— *Poësies de Monsieur de la Motte avec un discours sur la poësie en general, & sur l'ode en particuleur* (Suivant la copie de Paris, & se vend, à Bruxelles, chez les Frères t'Serstevens, 1707), 8°. List 390 ('12°.'). Theca 24.

—— (tr.), *L'Iliade, poeme, avec un Discours sur Homere, see* Homer [Iliad. 1714].

Lang, Joseph (*c.*1570–1615) (ed.), *see* Horace, *Odæ* (1604).

Lansdowne, George Granville, Baron (1667–1735), *Poems upon several occasions* (London: printed for J. Tonson, 1712), 8°. List 360. Theca 20. Leeds 273. ESTC T55586; cf. Foxon i. 314.

La Rue, Charles de (1643–1725) (ed.), *see* Virgil [Works. 1682].

Laughton, H. (ed.), *see* Virgil [Works. 1701].

Lawes, Henry (1596–1662) (composer), *see* Cartwright, William, *Comedies* (1651).

Le Bossu, René (1631–80), *Traité du poëme épique.* 2 vols. (Paris: M. Le Petit, 1675), 12°. List 61. Theca 12.

Le Bovier de Fontenelle, Bernard, *see* Fontenelle, M. de (Bernard Le Bovier).

Le Clerc, Jean (1657–1736) (ed.), *see* Menander, *Menandri et Philemonis reliquæ* (1709).

Lee, Nathaniel (1653?–1692), *The works of Mr. Nathaniel Lee in one volume* (London: printed for Richard Bentley and S. Magnes, 1687), 4°. List 358 (date of publication not given. Another possibility is the edition printed for R. Bentley, 1694). Theca 28. Wing L845 (1687) or L845A (1694); ESTC R230696 or R16027.

Lefebvre, Tannegui (1615–72), *Tanaquilli Fabri Epistolæ. Pars prima.* Edition altera priori emendatior (Salmurij: typis & sumptibus Isaaci Desbordes & Ioannis Lesnerii, 1674), 4°. List 241. Theca 22.

Lefèvre, Anne, *see* Dacier, Anne Lefèvre.

Lefèvre, Raoul (*fl.* 1460), *The destruction of Troy* (London: printed for Thomas Passenger, 1684), 4°. List 405 (edition not given; bound with 10 other miscellaneous 4° items; this edition is one of numerous English quarto translations published after the late sixteenth century). Theca 28. Wing L941A; ESTC R213964.

Lefèvre, Tannegui, *see* Lefebvre, Tannegui.

Leng, John (d. 1727) (ed.), *see* Terence [Comedies. 1701].

Le Noble, Eustache (1643–1711), *Abra-Mulè; or, A true history of the dethronement of Mahomet IV. Written in French by M. Le Noble. Made English by J. P.* (London: printed for R. Clavel, 1696), 8°. List 24 ('12°.'). Theca 8. Wing L1051; ESTC R13238.

—— *Le gage touchè, histoires galantes* (Paris: chez Jacques Desbordes, 1709). List 271 ('[Paris] 1711', possibly in error). Theca 26.

Le Roux, Philibert Joseph (d. *c.*1790), *Dictionnaire comique, satyrique, critique, burlesque, libre & proverbial* (Amsterdam: chez Michel Charles. Le Cène, 1718), 8°. List 176. Theca 23.

Le Roy, Marin, Sieur de Gomberville (1600?–74), *The history of Polexander: in five bookes. Done into English by William Browne* (London: printed by Tho. Harper, for Thomas Walkley and are to be sold at his shop, 1648), 2°. List 308, 486. Theca 2. Wing G1026; ESTC R21269.

Le Sage, Alain René (1668–1747), *Histoire de Gil Blas.* 2 vols. (Amsterdam: chez J. Oosterwyk, Steenhouwer & Uytwerf, 1715), 12°. List 298. Theca 26.

—— *The history and adventures of Gil Blas of Santillane.* 2nd edn. 3 vols. (London: printed for Jacob Tonson, 1725), 12°. List 307. Theca 6. ESTC T122955.

—— (tr.), *see* Boiardo, Matteo Maria, *Nouvelle traduction de Roland l'amoureux* (1717).

Leti, Gregorio (1630–1701), *L'Histoire de la vie du Pape Sixte Cinquième traduite de l'Italien.* 2 vols. (Anvers: chez la veuve de Barthelemy Foppens, 1704), 12°. List 299. Theca 11.

Lettres persanes, *see* Montesquieu, Charles Louis de Secondat, baron de.

Lettres sur les Anglois, *see* Muralt, Béat Louis de.

Lilly, William (1602–81), *England's propheticall Merline foretelling to all nations of Europe untill 1663* (London: printed by John Raworth, for John Partridge, and are to be sold at the Sun in Pauls Church yard, 1644), 4°. List 359. Theca 8. Wing L2221; ESTC R8902.

Linguæ Romanæ, *see* Littleton, Adam.

Lipsius, Justus (1547–1606), *Justi Lipsi De constantia libri duo* (Antverpiæ: apud Christophorum Plantinum, 1584), 4°. List 364. Theca 7.

Lisle, William (1569?–1637) (tr.), *see* Heliodorus, *The famous historie* (1638).

Littlebury, Isaac (tr.), *see* Herodotus, *The history* (1720).

Littleton, Adam (1627–94), *Linguæ Romanæ dictionarium luculentum novum. A new dictionary in five alphabets* (Cambridge: printed for W. Rawlins, T. Dring, R. Chiswell, C. Harper, W. Crook, I. Place, and the executors of S. Leigh, 1693), 4°. List 87. Theca 22. Wing L2565; ESTC R29945.

Livy (59 BC–AD 17), *Titi Livii Historiarum libri ex recensione J.F. Gronovii.* 3 vols. (Lugd. Batavorum [Leiden]: ex officinâ Elzevirianâ, 1654), 12°. List 363. Theca 5.

—— *Titi Livii Historiarum libri quod extat. Ex recensione I: F. Gronovii* (Amstel-odami: apud Danielem Elzevirium, 1678), 12°. List 362. Theca 6.

Lloyd, Nicholas (1630–80) (ed.), *see* Estienne, Charles, *Dictionarium historicum* (1686).

Locke, John (1632–1704), *Posthumous works... To which is added, VI. His new method of a common-place-book, written originally in French, and now translated into English* (London: printed by W.B. for A. and J. Churchill, 1706), 8°. List 349. Theca 33. ESTC T148785.

—— *An essay, concerning humane understanding, in four books.* 3rd edn. (London: printed for Awnsham and John Churchil, and Samuel Manship, 1695), 2°. List 348. Theca 9. Wing L2741; ESTC R20221.

Longinus, Dionysii (lst c.), *Dionysii Longini De sublimitate commentarius, ceter-aque quæ reperiri potuere... Jacobus Tollius... emendavit* (Trajecti ad Rhenum [Utrecht]: ex officinâ Francisci Halma, 1694), 4°. List 351. Theca 22.

Longus (*fl.* 2nd c.?), *Les Amours pastorales de Daphnis et Chloé. Avec figures. Ecrites en grec par Longus, & traduites en françois par Amiot.* Nouvelle edn. (Paris: Cramoisy, 1716?), 12°. List 20 (edition not given). Theca 25.

Lucan (39–65) [Pharsalia. 1635] *Lucans Pharsalia: or The civill warres of Rome, betweene Pompey the great, and Iulius Cæsar. The whole ten bookes, Englished by Thomas May.* 3rd edn. (London: printed by A.[ugustine] M.[athewes], and are to be sold by Will: Sheares, 1635), 8°. List 346, 402 ('12°'). Theca 6. STC 16889; ESTC S108867.

—— [Pharsalia. 1669] *M. Annæus Lucanus De bello civili, cum Hug: Grotii, Farnabii notis integris & variorum selectiss. Accurante Corn. Schrevelio* (Lugd. Batav. [Leiden] & Roterod.: ex officina Hackiana, 1669), 8°. List 344. Theca 7.

—— [Pharsalia. 1683] *La Pharsale de Lucain... en vers françois* (La Haye: chez Louïs & Henry van Dole, 1700), 12°. List 345, 489. Theca 24. Translated by Georges de Brébeuf.

—— [Pharsalia. 1718] *Lucan's Pharsalia. Translated into English verse by Nicholas Rowe, Esq.* (London, for Jacob Tonson, 1718 [1719]), 2°. List 343 (large paper), 521. Theca 16. Hornby Castle 1140. ESTC T114104; Foxon R293. List of subscribers includes Congreve.

Lucas, Paul (1664–1737), *Troisième voyage du sieur Paul Lucas, fait en M. DCCXIV, &c. par ordre de Louis XIV. Dans la Turquie, l'Asie, la Sourie, la Palestine, la Haute et la Basse Egypte, &c.* 3 vols. (Rouen: chez Robert Machuel le jeune, 1719), 8°. List 620 (12°). Theca 3. Hornby Castle 1218.

—— *Voyage de sieur Paul Lucas au Levant. On y trouvera entr'autre une description de la haute Egypte, suivant le cours du Nil, depuis le Caire jusques aux cataractes.* 2 vols. (La Haye: chez Guillaume de Voys, 1709), 12°. List 619. Theca 3.

—— *Voyage du sieur Paul Lucas, fait par ordre du roi dans la Grece, l'Asie Mineure, la Macédoine et l'Afrique.* 2 vols. (Amsterdam: aux dépens de la compagnie, 1714), 12°. List 618. Theca 3.

Lucian of Samosata (*c*.125–*c*.200), *Les œuvres de Lucian de Samosate autheur de nouveau traduites en François... par J. B.* [i.e. Jean Baudoin] (Paris: chez Jean Richer, [1613]), 4°. List 357 (date not given). Theca 14.

Lucian of Samosata *Loukianou Samosatéòs Theòn diàlogoi. Luciani Samosatensis deorum dialogi numero. 70. una cum interpretatione e regione latina: nusquam antea impressi. Contenta librorum partialium. 1 Deorum supernorum habet dialogos 26. 2 Deorum marinorum habet dialogos 14 3 Deorum infernorum habet dialogos 30* (Argentinae: Johannes Schottus, 1515), 4°. List 264. Theca 14.

—— *Lucien de la traduction de N. Perrot, sr. d'Ablancourt.* 2 vols. (Paris: chez A. Courbé, 1655), 4°. List 356. Theca 22.

Lucretius Carus, Titus (94?–55? BC) [De rerum natura. 1659] *Titi Lucretii Cari De rerum natura libri sex. Ad postremam Oberti Gifanii I. C. emendationem* (Leutetiæ Parisiorum: apud Guillemum de Luyne, 1659), 8°. List 354. Theca 7.

—— [De rerum natura. 1695] *Titi Lucretii Cari De rerum natura libri sex: quibus interpretationem et notas addidit Thomas Creech* (Oxonii: e Theatro Sheldoniano. Impensis Ab. Swall, & Tim. Child, 1695), 8°. List 353. Theca 7. Wing L3445; ESTC R37615.

—— [De rerum natura. 1712] *Titi Lucretii Cari De rerum natura libri sex* (Londini: sumptibus & typis Jacobi Tonson, 1712), 4°. List 352 (large paper). Theca 17. ESTC T50367 or T50368.

—— [De rerum natura. 1713] *Titi Lucretii Cari De rerum natura libri sex* (Londini: ex officinâ Jacobi Tonson, & Johannis Watts, 1713), 12°. List 355. Theca 24. ESTC T50364 (large paper) or N1181. Edited by Michael Maittaire.

Luna, Miguel de (*fl.* 1600), *The life of the most illustrious monarch Almanzor: and of the several revolutions of the mighty empire of the caliphs, and of the African kingdoms* (London: printed for Dan. Brown and Isaac Cleave, 1693), 8°. List 366 ('1695'). Theca 8. Wing L3484C; ESTC R10867.

Lydgate, John (1370?–1451?), *see* Chaucer, Geoffrey [Works. 1687].

Lyttelton, George, Baron (1709–73), *Bleinheim* (London: printed for J. Roberts, 1728), 2°. List 70. ESTC N15159; Foxon L330.

Mabbe, James (1572–1642?) (tr.), *see* Aléman, Mateo, *The rogue* (1630).

Macrobius, Ambrosius Theodosius (*fl. c.*400), *Aur. Theodosii Macrobii v. cl. & inlustris Opera. Ioh Isacius Pontanus secundò recensuit: adiectis ad libros singulos notis. Quibus accedunt Ioh. Meursi breviores notae* (Lugduni Batavorum [Leiden]: ex officinâ Joannis Maire, 1628), 8°. List 399. Theca 7.

Mailly, Chevalier de (d. *c.*1724), *Nouvelles toutes nouvelles* (Amsterdam: aux dépens d'Estienne Roger, 1710), 12°. List 425. Theca 26.

Maittaire, Michael (ed.), *see* Catullus, *Catulli, Tibulli, et Propertii* [Works. 1715].

—— *see* Florus [Epitome rerum romanorum. 1715].

—— *see* Horace [Works. 1715].

—— *see* Justinus, *Justini Historiarum ex Trogo Pompeio* (1713).

—— *see* Juvenal and Persius [Works. 1716].

—— *see* Lucretius Carus, Titus [De rerum natura. 1713].

—— *see* Nepos, Cornelius, *Excellentium imperatorum vitæ* (1715).

—— *see* Ovid [Works. 1715].

—— *see* Phaedrus, *Phædri Aug. liberti Fabularum Æsopiarum* (1713).

—— *see* Rufus, *Quinti Curtii Rufi De rebus gestis Alexandri Magni* (1716).

—— *see* Sallust [Works. 1713].

—— *see* Terence [Comedies. 1713].

—— *see* Virgil [Works. 1715].

Malebranche, Nicholas (1638–1715), *De la recherche de la verité.* 6th edn. 2 vols. (Paris: chez Michel David, 1712), 4°. List 382. Theca 2.

Malory, Thomas, Sir (*fl.* 1470) (tr.), *see Mort darthur* (1529).

Malthus, Francis, *A treatise of artificial fire-works both for warres and recreation . . . Newly written in French, and Englished by the authour Tho: Malthus* [i.e. Francis Malthus] (London: printed [by W. Jones] for Richard Hawkins, 1629), 8°. List 397. Theca 6. STC 17217; ESTC S109781.

Management of the war, see Hare, Francis (1711).

Mandelslo, Johann Albrecht von (1616–44), *Voyages aux Indes orientales.* In: Adam Olearius, *Relation du voyage* (1666).

—— *see also* Olearius, Adam, *The voyages and travells* (1669).

Mandeville, John, Sir (1300?–1372), *The voiage and travaile of Sir John Maundevile, kt. which treateth of the way to Hierusalem . . . Now publish'd entire from the original MS in the Cotton Library* (London: printed for J. Woodman, and D. Lyon, and C. Davis, 1725), 8°. List 641 ('4°.'). Theca 29. Leeds 391 (large paper). ESTC T100822.

—— *The voyages and travels of Sir John Mandeville, knight,* 4°. List 405 (edition not given; bound with 10 other miscellaneous 4° items). Theca 28. Cf. Wing M412+; there are a number of quarto editions recorded in the ESTC.

Manilius, Marcus (*fl.* 9), *The five books of M. Manilius, containing a system of the ancient astronomy and astrology: together with the philosophy of the Stoicks. Done into English verse. With notes* (London: printed for Jacob Tonson, 1697), 8°. List 385. Theca 20. Wing M430; ESTC R4238. Translated by Thomas Creech.

Manning, Francis (*fl.* 1695–1718) (tr.), *see* Cassius Dio Cocceianus, *History* (1704).

Marchand, Prosper (d. 1756) (ed.), *see* Bayle, Pierre, *Dictionnaire* (1720).

—— *see* Saint-Réal, M. l'abbé de, *Oeuvres* (1722).

Marguerite, queen, consort of Henry II, king of Navarre (1492–1549), *Contes et nouvelles de Marguerite de Valois, reine de Navarre mis en beau langage accomodé au goût de ce temps.* 2 vols. (Amsterdam: chez George Gallet, 'M.DCC.' [1699]), 8°. List 124. Theca 23.

Marini, Giovanni Ambrogio (1594–1650), *Il Calloandro fedele* (Venice, 1654?), 12°. List 113 ('Ven. 1654'; this edition not located). Theca 6.

Marino, Giambattista (1569–1625), *L'Adone, poema. Con gli argomenti del Conte Fortuniano Sanvitale, et l'allegorie di Don Lorenzo Scoto* (Parigi: Oliviero di Varano, 1623), 2°. List 2. Theca 1.

—— *L'Adone, poema heroico del C. Marino, con gli argomenti del Conte Sanvitale, et l'allegorie di Don Lorenzo Scoto . . . Di nuova ricorreto, e di figure ornatto.* 4 vols. (Amsterdam: nella stamperia del S.D. Elsevier, et in Parigi si vende appresso Thomaso Jolly, 1678), 32°. List 3 ('24°.'). Theca 5.

Massialot, François (*c.*1660–1733), *Le nouveau cuisinier royal et bourgeois; qui apprend à ordonner toute sorte de repas en gras & en maigre* (Paris: chez Claude Prudhomme, 1722). 8°. List 107. Theca 32.

Maucroix, François de (1619–1708) and **Jean de La Fontaine** (1621–95), *Ouvrages de prose et de poësis* (Amsterdam: chez Pierre Mortier, 1688), 12°. List 395. Theca 12.

May, Thomas (1595–1650) (tr.), *see* Lucan [Pharsalia. 1635].

Mayne, Zachary (*fl.* 1728), *Two dissertations concerning sense, and the imagination. With an essay on consciousness* (London: printed for J. Tonson, 1728), 8°. List 222. ESTC T117300.

Menander, of Athens and **Philemon** (3rd/4th century BC), *Menandri et Philemonis reliquæ quotquot reperiri potuerunt; Græce et Latine, cum notis Hugonis Grotii et Joannis Clerici* (Amstelodami: apud Thomam Lombrail, 1709), 8°. List 388. Theca 7.

Mendes Pinto, Fernando (1509–83), *The voyages and adventures of Ferdinand Mendez Pinto, a Portugal: during his travels for the space of one and twenty years in the kingdoms of Ethiopia, China, Tartaria, Cauchinchina, Calaminham, Siam, Pegu, Japan, and a great part of the East-Indies... Done into English by H. C.* [Henry Cogan] (London: printed by J. Macock, for Henry Herringman, 1663), 2°. List 463. Theca 2. Leeds 480. Wing M1706; ESTC R221803.

Meurs, Johannes van (1579–1639), *see* Chorier, Nicholas, *Joannis Meursii elegantiæ latini sermonis* (n.d.).

—— *see* Macrobius, *Opera* (1628).

Middleton, Thomas (1570?–1627), *A mad world, my masters*, 4°. List 407, 490 (edition not given; bound with 5 other miscellaneous 4° items). Theca 28. STC 17888 or 17889; ESTC S112578 or 112580.

Miege, Guy (1644–1718?), *The present state of Denmark* (London: printed for Tho. Basset, 1683), 8°. List 396 ('12°.'). Theca 8. Wing M2024; ESTC R214182.

Milbourne, Luke (1649–1720), *Notes on Dryden's Virgil. In a letter to a friend. With an essay on the same poet* (London: printed for R. Clavill, 1698), 8°. List 384. Theca 8. Wing M2035; ESTC R19804.

Milton, John (1608–74), *The poetical works of Mr. John Milton* (London: printed for Jacob Tonson, 1695). 2°. Wing M2162, M2163; ESTC R226434, R13029. Not listed in the catalogue of Congreve's library. Congreve's copy, signed 'Will: Congreve' on the title page: CLC: *fPR3550 C95.

—— *The poetical works of Mr. John Milton*. 2 vols. (London: printed for Jacob Tonson, 1705), 8°. Vol. 1: *Paradise lost*. 7th edn. Vol. 2: *Paradise regain'd*. 4th edn. List 381 ('3 Vols.'; large paper). Theca 19. ESTC T134227.

—— *The poetical works*. 2 vols. (London: printed for Jacob Tonson, 1720), 4°. List 380 (large paper). Theca 17. Hornby Castle 1153. ESTC T134621.

Minsheu, John (ed.), *see* Perceval, Richard, *A dictionarie in Spanish and English* (1599).

Miscellaneous poems and translations. By several hands (London: printed for Bernard Lintott, 1712), 8°. List 409. Theca 20. Case 260 (1a). ESTC T5777. Includes a number of poems by Alexander Pope, including the first printing of 'The Rape of the Lock' in two cantos.

Miscellany poems upon several occasions (London: printed for Peter Buck, 1692), 8°. List 411. Theca 20. Wing G733A; ESTC R21564. Case 197. Edited by Charles Gildon.

Moivre, Abraham de (1667–1754), *The doctrine of chances: or, a method of calculating the probability of events in play* (London: printed by W. Pearson for the author, 1718), 4°. List 205, 403. Theca 2. ESTC T33065.

Molière, Jean Baptiste Poquelin (1622–73), *Les Oeuvres de Monsieur de Molière. Reveuës, corrigées & augmentées. Enrichies de figures en taille-douce.* 8 vols. (Paris: chez Denys Thierry, Claude Barbin, et Pierre Trabouillet, 1697), 12°. List 393. Theca 25.

Molyneux, William (1656–98), *The case of Ireland's being bound by acts of parliament in England stated* (Dublin, 1698), 8°. List 387. Theca 8. There are two 8° Dublin editions of 1698 (Wing 2402, 2403; ESTC R30063; R32102).

Monmouth, Henry Carey, 2nd Earl of, *see* Carey, Henry, 2nd Earl of Monmouth.

Montagu, Charles, 1st Earl of Halifax (1661–1715), *An epistle to the Earl of Dorset.* In: John Sheffield, *A Collection of poems: viz. The temple of death* (1701).

Montaigne, Michel de (1533–92), [Essays. 1582] *Essais de messire Michel, Seigneur de Montaigne.* 2nd edn. 2 vols. in 1 (Bourdeaus: par S. Millanges, 1582), 8°. List 378 ('3 Tom 12°. Bourdeaux 1582'). Theca 6.

—— [Essays. 1657] *Essais... Avec augmentation de la version françoise des passages italiens* (Paris, 1657?), 2°. List 376 ('Fol. Paris 1658.'). Theca 15. There were at least 12 different issues of the 1657 Paris 2° edition (R.A. Sayce and David Maskell, *Montaigne's 'Essais'* (London, 1983), 31: 1657, pp. 146–53), but none dated 1658 is known to Sayce.

—— [Essays. 1659] *Les Essais.* Nouvelle édn. 3 vols. (Paris: chez Christophe Journel, 1659), 12°. List 377. Theca 5.

—— [Essays. 1685] *Essays of Michael, seigneur de Montaigne. In three books.... Now rendered into English by Charles Cotton.* 3 vols. (London: for T. Basset, and M. Gilliflower, and W. Hensman). 8°. List 379 ('Lond. 1695', is probably an error for either 1685 or 1693). Theca 12. Wing M2479 (vol. 1) and either M2480 or M2480A (vols. 2 and 3); ESTC R2740. Congreve's set with his signature on each title page was sold to Quaritch by Sotheby's, New York, 16 May 1981 (lot 35), but its present location is unknown.

Montesquieu, Charles Louis de Secondat, baron de (1689–1755), *Lettres persanes.* 2nd edn. 2 vols. (Cologne: chez Pierre Marteau, 1721), 12°. List 373. Theca 26.

Montfaucon de Villars, Abbé de, *see* Villars, Nicolas-Pierre-Henri de Montfaucon.

Moore, Jonas, Sir (1617–79) (tr.), *see* Moretti, Tomaso, *A general treatise of artillery.*

Morabin, Jacques (1687–1762), *Histoire de l'exil de Ciceron* (Paris: chez Lambert Coffin, 1725), 12°. List 324 (date not given; there was another Paris edition, 1726). Theca 30.

Morel, Fédéric (1552–1630) (commentator), *see* Strabo, *Strabonis Rerum geographicarum* (1620).

Moretti, Tomaso (d. 1675), *A general treatise of artillery: or, Great ordnance writ in Italian by Tomaso Moretii of Brescia ... Translated into English, with notes thereupon, and some additions out of French for sea-gunners. By Sir Jonas Moore, Kt. With an appendix of artificial fire-works for war and delight; by Sir Abraham Dager Kt. ingenieur* (London: printed by A.G. and J.P. for Obadiah Blagrave, 1683), 8°. List 386. Theca 8. Wing M2726; ESTC R37646.

Mort darthur [La Mort darthur. Translated from the French by Sir T. Malory] (London: printed by Wynkyn de Worde, 1529), 2°. List 13 ('wants ye Title'). Theca 2. STC 803.

The most delectable history of Reynard the Fox, see Shirley, John.

Motteux, Peter Anthony (1663–1718) (tr.), *see* Stanzani, Tomaso, *Arsinoe* (1705).

—— (tr.), *see* Rabelais, *Whole works* (1708).

Mulgrave, 3rd Earl of, *see* Buckingham, John Sheffield, Duke of.

Munday, Anthony (1553–1633) (ed.), *see* Stow, John, *The survey of London* (1633).

Muralt, Béat Louis de (1665–1749), *Lettres sur les Anglois et les François. Et sur les voiages* (Cologne, 1725), 12°. List 374. Theca 30.

Murtadá ibn al-Khafif (1154/5–1237), *The Egyptian history, treating of the pyramids, the inundation of the Nile, and other prodigies of Egypt, according to the opinions and traditions of the Arabians. Written originally in the Arabian tongue by Murtadi the son of Gaphiphus. Rendered into French by Monsieur Vattier ... and done into English by J. Davies, of Kidwelly* (London: printed by R[obert]. B[attersby]. for W. Battersby, 1672), 8°. List 238. Theca 3. Wing M3127 or 3128 (printed for Thomas Bassett); ESTC R213892 or R23142.

Musarum anglicanarum analecta. 2nd edn. 2 vols. (Oxon.: e theatro Sheldoniano, impensis Joh. Crosley, 1699), 8°. List 383 (large paper). Theca 19. Wing M3136; ESTC R32296. Vol. 2 edited by Joseph Addison.

Nepos, Cornelius, *Cornelii Nepotis excellentium imperatorum vitæ* (Londini: ex officinâ Jacobi Tonson, & Johannis Watts, 1715), 12°. List 132. Theca 24. Edited by Michael Maittaire. ESTC T83012.

Nereides, see Diaper, William.

Newton, Isaac, Sir (1642–1727), *The chronology of ancient kingdoms amended* (London: printed for J. Tonson, and J. Osborn and T. Longman, 1728), 4°. List 426. ESTC T30721 (large paper) or N2784.

—— *Opticks: or, a treatise of the reflexions, refractions, inflexions and colours of light* (London: printed for Sam. Smith, and Benj. Walford, 1704), 4°. List 421. Theca 2. Leeds 469. ESTC T82019.

—— *see also* Pemberton, Henry, *A view of Sir Isaac Newton's philosophy* (1728).

Nicole, Pierre (1625–95), *see* Arnauld, Antoine, *La logique* (1697).

Noris, Matteo (1640–1708), *Marzio Coriolano: drama per musica* (Venezia: per il Nicolini, 1698), 12°. List 392. Theca 30.

Le nouveau cuisinier, see Massialot, François.

Novilieri Clavelli, Guglielmo Allesandro de (tr.), *see* Cervantes, *Novelliere Castigliano* (1626).

Odassi, Lodovico (*fl.* 1497) (tr.), *see* Cebes, *Tabula* (1720).

Ogilby, John (1600–76), *Britannia depicta or Ogilby improv'd; being a correct coppy of Mr. Ogilby's Actual survey of all ye direct & principal cross roads in England and Wales*. 4th edn. (London: printed for and sold by Tho. Bowles, & I. Bowles, 1724), 4°. List 435 ('8° 1727'; this edition not located). Theca 4. ESTC T150741.

Oldham, John (1653–83), *The works of Mr. John Oldham together with his remains*. 4 pts. (London: printed for Jo. Hindmarsh, 1686), 8°. List 441. Theca 20. Leeds 479. Wing O228; ESTC R25172. Congreve's copy, signed 'Will: Congreve' on the title page and bearing the Leeds bookplate: Y: Ij/Ol1/C684b. On each of pages 44–53 of *Poems and Translations* (1684) Congreve has struck out the incorrect headline ('Horace *his Art of Poetry*') and written above it 'Imitation of Horace Book 1 Satyr 9'.

Oldisworth, William (1680–1734) (tr.), *see* Homer [Iliad. 1712].

Oldmixon, John (1673–1742), *Reflections on the stage and Mr. Collyer's Defense of the Short view* (London: printed for R. Parker, and P. Buck, 1699), 8°. List 102. Theca 8. Wing O262; ESTC R17325.

—— *The secret history of Europe*. 2 vols. (London: printed for the booksellers of London and Westminster, 1712), 8°. List 310, 588. Theca 8. ESTC T101010.

Olearius, Adam (1600?–71), *Relation du voyage d'Adam Olearius en Moscovie, Tartarie, et Perse… contenant le Voyage de Jean Albert de Mandelslo aux Indes orientales traduit de l'allemand par A. de Wicquefort*. 2 vols. (Paris: chez Jean du Puis, 1666), 4°. List 616. Theca 28.

—— *The voyages and travells of the ambassadors sent by Frederick Duke of Holstein, to the Great Duke of Muscovy, and the King of Persia. Begun in the year M.DC.XXXIII. and finish'd in M.DC.XXXIX…. Whereto are added the travels of John Albert de Mandelslo… from Persia, into the East-Indies… Faithfully rendered into English, by John Davies…* 2nd edn. corrected (London: for John Starkey, and Thomas Basset, 1669), 2°. List 4, 436. Theca 1. Leeds 480. Wing O270; ESTC R30756.

Orrery, 4th Earl of, *see* Boyle, Charles, 4th Earl of Orrery.

Osborne, Thomas, 1st Duke of Leeds (1631–1712), *Copies & extracts of some letters written to and from the Earl of Danby (now Duke of Leeds) in the years 1676, 1677, and 1678* (London: printed for John Nicholson, 1710), 8°. List 219. Theca 33. ESTC T132736.

Otway, Thomas (1652–85), *Alcibiades* [2nd edn.] (London, for R. Bentley and S. Magnes, 1687), 4°. List 444 ('Plays 4°. London 1687'). Theca 27. Leeds 484 (listing nine plays by Otway, bound in one volume). Wing O540; ESTC R10708. Congreve's copy, signed 'Will: Congreve' on the title page: Lady Eccles (Mary Hyde), Four Oaks Farm.

—— *The atheist: or, The second part of The souldiers fortune* (London: printed for R. Bentley and J. Tonson, 1684), 4°. List 444 ('Plays 4°. London 1687'). Leeds 484 (listing nine plays by Otway, bound in one volume). Theca 27. Wing O541; ESTC R10764. Congreve's copy: Lady Eccles (Mary Hyde), Four Oaks Farm.

—— *Don Carlos Prince of Spain*. 3rd edn. (London: printed for Richard Tonson, 1686), 4°. List 444 ('Plays 4°. London 1687'). Theca 27. Leeds 484 (listing nine plays by Otway, bound in one volume). Wing O544; ESTC R18569. Congreve's copy: Lady Eccles (Mary Hyde), Four Oaks Farm.

—— *Friendship in fashion* (London: printed by E[lizabeth]. F[lesher]. for R. Tonson, 1678), 4°. List 444 ('Plays 4°. London 1687'). Theca 27. Leeds 484 (listing nine plays by Otway, bound in one volume). Wing O548; ESTC R20912, R232829, R234472, or R234473. Congreve's copy: Lady Eccles (Mary Hyde), Four Oaks Farm.

—— *The history and fall of Caius Marius.* 2nd edn. (London: printed for R. Bentley, 1692), 4°. List 444 ('Plays 4°. London 1687'). Theca 27. Leeds 484 (listing nine plays by Otway, bound in one volume). Wing O550; ESTC R8583 or R232830. Congreve's copy: Lady Eccles (Mary Hyde), Four Oaks Farm.

—— *The orphan, or the unhappy-marriage* (London: printed for R. Bentley, 1691), 4°. List 444 ('Plays 4°. London 1687'). Theca 27. Leeds 484 (listing nine plays by Otway, bound in one volume). Wing O554; R7186. Congreve's copy: Lady Eccles (Mary Hyde), Four Oaks Farm.

—— *The souldiers fortune.* 2nd edn. (London: printed for R. Bentley and S. Magnes, 1687), 4°. List 444 ('Plays 4°. London 1687'). Theca 27. Leeds 484 (listing nine plays by Otway, bound in one volume). Wing O564; ESTC R6952. Congreve's copy: Lady Eccles (Mary Hyde), Four Oaks Farm.

—— *Titus and Berenice... With a farce called The cheats of Scapin* (London: printed for Richard Tonson, 1677), 4°. List 444 ('Plays 4°. London 1687'). Theca 27. Leeds 484 (listing nine plays by Otway, bound in one volume, Congreve's signature on the first title page). Wing O566; ESTC R9537. Congreve's copy: Lady Eccles (Mary Hyde), Four Oaks Farm.

—— *Venice preserv'd, or, A plot discover'd* (London: printed for Jos. Hindmarsh, 1682) 4°. List 444 ('Plays 4°. London 1687'). Theca 27. Leeds 484 (listing nine plays by Otway, bound in one volume). Wing O567; ESTC R9483 Congreve's copy: Lady Eccles (Mary Hyde), Four Oaks Farm.

Oughtred, William (1575–1660), *The circles of proportion and the horizontall instrument* (Oxford: printed by W. Hall for R. Davis, 1660), 8°. List 442. Theca 8. Leeds 485. Wing O572; ESTC R203065.

Ovid (43 BC–AD 18) [Works. 1715] *P. Ovidii Nasonis Opera.* 3 vols. (Londini: ex officinâ Jacobi Tonson, & Johannis Watts, 1715), 12°. List 433. Theca 24. Edited by Michael Maittaire. ESTC T100400.

—— [Amores. 1661] *P. Ovidii Nasonis Amorum libri tres. Cum interpretatione gallica et recentioribus notis* (Lutetiæ Parisorum: apud viduam Petri Lamy, 1661), 8°. List 432, 437 ('Ovidii Elegiarum sive Amorum Libri. 8°'; edition not given). Theca 6.

—— [Ars amatoria. 1684] *Ovid De arte amandi, and The remedy of love Englished. As also The loves of Hero and Leander* (London: printed in the year, 1684), 12°. List 434. Theca 20. Wing O653; ESTC R214548.

—— [Ars amatoria. 1709] *Ovid's Art of love. In three books... Translated into English verse by several eminent hands* (London: printed for Jacob Tonson, 1709), 8°. List 429 (large paper). Theca 28. Case 252. ESTC T099252. Includes Congreve's translation of Book III, as well as translations by John Dryden and Nahum Tate.

—— [Ars amatoria. 1709] *Ovid's Art of love. In three books… Translated into English verse by several eminent hands* (London: printed for Jacob Tonson, 1709), 8°. List 430 (small paper). Theca 20. Case 252. ESTC T099252. Includes Congreve's translation of Book III, as well as translations by John Dryden and Nahum Tate.

—— [Heroides. 1681] *Ovid's Epistles, translated by several hands*. 2nd edn. (London: printed for Jacob Tonson, 1681), 8°. List 431. Theca 20. Wing O660; ESTC R31057. With a preface by John Dryden.

—— [Metamorphoses. 1640] *Ovids Metamorphosis Englished, mythologiz'd, and represented in figures… By G[eorge] S[andys]*. (London: printed by J[ohn]. L[egat]. for Andrew Hebb, 1640), 2°. List 428, 547. Theca 15. STC 18968; ESTC S121931.

—— [Metamorphoses. 1717] *Ovid's Metamorphoses in fifteen books. Translated by the most eminent hands* (London: printed for Jacob Tonson, 1717), 2°. List 427 (large paper). Theca 16. Leeds 486 (large paper). ESTC T138611. Case 298. Includes Congreve's translation of part of Book X, as well as translations by John Dryden, Joseph Addison, and others.

Ovington, John (1653–1731), *A voyage to Suratt, in the year, 1689* (London: printed for Jacob Tonson, 1696), 8°. List 440, 638. Theca 28. Wing O701; ESTC R26896.

Oxford and Cambridge, see Fenton, Elijah (ed.), *Oxford and Cambridge miscellany poems* (1708).

Ozell, John (d. 1743) (tr.), see Homer [Iliad. 1712].

Ozinde, J.B., *Pratique de l'ortographe et de la prononciation de la langue françoise* (Londres: chez Henry Woodfall, 1725), 8°. List 447 ('4°.'). Theca 30. ESTC N39812.

P., J. (tr.), see Le Noble, Eustache, *Abra-Mulè* (1696).

Paris, John (b. 1683?), *Ramillies. A poem humbly inscrib'd to his grace the Duke of Marlborough. Written in imitation of Milton* (London: printed for Jacob Tonson, 1706). List 413, 485. Theca 15. ESTC N12720; Foxon P65. In: *A Collection of poems, occasionally written upon the victories of Blenheim and Ramillies* (1708).

Parker, Samuel (1681–1730) (tr.), see Cicero [De finibus. 1702].

Parnell, Thomas (1679–1718), *Poems on several occasions… published by Mr. Pope* (London: printed for B. Lintot, 1722 [1721]), 8°. List 475. Theca 20. ESTC T42652; cf. Foxon i. 554.

Patin, Guy (1601–72), *Lettres choisies*. 2 vols. (Paris: chez Jean Petit, 1692), 12°. List 477 ('3 Tom.'; a 1692 edition in 3 vols. was published at Cologne). Theca 12.

—— *Nouvelles lettres de feu de Gui Patin, tirées du cabinet de Mr. Charles Spon*. 2 vols. (Amsterdam: chez Steenhouwer & Uytwerf, 1718), 12°. List 478. Theca 12.

Patru, Olivier (1604–81), *Plaidoyers et œuvres diverses*. Nouvelle édn. 2 pts (Paris: chez Sebastien Mabre-Cramoisy, 1681), 8°. List 471. Theca 14.

Pausanias, *Pausaniou tes Hellados perigesis* [in Greek], hoc est, *Pavsaniæ accvrata Græciæ descriptio, qva lector cev manv per eam regionem circumdvcitur: a Gvilielmo Xylandro, Avgvstano, diligenter recognita & ab innumeris mendis repurgata* (Hanoviæ: typis Wechelianis, apud hæredes Claudii Marnii, 1613), 2°. List 457. Theca 15.

Pazzi, Alessandro de' (1483–*c*.1530) (ed.), *see* Aristotle [Poetics. 1542].

Pechey, John (1655–1715) (ed.), *see* Sydenham, Thomas, *The whole works* (1705).

Pemberton, Henry (1694–1771), *A view of Sir Isaac Newton's philosophy* (London: printed by S. Palmer, 1728), 4°. List 492. Hornby Castle 1149. ESTC T53471, N64146.

Perceval, Richard (1550–1620), *A dictionarie in Spanish and English, first published into the English tongue by Ric. Perciuale Gent. Now enlarged... by John Minsheu* (Imprinted at London by E. Bollifant, 1599), 2°. List 181, 401. Theca 2. STC 19620; ESTC S115747.

Persius, *see* Juvenal and Persius [Works. 1673, 1691, 1716].

Pétis, François (1622–95) (tr.), *Turkish tales... Written originally in the Turkish language, by Chec Zade, for the use of Amurath II. And now done into English* (London: printed for Jacob Tonson, 1708), 12°. List 604. Theca 30. ESTC N014225. A translation by K. William and others of *Histoire de la Sultane de perse et des visirs* by François Pétis, who claimed to have translated them from the original.

Pétis de la Croix, François (1653–1713) (tr.), *Les mille & un jour. Contes persans, traduits en françois.* 5 vols. (Paris: en la boutique de Claude Barbin, chez la veuve Ricœur, 1710–12), 12°. List 121. Theca 23.

Petronius Arbiter, Titus, *The satyr of Titus Petronius Arbiter, a Roman knight. With its fragments, recover'd at Belgrade. Made English by Mr. Burnaby of the Middle-Temple, and another hand* (London: printed for Samuel Briscoe, 1694), 8°. List 473. Theca 8. Wing P1881; ESTC R214727.

Phædrus (*c*.15 BC–*c*.AD 50), *Phædri Aug. liberti Fabularum Æsopiarum libri quinque* (Londini: ex officinâ Jacobi Tonson, & Johannis Watts, 1713), 12°. List 483. Theca 24. ESTC T140258. Edited by Michael Maittaire.

Philemon, *see* Menander, *Menandri et Philemonis reliquæ* (1709).

Philips, John (1676–1709), *Cyder, a poem* (London: printed for Jacob Tonson, 1708), 8°. List 88. Theca 28. ESTC T78744 (large paper); T78745; Foxon P237.

Phillippes, Henry (d. 1677?), *A Mathematical manual containing tables of logarithmes, for numbers, sines, and tangents* (London: printed by A. Clark for W. Fisher, E. Thomas, J. Northcot, and E. Hurlock, 1677), 8°. List 479 (format not given). Theca 6. Wing P2048A; ESTC R181768.

Pindar, *Pindarou periodos* [in Greek]*: hoc est Pindari lyricorum principis... Opera Erasmi Schmidii* ([Wittenberg]: sumptibus Zachariæ Schureri, 1616), 4°. List 464. Theca 21.

Pix, Mary Griffith (1666–1720), *Violenta, or the rewards of virtue: turn'd from Boccace into verse* (London: printed for John Nutt, 1704), 8°. List 628. Theca 8. ESTC T106756; Foxon P463. Based on the eighth tale of the second day of Boccaccio's *Decameron*.

Plato, *Les oeuvres de Platon traduites en françois, avec des remarques, et la vie de ce philosophe, avec l'exposition des principaux dogmes de sa philosophie.* 2 vols. (Paris: chez Jean Anisoon, 1699), 12°. List 480. Theca 12. Translated by André Dacier.

Plautus, Titus Maccius [Comedies. 1587] *M. Accius Plautus ex fide, atque auctoritate complurium librorum manscriptorum opera Dionys. Lambini emendatus & commentariis explicatus* (Lutetiæ [Paris]: apud Bartholomæum Macæum, 1587), 2°. List 451. Theca 16. Leeds 417.

—— [Comedies. 1684] *M. Acci Plauti Comoediæ. Accedit commentarius ex variorum notis & observationibus, ex recensione Joh. Frederici Gronovii. Edition novissima.* 2 vols. (Amstelodami: ex typographia Blaviana, 1684), 8°. List 448 ('4 vol.'). Theca 29.

—— [Comedies. 1694] *Plautus's Comedies, Amphitryon, Epidicus, and Rudens, made English* (London: printed for Abel Swalle and T. Child, 1694), 8°. List 450. Theca 20. Wing P2415; ESTC R4311. Translated and edited by Laurence Echard.

—— [Fables. 1604] *M. Acci Plauti, comici Fabulæ superstites XX. Ex recensione Dousica* (Francofurti: excudebat Joannes Sauris, impensis Petri Kopffij, 1604), 12°. List 452. Theca 5.

Playford, Henry (1657–1706?) (ed.), *Harmonia sacra: or, divine hymns and dialogues; with a through-bass for the theorbo-lute, bass viol, harpsichord, or organ. Composed by the best masters of the last and present age. The words by several learned and pious persons. The first book.* (London: printed by William Pearson for Henry Playford, 1703), 2°. List 283 ('2 Parts... 1703'). Theca 21. Cf. Leeds 455. ESTC T154450. Congreve probably had the 2nd edn. of part 1 (1703), and the 1st edn. of part 2 (1693). See Wing P2437; ESTC R231598: 'printed by Edward Jones, for Henry Playford'.

Pliny, the Elder, C. *Plinii Secundi Naturalis historiæ.* 3 vols. (Lugd. Batav. [Leiden], Roterdami: apud Hackios, 1669), 8°. List 474. Theca 4.

Plutarch, *Plutarch's Lives. Translated from the Greek, by several hands.* 5 vols. (London: printed by R. E[veringham]. for Jacob Tonson, 1693), 8°. List 470 (large paper). Theca 13. Wing P2635B/P2635BA, P2637, P2638bA, P2639A, P2640A; ESTC R188954/R217664, R216988, R219473, R217668, R220547 (each vol. recorded separately).

Polybius, *The history of Polybius the Megalopolitan.... Translated by Sir H. S[heeres]. To which is added, a character of Polybius and his writings: by Mr. Dryden.* 2 vols. (London: printed for Samuel Briscoe, 1693), 8°. List 312, 472. Theca 13. Wing P2786; ESTC R8400.

Pomey, François Antoine (1618–73), *Pantheum mythicum, seu Fabulosa deorum historia, hoc epitomes eruditionis volumine, breviter dilucidéque comprehensa.* 5th edn. (Ultrajecti [Utrecht]: apud Guiljelmum van de Water, 1697), 12°. List 476. Theca 24.

Pontanus, Johann Isaac (1571–1639) (ed.), see Macrobius, *Opera* (1628).

Pontis, Louis de, sieur de (1583–1670), *Memoirs of the Sieur de Pontis... Faithfully Englished by Charles Cotton, Esq.* (London: printed by F. Leach for James Knapton, 1694), 2°. List 468. Theca 15. Wing P2807; ESTC R33997.

Pope, Alexander (1688–1744), *The works* (London: printed by W. Bowyer for Bernard Lintot, 1717), 4°. List 467 (large paper). Theca 2. Hornby Castle 1172. ESTC T005385 or T005386 (variant).

—— (ed.), *see* Shakespeare, William [Works. 1723–5].

—— (ed.), *see* Swift, Jonathan, *Miscellanea* (1727).

Pope, Alexander (ed.), *see* Swift, Jonathan, *Miscellanies in prose and verse* (1711).
—— (tr.), *see* Homer [Iliad. 1715–20].
—— (tr.), *see* Homer [Odyssey. 1725–6].
—— *see also Miscellaneous poems and translations* (1712).
—— *see also* Parnell, Thomas, *Poems on several occasions* (1722).
Porphyry (*c*.234–*c*.305), *see* Iamblichus, *De mysteriis liber* (1678).
Portus, Æmilius (1550–1615) (ed.), *see Suidas, nunc primum integer Latinitate donatus* (1619).
Prateus, Ludovicus [i.e. Louis Desprez] (ed.), *see* Juvenal and Persius [Works. 1691].
Pratt, Samuel (1659?–1723), *The regulating silver coin, made practicable and easie, to the government and subject* (London: printed for Henry Bonwick, 1696), 8°. List 511. Theca 8. Wing P3184; ESTC R8943.
Prideaux, Humphrey (1648–1724), *The old and new Testament connected in the history of the Jews and neighbouring nations*. 2 pts. (London: printed for R. Knaplock and J. Tonson, 1717–18), 2°. List 449, 454. Theca 15. ESTC T88593, T88589. Probably the 3rd edn. of pt. 1 (1717) with the 1st edn. of pt. 2 (1718).
Prior, Matthew (1664–1721), *A Letter to Monsieur Boileau Depreaux; occasion'd by the victory at Blenheim* (London: printed for Jacob Tonson, 1704). List 413, 485. Theca 15. ESTC T62171; Foxon P1079. In: *A Collection of poems, occasionally written upon the victories of Blenheim and Ramillies* (1708).
—— *An Ode humbly inscrib'd to the Queen. On the late glorious success of her majesty's arms. Written in imitation of Spencer's stile* (London: printed for Jacob Tonson, 1706). List 413, 485. Theca 15. ESTC T41935; Foxon P1081. In: *A Collection of poems, occasionally written upon the victories of Blenheim and Ramillies* (1708).
—— *Poems on several occasions* (London: printed for Jacob Tonson, 1709), 8°. List 460. Theca 20. Leeds 521. ESTC N63550; cf. Foxon i. 641.
—— *Poems on several occasions* (London: printed for Jacob Tonson, and John Barber, 1718), 2°. List 458 (large paper). Theca 16. Leeds 523. ESTC T75639; cf. Foxon i. 641. List of subscribers includes Congreve.
—— *Poems on several occasions* (London: printed for Jacob Tonson, and John Barber, 1718), 2°. List 459 (small paper). Theca 15. Leeds 522. ESTC T75639; cf. Foxon i. 641. List of subscribers includes Congreve.
Propertius, Sextus, *see* Catullus [Works. 1680, 1686, 1691, 1702, 1715].
Purcell, Henry (1658–95), *Orpheus Britannicus. A collection of all the choicest songs for one, two, and three voices*. Vol. 1 (London: printed by J. Heptinstall for Henry Playford, 1698–1702); Vol. 2 (London: printed by William Pearson for Henry Playford, 1702). List 445, 462. Theca 21. Leeds 459 ('Congreve's copy, with his signature on the title of vol. I'). Wing P4218 (vol. 1). ESTC R231719; T153688. Resold for £9.10s. to Scribner's by Sotheby's, Harmsworth Sale, 9 May 1939 (lot 815), but present location is unknown.
Pythagoras (*c*.531–*c*.460 BC), *see* Dacier, André, *The life of Pythagoras* (1707).
Quevedo, Francisco de (1580–1645), *Les Oeuvres de Don Francisco de Quevedo Villegas…Seconde partie. Contenante les sept visions* (Brusselles: chez Josse de Grieck, 1699), 12°. List 494. Theca 29.

—— *Les Oeuvres de Don Francisco de Quevedo Villegas...traduit de l'espagnol par le Sr. Raclots parisien.* 2 vols. (Bruxelles: chez Joseph t'Serstevens, 1718), 12°. List 495. Theca 26.

Quillet, Claude (1602–61), *Callipædia. A poem...made English by N. Rowe* (London: printed for E. Sanger and E. Curll, 1712), 8°. List 89. Theca 20. ESTC T19836; Foxon R280. Rowe translated Book I, George Sewell Book II, Samuel Cobb Book III, and Cobb and William Diaper Book IV.

Quincy, John (d. 1722), *Pharmacopœia officinalis & extemporanea: or, a compleat English dispensatory* (London: printed for A. Bell, T. Varnam and T. Osborn, and W. Taylor, 1718), 8°. List 213, 498. Theca 4. ESTC T61384.

—— (ed.) *see* Royal College of Physicians in London [Pharmacopœia Londinensis. 1721].

—— (tr.) *see* Santorio, Santorio, *Medicina statica* (1712).

Quintilian, *M. Fabii Quintiliani Oratoris eloquentissimi, institutionum orationum libri XII* (Parisiis: ex officina Rob. Stephani typographi regii, 1542), 4°. List 493. Theca 22. Hornby Castle 1272.

Rabelais, François (1490–1553?), *The whole works of F. Rabelais, M.D....Done out of French, by Sir Thomas Urchard, Knight, Mr. Motteaux, and others.* 2 vols. (London: printed for James Woodward, 1708), 8°. List 506. Theca 28. ESTC T52476.

Racine, Jean Baptiste (1639–91), *Oeuvres.* 2 vols. (Paris: chez Claude Barbin 1697), 12°. List 514 (publisher not given).Theca 25.

Raclots (tr.), *see* Quevedo, *Oeuvres* (1718).

Ramsay, Allan (1685–1758), *The tea-table miscellany* (Edinburgh: printed by Thomas Ruddiman, for Allan Ramsay, 1724), 12°. List 415 ('24°'). Case 333. ESTC N45927.

Ramsay, Andrew Michael (1686–1743), *The travels of Cyrus.* 2 vols. (London, printed: and sold by T. Woodward and J. Peele, 1727), 8°. List 531. ESTC T82619.

Randolph, Thomas (1605–35), and **Richard Brathwait** (1588?–1673), *Cornelianum dolium. Comœdia lepidissima, optimorum judiciis approbata, & theatrali coryphœo, nec immeritò, donata, palma chorali apprimè digna. Auctore T.R[andolph and Richard Brathwait].* (Londini: apud Tho. Harperum, et væneunt per Tho. Slaterum & Laurentium Chapman, 1638), 12°. List 112 ('8°'). Theca 5. STC 20691; ESTC S115624.

Rapin, René (1621–87), *Oeuvres diverses du R.P.R. Racine, concernant les belles lettres.* 2 vols. (Amsterdam: chez Abraham Wolfgang, 1686), 12°. List 510 ('8°.'). Theca 12.

—— *Reflections on Aristotles treatise of poesie* (London: printed by T.N[ewcomb]. for H. Herringman, 1674), 8°. List 509. Theca 8. Wing R270; ESTC R10386. Translated by Thomas Rymer.

Ray, John (1627–1705), *Historia plantarum.* [Vol. I] (Londini: typis Mariæ Clark, prostant apud Henricum Faithorne, 1686), 2°; Vol. II. (Londini: typis Mariæ Clarke, prostant apud Henricum Faithorne, 1688). List 499 ('2 Vol.'; large paper). Theca 16. Wing R394, R395A; ESTC R219020, R217969. Hornby Castle 1181. Vol. 3 was not published until 1704.

Raymond, John, *An itinerary contayning a voyage, made through Italy, in the yeare 1646, and 1647* (London: printed for Humphrey Moseley, 1648), 12°. List 518. Theca 6. Leeds 532. Wing R415; ESTC R33233. Congreve's copy, signed 'Will: Congreve' on the title page, formerly owned by E.S. de Beer: WTu.

Regis, Pierre Silvain (1632–1707), *Cours entier de philosophie, ou systeme generale selon les principes de M. Descartes.* 3 vols. (Amsterdam: aux dépens des Huguetan, 1691), 4°. List 504. Theca 14.

Regnier Desmarais, abbé (François-Séraphin) (1623–1713) (tr.), see Cicero [De divinatione. 1711].

—— *see* Homer [Iliad. 1700].

The regulating silver coin, see Pratt, Samuel.

Retz, Jean François Paul de Gondi de (1613–79), *Mémoires du cardinal de Retz, contenant ce qui s'est passé de plus remarquable en France, pendant les premieres années du regne de Louis.* 5 vols. (Amsterdam [i.e. Rouen], 1718), 8°. List 516 ('12°.'). Theca 11. Hornby Castle 1292.

—— *Memoirs of the Cardinal du Retz...Done out of French.* 4 vols. (London: printed for Jacob Tonson, 1723), 8°. List 517. Theca 30. ESTC T88963. Translated by Peter Davall and dedicated by him to Congreve.

Riccoboni, Luigi (1676–1753), *Histoire du theatre Italien depuis la decadence de la comedie latine* (Paris: chez H.D. Chaubert [1727]), 8°. List 314 ('8° Lond.'; London edn. not located; Hodges suggests this Paris edn.).

Richelet, Pierre (1631–98), *Dictionnaire françois... corrigée augmentée* (Genéve: pour David Ritter, chez Vincent Miége, 1693), 4°. List 174. Theca 22. Edited by Etienne Souciet.

Richerius, Ludovicus Caelius (1450–1520), *Lvdovici Cælii Rhodigini Lectionum antiquarum libri triginta. Postrema editio* ([Frankfurt]: apud heredes Andreæ Wecheli, Claudium Marnium, & Ioannem Aubrium 1599), 2°. List 501. Theca 15. Congreve's copy, signed 'W^m: Congreve' on the title page, with Duke of Leeds bookplate and pencilled note 'bought at Hornby Castle' on inner front board: O: Vet.D1 c.58.

Riflé de Garouville, Savinien, *L'Amant oisif. Contenant cinquante nouvelles espagnoles* (Brusselles: chez George de Backer, 1711), 12°. List 28. Theca 26.

Roberti, Antonius (17th c.), *Clavis homerica, sive lexicon vocabularum omnium quæ in Iliade Homeri, nec non potissimâ Odysseæ parte contintentur* (Roterdami: ex officinâ Arnoldi Leers, 1655), 8°. List 111. Theca 7.

Rocoles, Jean Baptiste de (1620–96), *The history of infamous imposters... done into English* (London: printed for William Cademan, 1683), 8°. List 309. Theca 8. Wing R1766; ESTC R6847.

Rodelle, Pierre de (*fl.* 1683–95) (ed.), *see* Horace [Works. 1690].

Roergas de Serviez, Jacques (1679–1727), *Les femmes des douze cesars contenant la vie & les intrigues secretes des imperatrices & femmes des premiers empereurs romains; où l'on voit les traits les plus interessants de l'histoire romaine. Tirée des anciens auteurs grecs & latins, avec des notes historiques & critiques* (Paris: chez De Launay, 1718), 12°. List 251. Theca 11.

Rogers, Thomas (d. 1616), *The faith, doctrine, and religion, professed, and protected in the realm of England, and dominions of the same expressed in thirty-nine* *articles* (London: printed by John Field, and are to be sold by George Saw-bridge, 1661), 4°. List 505. Theca 14. Wing R1833; ESTC R30129.

Roland l'amoureux, see Boiardo, Matteo Maria.

Rolli, Paolo Antonio (1687–1765), *Remarks upon M. Voltaire's Essay on the epick poetry of the European nations* (London: printed and sold by Tho. Edlin, 1728), 8°. List 532. ESTC T109612.

Roscommon, Earl of, *see* Dillon, Wentworth.

Rosseto, Joannes (ed.), *see* Cæsar, Julius [Commentarii. 1571].

Rousseau, Jean Baptiste (1670–1741), *Oeuvres diverses. Nouvelle edition revüe & augmentée.* 2 vols. (Londres: de l'imprimerie de Jacob Tonson & Jean Watts, 1723), 4°. List 502 (large paper). Theca 17. Leeds 549. ESTC T139795.

—— *Les Oeuvres choisies du Sr. Rousseau, contenant ses odes, odes sacrées de l'edition de Soleure, & cantates,* 3 vols. (Rotterdam: chez Fritsch & Bohm, 1719), 12°. List 503. Theca 30.

Rowe, Nicholas (1674–1718) *A Poem upon the late glorious successes of her majesty's arms &c. Humbly inscrib'd to the right honourable the Earl of Godolphin, and High-Treasurer of England* (London: printed for Jacob Tonson, 1707). List 413, 485. Theca 15. ESTC T64244; Foxon R301. In: *A Collection of poems, occasionally written upon the victories of Blenheim and Ramillies* (1708).

—— (ed.), *see* Shakespeare, William [Works. 1709].

—— (tr.), *see* Dacier, André, *The life of Pythagoras* (1707).

—— *see* Lucan [Pharsalia. 1718].

—— *see* Quillet, Claude, *Callipædia* (1712).

Rowlands, Samuel (1570?–1630?), 'Dr. Merryman', 4°. List 405 (edition not given; bound with 10 other miscellaneous 4°. items). Theca 28. Cf. STC 21372.5–21377, Wing R2080A–R2083, and ESTC S124367, S2863, R229947, &c.

Royal College of Physicians of London [Pharmacopœia Londinensis. 1707] *Pharmacopœia Londinensis: or, the new London dispensatory. In VI. books. Translated into English. . . . By William Salmon.* 7th edn. (London: printed by J. Dawks for R. Chiswell, M. Wotton, J. Walthoe, G. Conyers, J. Nicholson, J. Sprint, and T. Ballard, 1707), 8°. List 216, 548. Theca 4. ESTC T132583. Edited and translated by William Salmon.

—— [Pharmacopœia Londinensis. 1718] *Doron medicum: or, a supplement to the New London dispensatory . . . By William Salmon* (London, 1718), 8°. List 217. Theca 4. 1718 edn. not located. Possibly *Pharmacopœia Londinensis: or, the new London dispensatory. In three books. Part the second. Or, doron medicum . . . The third edition, with additions, by William Salmon, M.D.* (London: printed by I. Dawks, for J. Walthoe, M. Wotton, G. Conyers, J. Nicholson, J. and B. Sprint, [and 5 others in London], 1717). ESTC N38858. Other possibilities are earlier edns. in 1683 and 1688.

—— [Pharmacopœia Londinensis. 1721] *The dispensatory of the Royal College of Physicians in London: with some notes . . . By John Quincy, M.D.* (London: printed by W. Bowyer for R. Knaplock, B. Took, D. Midwinter, R. Smith, W. and J. Innys, and J. Osborn, 1721), 8°. List 214. Theca 4. ESTC T61388.

—— *see also* Bate, George, *Pharmacopœia Bateana* (1713).

528   *Congreve's Library*

Royal College of Physicians of London *see also* Culpeper, Nicholas [Pharmacopœia Londinensis. 1654, 1675].

Ruæus, Carolus (1643–1725), *see* Virgil [Works. 1682].

Rufus, Quintus Curtius (*fl.* 50), *Quinte Curce, De la vie & des actions d'Alexandre le Grand. De la traduction de M. de Vaugelas* (Amsterdam: chez Henrij Wetstein, 1696), 8°. List 496 ('12°.'). Theca 11.

—— *Quinti Curtii Rufi De rebus gestis Alexandri Magni libri* (Londini: ex officinâ Jacobi Tonson, & Johannis Watts, 1716), 12°. List 497. Theca 24. ESTC T144572. Edited by Michael Maittaire.

Ruggle, G. (1575–1622), *Ignoramus. Comœdia coram Rege Jacopo.* 4th edn. (Londini: ex officina J[ohn]. R[edmayne]., 1668), 12°. List 333. Theca 5. Wing R2215; ESTC R33559.

Rutgers, Johannes (1589–1625) (ed.), *see* Horace [Works. 1699].

Rycaut, Paul, Sir (1628–1700), *The history of the present state of the Ottoman Empire.* 5th edn. (London: printed by T.N[ewcomb]. for Joanna Brome, 1682), 8°. List 313 (publisher not given). Theca 3. Wing R2403; ESTC R33568.

—— (tr.), *see* de la Vega, Garcilaso, *The royal commentaries of Peru* (1688).

Rymer, Thomas (1641–1713) (tr.), *see* Rapin, René, *Reflections on Aristotles treatise of poesie* (1674).

Saint-Évremond (1613–1703), *Oeuvres meslées de Mr. de Saint-Evremond.* 2 vols. (Londres: chez Jacob Tonson, 1705), 4°. List 233 ('3 Tom Grd. Papr'). Theca 17. Hornby Castle 1146. ESTC T123020. Edited by P. Silvestre and Pierre des Maizeaux.

Saint-Réal, M. l'abbé de (César Vichard) (1639–92), *Oeuvres de Mr. l'abbé de Saint-Real.* 5 vols. (La Haye: chez les frères Vaillant & Nicholas Prèvost, 1722), 12°. List 18, 565. Theca 30. Edited by Prosper Marchand.

—— *Conjuration des Espagnols contre la republique de Venise, en l'année M.D.C.XVIII* (Paris: chez Claude Barbin, 1683), 12°. List 129. Theca 24.

Sallust (86–34 BC) [Works. 1634] *C. Sallustius Crispus, cum veterum historicorum fragmentis* (Lugduni Batavorum [Leiden]: ex officina Elzeviriana, 1634), 24°. List 585. Theca 5. Edited by Marcus Zuerius Boxhorn.

—— [Works. 1684] *C. Sallustius Crispus cum veterum historicorum fragmentis* (Amstelædami: Janssonius, 1684), 24°. List 586 ('cum Catullo, Tibullo &c'). Theca 5.

—— [Works. 1713] *Caii Sallustii Crispi quæ extant* (Londini: ex officinâ Jacobi Tonson, & Johannis Watts, 1713), 12°. List 584. Theca 24. ESTC T111402. Edited by Michael Maittaire.

—— [Works. 1715] *C. Sallustii Crispi opera omnia quae extant, interpretatione et notis illustravit Daniel Crispinus* (Londini: ex officinâ typographicâ M. Matthews. Impensis Johannis Churchil, Henrici Clements, & Fletcheri Gyles, 1715), 8°. List 583. Theca 7. ESTC T152388.

Salmon, William (1644–1713) (ed., tr.), *see* Bate, George, *Pharmacopœia Bateana* (1713).

—— *see* Royal College of Physicians of London [Pharmacopœia Londinensis. 1707, 1718].

Sandisson, Monsieur de (pseud.), *see* Bignon, abbé (Jean Paul).

Sandys, George (1578–1644) (tr.), *see* Ovid [Metamorphoses. 1640].

Sannazaro, Jacopo (1458–1530), *Actii synceri Sannazarii... Opera latina omnia, et integra* (Amstelædami: apud Henricum Wetstenium, 1689), 12°. List 581 (format not given). Theca 5.

Sanson, Nicolas (1600–67) (ed.), *see* Cæsar, Julius [Commentarii. 1650].

Santorio, Santorio (1561–1636), *Medicina statica: being the aphorisms of Sanctorius, translated into English... By John Quincy* (London: printed for William Newton, 1712), 8°. List 419, 563. Theca 4. ESTC T100344.

Sanvitale, Fortuniano, conte, *see* Marino, Giambattista, *L'Adone* (1623, 1678).

Sappho, *see* Anacreon, *Les Poesies d'Anacreon et de Sapho* (1699).

Sarpi, Paolo (1552–1623), *The historie of the Councel of Trent... Written in Italian... translated into English by Nathanæl Brent* (London: printed by Robert Barker and John Bill, 1620), 2°. List 453. Theca 15. STC 21761; ESTC S116698.

Scala, Flaminio (*fl.* 1620), *Il Teatro delle favole rappresentative, ovvero, La ricreatione comica, boscareccia et tragica* (Venetia: appresso Gio: Battista Pulciani, 1611), 4°. List 600. Theca 14.

Scaliger, Joseph Juste (1540–1609) (ed.), *see* Catullus [Works. 1680].

—— *see* Virgil, *Publii Virgilii Maronis Appendix* (1572).

Scaliger, Julius Cæsar (1484–1558), *Poetices libri septem* ([Geneva]: apud Petrum Santandreanum, 1594), 8°. List 559 (place of publication not given). Theca 7.

Scapula, Johann (*c.*1540–*c.*1600), *Joan. Scapulæ lexicon Græco-Latinum... glossarium contractum*. Editio nova accurata. 2 pts. (Lugduni [Lyon]: sumptibus Joannis Antonii Huguetan, & Maroi Antonii Ravaud, 1663), 2°. List 539. Theca 15.

Scarron, Paul (1610–60), *The whole comical works... Translated by Mr. Tho. Brown, Mr. Savage, and others*. 3rd edn. (London: printed for J. Nicholson, J. and B. Sprint, R. Parker and Benj. Tooke, 1712), 8°. List 572. Theca 33. ESTC T129732.

—— *Les Nouvelles oeuvres tragi-comiques*. 2 vols. (Paris: chez Jean Baptiste Loyson, 1665), 12°. List 571. Theca 26.

—— *Le Romant comique*. 2 vols. (Paris: chez Guillaume de Luynes, 1655), 8°. List 569. Theca 3.

—— *Le Romant comique*. 3 pts. (Amsterdam: chez Pierre Mortier, 1695), 12°. List 570. Theca 26.

—— *see also* Furetière, Antoine, *Scarron's City romance* (1671).

Schmid, Erasmus (1560–1637) (ed.), *see* Pindar.

Schrevel, Cornelius (d. 1661) (ed.), *see* Lucan [Pharsalia. 1669].

Scoto, Lorenzo, *see* Marino, Giambattista, *L'Adone* (1623, 1678).

Scribonius Largus (*c.*1–*c.*50), *Scriboni Largi compositiones medicæ* (Patauii [Padua]: typis Pauli Frambotti bibliopolæ, 1655), 4°. List 589. Theca 1.

Scudéry, Georges de (1601–67), *Alaric, ou Rome vaincuë. Poëme heroïque* (Paris: chez Augustin Courbé, 1655), 12°. List 32, 579. Theca 6. Leeds 574 (signed 'Jean Driden' on the frontispiece). Evidently a gift from Dryden to Congreve; now at WF.

The secret history of Europe, *see* Oldmixon, John.

The secret history of the reigns of K. Charles II. and K. James II (Printed in the year 1690), 12°. List 311. Theca 6. Wing S2347; ESTC R225678. Sometimes attributed to Nathaniel Crouch and to John Phillips.

Segrais, Regnauld de (pseud.), *see* La Fayette, Madame de.

Seneca, Lucius Annæus (*c.*4 BC–AD 65), *L. Annæi Senecæ philosophi. Tomus secundus. In quo epistolæ, et quæstiones naturales* (Lugd. Batav. [Leiden]: apud Elsevirios, 1639), 24°. List 587 ('Senecæ Epistolæ'). Theca 5.

Les Sentimens, see Chapelain, Jean, *Les Sentimens de l'Académie françoise* (1703).

Settle, Elkanah (1648–1724), *A defense of dramatick poetry: being a review of Mr. Collier's View of the immorality, and profaneness of the English stage* (London: printed for Eliz. Whitlock, 1698), 8°. List 101. Theca 8. Wing S2675bA; ESTC R16098 or R20214.

Sewell, George (*c.*1690–1726) (tr.), see Quillet, Claude, *Callipædia* (1712).

Shadwell, Thomas (1642?–92), *The dramatick works*. 4 vols. (London: printed for J. Knapton and J. Tonson, 1720), 12°. List 566. Theca 33. Leeds 584. ESTC T119901, N64322.

Shakespeare, William (1564–1616) [Works. 1623] *Mr. William Shakespeares comedies, histories, & tragedies. Published according to the true originall copies* (London: printed by Isaac Jaggard, and Ed. Blount, 1623), 2°. List 541 (edition not given). Theca 21. STC 22273; ESTC S111228. Congreve's copy, signed 'Will: Congreve' on sig. ᵖAʳ, formerly at LLU, but sold in 1991 by Sotheby's to Mesei University Library, Japan. The main autograph annotations are on the outer margin (cropped) of sig. Q5ᵛ of *As You Like It*: (1) '<S>panish | fryar', against the lines ('Almost to bursting...innocent nose'); and (2) 'Anthony | <i>n all | <f>or Love | <by> Dryden', against the lines 'Left and abandoned... greazie Citizens,'.

—— [Works. 1709] *The works of Mr. William Shakespear; in six volumes... Revis'd and corrected, with an account of the life and writings of the author. By N. Rowe, Esq.* 6 vols. (London: printed for Jacob Tonson, 1709), 8°. List 544 ('9 Vols. wth Cuts/L. Paper'). Theca 19. Leeds 587 ('6 vol. in 9...large paper copy'). ESTC T138297, T138294. Congreve's copy: WF. Though lacking Congreve's signature, each volume has the bookplate of the Duke of Leeds. At vol. iv, p. 1171, the misprint 'ways' has been struck out and 'eyes' written against the line 'So common hackney'd in the ways of Men' (*1 Henry IV*, III. ii).

—— [Works. 1723–5] *The works of Shakespear. In six volumes. Collated and corrected by the former editions, by Mr. Pope.* 6 vols. (London: printed for J. Tonson, 1723–5), 4°. List 542 (large paper). Theca 29. Leeds 590. ESTC N26060. A reissue of the 1723 edition, with a cancel general title page: vol. 1 dated 1725; vols. 2–6 dated 1723. List of subscribers includes Congreve.

—— [Works. 1723–5] *The works of Shakespear. In six volumes. Collated and corrected by the former editions, by Mr. Pope.* 6 vols. in 12 (London: printed for J. Tonson, 1723–5), 4°. List 543 (small paper). ESTC N26060. List of subscribers includes Congreve. Hornby Castle 1277 ('6 vols. in 12', another copy, evidently specially bound for Congreve).

—— [Hamlet. 1720] *Hamlet, prince of Denmark* (London [i.e. The Hague]: printed for T. Johnson, 1720?), 8°. List 408, 491, 546 ('12°. Lond.—bound together Vizt. Merry Wives of Windsor, King Henry IV. 2 parts, Julius Cæsar—Hamlet & Othello Moor of Venice'). Theca 30. ESTC T65542. Though said to be 12°, this was probably the small 8° published by Thomas Johnson, 1720.

—— [Henry IV pt. 1. 1721] *K. Henry IV. With the humours of Sir John Falstaff* ... (London [i.e. The Hague]: printed for T. Johnson, 1721?), 8°. List 408, 491, 546 ('12°. Lond.—bound together Vizt. Merry Wives of Windsor, King Henry IV. 2 parts, Julius Cæsar—Hamlet & Othello Moor of Venice'). Theca 30. ESTC N27427. Though said to be 12°, this was probably the small 8° published by Thomas Johnson, 1721.

—— [Henry IV pt. 2. 1720?] *The sequel of Henry the Fourth. With the humours of Sir John Falstaff ... Alter'd from Shakespeare, by the late Mr. Betterton* (London: printed for W. Chetwood, and T. Jauncey [*c*.1720]), 8°. List 408, 491, 546 ('12°. Lond.—bound together Vizt. Merry Wives of Windsor, King Henry IV. 2 parts, Julius Cæsar—Hamlet & Othello Moor of Venice'). Theca 30. ESTC T62223.

—— [Julius Cæsar. 1720?] *Julius Cæsar. A Tragedy* (London [i.e. The Hague]: printed for the company of booksellers, [1720?]), 8°. List 408, 491, 546 ('12°. Lond.—bound together Vizt. Merry Wives of Windsor, King Henry IV. 2 parts, Julius Cæsar—Hamlet & Othello Moor of Venice'). Theca 30. ESTC T152104. Possibly the small 8° published by Thomas Johnson, 1720–1.

—— [Merry wives of Windsor. 1630?] *The merry wives of Windsor*, 4°. List 407, 490 (edition not given; bound with 5 other miscellaneous 4° items). Theca 28. Cf. STC 22301+; ESTC S111208+.

—— [Merry wives of Windsor. 1720?] *The merry wives of Windsor* (London [i.e. The Hague]: printed for the company, [1720?]), 8°. List 408, 491, 546 ('12°. Lond.—bound together Vizt. Merry Wives of Windsor, King Henry IV. 2 parts, Julius Cæsar—Hamlet & Othello Moor of Venice'). Theca 30. ESTC T14953. Possibly the small 8° published by Thomas Johnson, 1720–1.

—— [Othello. 1720?] *Othello, the moor of Venice* (London [i.e. The Hague]: printed for the company, [1720?]), 8°. List 408, 491, 546 ('12°. Lond.—bound together Vizt. Merry Wives of Windsor, King Henry IV. 2 parts, Julius Cæsar—Hamlet & Othello Moor of Venice'). Theca 30. ESTC T14955. Possibly the small 8° published by Thomas Johnson, 1720–1.

—— [Poems. 1709] *A Collection of poems, viz. I. Venus and Adonis. II. The rape of Lucrece. III. The passionate pilgrim. IV. Sonnets to sundry notes of musick* (London: printed for Bernard Lintott, [1709]). Small 8°. List 545 ('Collection of Poems in |Turkey Leather 12°'). Theca 27. ESTC T138085. Edited by Charles Gildon. The first one-volume edition. See 'Allusions' for 3 March 1711 for Congreve's connection with this edition.

Sheeres, Sir Henry (d. 1710) (tr.), *see* Polybius.

Sheffield, John, Duke of Buckingham, *see* Buckingham.

Shelton, Thomas (*fl.* 1612–1620) (tr.), *see* Cervantes [Don Quixote. 1620, 1652].

Sherley, Anthony, Sir (1565–1635?), *Sir Anthony Sherley his relation of his trauels into Persia* (London: printed [by Nicholas Okes] for Nathaniel Butter and

Joseph Bagfet, 1613), 4°. List 643 ('Blue paper 8°.'). Theca 29. STC 22424; ESTC S117262.

Shirley, James (1596–1666), *Six new playes, viz, The brothers. Sisters. Doubtfull heir. Imposture. Cardinall. Court secret. The five first were acted at the Private House in Black Fryers with great applause. The last was never acted.... Never printed before* (London: printed [by William Wilson and Thomas Warren] for Humphrey Robinson and Humphrey Moseley, 1653), 8°. List 552, 574. Theca 8. Wing S3486; ESTC R20878.

—— *Two playes* (London: printed for Joshua Kirton, 1657), 4°. List 551 ('Shirley's Plays: And also Caradoc the Great *or the Valiant Welchman.* 4°. 1663'). Theca 8. Wing S3490; ESTC R134123. Bound with Robert Anton's *The valiant Welshman* (1663).

Shirley, John (*fl.* 1680–1702), *The most delectable history of Reynard the Fox. Newly corrected and purged, from all grossness in phrase and matter* (London: printed by T. Ilive for Edward Brewster, 1701), 4°. List 529. Leeds 537. ESTC T60836.

Sidney, Philip, Sir (1554–86), *The countess of Pembroke's Arcadia.* 13th edn. (London: printed for George Calvert, 1674), 2°. List 455. Theca 15. Leeds 600. Wing S3770; ESTC R21446.

Sidonius, Caius Sollius Apollinaris (430?–487?), *C. Sollii Sidonii Apollinaris... Opera... Petri Colvi Brugensis in Sidonium notas edi curavit* (Parisiis: apud Ambrosium Drouart, 1578), 8°. List 560. Theca 7.

Silvestre, P. (ed.), *see* Saint-Évremond, *Oeuvres meslées* (1705).

Smith, John (1652–1742), 'Mezzo Tinto Prints by J. Smith', 2°. List 375 (large paper). Theca 10. Probably a miscellaneous collection made by Congreve.

Smith, Robert, *Court cookery: or, the compleat English cook.* 2nd edn. (London: printed for T. Wotton, 1725), 8°. List 109 ('Richd. Smith'), 550. Theca 32. ESTC N4772.

Somers, John, Baron Somers (1651–1716), *see* Demosthenes, *Several orations* (1702).

Sophocles (496–406 BC), *Tragedies grecques de Sophocle traduites en françois... Par André Dacier* (Amsterdam: chez George Gallet, 1693), 12°. List 197. Theca 25.

Sorel, Charles (1582?–1674), *Le berger extravagant* (Rouen: chez Jean Berthelin, 1639), 8°. List 54 ('1640'; so dated on engraved title page). Theca 3.

—— *The extravagant shepherd... written originally in French, and now made English* (London: printed by T. Newcomb for Thomas Heath, 1654), 2°. List 350. Theca 9. Wing S4704; ESTC R10519. Translated by John Davies.

—— *La vraie histoire comique de Francion.* 2 vols. (Leyde [&] Roterdam: chez les Hackes [1668]), 12°. List 296. Theca 26.

Souciet, Etienne (1671–1744) (ed.), *see* Richelet, Pierre, *Dictionnaire françois* (1693).

La Source des malheurs d'Angleterre, et de tous les maux, dont ce roiaume a été affligé depuis la regne de Jacques I. & qui ont causé la perte de Charles I. & la desertion de Jacques II (Cologne: chez Pierre Marteau, 1689), 12°. List 580 ('24°.'). Theca 5.

Southerne, Thomas (1660–1746), *Money the mistress* (London: printed for J. Tonson, 1726), 8°. List 590. ESTC T002471 & N066966.

Speght, Thomas (*fl.* 1600), (ed.), *see* Chaucer, Geoffrey [Works. 1687].

Spenser, Edmund (1552?–1599) [Works. 1679] *The works of that famous English poet, Mr. Edmond Spenser* (London: printed by Henry Hills for Jonathan Edwin, 1679), 2°. List 535. Theca 21. Wing S4965; ESTC R7177.

—— [Works. 1715] *The works of Mr. Edmund Spenser.... With a glossary explaining the old and obscure words. Publish'd by Mr. Hughes.* 6 vols. (London: printed for Jacob Tonson, 1715), 12°. List 536. Theca 19. Leeds 614 ('8*vo.*'). ESTC T61111 & N65235.

Spinoza, Benedictus de (1632–77), *A treatise partly theological, and partly political... Translated from the Latin of Spinoza* (London: printed in the year, 1689), 8°. List 602. Theca 14. Wing S4985; ESTC R21627.

Sponde, Jean de (1557–95) (tr.), *see* Homer [Works. 1606].

Stanhope, George (1660–1728) (tr.), *see* Charron, Pierre, *Of wisdom* (1697).

Stanyan, Abraham (1669?–1732), *An account of Switzerland* (London: printed for Jacob Tonson, 1714), 8°. List 556 (large paper). Theca 13. ESTC T134206.

Stanyan, Temple (1677?–1752), *The Grecian history. Volume the first* (London: printed for Jacob Tonson, 1707), 8°. List 555 (large paper). Theca 13. ESTC T102862. Vol. 2 was not published until 1739.

Stanzani, Tomaso, *Arsinoe, Queen of Cyprus. An opera, after the Italian manner* (London: printed for J. Tonson, 1705), 4°. List 36. ESTC N30676 or T126975. Translated by Peter Anthony Motteux.

Steele, Richard, Sir (1672–1729), *The Englishman: being the sequel of the Guardian* (London: printed by Sam. Buckley, 1714), 8°. List 234 (large paper). Theca 28. Leeds 620. ESTC T147727. A copy, signed 'W. Congreve' on the title page, was sold to Burnstead for 11*s.* at the Sir William Tite sale, 22 May 1874, but its present location is unknown.

—— *The Romish ecclesiastical history of late years* (London: printed for J. Roberts, 1714), 8°. List 567 ('1715'). Theca 8. ESTC T146635 & N064449.

—— (ed.), *Poetical miscellanies, consisting of original poems and translations. By the best hands. Publish'd by Mr. Steele* (London: printed for Jacob Tonson, 1714), 8°. List 414, 568. Theca 20. ESTC T133656. Case 279. Dedicated to Congreve.

Stephanus, Carolus, *see* Estienne, Charles, *Dictionarium historicum* (1686).

Stobæus, Johannes, *Ioannis Stobæi Eclogarum libri duo... interprete Gulielmo Cantero* (Antuerpiæ: ex officinâ Christophori Plantini, 1575), 2°. List 537. Theca 21.

—— *Ioannis Stobei Sententiae ex thesauris Graecorum delectae, quarum autores circiter ducentos & quinquaginta citat, & in sermones siue locos communes digestae, nun primum á Conrado Gesnero... in Latinu[m] sermonen traductae* (Tiguri [Zurich]: excudebat Christoph. Froscheverus, 1543), 2°. List 538. Theca 21.

Stow, John (1525?–1605), *The survey of London... Begunne first by the paines and industry of John Stow, in the yeere 1598. Afterwards inlarged by the care and diligence of A[nthony].M[unday]. in the yeere 1618. And now completely finished by the study and labour of A.M. H[umphrey]. D[yson]. and others, this present* *yeere 1633* ... (London: printed by Elizabeth Purslow, and are to be sold by Nicholas Bourne, 1633), 2°. List 534. Theca 15. Leeds 625 (signed 'Willm. Congreve'). STC 23345; ESTC S117597. The present location of Congreve's signed copy is unknown.

Strabo, *Strabonis Rerum geographicarum libri XVII. Isaacus Casaubonus recensuit* ... *Adiuncta est etiam Gulielmi Xylandri Augustani Latina versio ab eodem Casaubono recognita. Accessere Fed. Morelli* (Lutetiæ Parisiorum [Paris]: typis regiis, 1620), 2°. List 533. Theca 21. Hornby Castle 1272.

Suckling, John, Sir (1609–42), *Fragmenta aurea: a collection of all the incomparable peeces written by Sir John Suckling* (London: printed for Humphrey Moseley, 1648), 8°. List 558. Theca 20. Leeds 630 or 631. Wing S6127; ESTC R7002.

Suidas, nunc primum integer Latinitate donatus ... opera & studio Æmilii Porti. 2 vols. (Coloniæ Allobrogum [Geneva]: apud Petrum de la Rouiere, 1619), 2°. List 540. Theca 21. Greek and Latin.

Swift, Jonathan (1667–1745), *A tale of a tub. Written for the universal improvement of mankind.* 5th edn. (London: printed for John Nutt, 1710), 8°. List 554 (large paper), 611. Theca 19 and 29 (possibly a small-paper duplicate). ESTC T049835. Teerink-Scouten 222.

—— *Travels into several remote nations of the world. In four parts. By Lemuel Gulliver.* 2 vols. (London: printed for Benj. Motte, 1726), 8°. List 612 (edition not given, but probably the 1st). Theca 29. ESTC T139454, T139451, or T139452. Teerink-Scouten 289, 291.

—— and Alexander Pope (eds.), *Miscellanea. In two volumes.* (London: printed [for E. Curll], 1727), 12°. List 420 ('Miscellanies, Pope & Swift—3 vol. 8vo. Lond:1727.'). Theca 27. ESTC T039417.

—— and Alexander Pope (eds.), *Miscellanies in prose and verse* (London: printed for John Morphew, 1711), 8°. List 418, 553 (large paper). Theca 28. Leeds 638 (large paper). ESTC N044669.

—— see Temple, Sir William, *Miscellanea* (1701).

Sydenham, Thomas (1624–89), *Opera universa.* 3rd edn. (Londini: typis J. Heptinstall, impensis Walteri Kettilby, 1705), 8°. List 561. Theca 4. ESTC T136718.

—— *The whole works of that excellent practical physician.* 4th edn., corrected by John Pechey (London: printed for R. Wellington, 1705), 8°. List 562. Theca 4. ESTC T064459.

Sylvester, Joshua (1563–1618) (tr.), *The parliament of vertues royal (summoned in France; but assembled in England) for nomination, creation, and confirmation of the most excellent prince Panaretus a præsage of Pr. Dolphin: a pourtrait of Pr.— Henry: a promise of Pr. Charles. Translated & dedicated to His Highnes, by Iosuah Syluester* (London: printed by Humphrey Lownes, 1614), 8°. List 582 (edition, date and format not given). Theca 6. STC 23581; ESTC S118073.

Tachard, Guy (1651–1712), *Voyage de Siam des peres Jesuites, envoyés par le roy, aux Indes à la Chine.* 2 vols. (Amsterdam: chez Pierre Mortier, 1688–9), 12°. List 645. Theca 3.

Tacitus, Cornelius, *Les oeuvres de Tacite, de la traduction de N. Perrot, sieur d'Ablancourt.* 2 vols. (Amsterdam: chez Andre De Hoogenhuysen, 1691), 8°. List 606 ('12°.'). Theca 11.

Talbot, James (d. 1708) (ed.), *see* Horace [Works. 1699].

Tarteron, Jérôme (1644–1720) (tr.), *see* Horace [Works. 1710].

Tasso, Torquato (1544–95), *Aminta, favola boscareccia* (Amsterdam: nella stamperia del s. D. Elsevier. Et in Parigi si vende appresso Thomaso Jolly, 1678), 32°. List 29 ('24°.'). Theca 5.

—— *Godfrey of Bulloigne: or the recovery of Jerusalem. Done into English historical verse, by Edward Fairfax* (London: printed by J[ohn]. M[acock]. for H. Herringman, and are to be sold by Jos. Knight, and F. Saunders, 1687), 8°. List 266. Theca 19. Wing T174, 174A, or 174B; ESTC R220105, R30158, or R30159.

—— *Il Goffredo, overo Gierusalemme liberata.* 2 vols. (Amsterdam: nella stamperia del s. D. Elsevier. Et in Parigi si vende appresso Thomaso Jolly, 1678), 32°. List 267, 609 ('24°.'). Theca 5.

Tate, Nahum (1652–1715) (tr.), *see* Fracastero, Girolamo, *Syphilis* (1686).

—— *see* Ovid [Ars amatoria. 1709].

Temple, William, Sir (1628–99), *Miscellanea. The third part.... Published by Jonathan Swift* (London: printed for Benjamin Tooke, 1701), 8°. List 603. Theca 33. ESTC T136599.

Tenain, Mme de, *La religieuse interessée et amoureuse, avec l'histoire du comte de Clare* (Cologne: chez ***, 1695), 12°. List 520. Theca 26.

Terence (195?–159 BC) [Comedies. 1642] *Publii Terentii Comoediæ* (Parisiis: e typographia regia, 1642), 2°. List 592. Theca 16. Leeds 675.

—— [Comedies. 1694] *Terence's Comedies: made English... By several hands* (London: printed for A. Swall and T. Childe, 1694), 8°. List 595. Theca 20. Wing T749; ESTC R30657. Edited and probably for the most part translated by Laurence Echard. Congreve's copy, signed 'Will: Congreve' on the title page: University of Tennessee.

—— [Comedies. 1701] *Publii Terentii Afri Comoediæ* (Cantabrigiæ: typis academicis, impensis Jacobi Tonson, 1701), 4°. List 593 (large paper). Theca 17. ESTC T137034. Edited by John Leng. Congreve was one of the 'Subscribers for the Encouragement of this Undertaking': *see* Horace [Works. 1699].

—— [Comedies. 1706] *Les Comedies de Terence traduites en françois... par Madame Dacier.* 3 vols. (Amsterdam: aux dépens de Gaspar Fritsch, 1706), 12°. List 191. Theca 25.

—— [Comedies. 1713] *Publii Terentii carthaginiensis afri Comoediæ sex* (Londini: ex officinâ Jacobi Tonson, & Johannis Watts, 1713), 12°. List 594. Theca 24. ESTC T137033. Edited by Michael Maittaire.

Theobald, Lewis (1688–1744), *Double falsehood; or, The distrest lovers. A play... Written originally by W. Shakespeare; and now revised and adapted to the stage by Mr. Theobald* (London: printed by J. Watts, 1728), 8°. List 591. ESTC T034858.

Theophrastus, *Caracteres de Theophrastus traduit du grec; avec Les caracteres ou les moeurs de ce siecle. Par Mr. de La Bruière.* 7th edn. (Bruxelles: chez Jean Leonard, 1693), 12°. List 607. Theca 12.

—— *The moral characters of Theophrastus. Translated from the Greek, by Eustace Budgell, Esq.* (London: printed for Jacob Tonson, 1714), 12°. List 608. Theca 8. ESTC T086597.

Thompson, Aaron (b. 1682?) (tr.), *see* Geoffrey of Monmouth, *The British history* (1718).

Thucydides, *Eight bookes of the Peloponnesian warre ... Interpreted with faith and diligence immediately out of the Greeke by Thomas Hobbes* (London: imprinted [at Eliot's Court Press] for Richard Mynne, 1634), 2°. List 282. Theca 9. STC 24059; ESTC S117706.

—— *L'Histoire de Thucydide, de la guerre du Peloponese; continuée par Xenophon. De la traduction de N. Perrot, sr. d'Ablancourt* (Paris: chez Augustin Courbé, 1662), 2°. List 596. Theca 21.

Tibullus, *see* Catullus [Works. 1680, 1686, 1691, 1702, 1715].

—— *see also* La Chapelle, Jean de, *Les Amours de Tibulle* (1715).

Tillotson, John, Archbishop of Canterbury (1630–94), *The works of the most reverend Dr. John Tillotson ... containing fifty four sermons and discourses.* 4th edn. (London: printed for B. Aylmer. And W. Rogers, 1704), 2°. List 597. Theca 21. ESTC T118081.

—— *[Sermons:* volume titles vary] ... *published from the originals by Ralph Barker.* 14 vols. (London: printed for R. Chiswell, 1700–4), 8°. List 599 ('Sermons Posthumous | *14 Vols.* Pub. by his | Chaplain Ra. Barker ... 1704 &c.'). Theca 32.

—— *Six sermons* (London: printed for B. Aylmer and W. Rogers, 1694), 8°. List 598. Theca 32. Wing T1268; ESTC R9445.

Timoléon de Choisy, François, *see* Choisy, abbé de.

Tollius, Jacobus (d. 1696) (ed.), *see* Longinus, *De sublimatate commentarius* (1694).

Tormes, Lazarillo de (fictional name), *see* Hurtado de Mendoza, Diego, *La vie et avantures de Lazarillo de Tormes* (1698).

Two dissertations, see Mayne, Zachary.

Urchard, Thomas, *see* Urquhart.

Urquhart, Sir Thomas (1611–60) (tr.), *see* Rabelais, *Whole works* (1708).

Urry, John (1666–1715) (ed.), *see* Chaucer, Geoffrey [Works. 1721].

Vallemont, abbé de (Pierre Le Lorrain) (1649–1721), *Les elemens de l'histoire.* 2 vols. (Paris, 1699), 12°. List 239, 637. Theca 11.

Vattier, Pierre (1623–70) (tr.), *see* Murtadá ibn al-Khafif, *The Egyptian history* (1672).

Vaugelas, Claude Favre de (1585–1650) (tr.), *see* Rufus, Quintus Curtius, *De la vie & des actions d'Alexandre le Grand* (1696).

Velleius Paterculus, Gaius (*c.*19 BC–*c.*AD 30), *M. Velleii Paterculi Historiæ romanæ quæ supersunt* (Londini: ex officinâ Jacobi Tonson, & Johannis Watts, 1713), 12°. List 627. Theca 24. ESTC T110981.

Veneroni, sieur de (1642–1708), *Dictionaire italien et françois, contenant tout ce qui se trouve dans les autres dictionaires*, new edn. (Paris: chez Michel David, 1710), 4°. List 175. Theca 22.

Vernon, Edward (1669?–1743), *Corona civica. A poem to the right honourable the lord-keeper of the great seal of England* (London: printed: and sold by John Nutt, 1706). List 413, 485. Theca 15. ESTC T060953 or N060737; Foxon V36 or V37. In: *A Collection of poems, occasionally written upon the victories of Blenheim and Ramillies* (1708).

—— *The Union. A poem, inscrib'd to the right honourable lord Marquiss of Granby, one of her majesty's commissioners for the Scotch union* (London: printed: and sold by J. Morphew, 1707). List 413, 485. Theca 15. ESTC N014492; Foxon V38. In: *A Collection of poems, occasionally written upon the victories of Blenheim and Ramillies* (1708).

Vertot, abbé de (1655–1735), *Histoire des Chevaliers hospitaliers de S. Jean de Jerusalem, appellez depuis chevaliers de Rhodes, et aujourd'hui chevaliers de Malte.* 5 vols. (Paris: chez Rollin, Quillau Pere & Fils, Desaint, 1726), 12°. List 636.

—— *Histoire des révolutions arrivées dans le gouvernement de la République romaine.* 3 vols. (Paris: chez François Barois, 1719), 12°. List 525, 633. Theca 11.

—— *Histoire des revolutions de Portugal* (Paris: chez Michel Brunet, 1711), 12°. List 526, 634. Theca 11.

—— *Histoire des revolutions de Suede.* 2 vols. (Paris: chez Michel Brunet, 1695), 12°. List 527, 635. Theca 11.

La vie et avantures de Lazarillo de Tormes, see Hurtado de Mendoza, Diego.

Villars, Nicolas-Pierre-Henri de Montfaucon (*c.*1635–73), *Le Comte de Gabalis, ou Entretiens sur les sciences secretes* (Paris: chez Claude Barbin, 1670), 12°. List 119. Theca 29. Congreve's copy, signed 'Will Congreve': University of Tennessee.

Villiers, George, Duke of Buckingham, *see* Buckingham.

Vinnius, Arnoldus (tr.), *see* Justinian I, *Sacratissimi principis, institutionum* (1663).

Violenta, or the rewards of virtue, see Pix, Mary Griffith.

Virgil [Works. 1636] *P. Virgilii Maronis Opera; nunc emendatorium* (Lugd. Batavor. [Leiden]: ex officina Elzeviriana, 1636), 12°. List 626 ('24°.'). Theca 24. Congreve's copy is signed 'Ex libris Gul: Congreve' (J. Isaacs, *TLS* 2 September 1949); its present location is unknown.

—— [Works. 1682] *P. Virgilii Maronis Opera interpretatione et notis illustravit Carolus Ruæus* (Parisiis: apud Simonem Benard, 1682), 4°. List 613. Theca 22.

—— [Works. 1697] *The works of Virgil: containing his Pastorals, Georgics, and Æneis. Translated into English verse; by Mr. Dryden* (London: printed for Jacob Tonson, 1697), 2°. List 161 (large paper). Theca 10. Wing V616 or V616A; ESTC R26296 or R221907. List of subscribers includes Congreve. Hornby Castle 1180.

—— [Works. 1697] *The works of Virgil: containing his Pastorals, Georgics, and Æneis. Translated into English verse; by Mr. Dryden* (London: printed for Jacob Tonson, 1697), 2°. List 162 (small paper). Theca 9. Wing V616 or V616A; ESTC R26296 or R221907. List of subscribers includes Congreve.

Virgil [Works. 1701] *Publii Virgilii Maronis Bucolica, Georgica, et Æneis* (Cantabrigiæ: typis academici, impensis Jacobi Tonson, 1701), 4°. List 614 (large paper). Theca 17. ESTC T139222. Edited by H. Laughton. Congreve was one of the 'Subscribers for the Encouragement of this Undertaking': see Horace [Works. 1699].

—— [Works. 1704] *P. Virgilii Maronis Opera. Nic. Heins. . . . recensuit* (Ultrajecti [Utrecht]: apud Guil. van de Water, 1704), 12°. List 625. Theca 24.

—— [Works. 1715] *P. Virgilii Maronis Opera* (Londini: ex officinâ Jacobi Tonson, & Johannis Watts, 1715), 12°. List 624. Theca 24. ESTC T139212. Edited by Michael Maittaire.

—— *Publii Virgilii Maronis Appendix, cum supplemento multorum antehac nunquam excusorum poematum veterum. Iosephi Scaligeri in eandem appendicum commentarij & castigationes* (Lugduni [Lyon]: apud Guliel. Rovillium, 1572), 8°. List 622. Theca 7.

—— *Thesaurus P. Virgilii Maronis in communes locos olim digestus* (Parisiis, apud viduam Claudii Thiboust, et Petrum Esclassan, 1683), 12°. List 623. Theca 24.

Voiture, monsieur de (Vincent) (1597–1648), *Les oeuvres* (Paris: Augustin Courbé, 1650), 4°. List 615. Theca 2.

Voltaire, François Marie Arouet de (1694–1778), *An essay upon the civil wars of France . . . And also upon the epic poetry of the European nations, from Homer down to Milton*. 2nd edn. (London: printed for N. Prevost and Comp., 1728), 8°. List 650. ESTC T37630.

—— *La Henriade* (A Londres, 1728), 4°. List 649. Leeds 679. ESTC T137888 or T222176; Foxon V112. List of subscribers includes Congreve.

—— *La Henriade. Seconde édition revûe, corrigée, & augmentée de remarques critiques sur cet ouvrage* (Londres: chez Woodman & Lyon, 1728), 8°. List 648. Leeds 678? ESTC T130276; Foxon V113.

—— *see also* Rolli, Paolo Antonio, *Remarks upon M. Voltaire's Essay on the epick poetry* (1728).

von Hutten, Ulrich, *Epistolarum obscurorum virorum*, *see* Crotus Rubianus.

Vossius, Isaac (1618–89) (ed.), *see* Catullus [Works. 1691].

Voyage de Siam, *see* Tachard, Guy, *Voyage de Siam* (1688–9).

Waller, Edmund (1606–87), *Poems, &c. written upon several occasions, and to several persons*. 6th edn. (London: printed for H. Herringman, and sold by Jacob Tonson, 1694), 8°. List 653. Theca 20. Wing W519; ESTC R14123.

Walsh, William (1663–1708), *Ode for the thanksgiving day* (London: printed for Jacob Tonson, 1706). List 413, 485. Theca 15. ESTC T071924; Foxon W35. In: *A Collection of poems, occasionally written upon the victories of Blenheim and Ramillies* (1708).

Ward, John (1679?–1758) (ed.), *see* Kemp, John, *Monumenta* (1720).

Wee have brought our hogs to a fair market; or, Strange news from New-Gate: being a most pleasant and historical narrative of Captain J[ames] H[ind] (London: printed for George Horton, 1651), 4°. List 405 (edition not given; bound with 10 other miscellaneous 4° items). Theca 28. Wing W1178; but possibly Wing W1177; ESTC R203165.

Wicquefort, Abraham de (1606–82) (tr.), *see* Olearius, Adam, *Relation du voyage*.

Wild, Robert (1609–79), *Iter boreale, with large additions of several other poems* (London: printed for John Williams, 1670), 8°. List 655 ('12°.'). Theca 6. Wing W2137; ESTC R15239 or R234498.

Wilkins, John, Bishop of Chester (1614–72), *Mathematicall magick* (London: printed by M.F. for Sa. Gellibrand, 1648), 8°. List 654. Theca 8. Wing W2198, W2199, or W2199A; ESTC R6164, R227427, or R186578.

Willes, Richard (*fl.* 1558–78) (ed.), *see* Anghiera, Pietro Martire d', *The history of trauayle* (1577).

Willis, Thomas (1621–75), *Thomae Willis med. doct. opera omnia... Studio & opera Gerardi Blasii* (Amstelædami: apud Henricum Wetstenium, 1682), 4°. List 652. Theca 2. Hornby Castle 1244.

Wilmot, John, Earl of Rochester (1647–80), *Poems, &c. on several occasions: with Valentinian, a tragedy* (London: printed for Jacob Tonson, 1691), 8°. List 508. Theca 20. Wing R1756; ESTC R1390.

Wingfield, Anthony (1550?–1615?), *Pendantius* (1631), *see* Forsett, Edward.

Winstanley, William (1628?–1698), *The honour of the taylors; or, the famous and renowned history of Sir John Hawkwood* (London: printed by Alexander Milbourn, for William Whitwood, 1687), 4°. List 405 (edition not given; bound with 10 other miscellaneous 4° items). Theca 28. Wing H2599; ESTC R7888. Attributed to William Winstanley.

Wycherley, William (1640?–1716), *Miscellany poems* (London: printed for C. Brome, J. Taylor, and B. Tooke, 1704), 2°. List 651. Theca 21. Leeds 707 (large paper) or 708. ESTC T144864. Cf. Foxon i. 907. Leeds 707 is inscribed 'For My Lord High Treasurer, of England; from, His most obedient, and most humble Servant, W: Wycherly.' and was sold to Rosenbach for £200. It may have passed to Congreve on the death of Henrietta Godolphin's father-in-law in 1712, but it seems more likely that item 708 in the Leeds sale ('*panelled calf, back gilt, joints broken*' but bearing the Leeds bookplate) was Congreve's copy. It was sold by Sotheby's, London, to Starkie (lot 162) for £220 on 19 May 1975, but its present location is unknown.

Wynter, John (d. 1699), *Of bathing in the hot-baths, at Bathe; chiefly with regard to the palsie, and some diseases in women. In a letter, addressed to Doctor Freind* (London: printed for W. Innys and James Leake, at Bathe, 1728), 8°. List 656 ('two copies'). Leeds 659A. ESTC T042092.

Xenophon (*c*.430–*c*.354 BC), *La Cyropædie, ou l'histoire de Cyrus; traduite... François Charpentier*. 2 vols. in 1 (La Haye: pour Paul & Isaac Vaillant, 1717), 8°. List 159 ('12°') and 304. Theca 33.

—— *La vie de Socrate*. 3rd edn. (Amsterdam: aux dépens d'Etienne Roger, 1699), 8°. List 630. Theca 33. Translated by François Charpentier.

Xiphilinus, Joannes (11th c.), *see* Cassius Dio Cocceianus, *History* (1704).

Xylander, Wilhelm (1532–76) (ed.), *see* Pausanias, *Pausaniou tes Hellados perigesis* (1613).

—— (tr.), *see* Strabo, *Rerum geographicarum* (1620).

Young, Edward (1683–1765), *Ocean. An ode* (London: printed for Tho. Worrall, 1728), 8°. List 439 (format not given). ESTC T125535; Foxon Y94, Y95.

Young, Edward, *A Vindication of providence: or, a true estimate of human life.* 2nd edn. (London: printed for T. Worrall, 1728), 8°. List 658. ESTC T050833.

Zade, Chec (Shaik Zadah), *Turkish Tales* (1708), *see* Pétis, François.

SHELF LIST

NB. The Theca numbers against each entry in the manuscript catalogue of Congreve's library give the following arrangement. The figures within parentheses indicate only the number of that author's items on the shelf, not the number of volumes for any particular work.

Theca 1: Athenaeus of Naucratis, Beaumont and Fletcher, Blackmore (2), Blount, Gilbert Burnet, Thomas Burnet, Caesar (2), Chaucer (2), Corneille, Jonson, Marino, Olearius, Scribonius Largus.

Theca 2: Aléman, Balzac, Boccalini, Camõens, Cervantes, Comines, Gay, Jonson, Le Roy, Mendes Pinto, Malory, Newton, Perceval, Pope, Willis.

Theca 3: Gilbert Burnet, Calvi, Cervantes (2), Challes, Descartes, Exquemelin, Gemelli-Careri, Horace, Lucas (3), Murtadá ibn al-Khafif, Rycaut, Scarron, Sorel, Tachard.

Theca 4: Bate, Celsus (2), Chomel, Culpeper (2), Dale, Diemerbroeck, Gand, Halfpenny, Hippocrates, Ogilby, Pliny, Quincy, Royal College of Physicians (3), Sanctorius, Sydenham (2).

Theca 5: Aristotle, Bonarelli della Rovere, Busbecq, Catullus, Celimauro, Cluverius, Davenant, Earle, Erasmus, Forsett, Gellius, Guarini, Horace (2), Justinian, Livy, Marino, Montaigne, Plautus, Randolph, Ruggle, Sallust (2), Sannazaro, Seneca, Source des malheurs d'Angleterre, Tasso (2).

Theca 6: Thomas Browne, Burgersdijck, Cebes, Collection of Statutes, Colsoni, Crotus Rubeanus, Dufresny, Fuller, Homer, Kemp, Le Sage, Livy, Lucan, Malthus, Marini, Montaigne, Ovid, Phillippes, Aretino Pietro, Raymond, Scudéry, Secret History, Sylvester, Tachard, Wild.

Theca 7: Alexander, Busby, Catullus (2), Conti, Eustachius, Herodotus, Homer, Horace (2), Juvenal, Lipsius, Lucan, Lucretius (2), Macrobius, Menander, Roberti, Sallust, Scaliger, Sidonius, Virgil.

Theca 8: Anghiera, Anton, Aubrey, Bulstrode, Camus, Cervantes, Collier, Congreve (Amendments), Davenant, Dennis, English military discipline, Filmer, Fontenelle (2), Gildon, Le Noble, Lilly, Luna, Miege, Milbourne, Molyneux, Moretti, Oldmixon (2), Oughtred, Petronius, Pix, Pratt, Rapin, Rocoles, Settle, Shirley (2), Steele, Theophrastus, Wilkins.

Theca 9: Chardin, Cooper, Cotgrave, Cowley, Davenant, Dryden, Charles Estienne, Fables Ancient and Modern, Hobbes, Homer, Iamblichus, Killigrew, Locke, Sorel, Thucydides, Virgil.

Theca 10: Caesar, Chaucer, Dictionnaire universel François et Latin, Dryden, Juvenal, John Smith, Virgil.

Theca 11: Baudot de Juilly, Cervantes, Comines, Demosthenes, Fléchier, Gondi, Homer, Kennett (2), Leti, Roergas de Serviez, Rufus, Tacitus, Vallemont, Vertot d'Abeuf (3).

Theca 12: Aristotle, Bernier, Bouhours, Cicero, Dacier, Henri Estienne, Félibien des Avaux, Le Bossu, Maucroix, Montaigne, Patin (2), Plato, Rapin, Theophrastus.

Theca 13: Caesar, Dacier, Dio Cassius, Echard (2), Galfridus, Herodotus, Plutarch, Polybius, Abraham Stanyan, Temple Stanyan, Timoléon de Choisy.

Theca 14: Astell, Atterbury, Barclay, Blackmore, Book of Common Prayer, Thomas Burnet (2), Collins, Dodwell, Gaza, General collection of treatys, Hales, Hédelein, Lactantius, Lucian (2), Patru, Regis, Rogers, Scala, Spinoza.

Theca 15: Addison, Clay, Collection of Poems (Blenheim and Ramillies: includes Clay, Conduitt, Congreve, Fenton, Harison, Paris, Prior (2), Rowe, Vernon (2), Walsh), Henri Estienne, Garsilaso de la Vega, Montaigne, Ovid, Pausanius, Pontis, Prideaux, Prior, Richerius, Sarpi, Scapula, Sidney, Stow.

Theca 16: Bayle, Echard, Herodotus, Lucan, Ovid, Plautus, Prior, Ray, Terence.

Theca 17: Catullus (includes Propertius and Tibullus), Homer, Horace, Lucretius, Milton, Rousseau, Saint-Évremond, Terence, Virgil.

Theca 18: Athenaeus Naucratita, Dacier, Fénelon (4), Hardouin, Homer (3), Horace.

Theca 19: Boileau-Despréaux, Cowley, Dillon, Duke, Garth, Milton, Musarum anglicanarum analecta, Shakespeare, Spenser, Tasso.

Theca 20: Cartwright, Céspedes y Meneses, Chaucer, Collection of Poems (Montagu, Sheffield), Diaper, Donne (2), Egerton, Etherege, Fenton, Francastero, Garth, The Grove, Horace, Lansdowne, Manilius, Miscellaneous Poems (1712), Miscellany Poems (1693), Oldham, Ovid, Parnell, Plautus, Prior, Quillet, Steele, Suckling, Terence, Waller, Wilmot.

Theca 21: Bononcini, Eccles, Galliard, Homer, Pindar, Playford, Purcell, Shakespeare, Spenser, Stobaeus (2), Strabo, Suidas, Thucydides, Tillotson, Wycherley.

Theca 22: Aristotle (2), Bible, Demosthenes, Gellius, Homer, Lefèvre, Littleton, Longinus, Lucian, Quintilian, Richelet, Veneroni, Virgil.

Theca 23: Boccaccio, Boiardo, Caumont de La Force, Cervantes, Galland, La Fayette, Le Roux, Marguerite d'Angoulême, Pétis de la Croix.

Theca 24: Arnauld, Catullus (includes Propertius and Tibullus), Chapelain, Chifflet, Chorier, Cicero, Florus, Horace (2), La Motte, Justinus, Juvenal, La Chapelle, Lucan, Lucretius, Nepos, Ovid, Phaedrus, Pomey, Rufus, Saint-Réal, Sallust, Terence, Velleius Paterculus, Virgil (4).

Theca 25: Anacreon, Aristophanes, Fontenelle (6), Gherardi, La Fontaine (3), Longus, Molière, Racine, Sophocles, Terence.

Theca 26: Aulnoy, Baudot de Juilly, Bignon, Bourdeille, Bussy-Rabutin, J.D.D.C. (Monsieur, L'Honnête Homme), Caumont de La Force, Cervantes, Challes, Desjardins, Du Noyer, Garouville, Le Noble, Le Sage, Mailly, Quevedo Villegas, Scarron (2), Secondat, Sorel, Tenain, Vertot.

Theca 27: Congreve (Works, 1710 and 1719–20), Cowley, Dryden (6), Hédelin, Hopkins, Horace, Otway (9), Shakespeare, Swift, Villiers.

Theca 28: Addison, Aulnoy, Beaumont and Fletcher, Blackmore (2), Chapman, Congreve (Works, 1710, large paper), Deloney, Dennis, Famous life of Hercules, Gay, Greene, Hawkwood, Head, Life and death of Mother Shipton, Heliodorus, Homer, Jacob, Lee, Lefèvre, Mandeville, Middleton, Olearius, Ovid, Ovington, Philips, Rabelais, Rowlands, Shakespeare, Steele, Pope, We have brought our hogs.

Theca 29: Dunton, Frézier, Funnell, Idea, Mandeville, Plautus, Quevedo Villegas, Shakespeare, Sherley, Swift, Villars.

Theca 30: Boileau-Despréaux (2), Corneille (2), Daniel, Gondi, Gueulette (2), La Motte, La Fontaine, La Grange-Chancel, Morabin, Muralt, Noris, Ozinde, Rousseau, Saint-Réal, Shakespeare (6), Zade.

Theca 31: Cicero (8).

Theca 32: Cicero (5), L'escole parfaite, Jacob (2), Lamb, Massialot, Robert Smith, Tillotson (2).

Theca 33: Boccaccio, Boyle, Charron, Cicero, Dennis (2), Furetière, Hare, Labottière, Locke, Osborne, Scarron, Shadwell, Temple, Xenophon (2).

ABBREVIATIONS AND WORKS FREQUENTLY CITED

LL	*Love for Love*
MB	*The Mourning Bride*
OB	*The Old Batchelor*
WW	*The Way of the World*
W1	*The Works of Mr. William Congreve.* 3 vols. London: Printed for Jacob Tonson, 1710.
W2	*The Works of Mr. William Congreve.* 3rd edn. 2 vols. London: Printed for Jacob Tonson, 1719–20.
Ww	W1 and W2 as above

WORKS FREQUENTLY CITED AND OTHER ABBREVIATIONS

Addison, *Letters*: *The Letters of Joseph Addison*, ed. Walter Graham. Oxford: Clarendon Press, 1941.

Alleman, *Matrimonial Law*: Gellert Spencer Alleman, *Matrimonial Law and the Materials of Restoration Comedy*. Wallingford, Pa.: privately published, 1942.

Avery: William Congreve, *Love for Love*, ed. Emmett L. Avery. Regents Restoration Drama Series. London: Edward Arnold, 1967.

Avery, *Congreve's Plays*: Emmett L. Avery, *Congreve's Plays on the Eighteenth-Century Stage*. New York: Modern Language Association, 1951.

Baker: David Erskine Baker, *Biographia Dramatica, or, A Companion to the Playhouse*. New edn. 2 vols. London, 1782.

Barnard: William Congreve, *The Way of the World*, ed. John Barnard. Fountainwell Drama Texts. Edinburgh: Oliver and Boyd, 1972.

Bateson: *The Works of Congreve. Comedies: Incognita: Poems*, ed. F.W. Bateson. London: Peter Davies, 1930.

Beal: *Index of English Literary Manuscripts*. Volume II, Part I, A–K, Compiled by Peter Beal. London: Mansell Publishing, 1987.

Behn, *Works*: *The Works of Aphra Behn*, ed. Janet Todd. 7 vols. London: William Pickering, 1992–6.

Berger and Bradford: Thomas L. Berger and William C. Bradford, Jr., *An Index of Characters in English Printed Drama to the Restoration*. Englewood: Microcard Editions Books, 1975.

Berkeley: George-Monck Berkeley, *Literary Relics*. London, 1789.

Biog. Dict.: Philip H. Highfill, Jr., Kalman A. Burnim, and Edward A. Langhans, *A Biographical Dictionary of Actors, Actresses, Musicians, Dancers, Managers, and other Stage Personnel in London, 1660–1800*. 16 vols. Carbondale: Southern Illinois University Press, 1973–.

Biog. Dram.: *Biographia Dramatica; or a Companion to the Playhouse*, ed. David Erskine Baker (to 1764), Isaac Reed (to 1782), and Stephen Jones (to 1811). 3 vols. London, 1812.

Birdsall, *Wild Civility*: Virginia Ogden Birdsall, *Wild Civility: The English Comic Spirit on the Restoration Stage*. Bloomington and London: Indiana University Press, 1970.

Blount, *Law-Dictionary*: Thomas Blount, *Nomon-Lexicon: A Law-Dictionary* (1760).

Brett-Smith: William Congreve, *Incognita or Love and Duty Reconcil'd*, ed. H.F.B. Brett-Smith. The Percy Reprints. Oxford: Basil Blackwell, 1922.

Browne, *Pseudodoxia Epidemica*: Sir Thomas Browne, *Pseudodoxia Epidemica*, ed. Robin Robbins. 2 vols. Oxford: Clarendon Press, 1981.

Burnet: Gilbert Burnet, *History of His Own Time*. 2 vols. London, 1724–34.

Burney: Charles Burney, *A General History of Music. From the Earliest Ages to the Present (1789)*, ed. Frank Mercer. 2 vols. London: Foulis & Co., 1935.

Case: *A Bibliography of English Poetical Miscellanies 1521–1750*, ed. Arthur E. Case. Oxford: Oxford University Press for The Bibliographical Society, 1935.

Cibber, *Apology*: *An Apology for the Life of Mr. Colley Cibber, Written by Himself*. A new Edition with Notes and Supplement by Robert W. Lowe. 2 vols. London: John C. Nimmo, 1889.

Cibber, *Lives*: Theophilus Cibber [and Robert Shiels], *The Lives of the Poets*. 5 vols. London, 1753.

CJ: *The Journals of the House of Commons*.

Collier, *A Defence of the Short View*: Jeremy Collier, *A Defence of the Short View of the Profaneness and Immorality of the English Stage, &c. Being a reply to Mr. Congreve's Amendments*. London, 1699.

Collier, *Short View*: Jeremy Collier, *A Short View of the Immorality, and Profaneness of the English Stage*. London, 1698.

Craik: T.W. Craik, 'Congreve as Shakespearean', in *Poetry and Drama 1570–1700: Essays in Honour of Harold F. Brooks*, ed. Antony Coleman and Antony Hammond. London: Methuen, 1981. Pp. 186–99.

Crit. Herit.: *William Congreve: The Critical Heritage*, ed. Alexander Lindsay and Howard Erskine-Hill. London and New York: Routledge, 1989.

Crowne: *The Comedies of John Crowne*, ed. B.J. McMullin. Garland: New York and London, 1984.

CS: John Eccles, *A Collection of Songs for One, Two and Three Voices*. London: printed for I. Walsh, 1704.

Cunnington: C. Willett and Phillis Cunnington, *Handbook of English Costume in the Seventeenth Century*. 3rd edn. London: Faber, 1972.

D. & M.: C.L. Day and E. Murray, *English Song Books 1651–1702: A Bibliography with a First-line Index of Songs*. London: Oxford University Press, for The Bibliographical Society, 1940.

Danchin, *P/E*: *The Prologues and Epilogues of the Eighteenth Century. The First Part, 1700–1720*, ed. Pierre Danchin. 2 vols. Nancy: Presses Universitaires de Nancy, 1990. *The Second Part, 1721–1737.* 2 vols. Nancy: Presses Universitaires, 1993.

Davies: Thomas Davies, *Dramatic Miscellanies . . . With Anecdotes of Dramatic Poets, Actors, &c.*3 vols. London, 1783.

Davis: *The Complete Plays of William Congreve*, ed. Herbert Davis. Chicago: University of Chicago Press, 1967.

Dennis: *Letters upon Several Occasions* [by Dryden, Congreve, *et al.*], ed. John Dennis. London, 1696.

Dennis, *Works*: *The Critical Works of John Dennis*, ed. Edward N. Hooker. 2 vols. Baltimore: Johns Hopkins Press, 1939–43.

Dent: R.W. Dent, *Shakespeare's Proverbial Language. An Index.* Berkeley: University of California Press, 1981.

Dent, *PLED*: R.W. Dent, *Proverbial Language in English Drama exclusive of Shakespeare, 1495–1616: An Index.* Berkeley: University of California Press, 1984.

DL: Drury Lane Theatre.

Dictionary of the Canting Crew: B.E., *A New Dictionary of the Terms Ancient and Modern of the Canting Crew* [*c.*1699].

DM: *Deliciæ Musicæ: being, a Collection of the Newest and Best Songs Sung at Court and at the Publick Theatres.* The First Book. London: printed by J. Heptinstall, for Henry Playford, 1695.

DNB: *The Dictionary of National Biography*, ed. Sir Leslie Stephen and Sir Sydney Lee. 22 vols. Oxford: Oxford University Press, 1949–50.

Dobrée: William Congreve, *The Mourning Bride, Poems, & Miscellanies*, ed. Bonamy Dobrée. London: Oxford University Press, 1928.

Dobrée, *Comedies*: *Comedies by William Congreve*, ed. Bonamy Dobrée. London: Oxford University Press, 1925.

Downes, *Vanbrugh*: Kerry Downes, *Sir John Vanbrugh: A Biography* (London, 1987).

Drougge: Helen Drougge, *The Significance of Congreve's 'Incognita'.* Acta Universitatis Upsaliensis, 28. Uppsala: Universitets-biblioteket, 1976.

Dryden, *Letters*: *The Letters of John Dryden. With Letters Addressed to Him*, collected and ed. Charles E. Ward. Durham, NC: Duke University Press, 1942.

Dryden, *Poems*: *The Poems of John Dryden*, ed. James Kinsley. 4 vols. Oxford: Clarendon Press, 1958.

Dryden, *Works*: *The Works of John Dryden.* 20 vols. Berkeley and Los Angeles: University of California Press, 1956–2002.

ESTC: *Eighteenth-Century Short-Title Catalogue.* Now incorporated into the on-line *English Short-Title Catalogue.*

Etherege: *The Dramatic Works of Sir George Etherege*, ed. H.F.B. Brett-Smith. 2 vols. Oxford, 1927.

Evelyn, *Diary*: *The Diary of John Evelyn*, ed. Esmond S. de Beer. 6 vols. Oxford: Clarendon Press, 1955.

Ewald: *William Congreve*, ed. Alexander Charles Ewald. The Mermaid Series. London: Vizetelly, 1887.

Ewen, *Lotteries and Sweepstakes*: C.H.L'E. Ewen, *Lotteries and Sweepstakes*. London, 1932.

Familiar Letters: *Familiar Letters of Love, Gallantry, and Several Occasions.* London: printed for Sam. Briscoe, 1718.

Farmer and Henley: *Slang and Its Analogues Past and Present*, comp. and ed. J.S. Farmer and W.E. Henley. 7 vols. London: Routledge and Kegan Paul, 1890–1904.

Farquhar: *The Works of George Farquhar*, ed. Shirley Strum Kenny. 2 vols. Oxford: Clarendon Press, 1988.

Foxon: D.F. Foxon, *English Verse 1701–1750: A Catalogue of Separately Printed Poems with Notes on Contemporary Collected Editions*. 2 vols. Cambridge: Cambridge University Press, 1975.

Gay, *Dramatic Works*: John Gay, *Dramatic Works*, ed. John Fuller. 2 vols. Oxford: Clarendon Press, 1983.

Gay, *Letters*: *The Letters of John Gay*, ed. C.F. Burgess. Oxford: Clarendon Press, 1966.

Gay, *Poetry and Prose*: John Gay, *Poetry and Prose*, ed. Vinton A. Dearing, with the assistance of Charles E. Beckwith. 2 vols. Oxford: Clarendon Press, 1974.

Genest: John Genest, *Some Account of the English Stage, from the Restoration in 1660 to 1830*. 10 vols. Bath, 1832.

Gibbons: William Congreve, *The Way of the World*, ed. Brian Gibbons. The New Mermaids. London: Ernest Benn, 1971.

GJ: *The Gentleman's Journal*.

Gosse: Edmund Gosse, *The Life of William Congreve*. London: Walter Scott, 1888.

Grose: *Lexicon Balatronicum: A Dictionary of British Slang, University Wit and Pickpocket Eloquence*, comp. Francis Grose. London, 1811.

Halifax: *The Works of George Savile, Marquess of Halifax*, ed. Mark N. Brown. 3 vols. Oxford: Clarendon Press, 1989.

Harbage: Alfred Harbage, *Annals of English Drama 975–1700*, rev. S. Schoenbaum. London: Methuen, 1964.

Harvey, *Playford*: Douglas Ross Harvey, 'Henry Playford: A Bibliographical Study'. 3 vols. Ph.D. thesis, Victoria University of Wellington, 1985.

Hawkins: Sir John Hawkins, *General History of the Science and Practice of Music*. 5 vols. London, 1776.

Hédelin, *Whole Art*: François Hédelin, *The Whole Art of the Stage*. London, 1684.

Hodges, *Biography*: John C. Hodges, *William Congreve the Man: A Biography from New Sources*. London: Oxford University Press, 1941.

Hodges, *Documents*: *William Congreve Letters & Documents*, collected and ed. John C. Hodges. London: Macmillan, 1964.

Hodges, *Library*: *The Library of William Congreve*, ed. John C. Hodges. New York: The New York Public Library, 1955.

Holland: Peter Holland, *The Ornament of Action: Text and Performance in Restoration Comedy*. Cambridge: Cambridge University Press, 1979.

Holland, *Modern Comedies*: Norman H. Holland, *The First Modern Comedies: The Significance of Etherege, Wycherley and Congreve*. Cambridge, Mass.: Harvard University Press, 1959.

Hume: Robert D. Hume, *The Development of English Drama in the Late Seventeenth Century*. Oxford: Clarendon Press, 1976.

Hunt: *The Dramatic Works of Wycherley, Congreve, Vanbrugh, and Farquhar*, ed. Leigh Hunt. London, 1840.

Hunter: David Hunter, *Opera and Song Books Published in England 1703–1726*. London: The Bibliographical Society, 1997.

Jacob, *Account*: Giles Jacob, *An Historical Account of the Lives and Writings of our Most Considerable English Poets*. London, 1720.

Jacob, *Register*: Giles Jacob, *The Poetical Register: Or, The Lives and Characters of the English Dramatic Poets*. London, 1719.

Jeffares: *Congreve: Incognita and The Way of the World*, ed. A. Norman Jeffares. London: Edward Arnold, 1966.

Johnson, *Lives*: Samuel Johnson, *The Lives of the English Poets*, ed. George Birkbeck Hill. 3 vols. Oxford: Clarendon Press, 1905.

Jonson: *Ben Jonson*, ed. C.H. Herford and Percy and Evelyn Simpson. 11 vols. Oxford: Clarendon Press, 1925–52.

Kelsall: William Congreve, *Love for Love*, ed. M.M. Kelsall. The New Mermaids. London: Ernest Benn, 1969.

Ladies Dictionary: N.H., *The Ladies Dictionary, being a General Entertainment for the Fair-Sex*. London, 1694.

Langbaine, *Lives and Characters*: Gerard Langbaine, *The Lives and Characters of the English Dramatick Poets*, rev. Charles Gildon. London, 1699.

LC: Lord Chamberlain's Records at the Public Record Office, London.

Lee, *Works*: *The Works of Nathaniel Lee*, ed. Thomas B. Stroup and Arthur L. Cooke. 2 vols. New Brunswick: Scarecrow Press, 1954.

Leeds: *Catalogue of a Selected Portion of the Valuable Library at Hornby Castle, Bedale, Yorkshire, the Property of His Grace the Duke of Leeds*. London: Sotheby and Co., 1930.

LG: *London Gazette*.

LIF: Lincoln's Inn Fields Theatre.

Lillywhite: Bryant Lillywhite, *London Coffee Houses: A Reference Book*. London: Allen and Unwin, 1963.

LJ: *The Journals of the House of Lords*.

Locke: *An Essay Concerning Human Understanding*, ed. Peter H. Nidditch. Oxford: Clarendon Press, 1975.

Love: Harold Love, *Congreve*. Oxford: Basil Blackwell, 1974.

Lowe, *Betterton*: Robert W. Lowe, *Thomas Betterton*. London: Kegan Paul, Trench, Trübner, 1891.

LS: *The London Stage, 1660–1800*. Part 1: 1660–1700, ed. William Van Lennep, Emmett L. Avery, and Arthur H. Scouten. Carbondale: Southern Illinois University Press, 1965. Part 2: 1700–1729, ed. Emmett L. Avery. 2 vols. Carbondale: Southern Illinois University Press, 1960.

Luttrell: Narcissus Luttrell, *A Brief Historical Relation of State Affairs from September 1678 to April 1714*. 6 vols. Oxford, 1857.

Lynch: William Congreve, *The Way of the World*, ed. Kathleen M. Lynch. Regents Restoration Drama Series. London: Edward Arnold, 1965.

Lynch, *Gallery*: Kathleen M. Lynch, *A Congreve Gallery*. Cambridge, Mass.: Harvard University Press, 1951.

Lynch, *Social Mode*: Kathleen M. Lynch, *The Social Mode of Restoration Comedy*. London: Macmillan, 1926; reprinted, New York: Octagon Books, 1965.

Lynch, *Tonson*: Kathleen M. Lynch, *Jacob Tonson Kit-Cat Publisher*. Knoxville: University of Tennessee Press, 1971.

Macdonald: Hugh Macdonald, *John Dryden: A Bibliography of Early Editions and of Drydeniana*. Oxford: Clarendon Press, 1939.

Mann, *Concordance*: *A Concordance to the Plays of William Congreve*, ed. David Mann. Ithaca and London: Cornell University Press, 1973.

Marshall: *The Comedies of William Congreve*, ed. Norman Marshall. London: John Lehmann, 1948.

Memoirs: *Memoirs of the Life, Writings, and Amours of William Congreve, Esq.*, comp. Charles Wilson. London: printed for E. Curll, 1730.

Milhous & Hume: *A Register of English Theatrical Documents, 1660–1737*, comp. and ed. Judith Milhous and Robert D. Hume. Carbondale: Southern Illinois University Press, 1991.

MLN: *Modern Language Notes* (former title).

MM: *Mercurius Musicus: or, The Monthly Collection of New Teaching Songs, compos'd for the Theatres*. London: printed by William Pearson, for Henry Playford, J. Hare, and J. Young, [1699].

Montagu, *Essays and Poems*: Lady Mary Wortley Montagu, *Essays and Poems, and 'Simplicity, a Comedy'*, ed. Robert Halsband and Isobel Grundy. Oxford: Clarendon Press, 1977.

Montagu, *Letters*: *The Complete Letters of Lady Mary Wortley Montagu*, ed. Robert Halsband. 3 vols. Oxford: Clarendon Press, 1965–7.

Morris: *William Congreve*, ed. Brian Morris. Mermaid Critical Commentaries. London: Ernest Benn, 1972.

NA: National Archives (formerly Public Record Office).

N&Q: *Notes and Queries*.

Nichols, *Illustrations*: John Nichols, *Illustrations of the Literary History of the Eighteenth Century*. 8 vols. (1817–58).

Nicoll, *History*: Allardyce Nicoll, *A History of the English Drama, 1660–1900*. 6 vols. Cambridge: Cambridge University Press, 1955–9.

Novak: Maximillian E. Novak, *William Congreve*. New York: Twayne, 1971.

OBr: *Orpheus Britannicus*. The First Book. London: printed by J. Heptinstall, for Henry Playford, 1695.

OED: *Oxford English Dictionary*.

Otway: *The Works of Thomas Otway*, ed. J.C. Ghosh. 2 vols. Oxford: Clarendon Press, 1932.

Partridge, *Slang*: Eric Partridge, *A Dictionary of Slang and Unconventional English*. 7th edn. 2 vols. London: Macmillan, 1970.

PBSA: *Publications of the Bibliographical Society of America*.

Pepys, *Diary*: *The Diary of Samuel Pepys*, ed. Robert Latham and William Matthews. 9 vols. London: Bell, and Bell and Hyman, 1970–83.

Phillips, *World of Words*: Edward Phillips, *The New World of Words: Or, Universal English Dictionary*. 6th edn. London, 1706.

Piper, *Catalogue*: *Catalogue of Seventeenth-Century Portraits in the National Portrait Gallery, 1625–1714*, comp. David Piper (Cambridge, 1963).

POAS: *Poems on Affairs of State: Augustan Satirical Verse, 1660–1714*. General editor George de F. Lord. 7 vols. New Haven: Yale University Press, 1963–75. Volumes vi (1697–1704) and vii (1704–14), ed. Frank H. Ellis. New Haven: Yale University Press, 1970, 1975.

Pope: *The Works of Alexander Pope, Esq.*, vol. 5: *Containing an Authentic Edition of His Letters*. 2nd edn. London: printed for T. Cooper, 1737.

Pope, *Correspondence*: *The Correspondence of Alexander Pope*, ed. George Sherburn. 5 vols. Oxford: Clarendon Press, 1956.

Pope, *Poems*: *The Twickenham Edition of the Poems of Alexander Pope*, ed. John Butt *et al.* 11 vols. London: Methuen, 1961–9.

Price, *Purcell*: Curtis A. Price, *Henry Purcell and the London Stage*. Cambridge: Cambridge University Press, 1984.

Price, *Restoration Theatre*: Curtis A. Price, *Music in the Restoration Theatre, with a Catalogue of Instrumental Music in the Plays 1665–1713*. Studies in Musicology 4. Ann Arbor: UMI Research Press, 1979.

Prior, *Works*: *The Literary Works of Matthew Prior*, ed. H. Bunker Wright and Monroe K. Spears. 2 vols. Oxford: Clarendon Press, 1959.

PRO (Public Record Office), *see* NA.

RES: *Review of English Studies.*

Rochester: *The Works of John Wilmot, Earl of Rochester*, ed. Harold Love. Oxford: Oxford University Press, 1999.

Roscius Anglicanus: John Downes, *Roscius Anglicanus*, ed. Judith Milhous and Robert D. Hume. London: Society for Theatre Research, 1987.

Ross: William Congreve, *The Double Dealer*, ed. J.C. Ross. The New Mermaids. London: Ernest Benn, 1981.

Rump: *The Comedies of William Congreve*, ed. Eric S. Rump. Harmondsworth: Penguin Books, 1985.

Rymer: *The Critical Works of Thomas Rymer*, ed. Curt A. Zimansky. New Haven: Yale University Press, 1956.

SB: *Studies in Bibliography.*

Shakespeare: William Shakespeare, *The Complete Works*, ed. Stanley Wells and Gary Taylor. Oxford: Clarendon Press, 1986.

Smith: William C. Smith, *A Bibliography of the Musical Works Published by John Walsh during the Years 1695–1720*. London: The Bibliographical Society, 1968.

Snyder: *The Marlborough–Godolphin Correspondence*, ed. Henry L. Snyder. 3 vols. Oxford: Clarendon Press, 1975.

Southerne, *Works*: *The Works of Thomas Southerne*, ed. Robert Jordan and Harold Love. 2 vols. Oxford: Clarendon Press, 1988.

SP: *Studies in Philology.*

Spectator: *The Spectator*, ed. Donald F. Bond. 5 vols. Oxford: Clarendon Press, 1965.

Spence: Joseph Spence, *Observations, Anecdotes, and Characters of Books and Men Collected from Conversation*, ed. James M. Osborn. 2 vols. Oxford: Clarendon Press, 1966.

Spingarn: *Critical Essays of the Seventeenth Century*, ed. Joel E. Spingarn. 3 vols. Oxford: Clarendon Press, 1908–9.

STC: *A Short-Title Catalogue of Books Printed in England, Scotland, & Ireland and of English Books Printed Abroad, 1475–1640*. Comp. A.W. Pollard and G.R. Redgrave, 2nd edn. rev. and enlarged: begun by W.A. Jackson and F.S. Ferguson; completed by Katharine F. Pantzer, 3 vols. London: Bibliographical Society, 1976–91.

Steele, *Correspondence*: *The Correspondence of Richard Steele*, ed. Rae Blanchard. Oxford: Clarendon Press, 1941.

Steele, *Plays*: *The Plays of Richard Steele*, ed. Shirley Strum Kenny. Oxford: Clarendon Press, 1971.

Stephens: *The Guardian*, ed. John Calhoun Stephens. Lexington: University of Kentucky, 1982.

Stow: John Stow, *Survey of the Cities of London and Westminster*. Enlarged by John Strype. 2 vols. London, 1720.

Stratman: *Bibliography of English Printed Tragedy 1565–1900*, comp. and ed. Carl J. Stratman. Carbondale and Edwardsville: Southern Illinois University Press, 1966.

Summers: *The Complete Works of William Congreve*, ed. Montague Summers. 4 vols. London: Nonesuch Press, 1923.

Swift, *Correspondence*: *The Correspondence of Jonathan Swift*, ed. Sir Harold Williams. 5 vols. Oxford: Clarendon Press, 1963–5.

Swift, *Journal*: Jonathan Swift, *Journal to Stella*, ed. Harold Williams. 2 vols. Oxford: Clarendon Press, 1948.

Swift, *Poems*: *The Poems of Jonathan Swift*, ed. Harold Williams. 3 vols. Oxford: Clarendon Press, 1937.

Swift, *Prose*: *The Prose Writings of Jonathan Swift*, ed. Herbert Davis. 13 vols. Oxford: Basil Blackwell, 1939–62.

Tatler: *The Tatler*, ed. Donald F. Bond. 3 vols. Oxford: Clarendon Press, 1987.

Taylor: D. Crane Taylor, *William Congreve*. London: Oxford University Press, 1931.

TC: *The Term Catalogues, 1668–1709 A.D.*, ed. Edward Arber. 3 vols. London, 1903–6.

Teerink: Herman Teerink, *A Bibliography of the Writings in Prose and Verse of Jonathan Swift*. Oxford: Oxford University Press, 1964.

Tilley: Morris Palmer Tilley, *A Dictionary of the Proverbs in England in the Sixteenth and Seventeenth Centuries*. Ann Arbor: University of Michigan Press, 1950.

TM: John Hudgebutt, *Thesaurus Musicus*. Books I to 5. London: printed by John Heptinstall for John Hudgebutt, 1693–6.

Vanbrugh, *Works*: *The Complete Works of John Vanbrugh*, ed. Bonamy Dobrée and Geoffrey Webb. 4 vols. London: The Nonesuch Press, 1927.

Voris: W.H. Van Voris, *The Cultivated Stance: The Designs of Congreve's Plays*. Dublin: The Dolmen Press, 1965.

Walpole, *Correspondence*: *The Yale Edition of Horace Walpole's Correspondence*, ed. W.S. Lewis. New Haven: Yale University Press, 1937–83.

Walsh: William C. Smith, *A Bibliography of the Musical Works Published by John Walsh during the Years 1695–1720*. Oxford: Oxford University Press for The Bibliographical Society, 1948.

Williams, *Approach*: Aubrey L. Williams, *An Approach to Congreve*. New Haven and London: Yale University Press, 1979.

Wilson, *Memoirs*: *Memoirs of the life, writings, and amours of William Congreve, Esq interspersed with miscellaneous essays, letters, and characters, written by him: also some very curious memoirs of Mr. Dryden and his family, with a character of him and his writings, by Mr. Congreve. Compiled from their respective originals, by Charles Wilson.* London, 1730.

Wilson, *Proverbs*: *The Oxford Dictionary of English Proverbs.* 3rd edn., rev. F.P. Wilson, with an introduction by Joanna Wilson. Oxford: Clarendon Press, 1970.

Wing: *Short-Title Catalogue of Books Printed in England, Scotland, Ireland, Wales and British America and of English Books Printed in other Countries 1641–1700*, ed. Donald Wing. 3 vols. 2nd edn., revised and enlarged. 3 vols. New York: Modern Language Association of America, 1972–88.

Wycherley, *Plays*: *The Plays of William Wycherley*, ed. Arthur Friedman. Oxford: Clarendon Press, 1979.

Zimmerman: Franklin B. Zimmerman, *Henry Purcell, 1659–1695: An Analytical Catalogue of his Music.* London: Macmillan, 1963.

INDEX OF WORKS CITED

This is an index of works cited in commentary. Works referred to in Congreve's text or discussed in the introductionary discussion to the commentary for each work, are cited in the Main Index.

CUMULATIVE INDEX

Coverage of topics is selective; many titles are in short form; for literary
works cited in passing in the commentary, see Index of Works Cited